MICROECONOMIC
THEORY

IRWIN PUBLICATIONS IN ECONOMICS

Advisory Editor   Martin S. Feldstein *Harvard University*

Sixth Edition

MICROECONOMIC
THEORY

John P. Gould, Jr.   Edward P. Lazear

Both of
Graduate School of Business
The University of Chicago

1989

IRWIN

Homewood, IL 60430
Boston, MA 02116

TO THE LATE C. E. FERGUSON

Color photo: THE IMAGE BANK

© RICHARD D. IRWIN, INC., 1966, 1969, 1972, 1975, 1980, and 1989

All rights reserved. No part of this publication may be reproduced, stored in a retrieval system, or transmitted, in any form or by any means, electronic, mechanical, photocopying, recording, or otherwise, without the prior written permission of the publisher.

Acquisitions editor: *Gary L. Nelson*
Developmental editor: *Ann M. Granacki*
Project editor: *Joan A. Hopkins*
Production manager: *Irene H. Sotiroff*
Designer: *Michael Warrell*
Artist: *Benoit Design*
Compositor: *Beacon Graphics Corporation*
Typeface: *10/12 Times Roman*
Printer: *R.R. Donnelley & Sons Company*

LIBRARY OF CONGRESS
Library of Congress Cataloging-in-Publication Data

Gould, John P., 1939–
    Microeconomic theory/John P. Gould, Jr., Edward P. Lazear. —
6th ed.
        p.   cm.
    Bibliography: p.
    Includes index.
    ISBN 0-256-02996-2
    1. Microeconomics.   I. Lazear, Edward P. II. Title.
HB172.G64 1989
338.5–dc19   87–81574
                                                                          CIP

Printed in the United States of America
1 2 3 4 5 6 7 8 9 0 D O 5 4 3 2 1 0 9 8

Preface

Our goal has been to make this edition of Microeconomic Theory the most radical improvement of any revision to date. Because this book has always occupied a major part of the intermediate micro market and because many courses are constructed around earlier editions, we have been careful to retain almost all previous material. While users of past editions will feel comfortable with this version, the entire format of the book has been changed. That is immediately apparent. Gone is the traditional green and black cover, and color has replaced the somewhat staid black-and-white presentation. Another obvious change is that the author of previous versions, the late C. E. Ferguson, has been replaced by Edward Lazear.

Two new chapters have been added. The new chapter 1 is a short introduction to economics at a principles level. Because this book is often used as the main text in courses that are designed to bring students with no economic background up through an intermediate level, the first chapter eliminates the need to resort to a supplementary principles text. Chapter 1 may prove useful to M.B.A. students, for example, who must move from basics to advanced economics in a very short time. The other new chapter, chapter 19, introduces the economics of information to the reader in a digestible fashion. This area has received great attention in the economics literature over recent years, but it has not found its way into textbooks in any widespread or systematic manner. Chapter 19 recognizes the importance of this area by considering a number of information topics including job market signalling, pricing under uncertainty, and the economics of search.

The format has been changed to make the presentation livlier and to emphasize the significance of economics in day-to-day life. Most important, each chapter begins with a real-world example, generally pulled from a newspaper clipping that motivates the subsequent material. The seemingly complicated question posed by the example is answered using the theory developed in the chapter. Additionally, more examples have been added to make the text more readable. Robert Moore is responsible for these improvements.

This text has found its way into many intermediate micro classes, but it has been used at the graduate level as well. Chapter 19 and some of the more technical footnotes make it a good text for graduate students to work through in preparation for a theory general examination. Also, the addition of chapter 1, along with the real-world examples, make it ideal for M.B.A. students. Indeed, both authors have made the book the centerpiece of their M.B.A. courses taught at the University of Chicago.

This edition has corrected mistakes of the fifth edition and has clarified some presentations; in large part this is a result of suggestions made by users of the book. This is a continuing process, and we hope that readers of this edition will bring any errors, omissions, and suggestions to our attention. Such advice is of great value to us and other users and is much appreciated.

Finally, we wish to thank our many reviewers and readers who have made this version better than earlier ones. We owe special gratitude to William Chan, who patiently worked through the manuscript page by page and made many improvements. We also thank Maggie Newman for her cooperation in typing and assembling the final document so that we could meet our publication deadlines. Of course, the deepest debt is to the late Professor Ferguson who is, more than anyone, responsible for creating what we believe is a valuable text.

John P. Gould, Jr.

Edward P. Lazear

Contents

Contents

1

Demand, Supply, and Markets: An Introductory Look

Individuals play many roles in an economy. The same individual may be a buyer, a seller, a worker, and an employer all in a short period of time. For example, on any given day, an individual might stop at the local coffee shop to buy breakfast on his way to work at a large factory. When he returns home in the evening, he may conclude a transaction to sell his car. During the day, he might have hired the teenaged boy next door to mow his lawn.

Most of the time, it is the action rather than the identity of the individual that is essential in economics. When an individual is purchasing a good, he is a demander and what we are concerned about is the demand for the good in question. When he sells a good, he is a supplier and it is the supply of that good to the market that is generally of interest.

Individuals rarely take actions that have no impact on others. First of all, individuals tend to live in families and they must deal directly with other family members. Secondly, in a complex industrial society, work generally takes place at a common location where many individuals are simultaneously involved in the same production process. In fact, most of what this book is about relates to the ways in which individuals interact with one another in a market environment. The goal of a well-functioning market is to coordinate the actions of individual agents to bring about results that make all the trading parties better off.

Virtually all of the actions and interactions that are of interest in economics can be analyzed with the use of two simple constructs: demand and supply. Every action that an individual takes will affect either demand or supply, and what we must do is determine the manner in which they are influenced. Once this is done, it becomes possible to describe all of the important impacts on the rest of the economy.

Of course, there are many levels at which to address the tools associated with a study of demand and supply. At the simplest level, analysis is easy, and one moves quickly from the question to the answer. The drawback is that the most simple characterization of the problem leaves out the details. As the details become more important, it is necessary to understand more and more about demand and supply. This means that it will become necessary to go behind these constructs and search for the basic building blocks—in order to apply the tools to more complex situations. Still, much can be learned by thinking about demand and supply at their simplest levels and Chapter 1 is devoted to a preliminary exploration. ■

1 Demand, Supply, and Market Equilibrium

"You can make even a parrot into a learned economist — all it must learn are the two words *supply* and *demand*. [Anonymous] While this is a bit of an overstatement, all issues in economics can be reduced to questions about supply and demand.

This chapter introduces you to the key tools of the market demand curve and the market supply curve and to the concept of an equilibrium price and quantity. What causes the market demand curve or the market supply curve to shift? What determines the shape of these curves? If you can answer these questions, you will be able to answer many otherwise complex economic questions. In the "Applying the Theory" section you will consider the points made in a newspaper article that describes the effects of a rise in the price of sugar on a variety of interrelated markets. ■

Moonshiners in South Find Sales Are Down as Their Costs Go Up

My daddy, he made whiskey
My granddaddy did, too
We ain't paid no whiskey tax
Since 1792.

—from "Copper Kettle" by Albert F. Beddoe

HABERSHAM COUNTY, Ga. — When Joan Baez popularized the song "Copper Kettle" in the early 1960s, the verse quoted above described life in these North Georgia hills pretty accurately.

"There probably isn't a family around here that hasn't had at least one member involved with a still," observes Clyde Dixon, executive vice president of the Peoples Bank in Cleveland, Ga. "It hasn't been so long around here since moonshine was the only way to make money. My father made moonshine," Mr. Dixon says.

But two years ago the price of sugar—an essential ingredient in moonshine—tripled, and life in the laurel thickets changed rapidly. It takes at least 10 pounds of sugar to make a gallon of barnyard whiskey. With other inflationary factors added, moonshine that sold a few years ago for $6 a gallon at the still began pushing $15 a gallon.

At that price the moonshine market contracted severely, because for $15 plus retail markup, a customer can buy government whiskey. ("Government whiskey" is the hill country term for legal booze—stuff on which the tax has been paid. Unlike hastily made moonshine, its manufacture relies on slowly drawing natural sugars from the grain being distilled, and therefore its price is unaffected by the sugar market.)

Revenuers Look Elsewhere

The price squeeze on moonshine has forced new occupations on a lot of people who were engaged, one way or another, in what may have been, even as late as the 1950s, the largest industry in such counties as Habersham, Dawson, and Gilmer. Not all of those people whose employment depended on illegal booze were moonshiners, themselves, however.

Billy Corbin is a revenue agent with the Treasury Department's Bureau of Alcohol, Tobacco and Firearms (ATF). He chased moonshiners in North Georgia for 10 years and says his team of five agents used to bust up an average of 10 stills a month. Then, in December, he was transferred to a new office with emphasis on nonwhiskey violations. "When I left (the moonshine post) it was down to no more than one still a month," Mr. Corbin says.

Mr. Corbin's boss, Bill Barbary, agent in charge of ATF's Gainesville, Ga., office, says the 108 revenue agents in Georgia used to spend 75 percent of their time on liquor offenses, the rest on other crimes, mostly the unlicensed sale of firearms. Now, he says, agents spend only about 25 percent of their time on moonshine patrol. To help fill the slack, the Treasury Department this year reassigned its gambling tax enforcement to ATF from the Internal Revenue Service.

So, for the government, one beneficial by-product of the sugar inflation and moonshine depression is an increase in arrests for firearms violations and illegal wagering. Some 15 or 20 revenue agents from the countryside were reassigned to Atlanta this spring and broke up a big numbers ring there, federal officials say; they promised to follow up with the indictment of 30 or 40 gambling operators.

The Pot Shuttle

On the other hand, with the whiskey business in turmoil, many former moonshine overlords — Mr. Barbary says most of them — have simply reapplied their resourcefulness to trafficking in other illicit goods that are still profitable. They are suspected of being responsible for the recent big increase in the airlifting of drugs, particularly marijuana, from South America to small airstrips in Georgia and neighboring moonshine states.

For example, two long-reputed North Georgia moonshine czars, Garland "Bud" Cochran and Ben Kade "Junior" Tatum, were indicted in federal court in South Carolina last summer for allegedly masterminding a DC-4 pot shuttle from Colombia. Mr. Tatum was convicted and is appealing. Mr. Cochran — who the ATF says was shipping 7,000 gallons of moonshine a month into Atlanta in trailer trucks during the 1960s — has been a fugitive since the smuggling indictment came down. Officials believe he is in South America directing more smuggling operations.

Radical as the change in North Georgia life has been since the price of sugar rose, it actually is the culmination of an evolutionary change that began in the early 1940s.

Get you a copper kettle
Get you a copper coil
Cover with new-made corn mash
And never more you'll toil

Revenue agents agree that the old-time, 100 percent corn liquor made in pure copper stills — the fabled "white lightning" — was as good as or better than bonded whiskey. But when copper became scarce at the start of World War II, moonshiners turned to sheet metal vats, and in more recent times began cooling the liquor in automobile radiators instead of copper coils. The result often is a fatal dose of lead poisoning. In probably the most famous case of this, the late Fats Hardy, a Gainesville moonshine king, was sentenced to life in prison in the late 1950s after many persons died from drinking the moonshine he shipped to Atlanta.

"They just don't have professional pride anymore," observes Mr. Corbin, the revenue agent. "They aren't making drinking liquor. You find beer cans around those stills — they don't drink this stuff."

The people who do drink it, authorities say, are almost exclusively poor, urban

(continued on page 6)

(continued from page 5)
blacks. The biggest retail distribution centers are so-called "shot-houses," operated in private homes or stores in black neighborhoods of Atlanta, Macon, and other cities throughout the Southeast. Because the price of a shot has soared to 75 cents, almost the price of safer, stronger, legal bar whiskey, the ATF estimates that there are only a few hundred shot-houses in Atlanta now, down from a few thousand before the crunch.

Assistant U.S. Attorney Owen Forrester in Atlanta—who says his grandmother had a still on her land, though she didn't drink—says he doubts that even a new rise in sugar prices could wipe out moonshine entirely. "The revenue agents who work the shot-houses here tell me that there are still a lot of old-timers who like the taste of it," Mr. Forrester says. "There's a certain zang, or sizzle, going down."

How to Make It

Hill folks and revenue agents have described the methods moonshiners use to get that "zang" and "sizzle" in there.

First, there's a widespread belief, often put into practice, that horse manure added to the corn mash speeds its fermentation. In addition, sanitary conditions aren't always up to FDA standards. Mr. Dixon, the country banker, says "I've seen a hog get in (the vat) to drink some of that slop and drown. They just take the hog out and go ahead. They can't afford to lose all that money (by throwing out the contaminated mash). I'll tell you, Jack Daniel's does it a lot cleaner." Mr. Forrester, the prosecutor,

recalls a moonshiner who "put in dead possums at the end to flavor it."

Later, still other foreign matter is added. Moonshine usually is 110 proof when it's sold at the still to a "tripper," who usually is either an independent truck driver or an employee of an urban distributor. To stretch the product, the distributors usually water it down as much as 50 percent. Then, to make it look its original strength, they add beading oil, which simulates the swirls that alcohol makes in liquor.

If some parts of the "Copper Kettle" song were accurate once, sources here agree that one verse never was accurate:

> You just lay there by the juniper
> While the moon is bright
> And watch them jugs a-fillin'
> In the pale moonlight.

"It's damn hard work to make whiskey," Mr. Dixon says. "They have to hide the stills in laurel thickets on a mountain. You have your barrels and boxes of malt—it's corn meal mostly, some barley malt. They'll carry 200 or 300 pounds of sugar up that mountain at a time on their backs. All the time (the mash) is working it has to be stirred. That corn meal has a tendency to lump up. I've seen them get stark naked and get in there and mash it. If you don't think it's hard work, try it."

Much of the hard work, high price, and poor quality is caused by the revenue agents, whose presence puts constant pressure on moonshiners to finish their work fast and get out. Moonshiners need costly sugar because they must dash off each batch of their product in about 72 hours. Bonded distillers have controlled conditions and plenty of time, so they can apply even heat as required and wait out the two weeks or so it takes to get sugar out of the natural grains.

> *Build you a fire with hick'ry*
> *Hick'ry and ash and oak*
> *Don't use no green or rotten wood*
> *They'll get you by the smoke.*

Byron Davis of Gainesville, who retired in 1968 after 31 years as a revenue agent because "it's a young man's job," says he remembers capturing a lot of moonshiners by cruising the hills looking for smoke. In fact, he attributes the switch in still materials from copper to other metals at least in part to a switch in cooking fuels from wood to butane gas. The butane largely eliminated the telltale smoke trail, he says, but didn't work well with copper equipment.

Keeping tabs on sugar sales also has helped agents to corral a few moonshiners. "One of these little country stores starts selling 500 pounds of sugar a week, you smell a rat," Mr. Corbin says.

Nowadays, however, agents say they make most of their arrests through tips from informants. Moonshiners love to tell on each other, Mr. Corbin says. Certainly the ATF needed informants 18 months ago in order to discover a fabulous 2,000-gallon-a-week underground still, which was entered by opening the trunk of an old Ford sitting in a Habersham County junkyard, and climbing down a ladder. Agents believe that the operator obtained electric power for his still by tapping into nearby underground Tennessee Valley Authority lines.

On the whole, authorities say their problem is less in catching moonshiners than in obtaining justice afterwards.

Judges and juries just "didn't consider whiskey to be a crime," Mr. Forrester recalls of his moonshine trial days. The operator of the underground still beneath the old Ford, for example, pleaded guilty and received a suspended sentence, Mr. Forrester says.

Professional

So relaxed is the atmosphere at moonshine trials that one notorious moonshiner from Adairsville, Ga., used to feel comfortable attending them. Mr. Forrester recalls, "Every term he'd come to court with mash all over his pants and listen to testimony in other cases to learn new techniques."

A typical still operation is financed and overseen by a man with substantial income from legitimate business, such as a farm or store. He hires three to six still hands and one or two women who live with them while the still is in operation, to keep house and to make the group appear to be a normal family. While the still hands sometimes wind up serving a year or two in federal prison, the boss, if convicted, usually gets probation, often impressing the judge and jury with letters of commendation from leaders in the community.

* * * * *

Questions

1. Explain carefully (with the use of a supply and demand diagram) how the increase in the price of sugar affects

(continued on page 8)

APPLYING THE THEORY

(continued from page 7)

the equilibrium quantity and price of moonshine. Make sure to indicate which curve shifts and why.

2. How does the change in the moonshine market affect the market for legal whiskey? Again, indicate which curve shifts and why.

3. Suppose North Georgians always chew tobacco while sipping moonshine. Are tobacco and moonshine substitutes or complements? How does the rise in the price of sugar affect the chewing tobacco market?

4. The title indicates that total revenue (sales) of moonshine goes down as costs go up. What does this indicate to you about the price elasticity of demand for moonshine? Explain carefully.

5. Suppose the federal government imposes a federal excise tax on government whiskey of $3.40 per gallon. How would such a tax affect the equilibrium quantity and price of federal whiskey? How would the tax affect the whiskey market?

Solutions

1. Sugar is a factor of production. When its price rises, this is exactly equivalent to an increase in "labor and material costs" in the numerical example of the supply curve for shirts shown in this chapter. Such a change will shift the supply curve leftward at each P, or equivalently, upward at each Q. The equilibrium price of moonshine will rise and the equilibrium quantity of moonshine fall.

2. Legal whiskey and moonshine are substitutes. A rise in the price of moonshine will increase the demand for legal whiskey (at each P). The demand for legal whiskey shifts to the right, which results in a rise in both the equilibrium price and quantity of legal whiskey.

3. Complements—they are used together. When the price of sugar results in an increase in the price of moonshine, the demand for chewing tobacco in North Georgia decreases (or equivalently, shifts leftward at each P). The

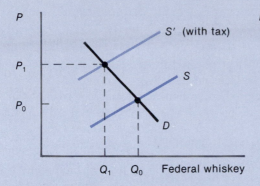

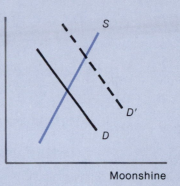

equilibrium price and quantity of chewing tobacco decrease.

4. In this case, an increase in the price of moonshine must have resulted in a proportionately larger decrease in the amount demanded. (Why?) As a result, we can infer that the price elasticity of demand in this price range must be greater than one. Another clue is the assertion in the article that legal whiskey is a good substitute for moonshine in the price range considered.

5. The tax would shift the supply curve of federal whiskey up by $3.40 (see

above at each Q) to reflect the higher cost per gallon as a result of the tax. The equilibrium price would rise and the equilibrium quantity fall (the exact amount of the price rise depends on the supply and demand curve price elasticities). The higher price of federal whiskey shifts the demand curve for moonshine to the right (at each P) because they are substitutes.

Source: Reprinted by permission of *The Wall Street Journal*. © Dow Jones & Company, Inc., July 30, 1975. All rights reserved.

The goal of this chapter is to show that the simple constructs of demand and supply can be used to answer many complex and important questions.

DEMAND CURVES
1.1

Demand curves are simply a graphical representation of preferences for a particular good. The shape of the demand curve tells the economist a good deal about the level of desire for the good in question. Some goods are so important that even large increases in prices do not result in a significant decrease in purchases. An example is a diabetic's demand for manufactured insulin. Other goods are less crucial, and a small rise in price will shift consumption from such a good toward others. An example is ABC laundry soap. A small increase in the price of ABC may cause a large number of consumers to shift from ABC brand to DEF brand. The consumer's desire for ABC over DEF is not as strong as the diabetic's desire for insulin over no insulin. Much more is made of this below, but it is time to derive some demand curves.

An Individual's Demand for a Product
1.1.a

Let us begin by considering Mr. Smith's preferences for some good, say shirts. A simple way to characterize his preferences is to ask, "How many shirts will Smith buy if the price of a shirt is $P?" By asking this question for a large number of potential prices, P, we can fill in an entire schedule of his preferences. Before attempting a graphical representation, let us examine his preferences in tabular form (Table 1.1).

Table 1.1 Smith's demand for shirts	
Price	**Quantity Purchased**
$100	0
90	0
80	1
70	2
60	3
50	5
40	7
30	12
20	15
10	20
5	30
0	30

At $100, Smith decides that shirts are too expensive and buys none during a period, say, a year. This holds until the price drops to $80, where he chooses to buy only one shirt. As the price falls, the number of shirts that he purchases rises because they are becoming less expensive. At a price of $10, he buys 20 shirts. If the price were to fall to $5, shirts would be so inexpensive he might buy some to give to friends. However, even at a price of $0 — i.e., even if shirts were given away freely — he would not take more than 30 shirts, because at that point it becomes a burden to unload them.

Although Smith's preferences may be typical, we do not expect all individuals to have the same preferences for shirts. People differ in a number of respects. In addition to having different inherent preferences, some individuals are richer than others. Personal wealth can affect the number of units that an individual demands at a given price. For example, consider Mr. Roberts, whose annual income is twice that of Mr. Smith. His preferences are described by Table 1.2. Mr. Roberts consumes more than Mr. Smith at every price because he is wealthier. This is not true of all goods. Later we discuss a more systematic way to describe when richer individuals consume more or less than poorer individuals. For the present it suffices to point out that the demand schedules are different.

It is a simple matter to move from the tabular representation of preferences to the more standard graphical one. Figure 1.1 plots Smith's quantity demanded against the announced price.[1] Similarly, Figure 1.2 plots Roberts' demand.

Table 1.2 Roberts' demand for shirts	
Price	**Quantity Purchased**
$100	1
90	2
80	2
70	3
60	5
50	8
40	9
30	15
20	30
10	35
5	35
0	35

---

[1]Mathematically inclined readers may be puzzled to find the independent variable, price, on the vertical axis and the dependent variable, quantity, on the horizontal axis. This is a convention that started many years ago in economics and, despite some awkardness at this point, provides some advantages later when we relate demand curve to the cost curves of the firm.

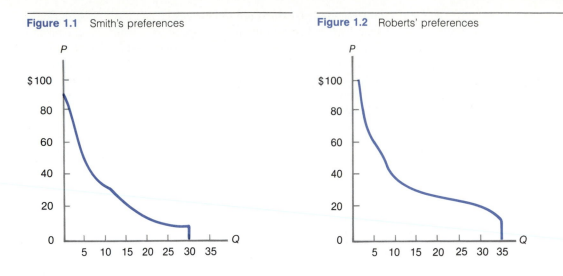

Figure 1.1 Smith's preferences

Figure 1.2 Roberts' preferences

The Market Demand Curve
1.1.b

Figure 1.3 plots the sum of the demand curves. Note that the sum is "horizontal"; i.e., for each price, we sum the quantities demanded by the individuals. This is because we want the total-demand curve to be interpreted as the quantity that the entire economy purchases at any given price. For example, at a price of $30, Smith consumes 12 and Roberts consumes 15, yielding a total demand of 27 units.

Usually, it is the economy-wide demand curve that is of interest. As economists, businessmen, or policymakers, we are generally less concerned about who buys what at a given price than we are about how much of a particular good is purchased at that price by consumers taken together.

Demand Curves and *"Ceteris Paribus"*
1.1.c

A term that finds frequent use in economics is *ceteris paribus*, which translates to: "other things equal." Whenever we consider any functional relationship, such as the one between the price of a good and the quantity purchased at that price, there are always other things that are held constant, either implicitly or explicitly. When we look at demand curves, we are varying the price of the good in question, but holding constant the consumer's income and the prices of other goods in the economy. Most important are the prices of close substitutes or complements.

A *close substitute* is a good that (in the consumer's mind) performs essentially the same function as the original, so that small increases in the price of one good may shift a large number of consumers toward consumption of the other good.

Part One   Demand, Supply, and Markets: An Introductory Look

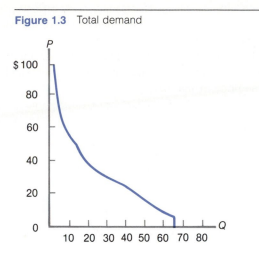

Figure 1.3 Total demand

The example given above was that of ABC and DEF laundry soaps. When the price of a DEF soap rises, the demand for ABC soap rises, as some consumers shift from DEF to ABC.

A *complement* is a good that is used in conjunction with the particular good in question. For example, a left shoe is a complement to a right shoe, and gasoline and automobiles are also complements. When a complement becomes more expensive, the demand for the product in question falls as well. If left and right shoes were purchased separately, then an increase in the price of left shoes would reduce the demand for right shoes, since what the consumer usually cares about is the price of a pair of shoes — and increases in the price of left shoes increase the price of a pair.

Movements along, versus Shifts in, the Demand Curve
1.1.d

When we say that there has been an increase in *the demand* for a good, as opposed to an increase in the amount demanded, we are talking about a shift in the entire demand curve. We have already examined one kind of demand shift. Roberts' entire demand curve lies to the right of Smith's because Roberts has twice as much income. If we think of Smith and Roberts as having identical tastes, with differences in their behavior relating to income differences, then Smith's demand curve would shift to Roberts' if Smith's income were to double. Thus, we would say that the effect of a doubling of income is to shift Smith's demand curve to the right. This represents an increase in demand (rather than an increase in the amount demanded) because the quantity demanded by Smith at any given price increases.

Changes in *the amount demanded* are associated with changes in the price of the good in question. When the price of shirts falls from $80 to $70, the amount demanded by Smith rises from 1 to 2 units. This reflects a movement along the demand curve associated with a change in the price of the good (rather than a shift in the curve itself).

Shifts in demand curves are caused by changes in income or in the prices of substitutes or complements. Movements along the demand curve are caused by changes in the price of that particular good.[2]

Substitutability and Narrowness of Definition
1.1.e

When there are other goods in an economy, it is possible that an increase in the price of a particular good will induce customers to buy more of other goods. It is important to know how responsive are purchases to changes in price. Before providing any formal definitions, one intuitive statement can be made:

The ability to substitute away from a good increases with the narrowness of its definition.

An example clarifies the point. Food is a broader category than meat, and meat is broader than hamburger. Suppose that the good in question were food. A rise in the price of food induces little substitution away from it because there exist only poor substitutes for food taken as a whole. If the good is meat, then better substitution possibilities exist. Vegetables are a relatively good substitute for meat, and certainly a better substitute than is, say, housing for food. As the definition of the good becomes even narrower (hamburger) the substitution possibilities are even better. Steak is a "closer" substitute for hamburger than are vegetables for meat. When the definition is extremely narrow (say hamburger purchased at ABC market) the ability to substitute becomes close to perfect. If ABC raises its price, consumers can switch to purchasing from DEF across the street.

Elasticity: A Concise Way to Describe Substitutability
1.1.f

It is desirable to express the amount of substitution away from a good in a concise fashion. The price elasticity of a good is defined as follows:

Price Elasticity of Demand: Price elasticity of demand is the percent of change in the quantity of a good demanded that is induced by a 1 percent change in price. A formal algebraic definition of price elasticity will be provided in Chapter 5.

---

[2]Algebraically, if the demand for good 1 is represented by

$$q_1 = f(P_1; y, P_2, P_3, \ldots, P_N)$$

where q_1 is the quantity of good 1, P_i is the price of good i, and y is income, then $\frac{\partial f}{\partial P_1} dP_1$ represents the movement along a demand curve and $\frac{\partial f}{\partial y} dy$, $\frac{\partial f}{\partial P_2} dP_2$, $\frac{\partial f}{\partial P_3} dP_3, \ldots, \frac{\partial f}{\partial P_N} dP_N$ are all shifts in the demand curve.

To see that this fits with the notions described above, consider the demand for food. Because there are few, if any, good substitutes for food, the price elasticity is very small, that is, close to zero. An increase in the price of food is likely to be accompanied by only trivial changes in the amount of good demanded because there is little that the consumer can do to avoid consumption of this increasingly expensive good. But an increase in the price of hamburger at ABC market is likely to induce some significant movement toward purchase of other types of meat or of hamburger at other markets. At the extreme, the price elasticity is infinite: an infinitesimally small change in the price of a good induces complete substitution away from that good and toward something else.

Although elasticity is not the same as the slope of the demand curve, slope is one of the ingredients in the determination of elasticity. At a given price/quantity point on the demand diagram, flatter demand curves have higher associated elasticities than steeper ones. At one extreme, a perfectly elastic demand curve is a horizontal line so that the smallest increase in the price drives the amount demanded to zero. At the other extreme no increase in price affects the amount demanded, so the demand curve is vertical.

Example
1.1.f.1

The concepts of demand curves and elasticity are important in many business decisions. One example follows:

Consider an entrepreneur who owns two movie theaters. One is located in the entertainment district of a large city. The other is located in a rural community that is 75 miles from the nearest city. The price per ticket is currently $4. The owner is considering a price increase and is trying to determine whether to raise prices in the urban theater, the rural theater, or both. A crucial ingredient to the decision is the effect of the price increase on the number of tickets sold. What are the major factors that the entrepreneur should consider?

A number of answers are possible, but two immediately come to mind and tend to operate in opposite directions. First, recall that the location of the demand curve depends on income. The average income of individuals in the city is likely to be higher than the average income of individuals in the rural community. If this is so and if wealthier people attend more movies, then the profit-maximizing price of movies in the city is almost certainly higher than the profit-maximizing price of movies in the rural community, other things equal. But other things are not equal.

Recall that the ability to substitute away from a good varies with the good in question. Large cities have a number of movie theaters and other entertainment attractions as well. The urban dweller can more easily substitute away from the increasingly expensive movie than can his rural counterpart. This works in the direction of a lower optimal price in the city, where there is a great deal of competition for the consumer's entertainment dollar, than in the country.

The fact that the net effect is ambiguous at this stage is unimportant. What is important is that demand curves and the concept of elasticity allow us to think more systematically about the kinds of issues that face decision makers and policy makers daily.

In the same way that demand curves describe buyers' preferences for a good, supply curves describe the seller's desire to make the good available. The basic idea is simple. Generally, the more someone is willing to pay for a good, the more interested is a seller in supplying it. What is most important in the discussion of supply curves and their shapes is the ease with which production can be expanded to a large scale. For example, a farmer with a great deal of idle land can respond to an increase in next year's price of wheat by expanding the acreage under cultivation. A farmer who has no idle land can expand production only by finding available land that he can rent or purchase. He is unlikely to go to the trouble unless the selling price goes up by a substantial amount. Supply curves are merely a graphical way to describe his willingness to respond with additional goods to an increase in the selling price.

The Individual Firm's Supply Curve and the Market Supply Curve
1.2.a

Consider the supply of shirts by Acron Clothiers. Given the current physical structure, it is straightforward for Acron to produce 10,000 shirts per year. Suppose that the labor and material cost associated with the production of 10,000 shirts in that one-year period were $100,000. Then at a price of $10 per shirt, the firm could just cover labor and material. If the price of shirts fell below $10, no shirts would be produced because the selling price would not even cover the cost of material and labor.[3] So the amount supplied by Acron is zero for any price under $10.

At a price of $10.01, the firm is willing to supply the 10,000 shirts, but if the price were to rise to $20, it might pay to convert some of the facilities previously used to make trousers to shirt production. Suppose that this would yield another 5,000 shirts. If the price were to rise to $50, it might then become profitable to rent sewing machines and move them into the vacant warehouse across the street. This yields another 15,000 shirts, so that the total produced at a price of $50 is 30,000. Table 1.2.1 describes the supply schedule for Acron Clothiers. Alternatively, the schedule can be presented in graphical form. This supply curve is shown in Figure 1.2.1.a.

---

[3]This ignores any complications that are introduced by possible effects of this year's production on next year's demand.

Part One   Demand, Supply, and Markets: An Introductory Look

Table 1.2.1	Acron's supply schedule

Price	Quantity Supplied
$5	0
8	0
10	10,000
20	15,000
30	20,000
40	25,000
50	30,000

Figure 1.2.1.a Acron supplier   **Figure 1.2.1.b** Dayton supplier

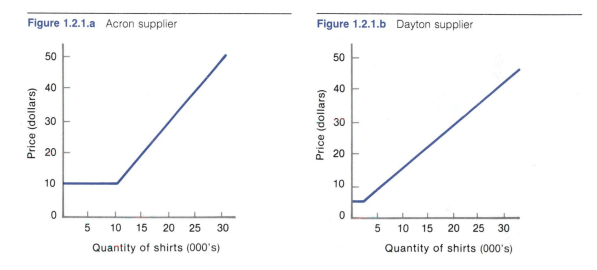

Other firms may face different production possibilities. Their supply schedules are shown in Figures 1.2.1.b and 1.2.1.c.

It is straightforward to go from the individual supply curves to the market supply curve in the manner that applied for demand curves. The horizontal sum of the supply curves of all the firms generates the market supply curve. This is because what we are interested in at the market level is the total amount supplied at any given price, and summing over quantities for a given price provides this information. For example, at a price of 10, Acron supplies 10,000, Dayton supplies 5,000, and Toledo supplies 7,000, implying a total supply of 22,000, given that there are no other shirtmakers in the market at this time (Figure 1.2.1.d).

One point to notice is that the market supply curve tends to be "smoother" than any of the individual supply curves. This is because some of the idiosyncracies in individual firms' behavior are ironed out at the aggregate level. This is analogous to the proposition that averages tend to be smoother than individual observations.

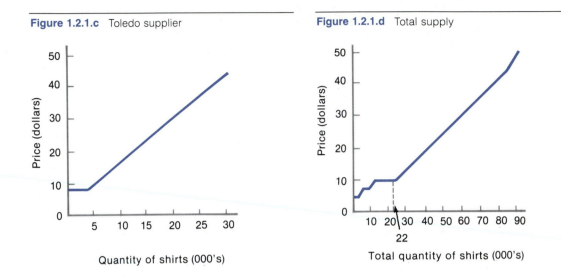

Figure 1.2.1.c Toledo supplier

Figure 1.2.1.d Total supply

Quantity of shirts (000's)

Total quantity of shirts (000's)

Movements along, versus Shifts in, the Supply Curve
1.2.b

As with demand curves, it is important to distinguish movements along a supply curve from shifts in the curve. An increase in the supply of a good refers to a shift in the entire schedule of supply, that is, to a shift in the supply curve. An increase in the amount supplied corresponds to movement that occurs as the price of the good in question increases. As such, it is a movement up the supply curve without any shifts implied. Above, movements along the supply curve occurred when the price of shirts changed. For example, when the price rose from $10 to $30 the number of shirts supplied by Acron increased from 10,000 to 20,000. This experiment holds, all other things being constant.

In the case of demand, the most important other things were (*a*) prices of substitutes and complements and (*b*) income. In the case of supply, the most important other things are (*a*) prices of the factors of production and (*b*) technology. First consider changes in the price of factors of production. Suppose, for example, that the price of labor and material fell from $10 per shirt to $7 per shirt. This means that Acron would be willing to supply the first 10,000 for $7. Additionally, it might also imply that Acron would convert facilities at $17 per shirt rather than at $20 per shirt, and so forth. This is reflected in a shift in supply curves as shown in Figure 1.2.2.

A similar shift could have occurred because of a change in technology, rather than in the prices of factors of production. For example, the price of labor and material could have remained the same, but some technological innovation might have made shirt production more rapid, lowering the amount of labor necessary per shirt. Suppose that this change in technology lowered labor usage sufficiently to reduce the cost of shirt production initially to $7 per shirt. Again, the shift that would occur is the one shown in Figure 1.2.2.

Part One   Demand, Supply, and Markets: An Introductory Look

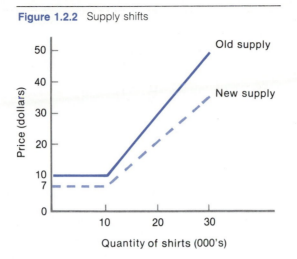

Figure 1.2.2 Supply shifts

Quantity of shirts (000's)

Elasticity of Supply
1.2.c

The elasticity of supply is analogous to the elasticity of demand. It describes the responsiveness of sellers to a change in the price of the product. The definition is:

Elasticity of Supply: The elasticity of supply is the percentage change in quantity supply induced by a 1 percent change in price.

The price elasticity of demand was a more precise way to discuss the consumer's willingness to substitute one good for another. The elasticity of supply is a precise way to describe the seller's ability to supply more of the product at nearly the same cost.

Let us consider two extreme cases: First, suppose that the good we are discussing is raw fish, which gourmets know must be eaten within hours of being caught or the quality deteriorates significantly. A fisherman brings his catch to the market and offers it for sale. If its price is $10 per pound, he will sell the entire catch. If the price rises to $15 per pound, he has no more to sell so he still supplies the same amount. Even if the price were to fall to $5, since the fish cannot be stored, the fisherman continues to supply the entire amount. His supply of fish is perfectly inelastic, that is, it is totally unresponsive to price because a 1 percent change in price induces no change in the quantity supplied. Figure 1.2.3.a shows that situation.

The opposite situation is shown in Figure 1.2.3.b. This corresponds to a good of which the supply is perfectly elastic. For example, suppose that this is the supply of GM stock by one brokerage house on Wall Street on October 17, 1989, at 2:03 P.M. If the market price of the stock at that point is $80, then this brokerage house is willing to supply not only one share, but two, three, five hundred, or ten

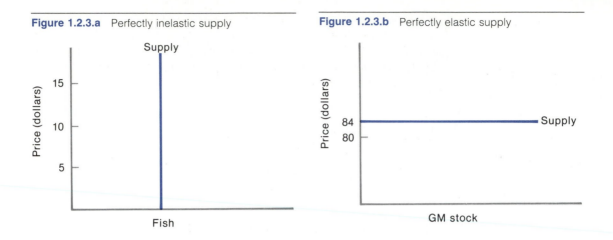

Figure 1.2.3.a Perfectly inelastic supply

Figure 1.2.3.b Perfectly elastic supply

thousand shares at that price plus brokerage fee because it can always acquire those shares to sell from the market. Thus, the supply is perfectly elastic because the seller can supply more of the good at the same cost.

Supply Elasticities in the Short and Long Run
1.2.d

The elasticity of supply tends to be greater in the long run than in the short run because it is easier to increase the amount produced when the firm has more time in which to do it. This is obvious if one considers agricultural products. Suppose that the price of tomatoes rises unexpectedly on a given day. There is little that farmers can do to supply more tomatoes because it takes considerable time to grow them. Thus, the supply of agricultural products tends to be very inelastic in the short run.

If the price increase were expected to persist, then farmers would respond to the change by allocating more acreage to tomato plants and less to other crops. Over a few-month period, the number of tomatoes to be sold could respond significantly to price increases.

Roughly speaking, then, supply curves tend to be flatter in the long run than in the short run. The long run offers opportunities to expand output that are not available instantaneously.

MARKET EQUILIBRIUM
1.3

Virtually all of the questions that are of interest in economics involve market equilibrium and how that equilibrium shifts with changes in factors that affect the supply or demand curves. Roughly speaking, equilibrium is the situation that results as supply and demand interact in the marketplace to determine a quantity

Part One   Demand, Supply, and Markets: An Introductory Look

bought and sold and a stable price. Much of the time, it is changes in prices that are of concern to planners, but just as frequently quantities sold are of importance. In fact, an equilibrium determines both simultaneously, and it is rarely sensible to talk about one without also being cognizant of the other.

We define market equilibrium as:

Market Equilibrium: A price–quantity combination that results from the interaction of the supply curve and the demand curve such that at the indicated price, the quantity demanded equals the quantity supplied. The equilibrium has the property that once the market settles on that point it stays there unless either supply or demand shifts. Additionally, a market that is not at the equilibrium price–quantity combination moves toward that point.

Market Equilibrium: A Graphical Representation
1.3.a

In Figure 1.3.1 the equilibrium in the shirt market is shown at point A. The equilibrium lies at the intersection of the supply and demand curves. As is often the case in economics, something magical occurs at the intersection of two curves, especially when they are supply and demand.

In Figure 1.3.1 the equilibrium price is P_0, and the equilibrium quantity is Q_0. Point A is an equilibrium because all sellers can sell as many shirts as they want to at the equilibrium price, P_0, and all consumers can buy as many shirts as they want to at price P_0. At price P_0, sellers want to supply Q_0 of shirts since point A is on the supply curve. At price P_0, consumers want to buy Q_0 of shirts since point A is on the demand curve. Supply equals demand, so there are no dissatisfied buyers and no dissatisfied sellers. This is the essence of an equilibrium.

This does not imply, of course, that consumers would not be happier if they could buy more at a lower price. Similarly, sellers would be happier if they were able to supply more goods at a higher price. But given that the price is P_0, all who want to sell can do so and all who want to buy can do so at that price.

There is no reason for the economy to move away from point A once that situation has been attained. Point A therefore meets the first condition for qualifying as an equilibrium: Once the market settles at that point it stays there. All agents are satisfied. But what if for some reason the price were not P_0, but rather P_1?

At P_1, suppliers want to supply S_1 of the good and consumers want to buy D_1 of the good. Since S_1 exceeds D_1, a *surplus* exists. Some suppliers who would like to sell shirts at price P_1 will be disappointed because there are not enough buyers to go around. But a disappointed seller has another course of action. Rather than go home with the shirt in his possession, he can compete by undercutting the price of those sellers who threaten to be successful. He can offer to sell a shirt at a price less than P_1 to a buyer who would have bought from another seller at P_1. This strategy is superior to not making a sale at all. But then the other seller is disappointed. He retaliates by cutting the price even lower. The price falls until it reaches P_0. At P_0 there are no disappointed sellers, nor are there disappointed

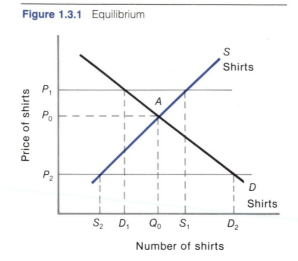

Figure 1.3.1 Equilibrium

buyers. Supply equals demand, so the market—previously not at an equilibrium—moves to the equilibrium at A.

Notice that the surplus that existed when the price was P_1 was eliminated by two forces. First, as the price fell from P_1 to P_0, sellers experienced a reduced desire to sell shirts. At the lower price of P_0, sellers wanted to sell Q_0 of the good rather than S_1. At the same time, the fall in price stimulated the desire by consumers to purchase the good. When the price was P_1, consumers wanted to purchase D_1 of the good. When the price fell to P_0, Q_0 of the good was desired. The increase in the amount demanded coupled with the reduction in the amount supplied eliminated the surplus that existed when price was P_1.

A similar situation applies at the other end of the spectrum. Suppose that price were P_2. At P_2, sellers only want to supply S_2 of the good, while consumers want to purchase D_2 of it. Thus, a *shortage* exists since demand exceeds supply. If the price of the good were to remain at P_2, some consumers would be frustrated. Rather than accept this fate, a dissatisfied consumer can offer a seller a price greater than P_2 and secure that shirt for himself. But this leaves another consumer frustrated. That consumer retaliates by offering an even higher price. The process continues until the price is driven up to P_0. At that price all those wanting to buy can and all those wanting to sell can. Thus, if the market starts at a price below the equilibrium, forces exist to move it back to the equilibrium price of P_0.

Note that the shortage was eliminated by the interaction of two forces. As the price rose from P_2 to P_0, sellers became more anxious to supply the good and the quantity supplied rose from S_2 to Q_0. At the same time, the rise in price dampened consumer desire for the good and the amount demanded fell from D_2 to Q_0. Both factors worked to eliminate the surplus, so supply equaled demand at price P_0.

Part One   Demand, Supply, and Markets: An Introductory Look

Again, a market at the equilibrium point remains there, and one that is not at an equilibrium moves there.

Effects of Changes in Demand on the Equilibrium
1.3.b

Armed with the concepts of supply, demand, and market equilibrium, it is now possible to answer the kinds of substantive questions that business leaders and policymakers ask of economists. The first kind of question is about changes in demand curves and the impact on market prices and quantities.

Suppose, for example, that we are concerned about what will happen to the price and quantity sold of automobiles as the economy moves from bad times to good times. The relevant variable that will change is income. As economic conditions improve, the wealth level of the average citizen rises. Along with this increase in income is an increase in the demand for most goods. Automobiles are one such good. Recall that the kind of change brought about by an increase in income is a shift in the entire demand schedule, rather than a movement along it. The situation is illustrated in Figure 1.3.2.

The demand for automobiles when times were bad was D_0. The supply curve of automobiles (assumed to be stable for now) is fixed at S. During bad times the equilibrium price and quantity were P_0 and Q_0, respectively. With the start of good times, the demand for automobiles shifts to D_1. (Note that there is nothing that requires that D_1 be parallel to D_0. This is a function of consumer preferences.) If the price were to remain at P_0, then a shortage equal to $Q' - Q_0$ would exist. D_0 is no longer relevant and with supply and demand curves S and D_1, shortages result at a price of P_0. A shortage implies that consumers compete for the scarce goods and drive the price up. This process continues until the price rises to P_1, the new equilibrium price and quantity is Q_1. Notice that Q_1 is smaller than Q'. Some of the increased demand is discouraged by the price increase that occurs. What is clear, however, is that an increase in demand can never result in a decrease in price or in a decrease in quantity sold.

What factors affect the magnitude of the price and quantity change? Obviously, the size of the demand shift will have a major impact. If D_1 were situated very close to D_0, then there would be little change in price. Additionally, the slope or elasticity of the supply curve plays a major role. If the supply curve were steeper than S, price would rise by more and quantity would rise by less than shown. In an extreme case, where supply is perfectly inelastic, all of the change in demand is manifested in a rise in price with no increase in quantity, as shown in Figure 1.3.3.a. At the other extreme, with a perfectly elastic supply curve, all of the increase in demand shows up as an increase in quantity sold, without any change in price. This is shown in Figure 1.3.3.b.

Although the shape of the supply curve has a major impact on the effects of demand changes on quantity and price, it is important to recognize that supply and demand curves are independent. The shift in demand did not bring about

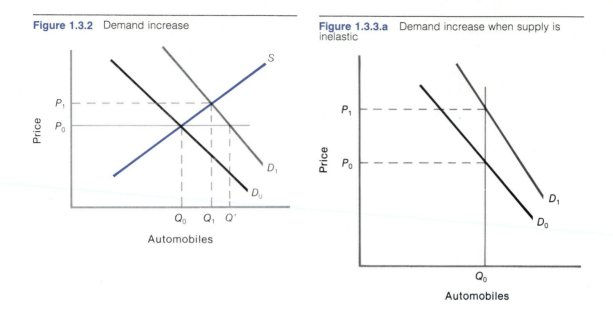

Figure 1.3.2 Demand increase

Figure 1.3.3.a Demand increase when supply is inelastic

a shift in supply. It changed the amount supplied because the equilibrium price is higher in the new situation than in the old, inducing firms to supply a larger quantity.

Effects of Changes in Supply on Equilibrium 1.3.c

Let us pursue the example of the automobile market. Suppose that we are concerned now about the effects of an increase in the price of steel on the price of automobiles and the amount of automobiles sold. Steel is an input into the production of automobiles, so an increase in its price shifts the supply curve. To induce producers to supply a given number of cars, a higher price must be offered. The change is shown by the shift from S_0 to S_1 in Figure 1.3.4.

Note that as with demand curves, there is no reason that the shift in the supply curve must be a parallel one. Later, when cost relationships are considered more explicitly, we can say more about the exact nature of the shift. For now, however, it suffices to recognize that the supply curve shifts leftward.

The equilibrium price rises from P_0 to P_1 and the equilibrium quantity falls from Q_0 to Q_1. At the old price of P_0, a shortage of $Q_0 - Q_1$ exists. Competition for the scarce goods drives the price up to P_1. Two forces act to eliminate the shortage. The higher price makes producers willing to supply more goods to the market. At the same time, the higher price makes some buyers unwilling to purchase the good as the market moves up the demand curve.

It is interesting that a decrease in supply reduces quantity sold, but increases price. Contrast this with a decrease in demand, which reduces quantity sold, but decreases price.

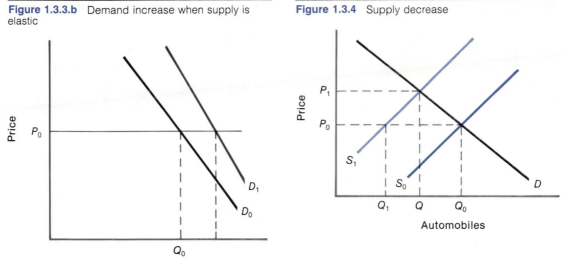

Figure 1.3.3.b Demand increase when supply is elastic

Figure 1.3.4 Supply decrease

As before, the shift in the supply curve changed the amount demanded, but did not shift demand. Demand and supply curves are independent. Of course, the shape of the demand curve is crucial in determining the amount of price change associated with a decrease in supply. If the demand curve were perfectly inelastic, then all of the change in supply would manifest itself in an increase in price. At the other extreme, if the demand curve were perfectly elastic, then the entire change would show up as a decrease in quantity sold, but the price would remain the same. The two extremes are illustrated in Figures 1.3.5.a and 1.3.5.b.

A Few Sample Questions
1.3.d

In this subsection, we illustrate the power of the simple supply and demand analysis by examining a few questions that might arise in the context of simple exchange, sophisticated business, or government.

A Barter Economy
1.3.d.1

To begin, consider what would happen in a primitive economy that did not have money as we usually think of it and exchange is of the simplest form. The society's products are limited, consisting, say, of rice, bananas, and beads. Suppose that there are 300 people on the island and suppose that in the initial equilibrium, 150 produce rice, 125 produce bananas, and 25 are artisans, fashioning beads into necklaces.

Suppose, for simplicity, that all islanders have equal ability and can enter any of the three occupations. Specialization occurs because more can be produced by

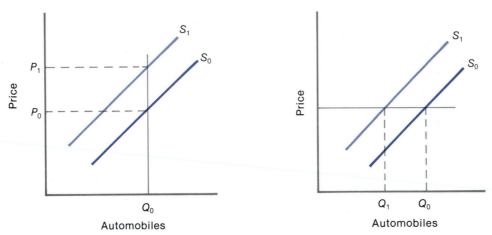

spending all of one's work time in one activity than by dividing time up over a number of different tasks. (For example, if half the day is spent growing rice and the other half is spent picking bananas, then time is wasted during the commute from the rice fields to the banana groves.)

In this initial equilibrium, it must be the case that all individuals have the same command over resources. This proposition, which will come up many times in the future, is true when individuals have identical abilities and can move freely from one occupation to another. If it were not true, occupational shifts would occur. For example, suppose that banana picking were more lucrative than rice growing. Individuals would enter banana picking and exit rice growing. This would reduce the supply of rice, driving its price up and increase the supply of bananas, driving its price down, until earnings were equated across occupations.

The question that we want to address has to do with crop failure in this economy. Suppose that a banana-craving insect unexpectedly infests the banana groves and destroys half of the banana crop. What does this do to the price of bananas, the price of rice, the price of beads, and to the income of banana growers in the short run?

The basic tools that we have developed in this chapter are sufficient to give a reasonably clear set of predictions. Although the developments of later chapters will assist in refining the analysis, much can be said already.

First, it is necessary to specify prices in terms of some commodity, arbitrarily chosen to be beads. The commodity in which prices are specified is called the *numéraire*. Suppose that, initially, one pound of rice traded for three beads, whereas one banana traded for two beads. The initial situations are shown in Figures 1.3.6.a and 1.3.6.b, where subscripts 0 refer to the situations *before* the crop failures. As stated, the prices, determined by the intersection of supply and demand are at 3 and 2, respectively.

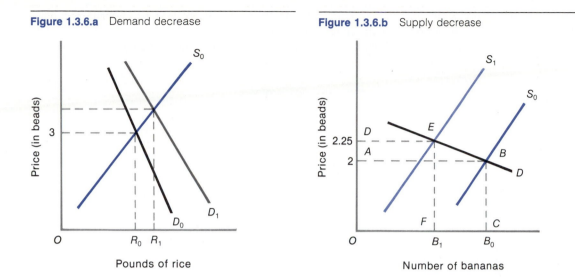

Figure 1.3.6.a Demand decrease

Figure 1.3.6.b Supply decrease

The first effect of the banana crop failure is to shift the supply curve in Figure 1.3.6.b from S_0 to S_1. This immediately raises the bead price of bananas from 2 to 2.25 and this is the primary effect. But in this economy, since there are only two types of food, rice is the only real substitute for bananas. An increase in the price of bananas affects the demand for rice in the same way that an increase in the price of margarine shifts some consumers toward butter. The demand for rice shifts out as a result of the increase in the price of bananas. This raises the bead price of rice as well. (Consequent effects on the demand for bananas are ignored.) Thus, the price of bananas rises, but the quantity of bananas falls. The price of rice rises, and the quantity supplied does as well. In the short run, the ability of rice producers to increase the amount of rice supplied to the market is limited, as reflected by the inelastic nature of the supply curve.

What happens to the income of the banana pickers? The total amount spent on bananas is measured by the price of bananas times the quantity sold. In the initial situation, this amount was given by area $OABC$. If each of the 125 banana pickers is identical, then each one received 1/125 of that amount. After the failure, the total revenue slipped to area $ODEF$, which is smaller than $OABC$. Therefore, 1/125 of $ODEF$ is smaller as well, so each picker's income falls.[4] By contrast, the rice growers benefit as a result of the banana crop failure. The price increase induces some who were eating bananas to eat rice and this causes the total revenue of rice growers to rise. If all rice growers are identical, each now receives 1/150 of a larger number.

---

[4] It is actually possible for the income of banana growers to increase as well. If the demand for bananas were inelastic, then a shift in the supply curve would increase total revenue of the pickers in terms of beads. The individuals who would suffer under these circumstances would be the artisans, whose products are shunned as the economy moves to depression conditions.

In the long run, movements from one occupation to another take place in response to different incomes available across occupations. The nature of these movements is quite complex, however, and we leave that analysis to later chapters.

An Example from the Corporate Sector
1.3.d.2

Let us move to a modern economy and a more current problem. The scene is the personal computer market, which has taken off in recent years. You are the president of Modern Computers, Inc. Your firm was the first to market personal computers on a large scale, but the market has become quite competitive, with 20 firms dividing total sales about equally. You anticipate two developments during the next year and you are interested in being able to predict what will happen to the price of personal computers this year as a result of those developments. The first is that the computer operators' union has agreed to major wage concessions. (Computer operators are used only with large, mainframe computers.) The second is that a new chip has been invented, which makes production of personal computers only about half as expensive as they were previously.

The initial situation is shown by the intersection of D_0 and S_0 in Figure 1.3.7.

The wage concession by computer operators is likely to reduce the price of using mainframe computers. Since mainframes are a substitute for personal computers, this reduction in mainframe price shifts the demand for personal computers to the left, reflecting a decrease in demand. This is illustrated by the shift to D_1.

The change in chip technology reduces the cost of producing personal computers. This does so not only for Modern Computers but also for all computer companies in the personal computer industry. The result is to cause an increase in the supply of personal computers, shifting the supply curve rightward. This is illustrated by the shift from S_0 to S_1.

The result of the two developments is unambiguous: Prices will necessarily fall over the year. Part of that price fall will be offset by cost reductions as a result of the new technology. But part is likely to imply a reduction in the profits of Modern Computers, because the decrease in demand caused by the wage concessions in the rival industry is not balanced by a concomitant cost reduction. Note further that although the direction of price movement is clear, the quantity sold may rise or fall, depending on the relative strengths of the supply and demand shifts.

Decision makers in business often encounter this kind of ambiguity in the problems they face. To translate this analysis into the concrete terms that are required in an actual business decision, it is necessary to obtain more precise estimates of the effects of the various economic forces involved. This often requires the personal judgment of the decision maker in addition to the use of various statistical techniques.

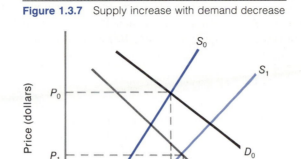

Figure 1.3.7 Supply increase with demand decrease

Government Policies
1.3.d.3

Many of the questions in which economists are interested center around government policy — its effects on output and its distribution. The policy that we
consider here is a subsidy on the production of milk. Suppose the government
is considering the following policy: For every gallon of milk that the dairy
farmer produces, he receives a direct payment of $.15 from the federal gov-
ernment. The government is interested in determining what this policy will do to
the price that consumers pay for milk. Additionally, the senator from Wisconsin
favors the policy while the senator from Florida opposes it. The Department of
Agriculture would like to understand why before proceeding with the subsidy.

The first question is what happens to the price of milk that consumers pay
and the quantity of milk sold. This is easily analyzed by an examination of Figure 1.3.8. The most obvious effect is that the supply curve of milk shifts from
S_0 to S_1. Note that the $.15 subsidy now is like an increase in the price that
producers receive, but not an increase in the price that consumers pay. Thus, with
the subsidy, farmers are willing to produce as much milk at a consumer-paid price
of $.85 as they would without the subsidy and a consumer-paid price of $1.00.
Our prediction about the shift in the supply curve is very precise because the only
direct effect of the subsidy is to change the amount received by producers for any
given price.

The quantity of milk sold will surely rise, but the extent of the rise depends
on the elasticity of demand for milk. The demand for milk is likely to be quite
inelastic so that most of the effect of the shift in supply is likely to be a decrease
in the price paid by consumers, rather than an increase in the amount of milk
produced.

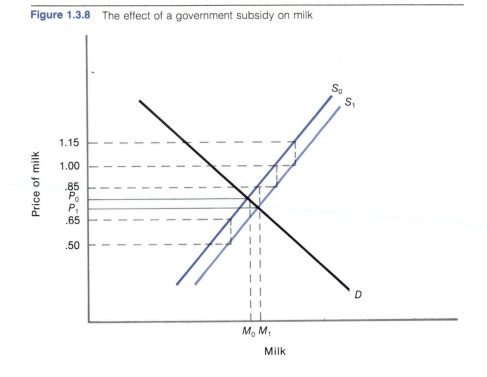

Figure 1.3.8 The effect of a government subsidy on milk

Even though the price has fallen, it is clear that producers are better off as a result of the subsidy. Before, they sold M_0 at a price of P_0. Now they sell M_1 (which exceeds M_0) at a price of P_1. Although P_1 is less than P_0, the price received by producers is $P_1 + \$.15$ or $\$.85$. That amount, $\$.85$, is larger than P_0, so producers must be better off. They always have the option to sell only M_0 at $\$.85$ and that clearly dominates selling M_0 at P_0. The fact they choose to sell M_1 must make them better off.

That the senator from Wisconsin favors the subsidy is now clear because Wisconsin is a milk-producing state. But why should the senator from Florida oppose it? There are two reasons. First, Florida engages in relatively little milk production so its population is not likely to benefit from the subsidy as producers. Furthermore, as will be shown in later chapters, the cost of the subsidy to Floridians necessarily exceeds the benefit received in lower milk prices. The second reason is that milk and orange juice are substitutes, at least to some extent, and Florida is a major producer of orange juice. A fall in the price of milk shifts the demand for orange juice to the left as shown in Figure 1.3.9. This implies a decrease in the quantity of orange juice sold and a decrease in the price at which it sells. Both of these effects make orange juice producers worse off.

Part One   Demand, Supply, and Markets: An Introductory Look

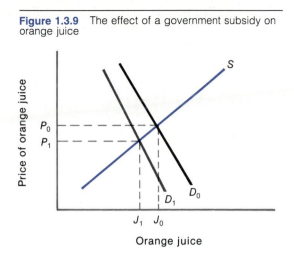

Figure 1.3.9 The effect of a government subsidy on orange juice

SYNOPSIS 1.4

This chapter illustrates that a large class of important questions can be answered with the simple tools of supply and demand. As the book progresses, the analyses become more sophisticated and complex. This allows us to answer more subtle questions with additional accuracy and detail. But the underlying theme is the same: There are no issues in economics that cannot be reduced to questions of supply and demand. At some level, these notions can incorporate all of the complications and difficulties that reality imposes on the analyst.

2 Theory of Utility and Preferences

According to a newspaper article included in the "Applying the Theory" section of this chapter, in 1981 England imposed two tax increases on cigarettes, which raised the tax by 30 percent. Will this decrease the quantity of cigarettes smoked in England? Would it have been more effective to increase the tax on cigarettes with high tar and nicotine, rather than on all cigarettes? To answer these questions, we will need to look behind the demand curve defined in the previous chapter. This chapter begins that process by examining consumer "preferences" (or tastes) in detail. It will be an important step toward answering the questions posed at the beginning of this paragraph. ■

APPLYING THE THEORY

Tax Increases Persuade Britons to Kick Expensive Smoking Habit

LONDON — After puffing doggedly through years of alarming reports on the risk to their health, hundreds of thousands of British smokers have kicked the habit in the past six months — persuaded by savage tax increases.

Tobacco company executives, reporting a 10 percent drop in sales, say this time smokers are sticking to their resolution.

A survey in *The Guardian* newspaper described it as "the biggest and most abrupt change in national smoking habits since cigarettes were introduced at the turn of the century," and estimated that 2 million of Britain's 17 million adult smokers have quit.

Their will was stiffened by two 1981 tax increases. In an austere March budget, the Conservative Government slapped an extra 30 cents on the tax for a pack of 20.

It followed with another increase in July, sending the tax up 30 percent in six months and the average price of a pack to the equivalent of about $2.50.

The tobacco companies, which report falling profits, are due to add an additional 3 cents in the fall.

The treasury collects 75 percent of the retail price. It will get an estimated $10 billion this year.

"I think any industry which has to carry this kind of burden is bound to be worried," said a spokesman for the Tobacco Advisory Council, which represents manufacturers.

Britons now pay up to three times more for cigarettes than do other Western Europeans. Smoking is considered the single biggest cause of premature deaths, killing at least 50,000 Britons a year, mainly through heart disease and lung cancer.

Since the mid-1960s, the health department has been reeling out statistics and eminent physicians' reports. It has been backed by compulsory health warnings on cigarette packs and "voluntary" agreements with tobacco corporations to curb advertising, including a ban on television ads.

Even so, cigarette consumption has fallen only gradually until now, but smokers' determination to quit has been aroused as never before by Chancellor of the Exchequer Sir Geoffrey Howe. The downturn is most marked among the professional classes — only 21 percent now smoke. A 1980 Government survey indicated that 39.5 percent of adult Britons smoked.

Herbert Bentley, assistant managing director of Imperial Tobacco, the largest British manufacturer, said there is no sign of recovery in consumption. He estimated the overall drop for the year will be between 8 and 15 percent.

Mr. Bentley estimates total sales of 107 billion cigarettes this year, compared with 121.5 billion in 1980. Retailers report a run on packs of 10 instead of 20s.

David Simpson, director of the independent, Government-financed anti-smoking organization Action on Smoking and

(continued on page 34)

APPLYING THE THEORY

(continued from page 33)
Health, has been skeptical of sales figures, maintaining that tobacco companies have reported slumps in the past to drum up Government concern about increasing unemployment.

But now Mr. Simpson says: "We are really quite thrilled. We are fairly optimistic there is a real change, which will be a lasting one as long as the chancellor moves to keep prices up."

Question

1. Suppose most smokers care more about whether they smoke than about which type of cigarette they smoke. Draw two separate diagrams of indifference curves for smokers: one set of indifference curves between cigarettes that are high in nicotine and tar and cigarettes that are low in nicotine and tar; a second set of indifference curves between cigarettes (all types) and other goods.

(Note: We will refer back to this article at the beginning of Chapter 3 and consider further questions at that time.)

Solution:

1. Low- and high-tar cigarettes are good substitutes for each other. There are few good substitutes for the general category of cigarettes. This leads to the following set of indifference curves:

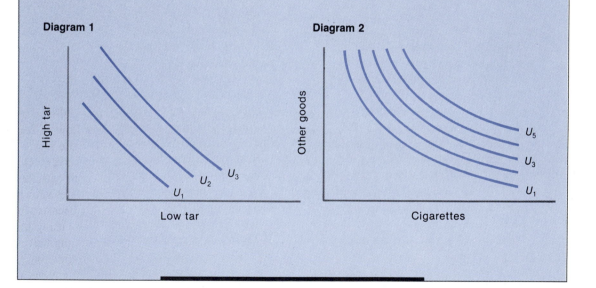

Diagram 1

Diagram 2

Each individual or household has a fairly accurate notion of what its money income will be for a reasonable planning period, say a year. It also has some notion—perhaps not too well defined—of the goods and services it wants to buy. The task confronting every household is to spend its limited money income so as to maximize its economic well-being. No individual or household, of course, actually succeeds in this task. To some extent this failure is attributable to the lack of accurate information; but there are other reasons as well, such as impulse buying. Yet in any event, the more or less conscious effort to attain maximum satisfaction from a limited money income determines individual demand for goods and services.

The last chapter presented a basic view of how economics could be used to answer some simple questions. As the questions become more complex, it becomes useful to call upon more sophisticated machinery. To do this, more formal definitions and deeper analyses are needed. We start by looking behind the demand curves, in search of basic elements with which a description of preferences can be constructed.

Often it is helpful, from a pedagogical point of view, to make simplifying assumptions so that the essence can be presented in the most straightforward manner. As the book proceeds, many of these assumptions are relaxed, and the reader will see that they rarely distort the important meaning of a particular analysis. Additionally, these assumptions rarely create a schism between analytics and economic reality.

The Nature of Commodities
2.1.a

The goods and services consumed by the household are generically called commodities. It is convenient to think of commodities as providing a flow of consumption services per unit of time. The objects of choice are then the services provided by the commodities rather than the commodities themselves. This allows us to handle durable goods such as automobiles, television sets, and houses in a manner strictly analogous to nondurable goods and services such as food, haircuts, and theater tickets. What at first glance might appear to be problems arising from product indivisibilities are easily handled by using this convention: it makes little sense to talk about an individual consuming half an automobile, but it is quite natural to think of using half (or any other fraction) of the services of an automobile per unit of time. Car pooling, rental, or any one of a number of other strategies can be used to adjust the service flow per unit of time.

There is nothing in the theory that severely limits the scope of what we call "commodities." The theory allows us to analyze choices involving where we live, the allocation of time between work and leisure, the amount of income given to charity, and many other dimensions of consumer behavior.

Full Knowledge
2.1.b

We assume that each consumer or family unit has complete information on all matters pertaining to its consumption decisions. A consumer knows the full range of goods and services available in the market; he knows precisely the technical capacity of each good or service to satisfy a want. Furthermore, he knows the exact price of each good and service, and he knows these prices will not be changed by his actions in the market. Finally, the consumer knows precisely what his money income will be during the planning period.

In point of fact, the assumptions introduced above are unnecessarily restrictive so far as demand theory is concerned. To derive demand functions and indifference curves (see below), it is only necessary to assume that (a) the consumer is aware of the existence of some goods and services; (b) he has some reactions to them, that is, he prefers some goods to others; and (c) he has some money income so as to make these reactions significant in the market. Actually, the more rigid set of assumptions contained in the previous paragraph are necessary only when we come to the theory of welfare economics (at the end of the book). But since an assessment of economic welfare resulting from competitive markets is a central task of microeconomic theory, the more restrictive assumptions are introduced at this time.

The Nature of Commodities
2.1.c

A household will consume a large variety of different commodities, and we will refer to this collection of different commodities as a *commodity bundle*. To attain its objective — maximization of satisfaction or utility for a given level of money income — the consuming unit must be able to rank different commodity bundles. That is, the consumer must be able to compare alternative commodity bundles and to determine his or her order of preference among them. To this end we assume that each consuming unit is able to make comparisons among alternative commodity bundles that satisfy the following conditions:

1. For any two commodity bundles, A and B, the consuming unit is able to determine which provides the most satisfaction. If A provides more satisfaction than B, then we say A is *preferred* to B, and if B provides more satisfaction than A, we say B is preferred to A. If both bundles provide the same satisfaction, we say the customer is *indifferent* between A and B.

2. If A is preferred to B and B is preferred to C, then A is preferred to C. Preference is a *transitive* relation. Similarly, if A is indifferent to B and B is indifferent to C, then A is indifferent to C.

An example will help to clarify these concepts.

Suppose there are only two goods, X and Y. The preferences of a given consumer are shown in Table 2.1.1 and illustrated in Figure 2.1.1. Commodity bundle A is preferred to all other bundles. The consumer is indifferent among

Table 2.1.1 Rank ordering of commodity bundles

Bundle	Amount of X	Amount of Y	Rank Order*
A	6	6	4
B	3	5	3
C	4	3	3
D	5	2	3
E	3	4	2
F	1	4	1
G	2	2	1
H	3	1	1

*More preferred bundles are assigned a higher number.

Figure 2.1.1 Ordering of bundles in Table 2.1.1

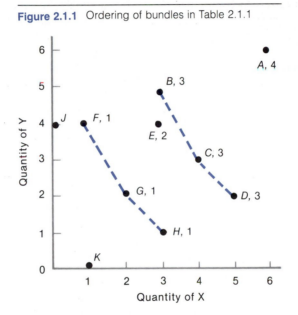

bundles B, C, and D, indicating that this consumer is willing to take less Y if he or she gets enough more X in return. Bundle B is preferred to E (the latter has less Y and the same amount of X). Similarly, E is preferred to F (the latter has less X and the same quantity of Y). Finally, G and H are indifferent to F, the consumer being willing to substitute X for Y in his or her consumption pattern.

Figure 2.1.1, which is often called a *commodity space*, is interpreted as follows: Each point in the space describes an allocation of X *and* Y, not X *or* Y. So at point F, the consumer is considering the allocation of one unit of X and four units of Y. To say that the consumer is indifferent between F and G implies that he is indifferent between the bundle 1X and 4Y and the bundle 2X and 2Y. It does not imply that he is indifferent between 4Y and 1X. That comparison would involve ranking point *J* against point *K*.

The assumptions necessary to analyze consumer behavior can be set out in the following compact form:

Assumptions: (*a*) Each consumer has exact and full knowledge of all information relevant to his consumption decisions — knowledge of the goods and services available and of their technical capacity to satisfy his wants, of market prices, and of his money income.

(*b*) Each consumer is able to make comparisons of commodity bundles such that (*i*) for any two bundles, *A* is preferred to *B*, *B* is preferred to *A*, or the consumer is indifferent between *A* and *B*; (*ii*) if *A* is preferred (indifferent) to *B* and if *B* is preferred (indifferent) to *C*, then *A* is preferred (indifferent) to *C*.

UTILITY AND PREFERENCE
2.2

The analysis of consumer behavior is greatly facilitated by the use of a utility function that assigns a numerical value or utility level to commodity bundles. The reader may find it difficult to accept the idea that the highly subjective phenomenon of consumer preference, which obviously depends on each person's physiological and psychological make-up, can be so quantified. For most of our purposes, however, the particular numerical values assigned to commodity bundles are not of significance in their own right. All that is required of the utility function is that it reflect the same rankings that the consumer assigns to alternative commodity bundles. If the consumer prefers bundle *A* to bundle *B*, the utility function has to assign a *larger* numerical value to bundle *A* than to bundle *B*, but the actual numerical values so assigned are themselves irrelevant. Similarly, if the consumer is indifferent between bundle *A* and bundle *B*, the utility function must assign the *same* numerical value to each bundle, but the particular value so assigned is irrelevant. For example, the rank order assigned to commodity bundles *A* through *H* in Table 2.1.1 can be thought of as the numerical values assigned to these bundles by some utility function. Any other set of numbers, such as 20, 10, 10, 10, 8, 5, 5, 5, which preserved this ranking would do equally well for our purposes. A utility function that assigned the values 10, 9, 8, 7, 6, 5, 4, 3 to bundles *A*, *B*, *C*, *D*, *E*, *F*, *G*, *H*, respectively, would *not* apply, however, since such an assignment of numbers would indicate that bundle *B* is preferred to bundle *C*, whereas the consumer is in fact indifferent between these bundles. In short, all we require of the utility function is that it provide an *ordinal* measurement of the utility provided by commodity bundles, not a *cardinal* measurement.[1]

---

[1]The original approach to utility theory treated utility as *cardinally* measurable. In subsection 2.2.c we review historical developments that led to the modern (ordinal) theory of utility.

The utility function is nothing more than an algebraic description of a consumer's preferences. Table 2.1.1 revealed the consumer's preferences in tabular form and Figure 2.1.1 did the same in graphical form. The algebraic notion of a utility function is somewhat more abstract, but often much easier to analyze and is an important tool of consumer theory.

The Utility Surface
2.2.a

Once it is recognized that only the ordinal properties of the utility function are important for our purposes, no harm is done by considering a specific utility function. Indeed, this is probably the most convenient way to gain an understanding of the ordinal properties in which we are interested. To illustrate with a concrete example, suppose the utility that Smith obtains from consumption of goods X and Y is given by the function

$$U = xy .$$

In words, the utility is the product of the quantities of X and Y consumed by Smith. Using this utility function, Smith derives 100 units of utility from a bundle consisting of 10 units of X and 10 units of Y ($100 = 10 \times 10$). Smith also derives 100 units of utility from a bundle consisting of 5 units of X and 20 units of Y or from a bundle consisting of 1 unit of X and 100 units of Y. Smith is thus *indifferent* among these bundles. However, he prefers any of these bundles to a bundle consisting of 5 units of X and 5 units of Y since the latter has utility of only 25 according to the above function.

Because we are concerned only with the ordinal properties of the utility function (that is, with the ranking assigned to the alternative bundles), there are many other utility functions that would represent Smith's preferences equally well. For example, the utility function

$$V = (xy)^2$$

gives the same preference ranking of the above-mentioned bundles. The bundle consisting of 10 units of X and 10 units of Y has utility of 10,000 with this new utility function, but so do the bundles consisting of 5 X and 20 Y, and 1 X and 100 Y. Hence both U and V tell us that Smith is indifferent among these three bundles even though the *cardinal* value of utility depends on the particular utility function (10,000 compared with 100).[2]

---

[2]Once we have one utility function that correctly reflects the consumer's ordinal preferences, we can construct an arbitrary number of alternative utility functions that reflect the same ordinal preferences. To see how, let $f(z)$ be any function such that $f(z_1) > f(z_0)$ whenever $z_1 > z_0$. Now consider any utility function U that correctly represents the consumer's ordinal preferences. Let $V = f(U)$. If bundle A is preferred to bundle B, then $U(A) > U(B)$, but then $V(A) = f[U(A)] > f[U(B)] = V(B)$, so V also ranks A higher than B. Similarly, if the consumer is indifferent between bundles C and D then $U(C) = U(D)$, but then $V(C) = f[U(C)] = f[U(D)] = V(D)$, so V also shows that the consumer is indifferent between C and D. Additional utility functions can easily be constructed by choosing different transformation functions like $f(z)$.

Utility functions can be represented geometrically by a utility surface such as the one shown in Figure 2.2.1. The utility surface is *OXZY*. Thus, if OX_1 units of X and OY_1 units of Y are consumed per period of time, utility is the vertical magnitude *PP'*. Similarly, if OX_2 and OY_2 are consumed per period of time, total utility is *QQ'*.

Although Figure 2.2.1 looks complicated, it is nothing more than the commodity space of Figure 2.1.1, augmented by a vertical axis that relates the utility associated with the bundle described by a point in the X,Y plane. *Q'* is a point in the X,Y plane and refers to the bundle consisting of OX_2 units of X and OY_2 units of Y. The vertical distance, *Q'Q*, measures the utility associated with bundle *Q'*. For most purposes, the vertical axis is suppressed because the numerical values of utility are unimportant. It is useful, however, to work through the three-dimensional diagram so that an understanding of what is implicit in the future can be gained.

Suppose the rate of consumption of X is fixed at OX_1. The curve *EPRD* then shows the total utility associated with OX_1 units of X and different amounts of Y. If consumption is OY_1, utility is *PP'*; if consumption is OY_2, ($>OY_1$), utility is *RR'* ($>PP'$), and so forth. In like manner, if the consumption of X is held fixed at OX_2 units per period of time, the curve *FSQC* relates total utility to the rate of consumption of Y. The same analysis can be applied to a fixed rate of consumption of Y and a variable rate for X. If the consumption of Y is fixed at OY_1, total utility is *PP'* if OX_1 units of X are consumed per period of time, *SS'* ($>PP'$) if the rate of consumption is OX_2 ($>OX_1$), etc. Thus the curve *GPSA* shows the level of total utility associated with OY_1 units of Y and various rates of consumption of X. Similarly, *HRQB* shows the same thing when the rate of consumption of Y is fixed at OY_2 units per period of time.

The Indifference Curve
2.2.b

The utility surface helps us to focus on the important concept of a constant utility contour or *indifference curve* which is the basis of the modern (ordinal) theory of consumer behavior. This concept may be explained by means of Figure 2.2.2. There are two goods, X and Y, and the total utility surface is *OXZY*, just as in Figure 2.2.1. If OX_1 units of X and OY_3 units of Y are consumed per period of time, total utility is *RR'*. If the consumption of X is greater — at the rate OX_2, for instance — the consumption of Y remaining unchanged, the level of utility is greater. But an essential feature of utility theory is that one commodity may be *substituted* for another in consumption in such a way as to leave the level of total utility unchanged. For example, in Figure 2.2.2, $OX_2 - OX_1$ units of X may be substituted for $OY_3 - OY_2$ units of Y without changing total utility because *P'* and *R'* yield the same utility level. If the rates of consumption are OX_1 of X and OY_3 of Y, total utility is *RR'*. If the rates are OX_2 of X and OY_2 of Y, total utility is *PP' = RR'*. Similarly, OX_3 of X and OY_1 of Y yield total utility of *SS' = PP' = RR'*.

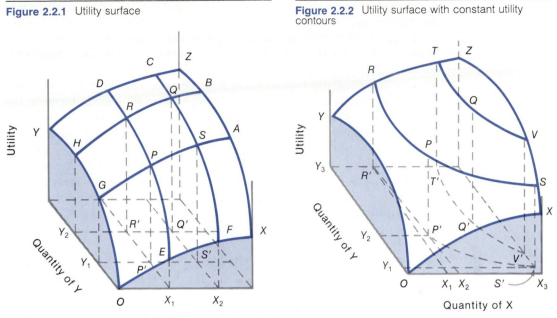

In other words, one may "slice" or intersect the utility surface at the level $RR' = PP' = SS'$ and determine all combinations of X and Y that will yield this constant level of utility. These combinations are shown by the dashed curve $R'P'S'$ in the X,Y plane. Since each combination of X and Y on $R'P'S'$ yields the same level of utility, a consumer would be indifferent to the particular combination he consumed. In like manner, all combinations of X and Y on the dashed curve $T'Q'V'$ yield the same total utility ($TT' = QQ' = VV'$). A consumer would thus be indifferent as to the particular combination consumed. But a consumer would *not* be indifferent between a combination of X and Y lying on $R'P'S'$ and a combination lying on $T'Q'V'$. Each combination on $T'Q'V'$ is preferred to any combination on $R'P'S'$ because the former yields a higher level of utility (for example, $TT' > RR'$).

Curves such as $R'P'S'$ and $T'Q'V'$ are called *indifference curves*.

Indifference Curve: An indifference curve is a locus of points in commodity space—or commodity bundles—among which the consumer is indifferent. Each point on an indifference curve yields the same total utility as any other point on that same indifference curve. If the utility function is given by $U(X_1, X_2, \ldots, X_n)$ where X_1 is the amount of good 1 consumed, X_2 the amount of good 2 consumed, and so on, then an indifference curve is defined as the set of all commodity bundles $(X_1, \ldots, X_n)$ that satisfy the equation $U(X_1, X_2, \ldots, X_n) = c$ where c is the constant level of utility for that indifference curve.

A partial set of indifference curves is shown in Figure 2.2.3. Graphs such as this are called *indifference maps*.[3]

The curve labeled I in Figure 2.2.3 might represent all combinations of X and Y that yield 10 "utils" of utility to a certain person. Similarly II, III, and IV represent all combinations yielding 19, 26, and 30 utils, respectively. The significance of the ordinal approach to utility is the recognition that the specific utility numbers attached to I, II, III, and IV are immaterial — the numbers could be 10, 19, 26, and 30, or 100, 190, 270, 340, or any other set of numbers that *increase*. The salient point is that for the theory of consumer behavior, only the shape of the *indifference map* matters — the underlying *utility surface* is immaterial. The indifference map may be defined on a psychological-behavioristic basis without making use of the concept of measurable utility. The indifference curves and the concept of preference are all that are required — all bundles situated on the same indifference curve are equivalent; if bundle A is preferred to bundle B, then A and B will be on different indifference curves.

Example: When $U(X,Y) = XY$, the indifference curves are given by

$$XY = c$$

where c is the constant value of utility along the indifference curve. It is easy to check that the points $X = 1$, $Y = 5$ and $X = 2.5$, $Y = 2$ are on the same indifference curve (with $c = 5$). Now suppose we change the *cardinal* values of utility by squaring the utility function (see subsection 2.2.a) so $V(X,Y) = [U(X,Y)]^2 = X^2Y^2$. Once again it is easy to check that the points $X = 1$, $Y = 5$ and $X = 2.5$, $Y = 2$ are on the same indifference curve (but now $c = 25$). This illustrates how the indifference curves remain unchanged (except for their numerical labels) under monotonic transformations of the utility function. In other words, the indifference curves convey the relevant *ordinal* information about consumer preferences.

Antecedents to the Modern Theory
2.2.c

It is impossible to find an area of intellectual endeavor, be it music, mathematics, physics, or economics, where theory does not change. Changes in theory are a response to new questions, new empirical findings, and new conceptual breakthroughs. Sometimes the new theory generalizes and extends the old theory and sometimes it replaces the old theory in the revolutionary sense. We can sometimes deepen our understanding of modern theory by examining its intellectual precursors. The historical development of the theory of consumer utility provides a good example.[4]

---

[3]An indifference map is generated by choosing different values for c in the expression

$$U(X_1, X_2, \ldots, X_n) = c.$$

[4]The following discussion is based in part on George Stigler's thoughtful essay "The Development of Utility Theory," *Journal of Political Economy* 58 (August and October 1950). The interested reader will wish to consult Stigler's paper for more detail.

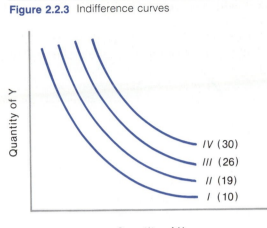

Figure 2.2.3 Indifference curves

Quantity of Y

IV (30)
III (26)
II (19)
I (10)

Quantity of X

Jeremy Bentham (1789) employed the concept of cardinally measurable utility in his attempt to develop a rational system of civil and criminal law. David Ricardo and other economists of Bentham's time did not pursue this approach and it was not until the work of Gossen (1854), Jevons (1871), and Walras (1874) that utility theory started to be generally accepted in economic analysis. Initially, utility was assumed to be measurable and additive, so that "utils" obtained from one commodity were not affected by the rate of consumption of other commodities. To illustrate, if a slice of bread yielded 2 utils and a flagon of beer 6 utils, the consumption of both bread and beer gave 8 utils. This approach is illustrated in Figure 2.2.4. Assume there are two commodities, X and Y, with utility functions for a given individual as shown in Panels A and B, respectively. If the individual consumes X_1 units of X, the measured utility is U_1 as seen in Panel A. Similarly, if Y_2 units of Y are consumed, measured utility is U_2. The additivity assumption says that if X_1 and Y_1 are both consumed in the period, total utility is $U_1 + U_2$. Algebraically, the measurable and additive utility function is expressed as

$$U = U_1(X_1) + U_2(X_2) + \ldots + U_n(X_n)$$

where $U_i(\cdot)$ $(i = 1, 2, \ldots, n)$ is the utility derived from commodity i and X_i is the quantity of commodity i.

While this formulation of utility theory provides certain analytical conveniences, it contains two basic weaknesses. First, it is not clear that utility can be cardinally measured—at least none of the early writers was able to suggest a convincing way of doing so.[5] Second, the idea that utility is independent and

---

[5]In 1918 Irving Fisher suggested that "wantability" might be a better term than "utility" and expressed the belief that in the future the science of measuring human wants would be developed. He proposed the word "wantab" as the *unit* of wantability that such a science would measure. See Irving Fisher, "Is 'Utility' the Most Suitable Term for the Concept It Is Used to Denote?" *American Economic Review* (June 1918).

Figure 2.2.4 Additive and measurable utility

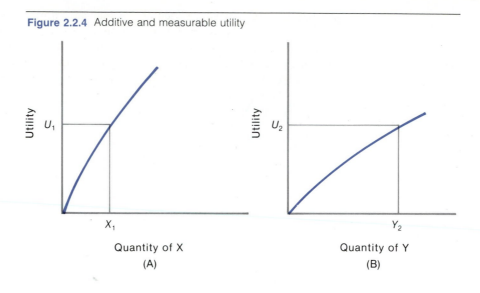

Quantity of X
(A)

Quantity of Y
(B)

additive is excessively restrictive — the utility of tennis balls must partially depend on tennis rackets.

The restriction of utility to additive functions was removed by the work of Edgeworth (1881), Antonelli (1886), and Irving Fisher (1892). These writers assumed that utility was measurable and depended on the quantities consumed but not necessarily in an additive fashion. Thus, the utility function was written

$$U = U(X_1, \ldots, X_n)$$

where X_i is the rate of consumption of commodity i. Total utility thus came to be represented as a surface such as that shown in Figure 2.2.1. Even though these writers were aware of indifference maps, they continued to think of utility as a cardinally measurable quantity. The critical step in removing the measurability assumption was provided by Vilfredo Pareto (1906). Pareto's great insight was to point out that it was not necessary to assume the existence of a unique measurable utility function to obtain indifference curves. Pareto argued that one could *start* with indifference curves, which in his view could be treated as a fact of experience, and derive from them directly all that was necessary for the theory of consumer equilibrium.[6] This was a truly felicitous discovery; it neither denied nor confirmed measurability of utility but showed that the measurability question did not have to be resolved in order to have a viable theory of consumer behavior. In short, the indifference curves depended only on ordinal preferences; because

___
[6]Pareto did not fully exploit his discovery, however. The derivation of consumer equilibrium was accomplished by Slutsky in a very important paper that was published in 1915. See E. E. Slutsky, "Sulla teoria del bilancio del consumatore," *Giornale degli economisti* (1915). The translation, "On the Theory of the Budget of the Consumer," appears in *Readings in Price Theory*, ed. G. Stigler and K. Boulding (Homewood, Ill.: Richard D. Irwin, 1952).

Part One   Demand, Supply, and Markets: An Introductory Look

the indifference curves provided all the relevant information for consumer demand theory, this theory could be built on an ordinal preference foundation.

Within the last 25 or so years, economists have become very interested in studying the effects of risk and uncertainty in economic behavior. As it turns out, efforts to deal with these questions have led to extensions of utility theory which reintroduce elements of cardinality to the analysis. Current research in economics reflects much less concern about the cardinality/ordinality issue than was the case 50 or 100 years ago.

Some of these extensions to situations involving risk will be considered in later chapters. For the present, we will examine consumer preference and demand theory in the certainty case — a model that continues to play a very prominent role in economic theory and analysis.

CHARACTERISTICS OF INDIFFERENCE CURVES
2.3

Indifference curves have certain characteristics that reflect assumptions about consumer behavior. In fact, one of the major uses of indifference curves is to examine the kinds of consumer behavior implied by different preferences, prices, and incomes. For simplicity, assume there are only two goods, X and Y.

Consider the assumptions about consumer behavior in subsection 2.1.c. The first assumption is that the consumer can compare any two bundles in the commodity space and decide that he or she prefers one of them or is indifferent between them. This means that *there is an indifference curve passing through each point in the commodity space.*[7]

Second, indifference curves cannot intersect. This is illustrated in Figure 2.3.1. In Figure 2.3.1, I and II are indifference curves, and the points P, Q, and R represent three different bundles. Bundles R and Q are on different indifference curves, so either R is preferred to Q or Q is preferred to R. Suppose R is preferred to Q. Note that P and Q are both on indifference curve I. By property (*ii*) of subsection 2.1.c, indifference is a transitive relation. Thus, if the consumer prefers R to Q, then by transitivity, P is also preferred to Q. But P and Q are on the same indifference curve so the consumer is indifferent between them. We thus arrive at a contradiction. A contradiction also arises if we assume Q is preferred to R. Hence, intersecting indifference curves, of the kind shown in Figure 2.3.1, are logically precluded by the transitivity assumption.

This does not imply that all consumers will always describe their preferences in a manner consistent with transitivity. For example, one might rank T, P, and R equally, but claim that he is indifferent between Q and S. This is logically

---

[7]Strictly speaking, in order to assure the existence of a continuous utility function that is suggested here, an additional assumption about the continuity of consumer preferences is needed. Readers interested in the conditions needed to establish the existence of a continuous utility function should consult Gerard Debreu, *The Theory of Value* (New York: John Wiley & Sons, 1959), chap. 4.

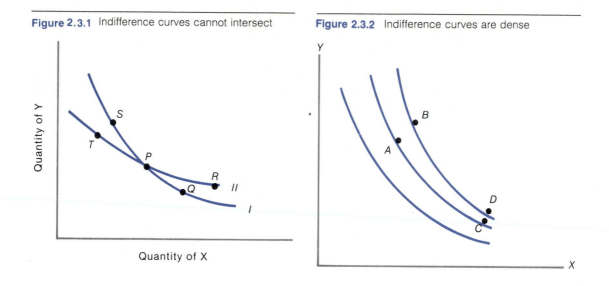

Figure 2.3.1 Indifference curves cannot intersect

Figure 2.3.2 Indifference curves are dense

inconsistent because it implies that S is preferred to T and therefore to P and R and therefore to Q. A consumer has only a limited ability to distinguish between different commodity bundles and might mistakenly describe his preferences in an inconsistent manner. Most consumers, however, when made aware of the inconsistency, straighten things out in an appropriate fashion. This merely points out that informational problems and difficulties of decision making are ignored in the most basic analyses. More advanced theory recognizes these difficulties.

Third (as a consequence of the first and second points made), it is not necessary that indifference curves be parallel in the usual sense. Figure 2.3.2 illustrates a perfectly reasonable indifference map where curves get closer together at the southeast part of the space.

The distance between A and B is larger than the distance between C and D. But if every point in the commodity space has an indifference curve through it, how can all the curves that fit between A and B also fit between C and D without crossing or overlapping?

The answer lies in the fact that indifference curves have no width. There is an infinite number of points between C and D as well as between A and B. The number of indifference curves that can be squeezed between A and B is infinite, but that same number fits between C and D! The confusion arises only because the line drawn on a sheet of paper has width to it, no matter how fine the pen point.

The assumptions of subsection 2.1.c apply to all indifference maps. In many applications, further assumptions are made about consumer preferences and, hence, the character of indifference curves. Some of these are discussed in the next two subsections.

Part One   Demand, Supply, and Markets: An Introductory Look

Negatively Sloped, Convex Indifference Curves — The Standard Case
2.3.a

In many problems of interest it is reasonable to assume that the commodity bundles consist of goods which the individual would like to consume in very large quantities if this were possible. In other words, it is often assumed that "more is better." In the next subsection we shall see that, for a given consumer, not all commodities necessarily have the property that more is better, so it is useful to have a special term when discussing those that do. The term we will use for this is "MIB."

MIB: If a consumer always prefers more units of a commodity to less, that commodity will be called a MIB (*more is better*). Whether a commodity is a MIB or not is strictly a characteristic of the individual *consumer's* preferences and it is conceivable that a given commodity will be a MIB for one consumer but not for another.

Consider two commodity bundles, *A* and *B*. Bundle *A* is said to be *strictly larger* than bundle *B* if it contains more units of every commodity. In the X,Y plane, *A* will be strictly larger than *B* if it lies to the northeast of *B*. If all commodities are MIBs, then a bundle that is strictly larger than another will be preferred by the consumer. It follows that *when the commodity bundles contain only MIBs the indifference curves will be negatively sloped.* The reason is that if both goods are MIB, then the individual can maintain the same level of satisfaction when acquiring more of X only by giving up some of Y.

Another property of indifference curves, which is *not* limited by the assumptions of subsection 2.1.c but which is often introduced for expository convenience, is that indifference curves are *convex*. Convexity means that the indifference curve lies above its tangent at each point, as illustrated in Panel A, Figure 2.3.3. The indifference curve in Panel B is not convex (it is concave).

Summary of Properties of Standard Case Indifference Curves
2.3.a.1

1. An indifference curve passes through each point in the commodity space.
2. Indifference curves cannot intersect.
3. Indifference curves are negatively sloped.
4. Indifference curves are convex.
5. The higher or further to the right is an indifference curve, the higher the bundles on that curve are in the consumer's preference ordering, that is, bundles on higher indifference curves are preferred to bundles on lower indifference curves.

Figure 2.3.3 Indifference curve convexity

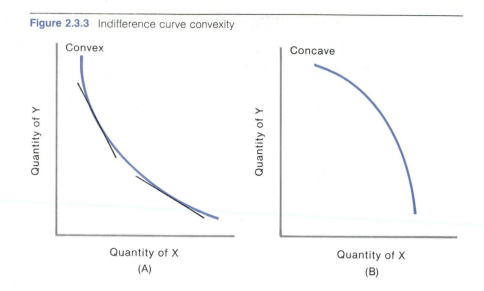

Convex

Quantity of Y

Quantity of X

(A)

Concave

Quantity of Y

Quantity of X

(B)

Characteristics of Indifference Curves—Some Nonstandard Cases 2.3.b

We noted in the last subsection that not all commodities are MIBs. Some commodities are "bads" rather than "goods." Pollution, illness, risk, and tedious work are often cited as examples of bads. Remember that commodities are classified in terms of the preferences of a particular consumer—thus a teetotaler regards wine as a bad, but for a gourmet it will be a good.

To illustrate, suppose that Smith enjoys steak and lobster but believes in moderation when it comes to eating seafood. Smith thinks that steak is a good (in the MIB sense), but that beyond three lobsters a day, eating seafood is a bad. Smith's indifference curves for steak and lobsters are shown in Figure 2.3.4. In this figure, indifference curve III is preferred to II and II is preferred to I. For three or fewer lobsters a day, both steak and lobsters are goods and the lower section of the curves have the standard properties described in subsection 2.3.a. Lobsters are a bad for Smith when consumption exceeds three of them a day. Beyond three lobsters a day the indifference curves have a positive slope because Smith needs more steak to compensate him for the loss of utility from the additional lobsters.

One might object that Smith would simply refuse to eat more than three lobsters a day. The trouble with this objection is that it fails to distinguish clearly between consumer *preferences* and consumer *behavior*. The indifference curves only indicate the consumer's subjective reactions to different potential bundles; they do not by themselves tell us which bundles will actually be chosen. To answer the latter question, we need information about the choices available to the consumer. Suppose, for example, that Smith were offered a choice among bundle *A*, bundle *B*, and bundle *C* in Figure 2.3.4 but only on the condition that

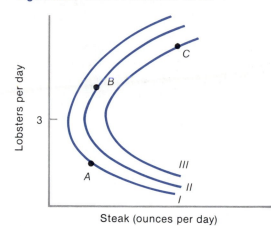

Figure 2.3.4 Smith's indifference curves

he does not throw away or give away any steak or lobster. Bundle C is on indifference curve III, so Smith prefers it to both A and B even though it contains more than three lobsters a day and, indeed, more lobsters than either A or B. This is because C has enough additional steak to compensate Smith for being forced to eat more lobster than he prefers.

A convenient trick to help remember the slope and shape of indifference curves is to imagine being able to walk around the commodity space and to locate oneself in the worst spot. From that vantage point, the indifference curves should look like a solid wall the center of which bends toward the eye. Thus, if both X and Y are goods, the worst location is at zero and looking out at them reveals a solid wall whose center bends toward the eye if they are shaped as in Figure 2.3.2. Suppose X were a bad, like tedious work, and Y were a good, like income. Then the worst spot is at A in Figure 2.3.5 and indifference curves form a curving wall with respect to that spot.

Indifference curves also may have the shape indicated in Figure 2.3.6. The right-angle indifference curves tell us that the consumer prefers to use commodities X and Y in strict proportion (like right- and left-hand gloves). For example, the consumer is indifferent between the bundle (X_0, Y_0) and the bundle (X_0, Y_1) even though $Y_1 > Y_0$. This is because the consumer finds no use for the additional Y without an increase in X. The slope of the ray that connects the origin with the point of right angle is the proportion at which Y must be consumed relative to X. For example, if X were bicycle frames and Y were wheels, the slope of that ray would be 2. For many applications the standard assumptions described in subsection 2.3.a are the most plausible and useful. The examples of this section illustrate how indifference curves can be used to represent nonstandard assumptions that may be of interest in some circumstances. Further examples can be found in the problems at the end of this chapter.

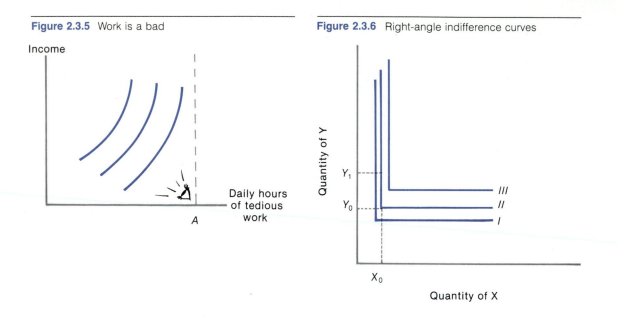

Figure 2.3.5 Work is a bad

Income

Daily hours
of tedious
work

A

Figure 2.3.6 Right-angle indifference curves

Quantity of Y

Y_1

Y_0

X_0

Quantity of X

III

II

I

MARGINAL RATE OF SUBSTITUTION
2.4

An essential feature of the subjective theory of value is that different combinations of commodities can yield the same level of utility.[8] This means that one commodity can sometimes be substituted for another in an amount such that the consumer remains as well off as before. In other words, substitutions of one commodity for another can be made in such a way that the consumer remains on the same indifference curve. It is of considerable interest to know the *rate* at which consumers are *willing* to substitute one commodity for another in their consumption patterns.

Consider Figure 2.4.1. An indifference curve is given by the curve labeled I. The consumer is indifferent between bundle R, containing OX_1 units of X and OY_1 units of Y, and the bundle P containing $OX_2 > OX_1$ units of X and $OY_2 < OY_1$ units of Y. The consumer is willing to substitute X_1X_2 units of X for Y_1Y_2 units of Y. The rate at which he is willing to substitute X for Y, therefore, is

$$\frac{OY_1 - OY_2}{OX_2 - OX_1} = \frac{RS}{SP}.$$

This ratio measures the average number of units of Y the consumer is willing to forgo in order to obtain one additional unit of X (over the range of consumption pairs under consideration). Stated alternatively, the ratio measures the amount of

---

[8]Some writers have questioned the existence of indifference loci on the grounds of the so-called psychological perception threshold. Notable among these is Professor Georgescu-Roegen. For references to some of his works, see the Advanced Readings at the end of Part 1.

Figure 2.4.1 The marginal rate of substitution

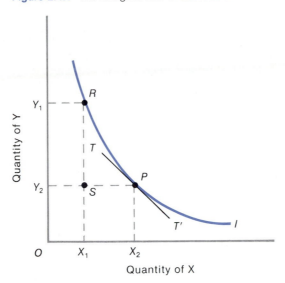

Y that must be sacrificed per unit of X gained if the consumer is to remain at precisely the same level of satisfaction.

The rate of substitution is given by the ratio stated above. But as the point R moves along I toward P, the ratio RS/SP approaches closer and closer to the slope of the tangent TT' at point P. In the limit, for very small movements in the neighborhood of P, the slope of I or of its tangent at P is called the *marginal rate of substitution* of X for Y.

Marginal Rate of Substitution (MRS): The marginal rate of substitution of X for Y measures the number of units of Y that must be sacrificed per unit of X gained so as to maintain a constant level of satisfaction. The marginal rate of substitution is the negative of the slope of an indifference curve at a point. It is defined only for movements along an indifference curve, never for movements among curves.[9]

---

[9]Let the utility function be $U(x, y)$. The change in utility arising from a small change in x (or y) is the *marginal utility* of x (or y). Hence the marginal utility of x is $\partial U / \partial x$ and the marginal utility of y is $\partial U\ \partial y$. As in footnote 3, an indifference curve is given by $U(x, y) = c$ where c is a constant. Taking the total derivative, one obtains

$$\frac{\partial U}{\partial x}\, dx + \frac{\partial U}{\partial y}\, dy = 0.$$

Solving for the slope of the indifference curve, dy/dx, given that $U(x, y) = c$, we find that

$$-\frac{dy}{dx}\bigg|_{u=c} = MRS_{x \text{ for } y} = \frac{\dfrac{\partial U}{\partial x}}{\dfrac{\partial U}{\partial y}}.$$

The marginal rate of substitution of x for y is the ratio of the marginal utilities of x and y.

The convexity of indifference curves implies that the marginal rate of substitution of X for Y diminishes as X is substituted for Y along an indifference curve. This is illustrated in Figure 2.4.2.

I is an indifference curve; and P, Q, and R are three bundles situated on this curve. The horizontal axis is measured so that $OX_1 = X_1 X_2 = X_2 X_3$. Consider first the movement from P to Q. If P is very close to Q, or the amount $X_1 X_2$ is very small, the marginal rate of substitution of X for Y at Q is

$$\frac{OY_1 - OY_2}{OX_2 - OX_1} = \frac{Y_1 Y_2}{X_1 X_2}.$$

Similarly, for a movement from Q to R, the marginal rate of substitution at R is

$$\frac{OY_2 - OY_3}{OX_3 - OX_2} = \frac{Y_2 Y_3}{X_2 X_3}.$$

By construction, $X_1 X_2 = X_2 X_3$; but very obviously, $Y_1 Y_2 > Y_2 Y_3$. Hence the marginal rate of substitution is less at R than at Q. This is also shown by the decreasing slopes of the tangents at P, Q, and R.

Convexity of indifference curves is often intuitively justified on the grounds that, as more and more of commodity X is taken away, the subjective value of an increment of X increases. Thus, as the quantity of X in the commodity bundle decreases, larger and larger increments of Y must be added to compensate the consumer for the loss of a given quantity of X. For example, if a consumer has 1,000 gallons of water a week he may be quite happy to trade an ounce of water for a crust of bread. If he has only a pint of water a week he may be reluctant to trade an ounce of it for a whole bakery.[10]

SYNOPSIS 2.5

■ The modern theory of consumer behavior assumes that individuals can compare commodity bundles and ordinally rank them according to how much satisfaction or utility they provide. This ranking is transitive: if bundle A is preferred (indifferent) to bundle B and if B is preferred (indifferent) to C, then A is preferred (indifferent) to C.

■ Utility functions that reflect the consumer's ordinal preferences can be constructed and are useful analytical and intuitive aids in economics. In the early development of the theory, utility and the associated utility functions were thought of as cardinally measurable and additive. These restrictions were eliminated (for the case of riskless choices) by the early

---

[10]The reader should be cautioned that decreasing marginal utility is neither a necessary nor sufficient condition for convexity of indifference curves. However, if marginal utilities are decreasing and if an increment in X does not diminish the marginal utility of Y, then convexity of the indifference curve is assured.

Part One   Demand, Supply, and Markets: An Introductory Look

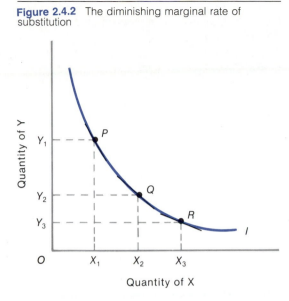

Figure 2.4.2 The diminishing marginal rate of substitution

part of the 20th century. Theoretical developments of the last 20 or 30 years dealing with choice behavior in the presence of risk have reintroduced a certain amount of cardinal measurability, but this is not a point of major concern in current research.

■ Indifference curves are loci of points in the commodity space such that all the commodity bundles on a given indifference curve provide the same satisfaction or utility. Each point in the commodity space is on one and only one indifference curve. In the standard case (discussed in subsection 2.3.a) the indifference curves are negatively sloped and convex.

■ Indifference curves contain all of the essential information about consumer preferences, and the theory of consumer demand can be developed directly in terms of the consumer's indifference map. This will be taken up in Chapter 3.

■ The marginal rate of substitution measures the trade-off between two commodities along an indifference curve. In the standard case, the marginal rate of substitution of X for Y diminishes as X is substituted for Y.

QUESTIONS AND EXERCISES

1. There are three commodities, X, Y, and Z. The following table contains a list of commodity bundles composed of different combinations of these three goods. Determine the rank order of the bundles and list them on a separate sheet. (In this problem all of the commodities are MIBs as described in subsection 2.3.a, and there are no bundles among which the consumer is indifferent.)

	Amount of		
Bundle	X	Y	Z
A	86	88	77
B	86	87	76
C	100	90	80
D	79	80	69
E	85	87	76
F	79	79	68
G	95	89	79
H	80	80	70
I	79	79	69
J	86	87	77

2. In the following table, four commodity bundles, each consisting of two commodities (X and Y), are listed. Also listed are six different utility functions, U_1 to U_6. Which of these six utility functions, if any, are consistent with the assumptions about consumer preferences in the standard case discussed in subsection 2.3.a? When inconsistencies are found, indicate which assumption(s) is violated. (Hint: Plot the bundles on the X,Y commodity space.)

	Amount of		Utility assigned by					
Bundle	X	Y	U_1	U_2	U_3	U_4	U_5	U_6
A	1	1	10	5	2	30	3	7
B	2	3	30	10	2	60	6	7
C	3	1	20	10	4	60	3	7
D	1	4	30	10	4	30	3	7

3. Explain the following statement: The distance between two indifference curves is immaterial; the only relevant issue is which is higher and which is lower.
4. Assume that Jones thinks pollution is bad and automobiles are good. Draw a typical indifference curve in the pollution–automobile commodity space for Jones.
5. Suppose there are two commodities, each of which causes a reduction in total utility beyond a certain rate of consumption (that is, marginal utility for each becomes negative beyond some point).[11] What would be the shape of a typical indifference curve and how would the utility surface look?
6. Two goods, X and Y, are said to be perfect substitutes if the marginal rate of substitution of X for Y is a constant that does not depend on the quantities of X and Y in the commodity bundle. Sketch a typical indifference map for two goods that are perfect substitutes. Can you think of any actual goods or services that are nearly perfect substitutes?
7. Consider a community of three individuals: Jones, Smith, and Brown. Three community projects are being considered, labeled A, B, and C. The table indicates the rank preference of each of the individuals.

---

[11]Marginal utility is defined in footnote 9.

Rank	Jones	Smith	Brown
1	A	C	B
2	B	A	C
3	C	B	A

Suppose community preferences are determined by a majority voting rule. Thus, in comparing project A and project B the community prefers A (Jones and Smith vote for A) to B (only Brown votes for B). Is this community preference rule consistent with the assumptions of subsection 2.1.c?[12]

Additional mathematical skills are assumed in the following problems.

8. Sketch an indifference curve for the utility function $U(X, Y) = 3X^{1/2}Y^{1/2}$. Does the utility function $V(X, Y) = 6 + 8XY + X^2Y^2$ represent the same ordinal preferences as $U(X, Y)$? Does the utility function $W(X, Y) = 3X^{1/3}Y^{2/3}$ represent the same ordinal preferences as either $U(X, Y)$ or $V(X, Y)$?

9. At each point along a given indifference curve in X,Y space, we can calculate the marginal rate of substitution

$$MRS = \frac{U_X}{U_Y} = -\frac{dY}{dX}\bigg|_{U=c}$$

where $U(X, Y)$ is the utility function, $U_X = \partial U/\partial X$, and $U_Y = \partial U/\partial Y$, and we also can calculate the ratio Y/X. In this fashion we can define a function with Y/X as the dependent variable and MRS as the independent variable.[13] In some situations we wish to know how Y/X changes as the MRS changes. The response of Y/X to changes in MRS along a given indifference curve is called the elasticity of substitution (σ) between Y and X and is mathematically defined by

$$\sigma = \frac{\% \text{ change } Y/X}{\% \text{ change } MRS_{x \text{ for } y}} = \frac{d(Y/X)/(Y/X)}{d(MRS)/(MRS)} = \frac{d(Y/X)}{d(MRS)} \cdot \frac{MRS}{Y/X}.$$

Note also that $dz/z = d \log z$, where "log" is the natural logarithm. Using this result, σ may also be written

$$\sigma = \frac{d \log(Y/X)}{d \log MRS_{x \text{ for } y}}.$$

---

[12]The problem of community or social choice has received substantial attention. It is interesting to note that majority ordering may be inconsistent even if individuals' preferences are consistent.

For a particularly important contribution, see Kenneth J. Arrow, *Social Choice and Individual Values* (New York: John Wiley & Sons, 1951).

[13]When the indifference curves are strictly convex and negatively sloped, each point on the indifference curve has a unique slope (*MRS*) and a unique value for Y/X. In unusual cases, the indifference curve may have the same *MRS* at two or more distinct values of Y/X, and in these cases the relation between Y/X and *MRS* is not a "function" as commonly defined.

a. When $U(X, Y) = A X^\alpha Y^{1-\alpha}$ with $A > 0$ and $0 < \alpha < 1$, show that $\sigma = 1$.

b. When $U(X, Y) = A[\alpha X^{-\rho} + (1 - \alpha)Y^{-\rho}]^{-1/\rho}$ with $A > 0$ and $0 < \alpha < 1$, show that

$$MRS_{x \text{ for } y} = \frac{\alpha}{1 - \alpha}\left(\frac{Y}{X}\right)^{(1+\rho)}$$

c. For $U(X, Y)$ in part (b), show that

$$\sigma = \frac{1}{1 + \rho}.$$

(Hint: Take the log of the expression for the marginal rate of substitution given in part (b), solve for $\log(Y/X)$ as a function of $\log MRS$, and apply the logarithmic form of the expression for σ.)

10. "I like both tea and biscuits, but prefer to avoid eating them together." Draw an indifference map that illustrates this proposition.

SUGGESTED READINGS

Henderson, James M., and **Quandt, Richard E.** *Microeconomic Theory: A Mathematical Approach.* 2nd ed. New York: McGraw-Hill, 1971, chap. 2, pp. 6–14.

Hicks, John R. *Value and Capital,* 2nd ed. Oxford: Oxford University Press, 1946, pp. 1–25.

Marshall, Alfred. *Principles of Economics.* Book III, 8th ed. London: Macmillan, 1920, chaps. 5–6, pp. 117–37.

Samuelson, Paul A. *Foundations of Economic Analysis.* Cambridge, Mass.: Harvard University Press, 1948, chap. V, pp. 90–96.

Stigler, George J. "The Development of Utility Theory, I." *Journal of Political Economy* 58 (August 1950), pp. 307–24.

Takayama, Akira. *Mathematical Economics.* Hinsdale, Ill.: Dryden Press, 1974, chap. 2, pp. 169–83.

3 Theory of Consumer Behavior

The theory of consumer behavior can help us answer the questions regarding the efficacy of various taxes on cigarettes posed at the beginning of Chapter 2. It can also be applied to the problem of how a student should decide to allocate his study time to various courses to maximize his grade point average. Both of these applications will be explored in this chapter. In the ensuing chapters, more extensive (and more subtle) applications will be explored. ■

Tax Increases Persuade Britons to Kick Expensive Smoking Habit (II)

(Refer to the article by the above title included at the beginning of Chapter 2.)

Questions

1. According to the article (second paragraph), the result of the two tax increases has been to reduce the quantity demanded of cigarettes by 10 percent. The current price is $2.50. Assuming the price of cigarettes before the recent tax increases was $2.00 per pack, is the price elasticity of demand for cigarettes elastic or inelastic over this price range?

2. Refer back to Diagram 2 in the Solutions to the "Applying the Theory" section. Show the effect of the higher price on the quantity demanded of (all) cigarettes. Given your answer to question 1 above, should the price–consumption curve be upward sloping or downward sloping in this diagram? Explain.

3. Now consider a tax *only* on cigarettes with high tar and nicotine (not discussed in the article) and refer back to Diagram 1 in the solutions. Show the effect of this tax on the equilibrium position of smokers in this diagram. Is the slope of your price–consumption curve positive or negative? What does this indicate about the price elasticity

of demand for cigarettes high in tar and nicotine? Is this consistent with the determinants of the price elasticity of demand for a good?

4. If your goal is to reduce cancer by eliminating smoking, which of the two taxes above would you prefer? If your goal is to eliminate smoking of high nicotine and tar cigarettes, which tax do you prefer? Explain.

Solutions

1. INELASTIC. The percentage price change can be approximated by the change in price (50¢) divided by the average price over this price range ($2.25). Thus, the price elasticity of demand over this price range = 10 percent/22 percent or .45. Since this is less than one, it is inelastic.

2. The price–consumption curve should be upward sloping if the price elasticity of demand is less than 1. That is, when the price of cigarettes increases, the quantity of "other goods" decreases, and thus, total expenditures on other goods decreases. For a given money income, this must mean that total ex-

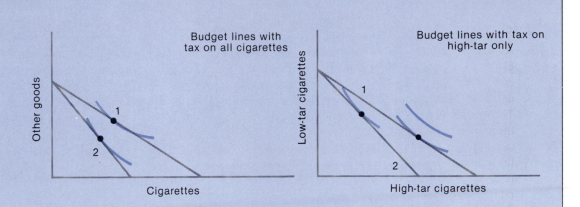

Budget lines with tax on all cigarettes

Budget lines with tax on high-tar only

penditures on cigarettes rose with the price rise. This means that the percentage change in price overwhelms the percentage decrease in quantity, and thus elasticity is less than one.

3. Given the high substitutability, we get a large decrease in the amount of high-tar cigarettes consumed and a large rise in the amount of low-tar cigarettes smoked. The slope of the price consumption curve is now negative, which indicates that the price elasticity of demand is greater than one. The key determinant of the price elasticity of demand is the availability of substitutes, so the shape of the price-consumption curve is consistent with

what economic theory predicts here.

4. To eliminate smoking, you will need to tax all cigarettes, and the amount of the tax will need to be much higher than currently in effect in Britain, despite the headline of the article in Chapter 2. Given the inelastic demand for cigarettes, this tax will mainly increase revenue rather than reduce the quantity demand of cigarettes.

To eliminate high-tar smoking, it would be much easier to tax high-tar cigarettes. The size of the tax necessary here would be more modest, given the depiction of the preferences of smokers in this problem, i.e. the easy substitutability of low-tar cigarettes.

This chapter uses the concepts of utility and indifference curves from Chapter 2 to explain the modern theory of consumer behavior. The fundamental work in the development of this theory was done by Slutsky (1915), Hicks and Allen (1934), Hotelling (1935), and Hicks (1939).

As Chapter 1 revealed, it is sufficient for many purposes to employ only the tools of supply and demand. There are some questions, however, that are difficult to answer without a somewhat more refined apparatus. For example, the effects of changes in a consumer's income on demand for a product are best understood through utility theory. Similarly, the effects of offering quantity discounts on consumption patterns are most readily seen on an indifference curve diagram. These tools do not replace demand curves, but underlie them. In fact, one section of this chapter is devoted to deriving demand curves from these more fundamental units.

In later chapters, the analogous constructs of production functions and isoquants are used to derive supply curves.

Maximization of Satisfaction
3.1.a

The theory of consumer behavior and demand is based on the assumption that consumers attempt to allocate limited money income among available goods and services so as to maximize satisfaction. The consumer makes purchases to maximize satisfaction subject to the constraint that these purchases do not exceed the consumer's limited money income. Given this assumption and the properties of indifference curves (developed in Chapter 2), individual demand curves can easily be determined. The usefulness of the theory lies in the fact that it helps us to understand how consumer demand responds to changes in prices and income. Although maximization may not always be attainable because of limited information, the theory gives a good approximation of the average consumer's behavior and is an important predictive device.

Limited Money Income
3.1.b

If each consumer had unlimited money income — in other words, if there were an unlimited pool of resources — there would be no problems of "economizing," nor would there be "economics." This utopian state does not exist, even for the richest members of our society.[1] People are compelled to determine their behavior in light of limited financial resources. For the theory of consumer behavior, this

---

[1] As Bunker Hunt remarked during testimony before the U.S. Congress, "a billion dollars isn't what it used to be."

means that each consumer has a maximum amount that can be spent per period of time. The consumer's problem is to spend this amount in the way that yields maximum satisfaction.

Begin by assuming that there are only two goods, X and Y, bought in quantities x and y. Each consumer is confronted with market-determined prices p_x and p_y of X and Y, respectively. Finally, the consumer in question has a known and fixed money income (I) for the period under consideration. Thus the maximum amount he or she can spend per period is I, and this amount can be spent only upon goods X and Y.[2] Thus the amount spent on X (xp_x) plus the amount spent on Y (yp_y) must not exceed the stipulated money income I. Algebraically,

$$I \geq xp_x + yp_y. \tag{3.1.1}$$

Expression (3.1.1) is an inequality that can be graphed in commodity space since it involves only the two variables, x and y. First consider the equality form of this expression:

$$I = xp_x + yp_y. \tag{3.1.2}$$

This is the equation of a straight line. Solving for y — since y is plotted on the vertical axis — one obtains

$$y = \frac{1}{p_y}I - \frac{p_x}{p_y}x. \tag{3.1.3}$$

Equation (3.1.3) is plotted in Figure 3.1.1. The first term on the right-hand side of equation (3.1.3), $(1/p_y)I$, shows the amount of Y that can be purchased if X is not bought at all. This is represented by the distance OA in Figure 3.1.1; thus $(1/p_y)I$ is the *ordinate intercept* of the equation.

The second coefficient on the right-hand side of equation (3.1.3), that is, $-(p_x/p_y)$ is the *slope* of the line. The slope of the line is the negative of the price ratio. The line in Figure 3.1.1 is called the *budget line*.

Budget Line: The budget line is the set of commodity bundles that can be purchased if the entire money income is spent. Its slope is the negative of the price ratio.[3]

---

[2] In more elaborate cases, *saving* may be considered as one of the many goods and services available to the consumer. Graphical treatment limits us to two dimensions; thus we ignore saving. This does *not* mean that the theory of consumer behavior precludes saving — depending upon his or her preference ordering, a consumer may save much, little, or nothing. Similarly, spending may in fact exceed income in any given period as a result of borrowing or from consuming assets acquired in the past. The I in question for any period is the total amount of money to be spent during the period. For a more sophisticated treatment of this problem, see Ralph W. Pfouts, "Hours of Work, Savings and the Utility Function," in *Essays in Economics and Econometrics in Honor of Harold Hotelling*, ed. Pfouts (Chapel Hill: University of North Carolina Press, 1960), pp. 113–32.

[3] The prices p_x and p_y are the prices of X and Y in terms of money. They are commonly referred to as the *nominal* prices or the *money* prices of the goods. The price ratio p_x/p_y is the *relative* price of X in terms of Y — it tells how many units of Y must be given up to get one unit of X. Similarly, the ratio p_y/p_x is the relative price of Y.

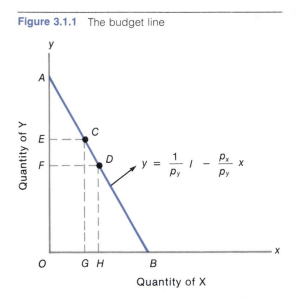

Figure 3.1.1 The budget line

$$y = \frac{1}{p_y} I - \frac{p_x}{p_y} x$$

The budget line is interpreted as the trade-off of Y for X that is imposed by having finite resources at given market prices. As already stated, consumption of no X allows consumption of *OA* of Y. Similarly, consumption of no Y permits consumption of *OB* of X. The consumer can trade *OA* of Y for *OB* of X. At point *C,* he or she has *OE* of Y and *OG* of X. Suppose that the vertical distance between *E* and *F* were 1 unit. (We can always select *C* and *D* to make this so.) By giving up one unit of Y, the consumer can move from *C* to *D* and acquire *GH* units of X. This implies that *GH* of X costs one unit of Y or its price in terms of Y is 1. But if 1 unit of Y is relinquished, this releases $(1)p_y$ of income to be spent on X and (p_y/p_x) of X can be purchased with that income. Thus, Y trades for X at p_y/p_x so X trades for Y at p_x/p_y and that is the interpretation of (minus) the slope of the budget line. The budget line is sometimes called the *budget constraint.*

The budget line is the graphical counterpart of equation (3.1.3), but it is not the graph of the inequality in expression (3.1.1). The latter includes the budget line, but it also includes all commodity bundles whose total cost is not as great as *I.* Inequality (3.1.1) is shown graphically in Figure 3.1.2 by the triangular shaded areas — it is the entire area enclosed by the budget line and the two axes. This area is called the *budget space.*[4]

---

[4]Mathematically, the budget space is defined by the following three inequalities:

$$I \geq xp_x + yp_y,$$

$$x \geq 0,$$

$$y \geq 0.$$

Part One   Demand, Supply, and Markets: An Introductory Look

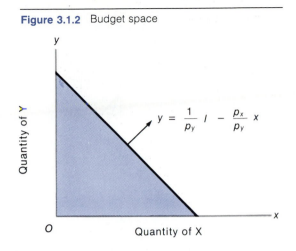

Figure 3.1.2 Budget space

$$y = \frac{1}{p_y} I - \frac{p_x}{p_y} x$$

Quantity of Y

O

Quantity of X

x

Budget Space: The budget space is the set of all commodity bundles that can be purchased by spending all or part of a given money income. It is a subset of the commodity space.

Shifting the Budget Line
3.1.c

In much of the analysis that follows, we are interested in *comparative static* changes in quantities purchased resulting from changes in price or money income. The latter changes are graphically represented by shifts in the budget line.

Consider an increase in money income from I to $I^* > I$, money prices remaining unchanged. The consumer can now purchase *more* — more of Y, more of X, or more of both. The maximum purchase of Y increases from $(1/p_y)I$ to $(1/p_y)I^*$, or from OA to OA' in Figure 3.1.3. Similarly, the maximum purchase of X increases from $(1/p_x)I$ to $(1/p_x)I^*$, or from OB to OB'. Since prices remain constant, the *slope* of the budget line does not change. Thus an increase in money income, prices remaining constant, is shown graphically by shifting the budget line upward and to the right. Since the slope does not change, the movement might be called a "parallel" shift. A decrease in money income is shown by a parallel shift of the budget line in the direction of the origin.

Figure 3.1.4 shows what happens to the budget line when the money price of X increases, the money price of Y and money income remaining constant. Let the price of X increase from p_x to p_x^*. Since p_y and I are unchanged, the ordinate intercept does not change — it is OA in each case. But the slope of the line, the negative of the price ratio, changes from $-p_x/p_y$ to $-p_x^*/p_y$. Since $p_x^* > p_x$, $-p_x^*/p_y < -p_x/p_y$. In other words, the slope of the budget line becomes *steeper*.

The price change can be explained as follows. At the original price p_x, the maximum purchase of X is $(1/p_x)I$, or the distance OB. When the price changes to p_x^*, the maximum purchase of X is $(1/p_x^*)I$, or the distance OB'. Thus an

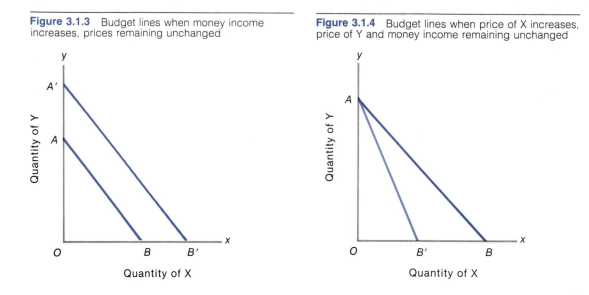

Figure 3.1.3 Budget lines when money income increases, prices remaining unchanged

Figure 3.1.4 Budget lines when price of X increases, price of Y and money income remaining unchanged

increase in the price of X is shown by rotating the budget line *clockwise* around the ordinate intercept. A decrease in the price of X is represented by a *counterclockwise* movement.

There is nothing that requires that Y be treated differently from X. The price of X might remain constant, but that of Y might rise or fall. A rise in the price of Y from p_y to p_y^* rotates the budget line counterclockwise around the X-axis intercept. This is shown in Figure 3.1.5 as the movement from AB to $A'B$. That point A', the Y-axis intercept, lies below A is easily seen. Since the budget line intersects the Y axis at I/P_y and I/P_y^*, respectively, and since $P_y^* > P_y$, the vertical intercept is lower in the second case. But the horizontal intercept is independent of P_y. To find it, merely set $y = 0$ and solve for the X on the budget line that corresponds to $y = 0$. This requires

$$0 = I/P_y - (P_x/P_y)x$$

or

$$I/P_x = x.$$

Thus, the X-axis intercept is independent of the price of Y.

It is important to emphasize that *relative* prices are crucial. If money income remains constant and the nominal prices of both commodities change proportionately, there is no change in relative price; the change in this case is tantamount to an increase in income (if prices decline) or a decrease in income (if prices rise). Similarly, let money income and the nominal price of Y remain constant. An increase in the nominal price of X is equivalent to a decrease in the relative price

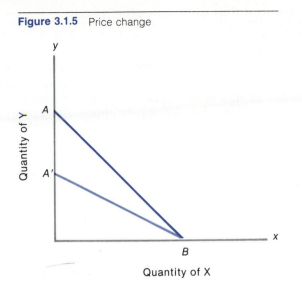

Figure 3.1.5 Price change

Quantity of Y

y

A

A'

B

x

Quantity of X

of Y, and vice versa. As we shall see, given money income, only relative prices
are relevant to a consumer's decision-making process. Hence the connections
among nominal money income, nominal prices, and relative prices deserve careful attention.

Relations: (*i*) An increase in money income, prices unchanged, is shown by
a parallel shift of the budget line—outward and to the right for an increase in
money income, and in the direction of the origin for a decrease in money
income. (*ii*) A change in the price of X, the price of Y and money income
constant, is shown by rotating the budget line around the ordinate
intercept—to the left for a price increase, and to the right for a decrease in
price. (*iii*) A change in the price of Y, the price of X and money income
constant, is shown by rotating the budget line around the X-axis intercept—up
for a price decrease and down for a price increase.

CONSUMER EQUILIBRIUM
3.2

The consumer's indifference map establishes a rank ordering of all bundles in the
commodity space. The budget space is established by relative prices and the
consumer's fixed money income. The assumption that each consumer attempts to
maximize satisfaction from a given money income simply means that the consumer selects the most preferred bundle of goods from those available in the
budget space.

The Relevant Part of Commodity Space
3.2.a

The consumer's problem is depicted in Figure 3.2.1. The entire X,Y plane is commodity space; the indifference map, represented by the five indifference curves drawn in that figure, indicates the consumer's preferences among all commodity bundles in this space. (There are, of course, an infinite number of indifference curves, but we merely depict five.) The consumer's budget space — the line *LM* and the shaded area enclosed by *LM* and the two axes — shows the bundles that the consumer can feasibly buy. Clearly, the consumer cannot purchase any bundles lying above and to the right of the budget line *LM*. The consumer would prefer such a bundle but does not have enough income to pay for it.

The choice is limited to those bundles lying in the budget space. We can eliminate most of these. In particular, no point in the interior of the budget space — below the budget line *LM* — can yield maximum satisfaction because a higher indifference curve can be reached by moving to the budget line. Hence, given the income constraint, the optimal bundle will be on the budget line.

Maximizing Satisfaction Subject to a Limited Money Income
3.2.b

The way in which a consumer maximizes satisfaction subject to a limited money income is illustrated in Figure 3.2.2. The budget line is *LM*, and the curves labeled I, II, III, and IV are a portion of an individual's indifference map. Because of the income constraint, the consumer cannot attain a position on any indifference curve, such as IV, that lies entirely beyond the budget line.

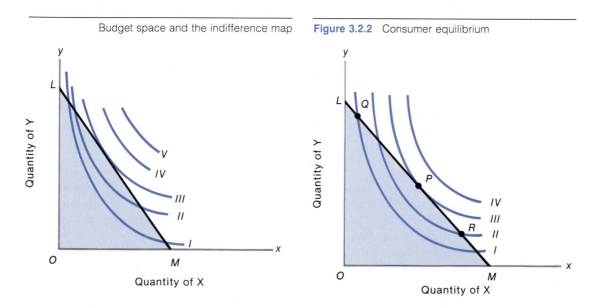

Budget space and the indifference map   **Figure 3.2.2**   Consumer equilibrium

Part One   Demand, Supply, and Markets: An Introductory Look

Three of the infinite number of attainable bundles on LM are represented by the points Q, P, and R. Each of these, and every other point on the budget line LM, is attainable with the consumer's limited money income.

Suppose the consumer, say Smith, were located at Q. Let Smith experimentally move to bundles just to the left and right of Q. Moving to the left from Q lowers Smith's satisfaction to some indifference curve below I. But moving to the right brings Smith to a higher indifference curve; and continued experimentation will lead Smith to move at least as far as P, because each successive movement to the right brings the consumer to a higher indifference curve.

By moving to the right of P, Smith would move to a lower indifference curve with its lower level of satisfaction. Smith would accordingly return to the point P.

Similarly, if a consumer were situated at a point such as R, experimentation would lead to a substitution of Y for X, thereby moving in the direction of P. The consumer would not stop short of P because each successive substitution of Y for X brings the consumer to a higher indifference curve. Hence the position of maximum satisfaction — or the point of consumer equilibrium — is attained at P, where an indifference curve is just tangent to the budget line.

As you will recall, the slope of the budget line is the negative of the price ratio, the ratio of the price of X to the price of Y. Also recall that the negative of the slope of an indifference curve at any point is called the marginal rate of substitution. Hence the point of consumer equilibrium satisfies the condition that the marginal rate of substitution equals the price ratio.

The interpretation of this proposition is straightforward. The marginal rate of substitution is the rate at which the consumer is willing to substitute X for Y. The price ratio shows the rate at which the consumer can substitute X for Y. Unless these two are equal, it is possible to change the combination of X and Y purchased so as to attain a higher level of satisfaction. For example, suppose the marginal rate of substitution is two — meaning the consumer is willing to give up two units of Y in order to obtain one unit of X. Let the price ratio be unity, meaning one unit of Y can be exchanged for one unit of X. Then, by giving up one unit of Y the consumer can get one more unit of X. Since the consumer was willing to give up as many as two units of Y for one unit more of X, this exchange increases the consumer's utility. Generalizing, unless the marginal rate of substitution and the price ratio are equal, some exchange can be made so as to push the consumer to a higher level of satisfaction.

Principle: The point of consumer equilibrium — or the maximization of satisfaction subject to a limited money income — satisfies the condition that the marginal rate of substitution of X for Y equals the ratio of the price of X to the price of Y.[5]

---

[5]Mathematically, the point of consumer equilibrium is the solution to the constrained maximization problem:

$$\max_{x,y} U(x,y)$$

We saw in footnote 9 of Chapter 2 that MU_x/MU_y, i.e., $(\partial U/\partial x)/(\partial U/\partial y)$, is the marginal rate of substitution of X for Y where MU_x and MU_y are the marginal utilities of X and Y, respectively. Thus, the point of consumer equilibrium can be expressed algebraically by the condition,[6]

$$MRS_{x \text{ for } y} = \frac{MU_x}{MU_y} = \frac{p_x}{p_y}$$

or, equivalently,

$$\frac{MU_x}{p_x} = \frac{MU_y}{p_y}.$$

If there are several goods, the above reasoning applies to every pair of them; the equilibrium condition may then be expressed as

$$\frac{MU_x}{p_x} = \frac{MU_y}{p_y} = \ldots = \frac{MU_z}{p_z}. \tag{3.2.1}$$

CHANGES IN MONEY INCOME
3.3

Changes in money income, prices remaining constant, usually result in changes in the quantities of commodities bought. For most goods, an increase in money income leads to an increase in consumption, and a decrease in money income

---

subject to:

$$p_x x + p_y y = I$$

where $U(x,y)$ is the consumer's utility function. The Lagrangian for this problem is $L(x, y; \lambda) = U(x, y) + \lambda(I - p_x x - p_y y)$ where λ is the Lagrangian multiplier. The first-order conditions are

$$\partial U/\partial x = \lambda p_x$$

and

$$\partial U/\partial y = \lambda p_y.$$

Eliminating λ from these last two equations, we get the equilibrium condition $(\partial U/\partial x)/(\partial U/\partial y) = p_x/p_y$. The left side is the $MRS_{x \text{ for } y}$ as noted in footnote 9 of Chapter 2, and the right side is the negative of the slope of the budget line.

[6] In some problems, the indifference curves of Figure 3.2.2 may intersect the vertical or horizontal axis (or both). Assuming negative quantities of X and Y are inadmissible, this may result in a situation known as a "corner solution" for which the consumer equilibrium theory presented here would not apply. We will not be greatly concerned with this possibility in this book; however, problem 5 of this chapter involves a case where corner solutions arise.

NUMERICAL EXERCISE

A certain college student who is cramming for final exams has only six hours study time remaining. Her goal is to get as high an average grade as possible in three subjects: economics, mathematics, and statistics. She must decide how to allocate her time among the subjects. According to the best estimates she can make, her grade in each subject will depend upon the time allocated to it according to the following schedule:

Economics		Mathematics		Statistics	
Hours of study	Grade	Hours of study	Grade	Hours of study	Grade
0	20	0	40	0	80
1	45	1	52	1	90
2	65	2	62	2	95
3	75	3	71	3	97
4	83	4	78	4	98
5	90	5	83	5	99
6	92	6	86	6	99

Questions

1. How should the student allocate her time? Why?
2. How does the solution relate to the equilibrium condition for the consumer (equation 3.2.1)?
3. Will a consumer generally purchase bundles of goods such that the *MU* is the same for all goods?

Solutions

1. To maximize her average grade, this student must calculate the addition to her grade from an extra hour of study in each course. Call this the marginal grade in the schedule* below: The principles in this chapter should lead you to recognize that if these marginal grades are not equal, then this student should reallocate her study hours toward the course that has a higher marginal grade. Such a move will increase her average grade. Thus, from two hours per course, this student should increase her study time in economics, since the third hour in economics has a marginal grade of 10 while her second hour in statistics has a marginal grade of 5. This move will increase her total grade by 5. At this allocation, the marginal grade in each course is the same (= 10), so

(continued on page 70)

NUMERICAL EXERCISE

(continued from page 69)

Economics		Math		Statistics	
Hours	**Marginal grade**	**Hours**	**Marginal grade**	**Hours**	**Marginal grade**
0	—	0	—	0	—
1	25	1	12	1	10
	(45 − 20)				
2	20	2	10	2	5
	(65 − 45)				
3	10	3	9	3	2
4	8	4	7	4	1
5	7	5	6	5	1
6	2	6	3	6	0

*This schedule is analogous to the *marginal utility* schedule.

this must be the maximum allocation. Thus, the final allocation should be three hours to economics, two hours to math, and one hour to statistics . . . for a total grade of (75 + 62 + 90) = 227 (or an average grade of 75.66). Any move away from this allocation will lower her average since the gain in grade by adding an additional hour to any course is less than the 10 points lower grade she must give up.

2. This solution relates to the equation 3.2.1 in that you can think of the "prices" of the three courses (goods) as equal. In such a situation, you would maximize utility by consuming amounts of the goods such that the *MU* (= marginal grades) were equal. (If they weren't, you could gain by buying the good with a higher *MU* and giving up a smaller *MU* from the unit of another good given up to purchase it.)

3. In general, no. The only time a consumer will be in equilibrium with the *MU* the same for all goods is when the prices of the goods are the same. What matters in equation 3.2.1 is the *MU* per dollar of the good (or the *MU/P*).

Part One   Demand, Supply, and Markets: An Introductory Look

leads to a decrease in consumption.[7] It is of considerable interest to analyze the effects on consumption of changes in income. To isolate the effects of income changes, we will hold nominal prices constant.

The Income-Consumption Curve
3.3a

As explained in subsection 3.1.c, an increase in money income shifts the budget line upward and to the right, and the movement is a parallel shift because nominal prices are assumed to be constant. In Figure 3.3.1, the price ratio is given by the slope of LM, the original budget line, and remains constant throughout.

With money income represented by LM, the consumer comes to equilibrium at point P on indifference curve I, consuming Ox_1 units of X. Now let money income rise to the level represented by $L'M'$. The consumer shifts to a new equilibrium at point Q on indifference curve II. The consumer has clearly gained. The consumer also gains when money income shifts to the level corresponding to $L''M''$. The new equilibrium is at point R on indifference curve III.

As income shifts, the point of consumer equilibrium shifts as well. The line connecting the successive equilibria is called the income–consumption curve. This curve shows the *equilibrium combinations* of X and Y purchased at various levels of money income, nominal prices remaining constant throughout.

Income–Consumption Curve: The income–consumption curve is a locus of points in the commodity space showing the equilibrium commodity bundles associated with different levels of money income for constant money prices.

The income–consumption curve in Figure 3.3.1 is rather flat at first and then becomes steep, i.e., it is a convex function. In this situation (although not always) this implies that the ratio of Y to X first falls as income increases, then rises. Diagrammatically, this means $y_3/x_3 > y_1/x_1 > y_2/x_2$. The ratio y_1/x_1 is given by the slope of the line that connects the origin with P(i.e., slope is $(y_1 - 0)/(x_1 - 0)$). Similarly, y_2/x_2 is the slope of the line that connects the origin with Q, and y_3/x_3 and R are analogously related. Line $\overline{OR}$ is steeper than $\overline{OP}$ which is steeper than $\overline{OQ}$. It is also true that if y/x is increasing with income, the Y's share of total expenditure, defined as $p_y y/\text{INCOME}$, is also increasing with income.[8]

---

[7]Goods for which changes in consumption are positively related to changes in income are said to be "normal" or "superior." "Inferior" goods are treated in Chapter 4. A formal definition of "normal," "superior," and "inferior" goods is given in subsection 3.3.d.

[8]If

$$\frac{y_1}{x_1} < \frac{y_3}{x_3}$$

then, since prices are positive,

$$\frac{p_y y_1}{p_x x_1} < \frac{p_y y_3}{p_x x_3}$$

(continued on page 72)

Figure 3.3.1 The income–consumption curve

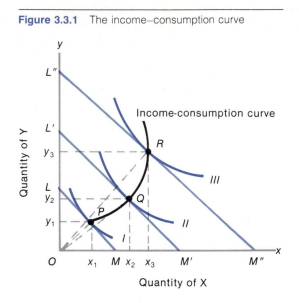

(continued from page 71)

or

$$\frac{p_x x_1}{p_y y_1} > \frac{p_x x_3}{p_y y_3}.$$

Thus,

$$\frac{p_x x_1}{p_y y_1} + 1 > \frac{p_x x_3}{p_y y_3} + 1$$

or

$$\frac{p_x x_1 + p_y y_1}{p_y y_1} > \frac{p_x x_3 + p_y y_3}{p_y y_3}.$$

The numerator of the left-hand side is income in situation 1 (I_1), and the numerator of the right-hand side is income in situation 3 (I_3). Thus,

$$\frac{I_1}{p_y y_1} > \frac{I_3}{p_y y_3}$$

or

$$\frac{p_y y_1}{I_1} < \frac{p_y y_3}{I_3}.$$

In this two-good case, it also implies that X's share is decreasing in income. Using the definition of I_1 and I_3, it follows that

$$\frac{p_x x_1 + p_y y_1}{I_1} = 1 = \frac{p_x x_3 + p_y y_3}{I_3}$$

so

$$\frac{p_x x_1}{I_1} - \frac{p_x x_3}{I_3} = \frac{p_y y_3}{I_3} - \frac{p_y y_1}{I_1}.$$

Since $p_y y_3 / I_3 > p_y y_1 / I_1$, the right-hand side is positive, which implies that $p_x x_1 / I_1 > p_x x_3 / I_3$.

Part One   Demand, Supply, and Markets: An Introductory Look

There is no requirement that income–consumption curves have such a shape or even be positively sloped. Two other possibilities are shown in Figures 3.3.2a and 3.3.2b. In the second figure, not only does the proportion y/x fall with income, but the absolute amount of Y falls as well. The actual shapes of income–consumption curves depend on the individual's preferences.

Engel Curves
3.3.b

The income–consumption curve may be used to derive Engel curves for each commodity.

Engel Curve: An Engel curve is a function relating the equilibrium quantity purchased of a commodity to the level of money income. The name is taken from Christian Lorenz Ernst Engel, a 19th-century German statistician.

Engel curves are important for applied studies of economic welfare and for the analysis of family expenditure patterns.

The Engel curve that corresponds to the income–consumption curve of Figure 3.3.1 is shown in Figure 3.3.3, Panel A. There X and I (Income) are on the axes rather than X and Y as in Figure 3.3.1. That is because Figure 3.3.1 is a commodity space. Panel A shows what level of X is purchased for any income, p_x and p_y held constant at their initial levels.

At point P in Figure 3.3.1, x_1 of X was consumed and income was I_1 (given by $p_y \cdot OL$ or, equivalently, by $p_x \cdot OM$). Thus, P in Figure 3.3.3, Panel A, corresponds to P in Figure 3.3.1. Similarly, at R in Figure 3.3.1 income was I_3 (equal to $p_y \cdot OL''$ or $p_x \cdot OM''$) and x_3 of X was consumed. Thus, R in Panel A corresponds to R in Figure 3.3.1. The change from x_1 to x_3 is the change in consumption of X that results when income rises from I_1 to I_3. The Engel curve is formed by connecting the points generated by repeating the process for all possible levels of money income.

Two basically different types of Engel curves are shown in Panels A and B, Figure 3.3.3. In Panel A, the Engel curve slopes upward rather gently, implying that changes in money income do not have a large effect upon consumption. An Engel curve with this property indicates that the quantity purchased does not expand rapidly as income increases. If "food" is treated as a single commodity, its Engel curve would look something like the curve in Panel A, even though the curve for "steak" as a separate commodity probably would not.

On the other hand, steak and many other types of goods give rise to Engel curves more nearly represented by the curve in Panel B. The relatively steep upward slope indicates that the quantity bought changes markedly with income.[9]

---

[9]The reader may associate "necessities" and "luxuries" with commodities whose Engel curves look like those in Panels A and B, respectively. One should be warned, however, that such associations are very rough and highly sensitive to the particular definitions of the commodities in question.

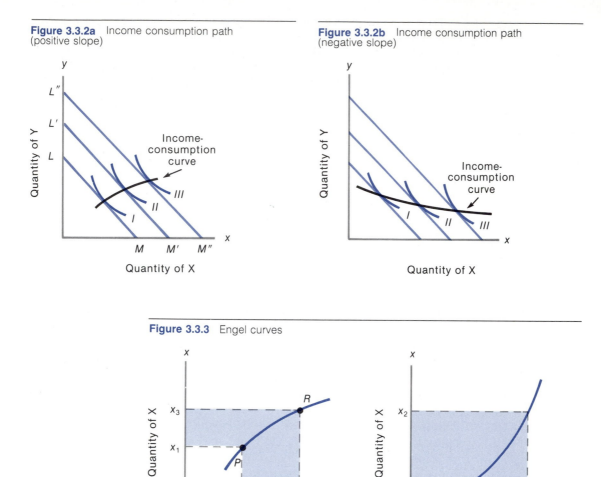

Figure 3.3.2a Income consumption path
(positive slope)

Income-
consumption
curve

Quantity of Y

L"
L'
L

I
II
III

M *M'* *M"*

x

Quantity of X

Figure 3.3.2b Income consumption path
(negative slope)

Quantity of Y

Income-
consumption
curve

I
II
III

x

Quantity of X

Figure 3.3.3 Engel curves

x

Quantity of X

x_3
x_1

R

P

O I_1 I_3 *I*

Income
(A)

x

Quantity of X

x_2

x_1

O I_1 I_2 *I*

Income
(B)

Engel Curves and Demand Curves
3.3.c

Recall that the demand curve describes what happens to x, the amount of X purchased, as the price of X changes, income and other prices constant. The Engel curve describes how x changes as income changes, the price of X and all other prices constant. The relation of the Engel curve to demand is shown in Figures 3.3.4a and 3.3.4b.

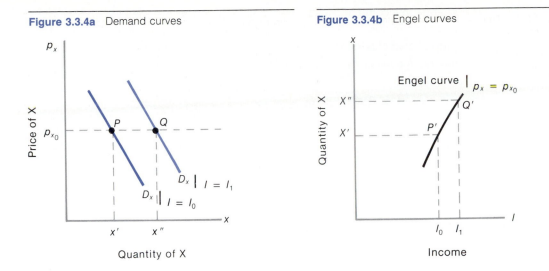

Figure 3.3.4a Demand curves

Figure 3.3.4b Engel curves

Figure 3.3.4a shows two demand curves corresponding to income levels I_0 and I_1. If the price of X were p_{x_0}, then an increase in income from I_0 to I_1 moves the individual from P to Q and consumption of X rises from x' to x''. This is also shown in Figure 3.3.4b as a move from P' to Q', where income rises from I_0 to I_1, and X rises from x' to x''. Note that p_x is held constant at p_{x_0}. There is another Engel curve for every price of X because the quantity of X purchased depends on price as well.[10]

Engel Curves and the Income Elasticity of Demand
3.3.d

The income elasticity of demand, which is discussed more thoroughly in Chapter 5, is defined as follows.

Income Elasticity of Demand: The income elasticity of demand is the proportional change in the consumption of a commodity divided by the proportional change in income. To obtain a more formal definition, let ΔI be the

---

[10]Algebraically, the demand for X can be written as

$$x = f(p_x; I; p_y, \ldots, p_z)$$

where $y, \ldots, z$ are the other goods in the economy. The traditional demand curve is the relation of X to p_x, i.e.,

$$x = f(p_x; \bar{I}; \bar{p}_y, \ldots, \bar{p}_z)$$

where the bar implies that the value is fixed at some arbitrary level.
   The Engel curve is the relation of X to I, i.e.,

$$x = f(\bar{p}_x; I; \bar{p}_y, \ldots, \bar{p}_z).$$

change in income and let Δx be the corresponding change in the consumption of good X. The *proportional change* in income is then $\Delta I/I$ and the proportional change in the consumption of X is then $\Delta x/x$. Using this notation, the income elasticity of demand is given by the expression

$$(\Delta x/x)/(\Delta I/I) = \frac{\Delta x}{\Delta I} \cdot \frac{I}{x}.$$

For small changes in ΔI (and hence Δx) the ratio $\Delta x/\Delta I$ is the slope (or derivative) of the Engel curve. The income elasticity (η_I) at a point on the Engel curve is given by the expression

$$\eta_I = \frac{dx}{dI} \cdot \frac{I}{x}.$$

Example: Suppose the Engel curve is given by the expression

$$x = I^2.$$

The slope of this Engel curve at income I is given by

$$\frac{dx}{dI} = 2I.$$

Thus income elasticity of demand is

$$\eta_I = \frac{dx}{dI} \cdot \frac{I}{x} = 2I\left(\frac{I}{I^2}\right) = 2.$$

In the example, income elasticity turned out to be a constant, independent of income. This is not true in general and we usually expect to see the income elasticity vary over the Engel curve. Income elasticities are used to classify goods as superior goods, normal goods, or inferior goods. The classification scheme is given in the following table:

Value of income elasticity	Classification of good
$\eta_I > 1$	Superior
$0 \leq \eta_I \leq 1$	Normal
$\eta_I < 0$	Inferior

As this table indicates, income elasticity can be negative; that is, an increase in income can in some cases lead to a reduction in the quantity consumed of the good. Notice that the words "inferior," "normal," and "superior" are used here only to describe the income elasticity of a good, no more and no less. Recall that it is possible that a given good will be inferior for one customer and normal or superior for some other customer. Also, for a given customer, a good may have $\eta_I > 0$ (superior or normal) for some values of income and $\eta_I < 0$ (inferior) for other values of income.

If the income elasticity of a commodity is greater than 1, then a consumer will increase the *fraction* of his or her income on that good when money income increases (prices remaining unchanged). Suppose at income I the individual consumes x and suppose that his or her consumption changes by dx when I increases by dI. Before the income change the fraction of income spent on x is $p_x x/I$ and after income changes this fraction is $p_x(x + dx)/(I + dI)$. The ratio of these fractions is

$$\frac{\dfrac{p_x(x + dx)}{I + dI}}{\dfrac{p_x x}{I}} = \left(\frac{x + dx}{x}\right)\left(\frac{I}{I + dI}\right) = \frac{1 + \dfrac{dx}{x}}{1 + \dfrac{dI}{I}} = \frac{\dfrac{I}{dI} + \dfrac{dx}{dI}\dfrac{I}{x}}{\dfrac{I}{dI} + 1}$$

and this last expression is greater than 1 if $\eta_I = (dx/dI)(I/x)$ is greater than 1. By the same reasoning the fraction of income spent on a good remains constant as income rises if income elasticity is unity, and the fraction decreases if income elasticity is less than unity.

Engel Curves in Economics
3.3.e

Now that the technical aspects of Engel curves have been described, it is useful to explain their role in economics. There are two major uses.

First, two individuals, say Smith and Jones, may be identical in virtually every relevant aspect except Smith's income may be $20,000 per year and Jones's $30,000. It is sometimes valuable to be able to predict Smith's purchases from other's behavior. Suppose, for instance, that a firm is trying to determine whether to market its good in Smith's neighborhood. Because of the fixed cost of setting up the operation, the firm might believe it not worthwhile unless the quantity of sales per consumer of Smith's type exceeds 22 per year. Jones consumes 25, and the Engel curve (say, previously estimated) is given by

$$x = 10 + I/2,000.$$

Smith is expected to consume

$$x = 10 + 20,000/2,000$$
$$= 20$$

so the estimated consumption is too low to warrant expansion into Smith's neighborhood.

Second, a firm may want to predict trends in demand for the product over time. If it holds its price constant, and average income rises from $30,000/year to $40,000/\text{year}$, over a five-year period, how large an increase in average quantity sold can it expect?[11]

Using the same Engel curve, average quantity sold would rise from

$$x = 10 + 30,000/2,000$$
$$= 25$$

to

$$x = 10 + 40,000/2,000$$
$$= 30.$$

CHANGES IN PRICE
3.4

The reaction of quantity purchased to changes in price is often even more important than the reaction to changes in money income. In this section we assume that money income and the nominal price of Y remain constant while the nominal price of X falls. We are thus able to analyze the effect of price upon quantity purchased without simultaneously considering the effect of changes in money income.

The Price–Consumption Curve
3.4.a

In Figure 3.4.1 the price of X falls from the amount indicated by the slope of the original budget line LM to the amount indicated by the slope of LM' and then to the amount represented by the slope of LM''.

With the original budget line LM, the consumer reaches equilibrium at point P on indifference curve I. When the price of X falls, the budget line becomes LM' and the new equilibrium is attained at Q on indifference curve II. Finally, when the price falls again, the new equilibrium is point R on indifference curve III and budget line LM''. The line connecting these successive equilibrium points is called the price–consumption curve.

Price–Consumption Curve: The price-consumption curve is a locus of points in the commodity space showing the equilibrium commodity bundles resulting from variations in the price ratio, money income remaining constant.

The Demand Curve
3.4.b

The individual consumer's demand curve for a commodity can be derived from the price–consumption curve, just as an Engel curve is derivable from an income–consumption curve.

---

[11] To be completely accurate, we must also assume that the prices of other goods do not change over the five-year period.

Part One   Demand, Supply, and Markets: An Introductory Look

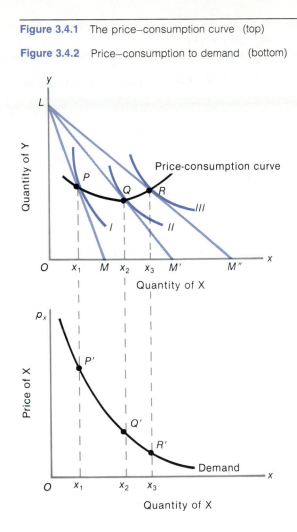

Demand Curve: The demand curve for a specific commodity relates equilibrium quantities bought to the market price of the commodity, nominal money income and the nominal prices of other commodities held constant.

When the price of X is given by the slope of *LM* in Figure 3.4.1, Ox_1 units of X are purchased. This price–consumption pair constitutes one point on the graph in Figure 3.4.2. Similarly, when the price of X falls to the level indicated by the slope of *LM'*, quantity purchased increases to Ox_2. This price–consumption pair is another point that can be plotted on Figure 3.4.2. Plotting all points so obtained and connecting them with a line generates the *consumer demand curve*, as shown in Figure 3.4.2. Its shape indicates an important principle, called the Law of Demand.

Principle: Quantity demanded varies inversely with price, nominal money income and nominal prices of other commodities remaining constant. This law (and one minor exception) will be established in the next chapter.

Note that Figure 3.4.2 has price on the vertical axis, whereas Figure 3.4.1 has Y on the vertical axis. Figure 3.4.1 is a commodity space so price depends on the slope of the budget line. Figure 3.4.2 shows the functional relation of X to p_x and price is read directly as the ordinate.

The Elasticity of Demand
3.4.c

The elasticity of demand is an important concept.

Price Elasticity of Demand: Price elasticity of demand or elasticity of demand is the proportional change in the consumption of a good divided by the proportional change in the price of the good. It may also be determined from the changes in price and in the money income spent upon a good. A formal algebraic definition of price elasticity will be provided in Chapter 5.

At this point it is helpful to review the relation between price elasticity of demand and changes in the total expenditure upon the good in question. First, suppose the nominal price of good X declines by 1 percent. The demand for X is said to be (a) price elastic, (b) of unitary price elasticity, or (c) price inelastic, according as the *quantity* of X demanded expands by more than 1 percent, exactly 1 percent, or by less than 1 percent.

Next, recall that the total expenditure upon a good is the product of price per unit and the number of units purchased. Given an initial price and quantity bought, a unique initial total expenditure is determined. Now let price fall by 1 percent. If demand is price elastic, quantity demanded expands by more than 1 percent. Thus total expenditure must expand when price falls and demand is price elastic. By the same argument, one finds (a) that total expenditure remains constant when price falls and demand has unitary price elasticity, and (b) that total expenditure declines when price falls and demand is price inelastic.

Exercise: Suppose the price of X increases rather than falls as in the above explanation. By an analogous argument, show that if total expenditure falls, then demand is price elastic; if total expenditure is unchanged, then demand has unitary elasticity; and if total expenditure rises, then demand is price inelastic.

Chapter 5 takes up the relationship of price elasticity and the demand curve in greater detail. In the next subsection we examine the relationship of demand elasticity and the price–consumption curve.

Elasticity of Demand and the Price–Consumption Curve
3.4.d

The elasticity of demand can be determined directly from the slope of the price–consumption curve. Consider Panel A, Figure 3.4.3. Let Y represent "all other goods," or what is frequently called "Hicks-Marshall" money. This is plotted on the vertical axis and labeled "money," whose price is unity. Thus money income is fixed at OM, and its price is fixed at 1. The original budget line is MN, and its slope is the price of $X(p_x/1 = p_x)$.[12]

The original equilibrium is at point P on the indifference curve II. At this point $Ox_1 = M_1P$ units of X and OM_1 units of "money" are bought. The slope of MN is (the negative of) MM_1/M_1P, so the price of X is MM_1/M_1P. The total amount spent on X is accordingly $M_1P(MM_1/M_1P) = MM_1$. When the price of X increases to the level given by the slope of MN', the quantity of X purchased drops to Ox_2, the amount of "money" bought remains constant at OM_1, and the amount spent on X remains unchanged. Price increases to MM_1/M_1Q, quantity purchased declines to M_1Q, and total expenditure on X is $M_1Q(MM_1/M_1Q) = MM_1$. The proportionate increase in the price of X is exactly offset by the proportionate decrease in the quantity of X bought. Consequently, demand has unitary elasticity over this range. And notice: the price–consumption curve is QP. Thus when the price–consumption curve is horizontal, price elasticity of demand for X is unitary.

In Panel B, an increase in the price of X (from that given by the slope of MN to that given by the slope of MN') is accompanied by a decrease in expenditure on X from MM_1 to MM_2. The proportionate increase in the price of X is more than offset by the proportionate reduction in quantity demanded. Demand is therefore elastic. The price–consumption curve is QP; hence when the price–consumption curve is negatively sloped, demand is elastic.

By the same reasoning, Panel C illustrates the price–consumption curve when demand is inelastic.

Thus we have the following:

Relations: Demand has unitary price elasticity, is price elastic, or is price inelastic according as the price–consumption curve is horizontal, negatively sloped, or positively sloped. Thus the price–consumption curve in Figure 3.4.1 reflects commodity demand that is first (at higher prices) elastic, becomes unitary at a point, and is inelastic thereafter.

---

[12]In microeconomic theory, a *price level* is not determined. That chore is left to macroeconomic theory. Thus we can take the "price" of Hicks-Marshall money to be whatever we wish it to be. Setting its price at unity is both logical and helpful. The determinants of the price level are determined and explained in course in macroeconomic theory and monetary theory. Here we concentrate exclusively upon relative prices.

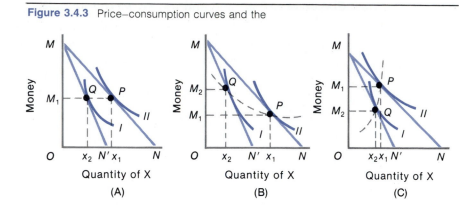

Figure 3.4.3 Price–consumption curves and the

Quantity of X (A)

Quantity of X (B)

Quantity of X (C)

- Consumers are assumed to allocate limited money income among available goods and services so as to maximize satisfaction. In the case of two goods, X and Y, the consumer's problem may be stated formally as that of finding values of x and y that maximize the consumer's utility function $U(x, y)$ while meeting the constraint that expenditures do not exceed total money income (that is, $I \geq p_x x + p_y y$ where I is total money income, and p_x and p_y are the nominal or money prices of X and Y, respectively).

- Given the problem stated above, the consumer will choose x and y to satisfy

$$\frac{MU_x}{MU_y} = \frac{p_x}{p_y}$$

where MU_x is the marginal utility of X and MU_y is the marginal utility of Y.[13] This condition states that in equilibrium the consumer will choose x and y such that the marginal rate of substitution of X for Y equals the price ratio.

- By varying money income, nominal prices held constant, one can find the consumer's income–consumption curve (subsection 3.3.a). The income–consumption curve can be used to derive the Engel curve for each commodity. Engel curves show the equilibrium quantity of the commodity that will be purchased at each level of money income. The income-elasticity of demand (η_I) is the proportional change in consumption of a commodity divided by the proportional change in income. Formally, η_I is

$$\eta_I = \frac{dx}{dI} \cdot \frac{I}{x}$$

[13]Exceptions to this condition are noted in question 5b of this chapter.

Part One   Demand, Supply, and Markets: An Introductory Look

where (dx/dI) is the slope of the Engel curve (subsection 3.3.d).

■ Goods with $\eta_I > 1$ are called "superior goods," goods with $0 \leq \eta_I \leq 1$ are called "normal goods," and goods with $\eta_I < 0$ are called "inferior goods." In principle a good may be classified as "superior" for some levels of income and "inferior" for other levels of income. A good may be inferior for one consumer and normal or superior for some other consumer.

■ By holding constant money income and one of the nominal prices while varying the other nominal price, a price–consumption curve can be derived (subsection 3.4.a). Given a price–consumption curve, a demand curve for a specific commodity can be derived. The demand curve shows the equilibrium quantity demanded of the commodity for different values of the nominal price of the commodity (subsection 3.4.b). The law of demand states that the quantity demanded of a commodity will vary inversely with its price, money income and the nominal prices of other commodities held constant.

■ The price elasticity of demand is the proportional change in the quantity of the good divided by the proportional change in the price of the good (subsection 3.4.c). If price elasticity is greater than 1 (elastic), the total expenditure on the good will increase when price falls. If price elasticity is exactly 1 (unitary), total expenditure remains constant when price falls, and if price elasticity is less than 1 (inelastic), total expenditure will decrease when price falls. Chapter 5 deals with the concept of price elasticity in more detail.

■ The analysis of this chapter can be generalized to the case of three or more commodities, but the fundamental conclusion remains: If individual consumers behave so as to maximize satisfaction from a limited money income, individual quantities demanded will vary inversely with price. In the following chapter this fundamental conclusion is explained more fully and one special exception is noted.

QUESTIONS AND EXERCISES

1. One of the basic assumptions underlying the theory of consumer behavior states that increases in utility tend to diminish as the consumption of a good increases.
   a. If you think this is true, show what role the assumption plays in the development of the theory and in its conclusions.
   b. If you think it is false, demonstrate that the main results of the theory of consumer behavior can be obtained anyway.

2. Both the marginal utility approach and the indifference curve approach yield the same equilibrium position for a rational consumer. Compare these explanations of equilibrium and discuss the relative advantage of the two approaches.

3. Comment on the following pair of statements:
   a. Consumer preferences are measured by relative prices.
   b. Consumer preferences are independent of relative prices.

4. Suppose a consumer in a two-good world has linear indifference curves with a slope that is everywhere equal to $-1/2$; that is, the marginal rate of substitution is $1/2$.

    a. What is the equilibrium consumption when $p_x = 1$ and $p_y = 1$ and income is $1,000? What is the equilibrium consumption when $p_x = 1$ and $p_y = 2$?

    b. In Chapter 2 it was noted that indifference curves are usually assumed to be convex. What would be the consumer equilibrium if the indifference curves were concave (as in Figure 2.3.2), given a budget constraint of the kind discussed in this chapter?

5. Consider a consumer in a two-commodity world whose indifference map is such that the slope of the indifference curves is everywhere equal to $-(y/x)$, where y is the quantity of good Y (measured along the vertical axis) and x is the quantity of good X (measured along the horizontal axis).

    a. Show that the demand for X is independent of the price of Y and that the price elasticity of demand for X is unitary. (Hint: Setting the marginal rate of substitution equal to the price ratio gives $(p_x/p_y) = (y/x)$, or $xp_x = yp_y$. Since $xp_x + yp_y = I$ where I is the given constant money income, one has $xp_x = (1/2)I$. Thus the demand function is $x = (1/2p_x)I$. Go on from here.)

    b. Explain precisely the meaning of the term "marginal rate of substitution." What is the value of the equilibrium MRS for this consumer, given that the price of X is $1, the price of Y is $3, and the consumer's income is $120?

    c. What does the Engel curve look like for X? What is the income elasticity of demand for X?

6. Suppose that a seller offers the following price policy for commodity X: The price of X is $2 a unit for the first 200 units and $1/2 a unit for all units purchased in excess of 200. Suppose commodity Y sells at a constant $1 a unit.

    a. Sketch the budget line when the consumer's income is $500.

    b. Is it possible to have more than one point of consumer equilibrium in this situation?

7. In the modern theory of finance, portfolios of securities are constructed with various combinations of riskiness and rates of return.[14] Given a set of securities, it can be shown that the set of available combinations of riskiness and rate of return looks like the shaded area in the following figure:

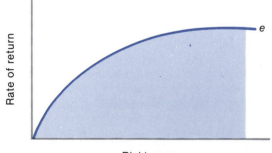

[14]The reader interested in more detail can consult E. Fama and M. Miller, *The Theory of Finance* (New York: Holt, Rinehart & Winston, 1972).

                                                                 Part One   Demand, Supply, and Markets: An Introductory Look

The efficient frontier, e, shows the maximum rate of return that can be achieved at each level of riskiness. Portfolios on or below e are feasible, but not those above e.

    a. Assuming that investors like larger rates of return but do not prefer greater risk, what is the shape of a typical indifference curve in the rate of return–riskiness space?

    b. Illustrate investor equilibrium graphically, using indifference curves of the kind obtained in part (*a*) of this question and treating the efficient frontier as a "budget" line.

8. Businessmen sometimes complain, "Inflation is killing me. My costs have risen and passing the increase along to consumers stifles demand." Define inflation as a proportionate increase in the price of all commodities in the economy in terms of money.

    a. Show the effects of inflation on a typical consumer budget line and on his demand curve.

    b. Is the businessman's statement correct?

    c. What kind of change is most likely to affect the businessman's profits?

SUGGESTED READINGS

Henderson, James M., and **Quandt, Richard E.** *Microeconomic Theory: A Mathematical Approach,* 2nd ed. New York: McGraw-Hill, 1971, pp. 14–31.

Hicks, John R. *Value and Capital,* 2nd ed. Oxford: Oxford University Press, 1946, pp. 26–30.

Samuelson, Paul A. *Foundations of Economic Analysis.* Cambridge, Mass.: Harvard University Press, 1947, pp. 96–100.

4 Topics in Consumer Demand

In this chapter we use the theory of consumer behavior from the previous two chapters to help us analyze a host of issues. Can we be sure the demand curve from Chapter 1 is downward sloping? What do we mean by the substitution and income effects of a price change? This question also relates to such present-day policy issues as whether a gas tax increase will necessarily reduce gas consumption. In the "Applying the Theory" section, two different tax increase schemes (from the Carter Administration and the present day) are considered and you will see how the consideration of the substitution and income effects helps in the analysis of the likely effects of these policies on gas consumption. We also see in this chapter that consumer theory is directly applicable to issues of labor supply (demand for leisure) and consumption versus saving decisions, among others. ∎

APPLYING THE THEORY

Rebates or Revenue?

By Tom Wicker

The architect of President Carter's energy program, James R. Schlesinger, has raised the distinct possibility that substantial revenues from the new energy-related taxes eventually would be diverted to tax and welfare reform programs.

That makes much sense but it's not exactly the impression that was at first created by Mr. Carter's energy messages. The President did concede, at his news conference last week, that he couldn't "certify today that every nickel of the taxes collected will be refunded to consumers." That, he said, was because "we still have to have some flexibility."

The question had been specifically asked, however — and repeated — whether there would be a diversion of the new revenues to welfare and other reforms. In the light of Mr. Schlesinger's remarks on the CBS "Face the Nation" program Sunday, Mr. Carter's news conference answers appear unresponsive, if not evasive.

The Administration did propose to rebate all energy-related tax revenues to the public "in the early years," Mr. Schlesinger said. But, he continued:

"We have not committed ourselves to the later years, because we want to integrate our energy proposals into welfare reform and into tax reform. . . . the President would like to have some flexibility."

Mr. Carter's vague response may have been politically more prudent, but what Mr. Schlesinger said makes more long-term

'A general rebate of the gasoline tax does not seem to promise much reduction in gas consumption.'

sense. Particularly as people become accustomed to the higher price of gasoline and plan their budgets and activities accordingly, the need to rebate every penny collected in additional gasoline taxes should diminish or even disappear.

Most earlier gasoline tax proposals, in fact, have included tax rebates only to low-income persons who had to depend on their automobiles for getting to and from work. Admittedly, making that kind of distinction among drivers — either by exempting a minimum amount of gas from the tax or by rebating only to low-income persons — would be more complex to administer and might be open to charges of inequity.

Nevertheless, it does not seem to make sense — to use an example provided by Steven Rattner of The Times Washington Bureau — for a family driving 17,558 miles on 1,255 gallons of gas per year in cars getting about 14 miles per gallon to make *a profit* on the proposed gasoline tax. If such a family continued driving as usual, they would pay $627.50 annually in taxes in 1985, when the full 50-cents-per-gallon tax presumably would be in effect — but

(continued on page 88)

(continued from page 87)
would get a rebate of $735, for a profit of $107.50.

In fact, to a layman at least, a general rebate of the gasoline tax does not seem to promise much reduction in gasoline consumption. The tax might give lower-income drivers a cash-flow problem since they would be paying higher prices all year, before a one-shot rebate at the end of the year. But drivers would not actually be paying *more* in the long run. So why curtail driving? As the oil companies like to say, where's the incentive?

Shouldn't driving, too, be made actually to cost what it's worth, if it's the aim of the Carter energy program to make *all* energy cost what it's worth? If so, it's hard to see the purpose of the promised gasoline tax rebates, other than to cushion early-year hardships, and to sustain low-income drivers — unless the promise of rebates is being held out now to make the tax more politically acceptable, while the long-range intention is to keep all or much of the revenue, as Dr. Schlesinger seemed to suggest.

If that *is* the ultimate aim, Mr. Carter might do better to fight the issue through now with Schlesingerian candor, and not just to avoid later charges of reneging on the rebates; it also makes more sense (*a*) to make driving costly enough to achieve real conservation, and (*b*) to tap the immense potential of revenues from what is essentially an increased user tax.

Those revenues, moreover, need not be used only to replace the costs of tax and welfare reform; they could also be legitimately invested in numerous energy and transportation projects. There is a difference only in degree in imposing a four-cent gas tax to build the interstate highway system, and raising that tax to 50 cents to help pay for mass transit or for rebuilding antiquated railway roadbeds.

Mr. Carter's political judgment may well be that the promise of full gasoline-tax rebates is needed to win public and Congressional approval even of the proposed standby tax. If so, the rebate legislation still could be limited in duration, to permit sensible reconsideration within a few years.

Questions

1. President Reagan and many Congressmen and Senators are now considering raising the excise tax on gasoline. Such a tax increase will increase the price of gasoline to consumers. Will it necessarily reduce gas consumption? (In your answer be sure to distinguish the substitution effect of this price rise from the income effect.)

2. In 1977, President Carter had proposed an increase in the gas tax, but with the added provision that the revenue raised would be returned "to the public." If the amount of this rebate is NOT related to the quantity of gas that an individual consumer individually purchases, how does this affect the income and substitution effects outlined in question 1? Does the income effect disappear? The substitution effect?

3. Refer to the paragraph "In fact, to a layman..." in the article. Is Mr. Wicker correct in his conclusion that there would be no incentive to curtail driving under the circumstances in question 2 above? Explain carefully.

4. If President Reagan asked for your help in determining how much gas consumption would be reduced as a result of his proposal to increase the gas tax, what economic concept from the previous chapters would you find most useful? Why? In your answer explain how you would use this concept.

Solutions

1. If gas is a "normal" good, then the increase in the price must necessarily reduce the quantity demanded, since both the substitution and income effect work in the same direction. The "income effect" of the price rise refers to the fact that as a result of the tax increase, the consumer can buy less of his total market basket of goods and services. This effect tends to reduce the consumption of all "normal" goods (although this effect is small if the taxed commodity does not account for a large part of the consumer's expenditures.) The "substitution" effect or the "relative price" effect results from the fact that the tax increase increases the price of gasoline relative to other goods. This effect *by itself always* causes the consumer to shift some of his consumption from the taxed commodity to other commodities.

2. The substitution effect is NOT offset, although the income effect may well be for any given consumer. An individual whose pre-tax purchasing power is restored will still have an incentive to consume less of the taxed commodity (and more of other commodities) due to this substitution effect or relative price effect.

3. Mr. Wicker is therefore incorrect. The substitution effect will still remain and provides an incentive to reduce gasoline consumption, although not quite as much as was the case where there is no rebate (assuming gasoline is a normal good).

4. The amount of the price increase from the tax increase is determined by the supply and demand elasticities. The price elasticity of demand would be most useful once we know the effect of the tax increase on the price rise. If we knew, for example, that in the range of prices under consideration, this price elasticity was .15, then we could use such information to determine the percentage decrease in gas consumption. Suppose the price increase as a result of the increased gas tax was 10 percent. Then, if the price elasticity of demand was .15, we would predict that gas consumption would decrease by 1.5 percent.

Source: *New York Times*, April 26, 1977. ©1977 by the New York Times Company. Reprinted by permission.

Despite Fare Rise, Taxi Fleets Report New Losses Again

The city's taxi fleets have found the fare increase granted last fall inadequate and are preparing to seek a new increase, according to Taxi News, the industry's paper.

The 17.5 percent fare increase that went into effect in November has produced only about a 10 to 11 percent increase in gross revenues rather than the 17.5 percent that the Taxi and Limousine Commission had predicted, the paper said. As a result, the paper said, the possibility of operational profit has been wiped out and losses are building up again, because "operating costs have continued to inflate."

The industry's paper said that the Metropolitan Taxicab Board of Trade, representing the city's 60 fleet owners, would probably demand that the Taxi Commission "live up to its commitment to give them

the fare increase that will provide the 17.5 percent increase in gross revenue.

"According to industry accountants, that can only be done by reshaping the fare upward to the 25 percent schedule they originally submitted," the paper added.

The Taxi News also suggested that the industry was expected to put forward a plan to offset the rising costs of gasoline. This might take the form of charging passengers 1 cent for each 2 cents per gallon of increased gasoline costs, the paper said. If gasoline costs dropped, it said, the procedure would be reversed, and 1 cent would be taken off the trip cost for each 2-cent reduction in the cost of gasoline.

The Metropolitan Taxicab Board of Trade has called a news conference for this morning to announce details of its plans

INTRODUCTION
4.1

The theory of consumer behavior was developed in Chapter 3, where it was noted that an individual consumer demand curve normally slopes downward to the right—that quantity demanded varies inversely with price. This chapter presents a closer analysis of consumer demand and of market demand for related commodities.

SUBSTITUTION AND INCOME EFFECTS
4.2

A change in the nominal price of a commodity actually exerts two influences on quantity demanded. In the first place, there is a change in *relative* price—a change in the terms at which a consumer *can* exchange one good for another. The change in relative price alone leads to a *substitution effect*. Second, a change in the nominal price of a good (nominal income remaining constant) causes a change and to document the fleet industry's needs, a spokesman said.

Questions

1. From the information in this article, is the demand for taxis elastic or inelastic over the price range in effect in the article? How do you know?
2. According to the Taxi and Limousine Commission, the 17.5 percent fare increase *was supposed* to generate an increase in "gross revenues" of 17.5 percent. For this to occur, what would the elasticity of demand for taxis have to be?
3. The MTBT, representing the city's 60 fleet owners, want a 25 percent fare increase in order to increase gross revenues by 17.5 percent. Does the MTBT agree with the Taxi and Limousine Commission regarding the elasticity of demand for taxis under the price range under consideration? Explain.

Solutions

1. Demand for taxis must be inelastic. As a result of the price *increasing*, total revenue went *up*.
2. They must have thought the elasticity was *zero*. That is, for a given price increase to generate a corresponding increase of the same amount in total revenue, there must be no reduction in quantity demanded. Note that if the elasticity was equal to 1, then there would be no increase in total revenue.
3. No. The MTBT feels the elasticity is less than 1, but greater than zero. The Taxi and Limousine Commission implicitly assumes it is zero.

in *real* income, or in the size of the bundle of goods and services a consumer can buy. If the nominal price of one good falls, money income and other nominal prices remaining constant, real income rises because the consumer can now buy more, either of the good whose price declined or of the other goods. In other words, the consumer's level of satisfaction must increase. This change in real income leads to an *income effect* on quantity demanded.

An application of the substitution and income effects (given in the "Applying the Theory" section) involves whether a rise in the gasoline tax (that is rebated) will necessarily decrease the amount of gasoline consumption. See the "Applying the Theory" section at the end of this chapter for more details.

The Substitution Effect in the Case of a Normal or Superior Good 4.2.a

When the price of one good changes, the prices of other goods and money income remaining constant, the consumer moves from one equilibrium point to another. In normal circumstances, if the price of a good diminishes, more of it is bought;

if its price increases, fewer units are taken. The overall change in quantity demanded from one equilibrium position to another is referred to as the *total effect*.

Total Effect: The total effect of a price change is the total change in quantity demanded as the consumer moves from one equilibrium to another.

The total effect of a price increase is illustrated in Figure 4.2.1. The original price ratio is indicated by the slope of the budget line LM. The consumer attains equilibrium at point P on indifference curve II, purchasing Ox_1 units of X. When the price of X rises, as indicated by shifting the budget line from LM to LM', the consumer moves to a new equilibrium position at R on indifference curve I. At this point Ox_3 units of X are purchased. The total effect of the price change is indicated by the movement from P to R, or by the reduction in quantity demanded from Ox_1 to Ox_3. In other words, the total effect is $Ox_1 - Ox_3 = x_1x_3$. This is called a negative total effect because quantity demanded is reduced by x_1x_3 units.

The total effect of a price change can be decomposed into two effects; the *substitution effect* and the *income effect*. Let us first examine the substitution effect. Consider Figure 4.2.1. When the price of X increases, the consumer suffers a decline in "real income," i.e., utility, as indicated by the movement from indifference curve II to indifference curve I. Suppose that coincident with the price rise the consumer were given an amount of (additional) money income just sufficient to compensate him for the loss in real income that would otherwise be sustained. That is, the consumer is given a compensatory payment just sufficient to remain on indifference curve II under the *new* price regime.

Graphically, this compensation is shown by constructing a fictitious budget line tangent to the *original* indifference curve, but whose slope corresponds to the *new* price ratio. The dashed line CC' in Figure 4.2.1 is the fictitious budget line for this example — it is tangent to the original indifference curve II at point Q; but it is parallel to the new budget line LM', thereby reflecting the new price ratio.

The substitution effect is represented by the movement from the original equilibrium position at P to the imaginary equilibrium position at Q, both points being situated on the original indifference curve. In terms of quantity, the substitution effect is the reduction in quantity demanded from Ox_1 to Ox_2, or by x_1x_2 units.

Substitution Effect: The substitution effect is the change in quantity demanded resulting from a change in relative price after compensating the consumer for the change in real income. In other words, the substitution effect is the change in quantity demanded resulting from a change in price when the change is restricted to a movement along the original indifference curve, thus holding real income constant.[1]

---

[1] As this statement implies, we will use total consumer satisfaction as indicated by the indifference curve as the measure of real income. Hence all points on the same indifference curve represent the same real income, higher indifference curves represent greater real income, and lower indifference curves represent smaller real income.

Part One   Demand, Supply, and Markets: An Introductory Look

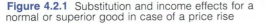

Figure 4.2.1 Substitution and income effects for a normal or superior good in case of a price rise

Figure 4.2.2 Substitution and income effects for a normal or superior good in case of a price decrease

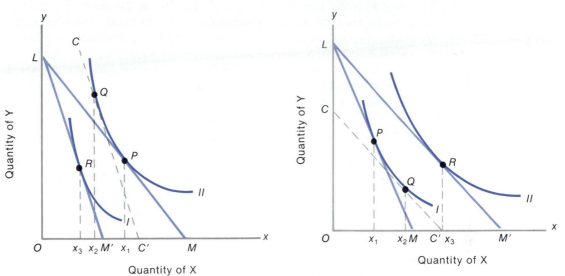

It is called a substitution effect because it is the change that occurs as the consumer attempts to substitute away from the relatively expensive good to the cheaper one. Even if his real purchasing power did not change, a consumer will (generally) shift away from more costly goods.

The substitution effect in the case of a price decline is illustrated in Figure 4.2.2. The original equilibrium is point P on indifference curve I, the price ratio being indicated by the original budget line LM. The price of X now declines to that indicated by the slope of LM'. In the absence of a compensatory payment, the consumer would enjoy an increase in real income, moving to equilibrium on indifference curve II. In this case, we compensate by imagining a decrease in money income by an amount just sufficient to maintain real income constant at the new price ratio. Graphically, this is illustrated by the dashed line CC'.

As a result of the price change alone, real income held constant, the consumer moves from the original equilibrium at P to the imaginary equilibrium at Q. The movement from P to Q along the original indifference curve represents the substitution effect. In quantity units, it is the expansion of quantity demanded from Ox_1 to Ox_2.

Comparing the cases in Figures 4.2.1 and 4.2.2, one readily sees that the *substitution effect by itself always implies that quantity demanded varies inversely with price.*[2] An increase in the price of X leads to a decrease in the quantity demanded of X if we keep real income constant (that is, if we keep the consumer on the same indifference curve).

---

[2]There is one extreme case, where X and Y are "perfect complements," where there can be no substitution effect at all.

Further insight may be gained into the proposition that income-compensated price increases result in a reduction in the quantity demanded by considering the following argument that does not depend directly on the use of indifference curves. In Figure 4.2.3, the initial budget line is LM. We know that the consumer, say Smith, chooses a point on (not below) LM.[3] Suppose Smith chooses bundle A. Now let the price of X increase so the budget line is LM'. We know that Smith is worse off after this price increase. Next assume we give Smith enough additional money income to compensate for this utility loss. Additions to money income result in parallel shifts in LM' to the northeast. We know that Smith will be *at least* as happy as before the price increase if we shift the budget line until it intersects LM at A, because at that point Smith could consume A even with the new prices. Accordingly, Smith will be just as happy as before the price increase when the budget line shifts to intersect LM at A or some point to the left of A. Suppose the increase in money income needed to compensate Smith for the price increase results in the new budget line DC'. The new consumption bundle must be on the segment DC because any point on the segment CC' could have been consumed at the old budget line LM, and we know Smith preferred A to any of these other consumption bundles. (This is the transitivity assumption *ii* of Chapter 2.) But all points on DC have less X than bundle A, so the quantity demanded of X decreases when there are income-compensated increases in the price of X (that is, when money income is raised just enough to offset the utility lost from the real-income reduction caused by the increase in the price of X). This result is thus seen to follow directly from the assumptions about consumer behavior in Chapter 3 and does not require the explicit use of indifference curves.

Note that the approach without indifference curves is identical to the approach with indifference curves. Given our definition of line DC' in Figure 4.2.3, it is identical to line CC' in Figure 4.2.1. Both are drawn such that the utility when Smith is at his optimum on the relevant budget line (DC' in Figure 4.2.3 and CC' in 4.2.1) is equal to the utility at R, the new optimum. Figure 4.2.3 is merely 4.2.1 without the indifference curves drawn in.

The method just described is usually attributed to Hicks, but there is another approach to deriving income and substitution effects that is associated with Slutsky. This method holds real income constant in a different way.

Again consider a price rise for X as shown in Figure 4.2.1. The substitution effect is defined as the change in consumption after compensating the consumer to hold real income constant. One way to compensate him is to give him enough money so that he could still buy the previous optimum bundle, at P, given that he faces the new set of prices. This is done in Figure 4.2.4 by giving him budget line DD'.

In some sense, income is held constant because the individual has point P available to him even though the price of X has gone up. For example, if $p_{x_0}=5$ and $Ox_1=4$, then an increase in p_x to $p_{x_1}=6$ implies that an increase in income

---

[3]We assume that X and Y are MIBs as defined in Chapter 2.

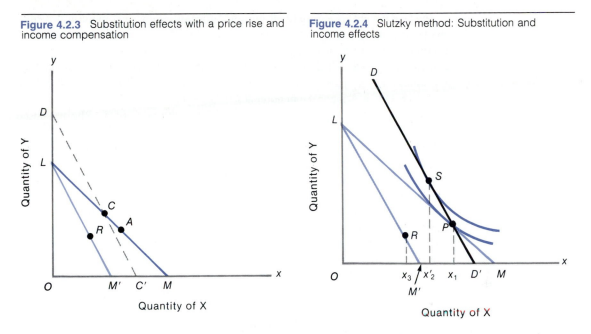

Figure 4.2.3 Substitution effects with a price rise and income compensation

Figure 4.2.4 Slutzky method: Substitution and income effects

of \$4 $(= 4 \times (6 - 5))$ would permit the individual to consume the same amount of X and Y even though the price of X has gone up.

Of course, given DD', the individual would no longer choose P. Instead he would substitute toward Y and away from X moving to some new point like S. The reduction in X from x_1 to x_2' is the substitution effect.

In general, $Ox_1 - Ox_2'$ in Figure 4.2.4 will not be equal to $Ox_1 - Ox_2$ in Figure 4.2.1. The reason is that real income is held constant in a different way in the two diagrams. As the change in price becomes small, the difference between the two methods disappears. Although no one approach is correct, most economists prefer to use the Hicksian method since it has a cleaner interpretation in most circumstances.

4.2.b The Income Effect in the Case of a Normal or Superior Good

In determining the substitution effect, one is constrained to movements along the original indifference curve. However, the total effect of a price change — money income and the prices of other commodities held constant — always entails a shift from one indifference curve to another, or a change in real income.

Income Effect: The income effect of a change in the price of one commodity is the change in quantity demanded resulting exclusively from a change in real income, all other prices and money income held constant.

Consider Figure 4.2.1. When the price of X rises, as indicated by the shift of the budget line from LM to LM', the consumer attains a new equilibrium on indifference curve I. The movement from P to Q along indifference curve II represents the substitution effect. Now let the consumer's real income fall from the level represented by the fictitious budget line CC'. The movement from the imaginary equilibrium position Q on indifference curve II to the actual new equilibrium position R on indifference curve I indicates the income effect. Since CC' and LM' are parallel, the movement does not involve a change in relative prices. It is a real-income phenomenon.

Real income declines as a result of the rise in the price of X. The reduction in quantity demanded from Ox_2 to Ox_3 measures the change in purchases attributable exclusively to the decline in real income, the change in relative price already having been accounted for by the substitution effect.

Similarly, in Figure 4.2.2, the decline in the price of X leads to an increase in real income. The substitution effect accounts for the movement from P to Q, and the income effect is represented by the movement from Q to R. Real income increases as a result of the price decrease, and quantity demanded increases from Ox_2 to Ox_3, *exclusively* as a result of the increase in real income.

From either graph one may readily see that the total effect of a price change is the sum of the substitution and income effects. In Figure 4.2.1, the total effect of the rise in the price of X is a reduction in quantity demanded from Ox_1 to Ox_3. The movement from Ox_1 to Ox_2 is attributable to the substitution effect, and the movement from Ox_2 to Ox_3 is the income effect. The same reasoning applies, *mutatis mutandis,* for the total effect shown in Figure 4.2.2. See the "Applying the Theory" section for an application of substitution and income effects.

4.2.c Normal or Superior Goods

As indicated by the subheadings above, the analysis has so far been restricted to the case of "normal" or "superior" goods, but a "normal" or "superior" good has not yet been defined except in terms of income elasticity of demand. We now have the tools necessary for a more refined definition.

Note from Figure 4.2.1 that when the price of a commodity rises, real income declines and the income effect causes a decrease in quantity demanded. On the other hand, a price decline (Figure 4.2.2) leads to an increase in real income and to an increase in quantity purchased attributable to the income effect. In both these cases the quantity demanded varies directly with real income: an increase in real income leads to an increase in quantity demanded and a decrease in real income reduces the quantity demanded.

Normal or Superior Goods: A normal or superior good is one for which the quantity demanded varies directly with real income.

Principle: For a normal or superior good the income effect reinforces the substitution effect. A price decrease means real income has increased and, for a normal or superior good, this means the quantity demanded will increase. But a price decrease also increases the quantity demanded because of the substitution effect, so both the income and substitution effects work in the same direction. Thus for a normal or superior good quantity demanded always varies inversely with price.

INFERIOR GOODS
4.3

Theory dictates and empirical studies show that for most goods the income effect is positive.[4] In certain unusual cases, however, the income effect may cause a switch from margarine to butter, from dried to fresh beans. Thus an increase in real income may result in a decrease in the consumption of certain commodities. These commodities are called inferior goods.

Inferior Goods: An inferior good is one for which the quantity demanded varies inversely with real income—increases in real income reduce the quantity demanded and decreases in real income increase the quantity demanded of inferior goods.

Inferior Goods and the Giffen Paradox
4.3.a.

An increase in real income may be attributable to an increase in money income, commodity prices remaining constant, or to a decline in prices, money income remaining constant. Figure 4.3.1 shows an increase in income from the level given by the budget line LM to that given by $L'M'$. The two budget lines are parallel, so no change in relative price has occurred. The increase from LM to $L'M'$ can come from an increase in money income, prices constant, or by uniform percentage reduction in both prices.

---

[4]The income effect is the change in x that results from a change in income. Since

$$I = p_x x + p_y y + \ldots + p_z z,$$

then for any change in income, irrespective of its cause,

$$dI = p_x \frac{\partial x}{\partial I} dI + p_y \frac{\partial y}{\partial I} dI + \ldots + p_z \frac{\partial z}{\partial I} dI.$$

Since $p_x, p_y, \ldots, p_z > 0$ and since the left-hand side is positive, in some "average" sense, the $\frac{\partial x}{\partial I} dI$, $\frac{\partial y}{\partial I} dI, \ldots, \frac{\partial z}{\partial I} dI$ on the right-hand side must be positive. In fact, the last expression can be rewritten as

$$1 = p_x \frac{x}{I} \frac{\partial x}{\partial I} \frac{I}{x} + p_y \frac{y}{I} \frac{\partial y}{\partial I} \frac{I}{y} + \ldots + p_z \frac{z}{I} \frac{\partial z}{\partial I} \frac{I}{z}$$

or

$$1 = s_x \eta_x + s_y \eta_y + \ldots + s_z \eta_z$$

where $s_q \equiv p_q q / I$ or the share of income spent on good q and $\eta_q \equiv \partial q/\partial I \cdot I/q$ or the income elasticity of good q. Thus, a weighted average of income elasticities must equal 1, and so income effects are positive, on average.

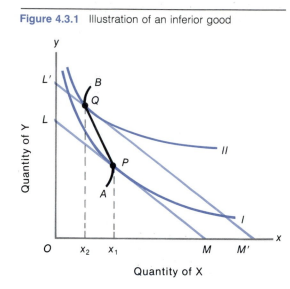

Figure 4.3.1 Illustration of an inferior good

In the change, the position of consumer equilibrium shifts from point P on indifference curve I to point Q on indifference curve II. As a result of the *increase* in real income at the constant *relative* prices, the quantity demanded of good X falls from Ox_1 to Ox_2. The income–consumption curve, over this range of real-income values, rises backward from P to Q; and the entire income–consumption curve might resemble the curve $APQB$.

Figure 4.3.1 illustrates an indifference map involving an inferior good (X).[5] The income effect is inverse, a rise in real income at a constant price ratio leading to a decline in quantity demanded. Similarly, if $L'M'$ is regarded as the original income level, LM represents a lower real income. In this case, a decline in real income would be accompanied by an increase in the quantity of X demanded.

Generally, the substitution effect of a price change is great enough to offset a negative income effect. But in one case, called the Giffen Paradox, the income effect is so strong that it more than offsets the substitution effect. Thus a decline in price leads to a decline in quantity demanded and a rise in price induces a rise in quantity demanded. Figure 4.3.2 is an illustration of the Giffen Paradox. The original price of X is given by the slope of LM. With given money income and a constant price of Y, the price of X falls to the level indicated by the slope of LM'. The position of consumer equilibrium shifts from point P on indifference

---

[5]The argument given in footnote 4 implies that both goods in a two-good world cannot be inferior. The intuition is that the increase in income must be spent on something, and if both were inferior, a decrease in expenditure on both would be implied. But this would imply that the individual is not spending all his income. This puts the consumer inside the budget line and cannot be optimal. Can both goods be superior in a two-good world?

Part One   Demand, Supply, and Markets: An Introductory Look

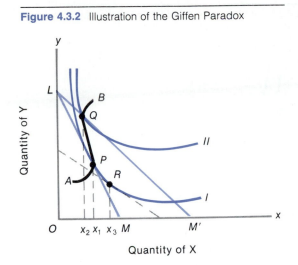

Figure 4.3.2 Illustration of the Giffen Paradox

curve I to point Q on indifference curve II. Over this range, the price–consumption curve is PQ, and throughout the entire range it might look like the curve $APQB$. In the case of the Giffen Paradox, the price–consumption curve is *backward rising* over a certain range.

The substitution effect associated with the fall in p_x is still positive (equal to $Ox_3 - Ox_1$) and shown by the move from P to R. But the income effect of $Ox_2 - Ox_3$ is not only negative; it is large enough to swamp the positive substitution effect so the net effect is negative, i.e., $Ox_2 - Ox_1 < 0$.

Giffen Paradox: Giffen Paradox refers to a good whose quantity demanded varies directly with price. A good must be an inferior good to belong in this category; but not all inferior goods conform to the conditions of the Giffen Paradox. The class of goods for which the Giffen Paradox holds constitutes the only exception to the law of demand.

While the Giffen Paradox is a legitimate theoretical exception to the law of demand, there is no persuasive empirical evidence that this phenomenon occurs to any measurable extent. There is evidence that some goods, such as oleomargarine, may have negative income elasticities and hence are classified as inferior goods, but there is virtually no evidence that the income effect is ever substantial enough in these cases to lead to the Giffen Paradox.[6]

---

[6]Frequently, one sees textbook "examples" of Giffen goods such as potatoes in 19th-century Ireland, but there does not appear to be any confirming evidence to support these examples. The interested reader may wish to consult George J. Stigler, "Notes on the History of the Giffen Paradox," *Journal of Political Economy* 55 (1947), pp. 152–56.

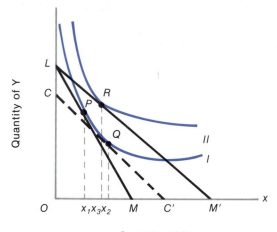

Figure 4.3.3 Income and substitution effects for an inferior good not subject to the Giffen Paradox

Quantity of X

Income and Substitution Effects for an Inferior Good
4.3.b

The relations described in subsection 4.3.a are shown more clearly by separating the total effect into its component parts. Figure 4.3.3 is an illustration of the income and substitution effects for an inferior good not subject to the conditions of the Giffen Paradox.

Exercise: Using a diagram analogous to Figure 4.3.2, show that X is an inferior good but is *not* subject to the Giffen Paradox.

SUBSTITUTION AND COMPLEMENTARITY
4.4

When an individual's demand schedule is constructed, his or her preference pattern, nominal money income, and the nominal prices of related commodities are held constant. Thus a demand schedule shows the relation between the nominal price of a commodity and the quantity of it demanded, all other demand influences held constant (or impounded in a *ceteris paribus* assumption). This partial equilibrium demand function is quite useful for some purposes, but much less useful for others. In some situations a general equilibrium view of the problem is required. So far as demand analysis is concerned, this means that one or more of the *ceteris paribus* assumptions must be relaxed.

More particularly, if the nominal prices of related commodities are allowed to vary, there will be definite repercussions on the quantity demanded of the commodity in question. By observing these repercussions, one is able to classify pairs of commodities as substitute or complementary goods. Historically, the first method of classification was based upon the *total effect* upon quantity demanded of good X resulting from a change in the price of good Y.

Classification by Cross-Elasticities
4.4.a

If all prices are allowed to vary, the quantity of good X demanded depends not only upon its own price but upon the prices of related goods as well. Instead of a demand *curve* there is a demand *surface* such as shown in Figures 4.4.1 and 4.4.2.

For illustrative purposes, suppose good X is related to only one other commodity, good Y. Schematically, the demand function can no longer be written as $q = h(p)$. Instead, one must write $q_x = f(p_x, p_y)$, where q and p represent quantity and price and the subscripts indicate the commodity in question.[7]

The price elasticity of demand, or "own" elasticity, is

$$\eta_{xx} = -\left(\frac{\Delta q_x}{q_x} \div \frac{\Delta p_x}{p_x}\right),$$

where Δ means "the change in." The direct price elasticity, in other words, is the proportional change in quantity demanded of good X resulting from a given proportional change in the price of good X. The elasticity formula is applicable whether the demand function has the form shown in the first or second equation. When the price of a related good enters the demand function, however, it is possible to define the price cross-elasticity of demand:

$$\eta_{xy} = \frac{\Delta q_x}{q_x} \div \frac{\Delta p_y}{p_y}.$$

The price cross-elasticity of demand is the proportional change in the quantity of X demanded resulting from a given change in the price of the related good Y.

According to the cross-elasticity classification, goods X and Y are substitutes or complements according as the price cross-elasticity of demand is positive or negative. As trivial examples, consider the following. An increase in the price of pork, the price of beef remaining constant, will tend to augment the quantity of beef demanded; η_{xy} is positive, and beef and pork are said to be substitute goods. On the other hand, an increase in the price of gin will tend to reduce the quantity of vermouth demanded (the price of vermouth remaining constant), because they are used in tandem for martinis; in this case η_{xy} is negative, and gin and vermouth are said to be complementary goods.

---

[7]Implicitly, this is always true, but when $\frac{\partial^2 x}{\partial p_x \partial p_y} = 0$, we tend to suppress it and write $q = f(p)$.

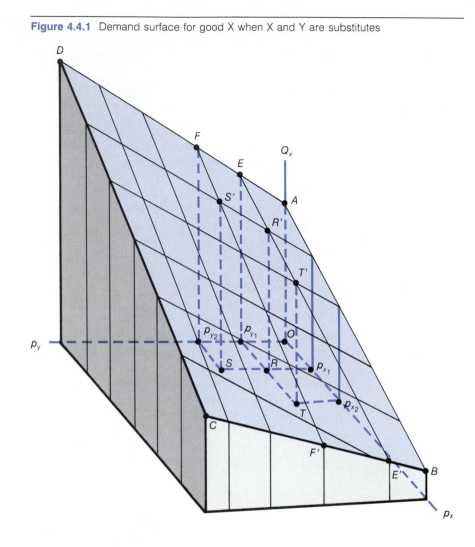

Figure 4.4.1 Demand surface for good X when X and Y are substitutes

Geometric Illustrations
4.4.b

Linear demand surfaces for the two-good case are shown in Figures 4.4.1 and 4.4.2. In each graph, the quantity of X demanded is plotted on the vertical or "height" axis, while the prices of X and Y are plotted on the "width" and "length" axes. In each case, the plane $ABCD$ is the demand surface.

Figure 4.4.1 shows a linear demand surface where goods X and Y are substitutes over the range of prices considered. Notice that the law of demand holds: as the price of X increases, its quantity demanded falls. Thus if the price of Y is held fixed at Op_{y_1}, an increase in the price of X from Op_{x_1} to Op_{x_2} causes a decline in quantity demanded from RR' to TT'. Now hold the price of X constant at Op_{x_1}. As the price of Y increases from Op_{y_1} to Op_{y_2}, the quantity of X demanded rises

Part One   Demand, Supply, and Markets: An Introductory Look

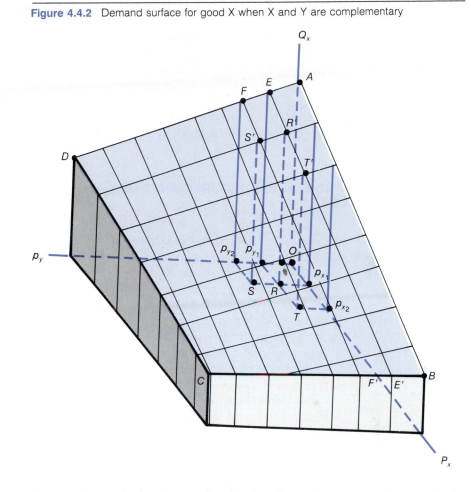

Figure 4.4.2 Demand surface for good X when X and Y are complementary

from RR' to SS' — an increase in the price of good Y causes an increase in the quantity of X demanded. To put it differently, an increase in the price of Y causes the demand curve in the Q_x, p_x plane to *shift* from EE' to FF'. Thus the coefficient η_{xy} is positive, and the goods are said to be substitutes.

Figure 4.4.2 shows the opposite relation over the range of prices considered. The law of demand again obtains. For a fixed price of Y, Op_{y_1}, an increase in the price of X from Op_{x_1} to Op_{x_2} causes a reduction in quantity demanded from RR' to TT'. But now hold the price of X constant at Op_{x_1}. An increase in the price of Y from Op_{y_1} to Op_{y_2} also causes a decline in the quantity of X demanded, from RR' to SS' in this case. Alternatively, one may say that the demand *curve* for X shifts from EE' to FF'. Accordingly, the coefficient of price cross-elasticity is negative and the commodities are said to be complementary goods.

The cross-elasticity approach to commodity classification directs attention to the change in quantity demanded resulting from a change in the price of a related good *without* compensating for the change in the level of real income. The *total effect* of a price change is thus the criterion used in this classification scheme. On an empirical level, this is the only feasible method of commodity classification because market demand functions can be computed while individual preference functions cannot (from readily available data).

In applied problems, one is usually interested in the *market* relation among commodities rather than the commodity relation as viewed by an individual consumer. Thus the cross-elasticity classification of commodity relations is the one most frequently encountered in applied studies. Indeed, reference to market cross-elasticities has even appeared in Supreme Court antitrust decisions.

APPLICATION OF INDIFFERENCE CURVE ANALYSIS: THE ECONOMIC THEORY OF INDEX NUMBERS
4.5

An interesting application of indifference curve analysis can be made in the field of index numbers. For simplicity, let us restrict our attention to a consumer who buys two commodities, X_1 and X_2, in two different time periods, 0 and 1. In time period 0 the consumer buys x_1^0 units of X_1 at price p_1^0 and x_2^0 units of X_2 at price p_2^0. Similarly, in period 1 the consumer purchases x_1^1 and x_2^1 units of X_1 and X_2 at prices p_1^1 and p_2^1 respectively. The essential problem of index numbers is as follows: Has the individual's standard of living increased or decreased in period 1 as compared with period 0?

To make the comparison of standards of living at all meaningful, it is necessary to assume that the consumer's taste (preference map) does not change over the time period under consideration. Given this assumption, information can sometimes be gained from indifference curve analysis.

Consider the budget lines given in Figure 4.5.1. In the original period (called the base period), the consumer's money income and prices p_1^0 and p_2^0 give rise to the budget line P_0P_0'. In period 1, prices (and possibly income) change so that the budget line becomes P_1P_1'. Is the consumer better off in period 1 compared with the base period in the sense of being on a higher indifference curve? The answer to this question, in the absence of direct knowledge of his or her indifference map, depends on the commodity bundles actually consumed in each period.

To see why, suppose first we observe that the consumer chooses bundle Q_0 in the base period and Q_1 in period 1. From the way the budget lines are drawn, it is clear that the consumer has the option of purchasing the base period bundle Q_0 in period 1. The reverse is not true; Q_1 could not be purchased at the base-year prices and income.

Thus, since Q_0 is still available in period 1 but is not chosen, the consumer must be better off in period 1.

If, instead of Q_0, the consumer had chosen Q_0' in the base period, we would not be able to use this reasoning to conclude that Q_1 makes the consumer better off. This is because Q_0' is not available to the consumer at the period 1 prices as Q_0 was. The reader should be able to see the ambiguity in this instance by imagining alternative sets of indifference maps imposed on Figure 4.5.1 — one

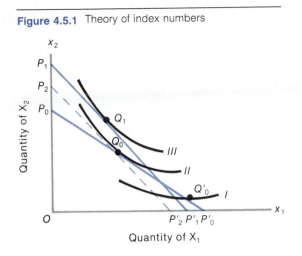

Figure 4.5.1 Theory of index numbers

set of indifference curves that puts Q_0' on a higher indifference curve than Q_1 and an alternative set of indifference curves that puts Q_1 on a higher indifference curve than Q_0'. Thus, unless we know something about the indifference map, we cannot determine which of the bundles Q_1 and Q_0' is preferred.

Information from the Budget Map
4.5.a

What we do know is that if the total expenditure in period 1 exceeds the cost of the base period bundle in terms of period 1 prices, then the consumer is better off in period 1. Thus, if

$$p_1^1 x_1^1 + p_2^1 x_2^1 > p_1^1 x_1^0 + p_2^1 x_2^0,$$

then Q_1 is preferred to Q_0. Writing this expression as a sum and suppressing subscripts, we know the individual is better off in period 1 when

$$\Sigma \, p^1 x^1 > \Sigma \, p^1 x^0. \tag{4.5.1}$$

By the same reasoning, if

$$\Sigma \, p^0 x^0 > \Sigma \, p^0 x^1, \tag{4.5.2}$$

then the individual is better off in the base period. This is because the inequality shows that the period 1 bundle was not chosen in the base period even though it could have been.

Index Numbers as Indicators of Individual Welfare Changes
4.5.b

The analysis can be pushed somewhat further by introducing three index numbers. The first of these index numbers measures the change in the consumer's income from the base year to the given year. Since it is assumed that income equals expenditure, the incomes of the base year and the given year are $\Sigma\, p^0 x^0$ and $\Sigma\, p^1 x^1$, respectively. Consequently, the index of money income change is

$$E = \frac{\Sigma\, p^1 x^1}{\Sigma\, p^0 x^0}. \qquad (4.5.3)$$

The next index number to be introduced is called the Laspeyre index. This index number measures the cost, relative to the base period, of purchasing the base-year quantities at the given-year prices. Since the cost of the base-year quantities at given-year prices is $\Sigma\, p^1 x^0$, the Laspeyre index is[8]

$$L = \frac{\Sigma\, p^1 x^0}{\Sigma\, p^0 x^0}. \qquad (4.5.4)$$

Finally, the Paasche index measures the cost of purchasing the given-year quantities at given-year prices relative to their cost at base-year prices. Since the cost of given-year quantities at base-year prices is $\Sigma\, p^0 x^1$, the Paasche index is

$$P = \frac{\Sigma\, p^1 x^1}{\Sigma\, p^0 x^1}. \qquad (4.5.5)$$

Now from expression (4.5.1), the individual is better off in period 1 if $\Sigma\, p^1 x^1 > \Sigma\, p^1 x^0$. Dividing both sides of this inequality by $\Sigma\, p^0 x^0$, we have that he or she is better off in period 1 if

$$\frac{\Sigma\, p^1 x^1}{\Sigma\, p^0 x^0} > \frac{\Sigma\, p^1 x^0}{\Sigma\, p^0 x^0}, \qquad (4.5.6)$$

or if

$$E > L. \qquad (4.5.7)$$

Similarly, from expression (4.5.2), the individual is better off in the base period if $\Sigma\, p^0 x^0 > \Sigma\, p^0 x^1$. Dividing both sides of this inequality by $\Sigma\, p^1 x^1$, we have that the consumer is better off in the base period if

$$\frac{\Sigma\, p^0 x^0}{\Sigma\, p^1 x^1} > \frac{\Sigma\, p^0 x^1}{\Sigma\, p^1 x^1}, \qquad (4.5.8)$$

or if

$$\frac{1}{E} > \frac{1}{P}, \qquad (4.5.9)$$

or if

$$E < P. \qquad (4.5.10)$$

---

[8] The familiar Consumer Price Index produced each month by the U.S. Bureau of Labor Statistics is an index of the Laspeyre form.

From this analysis, especially expressions (4.5.7) and (4.5.10), four cases can be distinguished.

1. E is greater than both P and L. By expression (4.5.7), the individual's standard of living increases from period 0 to period 1. By (4.5.10) the standard of living does not fall. Hence the individual is definitely better off in period 1.
2. E is less than both P and L. By expression (4.5.10), the individual was better off in the base period. By (4.5.7) the individual was not better off in the given period. An unequivocal answer is again obtained: the individual's standard of living falls from period 0 to period 1.
3. $L > E > P$. In this case neither expression (4.5.7) nor (4.5.10) is satisfied. $L > E$ implies that the consumer cannot be said to be better off in period 1. But $E > P$ implies that he cannot be said to be better off in period 0 either. Consequently, no conclusion can be drawn.
4. $P > E > L$. This situation is inconsistent. By expression (4.5.10), $P > E$ implies that the individual was better off in the base period. But $E > L$ implies, by (4.5.7), that the individual was better off in period 1. The individual's standard of living has both risen and fallen! Such a contradiction may reflect a change in the individual's preference pattern. In any event, it precludes an inference concerning the change in the individual's welfare.

This situation is illustrated in Figure 4.5.2. Base period prices are given by budget line $P_0 P_0'$ and period 1 prices by budget line $P_1 P_1'$.

Suppose that the individual chose S when the budget line was $P_0 P_0'$ and T when the budget line was $P_1 P_1'$. Since LL' lies below $P_1 P_1'$, but is parallel to it and since S is on LL' and T is on $P_1 P_1'$, it must be true that

$$\Sigma\, p_1 x_0 < \Sigma\, p_1 x_1$$

so that

$$\frac{\Sigma\, p_1 x_0}{\Sigma\, p_0 x_0} < \frac{\Sigma\, p_1 x_1}{\Sigma\, p_0 x_0}$$

or

$$L < E.$$

Also, since T is on MM', which has the same prices but lies below $P_0 P_0'$, on which S resides,

$$\Sigma\, p_0 x_0 > p_0 x_1$$

or

$$\frac{\Sigma\, p_0 x_0}{\Sigma\, p_1 x_1} > \frac{\Sigma\, p_0 x_1}{\Sigma\, p_1 x_1}$$

$$\frac{1}{E} > \frac{1}{P}$$

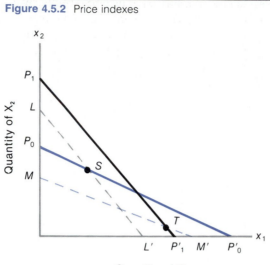

Figure 4.5.2 Price indexes

or

$$E < P.$$

Thus,

$$P > E > L.$$

That there is an inconsistency is obvious from the diagram because the consumer could have had T in the base period but chose S, implying that he prefers S to T. But in period 1, he could have had S, but chose T, implying that he prefers T to S. This is inconsistent unless tastes have changed.

In summary, it is sometimes possible to determine whether an individual's standard of living has increased or decreased by means of index number comparisons. In other situations, however, the results are inconclusive or contradictory.

APPLICATIONS OF INDIFFERENCE CURVE ANALYSIS: THE CHOICE BETWEEN LEISURE AND INCOME
4.6

The theory of consumer behavior as formulated above is quite general, and it leads to many interesting and important propositions concerning demand and consumer choice. One application involves the derivation of the worker's supply of labor to the market. This is equivalent to deriving his demand for leisure. To that end, let us aggregate expenditures on all goods and services into the simple term *income*. Since by our assumptions all income is spent on goods and services (which includes saving), this *income* is simply our familiar budget constraint.

Part One   Demand, Supply, and Markets: An Introductory Look

At the same time, the amount of income received by a consumer depends upon the amount of time allocated to work. The more one works, the greater is one's income. Yet the more one works, the less is one's leisure time. Leisure has utility to most people; therefore, each consumer is confronted with a fundamental trade-off between the consumption of goods and services and the consumption of leisure. This section analyzes this trade-off in some very simple cases.

The Income–Leisure Graph
4.6.a

Consider Figure 4.6.1. Income is plotted on the vertical axis, and leisure on the horizontal axis in the rightward direction. The unit of time in which leisure is measured is not relevant — it may be hours per day, weeks per year, or any other measurement unit. The essential point is that the total amount of time is fixed (say, 24 hours per day); and the sum of work time and leisure time must equal this fixed total time. Thus work time may be measured in a leftward direction along the horizontal axis. In Figure 4.6.1, OZ is the total time available. If OC hours per day are taken as leisure, then CZ hours are spent at work.

Now make two simplifying assumptions. First, assume the individual may work as many hours per day as he or she desires.[9,10] Second, assume the income per hour is the same irrespective of the number of hours worked. Thus, if the individual works CZ hours per day and receives income of $CE = OG$, the hourly wage is CE/CZ. But since CEZ and OAZ are similar triangles, $CE/CZ = OA/OZ$. Thus the slope of the straight line ZA represents the hourly wage rate.[11]

Exercise: Suppose an individual works CZ hours per day and receives income CF. Show that the slope of ZB represents the hourly wage rate.

Equilibrium between Income and Leisure
4.6.b

Since income (or consumption) and leisure are alternative sources of utility, the consumer's preference pattern between them may be represented by an indifference map such as that shown in Figure 4.6.2.[12] The indifference curves have all the properties of the usual indifference curves (Chapter 2). Thus the consumer is

---

[9]Recall that the unit of measurement of time is irrelevant. For the sake of brevity, we speak of hours per day. Any other time measurement may be substituted.

[10]This is not an unrealistic assumption — individuals can find part-time employment and they also can hold more than one job by "moonlighting" and other means. In a problem at the end of the chapter, we ask the reader to analyze the effect of restrictions on the number of hours that can be spent working.

[11]ZA is a straight line because we have assumed that the hourly wage is constant.

[12]This is the same as saying that goods X and Y are alternative sources of utility and that there must be a trade-off between them.

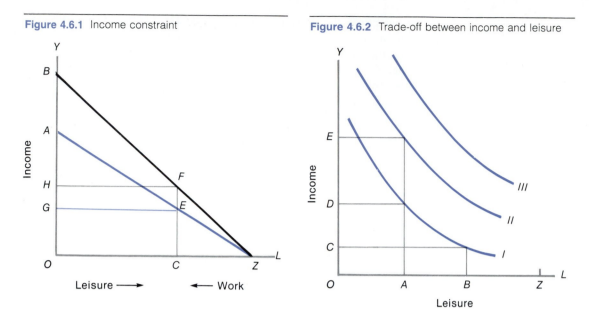

Figure 4.6.1 Income constraint

Figure 4.6.2 Trade-off between income and leisure

indifferent between OA hours of leisure and income OD, and OB hours of leisure and income OC. Of course, the higher the indifference curve, the greater is utility. For example, suppose that OA hours of leisure are taken. Then the consumer gains greater utility if income is OE than if it is OD.

Let us now put Figures 4.6.1 and 4.6.2 together, as shown in Figure 4.6.3. In the customary manner, we may determine the point of utility maximization (consumer equilibrium). The marginal rate of substitution is given by the (negative of the) slope of the indifference curve. The "price ratio" is given by the (negative of the) slope of ZA. Equilibrium is attained at point E on II, with CZ hours of work and income OB. Indifference curve III cannot be attained at the given wage rate. Any curve lower than II will result in less utility since there is a possible trade-off that will make the consumer-worker better off.

The Supply of Labor
4.6.c

It is now a simple matter to derive the supply of labor. Recall that demand curves are traced out by rotating the budget line to obtain the amount demanded at each price. Suppose that the wage rate rises. This implies that the budget line rotates clockwise around Z in Panel A of Figure 4.6.4.

When the wage rate is given by (minus) the slope of the line ZX, the individual chooses point R, demanding L_0 of leisure. When the wage rises to (minus) the slope given by line ZX', the individual chooses point S demanding L_1 of leisure. Those points are plotted in Panel B of Figure 4.6.4. If the process is repeated for all possible wage rates then the demand curve for leisure, DD', is traced out.

Part One   Demand, Supply, and Markets: An Introductory Look

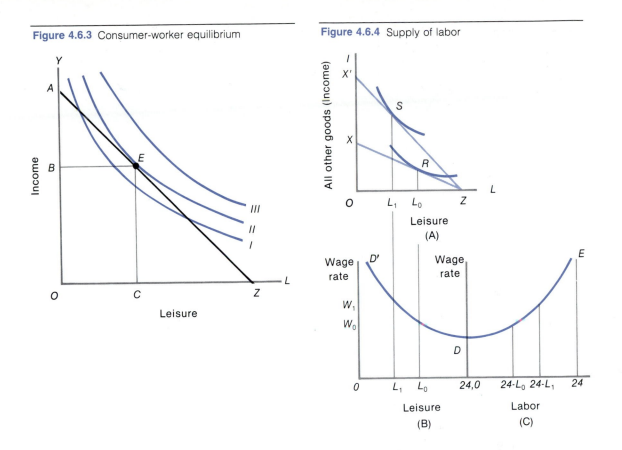

Figure 4.6.3 Consumer-worker equilibrium

Figure 4.6.4 Supply of labor

(A)

(B)

(C)

Now, Hours worked = 24 − Leisure so that once leisure is known, it is trivial to derive the hours of work. This is done in Panel C of Figure 4.6.4. When leisure equals 24, labor equals 0. When leisure equals L_0, labor equals $24 - L_0$, and so forth. Note that the labor supply curve, DE, is the reflection of the leisure demand curve, $D'D$ around the vertical line at leisure = 24 or labor = 0.

Exercise: Show that if the price–consumption curve in leisure and all other goods (Figure 4.6.4, Panel A) is positively sloped then the supply of labor is negatively sloped. Does this make any intuitive sense?

Overtime Rates
4.6.d

It is now customary that union–management contracts require extra pay for "overtime" work. In the situation represented by Figure 4.6.5, overtime is any work in excess of CZ hours per day. Further assume that the overtime wage is half again as great as the "straight-time" wage. Thus the slope of ZA represents

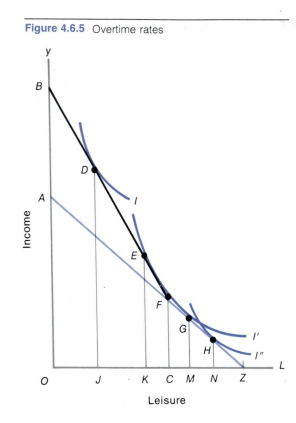

Figure 4.6.5 Overtime rates

the regular wage and the slope of *ZFB* represents the straight-time and overtime wage (where *CZ* hours of work is straight time). Finally, assume that the worker can choose the amount of overtime to be worked, if any.

It is clear from Figure 4.6.5 that the result of overtime pay for any individual is uncertain. A person with an indifference map represented by I will clearly choose to work overtime, while an individual with an indifference map represented by I″ will never voluntarily work overtime. An intermediate case is illustrated by the indifference curve I′. Such an individual is indifferent between working *KZ* hours for *KE* income or working *MZ* hours for *MG* income.

Suppose, however, that a worker chose to work *CZ* hours per day (consume *OC* of leisure) when offered only a straight-time wage as shown by *ZA* in Figure 4.6.6. This implies that there must be a tangency of an indifference curve to *ZA* at *F*(otherwise the worker would not demand *OC* of leisure). Now, offer him overtime after he works *CZ* hours. This gives him budget line *ZFB*. It is obvious from the diagram that the new optimum must lie to the left of *F*, so that the demand for leisure falls. In this case, it falls to *OD*, resulting from the choice of *E*. Thus, more hours are worked.

Why is it necessarily the case that workers who choose to supply *X* hours of labor with a straight-time wage will always supply more hours when they are offered overtime? The reason can be given in terms of income and substitution

Figure 4.6.6 Overtime implies increased hours of work

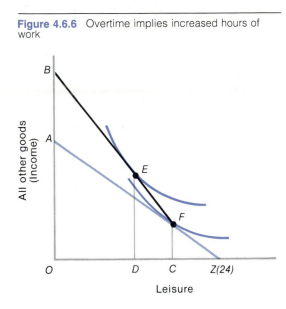

effects. At point F, the offer of overtime makes leisure more expensive, inducing a substitution away from leisure. The income effect works in the opposite direction because the option to work overtime makes the individual richer. But the income effect does not take hold until he supplies some overtime hours. That is, if the worker supplied only CZ hours, he is no richer than he is when overtime is not offered. Therefore, there is no income effect pushing against the substitution effect until more than CZ hours of labor are supplied. At F only the substitution effect is relevant, so fewer hours of leisure are demanded and more hours of labor are supplied. If overtime were paid before $24 - OC$ hours were worked, it would not *necessarily* be the case that hours would increase. Then the kink would lie on the FZ segment and a tangency with the highest indifference curve could result to the right of C.

Demand for General Assistance Payments[13]
4.6.e

Among many of the social welfare programs that have been proposed for adoption by the federal government is one that would provide a minimum annual income per family. This program has not yet been adopted; nonetheless we may analyze some potential economic consequences of it.

Refer to Figure 4.6.7. Suppose the wage rate is represented by the slope of ZA. In the absence of a guaranteed minimum income, an individual whose indifference map is given by I, II would attain equilibrium at B, working CZ hours and

---

[13]For a much more detailed discussion, see C. T. Brehm and T. R. Saving, "The Demand for General Assistance Payments," *American Economic Review* 54 (1964), pp. 1002–18.

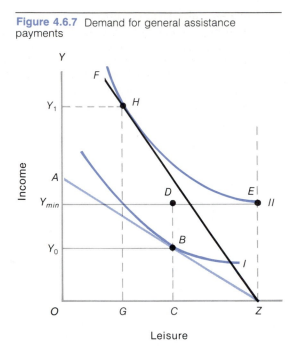

Figure 4.6.7 Demand for general assistance payments

receiving income OY_0. If a minimum income of $OY_{\min}$ is guaranteed by the government, this individual might still work CZ hours, earn income of OY_0, and receive supplementary payment from the government of $BD = OY_{\min} - OY_0$. In this case, however, the individual can attain a greater level of satisfaction by doing no work at all— by moving to point E on indifference curve II and receiving the minimum guaranteed income from the government.

From the point E the individual can be induced to work. In terms of Figure 4.6.7, if the wage rate should rise to ZF (or higher), the worker would forgo the government payment, work GZ hours, and receive income of OY_1. From this example it is clear that a guaranteed minimum income can never lead to an increase in labor time. When all individuals in the society are considered, it will also surely lead to a reduction in labor time (and, consequently, in national output). The exact result, however, depends upon the leisure–income preferences of individuals, the level of the minimum income, and the wage rate available to each individual in question.[14]

Exercise: Suppose an individual does not like to receive welfare payments. More specifically, assume that the person regards $1 in welfare payments as equivalent to $0.50 of earned income. Analyze the effects of a guaranteed minimum income under these circumstances.

---

[14]This ignores any effect that financing the government assistance payments may have on the amount of labor supplied.

Part One   Demand, Supply, and Markets: An Introductory Look

Exercise: There has recently been some policy discussion of a negative income tax. Under this scheme, a *base income* would be stipulated. A person earning more than the base income would pay a positive tax proportional to the difference between his or her earned income and the base income; one earning less than the base income would receive a subsidy proportional to the difference between the base income and his or her earned income. Suppose the factor of proportionality is 50 percent. (a) Analyze this welfare program by means of a graph such as Figure 4.6.7, and (b) compare the results of a negative income tax with the results of a guaranteed minimum income.

TIME PREFERENCE — CONSUMPTION AND SAVING OVER THE LIFE CYCLE
4.7

In the previous section, we investigated how a person might allocate time between work (earning income) and leisure. A related question concerns how an individual might decide between present and future consumption. Suppose we think of a person's life as being divided into two periods (for example, working years and retirement years) and that the individual receives income of y_1 in the first period and income of y_2 in the second period.[15]

By either borrowing or lending at a given interest rate, r, an individual can transfer current income into future income or future income into current income. For example, if $y_1 = \$100$ and $y_2 = \$50$, and the interest rate is 10 percent, the individual can lend (save) the current $100 of income and have a total wealth in period 2 of $160 (= 100[1.10] + 50) or the person can borrow against the collateral of future income and have $145.45 in period 1. In this last calculation, we use the fact that the $45.45 the individual borrows in period 1 accrues interest of $4.55 (at 10 percent) so the $50 income in period 2 is just enough to pay back the principal of $45.45 plus the accrued interest of $4.55. Algebraically, the individual's period 1 wealth (or the maximum possible income in period 1) is

$$y_1 + \frac{y_2}{(1 + r)}.$$

By either borrowing or lending, the individual can have as much as $160 to consume in period 2 (and nothing in period 1) or as much as $145.45 in period 1 (and nothing in period 2) or any linear combination of these extremes. The relationship between first and second period consumption is given by

$$c_2 = y_2 + (y_1 - c_1)(1 + r) \tag{4.7.1}$$

or

$$c_2 = y_2 + y_1(1 + r) - c_1(1 + r) \tag{4.7.2}$$

where c_1 can have any value between 0 and $y_1 + y_2/(1 + r)$. Equation (4.7.2) is the budget line between present and future consumption that is determined by the

---

[15]This analysis easily can be extended to more than two periods.

interest rate and the income in each of the two periods. As we have already seen, the individual moves along this budget line by either borrowing or lending (saving). If $y_1 - c_1$ is positive, then it represents the amount of saving the individual does in period 1 and $(y_1 - c_1)(1 + r)$ is the principal plus interest on this saving that is available for period 2 consumption. If $y_1 - c_1$ is negative, it represents the amount the individual borrows in period 1 and $(y_1 - c_1)(1 + r)$ is the principal plus interest that must be paid back to the bank out of period 2 income.

To find out how much the individual actually will save (borrow) and consume, we introduce a utility function $Y(c_1,c_2)$ representing the utility derived from consumption of c_1 in period 1 and c_2 in period 2. This utility function is represented in Figure 4.7.1 by indifference curves of the now familiar form. The budget line, BD, in Figure 4.7.1 is the linear equation (4.7.2) which has slope $-(1 + r)$. As shown, the individual has income of y_1 in period 1 and y_2 in period 2. The person consumes OC in period 1 and saves $Cy_1 (= Oy_1 - OC)$. In period 2, the individual has income of y_2 plus the amount $Ay_2 (= Cy_1[1 + r])$ and consumes OA.[16]

As can be inferred from Figure 4.7.1, the equilibrium condition is that the marginal rate of substitution between current and future consumption should equal (the negative of) the slope of the budget line which is $1 + r$. The term $1 + r$ is the relative price of period 2 dollars in terms of period 1 dollars (that is, a period 1 dollar will buy [by lending] $1 + r$ period 2 dollars). Thus, it is seen that interest rates act as prices at which income or assets can be transferred between different time periods.

Exercise: What do OD and OB represent in Figure 4.7.1?

To illustrate with a specific case, assume that the marginal rate of substitution is always given by c_2/c_1.[17] The equilibrium condition is then

$$\frac{c_2}{c_1} = 1 + r. \tag{4.7.3}$$

Solving (4.7.3) for c_2 and substituting in (4.7.2), we obtain the equilibrium c_1:

$$c_1 = \frac{1}{2}\left(y_1 + \frac{y_2}{1 + r}\right). \tag{4.7.4}$$

Equation (4.7.4) indicates that as income in *either* period increases, c_1 also increases and that as the interest rate r increases, c_1 decreases. The inverse relationship between the interest rate and c_1 in this example arises because a larger interest rate means savings in period 1 yield more consumption in period 2 than

---

[16]Because we have restricted the analysis to only two periods in this example, no saving for future consumption occurs in the second period.

[17]The utility function $U(c_1,c_2) = \alpha c_1 c_2 + \beta$, where α and β are given parameters, has this marginal rate of substitution.

Part One   Demand, Supply, and Markets: An Introductory Look

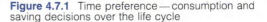

Figure 4.7.1 Time preference—consumption and saving decisions over the life cycle

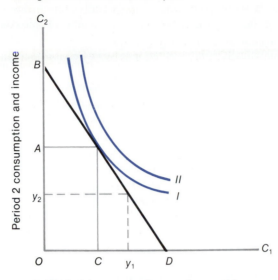

Period 1 consumption, saving, and income

before the increase, or, to use different language, the higher interest rate means it now costs more to transfer future income into current consumption. That is, the opportunity cost of consuming in period 1 goes up with the interest rate.

An increase in interest rates has both a substitution effect and a wealth effect (similar to the income effect discussed in section 4.2). The wealth effect occurs because an increase in interest rates means future income is worth less in present value. The wealth effect can, in theory, lead to cases where interest rate increases result in decreases in current saving.

Exercise: By use of indifference curves, show that it is possible that an increase in interest rates can reduce current savings (increase c_1).

Exercise: When the marginal rate of substitution is given by c_2/c_1, what is the expression (corresponding to [4.7.4]) for c_2? Show that in this case an increase in r will cause c_2 to increase. Also for this case, derive an expression for saving in period 1 and show that saving will decrease if y_2 increases.

MULTIPLE CONSTRAINTS—TIME AS AN ECONOMIC GOOD
4.8

Money income has been the only constraint on the consumer discussed so far. This is an important constraint that deserves emphasis, but there are other constraints that can affect consumer behavior. For example, during periods of general wage and price controls, governments sometimes introduce point-rationing schemes. In such circumstances, a five-pound bag of sugar has *both* a money price and a ration-point price. Analytically, this means there are two budget constraints faced by the consumer—the money income constraint and the ration-point constraint.

An analytically similar situation arises when it is recognized that consumption usually involves expenditures of time as well as money.[18] When you go to the theatre, take a vacation, or eat a meal, both physical (or money) resources and time resources are involved. To illustrate, suppose there are two goods, X and Y, with money prices p_x and p_y. Also suppose that the consumption of a unit of X takes t_x units of time, while consumption of Y takes t_y units of time. To analyze a problem like this, it is necessary to specify the total time available for consumption of X and Y. Actually, the total time a person has available for consumption is also an economic decision: by working less, more time is available for consumption activities. However, to start the analysis, we temporarily assume that the total amount of time for consumption of X and Y is a given amount T (specified in some convenient unit such as hours or minutes). Mathematically, the money income and budget constraints can be stated as:

$$p_x x + p_y y \leq M \tag{4.8.1}$$

$$t_x x + t_y y \leq T \tag{4.8.2}$$

$$x \geq 0$$

$$y \geq 0.$$

These inequalities together define the feasible region in the commodity space (that is, the subset from which the consumer can actually pick a consumption bundle). Figure 4.8.1 provides an example. In this figure, the line *ABE* is the familiar money income budget line. Bundles on and below this line satisfy the constraint (4.8.1). The line *DBC* represents the "time budget" line—points on and below *DBC* satisfy the constraint (4.8.2). If the individual consumed only good Y, the maximum possible consumption consistent with the amount of time available would be T/t_y ($= OD$). Similarly, given the time constraint, the maximum amount of X that would be consumed would be T/t_x ($= OC$). The bundle F (with x_1 units of X and y_2 units of Y) is consistent with the income constraint but violates the time constraint (4.8.2) because it is above *DBC*. Indeed, any bundle in the triangle *ABD* (except for points on *DB*) is not available to the consumer because such bundles violate the time constraint. Similarly, bundles in the triangle *BCE* are not attainable (except for those on the line *BE*), because they violate the money income constraint (4.8.1). Bundle G (with x_2 units of X and y_1 units of Y) is available to the consumer since it satisfies *both* the money and time budget constraints. It should now be clear that the set of bundles that are consistent with both (4.8.1) and (4.8.2) is represented by the area on and below

---

[18]A more elaborate development containing numerous interesting empirical insights may be found in Gary Becker, "A Theory of the Allocation of Time," *Economic Journal*, 75 (1965), pp. 493–517.

Part One   Demand, Supply, and Markets: An Introductory Look

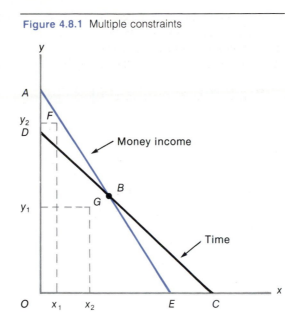

Figure 4.8.1 Multiple constraints

the kinked line *DBE* (and bounded by the horizontal and vertical axes, since $x \geq 0$ and $y \geq 0$ are also constraints). Thus, the set of bundles available to the consumer is given by the area enclosed by the irregular polygon *ODBE* (including its boundaries). Along the segment *DB*, time is the binding constraint ([4.8.2] is satisfied as an equality); and along the segment *BE*, money income is the binding constraint ([4.8.1] is satisfied as an equality).

Figure 4.8.2 shows the different equilibria that can arise. (In this figure, the segments *AB* and *BC* are eliminated for clarity, thus leaving only the boundary *DBE* of the feasible region.) In Panel A of Figure 4.8.2, the maximum utility that can be achieved consistent with the time and money income constraints is given by indifference curve II. This occurs at point *B*, the "kink" in *DBE*, indicating that both time and money are binding constraints. In Panel B, the equilibrium (point *V*) occurs along the segment *DB*, where the time constraint is binding but the money constraint is superfluous. In Panel C, the consumer is in equilibrium at point *R* along the segment BE, where money income is a binding constraint but the time constraint is superfluous.

The equilibria indicated in Panel B and Panel C do not make much sense in the broader problem where *T* is not treated as a given constant.[19] After all, money income and time are generally convertible: one can work more (overtime and moonlighting) or one can work less (part-time jobs), thereby trading money for time. Under these conditions, there never will be a superfluous constraint. To see

---

[19]If we interpret these diagrams as representing money income and ration-point (rather than time) constraints, the equilibria in Panels B and C do make sense, because it is usually illegal to exchange money for ration stamps.

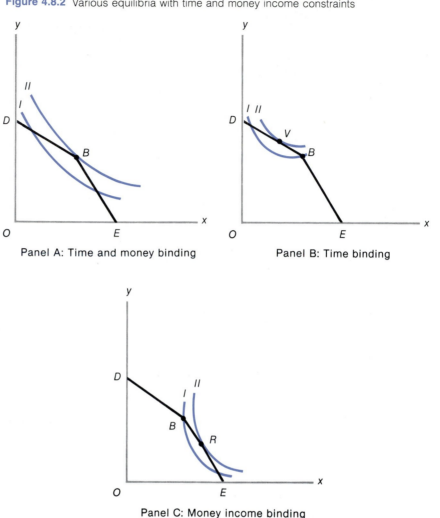

Figure 4.8.2 Various equilibria with time and money income constraints

Panel A: Time and money binding

Panel B: Time binding

Panel C: Money income binding

why, suppose that time is superfluous and money income is a binding constraint as in Panel C. By working a little more, money income can be increased. This must benefit the consumer because the extra time spent working has no alternative value (since time is superfluous at point *R* of Panel C), whereas the additional money income can provide more utility. Geometrically, this is equivalent to shifting *DBE* down a little in Figure 4.8.1 in order to shift up *ABE*. An upward shift of *BE* in Panel C of Figure 4.8.2 will allow the consumer to reach a higher indifference curve than II. Thus, when the consumer can freely adjust the number of hours worked so as to trade off time and money income, the final equilibrium

Part One   Demand, Supply, and Markets: An Introductory Look

Table 4.8.1		
	Cost to A	Cost to B
Baseball game	$ 3 + 6($100) = $603	$ 3 + 6($5) = $33
Wine drinking	$150 + .5($100) = $200	$150 + .5($5) = $152.50

will be of the type shown in Panel A of Figure 4.8.2. A problem at the end of this chapter shows how the usual budget line is modified when these considerations are taken into account.

Exercise: Explain how the consumer can improve the equilibrium in Panel B by adjusting the amount of time spent working.

By using this approach we can understand why different consumers prefer different kinds of commodities. Once it is recognized that there are two components to the cost of a good, its price can be written as

$$\pi_x = p_x + wt_x \tag{4.8.3}$$

where π_x is the good's total price, p_x is the price of purchasing the good, t_x is the time spent consuming it, and w is the wage rate, i.e., the opportunity cost of time.[20]

The point is best illustrated by an example. Consider two goods, going to a baseball game, X, and drinking a $150 bottle of wine, Y. Suppose there are two consumers, A and B, with wage rates $w_A = \$100/\text{hour}$ and $w_B = \$5/\text{hour}$, respectively. A baseball ticket costs $3 and the game takes 6 hours door to door. Wine drinking requires ½ hour. Table 4.8.1 above shows the relevant prices.

As B sees it, the total cost of wine drinking is much higher than the total cost of the baseball game ($152.50 > $33). As A sees it the reverse is true, with wine drinking being the bargain commodity ($200 < $603). It is no wonder that less wealthy individuals say they can't afford fancy wine, but frequently attend baseball games. Similarly, rich people will say that they cannot afford the time to go to a baseball game, but may think little of spending $150 on a bottle of wine.

Exercise: Using a table like 4.8.1, explain why children spend more time playing Frisbee than adults, while adults spend more time at expensive ski resorts.

---

[20]Problem 10 asks for a derivation of this expression for price.

The traditional approach to consumer theory treats goods as the direct source of utility. In recent years, some economists have considered a reformulation of consumer theory in which the characteristics or properties of goods, rather than the goods themselves, are the ultimate source of utility. Thus, a meal does not provide utility directly but has characteristics, such as nutrition and aesthetic appeal, which do enter the utility function. Professor Kelvin Lancaster summarizes the essence of this appeal as follows:[21]

1. The good, per se, does not give utility to the consumer; it possesses characteristics and these characteristics give rise to utility.

2. In general, a good will possess more than one characteristic and many characteristics will be shared by more than one good.

3. Goods in combination may possess characteristics different from those pertaining to goods separately.

In this book, we will not get involved in the details of this formulation of consumer theory, but it is worth noting that the theory provides some insights that are not intrinsic to the traditional theory. For example, by identifying the characteristics of goods, the new theory can predict which goods will be close substitutes and which will not. The new theory can also predict (at least in some cases) when an older product will be displaced from the market by new goods or by price changes.[22] These predictions of the new theory rest on the fairly strong assumption that goods possess multiple characteristics in fixed proportions.

The analytical techniques involved in this new theory are somewhat similar to the case of multiple constraints discussed in section 4.8. Linear constraints are used to represent the transformation (or decomposition) of goods into their underlying characteristics. Thus, at least part of the analysis takes place in "characteristics space" rather than the "goods space" that is used in the traditional analysis. Time constraints as well as money income constraints play a key role in the new theory.

SYNOPSIS
4.10

- The total effect on quantity demanded of a change in a nominal price can be decomposed into a substitution effect and an income effect. The substitution effect by itself always results in an inverse relationship

---

[21]The reader may wish to consult Professor Lancaster's paper, "A New Approach to Consumer Theory," *Journal of Political Economy* 74 (April 1966), pp. 132–57, for more detail. Points 1 to 3 in the text are quoted directly from Lancaster's paper.

[22]This new theory has attracted the interest of people involved in practical marketing problems where new product introductions are often a critical concern.

between nominal price changes and changes in the quantity demanded. The income effect for a normal or superior good reinforces the substitution effect, so, for normal and superior goods (the most common cases empirically), the total effect will exhibit an inverse relation between price and quantity demanded. If the good has a negative income elasticity (inferior good), the income effect runs counter to the substitution effect.

■ The cross-price elasticity between good X and good Y is

$$\eta_{xy} = \frac{\Delta q_x}{q_x} \div \frac{\Delta p_y}{p_y}.$$

This cross-elasticity will be nonzero if changes in the price of Y affect the demand for X. If η_{xy} is positive, the goods are called *substitutes*. If η_{xy} is negative, the goods are called *complements*.

■ Indifference curves can be useful analytical devices in a variety of applications, including index number theory, work–leisure choices, overtime wage rates, social welfare programs, and consumption–saving decisions. In later chapters, other examples of indifference curve analysis will be seen.

■ In some problems, there are additional constraints on consumer behavior beyond the usual money income constraint. As section 4.8 shows, it is not difficult to incorporate these additional constraints in the analysis. This provides additional implications for patterns of consumer demand.

QUESTIONS AND EXERCISES

1. *a.* Suppose the price of apples increases 5 percent and the income elasticity for apples is 0.5. What will happen to the quantity of apples demanded?
   b. Suppose the price of flour increases by 1 percent and the income elasticity for flour is −0.36. What will happen to the quantity of flour demanded?

2. It has been observed that the amount of services of domestic servants consumed in the United States declined in the first half of the 20th century while per capita income was increasing. Does this mean that domestic servants are an inferior good?

3. The following table lists three situations for an individual who consumes two goods X_1 and X_2. The table lists the prices of the goods p_1 and p_2, the quantities consumed of the goods, the consumer's nominal income M, and her utility level.

Situation	p_1	p_2	Quantity of X_1	Quantity of X_2	M	Utility
1	$1	$1	50	40	90	10
2	1	½	48	84	90	15
3	1	½	40	70	75	10

a. When the price of good 2 drops from $1 to $½, what is the change in the quantity demanded of X_2 when nominal income is constant at $90? What part of this change is due to the substitution effect and what part is due to the income effect? Is X_2 a normal or superior good or is it an inferior good?

b. Fill in the blanks in the following table and answer the questions in part (a) for this table.

Situation	p_1	p_2	Quantity of X_1	Quantity of X_2	M	Utility
1	$1	$1	50	—	70	10
2	1	½	52	—	70	15
3	1	½	—	36	60	10

4. Is it possible for all goods to be inferior goods? (Savings or cash balances are assumed to be goods.)

5. Mr. Jones spends all his income on two goods, X_1 and X_2. The prices of these goods, p_1 and p_2, and the quantity Mr. Jones consumed of each are shown in the following table for three separate years:

Year	p_1	p_2	Quantity of X_1	Quantity of X_2
1	$6	$3	10	50
2	4	4	20	30
3	4	3	24	28

a. What are the Laspeyre and Paasche indexes between years 1 and 2, between years 2 and 3, and between years 1 and 3?

b. Is Mr. Jones better off in year 1 or year 2? Is he better off in year 2 or year 3? Is he better off in year 1 or year 3?

6. Is is true that if two goods are substitutes, a fall in the price of one will lead to a fall in the price of the other? Does it matter whether the initial decline in price is demand-led or supply-led?

7. Suppose that upon graduation from college a person has the option of taking a job paying $10,000 per year or borrowing money to go through medical school. Why would anyone become a medical doctor?

8. Suppose Miss Smith, who is 22 years old, learns that she has received an inheritance that will pay her $100,000 on her 35th birthday. Using indifference curve analysis, explain what happens to her current consumption behavior.

9. a. Jeffrey, who is five years old, likes candy and hates spinach. He is allowed two candy bars a day, but his mother offers to give him one additional candy bar for every two ounces of spinach he eats each day. On these terms, Jeffrey eats three ounces of spinach and 3½ candy bars each day. Using indifference curves, analyze Jeffrey's equilibrium consumption of candy bars and spinach.

b. Suppose Jeffrey's mother did not give him his two "free" candy bars each day but offered a candy bar for each two ounces of spinach. Would his spinach consumption be greater or smaller than in part (a)?

10. Suppose money income M is given by $M = M_0 + w(24 - T)$, where M_0 is daily income from sources other than employment (and may be zero) and w is the hourly wage rate. The total hours at work during each 24-hour day will be $(24 - T)$, where T is the time, in hours, spent in consumption activities. Refer to the problem of section 4.8 and show algebraically (or give an economic argument) that, when T can be varied the relevant budget constraint for the consumer will be

$$(p_x + wt_x)x + (p_y + wt_y)y = M_0 + 24w.$$

   a. Show that this is the same as the usual money income constraint when $t_x = 0$ and $t_y = 0$.
   b. What is the economic interpretation of $(p_x + wt_x)$ and $(p_y + wt_y)$?
   c. How would this constraint be affected if overtime rates are paid for any work over eight hours per day?

11. Is the following empirical statement evidence of worker irrationality: "When a firm raises the straight-time wage of its workers, fewer hours of labor are supplied. But paying an overtime premium, which ends up costing less per hour worked, never fails to induce workers to supply the additional hours."

12. The number of people who travel by train rather than plane has fallen dramatically over time. Explain why.

SUGGESTED READINGS

Ben-Porath, Yoram. "Labor Force Participation Rates and the Supply of Labor." *Journal of Political Economy* 81 (May 1973), pp. 697–704.

Becker, Gary S. "A Theory of the Allocation of Time." *Economic Journal* 75 (1965), pp. 493–517.

Ferguson, C. E. "Substitution Effect in Value Theory: A Pedagogical Note." *Southern Economic Journal* 24 (1960), pp. 310–14.

Georgescu-Roegen, Nicholas. "A Diagrammatic Analysis of Complementarity." *Southern Economic Journal* 19 (1952), pp. 1–20.

Henderson, James M., and **Quandt, Richard E.** *Microeconomic Theory*, 2nd ed. New York: McGraw-Hill, 1971, pp. 32–49.

Hicks, J. R. *Value and Capital*, 2nd ed. Oxford: Oxford University Press, 1946, pp. 42–52.

Lancaster, Kelvin J. "A New Approach to Consumer Theory." *Journal of Political Economy* 74 (April 1966), pp. 132–57.

Samuelson, Paul A. *Foundations of Economic Analysis.* Cambridge, Mass.: Harvard University Press, 1947, pp. 100–107.

Staehle, Hans. "A Development of the Economic Theory of Price Index Numbers." *Review of Economic Studies* 2 (1935), pp. 163–88.

5 Characteristics of Market Demand

Will an increase in bus (and subway) fares increase or decrease total expenditures on these forms of transportation? The answer depends on the price elasticity of demand for bus and subway travel. In discussing the market demand curve in more detail, this chapter reexamines several influences on this curve. What is the price elasticity of demand, and what determines its size? What is the income elasticity of demand? The cross-price elasticity of demand? How do total expenditure changes depend on the price elasticity of demand? This last question is dealt with in detail in the "Applying the Theory" section of this chapter and the answer applies to the opening question here. Finally, this chapter discusses the marginal revenue schedule and how it differs from the market demand curve and describes the relevant demand curve facing a perfectly competitive seller. ■

Fare Rise Hit Buses Harder Than Subway, M.T.A. Says

By Edward C. Burks

Public buses lost one eighth of their passengers — far more than the subways — during the first full month of the new 50-cent fare compared with the same period in 1974, the Metropolitan Transportation Authority disclosed yesterday.

Comparing September 1975 and September 1974, the M.T.A. reported these changes on its transit and commuter facilities:

— Bus ridership declined 12.7 percent to 46.2 million from 53 million, an average daily loss of 225,000 riders.

— Subway ridership declined 5.2 percent to 79.3 million from 83.65 million, an average daily loss of 144,000 riders.

— The Long Island Rail Road, which had a 23 percent fare increase September 1, held its own in ridership, in fact had a tiny gain; but the Penn Central Harlem and Hudson Lines, with 25 percent fare increases September 1, had a 3.9 percent decline to 1.73 million riders from 1.8 million.

No Official Explanation

There was no official explanation of the falloff in bus ridership. Unofficially, however, M.T.A. people noted that there is a "greater element of discretion" in whether to take the bus. The bus passenger usually takes a much shorter ride than the subway rider and may elect to walk in good weather. Another theory was that subway ridership, after a steady decline for years, had almost "bottomed out" and most riders were using it to go to work or because they had to.

In raising the fare on September 1, the M.T.A. had sought to soften the blow with numerous bus-to-bus transfers for an extra 25 cents. That system saves many bus riders from paying double fares. Yet the ridership count plummeted.

Revenue Up 33.5 Per Cent

The increase in the transit fare from 35 to 50 cents produced a 33.5 percent gain in subway revenue in September compared with a year ago ($38.3-million compared with $28.7-million); and an 18.4 percent increase in bus revenue ($20.1-million compared with $17-million).

The M.T.A. also reported that Long Island Rail Road revenue was 16.3 percent higher in September 1975 than the year before while ridership increased from 5,068,000 to 5,070,000.

The declines in the transit ridership figures are all the more drastic when the comparison is between September, the first full month of the new fare, and June, the last previous 30-day month.

Subway ridership was 90.6 million in June, only 79.3 million in September, and the decline amounted to 373,000 fewer daily passengers on the average.

Bus ridership (both Transit Authority and Manhattan and Bronx Surface Transit Operating Authority) was 63.96 million in June, only 46.2 million in September.

(continued on page 128)

(continued from page 127)
The decline amounted to 590,000 fewer
daily riders.

Questions

1. Is the demand for bus transportation
   price elastic or price inelastic over the
   price range in the article? How do
   you know?

2. From the information in this article,
   how would you actually come up with
   a number for the price elasticity of
   demand "for bus transportation" when
   the price rose from 35¢ to 50¢? Why is
   such a number somewhat "arbitrary"?

3. Why do you think the price elasticity
   of demand for buses differs from that
   for subways? Which is greater? Are
   both greater than one? Explain.

4. Do you think the elasticity (with
   respect to price) will be greater in

the long run compared to the shorter
run? Why?

Solutions

1. When the price rose from 35¢ to 50¢,
   total revenue increased. This
   information implies that the price
   elasticity of bus transportation must be
   inelastic, or less than one, over this
   range. The quantity reduction must
   have been less than the price increase,
   in percentage terms.

2. Using the formula in the text for price
   elasticity (5.2.1)

$$-\frac{\Delta q}{q} \bigg/ \frac{\Delta p}{p}$$

$$= -\frac{46.2 - 53}{(1/2)(46.2 + 53)} \bigg/ \frac{50 - 35}{(1/2)(50 + 35)}$$

$$= \frac{13.7 \text{ percent}}{35.3 \text{ percent}} = 0.39$$

INTRODUCTION
5.1

The analysis in Part 1 has firmly established the proposition that individual
demand curves slope downward to the right—that quantity demanded varies
inversely with price. The only exception is a truly insignificant one, the Giffen
Paradox. But even if a few individuals are in a situation such that the Giffen
Paradox applies, it is doubtful that the *market* demand curve would show the
same properties.

This chapter considers in more detail some of the concepts introduced in
Chapter 1. In addition, it introduces a number of new ideas, which are important
for the description of behavior of markets that operate with different degrees of
competitiveness.

For the calculation of change in q, the values are taken from September 1974 to September 1975. Note that the calculation above uses the "average" Q and "average" P for q and p in the formula given in the text. Since the value of q and p isn't precisely defined, the value of the price elasticity of demand is somewhat "arbitrary."

3. The main reason cited in this chapter is the availability of substitutes. Presumably, there are fewer "substitutes" for subways. The article itself refers to the "greater element of discretion" in whether to take the bus — the much shorter ride, etc. To an economist, this says that there are fewer substitutes for subway travel. The greater the availability of substitutes, the greater the price elasticity of demand. Thus, this elasticity is greater for buses than subways, but both are less than one. (Why? Because total revenue (TR) increased for both when fares rose.)

4. Yes. Since it takes time to find substitutes, the price elasticity is greater in the long run than in short run. For example, some people might decide to purchase bikes in the longer run, or form carpools. They may not be able to do so in a short period of time, but may be able to do so in a longer period of time.

Source: *New York Times*, . © 1975 The New York Times Company. Reprinted by permission.

THE ELASTICITY OF DEMAND
5.2

The concept and computation of demand elasticities are familiar already; indeed, the measure of price cross-elasticity has been discussed in some detail in Chapter 4. However, the various demand elasticities are so important — on both the theoretical and the empirical level — that they are all discussed in this section.

Price Elasticity of Demand
5.2.a

As noted above, the quantity of a commodity demanded depends upon its price. It is of interest to measure the relative change in quantity demanded resulting from a given proportional change in price. This measure is called the price elasticity of demand.

Price Elasticity of Demand: The price elasticity of demand is the relative responsiveness of quantity demanded to changes in commodity price; in other words, price elasticity is the proportional change in quantity demanded divided by the proportional change in price.

Because quantity demanded and price vary inversely, a positive change in price will be accompanied by a negative change in quantity demanded. Thus, in order to make the coefficient of price elasticity positive, a "minus" sign is introduced into the formula:[1]

$$\eta_{xx} = -\frac{\Delta q}{q} \div \frac{\Delta p}{p} = -\frac{\partial q}{\partial p}\frac{p}{q} . \tag{5.2.1}$$

Equation (5.2.1) gives the formula for what is called "point" price elasticity of demand. This means that the coefficient computed is valid for very small movements only.

As an example, suppose we have the following information:

Price	Quantity demanded
$29.001 ($p_1$)	2,999 (q_1)
29.000 (p_2)	3,000 (q_2)

Obviously, $\Delta p = -\$0.001$ and $\Delta q = +1$. In the formula for point elasticity, one must also use p and q; but a question could arise: should one use p_1 and q_1 or p_2 and q_2? For very small changes such as these, it is immaterial — either may be used, so the point elasticity formula is applicable. This may be seen from the following calculations:

$$\eta = -\frac{\Delta q}{\Delta p}\frac{p_1}{q_1} = -\frac{+1}{-0.001}\frac{29.001}{2,999} = +9.67022,$$

---

[1]Let the demand curve for commodity i be

$$q_i = f(p_1, p_2, \ldots, p_n, I)$$

where q_i is the quantity demanded, p_j is the price of the jth commodity, I is income, and we assume there are n commodities. By definition, the direct, or "own," price elasticity of demand is

$$\eta_{ii} = -\frac{\partial q_i}{\partial p_i}\frac{p_i}{q_i} = -\frac{\partial \log q_i}{\partial \log p_i}$$

where log denotes logarithms to the base e.

$$\eta = -\frac{\Delta q}{\Delta p}\frac{p_2}{q_2} = -\frac{+1}{-0.001}\frac{29.000}{3,000} = +9.66667.$$

The difference in the two computed elasticities is very small, only 0.00355 in a magnitude exceeding 9.

Of course, the demand curve is a function and there is no reason to expect that the elasticity at one point is the same as the elasticity at another. As already discussed in Chapter 1, elasticity of demand need not be constant across consumer types. Nor must it be constant for the same consumer at different points on his or her demand curve. Consider Figure 5.2.1.

Suppose that D_1 is Mr. Smith's demand for shirts when his income is $30,000 per year. If he were to receive an inheritance that brought his income level to $50,000 per year, then his demand would shift to D_2. Suppose that by coincidence, D_2 is parallel to D_1 and that D_1 and D_2 are linear. Then the slope is the same at every point on D_1 and D_2. The elasticity of demand at A, B, and C are all different, even though the slopes are the same at all of those points.

The reason is that elasticity is not slope, but includes also the ratio of price to quantity. In fact equation (5.2.1) can be rewritten as[2]

$$\eta_{xx} = \left(\frac{-1}{\text{Slope of demand curve}}\right)\left(\frac{p}{q}\right). \qquad (5.2.2)$$

Although the slope is the same at A, B, and C, so that $-1/\text{slope}$ is the same at all these points, p/q is different. First, note that in comparing C to A, the price is lower and the quantity higher at C than at A. Therefore, the elasticity of demand is higher at A than at C. Second, note that price is the same, but quantity is greater at B than at A. Therefore, the elasticity of demand is higher at A than at B. What of B relative to C? The quantity is the same, but the price is higher at B than at C. Therefore, the elasticity of demand is higher at B than at C.

This result is not surprising when it is remembered that elasticity refers to percentage rather than absolute change. A given absolute change implies different percentage amounts if the base levels are different. To understand this, consider two extreme cases, as shown in Figure 5.2.2.

The elasticity at point A is infinite, because the smallest reduction in price implies that quantity demanded increases from zero to some positive amount. Because the previously demanded quantity was zero, the increase is infinite in percentage terms. Conversely, at point B, any increase in price from zero to a

---

[2]In reality, demand curves are drawn as "inverse" demand curves. If one understands the slope of the demand curve to be $\Delta q/\Delta p$, then (5.2.2) becomes

$$\eta_{xx} = (-\text{Slope of demand})(p/q).$$

It is only because p is on the vertical axis and slope is $\Delta p/\Delta q$ that it is necessary to think in terms of $(-1/\text{slope})$. In any event there is no ambiguity if we write

$$\eta_{xx} = (\Delta q/\Delta p) \cdot (p/q).$$

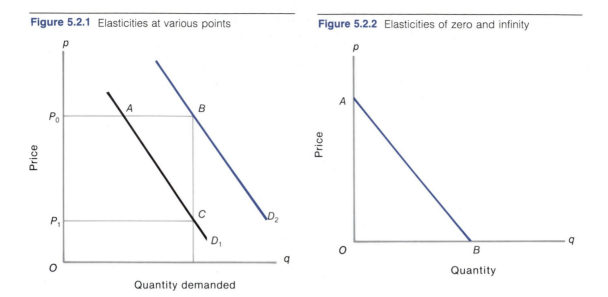

Figure 5.2.1 Elasticities at various points

Figure 5.2.2 Elasticities of zero and infinity

positive number is an infinite percent increase because the price was previously zero. Therefore, any finite change in quantity associated with this infinite change in price implies that elasticity must be zero at this point.

Coefficient of Price Elasticity
5.2.b

Demand is classified as price elastic, of unitary price elasticity, or as price inelastic, depending upon the value of η. If $\eta > 1$, demand is said to be *elastic* — a given percentage change in price will result in a greater percentage change in quantity demanded. Thus small price changes will result in much more significant changes in quantity demanded.

When $\eta = 1$, demand has unit elasticity, meaning that the percentage changes in price and quantity demanded are precisely the same. Finally, if $\eta < 1$, demand is inelastic. A given percentage change in price results in a smaller percentage change in quantity demanded.

Elastic, Inelastic, and Unitary Elasticity: Commodity demand is elastic or inelastic accordingly as the coefficient of price elasticity is greater than or less than unity. If the coefficient is exactly one, demand is said to have unitary price elasticity.

Elasticity and Total Revenue
5.2.c

The relation of price elasticity to one is important for another reason. The total amount spent on a good varies directly with the change in price when elasticity is less than one, and inversely with the price when elasticity is greater than one.

Part One   Demand, Supply, and Markets: An Introductory Look

The intuition behind this result is straightforward: A price increase means that more is spent on each good purchased, which tends to increase the amount spent. Offsetting this is the fact that fewer goods are purchased at the higher price. If the price effect outweighs the quantity effect, then total expenditure rises. If the quantity effect outweighs the price effect, then total expenditure falls.

Elasticity is a measure of the relative strengths of the two effects. If the elasticity of demand is less than 1, then a 1 percent increase in price induces less than a 1 percent decrease in quantity demanded. Thus, the price effect swamps the quantity effect, and expenditure rises. But when elasticity exceeds one, a small increase in price induces a larger decrease in quantity, so the quantity effect dominates and revenue falls.[3] (See the solution to question 4 from the Moonshine news article on p. 9 in Chapter 1. This relationship is also seen in the "Applying the Theory" section of this chapter.)

Factors Affecting Price Elasticity
5.2.d

Whether demand is elastic or inelastic is an important consideration, especially for government policy in individual commodity markets. For example, suppose the demand for wheat were highly price elastic. An increase in the price of wheat would accordingly result in a proportionately greater reduction in quantity demanded. Total dollar expenditures on wheat would decline. Now suppose the government establishes a minimum wheat price above the market equilibrium price. Wheat sales would be reduced, and so too would farmers' incomes, unless the price support were accompanied by a minimum-sales guarantee.

This is but one example; a large book could be filled with similar ones. The policy importance of price elasticity has led to many statistical studies designed to estimate numerical values of price elasticity. Table 5.2.1 reproduces some of these estimates.

As you see from the table, price elasticities range quite widely. The major factor that determines elasticity is the availability of substitute goods. This explains the variations observed in Table 5.2.1.

The more and better are the substitutes for a specific good the greater its price elasticity will tend to be. Goods with few and poor substitutes — food and fuel, for example — will always tend to have low price elasticities. Goods with many substitutes will have higher elasticities.

---

[3]Formally, this is seen as follows:

$$\text{Revenue} = p \cdot q$$

$$\frac{d(\text{Revenue})}{d(\text{Price})} = q + \frac{\partial q}{\partial p} \cdot p$$

$$= q\left(1 + \frac{\partial q}{\partial p} \cdot \frac{p}{q}\right)$$

$$= q(1 - \eta_{xx}).$$

So the change in revenue has the same sign as the change in price when $\eta_{xx} < 1$ and has the opposite sign when $\eta_{xx} > 1$.

Table 5.2.1 Estimated price elasticity of demand for selected broad commodities

Commodity	Average reported elasticity
Food	−.253
Clothing	−.466
Housing	−.327
Fuel	−.249
Tobacco/Alcohol	−.489
Transportation & Communication	−.794
Household durables	−.627

Source: These are averages compiled from a number of studies. The references are: Abbott and Ashenfelter (1976), Barten and Geyskens (1975), Deaton (1975), Deaton and Muelbauer (1980, 1982), Lluch and Powell (1975), and Powell (1974).

Price Cross-Elasticity of Demand
5.2.e

The measurement of price cross-elasticity of demand has been discussed in connection with the definition of substitute and complementary goods (Chapter 4, subsection 4.4.a). The definition is repeated at this point.

Price Cross-Elasticity: The price cross-elasticity of demand measures the relative responsiveness of quantity demanded of a given commodity to changes in the price of a related commodity. In other words, it is the proportional change in the quantity demanded of good X divided by the proportional change in the price of good Y.

Using this definition, the coefficient of price cross-elasticity of demand is defined as

$$\eta_{xy} = \frac{\Delta q_x}{q_x} \div \frac{\Delta p_y}{p_y} = \frac{\Delta q_x}{\Delta p_y} \frac{p_y}{q_x}. \tag{5.2.3}$$

As you will recall, goods may be classified as substitutes or complements according as $\eta_{xy} \gtrless 0$.

The interrelations of demand have been investigated in some statistical studies. A few illustrative coefficients are presented in Table 5.2.2.

Note that some goods have negative cross-elasticities with one another (they are complements), whereas others have positive cross-elasticities (they are substitutes). Food and drink and tobacco appear to be close complements, whereas food and clothing are not closely related at all. Fuel and housing also exhibit a significant degree of complementarity. Clothing and drink and tobacco are substitutes, although not strongly so.

Table 5.2.2 Selected cross-elasticities of demand

Commodity	Cross-Elasticity with respect to price of	Coefficient
Food	Drink and tobacco	−.629
Food	Clothing	+.022
Clothing	Drink and tobacco	+.215
Fuel	Drink and tobacco	−.046
Fuel	Housing	−.287

Source: Deaton and Muelbauer (1982).

Own- and Cross-Price Elasticities
5.2.f

As might seem plausible, own-price and cross-price elasticities of demand are not totally independent of one another. For example, suppose that there were only two goods in an economy, X and Y. Suppose further that a consumer's own-price elasticity for X was less than 1, say ½. Then, from the discussion in subsection 5.2.c, it is clear that expenditure on X must rise when the price of X rises. But this implies that expenditure on Y must fall because neither the price of Y nor money income has changed. Thus, the cross elasticity of Y with the price of X is negative; as X's price rises, the quantity of Y demanded falls. Thus, X and Y are complements.

A converse argument holds when the own-price elasticity of demand for X is greater than 1. And this is as it should be: To say that $\eta_{xx} > 1$ is to say that the demand for X is elastic, that is, that a price increase causes substantial substitution away from X. But if this is so, there must be other goods which are substitutable for X. In this case, the demand for Y moves with the price of X, implying that X and Y are substitutes.

These relationships can be extended to economies with any number of goods, but the same logic applies: If the own-price elasticity exceeds one, then in some average sense, the other goods are substitutes for X. If the own-price elasticity is less than one, then in that same sense, the other goods are complements.[4]

---

[4]The formal derivation of this proposition follows: The budget constraint implies that

$$I = p_1 x_1 + p_2 x_2 + \ldots + p_N x_N$$

where I is income, x_i the quantity consumed of good i, and P_i the price of good i. Differentiating with respect to p_1 yields

$$\frac{\partial I}{\partial p_1} = 0 = \frac{\partial x_1}{\partial p_1} p_1 + x_1 + \frac{\partial x_2}{\partial p_1} p_2 + \ldots + \frac{\partial x_N}{\partial p_1} \cdot p_N$$

(continued on page 136)

INCOME ELASTICITY OF DEMAND
5.3

The purchase of certain commodities are very sensitive to changes in nominal and real-money income. Thus it is sometimes desirable to relax the assumption that money income is held constant. In a simple case, the demand function can then be written as

$$q = f(p, I),\tag{5.3.1}$$

where I is money income. Following the concepts of elasticity already developed, the income elasticity of demand is given by the following.

Income Elasticity of Demand: The income elasticity of demand is the relative responsiveness of quantity demanded to changes in income. In other words, it is the proportional change in quantity demanded divided by the proportional change in nominal income.
Symbolically,

$$\eta_M = \frac{\Delta q}{q} \div \frac{\Delta I}{I} = \frac{\Delta q}{\Delta I}\frac{I}{q}.\tag{5.3.2}$$

Certain writers have suggested that commodities can be classified as "necessities" and "luxuries" on the basis of income elasticity. If income elasticity is very low (certainly less than one), quantity demanded is not very responsive to changes in income. Consumption remains about the same, irrespective of income level. This suggests that the commodity in question is a necessity. On the other hand, an income elasticity greater than one indicates that the commodity is more or less a luxury. Indeed, certain empirical "laws of consumption" were developed in the 19th century by the German statistician Christian Lorenz Ernst Engel. According to Engel, the income elasticity of demand for food is very low;

(continued from page 135)

which can be rewritten as

$$x_1 = \frac{-\partial x_1}{\partial p_1}P_1 - \frac{\partial x_2}{\partial p_1}P_2 - \ldots - \frac{\partial x_N}{\partial p_1}p_N$$

or dividing by x_1 and multiplying and dividing, where necessary, by $\frac{p_1}{x_j}$,

$$1 = \frac{-\partial x_1}{\partial p_1}\frac{p_1}{x_1} - \left(\frac{\partial x_2}{\partial p_1}\cdot\frac{p_1}{x_2}\right)\frac{x_2}{p_1}\cdot\frac{p_2}{x_1} - \ldots - \left(\frac{\partial x_N}{\partial p_1}\cdot\frac{p_1}{x_N}\right)\frac{x_N}{p_1}\cdot\frac{p_N}{x_1}$$

$$= \eta_{11} - \Sigma_{j=2}^N\left(\frac{\partial x_j}{\partial p_1}\cdot\frac{p_1}{x_j}\right)\frac{E_j}{E_1}$$

where η_{11} is the own-price elasticity of demand and E_j is expenditure on good j.

Note that $\left(\frac{\partial x_j}{\partial p_1}\cdot\frac{p_1}{x_j}\right)$ is the cross-elasticity of x_j with price 1. Thus, a weighted sum of cross-price elasticities plus the own-price elasticity equals 1. So if $\eta_{11} > 1$, then the weighted sum of cross-price elasticities must be positive, implying that they are, on average, substitutes. Conversely, for $\eta_{11} < 1$.

Table 5.3.1	
Commodity	**Income elasticity**
Food	.520
Clothing	1.559
Housing	.535
Fuel	1.400
Tobacco and drink	1.149
Transportation and communication	1.349
Household durables	1.683

Source: See Table 5.2.1.

those for clothing and shelter are about unity; while recreation, medical care, and other luxury goods have income elasticities in excess of unity. Therefore, according to Engel, the percentage of income spent on food by a family or a nation is a very good index of welfare—the poorer a family or a nation, the larger the percentage of expenditure that must go for food.

The latter generalization is somewhat crude; nonetheless, it does provide a rough measure of welfare. Some of Engel's specific statements regarding income elasticity, however, presumably no longer hold, as may be seen from the selected estimates of income elasticity presented in Table 5.3.1.

Although food and shelter have the lowest income elasticities, clothing is considerably above one. The good that is most luxurious in the set is "household durables," which is not counter-intuitive.

Despite some empirical deviations from Engel's original statement, many modern studies continue to use his basic insight. These studies are quite important in the context of government welfare programs. Many programs transfer income to families based on some standard of need. Since need is not easily defined, the Engel approach is often used as a guide. For example, a family of four living on income of $10,000 per year may be worse off than a family of five living on $12,500 per year even though income-per-person is the same. Under some circumstances, the Engel method allows us to calculate comparable living allowances for families of different sizes.

MARGINAL REVENUE
5.4

Having developed the concept of market demand and of its price, cross, and income elasticities, our attention can be directed to a closely related concept: marginal revenue.

Marginal revenue is important for a number of reasons. It is crucial for the study of different market structures and to analyze how the structure influences prices and quantities.

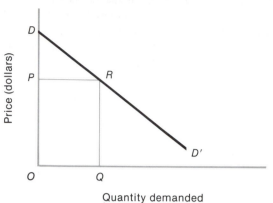

Figure 5.4.1 The measurement of total revenue

The market demand curve shows for each specific price the quantity of the commodity that buyers will take. For example, consider Figure 5.4.1. At the price *OP* per unit, *OQ* units are demanded and sold. From the standpoint of sellers, *OP* × *OQ*, or price times sales, is the *total revenue* obtainable when a price of *OP* per unit is charged. Thus total revenue is the area of the rectangle *OPRQ* in Figure 5.4.1.

Of perhaps greater importance than total revenue is the variation in total revenue incident to an expansion or contraction of sales. In the now familiar terminology of economics, this is called *marginal revenue*.

Marginal Revenue: Marginal revenue is the change in total revenue attributable to a one-unit change in output. Marginal revenue is calculated by dividing the change in total revenue by the change in output. Thus, marginal revenue *MR* is:

$$MR = \frac{\Delta TR}{\Delta Q}$$

where *TR* is total revenue.

Calculation of Marginal Revenue
5.4.a

Consider carefully the definition of marginal revenue (*MR*); namely, the change in total revenue (*TR*) attributable to a one-unit change in output. For the first unit sold, total, average, and marginal revenue are identical; for a quantity sold of one, each is precisely equal to price. To expand sales to the rate of two units per period of time, price must be reduced. The marginal revenue of the second unit is equal to total revenue from the sale of two units *minus* total revenue from the sale of one unit.

The marginal revenue function incorporates two effects. To expand the quantity sold, price must fall. (This is the essence of a downward sloping demand curve.) At first, the fall in price is more than offset by the increase in quantity. But eventually the fall in price is likely to dominate.

Marginal revenue can be best understood by reference to Table 5.4.1:

Table 5.4.1 Demand, total revenue, and marginal revenue

Price	Quantity	Total revenue	Marginal revenue	Sum of MR entries
$11	0	$ 0	—	—
10	1	10	$10	$10
9	2	18	8	18
8	3	24	6	24
7	4	28	4	28
6	5	30	2	30
5	6	30	0	30
4	7	28	−2	28
3	8	24	−4	24
2	9	18	−6	18
1	10	10	−8	10

The first two columns of this table contain price and quantity figures — the ingredients determining the demand curve (D) in Figure 5.4.2. The third column shows total revenue, the product of the corresponding entries in columns 1 and 2. The data in this column give rise to the TR curve in the figure. Column 4 contains the figures for marginal revenue calculated, according to the definition, as[5]

$$MR_1 = \Delta TR_1 = TR_1 - TR_0,$$

$$MR_2 = \Delta TR_2 = TR_2 - TR_1,$$

. . . .

$$MR_{10} = \Delta TR_{10} = TR_{10} - TR_9.$$

---

[5]The graph in Figure 5.4.2 contains a slight inaccuracy that may trouble the mathematically trained student. The example upon which the graph is based contains discrete data. The TR curve is obtained by plotting the points and connecting them by straight-line segments. The D and MR curves are obtained in the same manner. But here is where the inconsistency enters: Over any range of values for which total revenue is linear, marginal revenue is constant; and when marginal revenue is constant, so too is the demand function. To be exactly correct, the D and MR curves should be drawn as step-decreasing functions rather than as continuous functions with continuous first derivatives. However, the example is *merely illustrative;* and it seems better to illustrate a more general situation. To compensate some for this inconsistency, the values of MR are plotted at the midpoint of each interval.

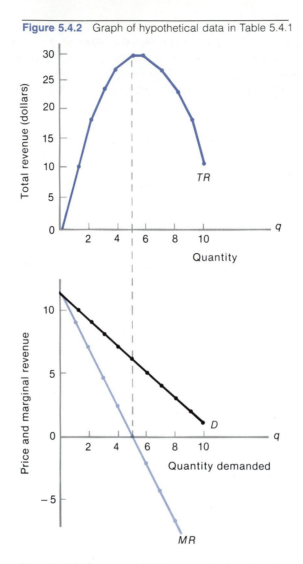

Figure 5.4.2 Graph of hypothetical data in Table 5.4.1

Note: In this figure marginal revenue is plotted at the midpoint of each interval on the quantity axis as explained in text footnote 5.

The final column is a check calculation to show that the sum of marginal revenue figures equals the associated total revenue. Using the notation employed above:

$$TR_1 = MR_1,$$

$$TR_2 = MR_1 + MR_2,$$

$$\ldots\ldots\ldots\ldots$$

$$TR_{10} = MR_1 + MR_2 + \ldots + MR_{10}.$$

This relation enters in an important way in the following subsection.

The data for marginal revenue are plotted in Figure 5.4.2 as the curve labeled *MR*. This curve has two crucial features. First, at the "outset" marginal revenue equals demand or average revenue. In this discrete example, $D = MR$ at quantity one and price \$10. (There is a slight difference between D and MR at quantity one on Figure 5.4.2 because of the convention of plotting MR at the midpoint of each interval on the quantity axis.) In a continuous case, the two are equal when they are infinitesimally close to the vertical axis. Second, $MR = 0$ when total revenue is at its maximum. When marginal revenue is *positive,* total revenue increases; and when marginal revenue is *negative,* total revenue declines. Naturally enough, when the *addition* to total revenue is zero, total revenue must be at its maximum. This is when the price effect exactly balances the quantity effect.

The Geometry of Marginal Revenue Determination 5.4.b

When the demand curve is linear, it is easy to find the associated marginal revenue curve. For example, suppose the demand curve is represented by the expression

$$p = 1000 - 3q . \tag{5.4.1}$$

This will mean that total revenue is

$$TR = pq = 1000q - 3q^2.$$

Marginal revenue is the change in total revenue per unit change in q. For extremely small changes in q, the marginal revenue is the slope (or derivative) of the total revenue curve. Formally,

$$MR = d(TR)/dq = 1000 - 6q. \tag{5.4.2}$$

Equation (5.4.2) gives marginal revenue as a function of q. Comparing it with (5.4.1), we see that it has the same intercept (1000) and a slope twice as large in absolute value (6 compared with 3). This will be true for any linear demand curve. In other words, if the demand curve[6] is represented by

$$p = a - bq \tag{5.4.3}$$

where a and b are the intercept and slope, respectively, then

$$TR = aq - bq^2 \tag{5.4.4}$$

and

$$MR = a - 2bq.$$

---

[6] Actually (5.4.3) is the "inverse" demand curve of the linear demand curve

$$q = \frac{a}{b} - \frac{p}{b}.$$

In general, the marginal revenue curve is simply given by

$$MR(q) = \frac{d}{dq}(TR) = \frac{d}{dq}(pq) = p + \frac{dp}{dq}q,$$

where dp/dq is the slope of the demand curve at the relevant point. Because demand curves are negatively sloped, marginal revenue is always lower than price.

The Marginal Revenue Curve Lies below the Demand Curve
5.4.c

In general, the marginal revenue curve lies below the demand curve. The reason is that to sell more units the price must be lowered, not just on the last unit, but on all prior units as well. Thus, the marginal revenue associated with selling the third unit derives from two factors: (*a*) the price that is obtained for the third unit and (*b*) the loss associated with charging a lower price on the two previous units. Since we are adding a loss — a negative number — to the price, marginal revenue is less than price. But for a given quantity, price measures the height of the demand curve. Since marginal revenue is less than price, the marginal revenue curve is below the demand curve.

Elasticity and Marginal Revenues
5.4.d

In subsection 5.2.c, we discussed the relation of elasticity to total revenue. Because total revenue and marginal revenue are related, there must also be a relationship between elasticity and marginal revenue.

To review the important content of Figure 5.4.2, when total revenue rises, marginal revenue is positive; when total revenue declines, marginal revenue is negative; when total revenue is constant, marginal revenue is zero. Notice that marginal revenue is zero when total revenue is at its maximum point. On the basis of these relations, we are able to construct Table 5.4.2.

The logic is this: When marginal revenue is positive, total revenue increases as we move down the demand curve. When a movement down the demand curve increases total revenue, elasticity must exceed one because the increased-quantity effect swamps the reduced-price effect. Thus, positive marginal revenue and

Table 5.4.2 Relation between marginal revenue and price elasticity of demand

Marginal revenue positive	Marginal revenue zero	Marginal revenue negative
Elastic demand	Unitary elasticity	Inelastic demand

Part One   Demand, Supply, and Markets: An Introductory Look

price elasticity greater than one go hand in hand. Conversely, when movement down the demand curve reduces total revenue, elasticity must be less than one because the falling-price effect swamps the rising-quantity effect. Thus, negative marginal revenue corresponds to elasticity less than one.[7]

THE FIRM'S DEMAND CURVE
5.5

In Chapter 1, we showed how individual consumers' demand curves could be summed to get a market demand. But what of the demand curve that faces an individual firm? Generally, it is not true that each firm gets a certain number of consumers assigned to it. The firm may not choose price independent of other sellers in the economy. The market structure influences the demand curve faced by the individual firm.

Demand Curve for a Firm in Perfect Competition
5.5.a

All the relations thus far developed can be used to describe the demand curve facing an individual producer in a perfectly competitive market.

Suppose that Panel A, Figure 5.5.1, depicts the equilibrium of a market in which there are a large number of sellers, each of approximately the same size. DD' and SS' are the market demand and market supply curves. Their intersection determines the equilibrium price $O\overline{P}$ and quantity demanded $O\overline{Q}$.

Let us now be more specific and stipulate that there are 25,000 sellers (say wheat farmers) of approximately the same size in the market. If any one seller increases output and sales by 100 percent, the total market sales will increase by only $\frac{1}{250}$ of 1 percent. Such a change is both graphically and *economically* so small as to have an imperceptible influence on price. Thus each individual firm may assume with confidence that variations in its *own* output and sales will have

---

[7]More formally, the approach is analogous to that of footnote 3:

$$\text{Total revenue} = pq$$

$$\text{Marginal revenue} = \frac{d(pq)}{dq}$$

$$= p + \frac{dp}{dq}q$$

$$= p\left(1 + \frac{dp}{dq} \cdot \frac{q}{p}\right)$$

$$= p\left(1 - \frac{1}{\eta}\right).$$

Thus, when $\eta > 1$, marginal revenue is positive, and when $\eta < 1$, marginal revenue is negative.

Figure 5.5.1 Derivation of demand for a perfectly competitive firm

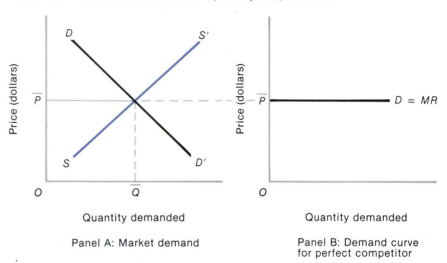

Panel A: Market demand

Panel B: Demand curve for perfect competitor

a negligible effect upon market price. Concerted action by a large number of firms can influence market price; but one firm acting alone cannot. The individual firm may therefore assume that the demand curve facing *it* is a horizontal line at the level of price established by demand and supply equilibrium in the market.

The demand curve for a perfectly competitive firm is shown in Panel B, Figure 5.5.1. The shape of the curve shows that the firm believes changes in its volume of output will have no perceptible effect upon market price. And if the firm is in fact in a perfectly competitive market, its belief is well-founded. A change in its rate of sales per period of time will change its total revenue, but it will not affect market price.[8]

The firm in a perfectly competitive market, therefore, does not have to reduce its price in order to expand its rate of sales. Any number of units per period of time can be sold at the market equilibrium price. If the firm were to charge a higher price, it could sell nothing. A lower price would result in a needless loss of revenue. It thus charges the market price for whatever quantity it wishes to produce and sell.

Since price remains constant, each additional unit sold increases total revenue by its (constant) price. In this special case, therefore, price and marginal revenue are equal at every level of sales. Therefore, the demand curve and the marginal revenue curve are identical for a firm in a perfectly competitive market. For this reason, the curve in Panel B is labeled $D = MR$.

_____

[8]The rationale used here to argue that each producer has no effect on market price is commonly employed for expository convenience. Under certain reasonable conditions, in a general equilibrium context, the absence of the individual producer's influence on market price is not simply a close approximation, it is literally true. The details of the argument can be found in E. Fama and A. Laffer, "The Number of Firms and Competition," *American Economic Review* 63 (1972), pp. 670–74.

Part One Demand, Supply, and Markets: An Introductory Look

When the demand curve is horizontal, demand is said to be perfectly elastic, meaning that the coefficient of price elasticity increases without bound as the percentage change in price becomes smaller and smaller. Take a numerical example: Suppose the market equilibrium price is $5 and a particular firm is selling 1,000 units at that price. If it increased its price to $5.01, its sales would fall to zero. Thus

$$\frac{\Delta q}{q} = \frac{-1,000}{1,000} \quad \text{and} \quad \frac{\Delta p}{p} = \frac{1}{500}.$$

The coefficient of price elasticity would be

$$\eta = -\frac{\Delta q}{q} \div \frac{\Delta p}{p} = 1 \div \frac{1}{500} = 500.$$

If it increased the price to only $5.001, its sales would also fall to zero and η would be 5,000. Thus one generalizes by saying that for infinitesimally small price changes the coefficient of price elasticity approaches infinity under conditions of perfect competition.

The results of this section may be summarized as follows:

Relations: The demand for a firm in a perfectly competitive market is a horizontal line at the level of the market equilibrium price. The output decisions of the seller do not affect market price. In this case, the demand and marginal revenue curves are identical; demand is perfectly elastic and the coefficient of price elasticity approaches infinity.

This is not the same as dividing the market demand by the number of sellers to get each seller's individual demand. For example, if there are 100 sellers, and the market demand and supply are given by D and S in Figure 5.5.1, then the equilibrium price is 10 and the market quantity is 1000. This implies that each producer sells 10 items. It does not imply, however, that if one firm raised its price to 12, it would sell 5 items. In fact, it would sell zero so long as all other firms kept price at 10. That is the meaning of Figure 5.5.1. Only if the market equilibrium price rose to 12, say because the supply was shifted, would the firm sell 5. But then its demand would be perfectly elastic at the new price of 12.

SYNOPSIS 5.6

■ There are four important determinants of demand. The *price of the commodity* determines the quantity demanded, given the level of the demand curve. Changes in price result in movements *along* the negatively sloped demand curve. Changes in *money income* result in an increase or upward shift in the entire demand curve if the good is normal or superior, and a decrease or downward shift if the good is inferior. *Taste* also determines demand in the sense of affecting where the demand curve lies and what its shape will be. Taste reflects consumer preferences (the utility function) and sometimes can be accounted for by observable variables such as age, sex, weather conditions, educational level, and so on. Finally, *prices of related commodities* determine the level of demand. When the price of a complementary good rises, the demand curve will shift downward; and when the price of a substitute good rises, the demand curve will shift upward.

■ Market demand is the horizontal summation of individual demand curves. The market demand curve shows total demand for the commodity by all consumers at each price.

■ Price elasticity measures the responsiveness of demand to changes in the commodity's price. The coefficient of price elasticity is given by

$$\eta = -\frac{\Delta q}{\Delta p} \frac{p}{q}.$$

The point elasticity represents elasticity at a single point on the demand curve. Mathematically, it amounts to replacing $\Delta q/\Delta p$ in the last formula with the derivative dq/dp.

■ Price cross-elasticity of demand measures the response in the quantity demanded of commodity X to changes in the price of commodity Y. The coefficient of price-cross elasticity is

$$\eta_{xy} = \frac{\Delta q_x}{\Delta p_y} \frac{p_y}{q_x}.$$

■ Income elasticity measures the response in the quantity demanded of a commodity to changes in money income. The coefficient of income elasticity is

$$\eta_I = \frac{\Delta q}{\Delta I} \frac{I}{q}.$$

■ Marginal revenue is the change in total revenue attributable to a one-unit change in quantity. If *TR* is total revenue and q is quantity, then marginal revenue, *MR*, is

$$MR = \frac{\Delta TR}{\Delta q}.$$

■ Marginal revenue is related to price elasticity by the equation

$$MR = \frac{\Delta TR}{\Delta q} = p\left(1 - \frac{1}{\eta}\right).$$

Thus, when demand is elastic ($\eta > 1$), *MR* is positive; when demand is inelastic ($\eta < 1$), *MR* is negative; and when demand has unit elasticity, $MR = 0$.

■ In perfect competition the demand curve perceived by any individual firm is essentially horizontal, even though market demand will usually have a price elasticity that is greater than zero.

Part One   Demand, Supply, and Markets: An Introductory Look

QUESTIONS AND EXERCISES

1. The following table gives hypothetical data for a consumer. Compute all meaningful elasticity coefficients (price, cross, and income). Remember that income must be constant when price elasticities are computed, and prices must be constant when income elasticity is computed.

Year	Price of X	Quantity purchased	Income	Price of Y
1	$1.00	100	$5,000	$0.50
2	1.01	95	5,000	0.50
3	1.01	100	5,500	0.51
4	1.01	105	5,500	0.52
5	1.00	100	5,500	0.50
6	1.00	105	5,500	0.51
7	1.00	100	5,000	0.51
8	1.02	105	5,500	0.51
9	1.02	95	5,500	0.50
10	1.03	90	5,500	0.50
11	1.03	100	6,500	0.51
12	1.03	105	7,000	0.51

2. The following table gives hypothetical data for market demand. Compute total revenue, marginal revenue, and the price elasticity of demand on a separate sheet. Plot the demand, total revenue, and marginal revenue curves.

Price	Quantity demanded	Price	Quantity demanded
$70.00	1	$23.33	7
50.00	2	20.00	8
40.00	3	17.50	9
35.00	4	15.00	9
30.00	5	12.50	11
26.67	6	10.00	12

3. Answer "true," "false," or "uncertain," and give a defense of your answer:

   a. If the income elasticity of demand for a commodity exceeds one, the relative price of that commodity will rise as real per-capita income increases, that is, will rise relative to the goods whose income elasticity is less than one.

   b. If the utility of each good is independent of the quantities of all other goods consumed, then all goods must have positive income elasticities (that is, all goods are normal goods).

   c. If total consumer expenditures are the same before and after a tax, then an excise tax on a consumer good with elastic demand will lead to an increase in consumption spending on other consumer goods, while an excise tax on a good whose demand is inelastic will lead to a decrease in consumption spending on other goods.

   d. An individual spends all her income on two goods, X and Y. She spends one fourth of her income on good X, and the income elasticity for this good is 5.

Thus, good Y is now an inferior good to her. (Additional exercise: Determine the exact income elasticity for Y.)

e. If each of 100 buyers has an elasticity of demand for a commodity equal to 3, then the elasticity of demand by the 100 buyers taken together is 0.03.

f. Two consumers each buy positive amounts of commodities X and Y at given market prices. In equilibrium they will have the same marginal rate of substitution between goods X and Y even if they consume different amounts of these goods.

4. If half of the total quantity demanded of a good is purchased by 75 consumers, each of whom has demand elasticity of 2, and the other half is purchased by 25 consumers, each of whom has demand elasticity of 3, what is the elasticity of the 100 buyers taken together?

5. An individual spends all his income on two goods, X and Y. If a $2 increase in the price of X does not change the amount consumed of Y, what is the price elasticity of good X?

6. The following statement is taken from *The Wall Street Journal,* March 30, 1966: "A retired Atlanta railroad conductor complains that he can no longer visit his neighborhood tavern six times a week. Since the price of his favorite beer went up to 30 cents a glass from 25 cents, he has been dropping in only five times a week." Assuming the man in question consumed the same amount of beer *per visit* before and after the price change, calculate the elasticity of his demand for tavern-dispensed beer.

7. "The experience with rail passenger transport indicates that traffic is negatively related to income — the richer one gets, the less he wants of the rails. For the trains that have survived, a mixture of the aged and low-income groups is the ideal combination; not surprisingly, the patronage on East Coast–Florida trains holds up better than on almost any others. The Illinois Central's *City of New Orleans,* running the length of Mississippi, is typically one of the strongest trains in the country, and passenger service in prosperous California is sick unto the death." (G. W. Hilton, "What Went Wrong," *Trains* 27 [January 1967], p. 39.)

a. From this statement, what can you say about the income elasticity of demand for rail passenger service? What type of good is rail passenger service?

b. If (say) the Grand Trunk Western lowers its passenger fares, can you say anything about the income and substitution effects?

c. Suppose a person gets a salary increase and accordingly uses the trains less. Using his indifference curves, show this response to his increased income.

SUGGESTED READINGS

Marshall, Alfred. *Principles of Economics.* 8th ed. New York: Macmillan, 1920, pp. 92–113.

Robinson, Joan. *The Economics of Imperfect Competition.* London: Macmillan, 1933, pp. 29–40.

2 Theory of Production and Cost

In older textbooks it was conventional to define production as "the creation of utility," where utility meant "the ability of a good or service to satisfy a human want." In one respect this definition is too broad to have much specific content. On the other hand, it definitely points out that "production" embraces a wide range of activities and not *only* the fabrication of material goods. Rendering legal advice, writing a book, showing a motion picture, and servicing a bank account are all examples of "production." It is rather difficult to specify the inputs used in producing the outputs of these illustrative cases. Nevertheless, most people would agree that some kinds of technical and intellectual skills are required to perform the services.

Thus while "production" in a general sense refers to the creation of any *good or service* people will buy, the concept of production is much clearer when we speak only of *goods*. In this case it is simpler to specify the precise inputs and to identify the quantity and quality of output. Producing a bushel of wheat requires, in addition to suitable temperature and rainfall, a certain amount of arable land, seed, fertilizer, the services of agricultural equipment such as plows and combines, and human labor.

Even in our presently advanced state of automation, every act of production requires the input of human resources. Other inputs are usually required as well. In particular, production normally requires various types of capital equipment (machines, tools, conveyors, buildings) and raw or processed materials. The theory of production consists of an analysis of *how* the entrepreneur — given the "state of the art" or technology — combines various inputs to produce a stipulated output in an economically efficient manner.

Since the concept of production is clearer when applied to goods rather than services, our discussion will be restricted to production in agricultural and manufacturing industries. The reader should be aware, nevertheless, that problems of resource allocation in service trades and government are not less important because they are less discussed in this text. Indeed, as the population becomes more and more concentrated in the under 20 and over 65 age groups, the importance of services relative to goods increases. The principles of production studied here are as applicable to the output of services as to the output of goods.

The same statement applies to the theory of cost. The theory of cost consists of an analysis of the costs of production — how costs are determined from a knowledge of the production function, the effects of diminishing returns, cost in the short and long runs, the "four cost curves," and so on. But more importantly, it establishes the basis for study of the pricing practices of business firms, which occupies Part 3. ∎

6 Production with One Variable Input

This chapter begins the treatment of production and cost, which will have many applications in the next few chapters. What is meant by the following terms: short run versus long run, production function, total product, marginal product, average product, law of diminishing returns? How are the total product, marginal product, and average product schedules related to one another? ■

Production processes typically require a wide variety of inputs. These are not as simple as "labor," "capital," and "materials"; many qualitatively different types of each input are normally used to produce an output. To clarify the analysis, this chapter introduces some simplifying assumptions whose purpose is to cut through the complexities of dealing with hundreds of different inputs. Our attention can be focused upon the essential principles of production, and the analysis generalizes directly to more complex production technologies.

Specifically, we assume that there is only one *variable input*. In subsequent discussion, this variable input is usually called "labor," although any other input could just as well be used. Second, we assume that this variable input can be combined in different proportions with one *fixed input* to produce various quantities of output. The fixed input is called "land"; our discussion employs one specific example of production: agricultural output.

Fixed and Variable Inputs, the Short and Long Runs
6.1.a

In analyzing the process of physical production and the closely related costs of production, it is convenient to introduce a somewhat arbitrary distinction: the classification of inputs as fixed and variable. Accordingly, a *fixed input* is defined as one whose quantity cannot readily be changed when market conditions indicate that an immediate change in output is desirable. To be sure, no input is ever *absolutely* fixed, no matter how short the period of time under consideration. But frequently, for the sake of analytical simplicity, we hold some inputs fixed, reasoning that while these inputs are in fact variable, the cost of immediate variation is so great as to prohibit such action for the particular decision at hand. Buildings, major pieces of machinery, and managerial personnel are examples of inputs that cannot be rapidly augmented or diminished. A *variable input,* on the other hand, is one whose quantity may be changed almost instantaneously in response to desired changes in output. Many types of labor services and the inputs of raw and processed materials fall in this category.

Corresponding to the distinction of fixed and variable inputs, economists introduce another distinction: the short and long runs. The *short run* refers to that period of time in which the input of one or more productive agents is fixed. Therefore, changes in output must be accomplished exclusively by changes in the usage of variable inputs. Thus, if a producer wishes to expand output in the short run, this usually means using more hours of labor service with the existing plant and equipment. Similarly, if the producer wishes to reduce output in the short run, certain types of workers may be discharged; but one cannot immediately "discharge" a building or a diesel locomotive, even though its usage may fall to zero.

In the long run, however, even this is possible, for the *long run* is defined as that period of time (or planning horizon) in which all inputs are variable. The long run, in other words, refers to that time in the future when output changes can be achieved in the manner most advantageous to the entrepreneur. For example, in the short run a producer may be able to expand output only by operating the existing plant for more hours per day. This, of course, entails paying overtime rates to workers. In the long run, it may be more economical to install additional productive facilities and return to the normal workday.

In this chapter we are mostly concerned with the short-run theory of production, combining different quantities of variable inputs with a specific quantity of fixed input to produce various quantities of output. The long-run organization of production is largely determined by the relative cost of producing a desired output by different input combinations. Discussion of the long run is thus postponed until Chapters 7 and 8.

Fixed or Variable Proportions
6.1.b

As already indicated, the initial discussion focuses largely upon the use of a *fixed* amount of one input and a *variable* amount of another to produce *variable* quantities of output. This means that our attention is restricted mainly to production under conditions of *variable proportions*. The *ratio of input quantities* may vary; the entrepreneur, therefore, must determine not only the level of output to produce but also the optimal proportion in which to combine inputs (in the long run).

There are two different ways of stating the principle of variable proportions. First, variable-proportions production implies that output can be changed in the short run by changing the amount of variable inputs used in cooperation with the fixed inputs. Naturally, as the amount of one input is changed, the other remaining constant, the *ratio* of inputs changes. Second, when production is subject to variable proportions, the *same* output can be produced by various combinations of inputs — that is, by different input ratios. This may apply only to the long run, but it is relevant to the short run when there is more than one variable input. For example, wheat can be produced with a great deal of labor and very little machinery, or it can be produced with very little labor and a tractor, which can be leased on a weekly basis.

Most economists regard production under conditions of variable proportions as typical of both the short and long run. There is certainly no doubt that proportions are variable in the long run. When making an investment decision, an entrepreneur may choose among a wide variety of different production processes. As polar opposites, an automobile can be almost handmade or it can be made by assembly-line techniques. In the short run, however, there may be some cases in which output is subject to fixed proportions.

Fixed-proportions production means there is one, and only one, ratio of inputs that can be used to produce a good. If output is expanded or contracted, all inputs must be expanded or contracted so as to maintain the fixed input ratio. This is the technology that is common in baking a cake. If the recipe calls for ½ cup of milk and 3 cups of flour, one cannot produce the same cake by using, say, 2 cups of milk and 2 cups of flour. However, one can produce two cakes with 1 cup of milk and 6 cups of flour. Factors are used in fixed proportions.

At first glance this might seem the usual condition: one person and one shovel produce a ditch; two parts hydrogen and one part oxygen produce water. Adding a second shovel or a second part of oxygen will not augment the rate of production. But, in actuality, examples of fixed-proportions production are hard to come by. Even the production of most chemical compounds is subject to variable proportions. It is true, for example, that hydrogen and nitrogen must be used in the fixed ratio 3 : 1 to produce ammonia gas. But if three volumes of hydrogen and one volume of nitrogen are mixed in a glass tube and heated to 400° C, only minute traces of ammonia will be found (and that only after heating for a very long time). However, if finely divided iron is introduced into the tube under the same conditions, almost the entire amount of hydrogen and nitrogen are converted to ammonia gas within minutes. That is to say, the *yield* of ammonia for any given amount of hydrogen and nitrogen depends upon the amount of the catalyst (finely divided iron) used. Proportions are indeed variable from the standpoint of the catalyst, not only in this instance but in the production of almost every chemical compound.

THE PRODUCTION FUNCTION
6.2

The discussion so far, especially in subsection 6.1.b, has emphasized that the quantity of output depends upon, or is a function of, the quantities of the various inputs used. This relation is formally described by a *production function* associating physical output with input.

Production Function: A production function is a schedule (or table, or mathematical equation) showing the maximum amount of output that can be produced from any specified set of inputs, given the existing technology or "state of the art." In short, the production function is like a "recipe book" showing what outputs are associated with which sets of inputs.

Total Output or Product
6.2.a

The production function may be shown as a table, a graph, or as a mathematical equation. In any case, the short-run production function gives the total (maximum) output obtainable from different amounts of the variable input, given a specified amount of the fixed input and the required amounts of the ingredient inputs.

As an example, consider an experiment in the production of wheat on 10 acres of land. The fixed input is land, the variable input is labor time, and the output is bushels of wheat (we ignore seed, fertilizer, and other variable inputs). An agricultural experiment station blocks off eight tracts of land, each containing 10 acres. The first tract is worked for a producing season by one person; the second tract is worked by two people; and so on until the eighth tract is worked by eight people. Total output on the various tracts of land might be as shown in Table 6.2.1.

The hypothetical data in Table 6.2.1 are graphed in Figure 6.2.1. Output is plotted on the vertical axis and input, in this case the number of workers, is plotted on the horizontal axis. Joining the successive points by straight-line segments, one obtains the total product curve. Note that the curve first rises slowly, then more rapidly, and then more slowly again until it finally reaches a maximum and begins to decrease. This curvature reflects the principle of diminishing marginal physical returns to be discussed in subsection 6.2.c.

Average and Marginal Products
6.2.b

Table 6.2.2 is an expanded version of Table 6.2.1. The first two columns still indicate the tract number and the number of workers on each tract. The third column reports the total output for each tract of land, while the fourth column shows the average output per worker, or the output-labor ratio. Finally, the fifth column contains the entries for marginal product.

Average Product: The average product of an input is total product divided by the amount of the input used to produce this output. Thus, average product is the output–input ratio for each level of output and the corresponding volume of input.

Marginal Product: The marginal product of an input is the addition to total product attributable to the addition of one unit of the variable input to the production process, the fixed input remaining unchanged.[1]

Table 6.2.2 and the graph of its data (Figure 6.2.2) illustrate several important features of a typical production process. First, both average and marginal products initially rise, reach a maximum, and then decline. In the limit, average product could decline to zero because total product itself could conceivably decline to this point. Marginal product, on the other hand, may actually become negative — indeed, many economists suggest that the marginal product of agri-

---

[1]Consider the production function $f(x \mid y)$ where x is the variable input and y is the fixed input and where the vertical bar means "given." The average product of the variable input x is

$$\frac{q}{x} = \frac{f(x \mid y)}{x}$$

and the marginal product is the derivative,

$$\frac{dq}{dx} = \frac{df(x \mid y)}{dx}.$$

Table 6.2.1 Output of wheat on ten-acre tracts of land (bushels)

Tract number	Number of workers	Total output
1	1	10
2	2	24
3	3	39
4	4	52
5	5	61
6	6	66
7	7	66
8	8	64

Figure 6.2.1 Total product curve obtained from hypothetical data in Table 6.2.1

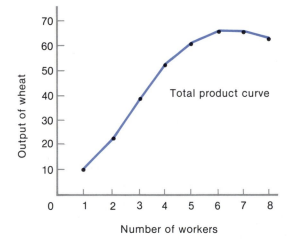

Table 6.2.2 Average and marginal products and the input ratio for ten-acre tracts

Tract number	Number of workers	Total output	Average product of labor	Marginal product of labor
1	1	10	10.0	—
2	2	24	12.0	14
3	3	39	13.0	15
4	4	52	13.0	13
5	5	61	12.2	9
6	6	66	11.0	5
7	7	66	9.4	0
8	8	64	8.0	-2

Part Two   Theory of Production and Cost

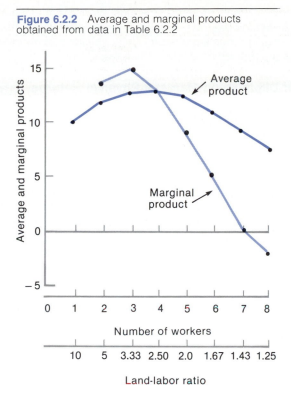

Figure 6.2.2 Average and marginal products obtained from data in Table 6.2.2

cultural workers in some underdeveloped countries is in fact negative. Workers may be so numerous that the addition of a worker merely causes confusion as individuals trip over one another's output.

In the present example, the marginal product of labor becomes negative because the variable input is used too intensively with the fixed input (land).

A second feature of significance is that marginal product exceeds average product when average product is rising, equals average product when average product is at maximum, and lies below average product when average product is falling. This proposition follows readily from the definitions of marginal and average product, and is true of all marginal and average relationships. Consider a student who has an average of 78 percent on six Economics 1 quizzes. If the score on the seventh quiz exceeds 78 percent, then the average rises. If it is below 78 percent, the average falls. Similarly with production.

So long as the increment is greater than the previous average, the average must increase. If the increment is less than the previous average, the newly computed average must be less. The two curves must intersect at the point where the average curve reaches its maximum, because an increment equal to the average does not change the average. The average product schedule must be flat at that point, in this case implying a maximum.

Relations: Both average and marginal products first rise, reach a maximum, and decline thereafter. When average product attains its maximum, average and marginal products are equal. These relations apply only to variable-proportions production functions.

Law of Diminishing Marginal Physical Returns
6.2.c

The shape of the marginal product curve in Figure 6.2.2 graphically illustrates an important principle: the "law" of diminishing marginal physical returns.

Comparing the outputs of tracts 1 and 2 (Table 6.2.2), one sees that using two workers rather than one increases output by 14 bushels, the marginal product of labor when there are two workers. Similarly, comparing tracts 2 and 3, the use of a third worker augments output by 15 bushels. The marginal physical product of labor increases as the number of workers increases. This may well happen when the land-labor ratio is very high.

Ultimately, however, as the input ratio declines so also must the marginal product of the variable input. When the number of units of the variable input increases, each unit, so to speak, has on the average fewer units of the fixed input with which to work. At first, when the fixed input is relatively plentiful, more intensive utilization of fixed inputs by variable inputs may increase the marginal output of the variable input. Nonetheless, a point is reached beyond which an increase in the intensity of use of the fixed input yields progressively less and less additional returns. Psychologists have even found that this holds true for consecutive study time.

Principle (The Law of Diminishing Marginal Physical Returns): As the amount of a variable input is increased, the amount of other (fixed) inputs held constant, a point is reached beyond which marginal product declines. It might be well at this point to emphasize that the "law of diminishing returns" is actually an *empirical assertion*. It is not a theorem derived from an axiom system; it is not a logical proposition that is susceptible of mathematical proof or refutation. It is a simple statement concerning physical relations that have been observed in the real economic world.[2]

THE GEOMETRY OF AVERAGE AND MARGINAL PRODUCT CURVES
6.3

The discussion has so far focused upon one specific, discrete production function given in tabular form. We turn now to a more general formulation in which both discrete and continuous production functions are used.

---

[2]Using the notation of footnote 1 of this chapter, the law of diminishing returns says there is some $\hat{x}$ such that

$$\frac{d^2f(x \mid y)}{dx^2} < 0$$

for all $x > \hat{x}$. That is, the production function is concave for inputs larger than $\hat{x}$.

Geometry of Average Product Curves
6.3.a

A typical form of the (continuous) total product curve is shown in Figure 6.3.1. In this, as in all other one-variable-input product graphs, units of the variable input are plotted on the abscissa and total product is plotted on the ordinate.

Given the total product curve *TP*, we wish to find average product. First, from its definition, average product is total product divided by the number of units of the variable input used to produce it, or the output-variable input ratio. Producing total output $OR = DA$ requires OD units of the variable input. Thus the average product of OD units of variable input is DA/OD. Similarly, the average product of OF units of variable input is FG/OF and of OH units is HJ/OH. In each case, to obtain the average-product corresponding to a given point on the total product curve, we found the slope of the line joining the origin with the point in question. In other words, we found the tangent of the angle formed by the abscissa and the line from the origin to the given point on the total product curve. Average product is equal to the slope of the line that connects the origin with the total product curve. This implies that the average product of F units of input is smaller than the average product of H units of input because $\overline{HJ/OH} > \overline{FG/OF}$.

As we have seen, the average product corresponding to point A is DA/OD, but this is precisely the slope of the line OA, or the tangent of the angle β. Notice also that average product must be the same for OH as for OD units of the variable input because the slopes of OJ and of OA are identical (in each case, average product is the tangent of angle β). Since average product is rising for movements along TP from the origin to point J, and since it is falling for movements from A to B, there is reason to suspect that average product reaches its maximum at a point between J and A on the total product curve.

Average product does, in fact, attain its maximum at an intermediate point, as may be seen more clearly in Figure 6.3.2. Points Q and R in Figure 6.3.2

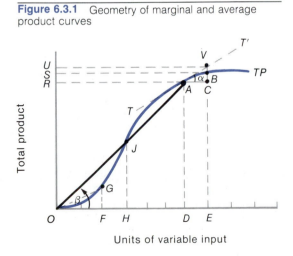

Figure 6.3.1   Geometry of marginal and average product curves

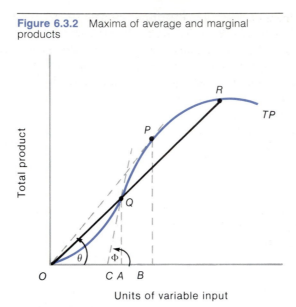

Figure 6.3.2 Maxima of average and marginal products

correspond to points J and A, respectively, in Figure 6.3.1, in that each pair of points lies on a common ray from the origin. Thus the average product at point Q is equal to the average product at point R. Since average product is the slope of a ray from the origin to a point on the curve, average product is a maximum when the slope of the line is steepest. This occurs, of course, when the line from the origin is just tangent to the total product curve, at point P with angle θ in Figure 6.3.2.

As one moves from point Q toward point P, the line from the origin to the curve becomes steeper. Similarly, as one moves from point P toward point R, the line moves downward, becoming less steep. Thus we have the following important points:

Relations: Average product corresponding to any point on the total product curve is given by the slope of a ray from the origin to the point in question. When average product attains its maximum value, this line is tangent to the total product curve.

Geometry of Marginal Product Curves 6.3.b

Using Figures 6.3.1 and 6.3.2 again, similar qualitative and quantitative relations may be found for the marginal product curve.

Turn first to Figure 6.3.1. By definition, marginal product is the addition to total product attributable to the addition of one unit (or a small amount) of the variable input to a given amount of the fixed input. Let the amount of variable input increase from OD to OE, or by the amount $DE = AC$. Output consequently increases from OR to OS, or by the amount $RS = CB$. Marginal product is, therefore, BC/AC. In this discrete case, there is no convenient slope measurement because the arc AB is not linear. That is, a unique slope measure cannot be obtained because the slope of the angle formed by arc AB and line AC changes over the interval $DE = AC$.

But let us suppose for a minute that the total product curve were linear from A to the point V. Then an increment of amount DE in the variable input would cause output to increase from OR to OU, or by $RU = CV$. In this case, marginal product would be CV/AC, or the tangent of angle α. The measure CV/AC overstates the true magnitude of marginal product, CB/AC. However, as the increment of variable input becomes smaller and smaller, the approximation becomes better and better. In the limit, for a very tiny increase in variable input the slope of the tangent to point A, labeled TT', approaches the true slope of the total product curve. Hence for sufficiently small changes in the variable input, the slope of the total product curve at any point is a good approximation of marginal product.[3]

The slope of a curve at any point is given by the slope of its tangent at that point. Thus the marginal product corresponding to point Q in Figure 6.3.2 is the slope of the line CQ, or the tangent of angle $\phi = AQ/CA$. As Figure 6.3.2 is constructed, marginal product is a maximum when OA units of variable input are used. This is true because the slope of the tangent to the total product curve is steeper at point Q, the inflexion point, than at any other point.

Other interesting relations can be determined from Figure 6.3.2. First, recall that maximum average product is associated with OB units of variable input and corresponds to point P. Hence, marginal product attains its maximum at a lower level of variable input usage than does average product. Second, notice that the tangent to the total product curve at point P — the line whose slope gives marginal product corresponding to point P — is the line OP. We have already seen in subsection 6.3.a that the slope of OP also gives average product associated with point P and that average product attains its maximum value at that point. Hence, as we have seen previously, marginal product equals average product when the latter is at its maximum.

---

[3]Let $q = f(x)$ be the production function. If the increment of variable input is denoted Δx, the new output is $f(x + \Delta x)$. Thus, by definition, marginal product is

$$MP = \frac{f(x + \Delta x) - f(x)}{\Delta x}.$$

But also by definition, the derivative of $f(x)$ is

$$\frac{dq}{dx} = \lim_{\Delta x \to 0} \frac{f(x + \Delta x) - f(x)}{\Delta x}.$$

Hence, in the limit, marginal product *is* the slope (dq/dx) of the total product curve. For finite changes, the slope is an approximation of marginal product.

The principal information contained in this subsection can be summarized as follows:

Relations: Marginal product corresponding to any point on the total product curve is given by the slope of the tangent to the curve at that point. Marginal product attains its maximum value when the slope of the tangent is steepest. The point of maximum marginal product occurs at a smaller level of variable input usage than does maximum average product; and marginal product equals average product when the latter attains its maximum value.

Total, Average, and Marginal Products
6.3.c

The relations discussed in the two preceding subsections are illustrated in Figure 6.3.3.[4] In this figure one can see not only the relation between marginal and average products but also the relation of these two curves to total product.

Consider first the total product curve. For very small amounts of the variable input, total product rises gradually. But even at a low level of input it begins to rise quite rapidly, reaching its maximum slope (or rate of increase) at point 1. Since the slope of the total product curve equals marginal product, the maximum slope (point 1) must correspond to the maximum point on the marginal product curve (point 4).

After attaining its maximum slope at point 1, the total product curve continues to rise. But output increases at a decreasing rate, so the slope is less steep. Moving outward along the curve from point 1, soon the point is reached at which a ray from the origin is just tangent to the curve (point 2). Since tangency of the ray to the curve defines the condition for maximum average product, point 2 lies directly above point 5.

As the quantity of variable input is expanded from its value at point 2, total product continues to increase. But its rate of increase is progressively slower until point 3 is finally reached. At this position total product is at a maximum; thereafter it declines until it (conceivably) reaches zero again. Over a tiny range around point 3, additional input does not change total output. The slope of the total product curve is zero. Thus marginal product must also be zero. This is shown by the fact that points 3 and 6 occur at precisely the same input value. And since total product declines beyond point 3, marginal product becomes negative.

Most of the important relations have so far been discussed with reference to the total product curve. To emphasize certain relations, however, consider the marginal and average product curves in Figure 6.3.3. Marginal product at first increases, reaches a maximum at point 4 (the point of diminishing marginal physical returns), and declines thereafter. It eventually becomes negative beyond point 6, where total product is at its maximum.

---

[4]This graph is constructed under the assumption that output is zero if the input of the variable factor is zero. Thus if the production function is $q = f(x \mid y)$, we assume that $f(0 \mid y) = f(x \mid 0) = f(0 \mid 0) = 0$. For an alternative approach, see Frank Knight, *Risk, Uncertainty, and Profit*, Reprints of Economic Classics (New York: Augustus M. Kelley, 1964), p. 100.

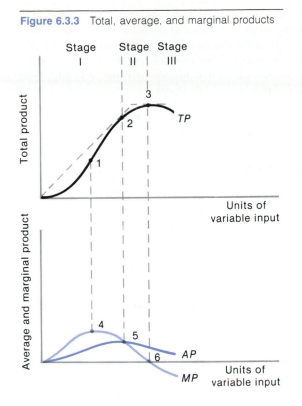

Figure 6.3.3 Total, average, and marginal products

Average product also rises at first until it reaches its maximum at point 5, where marginal and average products are equal. It subsequently declines, conceivably becoming zero when total product itself becomes zero. Finally, one may observe that marginal product exceeds average product when the latter is increasing and is less than average product when the latter is decreasing.

The Three Stages of Production
6.3.d

Using Figure 6.3.3, we can identify three stages of production. The first stage corresponds to usage of the variables input to the left of point 5 where average product achieves its maximum. Stage II corresponds to usage of the variable input between point 5 and point 6, where the marginal product of the variable input is zero. Finally, stage III corresponds to usage of the variable input to the right of point 6 where the marginal product of this input is negative.

Clearly, the producer would never produce in stage III, since in this stage more output can be obtained by using *less* of the variable input. Such inefficiencies in the use of scarce production factors will always be avoided. In stage I, average product of the variable factor is increasing. As we shall see in Chapter 8, when the unit cost of the variable factor (for example, the wage rate) is a constant, increasing average product of the variable factor implies that the unit cost of producing output decreases as output is increased. If the firm is in a competitive industry (refer back to the discussion in subsection 5.5.a), it would never produce in this stage because by expanding output it can reduce unit costs while receiving the same price for each additional unit sold, and this means that total profits must increase.[5] Thus we see that efficient production occurs in stage II.[6]

Example: Consider two identical wheat farms, each having 100 acres of land. The production schedule for each is given by the following table:

Total number of workers	Total product (in 000 bushels)
1	10
2	22
3	35
4	50
5	60
6	67
7	72
8	74
9	75
10	74

Suppose that both farms are owned by the same individual. How should labor be allocated across farms?

The answer depends on how many units of labor are to be employed. Although this is itself a question that is considered below, for now let us suppose that we have available no more than a certain number of workers.

Suppose that two workers are available. By using both on one farm, total output is 22 and average product is 11. If they are split between the farms, total output is $2 \times (10) = 20$ and average product is 10.

If three workers are available, employing them on one farm yields 35 units of output. If two are assigned to one farm and one to the other, output is only $22 + 10 = 32$. Again, putting all workers on one farm is the solution.

If four workers are available, they again should all be used on one farm. Then 50 is produced. If they were divided into two pairs of 2, $2 \times (22) = 44$ could be produced. If three work on one farm while one works on the other, then $35 + 10 = 45$ is produced. Note average product is 12 ½.

If five workers are available, placing all five on one farm yields 60 units. So does putting four on one farm and one in the other. Splitting them into three and two yields 57. Note that average product is 12.

If six workers are available, splitting them up is optimal. Placing four on one farm and two on the other yields 72 units and is better than any other allocation.

---

[5]An even stronger statement can be made when the production function exhibits constant returns to scale (see section 6.4): in this case, the marginal product of the fixed factor will be negative in stage I.

[6]As we shall see, however, a monopolist may decide, in some cases, to produce in stage I.

The point is that workers are not moved over to the second farm until we are in the range where average product is falling. This illustrates the relevance of production in stage II.

LINEARLY HOMOGENEOUS PRODUCTION FUNCTIONS
6.4

"Linear homogeneity," "homogeneous of degree one," and "constant returns to scale" are interchangeable terms when used to describe a production function. All get at the essential concept: if all inputs are expanded in the same proportion, output is expanded in that proportion. Consider the simple Cobb-Douglas function:

$$q = f(x,y) = Ax^{\alpha}y^{1-\alpha}, \tag{6.4.1}$$

where A and α are positive constants and $0 < \alpha < 1$. Now let both x and y be increased in the proportion λ. One then has

$$f(\lambda x, \lambda y) = A(\lambda x)^{\alpha}(\lambda y)^{1-\alpha} = A\lambda^{\alpha}\lambda^{1-\alpha}x^{\alpha}y^{1-\alpha}$$
$$= A\lambda x^{\alpha}y^{1-\alpha} = \lambda(Ax^{\alpha}y^{1-\alpha}) = \lambda f(x,y) = \lambda q. \tag{6.4.2}$$

Thus if the usage of all inputs is expanded in the same proportion, output expands in that proportion. This is precisely what is meant by "constant returns to scale."

The other essential feature of linearly homogeneous production functions is as follows: the average and marginal products depend upon the *ratio* in which the inputs are combined, but their values are *independent* of the absolute magnitudes of the inputs. Again consider the Cobb-Douglas function. Divide both sides of equation (6.4.1) by x to obtain the average product of X:

$$\frac{q}{x} = Ax^{\alpha-1}y^{1-\alpha} = A\left(\frac{y}{x}\right)^{1-\alpha} \tag{6.4.3}$$

This clearly shows that the average product of X depends upon the factor input ratio or factor proportions. For example, suppose $A = 100$ and $\alpha = \frac{1}{2}$. If $y = 4$ and $x = 1$, the average product of X is 200. If $y = 400$ and $x = 100$, the ratio is the same and so is the magnitude of the average product.

The same situation may be shown for the marginal product. If y is held constant, the Cobb-Douglas function (6.4.1) can be thought of as a relation between output, q, and the variable input, x. We have noted that marginal product is the slope or derivative of the total product function with respect to the variable input. The derivative of (6.4.1) with respect to x is thus the marginal product function we seek, or

$$\frac{dq}{dx} = \alpha A\left(\frac{y}{x}\right)^{1-\alpha} \tag{6.4.4}$$

which shows that the marginal product depends on the input ratio only.[7]

---

[7]When we consider the possibility that y can also vary, a more appropriate mathematical statement would replace the left side with the partial derivative symbol $\partial q/\partial x$.

The essential features of linearly homogeneous production functions may be summarized as follows:

Relations: If the production function is homogeneous of degree one, (*i*) there are constant returns to scale, that is, a proportional expansion of all inputs expands output by the same proportion; and (*ii*) the marginal and average product functions depend only upon the ratio in which the inputs are combined and, in particular, they are independent of the absolute amounts of the inputs employed.

SYNOPSIS 6.5

- Production functions show the relation between outputs and inputs. In the *short run* it is usually assumed for expositional convenience that there is one *variable input* and one *fixed input*. (By relying on mathematics more heavily, however, this analysis can be generalized to deal with a large number of inputs.)

- Average product (of input x) is $\frac{q}{x}$ where q is output and x is the amount of the input in question. Marginal product of input x is $\frac{\Delta q}{\Delta x}$ (or $\frac{dq}{dx}$ in continuous notation — for example, the change in output associated with a unit change in the input of x, all other inputs remaining constant).

- The law of diminishing returns says that beyond some point, increases in the amount of a variable input (all other inputs held fixed) lead to *decreases* in the marginal product of that input. In short, the production function ultimately becomes concave as the amount of the variable input is increased.

- Total product, marginal product, and average product are closely related. When marginal product (*MP*) is larger than average product (*AP*), average product is rising. When *MP* is smaller than *AP*, *AP* is falling. When *AP* is at its maximum, $MP = AP$. These relations are examined in more detail in the Appendix here.

APPENDIX* 6.A

Chapter 6 dealt with the relations among total product, average product, and marginal product. Chapter 5 dealt with similar relations among total revenue, average revenue (or, the demand curve), and marginal revenue. In Chapter 8, we will consider total cost, average cost, and marginal cost. These are all examples

---

*This appendix can be skipped without loss of continuity.

of the general relation among total magnitudes, average magnitudes, and marginal magnitudes. It is useful to consider the mathematical and geometric characteristics of these general relations; that is the subject of this appendix.

Let $TX(q)$ be the total X function (where X can be "product," "revenue," "cost," or just about any other magnitude of interest) stated as a function of a single quantity or output variable q. The average X function, $AX(q)$ is then defined as

$$AX(q) = \frac{TX(q)}{q},$$

and the marginal X function, $MX(q)$, is defined as the derivative

$$MX(q) = \frac{dTX(q)}{dq} = TX'(q).$$

If we differentiate $AX(q)$, we obtain:

$$\frac{dAX(q)}{dq} = AX'(q) = \frac{qTX'(q) - TX(q)}{q^2} = \frac{MX(q) - AX(q)}{q}$$

Rearranging the last equation, we get

$$MX(q) = AX(q) + AX'(q)q \qquad (6.A.1)$$

where $AX'(q)$ is the slope of the average X function at quantity q. From equation (6.A.1) we get the following propositions:

Proposition 1: If $MX(q) > AX(q)$, then (assuming $q > 0$), $AX'(q) > 0$ (that is, average X is rising).

Proposition 2: If $MX(q) < AX(q)$, then (assuming $q > 0$), $AX'(q) < 0$ (that is, average X is falling).

Proposition 3: If $AX(q)$ is at a maximum (or minimum) with $AX'(q) = 0$, then $AX(q) = MX(q)$.

Proposition 4: If $TX(0) = 0$, then $MX(0) = AX(0)$. The condition $TX(0) = 0$ is needed to assure that $AX(0)$ is not infinite. In some cases (for example, certain total cost functions discussed in Chapter 8), $TX(0)$ is not zero, so some care is needed in applying this proposition.

The geometry of (6.A.1) is shown in Figure 6.A.1. Given $AX(q)$, equation (6.A.1) can be used to locate $MX(q)$ for given values of q. For example, at q_0 the slope of $AX(q)$ is the tangent of θ. That is, θ is the slope of the line HH', which is tangent to $AX(q)$ at q_0. From equation (6.A.1), we know that $MX(q_0) = AX(q_0) + AX'(q_0)q_0$. Thus, to find $MX(q_0)$, we construct a line with origin at $AX(q_0)$ and constant slope $AX'(q_0)$ — this is the line $AX(q_0)G$ in Figure 6.A.1. It is simply a line parallel to HH' with origin $AX(q_0)$. By construction, at q_0, this line gives the desired value of MX. In other words, if we draw a perpendicular from q_0 up to the line $AX'(q_0)G$, the point at which the perpendicular intersects $AX(q_0)G$ is $MX(q_0)$. By repeating this procedure, values of $MX(q)$ for different values of q can be found.

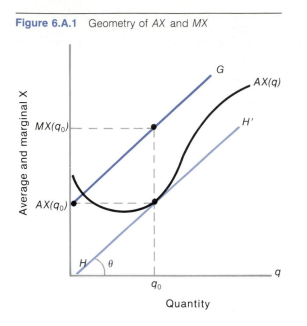

Figure 6.A.1 Geometry of *AX* and *MX*

QUESTIONS AND EXERCISES

Below are hypothetical data for a manufacturer possessing a fixed plant which produces a commodity that requires only one variable input. Total product is given. Compute and graph the average and marginal product curves. Make your basic calculations and set them up in tabular form, using the following information for the stub and column (1) entries and your calculations for average product in column (2) and marginal product in column (3). Save them, as they form the basis for a subsequent problem in Chapter 7. After completing the table and graph, answer the following questions:

1. When marginal product is increasing, what is happening to average product?
2. Does average product begin to fall as soon as marginal product does? That is, which occurs first, the point of diminishing marginal or average returns?
3. When average product is at its maximum, is marginal product less than, equal to, or greater than average product?
4. Does total product increase at a decreasing rate: (*a*) when average product is rising? (*b*) when marginal product is rising? (*c*) when average product begins to fall? (*d*) when marginal product passes its maximum value?
5. When average product equals zero, what is total product?
6. What is the precise relation between a two-factor production function and the marginal product curve for one factor?
7. Beginning with a production function or schedule involving two inputs, explain how one derives the total, average, and marginal products for a single factor.

8. Comment on the following statement: If the production of wheat requires only land and labor, if there are constant returns to scale, and if labor has an increasing average product, then the world's wheat supply could be grown in a flower pot, provided the pot were small enough.

Units of variable input	Total product (1)	Average product (2)	Marginal product (3)
1	100		
2	250		
3	410		
4	560		
5	700		
6	830		
7	945		
8	1,050		
9	1,146		
10	1,234		
11	1,314		
12	1,384		
13	1,444		
14	1,494		
15	1,534		
16	1,564		
17	1,584		
18	1,594		

SUGGESTED READINGS

Clark, J. M. "Diminishing Returns," *Encyclopaedia of the Social Sciences* 5. New York: Macmillan, 1931, pp. 144–46.

Ferguson, C. E. *The Neoclassical Theory of Production and Distribution.* London and New York: Cambridge University Press, 1969, chaps. 1–6.

Henderson, James M., and **Quandt, Richard E.** *Microeconomic Theory: A Mathematical Approach,* 2nd ed. New York: McGraw-Hill, 1971, pp. 52–58.

Knight, Frank H. *Risk, Uncertainty, and Profit.* Boston: Houghton Mifflin, 1921, pp. 94–104.

Machlup, Fritz. "On the Meaning of the Marginal Product," *Explorations in Economics.* New York: McGraw-Hill, 1936, pp. 250–63. Reprinted in American Economic Association, *Readings in the Theory of Income Distribution.* Philadelphia: Blakiston, 1951, pp. 158–74.

CHAPTER

7 Production and Optimal Input Proportions: Two Variable Inputs

According to the newspaper account given in the article at the beginning of this chapter ("Cheap Mexican Labor . . ."), workers who sort and box shrimp in the Tex-Mex Storage Co. in Brownsville, Texas, are paid the minimum wage, which is well above the 99¢ per hour paid to similar workers at Camarones, Selectos, S.A., a Mexican firm just across the U.S.–Mexican border. How does this difference in the price of labor affect the combination of workers and machinery used in the two firms? What accounts for the greater amount of shrimp peeled per hour by the workers in the U.S. firm? This chapter develops the tools to answer such questions. It derives the rule that a cost-minimizing firm will use to determine how to combine inputs to produce a given level of output. What is this rule? What are isoquants? Isocosts? What is the marginal rate of technical substitution? How do these concepts help explain the different proportions of workers to machinery used by Tex-Mex Co. and Camarones, Selectos, S.A.? ∎

APPLYING THE THEORY

Cheap Mexican Labor Attracts U.S. Companies to the Border

By James P. Sterba
Special to the *New York Times*

BROWNSVILLE, Tex., May 9 — The 35 women who sort and box shrimp at Tex-Mex Cold Storage Inc. are quick with their hands. With the help of machines, they can grade and package for freezing about 6,000 pounds of shrimp an hour. Their base pay is $2.30 an hour; their take-home pay: $2.12 an hour.

The 160 women who peel and devein shrimp at Camarones Selectos S.A., just across the border in Matamoros, Mexico, are also quick with their hands. Without machines, they can remove the shells and back veins from about 2,000 pounds of shrimp an hour. Their base pay: 99 cents an hour; their take-home pay: 65 cents an hour.

It is that basic disparity in wages that both lures Mexican workers into the United States and propels United States labor-intensive industries into Mexico. United States labor union officials charge that both movements are costing United States workers jobs at a time when unemployment rates remain high.

Hundreds of United States companies have closed factories in other parts of the country over the last decade and set up new plants along the border to take advantage of low labor costs on the Mexican side and abundant minimum-wage labor on the United States side. The border, in fact, has become an open sore in the Carter Administration's efforts to put Americans back to work, formulate a new immigration policy and deal with pressures for trade embargoes.

Although many companies have simply moved their labor-intensive jobs to such places as South Korea, Taiwan and Hong Kong, American union officials have focused much of their attention on Mexican workers, saying that they in particular are stripping jobs away from American workers.

But a look at the shrimp industry around Brownsville, which calls itself "Shrimp Capital of the World," shows a different picture. Virtually all the jobs requiring labor are performed by men and women of Mexican origin. Some are United States citizens. Many are Mexican citizens living legally on this side of the border. Some are Mexican citizens who live in Mexico and commute to jobs here or work in factories set up in Mexico by United States companies.

Shrimp boat owners and shrimp company processors contend that they simply cannot find many United States citizens who are willing to work at jobs, which are often part time, for wages at the Federal minimum of $2.30 an hour or slightly higher. At the same time, they say there is an abundant supply of Mexicans who are eager to take those jobs and grateful to get them.

But for the most labor-intensive chores of peeling and deveining shrimp, pro-

(continued on page 172)

(continued from page 171)

cessors avoid even United States minimum wages by trucking their shrimp across the border into Mexico. Wages of 99 cents an hour seem paltry by United standards, but they are above average for workers in Mexico. Americans and Mexicans who run processing plants, as well as a variety of other factories on the Mexican side of the border, contend that these plants actually save jobs in the United States. Without them, they contend, many American companies would be forced to move their entire operation to foreign soil in order to remain competitive.

To illustrate how this works, one can follow the circuitous path of a load of shrimp caught the other day in the Gulf of Mexico.

With a permit that costs $2,006 a year, United States shrimp boats can net shrimp in Mexican waters. The boats have threeman crews of a captain, rig man, and header. Many of the rig men are Mexican-Americans. Most of the headers, who remove the heads from shrimp and clean the boats, are Mexicans.

The boats from Brownsville are unloaded usually by Mexican workers. Boat maintenance and cleanup crews at the port are also usually Mexicans.

Shrimp Processor's View

Lawrence Touchet, manager of Gulf Shrimp Processors, hires 50 to 60 Mexicans in the peak season to unload the boats, ice the shrimp and load them onto trucks.

"I don't care how many people are supposed to be out of work, you just can't get Americans to do this work," he said.

The shrimp are then trucked to Tex-Mex Cold Storage for sorting, sizing, boxing and freezing. Ed Walker, the company's production manager agrees with Mr. Tochet.

Questions

1. The article indicates that shrimp peelers on the U.S. side of the border get $2.30 per hour (the minimum wage in the United States at the time), while shrimp peelers in Mexico (across the border) receive 99¢ per hour. How would you predict this difference in the price of labor affects the relative factor proportions of shrimp peelers versus machinery (capital) in firms on the U.S. side of the border versus firms on the Mexican side of the border? (Hint: use the principle that $MRTS$ = ratio of the input prices for cost minimization at any given output level.)

2. What can you say about the marginal product of the last shrimp peeler hired in the U.S. firm versus the marginal product of the last shrimp peeler hired in the firms on the Mexican side of the border? Is there any evidence in the article backing up your conclusion?

3. Why do you think the marginal productivity of the workers are different, depending on which side of the border the firm is located? Explain.

4. The U.S. minimum wage law applies to most workers, but not all workers.

Demonstrate that a *selective* minimum wage law that applies to manufacturing workers but not agricultural workers is NOT pareto optimal. Make sure to demonstrate how it would be possible to increase the total amount of output by rearrangeing factor proportions in the manufacturing and agricultural sectors. In which sector would it be necessary to increase the number of workers? (Note: you might want to come back to this question after completion of Chapter 17.)

Solutions

1. For any given output level, the $MRTS_{L,K}$ must equal the ratio of factor prices, or the slope of the isoquant must equal the slope of the isocost. In symbols, U.S. firms will employ workers and machinery (K) until

$$\frac{MP_L}{p_{L_{(U.S.)}}} = \frac{MP_K}{p_K}, \quad \text{or equivalently}$$

$$MRTS_{L,K} = \frac{MP_L}{MP_K} = \frac{p_{L(U.S.)}}{p_K}$$

Producers of shrimp in Mexico will hire workers such that

$$\frac{MP_L}{p_{L(Mexico)}} = \frac{MP_K}{p_K}, \quad \text{or equivalently}$$

$$\frac{MP_L}{MP_K} = \frac{p_{L(Mexico)}}{p_K}$$

Therefore, given the higher (minimum) wage faced by producers in the United States, it is not surprising to find that

they use less labor and more capital than producers in Mexico.

2. Based on the solution in (1) above, the MP_1 in the United States must be higher because of the relatively higher price of labor. We are told that U.S. shrimp peelers shell approximately 6,000 pounds of shrimp per hour. Since there are 35 workers, this comes out to 171 pounds per hour per person.

   In Mexico the 160 workers who peel shrimp can produce 2,000 pounds per hour, or 12.5 pounds per hour.

3. The U.S. workers each have more machinery to work with than the Mexican workers, thus their marginal productivity is greater. This is a direct result of the relative factor proportions used of the two factors, which in turn is a result of the difference in the relative prices of labor and machinery on the two sides of the border.

4. The minimum wage has resulted in an inefficiency in the allocation of factors. Assuming that workers in both the U.S. and Mexican plants are of equal skill, we find that a transfer of workers from Mexican plants to U.S. plants would result in an increase in total output. This transfer should continue (from an efficiency standpoint) until the ratio of the marginal products of workers to capital were equal in the U.S. and Mexico. Under the minimum wage, the condition for factor substitution is violated because the price of labor faced by producers in the

(continued on page 174)

(continued from page 173)
United States is different (greater) than the price of labor faced by producers in Mexico. As a result,

$$MRTS_{L,K}^{U.S.} = \left[\frac{MP_L}{MP_K}\right]^{U.S.} \text{ is greater}$$

than $\left[\dfrac{MP_L}{MP_K}\right]^{Mexico} = MRTS_{L,K}^{Mexico}$

Stating it differently, the same amount of shrimp could be peeled using fewer resources if there were not an artificially higher wage in the United States by increasing the number of shrimp peelers in the United States (and increasing the amount of machinery in Mexico).

(If you substitute "manufacturing output" for U.S. shrimp and "agricultural output" for Mexican shrimp, the above situation is exactly analogous to the operation of a selective minimum wage law in the U.S.)

Source: *New York Times*, May 13, 1977. © 1977 The New York Times Company. Reprinted by permission.

INTRODUCTION
7.1

The fundamental physical relations of production were discussed in Chapter 6 under the assumption that there is only one variable input. The analysis is continued in this chapter for a more general case. Graphically, production is studied under the assumption that there are two variable inputs. One may regard these inputs either as cooperating with one or more fixed inputs or as the only two inputs. The latter situation, of course, is relevant only for the long run. In either case, however, the results of the two-input model are easily extended to cover multiple inputs.

Production Table
7.1.a

The land-labor example used in Chapter 6 may be expanded to introduce the theory of production with two variable inputs. In the illustration we considered an agricultural experiment in which 10-acre tracts of land made up the fixed input. Labor was the variable input, and we obtained eight sample observations corresponding to the cultivation of the 10-acre tracts by one worker, two workers, and so on. In the present example the agricultural experiment is pushed further so as to obtain 64 sample observations. Land is, in a sense, still the fixed input; but now we suppose that there are eight 1-acre tracts, eight 2-acre tracts, and so on up to eight 8-acre tracts. Each of the sets of 8 constant-acre tracts is cultivated by one worker, two workers, etc., up to eight workers. Thus we have samples ranging from one worker on 1 acre to eight workers on 8 acres. The data for this example are listed in Table 7.1.1.

The entries in the row corresponding to 3-acre tracts of land are exactly the same as the entries in Table 6.2.2. Indeed, in every respect this table is just a "larger" example of the hypothetical experiment in Chapter 6.

In the spirit of Chapter 6, consider land as the fixed input. The entries in each row show the total outputs produced on the stipulated acreage when different numbers of workers cultivate the land. By successive subtractions along each row, the marginal product of labor is obtained. Next, by going to successively higher rows one sees that the total, average, and marginal products of labor increase as larger and larger tracts of land are used — that is, as the fixed input is expanded relative to the variable input.

Up to a point! But just as too many workers per acre of land make cultivation too intensive, too many acres of land per worker make cultivation too extensive. Instead of viewing acres per tract as the fixed input, we can regard workers per

Table 7.1.1 Data from hypothetical agricultural experiment*

Acres per tract	Output in bushels							
8	9	46	69	92	109	124	136	144
7	13	46	69	91	108	123	134	140
6	16	42	66	88	106	120	128	132
5	15	37	60	80	100	113	120	121
4	13	31	54	72	85	93	95	95
3	10	24	39	52	61	66	66	64
2	6	12	17	21	24	26	$25\frac{1}{2}$	$24\frac{1}{2}$
1	3	6	8	9	10	10	9	7
	1	2	3	4	5	6	7	8

Workers per tract of land

*Notice that this production schedule does not represent a production function homogeneous of degree one. Linear homogeneity implies that the diagonal elements are multiples of one another. For example, since (1,1) is 3, (2,2) should be 6, rather than 12, and so forth.

tract as fixed and the number of acres per tract as variable. We then read up the columns rather than across the rows; but the same fundamental physical relations are exhibited.

With one worker per tract, output increases as the size of the tract increases until 6 acres per tract is reached. Thereafter, total output declines and the marginal product of land is negative. As the number of workers per tract is expanded, thus diminishing the land–labor ratio for each given acreage, total product expands continuously beyond 3-acre tracts. Total product in these cases does not reach a maximum in the range shown in this example. But in each case the point of diminishing marginal returns is reached; thereafter, output expands at a decreasing rate.

Input Substitution
7.1.b

Table 7.1.1 illustrates that the basic empirical principles of physical production hold whether workers per tract are varied with acres per tract constant or whether acres per tract are varied with workers per tract constant. It also depicts another very important physical relation between inputs: the same amount of total output may be produced by different input combinations. For example, an output of 66 bushels can be produced by using six workers on 3 acres of land or by using three workers on 6 acres. Similarly, 120 bushels can be produced either by seven workers on 5 acres or by six workers on 6 acres.

In this example no more than two different input combinations can be used to produce the same output. In a more general, continuous case, however, a given level of output can be produced by a wide variety of different input combinations. In other words, one input may be *substituted* for another in producing a specified volume of output. One of the important tasks of the entrepreneur is to select the particular input combination that minimizes the cost of producing any given level of output. The chief purpose of this chapter is to show how this is done. A real-world example is provided in the newspaper article at the beginning of this chapter.

Example: As already mentioned, the theory of production can be used to describe services as well as goods. That is pursued in this example.

Consider a law firm that specializes in writing contracts between merging firms. Writing these contracts requires two skills. First, economic issues must be addressed. For example, it is important to know whether sharing profits equally will provide each division with the appropriate incentives to hold up its end. Second, the terms must be carefully worded so that they are understood by both parties and leave no room for error later.

Economists are best suited to deal with the first set of issues and lawyers are best able to deal with the last. Still, each can work on the other's area, at least to some extent. Thus, we can think of two variable factors as economist-hours worked and lawyer-hours worked. The technology of contract production can be written as

$$\text{Number of contracts} = (\text{Economist-hours})^{1/2} (\text{Lawyer-hours})^{1/2}$$

Table 7.1.E.1 Output of contracts

Economist-hours	Lawyer-hours									
	1	2	3	4	5	6	7	8	9	10
1	1.0	1.4	1.7	2.0	2.2	2.4	2.6	2.8	3.0	3.2
2	1.4	2.0	2.4	2.8	3.2	3.5	3.7	4.0	4.2	4.5
3	1.7	2.4	3.0	3.5	3.9	4.2	4.6	4.9	5.2	5.5
4	2.0	2.8	3.5	4.0	4.5	4.9	5.3	5.7	6.0	6.3
5	2.2	3.2	3.9	4.5	5.0	5.5	5.9	6.3	6.7	7.1
6	2.4	3.5	4.2	4.9	5.5	6.0	6.5	6.9	7.3	7.7
7	2.6	3.7	4.6	5.3	5.9	6.5	7.0	7.5	7.9	8.4
8	2.8	4.0	4.9	5.7	6.3	6.9	7.5	8.0	8.5	8.9
9	3.0	4.2	5.2	6.0	6.7	7.3	7.9	8.5	9.0	9.5
10	3.2	4.5	5.5	6.3	7.1	7.7	8.4	8.9	9.5	10.0

Table 7.1.E.1 presents some outcomes of different choices of each type of worker's hours. For example, if 5 hours of lawyer time is used and 3 hours of economist time is used, 3.9 contracts can be written.

Suppose that lawyers' and economists' time cost the same amount. Then the efficient output is given along the diagonal. To see this, note that the 3.9 contracts produced required 8 hours of labor. But if the same 8 hours were made up of 4 hours of economist's time and 4 hours of lawyer's time (instead of the 3 and 5 hours), 4.0 contracts could be produced. The cost would be the same since all hours cost the same amount, but the amount produced would be greater. It is not generally true that efficient production implies use of inputs in equal proportion; but in this case, where hours cost the same and the production function is symmetric, that is the outcome.

Two points are illustrated: First, it is as easy to use production theory to discuss services as it is to use it to discuss goods. Second, production theory can assist us in understanding the way to achieve the highest level of productivity for a given cost. Alternatively, it allows us to understand how firms choose input allocations from a very larger number of possibilities.

PRODUCTION SURFACE
7.2

Selection of the least-cost input combination requires knowledge of substitution possibilities and of relative input prices. For an individual producer, the input prices are given by market forces of supply and demand. Input substitution is the center of our interest. To get at an explanation requires the use of a device much like the one used in Part 1 to describe a consumer's preference surface. In the theory of consumer behavior we used equal-satisfaction contour lines, or indifference curves. Here we use equal-output contours, or *isoquants*.

Production Surface for Discrete Case
7.2.a

As an introduction, first look at the total production surface. Figure 7.2.1 is a graph of the discrete production function given earlier in Table 7.1.1. The height of the rectangular blocks indicates the volume (bushels of output). By following the heights visually in either "horizontal" direction, one may see how the total product curve is shaped for a fixed amount of one input and variable amounts of the other. But as we have already observed in this example, substitution possibilities are very limited. In certain cases two different input combinations yield the same output. However, this example is *too* discrete to illustrate a wide range of production possibilities.

Production Surface for Continuous Case
7.2.b

For this purpose a *continuous* production function is required. Let us imagine a manufacturing process that requires two inputs — labor and capital — to produce a specific commodity. The production function for this good is continuous; it cannot, therefore, be shown conveniently in tabular form. However, either a mathematical or a graphical representation is suitable.[1] We have already introduced a mathematical version of a continuous production function in Example 7.1.

A continuous production function is shown in Figure 7.2.2, a three-dimensional diagram in which height measures quantity of output and the two "flat" or "horizontal" dimensions measure quantities of the two inputs.[2]

The production surface is $OKQL$. Any point on this surface represents a particular quantity of output. Dropping perpendiculars from the point to the axes shows the quantities of inputs required. For example, P is a point on the surface and PP' is the associated volume of output. Drawing perpendiculars to the axes, $OL_1 (= K_1 P')$ units of labor and $OK_1 (= L_1 P')$ units of capital are required to produce the amount PP' at this particular point.

The production surface may be viewed in a different manner. Hold the capital input constant at the amount OK_1. The total product curve for OK_1 units of capital and variable inputs of labor is $K_1 PF$. At labor input OL_1, total output is PP'; and at labor input OL, total output is FG. The total product curve $K_1 PF$ rises rapidly for small quantities of labor input, reaches a point of maximum slope (the point of diminishing marginal physical returns to labor for the given capital input OK_1), and thereafter increases at a decreasing rate.

The same statement applies to a typical total product curve for a fixed labor input and variable capital usage. Hold the input of labor constant at OL_1 units.

---

[1]Let Q, K, and L represent the quantities of output, capital, and labor, respectively. The production function may be written $Q = f(K,L)$, where $\partial Q//\partial K$ and $\partial Q/\partial L$ are the marginal products of capital and labor, respectively.

[2]In constructing Figure 7.2.2 we have assumed that $f(K,0) = f(0,L) = f(0,0) = 0$.

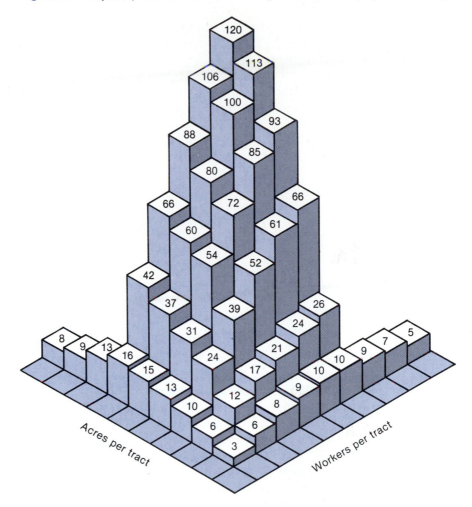

L_1PD is the curve of total output resulting from variable inputs of capital. For example, when OK_1 units of capital are used, output is PP'; when OK units are employed, output is DE.

Production Isoquants
7.2.c

Still using Figure 7.2.2, let us determine all the different input combinations capable of producing PP' units of output. To do this, we slice (or "intersect") the production surface $OKQL$ at the height $PP' = AA' = BB'$. This slicing process generates the curve APB, a locus of points equidistant ($AA' = PP' = BB'$) from

Figure 7.2.2 Physical production surface for a continuous production function

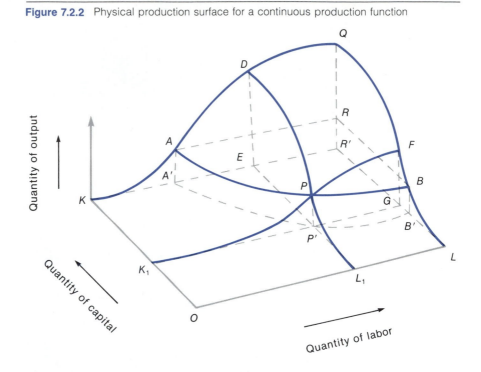

the *K,L* plane. By dropping perpendiculars from each point on the *APB* curve to the *K,L* plane, one obtains the input combinations associated with each point. In other words, the curve *APB* is projected onto the *K,L* plane, generating the curve *A′P′B′*. The latter is a locus of points each of which represents a combination of inputs capable of producing the stipulated quantity of output *PP′* = *AA′* = *BB′* = *RR′*. For examples, the following three combinations of capital and labor are points on the curve *A′P′B′*: *OK, KA′*; *OK₁, OL₁*; *LB′, OL*.

The curve *A′P′B′* is called an *isoquant*.

Isoquant: An isoquant is a curve in input space showing all possible combinations of inputs physically capable of producing a given level of output. The entire three-dimensional production surface can be exactly depicted by a two-dimensional isoquant map. The word derives from the root "iso" for constant and "quant," which is short for quantity.

A portion of an isoquant map, derived from a production surface such as *OKQL* in Figure 7.2.2, is shown in Figure 7.2.3.[3] The two axes measure the

---

[3]The excluded portion of the isoquant map is discussed in subsection 7.3.c.

Figure 7.2.3 Typical set of isoquants

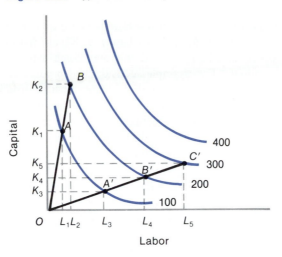

quantities of inputs, and the curves show the different input combinations that can be used to produce 100, 200, 300, and 400 units of output, respectively. The further northeast a curve lies, the greater is the output associated with it.

Consider first the isoquant for 100 units of output. Each point on this curve shows a capital–labor combination that can produce 100 units of output. For example, OK_1 units of capital and OL_1 units of labor may be used, or OK_3 units of capital and OL_3 units of labor, or any other input combination found by dropping perpendiculars to the axes from a point on the curve.

A ray from the origin, such as OAB or $OA'B'C'$, defines a constant capital–labor input ratio. In particular, the slope of the ray is the input ratio. For example, at points A and B, 100 and 200 units of output, respectively, are produced at the capital–labor ratio $OK_1/OL_1 = OK_2/OL_2$. Similarly, at points A', B', and C', 100, 200, and 300 units of output, respectively, are produced at the capital–labor ratio $OK_3/OL_3 = OK_4/OL_4 = OK_5/OL_5$.

Along the ray OAB, various levels of output are producible by the same input ratio; the magnitude of the inputs increases as one moves out along the ray but the capital–labor ratio remains unchanged. This contrasts clearly with movements along an isoquant. In this case the level of output remains unchanged and the capital–labor ratio changes continuously.

These points may be summarized as follows.

Relations: An isoquant represents different input combinations, or input ratios, that may be used to produce a specified level of output. For movements *along an isoquant,* the level of output remains constant and the input ratio changes continuously. A ray from the origin defines a specific, constant input ratio. For movements *along a ray,* the level of output changes continuously and the input ratio remains constant.

Fixed-Proportions Production Functions
7.2.d

Using isoquants, it is easy to illustrate the case of fixed-proportions production functions, briefly mentioned in Chapter 6. Recall that production is subject to fixed proportions when one, and only one, combination of inputs can produce a specified output.[4] For example, consider the production process illustrated in Figure 7.2.4. Two inputs, capital and labor, must be used in the fixed ratio 2 : 3. That is, 2 units of capital and 3 units of labor are required to produce 100 units of output. Fixed-proportions technology does not imply constant returns to scale; it implies only that to produce 100 units 2 units of capital and 3 units of labor must be used. There is no possibility of using, say, 3 units of capital and 2 units of labor.

It might be the case that 4 units of capital and 6 units of labor must be used to produce 150 units of output. Fixed proportions would be required, but there would be diminishing returns to scale because a doubling of inputs resulted in less than a doubling of output. Constant returns to scale, in addition to fixed-proportions technology, implies that 4 units of capital and 6 units of labor can produce 200 units of output; 6 units of capital and 9 units of labor can produce 300 units; and so on.

The required capital–labor ratio is shown by the slope of the ray *OR* in Figure 7.2.4. Isoquants are constructed for 100, 200, and 300 units of output. Rather than taking the more conventional shape shown in Figure 7.2.3, the isoquants for fixed-proportions processes are L-shaped curves. This illustrates, for example, that if 3 units of labor and 2 units of capital are employed, 100 units of output are obtainable. However, if the quantity of capital is expanded and labor input is held constant, no additional output can be obtained. Similarly, if capital input is held constant and labor expanded, output is unchanged. In other words, the marginal product of either labor or capital is zero if its usage is expanded while the other input is held constant. But since we usually think of fixed-proportions technologies as also having constant returns to scale, doubling inputs at the required ratio doubles output; trebling inputs at the required ratio trebles output, etc.[5]

A rather realistic case is that in which many, but not an infinite number of, different fixed-proportions processes are available. For example, Table 7.2.1 contains an example of the production of a commodity for which five different

---

[4]A fixed-proportions, constant-returns-to-scale, production function, which is frequently called a Leontief function, may be represented by

$$Q = \text{minimum } [(K/\alpha), (L/\beta)],$$

where α and β are constants and "minimum" means that Q equals the smaller of the two ratios. For a detailed treatment of the fixed-proportions case, see C. E. Ferguson, *The Neoclassical Theory of Production and Distribution* (London and New York: Cambridge University Press, 1969), chaps. *ii–iii*.

[5]It is readily seen from the Leontief function in footnote 4 that such fixed-proportions production functions are homogeneous of degree one; that is, these functions reflect constant returns to scale.

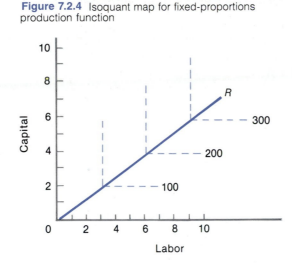

Figure 7.2.4 Isoquant map for fixed-proportions production function

Table 7.2.1 Production when several fixed-proportions processes are available

Ray	Capital labor ratio	Capital input	Labor input	Total output
OA	11:1	11	1	100
		22	2	200
OB	8:2	8	2	100
		16	4	200
OC	5:4	5	4	100
		10	8	200
OD	3:7	3	7	100
		6	14	200
OE	1:10	1	10	100
		2	20	200

fixed-proportions processes are available. The 100-output isoquants, together with the capital–labor ratio rays, are plotted in Figure 7.2.5.

Heavily shaded straight lines have been drawn to connect the different possible input combinations. Each of the points on this kinked line represents an input combination capable of producing 100 units of output. The kinked line *ABCDE* looks very much like the "normal" isoquant shown in Figure 7.2.3. It is different, however, in that no input combination lying on the arc between *A* and *B*, *B* and *C*, etc., is itself *directly* a feasible input combination. For example, it is not possible to produce 100 units of output by *one* process using 7.25 units of capital and 2.5 units of labor.

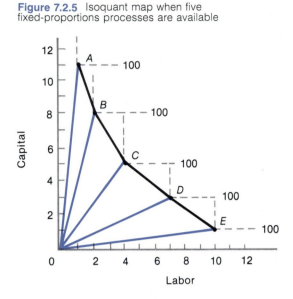

Figure 7.2.5 Isoquant map when five fixed-proportions processes are available

On the other hand, if input units are sufficiently divisible, any particular input ratio — represented by a point on the kinked line — can be achieved. All that is required is the proper combination of the two fixed-proportions processes with which it is most closely associated. For example, suppose a producer wished to obtain 100 units of output by using 7.25 units of capital and 2.5 units of labor. This could be achieved by producing 75 units of output by the process represented by the ray OB and 25 units by the process OC. To produce 75 units at the 8:2 ratio requires 6 units of capital and 1.5 units of labor. Producing 25 units at the 5:4 ratio requires 1.25 units of capital and 1 unit of labor. Thus 100 units of output can be produced at the desired ratio 7.25:2.5 by combining the two processes represented by the rays OB and OC.

Finally, suppose there are many fixed-proportions processes by which a given level of output can be produced. Instead of the five points in Figure 7.2.5, there would be many points. Similarly, there would be many straight-line facets of the type AB, BC, etc. As the number of processes increases, the kinked line looks more and more like a typical isoquant. Indeed, an isoquant depicting a variable-proportions production function is just the limiting case of fixed-proportions processes as the number of processes increases without bound.

This argument, in fact, constitutes one rationale for the use of smooth isoquants and variable-proportions production functions in economic theory. Many manufacturing processes may be characterized by fixed, or almost fixed, proportions; however, many different fixed-proportions processes are available. Constructing smooth isoquants rather than multiple facet lines simplifies analysis while leading to relatively unimportant departures from real-world conditions.

One of the chief features of production under conditions of variable proportions — or a large number of alternative fixed-proportions processes — is that different combinations of inputs can produce a given level of output. In other words, one input can be *substituted* for another in such a way as to maintain a constant level of output. Great theoretical and practical importance attaches to the *rate* at which one input must be substituted for another so as to keep output constant and to the proportionate change in the input ratio induced by a given proportionate change in the rate of substitution.

Marginal Rate of Technical Substitution
7.3.a

Consider a representative isoquant I_1 in Figure 7.3.1. P and R are two of the many different input combinations that may be used to produce the I_1 level of output. If production occurs at P, OK_1 units of capital and OL_1 units of labor are required. OK_2 units of capital and OL_2 units of labor are required for production at R. Thus, P is associated with the capital–labor ratio given by the slope of $OP = OK_1/OL_1$ and R with the capital–labor ratio given by the slope of $OR = OK_2/OL_2$.

If there is a change from P to R, the same level of output is produced by using *more* labor and less capital — labor can be substituted for capital by moving from P to R, and vice versa. The rate at which labor can be substituted for capital over the arc PR is given by

$$-\frac{OK_1 - OK_2}{OL_1 - OL_2} = \frac{PS}{SR},$$

where the minus sign is affixed so as to yield a positive number. Stated alternatively, the rate of substitution is the change in capital usage divided by the change in labor usage.

As the distance from P to R diminishes, the slope of the curvilinear segment PR approaches the slope of the tangent TT' at point P. In the limit, for a very tiny movement in the neighborhood of P, the slope of the tangent at P measures the rate of substitution. In this case — for small movements along I_1 — it is called the *marginal rate of technical substitution,* just as the slope of a consumer's indifference curve is called the marginal rate of substitution in consumption.

Next, suppose labor input is held constant at the OL_1 level while the input of capital is increased from OK_2 to OK_1. Output would increase from the I_2 level (say Q_2) to the I_1 level (say Q_1). The marginal product of capital is, of course, the increase in output per unit increase in input, or

$$\frac{Q_1 - Q_2}{OK_1 - OK_2}.$$

Figure 7.3.1 Marginal rate of technical substitution

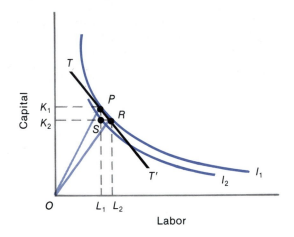

Since $OK_1 - OK_2 = PS$, the marginal product of capital is

$$\frac{Q_1 - Q_2}{PS}.$$

Now return to the I_2 level and hold capital input constant at OK_2 while increasing labor input from OL_1 to OL_2, or by the amount SR. The marginal product of labor for this change is

$$\frac{Q_1 - Q_2}{SR}.$$

The ratio of the marginal product of labor to that of capital is

$$\frac{Q_1 - Q_2}{SR} \div \frac{Q_1 - Q_2}{PS} = \frac{PS}{SR},$$

the rate of substitution of labor for capital. Thus in the limit, as the distance from P to R becomes very small, the marginal rate of technical substitution of labor for capital is equal to the ratio of the marginal product of labor to the marginal product of capital.

These results may be summarized as follows:

Relations: The marginal rate of technical substitution measures the reduction in one input per unit increase in the other that is just sufficient to maintain a constant level of output. The marginal rate of technical substitution of input X for input Y at a point on an isoquant is equal to the negative of the slope of the isoquant at that point. It is also equal to the ratio of the marginal product of input X to the marginal product of input Y.

Diminishing Marginal Rate of Technical Substitution
7.3.b

As already defined, the marginal rate of technical substitution is the ratio of the marginal product of labor to the marginal product of capital. As labor is substituted for capital, the marginal product of labor declines and the marginal product of capital increases.[6] Hence the marginal rate of technical substitution of labor for capital declines as labor is substituted for capital so as to maintain a constant level of output. This may be summarized as follows:

Relation: As labor is substituted for capital along an isoquant (so that output is unchanged), the marginal rate of technical substitution declines.

The fact that the marginal rate of technical substitution falls as labor is substituted for capital means that isoquants must be convex (that is, in the neighborhood of a point of tangency, the isoquant must lie above the tangent line).[7] This is illustrated in Figure 7.3.2.

Q, R, S, and T are four input combinations lying on the isoquant I. Q has the combination OK_1 units of capital and 1 unit of labor; R has OK_2 units of capital and 2 units of labor; and so on. For the movement from Q to R, the marginal rate of technical substitution of labor for capital is, by formula,

$$-\frac{OK_1 - OK_2}{1 - 2} = OK_1 - OK_2.$$

Similarly, for the movements from R to S and S to T, the marginal rates of technical substitution are $OK_2 - OK_3$ and $OK_3 - OK_4$, respectively.

Since the marginal rate of technical substitution of labor for capital diminishes as labor is substituted for capital, it is necessary that $OK_1 - OK_2 > OK_2 - OK_3 > OK_3 - OK_4$. Visually, the amount of capital replaced by successive units of labor will decline if, and only if, the isoquant is convex. Since the amount *must* decline, the isoquant must be convex.

Relation: Isoquants must be convex at every point in order to satisfy the principle of diminishing marginal rate of technical substitution.

Economic Region of Production
7.3.c

Many production functions lead to initial isoquant maps such as shown in Figure 7.2.3. Others, however, generate an isoquant map such as that shown in Figure 7.3.3. It is like the map in Figure 7.2.3 in that the isoquants do not

---

[6]This is not universally true but it will typically be the case in the economic region of production as will be seen shortly.

[7]Although it is not true that isoquants must be convex, the nonconvex portion of the isoquant is irrelevant since the firm never chooses an allocation of capital and labor in that region. It can always do better by skipping over the nonconvexity.

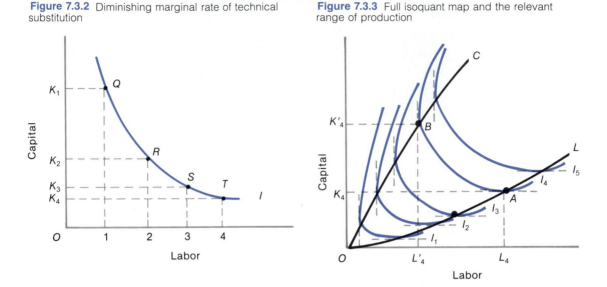

Figure 7.3.2 Diminishing marginal rate of technical substitution

Figure 7.3.3 Full isoquant map and the relevant range of production

intersect; the higher the isoquants the greater the level of output; and over a range of input values they are negatively sloped. The only difference lies in the fact that the isoquants in Figure 7.3.3 "bend back upon themselves," or have positively sloped segments.

The parallel dashed lines in Figure 7.3.3 indicate the points at which the isoquants bend back upon themselves. The lines OC and OL join these points and form, as we will see, the boundaries for the economic region of production (or the stage II region).

Suppose the quantity represented by isoquant I_4 is to be produced. Producing this amount requires a *minimum* of OK_4 units of capital, inasmuch as any smaller amount would not permit one to attain the I_4 level of output. With OK_4 units of capital, OL_4 units of labor must be used. Beyond this level of input, additional units of labor in combination with OK_4 units of capital would yield a smaller level of output. To maintain the I_4 level of output with a greater labor input would require a greater input of capital as well—a palpably uneconomic use of resources.

Since an expansion of labor input beyond OL_4, in the face of the constant capital input OK_4, reduces total output, point A on I_4 represents the intensive margin for labor. Its marginal product is zero, and hence the marginal rate of technical substitution of capital for labor is zero. This is shown by the horizontal tangent at point A. At this point labor has been substituted for capital to the maximum extent consistent with the level of output I_4.

Similarly, producing at the I_4 level requires a certain minimum input of labor, OL_4' in Figure 7.3.3. The I_4 level cannot be attained without at least this much labor; and with this minimum amount additions to capital input beyond OK_4'

would reduce rather than augment output. Thus the marginal product of capital is zero at point B and negative for quantities in excess of OK'_4 units (in combination with OL'_4 units of labor). Since the marginal product of capital is zero, the marginal rate of substitution of labor for capital is infinite or undefined at this point; capital is used to its intensive margin.

By connecting the points of zero marginal labor product, the line OL is formed. Similarly, OC is the locus of points for which the marginal product of capital is zero. Production must take place within this range. Hence the "ridge" lines OL and OC separate the economic from the uneconomic regions of production. To summarize:

Relations: If the production function is such that the total isoquant map is like the one in Figure 7.3.3, then only those portions of the isoquants lying between the ridge lines (the loci of zero marginal products) are relevant to production. These economic portions of the isoquants are uniquely associated with stage II production of each input.

Stage I production for any input conforms to the region of rising average product; and if average product rises, marginal product must exceed average product. Since a stage I area must be present to generate the isoquant map shown in Figure 7.3.3, the "normal" set of product curves — as shown in Figure 7.3.3 — must be associated with the production function giving rise to this isoquant map. This "normal" set of product curves is reproduced in Panel A, Figure 7.3.4.[8]

Some production functions, however, generate isoquant maps such as that in Figure 7.2.3. There is neither a stage I nor a stage III range for either input. The entire production function represents stage II, or the economic region. Marginal and average products decline continuously, but neither reaches zero because there is not a maximum point on the total product curve. Such a production function is shown in Panel B, Figure 7.3.4. The average and marginal product curves begin some distance from the origin. This is a mere convenience. They are both defined for infinitesimally small amounts of input; but at input levels less than unity, average and marginal products exceed total product.

The importance of production functions giving rise to the product curves of Panel B is an empirical question. For expository purposes, production functions of the type shown in Panel A are generally used. In empirical, statistical, and econometric applications, however, a broad class of production functions such as shown in Panel B are most often used. The distinction, in fact, is relevant only in theory because observed production relations are always those of stage II.

---

[8]We "superimpose" total product, average product, and marginal product curves on the same graph for purposes of comparison. Since these are measured differently (total product is units of output while average and marginal product are units of output per unit of input of the productive factor), we are using different scales on the vertical axis.

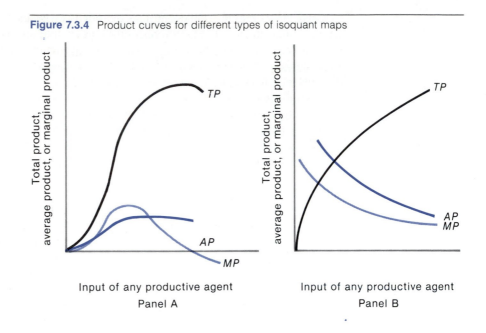

Figure 7.3.4 Product curves for different types of isoquant maps

Panel A:
- y-axis: Total product, average product, or marginal product
- Curves labeled TP, AP, MP
- x-axis: Input of any productive agent
- Panel A

Panel B:
- y-axis: Total product, average product, or marginal product
- Curves labeled TP, AP, MP
- x-axis: Input of any productive agent
- Panel B

OPTIMAL COMBINATION OF RESOURCES
7.4

So far, the theory of production has been analyzed from the standpoint of an individual entrepreneur. However, nothing has been said regarding the *optimal* way in which the entrepreneur should combine resources. Any desired level of output can normally be produced by a number of different combinations of inputs. Our task now is to examine how the producer selects a specific input combination.

Input Prices and Isocosts
7 4.a

Inputs, just as outputs, bear specific market prices. In determining the *operating* input combination, a producer must pay heed to relative input prices in order to minimize the cost of producing a given output or maximize output for a given level of costs. In the long run the producer must do this to obtain the *maximum* attainable profit.

We have already hinted at the importance of input prices for the determination of input choice in Example 7.1. There, we assumed that both types of labor cost the same amount per hour of use, so that the problem boiled down to selecting the most productive allocation in physical terms. That is not true in general. For example, if economist time cost twice as much as lawyer time, economists would have to be at least twice as productive to justify their use.

Part Two   Theory of Production and Cost

Input prices are determined, just as the prices of goods are, by supply and demand in the market. For producers who are not monopsonists or oligopsonists, input prices are given by the market. Let us now concentrate upon a producer who is a perfect competitor in the input market, but possibly a monopolist or an oligopolist in the output market. (Consideration of monopsony and oligopsony is deferred to Chapter 15.)

Let us continue to assume that the two inputs are labor and capital, although the analysis applies equally well to any two productive agents. Denote the quantity of capital and labor by K and L, respectively, and their unit prices by r for rent and w for wage.[9] The total cost, C, of using any volume of K and L is $C = rK + wL$, the sum of the cost of K units of capital at r per unit and of L units of labor at w per unit.

To take a more specific example, suppose capital costs $1,000 per unit ($r = \$1,000$) and labor receives a wage of $2,500 per labor-year ($w = \$2,500$). If a total of $15,000 is to be spent for inputs, the following combinations are possible: $\$15,000 = \$1,000K + \$2,500L$, or $K = 15 - 2.5L$. Similarly, if $20,000 is to be spent on inputs, one can purchase the following combination: $K = 20 - 2.5L$. More generally, if the fixed amount $\overline{C}$ is to be spent, the producer can choose among the combinations given by

$$K = \frac{\overline{C}}{r} - \frac{w}{r}L .$$

This is illustrated in Figure 7.4.1. If $15,000 is spent for inputs and no labor is purchased, 15 units of capital may be bought. More generally, if $\overline{C}$ is to be spent and r is the unit cost, $\overline{C}/r$ units of capital may be purchased. This is the vertical-axis *intercept* of the line. If 1 unit of labor is purchased at $2,500, 2.5 units of capital must be sacrificed; if 2 units of labor are bought, 5 units of capital must be sacrificed; and so on. Thus as the purchase of labor is increased, the purchase of capital must be diminished. For each additional unit of labor, w/r units of capital must be forgone. In Figure 7.4.1, $w/r = 2.5$. Attaching a negative sign, this is the *slope* of the straight lines constructed in this graph.

The solid lines in Figure 7.4.1 are called *isocost curves* because they show the various combinations of inputs that may be purchased for a stipulated amount of expenditure. In summary:

Relation: At fixed input prices r and w for capital and labor, respectively, a fixed outlay $\overline{C}$ will purchase any combination of capital and labor given by the following linear equation:

$$K = \frac{\overline{C}}{r} - \frac{w}{r}L .$$

---

[9]Various interpretations may be used. One simple interpretation is to suppose that capital is rented and r is the rental price. Even if capital is owned rather than rented, this interpretation is useful because by using it rather than renting it to someone else, the entrepreneur forgoes a rental payment of rK. This concept of "opportunity" cost will be discussed in Chapter 8.

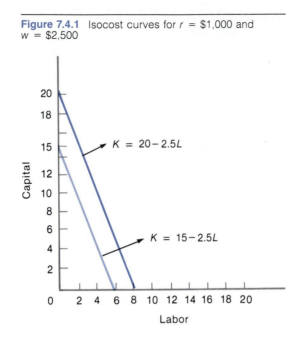

Figure 7.4.1 Isocost curves for $r = \$1,000$ and $w = \$2,500$

$K = 20 - 2.5L$

$K = 15 - 2.5L$

This is the equation for an isocost curve, whose intercept ($\overline{C}/r$) is the amount of capital that may be purchased if no labor is bought and whose slope is the negative of the input–price ratio (w/r).

Maximizing Output for a Given Cost
7.4.b

Suppose at given input prices r and w, a producer can spend only $\overline{C}$ on production. Subject to this input cost, the producer wishes to operate efficiently by producing the maximum attainable output. Thus, among all input combinations that can be purchased for the fixed amount $\overline{C}$, the producer seeks the one that results in the largest level of output.

Let the given level of cost $\overline{C}$ be represented by the isocost curve KL in Figure 7.4.2. The slope of KL is equal to the (negative) ratio of the price per unit of labor to the price per unit of capital. I_1, I_2, and I_3 are isoquants representing various levels of output. First, observe that the I_3 level of output is not obtainable because the *available* input combinations are limited to those lying on or beneath the isocost curve KL.

Next, the producer could operate at points such as R and S. At these two points, the input combinations *required* to produce the I_1 level of output are *available* for a given cost represented by the isocost KL. In this case, however, output can be increased without incurring additional cost by the selection of a

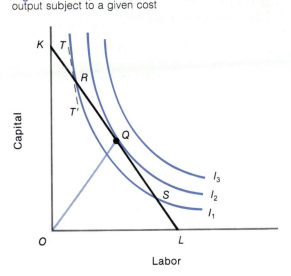

Figure 7.4.2 Optimal input combination to maximize output subject to a given cost

more appropriate input combination. Indeed, output can be expanded until the I_2 level is reached — the level at which an isoquant is just tangent to the specified isocost curve. A greater output is not obtainable for the given level of expenditure; a lesser output is inefficient because production can be expanded at no additional cost. Hence the input combination represented by the slope of the ray OQ is optimal because it is the combination that maximizes output for the given level of cost.

After studying the theory of consumer behavior, this proposition should be more or less obvious. However, a sound reason lies behind it. For a moment, suppose the entrepreneur contemplated producing at point R. The marginal rate of technical substitution of labor for capital — given by the slope of the tangent TT' — is relatively high. Suppose it is $3:1$, meaning that one unit of labor can replace 3 units of capital at that point. The relative input price, given by the slope of KL, is much less, say $1:1$. In this case, 1 unit of labor costs the same as 1 unit of capital but it can replace 3 units of capital in production. The producer would obviously be better off by substituting labor for capital. The opposite argument holds for point S, where the marginal rate of technical substitution is less than the input–price ratio.

Following this argument, the producer reaches equilibrium (maximizes output for a given level of cost) only when the marginal rate of technical substitution of labor for capital is equal to the ratio of the price of labor to the price of capital. The market input–price ratio tells the producer the rate at which one input can be substituted for another *in purchasing*. The marginal rate of technical substitution is the rate at which *inputs can be substituted in production*. So long as the two are not equal, a producer can achieve either a greater output or a lower cost by moving in the direction of equality.[10]

Principle: To maximize output subject to a given total cost and given input prices, the producer must purchase inputs in quantities such that the marginal rate of technical substitution of capital for labor is equal to the input–price ratio (the price of labor to the price of capital). Thus

$$MRTS_{L \text{ for } K} = \frac{MP_L}{MP_K} = \frac{w}{r}.$$

Minimizing Cost Subject to a Given Output
7.4.c

As an alternative to maximizing output for a given cost, an entrepreneur may seek to minimize the cost of producing a stipulated level of output. The problem is solved graphically in Figure 7.4.3. The isoquant I represents the stipulated level of output, while C_1, C_2, and C_3 are isocost curves with the same slope (input–price ratio).

First, notice that the level of cost represented by C_1 is not feasible because the I level of output is not physically producible by any input combination available for this outlay. Next, the I level could be produced, for example, by the input combinations represented by the points R and S, both at the cost level C_3. But by moving either from R to Q or from S to Q, the entrepreneur can obtain the same output at lower cost.

---

[10]Let MP_K be the marginal product of K and let MP_L be the marginal product of L. If capital is changed by a small amount ΔK, the resulting change in output will be

$$MP_K \Delta K$$

and capital costs will change by $r\Delta K$. If total cost is to remain constant, the change in labor costs must exactly offset this change in capital costs or

$$w\Delta L = -r\Delta K.$$

The change in output resulting from this change in labor input will be

$$MP_L \Delta L = -\frac{r}{w} MP_L \Delta K .$$

The net change in output is the sum of these two changes or

$$\Delta Q = \left(MP_K - \frac{r}{w} MP_L \right) \Delta K .$$

If the bracketed expression is positive, an increase in K will increase output; and if the bracketed expression is negative, a decrease in K will increase output. Hence, at maximum output, the bracketed expression must be zero or

$$\frac{MP_L}{MP_K} = \frac{w}{r} .$$

By definition, the left side of this expression is $MRTS_{L \text{ for } K}$ as stated in the text.

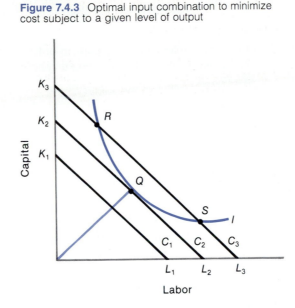

Figure 7.4.3 Optimal input combination to minimize cost subject to a given level of output

By the very same arguments used in subsection 7.4.b, a position of equilibrium is attained only at point Q where the isoquant is just tangent to an isocost curve. Thus in equilibrium the marginal rate of technical substitution of labor for capital must equal the ratio of the price of labor to the price of capital. The previous principle may thus be elaborated.

Principle: In order either to maximize output subject to a given cost or to minimize cost subject to a given output, the entrepreneur must employ inputs in such amounts as to equate the marginal rate of technical substitution and the input–price ratio.

THE EXPANSION PATH
7.5

The object of an entrepreneur is to maximize profit. Among other things, this involves organizing production in the most efficient or economical way. This requires, as we have now seen, adjusting factor proportions until the marginal rate of technical substitution equals the factor–price ratio — or what is the same, adjusting factor proportions until the marginal product of a dollar's worth of each input is the same. When this task is accomplished, equilibrium is attained at a point such as Q in Figures 7.4.2 and 7.4.3.

Now let us digress for a moment to recall the procedure we used when studying the theory of consumer behavior. First, the position of consumer equilibrium was established. Then we posed and answered the following question: How will the

NUMERICAL EXERCISES

According to the principles in this chapter, in order to minimize cost for any given output level, a producer should combine inputs such that

$$MRTS = \frac{MP_L}{MP_K} = \frac{P_L}{P_K}$$

or equivalently,

$$\frac{MP_L}{P_L} = \frac{MP_K}{P_K}.$$

This latter formula gives rise to the statement that "factor proportions should be adjusted until the marginal product (MP) of a dollar's worth of each input is the same."

Questions

1. Suppose you produce a product (Q) using inputs of labor (L) and machines (K). Your chief engineer comes to you and reports the following information about your production situation.

Q	K	L	Q	K	L
490	15	99	470	14	100
500	15	100	500	15	100

   If the price of L is $5 per unit, and the price of K is $10 per unit, does the input combination of 15 K and 100 L represent the least-cost method of producing output of 500? If not, should you use more L and less K, or less L and more K?

2. Suppose you inform the engineer of your analysis and decision. A month later he comes back with the following information about your production situation:

Q	K	L	Q	K	L
487.5	17	89	475	16	90
500	17	90	500	17	90

Is the combination of 17 K and 90 L the cost-minimizing proportions of L and K to use to minimize the cost of producing 500? If so, demonstrate that the total cost (TC) of producing Q of 500 has been reduced. Also illustrate the situation on the isocost-isoquant diagram of question 1.

Solutions

1. From this information, the MP of your 100th worker equals 10 (output increased from 490 to 500 when L was increased from 99 to 100, the number of machines held constant). The MP of your 15th machine was 30 (output increased from 470 to 500 when the number of machines went from 14 to 15, with workers held constant at 100). This implies that the extra output per dollar worth of labor equals 2 (10/5), while the extra output per dollar worth of machinery was 3. (30/10). As a result, you are not cost minimizing. Alternatively, the $MRTS_{L,K} = 10/30$, while the ratio input prices equals 5/10, or 1/2. As a result, you should use more of the input where the extra output per dollar is greater and less of the input where the extra output per dollar is less. In this case, this implies that you should produce output of 500 using more than 15 units of K and less than 100 units of L. Diagrammatically, the current situation is at point A in the diagram below:

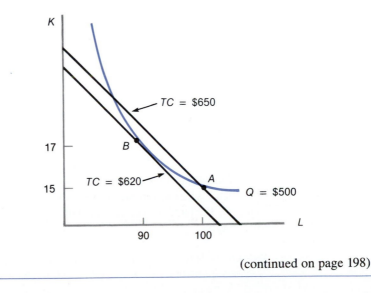

(continued on page 198)

(continued from 197)

Since the slope of the isoquant is less than the slope of the isocost at the current input combination, you should move along the isoquant until the *MRTS* increases to the ratio of the input prices. This requires more K and less L.

2. The *MP* of the 90th worker now equals 12.5, while the *MP* of the 17th machine equals 25. As a result, the ratio of the *MP* of L to K is just equal to the ratio of these input prices. Thus, 90L and 17 K must be the cost-minimizing combination of inputs to use to produce output of 500. Total cost in question 1 was equal to 100 × $5 + 15 × $10, or $650 (Why?) Total cost in question 2 equals 90 × $5 + 17 × $10, or $620. You have moved from point *A* along the isoquant (500) to point *B*. As a result you are now producing on the isocost associated with total cost equal to $620.

combination of goods be changed when price or income changes? We now pose the same type of question from the standpoint of a producer: How will factor proportions change when output changes?

Isoclines
7.5.a

Consider Panel A, Figure 7.5.1. The curves I, II, and III are isoquants depicting a representative production function. T_1, T_2, and T_3 are tangents to I, II, and III, respectively; and the tangents have been constructed so that they are parallel to one another. That is, the marginal rate of technical substitution of labor for capital is the same at points A, B, and C. These points have been connected by a smooth curve labeled *OS*, which is called an *isocline*.

Isocline: An isocline is a locus of points along which the marginal rate of technical substitution is constant.

In general, isoclines may have almost any shape. The one in Panel A has been constructed so as to ramble through the isoquant map. The *special* isoclines in Figure 7.3.3 have a very regular shape. We may now pause to point out the following:

Relation: The "ridge lines" defining the economic region of production are isoclines inasmuch as the marginal rate of technical substitution is constant along the lines. In particular (see Figure 7.3.3), OC is the isocline along which the marginal rate of technical substitution of labor for capital is infinite; OL is the isocline along which it is zero.

Now turn to Figure 7.5.1, Panel B. The difference between this and Panel A is that the isoclines are rays from the origin. An isoquant (or indifference curve) map that displays this property is said to be *homothetic*. All production functions that have constant returns to scale are homothetic and have isoclines that are rays from the origin. The isoquants are parallel in that the slope of the isoquant along any ray from the origin is the same on all points along that ray. This leads to the following:

Relations: The isoclines associated with production functions homogeneous of degree one are straight lines. Therefore, since ridge lines are special isoclines, the ridge lines associated with linearly homogeneous production functions are straight lines (providing, of course, that the function under consideration gives rise to an uneconomic region).[11]

---

[11]All production functions that are homogeneous of any degree exhibit homotheticity. To see this, note that a production function, $f(K, L)$ is homogeneous of degree h if

$$f(\lambda K, \lambda L) = \lambda^h f(K, L).$$

Let $\lambda = 1/L$ so that

$$f(\lambda K, \lambda L) = f(K/L, 1) = g(K/L).$$

Now, since output, $Q = f(K, L)$,

$$dQ = (\partial f / \partial K)\, dK + (\partial f / \partial L)\, dL\ .$$

Since Q is constant along an isoquant, $dQ = 0$, so

$$\left. \frac{dK}{dL} \right|_Q = \frac{-\partial f/\partial L}{\partial f/\partial K} \equiv -MRTS_{L \text{ for } K}\ .$$

Also, since $\lambda = 1/L$,

$$f(K, L) = \frac{1}{\lambda^h} g(K/L)$$

$$= L^h g(K/L)\ .$$

Thus,

$$\frac{\partial f}{\partial L} = L^h g'(K/L)(-K/L^2) + hL^{h-1} g(K/L)$$

and

$$\frac{\partial f}{\partial K} = L^h g'(K/L) \left(\frac{1}{L} \right)$$

so

$$\left. \frac{dK}{dL} \right|_Q = \frac{K}{L} - \frac{hg(K/L)}{g'(K/L)}$$

which is constant for any given K/L. Therefore, the slope along an isoquant depends only on the capital-labor ratio and is therefore constant along any ray from the origin. Thus, it is homothetic.

Figure 7.5.1 Isoclines

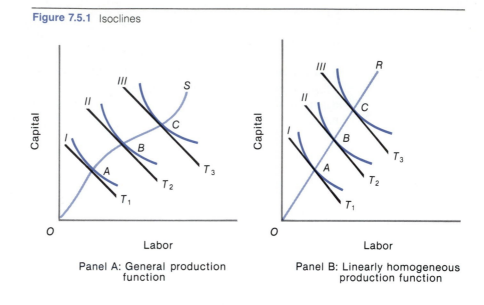

Panel A: General production
function

Panel B: Linearly homogeneous
production function

Changing Output and the Expansion Path
7.5.b

Turn now to Panel A, Figure 7.5.2. Given the input prices, the output correspond-ing to isoquant I can be produced at least cost at point A, where the isoquant is tangent to the isocost curve KL. This is the position of producer equilibrium. With input prices remaining constant, suppose the entrepreneur wishes to expand output to the level corresponding to the isoquant II. The new equilibrium is found by shifting the isocost curve until it is tangent to II. Since factor prices remain constant, the slope of the isocost curve does not change. Hence it shifts from KL to $K'L'$. Similarly, if the entrepreneur wished to expand output to the amount corresponding to the isoquant III, production would be at point C on III and $K''L''$.

Connecting all points such as A, B, and C generates the curve OE. Now let us assemble some facts. First, factor prices have remained constant. Second, each equilibrium point is defined by equality between the marginal rate of technical substitution and the factor–price ratio. Since the latter has remained constant, so has the former. Therefore, OE is an isocline, a locus of points along which the marginal rate of technical substitution is constant. But it is an isocline with a special feature. Specifically, it is the isocline along which $MRTS_{L \text{ for } K}$ equals the existing factor–price ratio. Accordingly, we may formulate this result as a definition.

Expansion Path: The expansion path is the particular isocline along which output will expand when factor prices remain constant. The expansion path thus shows how factor proportions change when output or expenditure changes, input prices remaining constant throughout.

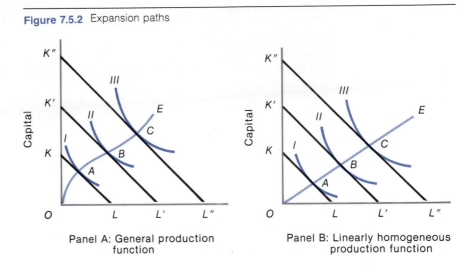

Figure 7.5.2 Expansion paths

Panel A: General production
function

Panel B: Linearly homogeneous
production function

Turn now to Panel B. Since the isoclines of a homothetic production function are straight lines, the expansion path is also. This permits the following statement:

Relation: The expansion path corresponding to a production function with constant returns to scale is a straight line. This reflects the fact that with homogeneity, factor proportions depend only upon the factor–price ratio (the slope of the isocost curve); and, in particular, factor proportions are independent of the level of output.

As we shall see in Chapter 8, the expansion path is crucial in determining the long-run cost of production.

Expenditure Elasticity[12]
7.5.c

In Chapters 3 and 5 the income elasticity of commodity demand was discussed. In particular, income elasticity was related to the income–consumption curve; and commodities were classified as superior, normal, or inferior according as income elasticity exceeds unity, lies in the unit interval, or is negative. The expenditure elasticity of a factor of production is an analogous concept: its measurement is restricted to the expansion path; and factors are classified as superior, normal, or inferior according as the corresponding expenditure elasticity exceeds unity, lies in the unit interval, or is negative.

Let us begin with the following:

---

[12]For a mathematical elaboration of this subsection, see C. E. Ferguson and Thomas R. Saving, "Long-Run Scale Adjustments of a Perfectly Competitive Firm and Industry," *American Economic Review* 59 (1969), pp. 774–83.

Expenditure Elasticity: Consider a factor of production, X. The expenditure elasticity of X is the relative responsiveness of the usage of X to changes in total expenditure. In other words, the expenditure elasticity of X is the proportional change in the usage of X divided by the proportional change in total expenditure. In this definition changes in total expenditure *are restricted to movements along the expansion path.*

Symbolically, the formula for the expenditure elasticity is

$$\eta_x = \frac{dx}{x} \div \frac{dc}{c} = \frac{dx}{dc}\frac{c}{x},$$

where x is the usage of factor X and c is total expenditure on factors of production. Next we introduce another definition.

Superior, Normal, and Inferior Factors: A factor of production is said to be superior, normal, or inferior according as its expenditure elasticity exceeds unity, lies in the unit interval, or is negative.

This definition is illustrated schematically in Figure 7.5.3. Consider the expansion path and concentrate on factor X. Along ray *OR* both inputs expand proportionally. At points such as *A* the usage of factor X expands proportionally more than total expenditure along the expansion path. At all such points the factor is superior. At points such as *B* factor usage expands proportionally less than total expenditure. Expenditure elasticity lies in the unit interval, and the factor is said to be normal. At *D* the change in usage of both inputs is proportional and the expenditure elasticity is unity. Analysis is the same along any ray from the origin.

In certain — presumably unusual — cases, the usage of a factor may decline when output and resource expenditure are increased. At point *C* in Figure 7.5.3 the expenditure elasticity of X is instantaneously zero. Beyond point *C*, the expansion path "bends back" on itself. The usage of X diminishes as expenditure is increased beyond point *C*. Over this range of expenditure and output, X is an inferior factor. For example, when the level of farm production goes beyond a certain level, employment of labor might actually decrease as the farmer switches from farming by hand to mechanized farming. The concept of expenditure elasticity is used in Chapter 8 to analyze the changes in cost curves that result from changes in factor price.

A LOOK AHEAD
7.6

It is tempting at this time to use the analytical structure of this chapter to derive the producer's demand curves for factors of production along the lines used in Part 1 to determine the consumer's demand functions. This temptation must be

Part Two   Theory of Production and Cost

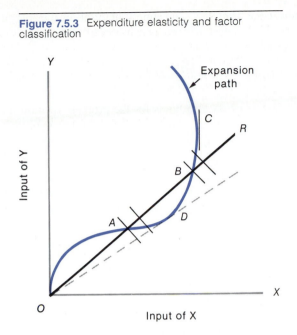

Figure 7.5.3 Expenditure elasticity and factor classification

resisted, however, because there is more to be considered in the case of the producer. In particular, this chapter treats output (or total cost) as fixed; however, as we shall see in the next two chapters, output will typically change in response to changes in factor prices. We must, therefore, defer the analysis of the demand for inputs until Chapters 14 and 15 when additional analytical tools will be available.

Chapters 6 and 7 contain an explanation of the theory of production and of the optimal combination of inputs when input prices are constant. Next, in Chapter 8, we turn to the theory of cost, which relies upon the physical laws of production and upon the prices the entrepreneur must pay for inputs.

SYNOPSIS 7.7

- Production isoquants are curves in input space showing all possible combinations of inputs capable of producing a given level of output. The negative of the slope of an isoquant is called the marginal rate of technical substitution.

- To maximize output subject to a given total cost and given input prices, the producer must purchase inputs in quantities such that the marginal rate of technical substitution of labor for capital ($MRTS_{L \text{ for } K}$) is equal to the ratio of the price of labor (w) to the price of capital (r). It can be shown that $MRTS_{L \text{ for } K}$ is simply the ratio of the marginal product of labor (MP_L) to the marginal product of capital (MP_K). Thus, the maximizing condition is

$$MRTS_{L \text{ for } K} = \frac{MP_L}{MP_K} = \frac{w}{r}.$$

- The last equation also holds for the problem of minimizing the total cost of producing a given output.
- The expansion path indicates how input factor proportions (and levels) change when output or expenditure changes, input prices remaining constant throughout. The expansion path is central to the determination of long-run cost functions, as we will see in Chapter 8. When the production function has constant returns to scale, the expansion path is a straight line and factor proportions are independent of the level of output.

QUESTIONS AND EXERCISES

1. Suppose that Transport Service must produce a certain output of cargo and passenger service per year. The service is confronted with the following combinations of HC100 aircraft and mechanics which can be used to yield this required output over its route pattern and meet schedule requirements.

Combination number	Number of aircraft	Number of mechanics
1	60	1,000
2	61	920
3	62	850
4	63	800
5	64	760
6	65	730
7	66	710

a. If Transport Service is using 60 aircraft and 1,000 mechanics, how many men can it dispense with and still maintain its output if it acquires an additional HC100 aircraft?

b. Your answer in (a) is called the _____ _____ of _____ in economic theory.

c. If the additional annual cost resulting from the operation of another HC100 is $250,000, and if mechanics cost Transport Service $6,000 each annually, should the service acquire a 61st HC100?

d. Which combination of aircraft and mechanics should Transport Service use to minimize its costs?

e. Suppose the *annual* cost of an HC100 drops to $200,000 and the cost of mechanics rises to $7,000 per year. What combination should now be employed to minimize annual costs?

f. Can the data presented above be used to illustrate the law of diminishing returns? Why or why not?

2. Suppose that a product requires two inputs for its production. Then is it correct to say that if the prices of the inputs are equal, optimal behavior on the part of producers will dictate that these inputs be used in equal amounts?

3. The Norfolk and Western Railway did not change from steam to diesel locomotives until nearly all other railroads had done so. This was probably because: (*a*) the N & W wanted to conserve national oil reserves for future generations; (*b*) since the railroad ran through the heart of the Appalachians, coal was cheap relative to diesel fuel; (*c*) N & W management — like some economics professors — couldn't bear to part with the "Iron Horse"; (*d*) all of the above.

4. A railroad would be most likely to substitute expensive signaling systems for multiple track operation if: (*a*) second and third tracks were heavily taxed by the counties through which they passed; (*b*) signaling equipment was produced by a monopolist; (*c*) all railroad officers took Principles of Economics; (*d*) none of the above.

5. Answer true or false and explain your choice.
   a. Two factors of production, say A and B, have the same price. The least-cost combination of A and B for producing a given output will be at the point where the isoquant has a slope of minus 1.
   b. Assume only two factors A and B are used to produce output X. A decrease in the price of A leads to less of B being used.
   c. If the marginal product of A is 5 and its price is $2, then the additional cost of one more unit of output obtained by employing more of factor A is $2.
   d. At current levels of employment of factors A and B, the marginal product of A is 3 and the marginal product of B is 2. The price of A is $5 a unit, and the price of B is $4 a unit. Because B is the less expensive factor of production, the firm can produce the same output at lower cost by reducing the employment of A and increasing the employment of B.

6. *a.* If the marginal product of L is $MP_L = 100K - L$ and the marginal product of K is $MP_K = 100L - K$, then what is the maximum possible output when the total amount that can be spent on K and L is $1,000 and the price of K is $5 and the price of L is $2?
   b. Answer part (*a*) when the price of K is $5 and the price of L is $5.
   c. (Advanced) When the price of K is P_K and the price of L is P_L, what is the expenditure elasticity for K? For L? (Hint: Use the marginal productivity equilibrium conditions to derive a relationship that expresses L in terms of K, P_K, P_L, and the parameters of MP_K and MP_L. Use this expression to substitute for L in the cost equation $C = P_K K + P_L L$.)
   d. (Advanced) If total output is zero when K and L are zero, what is the production function $f(K, L)$?

SUGGESTED READINGS

Borts, George H., and **Mishan, E. J.** "Exploring the 'Uneconomic Region' of the Production Function." *Review of Economic Studies* 29 (1962), pp. 300–312.

Cassels, John M. "On the Law of Variable Proportions," *Explorations in Economics*. New York: McGraw-Hill, 1936, pp. 223–36.

Ferguson, C. E. *The Neoclassical Theory of Production and Distribution*. London and New York: Cambridge University Press, 1969, chaps. 1–6.

Ferguson, C. E., and **Saving, Thomas R.** "Long-Run Scale Adjustments of a Perfectly Competitive Firm and Industry." *American Economic Review* 59 (1969), pp. 774–83.

Henderson, James M., and **Quandt, Richard E.** *Microeconomic Theory: A Mathematical Approach*, 2nd ed. New York: McGraw-Hill, 1971, pp. 58–67.

Hicks, John R. *Value and Capital*, 2nd ed. Oxford: Oxford University Press, 1946, pp. 78–98.

Samuelson, Paul A. *Foundations of Economic Analysis*. Cambridge, Mass.: Harvard University Press, 1947, pp. 57–76.

8 Theory of Cost

How do you derive a total cost schedule from a production function and the prices of the factor inputs? How do you derive marginal and average cost from total cost, both in the short run and the long run? What is the difference between fixed and variable costs, and the difference between "cost" to an economist and to an accountant? In this chapter you will learn the answers to these questions and others. These answers will be crucial to the material in the next chapter where we investigate how a firm decides how much to produce in order to maximize profits, and more specifically (in the "Applying the Theory" section), how an airline should decide whether to run an additional flight, and how a mink farmer should decide about staying in business. ■

The physical conditions of production, the price of resources, and the economically efficient conduct of an entrepreneur jointly determine the cost of production of a business firm. The production function furnishes the information necessary to trace out the isoquant map. Resource prices establish the isocost curves. Finally, efficient entrepreneurial behavior dictates the production of any level of output by that combination of inputs which equates the marginal rate of technical substitution and the input–price ratio. Each position of tangency therefore determines a level of *output* and its associated *total cost*. From this information, one may construct a table, a schedule, or a mathematical function relating total cost to the level of output. This is the cost schedule or cost function that is one of the subjects of this chapter.

It is not the only subject, however, because in the short run, by definition, all inputs are not variable. Some are fixed, and the entrepreneur cannot instantaneously achieve the input combination that corresponds to economic efficiency (that is, the one that equates the marginal rate of technical substitution with the input–price ratio). In the short run, a point on the expansion path will generally not be attained. We must thus analyze not only long-run cost but short-run cost as well.

In many respects, the level of analysis in this chapter is less microscopic than the level of analysis of the previous chapter. For many purposes, it is unnecessary to consider isoquant and isocost relationships. Much of the time, to understand business behavior, it is sufficient to understand cost curves and how they shift when prices of inputs and technology change. There is, however, an isoquant-isocost representation of any issue that can be discussed with cost curves.

Before turning to the mechanics of cost analysis, however, we need to pause for a somewhat broader view and to pose the question, "Just *what* constitutes the legitimate costs of production." There are two answers to this question which, under ideal circumstances, happen to become one and the same. At present we must be content with the two; but in Chapter 17 we set out the conditions under which the answers are the same.

Social Cost of Production
8.1.a

Economists are interested in the social cost of production, the cost a society incurs when its resources are used to produce a given commodity. At any point in time a society possesses a pool of resources either individually or collectively owned, depending upon the political organization of the society in question. From a social point of view the object of economic activity is to get as much as possible from this existing pool of resources. What is "possible," of course, depends not only upon the efficient and full utilization of resources but upon the specific list of commodities produced. A society could obviously have a greater output of automobiles if only small compact cars were produced. Larger, more luxurious cars require more of almost every input. But in their private evaluation schemes, some members of the society may attach much greater significance to luxury cars than to compact cars.

Balancing the relative resource cost of a commodity with its relative social desirability entails a knowledge of both social valuations and social cost. This broad problem is deferred to Chapter 17 so that our attention can now be directed exclusively to social cost.

The social cost of using a bundle of resources to produce a unit of commodity X is the number of units of commodity Y that must be sacrificed in the process. Resources are used to produce both X and Y (and all other commodities). Those resources used in X production cannot be used to produce Y or any other commodity. To illustrate with a simple example, think of Robinson Crusoe living alone on an island and sustaining himself by fishing and gathering coconuts. The cost to Crusoe of an additional fish is measured by the number of coconuts he has to forgo because he spends more time fishing.

This concept of cost, or as it is more frequently called, the *alternative* or *opportunity* cost of production, captures much of the essence of what economics is about. Unfortunately, this concept of cost is often overlooked in popular discussions of public and private policy issues. For example, congressional spokesmen often argue against the policy of an all-volunteer armed force on the grounds that it "costs" too much relative to a policy of conscription. The error in this reasoning is that the cash payments by the government to individuals who are drafted into military service are not the appropriate measure of the social cost of the draft. The individuals drafted into military service are often taken out of civilian jobs where they are producing goods and services — such as houses and automobiles, and health care and educational services. By drafting people into the armed services, society must give up some of these goods and services and this forgone production is the appropriate measure of the cost of conscription.

Opportunity Cost: The *alternative* or *opportunity* cost of producing one unit of commodity X is the amount of commodity Y that must be sacrificed in order to use resources to produce X rather than Y. This is the social cost of producing X.

Private Cost of Production
8.1.b

There is a close relation between the social cost of producing commodity X and a calculation the producer of X himself must make. The use of resources to produce X rather than Y entails a social cost, but there is a private cost as well, because the entrepreneur must pay a price to get the resources used in production.

The entrepreneur pays a certain amount to purchase resources, uses them to produce a commodity, and sells the commodity. The entrepreneur can compare the receipts from sales with the cost of the resources and determine whether there is an accounting profit. But an economist would be quick to tell this entrepreneur to make some further calculations. The entrepreneur invested time and money in this business and these resources could be used elsewhere — in another line of business, perhaps, or by purchasing securities or going to work as an employee of another entrepreneur.

The producer of X incurs certain explicit costs by purchasing resources. But implicit costs are also incurred, and a full accounting of profit or loss takes these implicit costs into consideration. The pure economic profit earned by producing commodity X may be thought of as accounting profit minus what could be earned in the best alternative use of the entrepreneur's time and money, which is defined as the implicit cost of production.

Implicit Costs: The implicit costs incurred in producing a specific commodity consist of the amounts that could be earned in the best alternative use of the entrepreneur's time and money. A *pure economic profit* is earned in the production of X if, and only if, total receipts exceed the sum of the entrepreneur's explicit and implicit costs.

Implicit costs are a fixed amount (in the short run) that must be added to explicit costs in a reckoning of pure economic profit.

The notion of opportunity cost is important for private decisions as well. For example, consider an individual who is thinking about leaving the labor force to return to school. The opportunity cost of attending school consists of two components: Explicit costs comprising tuition, book costs, and the additional cost associated with having to live near the school (rather than in some perhaps less expensive area) are only part of the cost. To this must be added implicit costs. The individual forgoes the opportunity to work while attending school. If he or she would have earned $14,000 per year, then the implicit cost of going to school is $14,000 per year, because the individual declined the opportunity to earn that money in the labor market.

SHORT AND LONG RUNS
8.2

In Chapter 6 a convenient analytical fiction was introduced, namely the *short run,* defined as a period of time in which certain types of inputs cannot be increased or decreased. That is, in the short run there are certain inputs whose usage cannot be changed regardless of the level of output. Similarly, there are other inputs, variable inputs, whose usage can be changed. In the long run, on the other hand, all inputs are variable — the quantity of all inputs can be varied so as to obtain the most efficient input combination.

The definition of the long run is reasonably clearcut; it is a period of time sufficiently long such that all factors of production can be fully adjusted. The short run is a more nebulous concept. In one nanosecond virtually nothing can be changed in the production process. In a day it may be possible to intensify the usage of certain machines; in a month the entrepreneur may be able to rent some additional equipment; in a year it may be feasible to build a new plant. There are

Part Two   Theory of Production and Cost

Question

Suppose Peter Zah opened his own submarine sandwich shop. To do so he quit his own job where he was earning $8,000 per year. He also bought a special oven for $1,000 by cashing in his savings account, which would have earned 5 percent interest otherwise. Finally, he took over a store building owned by his wife which had previously been rented out for $500 per month. Furthermore, he could expect to incur these additional expenses for the year: $50,000 for food; $15,000 for extra help; $2,000 for gas and electricity. If he were to sell 85,000 sandwiches during the year for $1 each, what would be his expected *explicit costs* for the year? What would be his *implicit costs* for the year? What would be his expected *pure economic profit* for the year?

Solution

Explicit costs would include the $50,000 for food, $15,000 for extra help, and $2,000 for gas and electricity, as these are expenses for purchasing resources. Peter also incurs implicit costs of $6,000 for the use of his wife's building, since the family would have collected rent of this amount over the year if he did not open his submarine shop. In addition, the $8,000 lost wages is an implicit cost since he no longer has the opportunity to work elsewhere if he opens the submarine shop. By purchasing the oven he has exchanged his savings of $1,000 for an asset that is worth $1,000 at the time it is new. He thereby forgoes the interest income of $50 (5 percent of $1,000) he would otherwise receive on this savings account, and since the oven will depreciate in value over the year, this depreciation must also be included as a "cost" of business. Suppose at the end of the year, the oven could be sold for $500. Then depreciation of $500 must also be included in implicit costs. The total costs (explicit + implicit) therefore equal the sum of $67,000 explicit costs and $14,550 ($6,000 + $8,000 + $50 + $500) implicit costs, or $81,550. Pure economic profit is the difference between total revenue and total economic costs, or $85,000 − $81,550 = $3,450.

obviously many "short runs," and the longer the time the greater the possibilities for factor substitution and adjustment. Costs of producing a given output will clearly depend on the time available to make adjustments in amounts used of the productive factors. Before going into detail about long- and short-run costs, we provide a general overview by examining the relationship between production functions and costs.

Long-Run Costs and the Production Function
8.2.a

The tools of Chapter 7 allow us to relate costs to outputs. That is, for any given output, we can determine the minimum cost at which that output can be produced, given factor prices and the production function. This is illustrated in Panel A of Figure 8.2.1 for three different output levels. At output level Q_1, the minimum total cost is determined by the cost associated with isocost line C_1. At output level Q_2, the minimum total cost is determined by isocost line C_2. The isocost line for Q_2 is above and to the northeast of the isocost line for Q_1, which means, as we expect, that costs increase with output.

It is easily seen that by repeating this procedure at all isoquants along the expansion path E, it is possible to derive the long-run cost schedule for the firm — that is, the schedule which shows the cost of producing each output after all factors of production have been fully adjusted. This is illustrated in Panel B of Figure 8.2.1. From Panel A we see that output Q_1 is produced at total cost C_1, and these two values are used as coordinates to plot a point on the total output–total cost graph of Panel B. Similarly, Q_2 is produced at total cost C_2, and Q_3 is produced at total cost C_3. These points are also plotted on the Panel B graph. Repeating this procedure for all other outputs, the long-run total cost schedule *LRTC* of Panel B is derived.

Relation: The long-run total cost schedule is directly related to the expansion path; indeed, the long-run total cost schedule or function is simply the cost–output equivalent of the expansion path.

Short-Run Costs and the Production Function
8.2.b

We have observed that there are really a large number of "short" runs, depending on the time period involved. Each such short run is characterized by the fact that not all factors of production can be fully adjusted in the given time period. To see the significance of this, suppose a firm wishes to increase output and must acquire 150 more milling machines to do so at lowest cost (that is, the long-run optimum requires 150 more machines). To be concrete, we assume there are four "short" runs, each of which is 3 months longer than the previous one. Because of delivery lags, no new milling machines can be added in the first 3 months, but delivery schedules permit the delivery of 50 additional machines in each of the next 3-month periods. Hence, the long-run adjustment (1 year in this case) involves an addition of 150 milling machines, but these are added in three steps. In the shortest run (3 months) no new machines are available, in the 6-month "run" there are 50 new milling machines, in the 9-month "run" there are 100 new

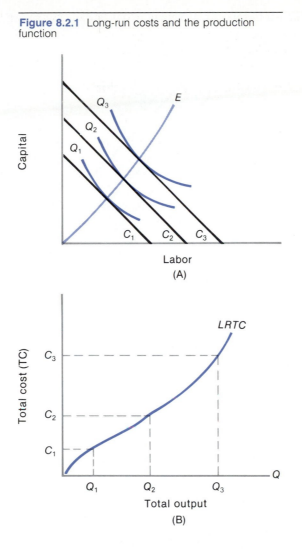

Figure 8.2.1 Long-run costs and the production function

(A)

Capital (vertical axis), Labor (horizontal axis)

(B)

Total cost (TC) (vertical axis), Total output (horizontal axis)

milling machines, and in the long run (12 months) there are 150 new machines. To produce at the new output level, different amounts of labor are needed in each 3-month period. We assume that man-hours can be freely adjusted at all times by using overtime and part-time employment. (For simplicity of exposition we also assume that the wage rate does not increase for overtime hours.) This situation is illustrated in Figure 8.2.2, Panel A.

In this figure, initial output is given by the isoquant Q_0 and the new higher output is shown by the isoquant Q_1. During the first 3-month period (the "shortest" run) the output Q_1 is produced with the current stock of milling machines ($K_1 = K_0 = 30$) and L_1 man-hours. Total cost to the entrepreneur in this period is given by the isocost line C_1. Note that the isocost line is *not* tangent

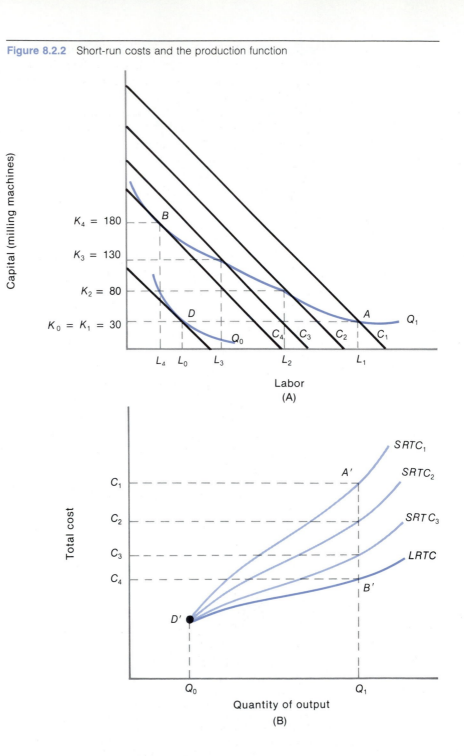

Figure 8.2.2 Short-run costs and the production function

Capital (milling machines)

$K_4 = 180$
$K_3 = 130$
$K_2 = 80$
$K_0 = K_1 = 30$

B

D

Q_0

C_4 C_3 C_2 C_1

A Q_1

L_4 L_0 L_3 L_2 L_1

Labor
(A)

Total cost

C_1
C_2
C_3
C_4

$SRTC_1$
A'
$SRTC_2$
$SRTC_3$
$LRTC$
B'

D'

Q_0 Q_1

Quantity of output
(B)

to Q_1 at point A. This is because of the inability of the firm to get any additional milling machines in the first 3 months. Given the existing stock of 30 milling machines, the cheapest way to get output Q_1 is by a substantial increase in man-hours (from L_0 to L_1).[1]

During the next 3 months, 50 new milling machines are delivered, so the total stock of milling machines rises to K_2 ($K_2 = 80 = K_1 + 50$). This allows the entrepreneurs to cut overtime and part-time labor hours to L_2. It also reduces the cost of producing output Q_1 because, as may readily be seen in Figure 8.2.2, the C_2 isocost line is to the southwest of isocost line C_1. Because capital stock is below the long-run optimum of 180 machines, however, it is still true that the C_2 isocost line is not tangent to Q_1. The next 3 months bring 50 more milling machines and a further shift in the isocost line to C_3.

Equilibrium is finally reached in one year when 180 milling machines are available. At this level, the isocost line C_4 is tangent to Q_1, and Q_1 is being produced at the lowest possible total cost, given factor prices and the production function.

There is a diagram in cost–output space that corresponds to Panel A of Figure 8.2.2. It is shown in Panel B. Point A' corresponds to point A in Panel A. There the cost is C_1 and output is Q_1. Point B' corresponds to B in Panel A. There output is Q_1 again, but cost is only C_4. Thus, $LRTC$ gives the total cost relationship when all factors are variable. $SRTC_1$ gives the cost relationship when only labor is variable. The other curves, $SRTC_2$ and $SRTC_3$, are the intermediate cases, showing what total cost would be if capital can be expanded some, but not to the desired extent. Note that all curves coincide at point D'. The reason is that the short-run and long-run solutions are the same at that point because even if the firm could alter capital, it would select the current level of 30 units of capital to produce Q_0 level of output.

This example illustrates the key point that the shorter the run, the more costly it is to produce outputs other than the output for which the current capital stock is optimal (that is, the output given by Q_0 in this example). Long-run costs for producing a given output will never exceed short-run costs of producing that output.

The dynamic theory of short- and long-run costs can be derived in several ways. For example, it is possible to introduce adjustment costs explicitly and obtain models of optimal capital accumulation.[2] However, in order to concentrate on important comparative static results, we will adhere to the traditional dichotomy between the short run and the long run. *In other words, while we recognize that there are many short runs, we will focus our attention on a given short-run period for expository convenience.*

---

[1] The entrepreneur would not want to operate with less than 30 milling machines in the short run because to produce Q_1 even more labor than L_1 then would be needed, and this would shift the isocost line further to the northeast.

[2] See for example, J. P. Gould, "Adjustment Costs in the Theory of Investment of the Firm," *Review of Economic Studies* 35 (1968), pp. 47–55.

Fixed and Variable Costs in the Short Run
8.2.c

Corresponding to fixed inputs are short-run fixed costs. The various fixed inputs have unit prices; the fixed explicit cost is simply the sum of unit prices multiplied by the fixed number of units used. In the short run, implicit cost is also fixed; thus it is an element of fixed cost. In the example of subsection 8.2.b, the fixed costs in the short run are the costs of the given stock of milling machines. In more complicated examples there will be many such fixed inputs with corresponding fixed costs.

Total Fixed Cost: Total fixed cost is the sum of the short-run explicit fixed cost and the implicit cost incurred by an entrepreneur.

Inputs that are variable in the short run give rise to short-run variable cost. Since input usage can be varied in accordance with the level of output, variable costs also vary with input. If there is zero output, no units of variable input need be employed. Variable cost is accordingly zero, and total cost is the same as total fixed cost. When there is a positive level of output, however, variable inputs must be used. This gives rise to variable costs, and total cost is then the sum of total variable and total fixed cost.

Total Variable Cost: Total variable cost is the sum of the amounts spent for each of the variable inputs used.

Total Cost (Short Run): Total cost in the short run is the sum of total variable and total fixed cost.

THEORY OF COST IN THE SHORT RUN
8.3

Our analysis of cost begins with the theory of short-run cost; we then move to the "planning horizon" in which all inputs are variable and study the theory of cost in the long run, when the optimal input combination can be obtained.

Total Short-Run Cost
8.3.a

Analysis of total short-run cost depends upon two propositions already discussed in this chapter: (*a*) the physical conditions of production and the units prices of inputs determine the cost of production associated with each possible level of output; and (*b*) total cost may be divided into two components, fixed cost and variable cost.

Table 8.3.1 Fixed, variable, and total cost

Quantity of output	Total fixed cost	Total variable cost	Total cost
0	$100	–0–	$ 100.00
1	100	$ 10.00	110.00
2	100	16.00	116.00
3	100	21.00	121.00
4	100	26.00	126.00
5	100	30.00	130.00
6	100	36.00	136.00
7	100	45.50	145.50
8	100	56.00	156.00
9	100	72.00	172.00
10	100	90.00	190.00
11	100	109.00	209.00
12	100	130.40	230.40
13	100	160.00	260.00
14	100	198.20	298.20
15	100	249.50	349.50
16	100	324.00	424.00
17	100	418.50	518.50
18	100	539.00	639.00
19	100	698.00	798.00
20	100	900.00	1,000.00

Suppose an entrepreneur has a fixed *plant* that can be used to produce a certain commodity. Further suppose this plant cost $100. Total fixed cost is, therefore, $100 — it is constant irrespective of the level of output. This is reflected in Table 8.3.1 by the column of $100 entries labeled "Total fixed cost." It is also shown by the horizontal line labeled *TFC* in Figure 8.3.1. Both table and graph emphasize that fixed cost is indeed fixed.

Variable inputs must also be used if production exceeds zero. In the spirit of Chapter 6, you might suppose there is only one variable input; alternatively, the multiple-input approach of Chapter 7 may be adopted. The choice is not material, because an increase in the level of output requires an increase in the usage of inputs — whether this be one variable input or many variable inputs used in the optimal combination. In either case, the greater the level of variable input the greater the total variable cost of production. This is shown in column 3 of Table 8.3.1 and by the curve labeled *TVC* in Figure 8.3.1.

Summing total fixed and total variable cost gives total cost, the entries in the last column of Table 8.3.1, and the curve labeled *TC* in Figure 8.3.1. From the figure, one may see that *TC* and *TVC* move together and are, in a sense, parallel. That is to say, the slopes of the two curves are the same at every output point; and at each point, the two curves are separated by a vertical distance of $100, the total fixed cost. The curves appear to get closer together, but this is because the

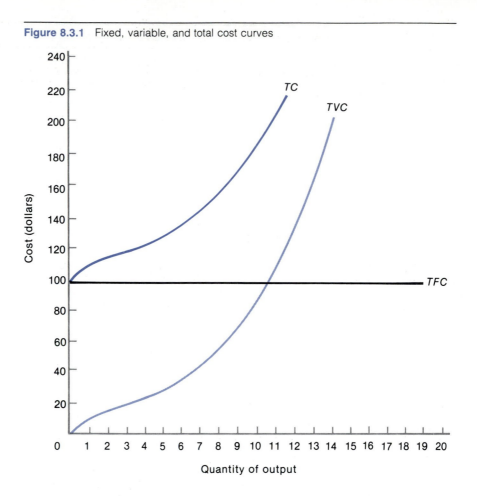

Figure 8.3.1 Fixed, variable, and total cost curves

eye focuses on the shortest distance between the curves, not the vertical distance. The vertical distance does, in fact, stay constant since the cost that separates them, total fixed cost, does not change with output.

Average and Marginal Cost
8.3.b

The total cost of production, including implicit cost, is very important to an entrepreneur. However, one may obtain a deeper understanding of total cost by analyzing the behavior of various average costs and of marginal cost.

The illustration of Table 8.3.1 is continued in Table 8.3.2. Indeed, the first four columns of the latter exactly reproduce Table 8.3.1. The remaining four columns show the new concepts to be introduced.

First consider the column labeled "Average fixed cost."

Table 8.3.2 Average and marginal cost calculations

(1) Quantity of output	(2) Total fixed cost	(3) Total variable cost	(4) Total cost	(5) Average fixed cost	(6) Average variable cost	(7) Average Total cost	(8) Marginal cost
1	$100	$ 10.00	$ 110.00	$100.00	$10.00	$110.00	$ 10.00
2	100	16.00	116.00	50.00	8.00	58.00	6.00
3	100	21.00	121.00	33.33	7.00	40.33	5.00
4	100	26.00	126.00	25.00	6.50	31.50	5.00
5	100	30.00	130.00	20.00	6.00	26.00	4.00
6	100	36.00	136.00	16.67	6.00	22.67	6.00
7	100	45.50	145.50	14.29	6.50	20.78	9.50
8	100	56.00	156.00	12.50	7.00	19.50	10.50
9	100	72.00	172.00	11.11	8.00	19.10	16.00
10	100	90.00	190.00	10.00	9.00	19.00	18.00
11	100	109.00	209.00	9.09	9.91	19.00	19.00
12	100	130.40	230.40	8.33	10.87	19.20	21.40
13	100	160.00	260.00	7.69	12.31	20.00	29.60
14	100	198.20	298.20	7.14	14.16	21.30	38.20
15	100	249.50	349.50	6.67	16.63	23.30	51.30
16	100	324.00	424.00	6.25	20.25	26.50	74.50
17	100	418.50	518.50	5.88	24.62	30.50	94.50
18	100	539.00	639.00	5.56	29.94	35.50	120.50
19	100	698.00	798.00	5.26	36.74	42.00	159.00
20	100	900.00	1,000.00	5.00	45.00	50.00	202.00

Average Fixed Cost: Average fixed cost is total fixed cost divided by output.

The calculation is very simple. When one unit of output is produced, *AFC* is $100/1 = $100. When two units are produced, *AFC* = $100/2 = $50; and so on. Graphically, average fixed cost is shown by the curve designated *AFC* in Figure 8.3.2. Cost in dollars is plotted on the vertical axis and output on the horizontal axis. The *AFC* curve is negatively sloped throughout because as output increases the ratio of fixed cost to output must decline.[3] Mathematically, the *AFC* curve is a rectangular hyperbola.

Next, move to column 6, Table 8.3.2. This column is labeled "Average variable cost," a concept that is entirely analogous to average fixed cost.

Average Variable Cost: Average variable cost is total variable cost divided by output.

---

[3]Let the cost function be $C = A + g(q)$, where A is total fixed cost and $g(q)$ gives the total variable cost associated with each level of output. Thus, average fixed cost is A/q and its slope is $-A/q^2$.

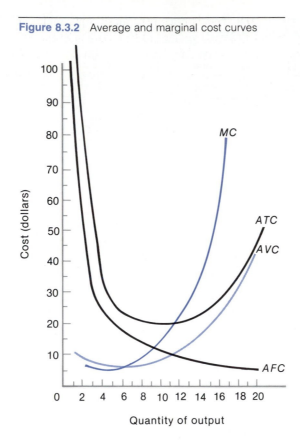

Figure 8.3.2 Average and marginal cost curves

Again the calculation is simple and gives rise to the curve labeled *AVC* in Figure 8.3.2. But now there is a great difference between *AVC* and *AFC*: the former does not have a negative slope throughout its entire range. Indeed, in this illustration *AVC* first declines, reaches a minimum, and rises thereafter.

The reason for this curvature lies in the theory of production. Total variable cost equals the number of units of variable input used (*V*) multiplied by the unit price of the input (*P*). Thus in the one-variable-input case, *TVC* = *PV*.

Average variable cost is total variable cost *TVC* divided by output *Q*, or

$$AVC = \frac{TVC}{Q} = P\frac{V}{Q}.$$

Consider the term *V/Q*, the number of units of input divided by the number of units of output. In Chapter 6, average product (*AP*) was defined as total output (*Q*) divided by the number of units of input (*V*). Thus

$$AVC = P\left(\frac{V}{Q}\right)$$

$$= P\left(\frac{1}{AP}\right)$$

since $AP = Q/V$. This is price per unit of input multiplied by the reciprocal of average product. Since average product normally rises, reaches a maximum, and then declines, average variable cost normally falls, reaches a minimum, and rises thereafter.

Relation: A production function such as that shown in Figure 6.2.1 gives rise to the average product curve shown in Figure 6.2.2. This type of production function also determines a total variable cost curve such as that in Figure 8.3.1 and the average variable cost curve shown in Figure 8.3.2.

Column 7, Table 8.3.2, contains the entries for average total cost, which may also be called average cost or unit cost.

Average Total Cost: Average total cost is total cost divided by output.

In light of this definition, ATC may be computed by dividing the entries in column 4 by the corresponding entries in column 1.

However, since

$$TC = TFC + TVC,$$

$$ATC = \frac{TC}{Q} = \frac{TFC}{Q} + \frac{TVC}{Q} = AFC + AVC.$$

Thus one may calculate average cost as the sum of average fixed and average variable cost.

This method of calculation also explains the shape of the average total cost curve in Figure 8.3.2. Over the range of values for which both AFC and AVC decline, ATC must obviously decline as well. But even after AVC turns up, the marked decline in AFC causes ATC to continue to decline. Finally, however, the increase in AVC more than offsets the decline in AFC; ATC therefore reaches its minimum and increases thereafter.

Finally, column 8 of Table 8.3.2 contains the entries for marginal cost.

Marginal Cost: Marginal cost is the addition to total cost attributable to the addition of one unit to output.

Marginal cost is thus calculated by subtracting successively the entries in the "Total cost" column.[4] For example, the marginal cost of the second unit produced is $MC_2 = TC_2 - TC_1$. Since only variable cost changes in the short run, however, marginal cost may be computed by successive subtraction of the entries in the "Total variable cost" column. Thus the marginal cost of the second unit is also $MC_2 = TVC_2 - TVC_1$.

---

[4]Let the cost function be defined as in footnote 3. For infinitesimally small changes in output,

$$MC = dc/dg = g'(q).$$

As shown in Figure 8.3.2, *MC*— like *AVC* —first declines, reaches a minimum, and rises thereafter. The explanation for this curvature also lies in the theory of production. Let Δ denote "the change in." As shown just above, $MC = \Delta(TVC)$ for a unit change in output. More generally, if output does not change by precisely one unit, $MC = \Delta(TVC)/\Delta Q$. In our previous notation, $TVC = PV$. Thus $\Delta TVC = P(\Delta V)$ for an entrepreneur who is a perfect competitor in the input market (input price is given by market demand and supply and changes in his purchases do not affect the price).

Using the two relations,

$$MC = P\frac{\Delta V}{\Delta Q}.$$

In Chapter 6, marginal product (*MP*) was defined as the change in output attributable to a change in input, or $MP = \Delta Q/\Delta V$. Thus

$$MC = P\left(\frac{1}{MP}\right).$$

Since marginal product normally rises, reaches a maximum, and declines, marginal cost normally declines, reaches a minimum, and rises thereafter.

Relation: A production function such as that shown in Figure 6.2.1 gives rise to the marginal product curve shown in Figure 6.2.2. This type of production function also determines a total cost curve such as that in Figure 8.3.1 and the marginal cost curve shown in Figure 8.3.2.

Geometry of Average and Marginal Cost Curves
8.3.c

In Chapter 8 the average and marginal product curves were derived geometrically from the total product curve. Similarly, the average and marginal cost curves may be derived from the corresponding total cost curve.

Figure 8.3.3 illustrates the derivation of average fixed cost. (Note: Vertical axes of Panels A and B have different scales.) In Panel A, total fixed cost is plotted and the outputs Oq_1, Oq_2, and Oq_3 are measured so that $Oq_1 = q_1q_2 = q_2q_3$. Since $AFC = TFC/Q$, average fixed cost is given by the slope of a ray from the origin to a point on the *TFC* curve. For output Oq_1, *AFC* is the slope of the ray *OP*, or q_1P/Oq_1. Similarly, for output Oq_2, *AFC* is q_2S/Oq_2, and so on. Since *TFC* is always the same, $q_1P = q_2S = q_3R$. By construction, $Oq_2 = 2Oq_1$, and $Oq_3 = 3Oq_1$. Thus *AFC* for output Oq_2 is $q_2S/Oq_2 = q_1P/2Oq_1 = \frac{1}{2}$ $(q_1P/Oq_1) = \frac{1}{2} AFC$ for output Oq_1. This is shown in Panel B by the difference in *OP'* and *OS'* —more specifically, $OS' = \frac{1}{2} OP'$. Similarly, as you can demonstrate for yourself, $OR' = \frac{1}{3} OP'$. The remaining points on *AFC* are determined in the same way.

In general, the average cost associated with output Oq_j where $Oq_j = j(Oq_1)$ is given by $(1/j) (OP')$. This is the equation of a rectangular hyperbola that is asymptotic to zero as j gets large.

Figure 8.3.3 Derivation of the average fixed cost curve

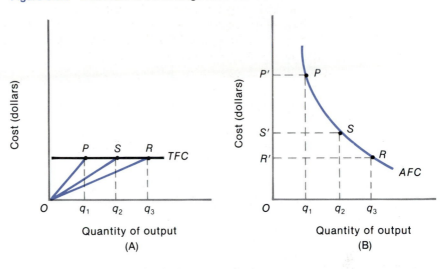

Cost (dollars)

TFC

P S R

O q_1 q_2 q_3

Quantity of output

(A)

Cost (dollars)

P'   P

S'   S

R'   R

AFC

O q_1 q_2 q_3

Quantity of output

(B)

Figure 8.3.4 shows how *AVC* is derived from *TVC*. As is true of all "average" curves, the average variable cost associated with any level of output is given by the slope of a ray from the origin to the corresponding point on the *TVC* curve. As may easily be seen from Panel A, the slope of a ray from the origin to the curve steadily diminishes as one passes through points such as *P*; and it diminishes until the ray is just tangent to the *TVC* curve at point *S*, associated with output Oq_2. Thereafter the slope increases as one moves from *S* toward points such as *R*. This is reflected in Panel B by constructing *AVC* with a negative slope until output Oq_2 is attained. After that point, the slope becomes positive and remains positive thereafter.

Exactly the same argument holds for Panels A and B of Figure 8.3.5, which show the derivation of *ATC* from *TC*. The slope of the ray diminishes as one moves along *TC* until the point *S'* is reached. At *S'* the slope of the ray is least, so minimum *ATC* is attained at the output level Oq_2'. Thereafter, the slope of the ray increases continuously, and the *ATC* curve has a positive slope. (Note: The output level Oq_2' does not represent the same quantity in Figures 8.3.3–8.3.6.)

The difference between average total cost and average variable cost is average fixed cost. Since average fixed cost becomes very small as output gets large, average variable cost and average total cost converge. This is another way of saying that when output is very large, most of total cost is made up of the variable component so that fixed cost does not matter very much.

Finally, the derivation of marginal cost is illustrated in Figure 8.3.6. Panel A contains the total cost curve *TC*. As output increases from Oq_1 to Oq_2, one moves from point *P* to point *V*, and total cost increases from TC_1 to TC_2. Marginal cost is thus

$$MC = \frac{TC_2 - TC_1}{Oq_2 - Oq_1} = \frac{VR}{PR}.$$

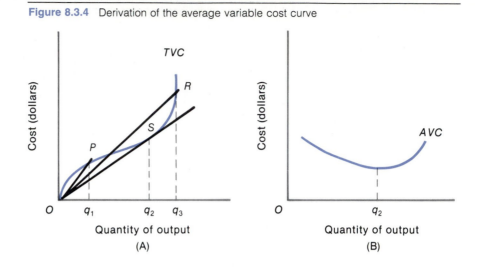

Figure 8.3.4 Derivation of the average variable cost curve

Cost (dollars) — TVC — R — S — P

Cost (dollars) — AVC

Quantity of output
(A)

O q_1 q_2 q_3

Quantity of output
(B)

O q_2

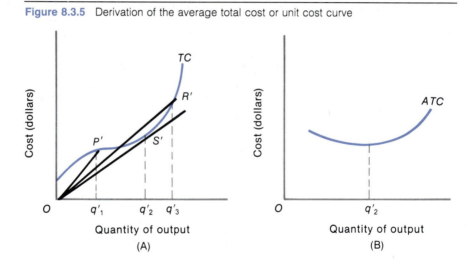

Figure 8.3.5 Derivation of the average total cost or unit cost curve

Cost (dollars) — TC — R' — P' — S'

Cost (dollars) — ATC

Quantity of output
(A)

O q'_1 q'_2 q'_3

Quantity of output
(B)

O q'_2

Now let the point P move along TC toward point V. As the distance between P and V becomes smaller and smaller, the slope of the tangent T at point V becomes a progressively better estimate of VR/PR. And in the limit, for movements in a tiny neighborhood around point V the slope of the tangent is marginal cost.

As one moves along TC through points such as P and V, the slope of TC diminishes. The slope continues to diminish until point S is reached at output Oq_3. Thereafter the slope increases. Therefore, the MC curve is constructed in Panel B so that it decreases until output Oq_3 is attained and increases thereafter.

One final point should be noted about Figures 8.3.4 and 8.3.6. As already shown, TC and TVC have the same slope at each output point; TC is simply TVC displaced upward by the constant amount TFC. Since the slopes are the same, MC

Figure 8.3.6 Derivation of the marginal cost curve

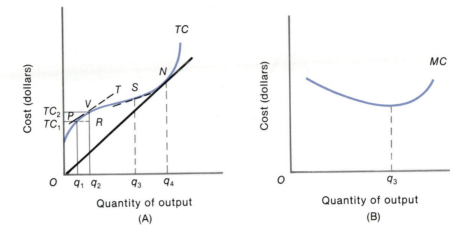

(A) — axes: Cost (dollars) vs Quantity of output
(B) — axes: Cost (dollars) vs Quantity of output

is given by the slope of either curve. In Panel A, Figure 8.3.4, the slope of the ray OS gives minimum AVC. But at this point the ray OS is just tangent to TVC; hence it also gives MC at this point. Thus $MC = AVC$ when the latter attains its minimum value. Similarly, in Panel A, Figure 8.3.6, the slope of the ray ON gives minimum ATC. But at this point the ray is tangent to TC; thus its slope also gives MC. Consequently $MC = ATC$ when the latter attains its minimum value. Again, this illustrates the notion that when the marginal exceeds the average, it pulls the average up and when it falls short of the average, it pulls the average down.

Short-Run Cost Curves
8.3.d

The properties of the average and marginal cost curves, as derived in subsection 8.3.c, are illustrated by the "typical" set of short-run cost curves shown in Figure 8.3.7. The properties may be summarized as follows:

Relations: (*i*) AFC declines continuously, approaching both axes asymptotically, as shown by points 1 and 2 in the figure. AFC is a rectangular hyperbola. (*ii*) AVC first declines, reaches a minimum at point 4, and rises thereafter. When AVC attains its minimum at point 4, MC equals AVC. As AFC approaches asymptotically close to the horizontal axis, AVC approaches ATC asymptotically, as shown by point 5. (*iii*) ATC first declines, reaches a minimum at point 3, and rises thereafter. When ATC attains its minimum at point 3, MC equals ATC. (*iv*) MC first declines, reaches a minimum at point 6, and rises thereafter. MC equals both AVC and ATC when these curves attain their minimum values. Furthermore, MC lies below both AVC and ATC over the range in which the curves decline; it lies above them when they are rising.

Figure 8.3.7 Typical set of cost curves

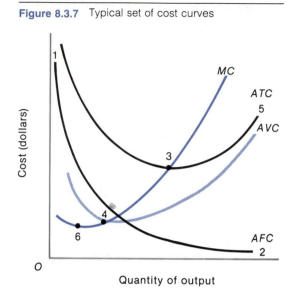

Example 8.3: To see how cost curves are used in business, consider a Caribbean cruise operator who is trying to determine the cost of putting different numbers of passengers on one-week cruises. The fixed cost in this case is the cost of the ship, which is at $1,000 per week. (That is, the interest payment on the loan taken to finance the purchase of the ship is $1,000 per week.)

The variable cost of taking aboard another passenger is

$$VC = Q^3 + 10,000Q^{.5}$$

where Q is the total number of passengers.

Table 8.3.E.1 produces all of the relevant information from the facts given above and from the following relationships:

$$AVC = VC/Q$$
$$TC = VC + FC = VC + 1,000$$
$$AC = TC/Q$$
$$MC = VC(Q) - VC(Q - 1) = TC(Q) - TC(Q - 1)$$

A few things are noteworthy. First, marginal (MC), average variable (AVC), and average (total) cost (ATC) all decline and then rise. Marginal cost begins to rise before either of the other two. Furthermore, marginal cost equals average variable cost at average variable cost's minimum point (22.87 passengers). Similarly, marginal cost equals average cost at average cost's minimum point (23.24 passengers).

First, the variable and total cost increase as the number of passengers increases. Adding passengers cannot reduce the cost of operating the cruise. However, the average variable and average total cost falls as passengers increase from 1 to 23 passengers. Therefore, the level of operation that yields minimum cost per unit is 23 passengers.

226   *Part Two   Theory of Production and Cost*

Table 8.3.E.1

Q	VC	TC	MC	AVC	ATC
1	$ 10001	$ 11001	$10001	$10001	$11001
2	14150	15150	4149	7075	7575
3	17348	18348	3197	5783	6116
4	20064	21064	2716	5016	5266
5	22486	23486	2422	4497	4697
6	24711	25711	2225	4118	4285
7	26801	27801	2090	3829	3972
8	28796	29796	1996	3600	3725
9	30729	31729	1933	3414	3525
10	32623	33623	1894	3262	3362
11	34497	35497	1874	3136	3227
12	36369	37369	1872	3031	3114
13	38253	39253	1883	2943	3019
14	40161	41161	1908	2869	2940
15	42105	43105	1944	2807	2874
16	44096	45096	1991	2756	2819
17	46144	47144	2048	2714	2773
18	48258	49258	2114	2681	2737
19	50448	51448	2190	2655	2708
20	52721	53721	2273	2636	2686
21	55087	56087	2365	2623	2671
22	57552	58552	2465	2616	2661
23	60125	61125	2573	2614	2658
24	62814	63814	2688	2617	2659
25	65625	66625	2811	2625	2665
26	68566	69566	2941	2637	2676
27	71645	72645	3078	2654	2691
28	74867	75867	3222	2674	2710
29	78241	79241	3374	2698	2732
30	81772	82772	3532	2726	2759
31	85469	86469	3696	2757	2789
32	89337	90337	3868	2792	2823
33	93383	94383	4046	2830	2860
34	97614	98614	4231	2871	2900
35	102036	103036	4422	2915	2944
36	106656	107656	4620	2963	2990
37	111481	112481	4825	3013	3040
38	116516	117516	5035	3066	3093
39	121769	122769	5253	3122	3148
40	127246	128246	5477	3181	3206

Does the fact that average cost is minimized at 23 passengers imply that the line should stop selling tickets at 23? In general, the answer is no. What the producer cares about is maximizing profit, not minimizing average cost. As we shall see in more detail in Chapter 9, these are not the same in the short run.

For example, suppose that a ticket could be sold for $3,200. The cost of adding the 24th passenger is only $2,688 (see the marginal cost of the 24th passenger) so that profit can be made by selling the ticket. In this case, $512 above cost is collected. The same is true for each additional passenger up to the 28th. That passenger costs $3,222. If the ticket can only be sold for $3,200, it does not pay to take him aboard.

The point that is illustrated is that minimizing cost is not the only factor at work in the determination of production. Cost conditions are key. But, with the exception of the long run when all factors are variable, selecting output levels that correspond to minimum average cost is not generally the appropriate strategy. This will become clearer in Chapter 9.

LONG-RUN THEORY OF COST
8.4

The conventional definition of the long run given in Chapter 6 and elsewhere is "a period of time of such length that all inputs are variable." Another aspect of the long run has also been stressed—an aspect that is, perhaps, the most important of all. The long run is a *planning horizon*. All production, indeed all economic activity, takes place in the short run. The "long run" refers to the fact that economic agents—consumers and managers—can plan ahead and choose many aspects of the "short run" in which they will operate in the future. Thus in a sense, the long run consists of all possible short-run situations among which an economic agent may choose.

As an example, *before* an investment is made, a manager is in a long-run situation and may select any one of a wide variety of different investments. After the investment decision is made and funds are congealed in fixed capital equipment, the firm operates under short-run conditions. Thus perhaps the best distinction is to say that an economic agent *operates* in the short run and *plans* in the long run.

Short Run and the Long
8.4.a

To begin with a highly simplified situation, suppose technology is such that plants in a certain industry can have only three different sizes. That is, the fixed capital equipment comprising the "plant" is available in only three sizes—small, medium, and large.

The plant of smallest size gives rise to the short-run average cost curve labeled SAC_1 in Figure 8.4.1; the medium-size plant has short-run average cost given by SAC_2; and the large plant has an average cost given by SAC_3. In the long run, a manager has to choose among the three investment alternatives represented by the three short-run average cost curves. The manager's choice of plant will depend

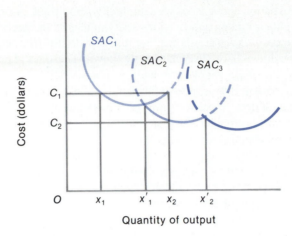

Figure 8.4.1 Short-run average cost curves for plants of different size

on planned or expected output. Thus, if the firm plans to produce output Ox_1, the smallest plant will be selected. If expected output is Ox_2, the medium plant is selected, and so forth. Such decisions would be made because the manager chooses the plant capable of producing the planned output at the lowest unit cost. (Note: At the time of the decision to build the plant, planned output is taken as given. Thus, choosing the plant with lowest unit or average cost is equivalent to choosing the plant with the lowest total cost for the planned output.)

If planned output is either Ox_1' or Ox_2', the decision involves some ambiguity. At each of these points, two plants have the same average cost. A manager might select the larger plant in order to meet a possible expansion of demand. On the other hand, the smaller plant would be preferred if a contraction of demand were possible. In these two examples, the decision would involve considerations other than least-cost output.

Suppose planned output is Ox_1. There is no ambiguity in this case and the plant represented by SAC_1 will be built. Now suppose that it actually turns out to be desirable to produce Ox_2 units. This can be done with the existing plant at an average cost of OC_1 per unit. In the short run, there are no other options and this is the only way to produce Ox_2. But the entrepreneur can plan for the future. When the old plant has "worn out," it can be replaced with a new one—and it will be a medium-size plant because Ox_2 can be produced for an average cost of OC_2 per unit, substantially less than with the small plant.

In the short run, a manager must operate with SAC_1, SAC_2, or SAC_3. But in the long run, it is possible to build a plant whose size leads to the least average cost for any output. Thus, as a planning device, the solid, scalloped curve is the long-run average cost curve, because this curve shows the long-run average cost of producing each possible output. This curve is frequently called the "envelope curve."

Long-Run Average Cost Curve
8.4.b

The illustration above is, as we said, highly simplified. A firm is normally faced with a choice among quite a wide variety of plants. In Figure 8.4.2, six short-run average cost curves are shown; but this is really far from enough. Many curves could be drawn between each of those shown. These six plants are only representative of the wide variety that could be constructed.

These many curves, just as the three in subsection 8.4.a, generate *LAC* as a planning device. Suppose a manager thinks the output associated with point *A* will be most profitable. The plant represented by SAC_1 will then be built because it will produce this output at the least possible cost per unit. With the plant whose short-run average cost is given by SAC_1, unit cost could be reduced by expanding output to the amount associated with point *B*, the minimum point on SAC_1. If demand conditions were suddenly changed so this larger output were desirable, the manager could easily expand — and would add to profitability by reducing unit cost. Nevertheless, when setting future plans the manager would decide to construct the plant represented by SAC_2 because this would reduce unit costs even more. The plant would operate at point *C*, thereby lowering unit cost from the level of point *B* on SAC_1.

It is interesting to note that point *B* is where plant of type 1 is operated most efficiently (i.e., at lowest unit cost). Still, it pays to shift to plant type 2, even though 2 is not operated at its most efficient level. In fact, all plants smaller than type 4 are only used when they are operating at less than the efficient level. The reason is that it is not efficiency for a given plant that matters, but efficiency overall. If plant 1 can be replaced by plant 2 and cost can be reduced, it is irrelevant that plant 1 would have been operated at peak efficiency. Since a cost-saving move cannot be made at point *A*, it is also irrelevant that *A* is not as efficient as *B*. This point is related to, but is not the same as that made in Example 8.3.

The long-run planning curve, *LAC*, is a locus of points representing the least unit cost of producing the corresponding output. This curve is the long-run average cost curve. The manager determines the size of plant by reference to this curve, selecting that short-run plant which yields the least unit cost of producing the anticipated volume of output.[5]

Long-Run Marginal Cost
8.4.c

A marginal cost curve may be constructed for the planning curve or the long-run average cost curve. This is illustrated in Figure 8.4.3. Consider the plant repre-

---

[5]It is important to recall that we are operating under the assumption that the "short" run is a well-defined period of time. That is, for expository purposes, we have adopted the analytical fiction that there is only *one* short run. If we were to account for the more realistic case of many short runs, each corresponding to a different length of time (as in subsection 8.2.b), we would have to replace each *SAC* curve in Figure 8.4.2 with a nested set of short-run average cost curves.

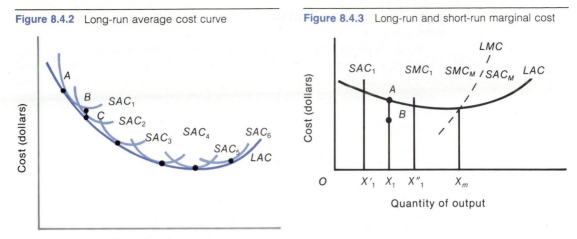

Figure 8.4.2 Long-run average cost curve

Figure 8.4.3 Long-run and short-run marginal cost

sented by the short-run average cost curve SAC_1 with the associated short-run marginal cost curve SMC_1. At point A, corresponding to output Ox_1, SAC and LAC are equal. Hence short-run and long-run total cost are also equal.

For smaller outputs, such as Ox_1', SAC_1 exceeds LAC, so short-run total cost is greater than long-run total cost. Thus for an expansion of output toward Ox_1, long-run marginal cost—whatever it may be—must exceed the known short-run marginal cost. That is, we have moved from a point where short-run total cost exceeds long-run total cost to a point where they are equal. The addition to total cost, or marginal cost, must consequently be smaller for the short-run curve than for the long-run curve. Therefore LMC is greater than SMC to the left of point A.[6]

For an expansion of output from Ox_1 to Ox_1'', the opposite situation holds. SAC_1 is greater than LAC at Ox_1'', so short-run total cost exceeds long-run total cost at this point. Now we have moved from a point where short-run and long-run total cost are equal (Ox_1) to a point where short-run total cost exceeds long-run total cost (Ox_1''). Therefore, the addition to total cost, or marginal cost, must be greater for the short-run curve than for the long-run curve. Whatever LMC might be, it must be less than SMC_1 to the right of Ox_1.

Now we have the information to find one point on the LMC curve. LMC must exceed SMC_1 to the left of Ox_1 and it must be less than SMC_1 to the right of Ox_1. Therefore, LMC must equal SMC_1 at output Ox_1. This gives us point B on the LMC curve. To find all the other points, this process is repeated. Take the next short-run average cost curve, together with its known short-run marginal cost. LMC must equal this SMC for the output at which the SAC curve is tangent to LAC. Performing this process for all plant sizes generates the LMC curve.

---

[6]It might be well to emphasize this point by means of a simple numerical example. Refer to Figure 8.4.3. At output Ox_1', since $SAC_1 > LAC$, let short-run total cost be $100 and long-run total cost be $90. At output Ox_1, they are equal, say, $110. Thus, over the range Ox_1' to Ox_1 short-run marginal cost is $10, while long-run marginal cost is $20.

It is important to notice that LMC intersects LAC when the latter is at its minimum point. There will be one, and only one, short-run plant size whose minimum short-run average cost coincides with minimum long-run average cost. This plant is represented by SAC_M and SMC_M in Figure 8.4.3. SMC_M equals SAC_M at the minimum point on the latter curve. SAC_M is tangent to LAC at their common minimum; and as we have shown, LMC equals SMC at the point where SAC and LAC are tangent. Therefore, LMC must pass through the minimum point on LAC.

At the risk of belaboring the obvious, let us emphasize that *optimal* adjustment is always preferable to *suboptimal* adjustment. This leads to a slightly different view of LAC and LMC.

Long-Run Average Cost Curve: The long-run average cost curve shows the *minimum unit cost* of producing every feasible level of output; the long-run marginal cost curve shows the *minimum amount* by which the cost is increased when output is expanded and the *maximum amount* that can be saved when output is reduced.

The Envelope Curve and the Expansion Path 8.4.d

We have just discussed the concept of the long-run average cost curve as the envelope of a set of short-run curves. Earlier, in subsection 8.2.a, the relationship between the expansion path and the long-run total cost curve was explained. Since long-run average costs are simply long-run total costs divided by output, these two approaches to long-run costs are really one and the same. In subsection 8.2.b, we saw that producing a given output with factor combinations other than those along the expansion path always meant that short-run total costs were higher than long-run total costs. This means, of course, that short-run average costs must exceed long-run average costs except at points corresponding to factor usage along the expansion path. The points on the expansion path are thus related on a one-to-one basis with the points of tangency of the short-run average cost curves and the long-run average cost curve in Figure 8.4.2.

This situation is illustrated in Figure 8.4.4. Suppose the short-run capital stock is fixed at K_0. The long-run equilibrium output for this capital stock obtains at point B where the isocost line C is tangent to isoquant Q at the given (fixed) capital stock K_0. This is a point on the expansion path E. To produce output Q' with capital stock K_0, the isocost line is shifted to C'. Note that point A, where the isoquant Q' intersects the expansion path E, is the long-run equilibrium for output Q'. In the short run, with K_0 fixed, the entrepreneur is on a higher isocost line than if capital stock could be adjusted. Thus, short-run costs (average and total costs) are greater than the long-run costs of producing Q'.

The same reasoning applies to the output Q'' where the short-run costs are given by the isocost line C''. When capital stock can be fully adjusted (downward in this case), equilibrium will occur at point D on the expansion path, and this

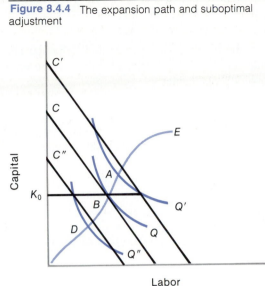

Figure 8.4.4 The expansion path and suboptimal adjustment

will be on a lower isocost line. Once again short-run costs exceed long-run costs. Only on the expansion path is $SAC = LAC$.

A very important relationship between the production function and the long-run total cost curve may now be established. We begin by introducing the concept of the function coefficient.

The Function Coefficient
8.5.a

The function coefficient is defined for every production function as follows:

Function Coefficient: The *function coefficient* (ε) shows the proportional change in output that results when all inputs are expanded in the same proportion.

The function coefficient may be expressed as a formula. The proportional change in output is $\Delta q/q$. Let all inputs be expanded in the proportion λ. Then, by definition

$$\varepsilon = \frac{\left(\dfrac{\Delta q}{q}\right)}{\lambda}.$$

(8.5.1)

NUMERICAL EXERCISES

Suppose the law firm of Freeman and Bella specializes in the writing of contracts of merging firms, according to the production function in Example 7.1 of Chapter 7,

$$Q = (E)^{1/2} (L)^{1/2}$$

where Q equals the number of contracts, E equals the number of hours put in by economists, and L the number of hours put in by lawyers.

It turns out that for this production function, the marginal product of economists is given by the formula:

$$MP_E = \tfrac{1}{2} \sqrt{L/E}$$

The marginal products of lawyers is given by the formula:

$$MP_L = \tfrac{1}{2} \sqrt{E/L}$$

Also assume that Freedman and Bella face giver input prices of $4 per hour for the use of economists, and $1 per hour for the use of lawyers.

Questions

1. Using the material in Chapters 7 and 8, what is the *long run cost-minimizing* number of hours of economist and lawyer time the firm will employ to produce 1 contract, 2 contracts, 3 contracts, 4 contracts, and 5 contracts?

2. From your result in question 1, calculate the total cost (TC), average cost (AC), and marginal cost (MC) for each of the five contract levels. Note that these are all long-run costs.

3. Now assume that the law firm has already hired on contract four hours of lawyer time and cannot alter this amount in the short run. Given this amount of lawyer time, what is the amount of economist time to be used to produce contract levels of 1, 2, 3, 4, 5?

4. Referring to question 3, calculate the short-run total cost, average cost, and marginal cost for each contract level.

5. Can the total cost and average cost in question 4 ever be less than the total cost and average cost determined in the second question? Explain.

Solutions

1. To find the cost-minimizing levels of inputs for any output level, set the *MRTS* equal to the ratio of the input prices, or

$$\frac{MP_E}{MP_L} = \frac{\$4}{\$1}, \quad \text{or equivalently,} \quad L/E = 4, \quad \text{or} \quad L = 4E.$$

To produce 1 contract, substitute into the production function this value for *L* and solve for *E*:

$$1 = (E)^{1/2} (4E)^{1/2}, \quad \text{or} \quad E = \tfrac{1}{2}, \quad \text{and} \quad L = 2$$

2. Similar calculations for $Q = 2, 3, 4, 5$ result in the combinations in the table below.

Q	E	L	LRTC ($4E + $1L)	LRAC	LRMC
1	$\frac{1}{2}$	2	4	$4	$4
2	1	4	8	4	4
3	3/2	6	12	4	4
4	2	8	16	4	4
5	5/2	10	20	4	4

3. For questions 3 and 4, we cannot use the table above because we are restricted in the use of lawyers' time to 4 hours. Thus, we are in the *short run*. In order to calculate the amount of economist time required to produce contract levels of 1, 2, 3, 4, 5 we again substitute into the production function, but set $L = 4$. This results in the combinations of *E* and *L* in the table below:

Q	E	L	SRTC ($4E + $1L)	SRAC	SRMC
1	1/4	4	$5	$5	$1
2	1	4	8	4	3
3	9/4	4	13	13/3	5
4	4	4	20	5	7
5	25/4	4	29	29/5	9

(continued on page 236)

4. See columns above headed *SRTC*, SRAC, and *SRMC*.
5. Notice that it is impossible for *LAC* to exceed *SAC*, or *LRTC* to exceed *SRTC*, because in the long run we could use the best short-run combination, but most of the time the short-run combination will not be cost minimizing in the long run. In our example, there is only one contract level where *SRAC* = *LRAC*, and that occurs at contract level 2, where $4L$ is indeed the best long-run amount of L to use to produce contract level 2. This is the reason for the diagrams in Figures 8.4.1 and 8.4.2.

If the function coefficient is unitary ($\varepsilon = 1$), then the proportional change in inputs leads to the same proportional change in output, and we say there are *constant returns to scale*. If the function coefficient is less than 1 ($\varepsilon < 1$), then the proportional change in output is less than the proportional change in inputs and we say there are *decreasing returns to scale*. Finally, when $\varepsilon > 1$, we say there are *increasing returns to scale*.

Let the production function be $q = f(x, y)$; then for a small change in x, denoted Δx, output will change by $MP_x \Delta x$, which is the marginal product of x times the change in x. Similarly, for a small change in y, output will change by $MP_y \Delta y$ where MP_y is the marginal product of y. For small changes in x and y, then, the output change is

$$\Delta q = MP_x \Delta x + MP_y \Delta y. \tag{8.5.2}$$

Simple algebra shows that equation (8.5.2) is equivalent to

$$\frac{\Delta q}{q} = \frac{x}{q} MP_x \frac{\Delta x}{x} + \frac{y}{q} MP_y \frac{\Delta y}{y}. \tag{8.5.3}$$

Now suppose x and y increased in the same proportion λ (that is, let $\Delta x/x = \Delta y/y = \lambda$), and we have from (8.5.3):

$$\frac{\Delta q}{q} = \left(MP_x \frac{x}{q} + MP_y \frac{y}{q} \right) \lambda$$

or

$$\varepsilon = \frac{\frac{\Delta q}{q}}{\lambda} = MP_x \frac{x}{q} + MP_y \frac{y}{q}. \tag{8.5.4}$$

Since q/x is the average product of x, and q/y is the average product of y, one can rewrite (8.5.4) as

$$\varepsilon = \frac{MP_x}{AP_x} + \frac{MP_y}{AP_y}.$$

(8.5.5)

This result is easily understood if x is the only factor. Then the function coefficient is the ratio of marginal to average product of x. Now, the average product of x tells the average productivity of x on all past units. The marginal product tells the productivity on the next unit. If the productivity on the next unit exceeds the productivity on previous units, then the firm is becoming more productive with expanding output, or there are increasing returns to scale. Conversely, if marginal product is less than average product, then the firm is becoming less productive with increasing output, or there are decreasing returns to scale. If marginal product equals average product, then there are constant returns to scale.

This result is useful in the following subsection.

Cost Elasticity
8.5.b

The results of interest require some *tedious but straightforward* manipulation of symbols that is relegated to a footnote.[7] This symbol manipulation leads to the following:

---

[7]Start with equation (8.5.4) in the text and let the prices of the two inputs be p_x and p_y. Multiply and divide the first term on the far right-hand side of (8.5.4) by p_x, the second term by p_y. One thus obtains

$$\varepsilon = \frac{MP_x}{p_x}\frac{xp_x}{q} + \frac{MP_y}{p_y}\frac{yp_y}{q}.$$

(8.7.1)

In Chapter 7 we found that the expansion path is defined by equality between the marginal rate of technical substitution and the input–price ratio. Further, we saw that this may always be expressed by saying that the marginal product of a dollar's worth of each input must be the same. Symbolically,

$$\frac{MP_x}{p_x} = \frac{MP_y}{p_y}.$$

(8.7.2)

Substituting equation (8.7.2) in (8.7.1), write

$$\varepsilon = \frac{MP_x}{p_x}\left(\frac{xp_x}{q} + \frac{yp_y}{q}\right) = \frac{MP_x}{p_x}\left(\frac{xp_x + yp_y}{q}\right).$$

(8.7.3)

Finally, we need some information from this chapter. First, by definition, total cost (C) is the sum of payments to all inputs, that is, the price of each input multiplied by the number of units employed and summed over all inputs. Thus

$$C = xp_x + yp_y.$$

(8.7.4)

Further, we defined average cost as $AC = C/q$. Substitution in equation (8.7.3) gives

$$\varepsilon = \frac{MP_x}{p_x}(AC).$$

(8.7.5)

(continued on page 238)

Relation: The function coefficient is equal to the ratio of long-run average cost to long-run marginal cost; in symbols,

$$\varepsilon = \frac{AC}{MC}.$$
(8.5.6)

The implications of this relation are worth exploring in some detail. First, recall that there are increasing, constant, or decreasing returns to scale according as the function coefficient exceeds, equals, or is less than one. For example, suppose $\varepsilon > 1$. This implies that a proportional expansion of inputs causes output to expand in greater proportion. Now if $\varepsilon > 1, AC/MC > 1$, this implies that a proportional increase in output causes cost to expand in smaller proportion. The reason is clear: since there are increasing returns to scale, the given proportional expansion of output can be achieved by a smaller proportional increase in input usage. At constant input prices, cost therefore increases by proportionately less than output.

Exercise: Carry out this type of argument for the case in which $\varepsilon < 1$.

Now continue to assume that $\varepsilon > 1$. If total cost increases in smaller proportion than output, average cost declines. Thus over the range in which the production function exhibits increasing returns to scale, the long-run average cost curve declines (see Figure 8.5.1). On the other hand, when there are decreasing returns to scale ($\varepsilon < 1$), the total cost function is elastic. This means that cost increases by proportionately more than output, so that average cost rises. Again the reason is clear: when $\varepsilon < 1$, a given proportional increase in output requires inputs to be increased in greater proportion. At constant factor prices, total cost expands by proportionately more than output and average cost increases.

These results may be summarized as the following:

Relation: Long-run average cost decreases or increases according as there are increasing or decreasing returns to scale; this relation holds if, and only if, factor prices are constant throughout.

(continued from page 237)

Note that MP_x is $\Delta Q/\Delta X$ and p_x is simply the change in cost associated with a change in x or $\Delta C/\Delta X$ (see 8.7.4). Therefore,

$$\frac{MP_x}{p_x} = \frac{\Delta Q/\Delta X}{\Delta C/\Delta X} = \frac{\Delta Q}{\Delta C}.$$

But $\Delta C/\Delta Q$ is marginal cost, so $\frac{MP_x}{p_x} = \frac{1}{MC}$, which implies that

$$\varepsilon = \frac{AC}{MC}.$$

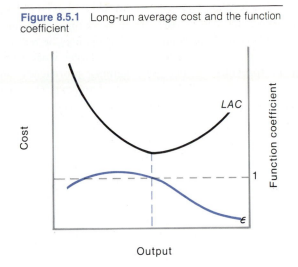

Figure 8.5.1 Long-run average cost and the function coefficient

Cost

LAC

Function coefficient

1

ϵ

Output

SHAPE OF *LAC*
8.6

The short- and long-run average cost curves are alike in that each has been drawn with a ∪ shape. The reasons for this shape, however, are quite different. *SAC* is ∪-shaped because the decline in average fixed cost is ultimately more than offset by the rise in average variable cost—the latter occurring because average product reaches a maximum and declines. But this has nothing at all to do with the curvature of *LAC*. Increasing or decreasing returns to scale in the production function and certain financial economies and diseconomies of scale are the factors governing the shape of *LAC*.

Economies of Scale
8.6.a

As the size of plant and the scale of operation become larger, considering expansion from the smallest possible plant, certain economies of scale are usually realized. That is, after adjusting *all* inputs optimally, the unit cost of production can be reduced by increasing the size of plant.

Adam Smith gave one of the outstanding reasons for this: specialization and division of labor. When the number of workers is expanded, fixed inputs remaining fixed, the opportunities for specialization and division of labor are rapidly exhausted. The marginal product curve rises, to be sure, but not for long. It very quickly reaches its maximum and declines thereafter. When workers and equipment are expanded together, however, very substantial gains may be reaped by division of jobs and the specialization of workers in one job or another.

Proficiency is gained by concentration of effort. If a plant is very small and employs only a small number of workers, each worker will usually have to perform several different jobs in the production process. In doing so he is likely to have to move about the plant, change tools, and so on. Not only are workers not highly specialized but a part of their work time is consumed in moving about and changing tools. Thus, important savings may be realized by expanding the scale of operation. A larger plant with a larger work force may permit each worker to specialize in one job, gaining proficiency and obviating time-consuming interchanges of location and equipment. There naturally will be corresponding reductions in the unit cost of production.

Technological factors constitute a second force contributing to economies of scale. Purchasing and installing larger machines is usually proportionately less than the cost of smaller machines for technological reasons. For example, a printing press that can run 200,000 papers per day does not cost 10 times as much as one that can run 20,000 per day — nor does it require 10 times as much building space, 10 times as many people to work it, and so forth. Again, expanding size tends to reduce the unit cost of production.

Thus two broad forces — specialization and division of labor and technological factors — enable producers to reduce unit cost by expanding the scale of operation.[8] These forces give rise to the negatively sloped portion of the long-run average cost curve.

But why should it ever rise? After all possible economies of scale have been realized, why does the curve not become horizontal?

Diseconomies of Scale
8.6.b

The rising portion of *LAC* is usually attributed to "diseconomies of scale," which essentially means limitations to efficient management. Managing any business entails controlling and coordinating a wide variety of activities — production, transportation, finance, sales, etc. To perform these managerial functions efficiently, the manager must have accurate information; otherwise the essential decision making is done in ignorance.

As the scale of plant expands beyond a certain point, top management necessarily has to delegate responsibility and authority to lower-echelon employees. Contact with the daily routine of operation tends to be lost and efficiency of operation to decline. Red tape and paperwork expand; management is generally not as efficient. This increases the cost of performing the managerial function and, of course, the unit cost of production.

It is very difficult to determine just when diseconomies of scale set in and when they become strong enough to outweigh the economies of scale. In businesses where economies of scale are negligible, diseconomies may soon become of paramount importance, causing *LAC* to turn up at a relatively small volume of output. Panel A, Figure 8.6.1, shows a long-run average cost curve for a firm

---

[8]This discussion of economies of scale has concentrated upon physical and technological forces. There are financial reasons for economies of scale as well. Large-scale purchasing of raw and processed materials may enable the buyer to obtain more favorable prices (quantity discounts). Sometimes the source of these discounts is technological. In other instances, however, they may reflect the optimum pricing policy of a monopolistic seller of factors of production.

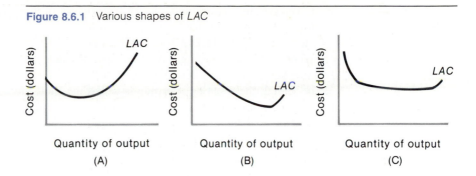

Figure 8.6.1 Various shapes of *LAC*

Cost (dollars) / Quantity of output
(A)

Cost (dollars) / Quantity of output
(B)

Cost (dollars) / Quantity of output
(C)

of this type. In other cases, economies of scale are extremely important. Even after the efficiency of management begins to decline, technological economies of scale may offset the diseconomies over a wide range of outputs. Thus the *LAC* curve may not turn upward until a very large volume of output is attained. This case, typified by the so-called natural monopolies, is illustrated in Panel B, Figure 8.6.1.

In many actual situations, however, neither of these extremes describes the behavior of *LAC*. A very modest scale of operation may enable a firm to capture all of the economies of scale; however, diseconomies may not be incurred until the volume of output is very great. In this case, *LAC* would have a long horizontal section, as shown in Panel C. Many economists feel that this type of *LAC* curve describes most production processes in the American economy.

CONCLUSION 8.7

The physical conditions of production and resource prices jointly establish the cost of production. This is very important to individual business firms and to the economy as a whole. But it is only half the story. Cost represents one aspect of economic activity: to the entrepreneur, it represents obligations to pay out funds; to society, it represents the resources that must be sacrificed to obtain a given commodity. The other aspect is revenue or demand. To the individual entrepreneur, revenue is the flow of funds from which the firm's obligations may be met. To society, demand represents the social valuation placed on the commodity.

Both demand and cost must be taken into consideration. It is to the demand side that we turn in Part 3.

SYNOPSIS 8.8

■ Cost involves both the explicit payments to purchase factors and the implicit costs represented by the forgone alternative uses of the entrepreneur's time and money. Pure economic profit may be thought of as accounting profit minus these implicit costs.

- Given the production function and factor costs, it is possible to derive total cost schedules that show the minimum total cost at which each total output can be produced. When all factors can be varied, the resulting schedule is called the long-run total cost schedule or function. When the time period involved is so short that only some factors of production can be varied, the resulting schedule is called the short-run cost schedule.

- In the short run, costs can be classified as fixed and variable. Given the total fixed costs and the total variable cost schedule, one can derive the average fixed cost schedule and short-run average variable cost and marginal cost schedules. These schedules have certain geometric relations similar to those discussed in the Appendix to Chapter 6.

- In the long run, there are no fixed costs. The long-run average cost schedule is, in effect, an envelope curve for the short-run average cost schedules. The long-run average cost schedule is a planning device in the sense that it represents the cost opportunities available to the entrepreneur before any actual plant has been built. Corresponding to the long-run average cost schedule is a long-run marginal cost schedule.

- When there are constant returns to scale, the long-run average cost schedule will be a horizontal line. A decreasing long-run average cost schedule occurs when there are economies of scale; and an increasing long-run average cost schedule reflects diseconomies of scale.

QUESTIONS AND EXERCISES

Return to the problem at the end of Chapter 6. Total product column (1) is given; and you have computed average product column (2) and marginal product column (3). You are also given the following information:

1. Total fixed cost (total price of fixed inputs) is $220 per period.
2. Units of the variable input cost $100 per unit per period. Using this information, add to your table entries for the new categories shown below in columns (4) through (10).

Units of variable input (1)	Total product (1)	Average product (2)	Marginal product (3)	Total fixed cost (4)	Total variable cost (5)	Total cost (6)	Average fixed cost (7)	Average variable cost (8)	Average total cost (9)	Marginal cost (10)

I. Graph the total cost curves on one sheet and the average and marginal curves on another.

II. By reference to table and graph, answer the following questions.

1. When marginal product is increasing, what is happening to:
   a. Marginal cost?
   b. Average variable cost?

2. When marginal cost first begins to fall, does average variable cost begin to rise?

3. What is the relation between marginal cost and average variable cost when marginal and average products are equal?
4. What is happening to average variable cost while average product is increasing?
5. Where is average variable cost when average product is at its maximum? What happens to average variable cost after this point?
6. What happens to marginal cost after the point where it equals average variable cost?
    a. How does it compare with average variable cost thereafter?
    b. What is happening to marginal product thereafter?
    c. How does marginal product compare with average product thereafter?
7. What happens to total fixed cost as output is increased?
8. What happens to average fixed cost as:
    a. Marginal product increases?
    b. Marginal cost decreases?
    c. Marginal product decreases?
    d. Marginal cost increases?
    e. Average variable cost increases?
9. How long does average fixed cost decrease?
10. What happens to average total cost as:
    a. Marginal product increases?
    b. Marginal cost decreases?
    c. Average product increases?
    d. Average variable cost decreases?
11. Does average total cost increase:
    a. As soon as the point of diminishing marginal returns is passed?
    b. As soon as the point of diminishing average returns is passed?
12. When does average cost increase? Answer this in terms of:
    a. The relation of average cost to marginal cost.
    b. The relation between the increase in average variable cost and the decrease in average fixed cost.

III. Do these problems on the theory of cost.
1. Consider the point where $SAC = LAC$. Explain precisely why LMC exceeds SMC for a decrease in output. (Hint: Both MCs show the reduction in cost attributable to the reduction in output.)
2. Comment on the following statement: long-run average cost is a meaningless concept since in this period most conditions underlying the cost function will probably change in unpredictable ways.
3. Beginning with a production function or schedule involving two variable inputs, explain how one derives both the short- and long-run average cost curves and the short-run marginal cost curve.
4. Given constant input prices and completely divisible and adaptable inputs, are the customary ∪-shaped short-run average variable cost curves consistent with a constant-returns-to-scale production function? Answer the same question for long-run average cost.
5. What are the relations between increasing returns to scale and decreasing long-run average cost? More generally, what relations, if any, exist between "returns to scale" and the shape of the long-run average cost curve?

6. The Southern Railway's lines from East St. Louis (Ill.) and Evansville (Ind.) to grain-consuming destinations in Georgia had substantial excess trackage capacity. In deciding whether to invest in a sizable fleet of giant cars for carrying grain to these destinations and in setting rates for this traffic, Southern would rationally consider (*a*) fully allocated costs of the trackage, crew and fuel costs; (*b*) fully allocated cost of the trackage, extra equipment costs, crew and fuel costs; (*c*) cost of the new equipment, crew and fuel costs; (*d*) none of the above.

7. In the late 1950s, the development of trilevel railroad "rack" cars for carrying new automobiles substantially lowered the costs of hauling such traffic. This represented (*a*) a change in demand for railroad services, (*b*) a change in supply of railroad services, (*c*) a change in supply of trucking services for new automobiles, (*d*) all of the above.

8. Forty years ago, several trains used the Monon Railroad Station in Lafayette, Ind., each day; eight years ago (and today), the station was used by one train per day in each direction. In deciding whether to tear down its older large station and replace it with a smaller building, the Monon probably considered whether (*a*) the total cost of the old building was greater than the total cost of the new building, (*b*) the variable cost of operating the old building was greater than the total cost of the new building, (*c*) the variable cost of the old building was greater than the variable cost of the new building, (*d*) the total cost of the old building was greater than the variable cost of the new building.

9. Suppose that the employees of a certain firm established a labor union and are able to negotiate an *effective* featherbedding contract (that is, the firm must employ more workers than dictated by the conditions of optimal resource utilization). Determine how this featherbedding contract changes the short-run cost curves of the firm. Hold your answer to this exercise for a related exercise in Chapter 10.

SUGGESTED READINGS

Clark, J. M. *The Economics of Overhead Costs.* Chicago: University of Chicago Press, 1923, chaps. 4–6.

Ferguson, C. E. *The Neoclassical Theory of Production and Distribution.* London and New York: Cambridge University Press, 1969, chap. 7.

Ferguson, C. E., and **Saving, Thomas R.** "Long-Run Scale Adjustments of a Perfectly Competitive Firm and Industry." *American Economic Review* 59 (1969), pp. 774–83.

Henderson, James M., and **Quandt, Richard E.** *Microeconomic Theory: A Mathematical Approach,* 2nd ed. New York: McGraw-Hill, 1971, pp. 70–79.

Robinson, Joan. "Rising Supply Price," *Economica (New Series),* 8 (1941), pp. 1–8.

Viner, Jacob. "Cost Curves and Supply Curves," *Zeitschrift für Nationalökonomie* 3 (1931), pp. 23–46. Reprinted in American Economic Association, *Readings in Price Theory.* Homewood, Ill.: Richard D. Irwin, 1952, pp. 198–232.

PART

3

Theory of the Firm and Market Organization

The theory of business operation within an organized but uncontrolled market brings together the topics covered in Parts 1 and 2. Demand, the broad topic of Part 1, establishes the *revenue side* of business operation. Product demand determines either the quantity a firm can sell at any price it selects or the price a firm can obtain for any quantity it wishes to market. Market demand also helps to determine the type of industry structure that is likely to emerge in response to market conditions—whether the industry is likely to be competitive, monopolistic, or what have you.

The technical conditions of production and their reflection in business operating costs, the subject of Part 2, establish the *cost side* of business operation and the *supply conditions* of the industry. Brought together, revenue and cost for the individual business concern and demand and supply for the entire market determine the market price and output of the firm and the industry. These forces accordingly determine the allocation of resources among industries as well.

The general purpose of Part 3 is to discover how the price–output decisions of individual entrepreneurs and the structure of the market jointly determine the allocation of resources. This inquiry inevitably entails an appraisal of the *efficiency* with which resources are allocated.

Given the conditions of demand and supply, or of revenue and cost, our analysis is based upon two fundamental assumptions.

Free Market. First, we assume that each market operates freely in the sense that there is no external control of market forces and resources can move in and out of the market in response to changing incentives. In an economy where competition is the basic force, this assumption is a good one. In the American economy of the 1980s, the assumption is valid for the most part, but there are exceptions.

The first exception is that government intervention can change the rules under which markets operate. For example, wage and price controls prevent the market from establishing its own price. Another example is that public utilities, such as the electric company, cannot choose their prices and supply service in accord with their own choosing. Instead, they must answer to some regulatory commission. Later, we will examine the pros and cons of such intervention, but at least initially, we analyze markets that are not affected by government regulation.

A second exception is that, occasionally, firms may attempt to set price collectively, preventing the market from operating by the strict laws of supply and demand. As Adam Smith once said,

> People of the same trade seldom meet together, even for merriment and diversion, but the conversation ends in a conspiracy against the public, or in some contrivance to raise prices.[1]

The key here is that a sufficiently small number of producers exist so that a cartel of the kind described can form and enforce agreements. As we shall see, the forces of competition are strongly destabilizing to collusive behavior, especially when the number of producers rises above a small number or when buyers have strong bargaining power. For these reasons, most of the economy is not governed by the rules of cartel behavior and that will be the maintained hypothesis for this section of the book. Later, we will consider how things change if that assumption is dropped.

Thus, while many markets are not "free" in the sense used here, a vast number are. The object is to analyze the efficiency of resource allocation in free markets. In case a market is not free, one is able to draw important inferences concerning the relative efficiency of free as against controlled markets.

Profit Maximization. The second fundamental assumption used in Part 3 is that firms attempt to maximize profits. At some level, this is tautologically true. But there are two real-world caveats that immediately come to mind.

First, firms may not have all the information necessary to maximize profits. Profit maximization may be a difficult process that requires much analysis by entrepreneurs in a situation where time is costly, so decisions must be made quickly.

Second, managers may not have the same interests as the owners of the firm and may do things that maximize their utility, but not necessarily the firm's profits. For example, we might expect the manager to spend the firm's resources on a plush office, even if the decor is not cost effective.

Both of these criticisms have given rise to a large body of literature in economics, some of which is discussed later. But for the most part, the notion that firms maximize profit is a good working assumption that generally leads to the correct conclusions. As such, we maintain that firms maximize profits throughout most of the analysis.[2] ■

---

[1] Adam Smith, *Wealth of Nations* (Cannan ed.; London: Methuen, 1904), vol. 1, p. 130. This book was written in 1776. Antitrust laws of the late 19th century and early 20th century have made such conspiracies illegal, and price fixing is far less common now than it was at the time Smith wrote his famous treatise.

[2] In dynamic multiperiod models, economists usually take the profit-maximization assumption to mean that the firm is managed so as to maximize the present value of all future net cash flows.

9 Theory of Price in Perfectly Competitive Markets

The model of perfect competition is probably used by economists today more than ever before. This chapter combines the previous material in Parts 1 and 2 for use in analyzing markets described by the model of perfect competition. What is meant by perfect competition? How does a firm choose an output level that maximizes its profit? How is the marginal cost curve of the previous chapter related to the competitive firm's supply curve? Where does the industry supply curve come from? How does a competitive industry adjust in the long run in response to the existence of economic profits (or losses)? In "Airline takes the marginal route" (see "Applying the Theory" section at the beginning of this chapter) you will see how an airline economist from Continental Air Lines uses such theoretical concepts as fixed versus variable cost, marginal cost, and average cost to decide which flights his firm should undertake in order to maximize its profits. The principles he describes as being so foreign to some of his fellow employees should be no surprise to the student (in answering the questions posed) who has mastered the principles in this chapter. You will also be asked to describe in detail how the competitive mink-farming industry (and the representative firm) would respond to an increase (and decrease) in the demand for mink, and to an increase in the price of some of its inputs, in your reading of the article, "Mink farming is growing more scarce as costs rise and fur demand declines" at the end of this chapter. Once again, the article's description of this adjustment should come as no surprise. ■

Airline Takes the Marginal Route

Continental Air Lines, Inc., last year filled only half the available seats on its Boeing 707 jet flights, a record some 15 percentage points worse than the national average.

By eliminating just a few runs—less than 5 percent—Continental could have raised its average load considerably. Some of its flights frequently carry as few as 30 passengers on the 120-seat plane. But the improved load factor would have meant reduced profits.

For Continental bolsters its corporate profits by deliberately running extra flights that aren't expected to do more than return their our-of-pocket costs—plus a little profit. Such marginal flights are an integral part of the over-all operating philosophy that has brought small, Denver-based Continental—tenth among the 11 trunk carriers—through the bumpy postwar period with only one loss year.

Chief Contribution

This philosophy leans heavily on marginal analysis. And the line leans heavily on Chris F. Whelan, vice-president in charge of economic planning, to translate marginalism into hard, dollars-and-cents decisions.

Getting management to accept and apply the marginal concept probably is the chief contribution any economist can make to his company. Put most simply, marginalists maintain that a company should undertake any activity that adds more to revenues than it does to costs—and not limit itself to those activities whose returns equal average or "fully allocated" costs.

The approach, of course, can be applied to virtually any business, not just to air transportation. It can be used in consumer finance, for instance, where the question may be whether to make more loans—including more bad loans—if this will increase net profit. Similarly, in advertising, the decision may rest on how much extra business a dollar's worth of additional advertising will bring in, rather than pegging the advertising budget to a percentage of sales—and, in insurance, where setting high interest rates to discourage policy loans may actually damage profits by causing policyholders to borrow elsewhere.

Communication

Whelan finds all such cases wholly analogous to his run of problems, where he seeks to keep his company's eye trained on the big objective: net profit.

He is a genially gruff, shirt-sleeves kind of airline veteran, who resembles more a sales-manager type than an economist. This facet of his personality helps him "sell" ideas internally that might otherwise be brushed off as merely theoretical or too abstruse.

Last summer, Whelan politely chewed out a group of operational researchers at an international conference in Rome for being incomprehensible. "You have failed to educate the users of your talents to the potential you offer," he said. "Your studies, analyses, and reports are couched in tables that sales, operations, and maintenance personnel cannot comprehend."

Full-time Job

Whelan's work is a concrete example of the truth in a crack by Prof. Sidney Alexander of MIT—formerly economist for Columbia Broadcasting System—that the economist who understands marginal analysis has a "full-time job in undoing the work of the accountant." This is so, Alexander holds, because the practices of accountants —and of most businesses—are permeated with cost allocation directed at average, rather than marginal, costs.

In any complex business, there's likely to be a big difference between the costs of each company activity as it's carried on the accounting books and the marginal or "true" costs that can determine whether or not the activity should be undertaken.

The difficulty comes in applying the simple "textbook" marginal concept to specific decisions. If the economist is unwilling to make some bold simplifications, the job of determining "true" marginal costs may be highly complex, time-wasting, and too expensive. But even a rough application of marginal principles may come closer to the right answer for business decision-makers than an analysis based on precise average-cost data.

Proving that this is so demands economists who can break the crust of corporate habits and show concretely why the typical manager's response—that nobody ever made a profit without meeting all costs—

is misleading and can reduce profits. To be sure, the whole business cannot make a profit unless average costs are met; but covering average costs should not determine whether any particular activity should be undertaken. For this would unduly restrict corporate decisions and cause managements to forgo opportunities for extra gains.

Approach

Management overhead at Continental is pared to the bone, so Whelan often is thrown such diverse problems as soothing a ruffled city council or planning the specifications for the plane the line will want to fly in 1970. But the biggest slice of his time goes to schedule planning—and it is here that the marginal concept comes most sharply into focus.

Whelan's approach is this: He considers that the bulk of his scheduled flights have to return at least their fully allocated costs. Overhead, depreciation, insurance are very real expenses and must be covered. The out-of-pocket approach comes into play, says Whelan, only after the line's basic schedule has been set.

"Then you go a step farther," he says, and see if adding more flights will contribute to the corporate net. Similarly, if he's thinking of dropping a flight with a disappointing record, he puts it under the marginal microscope: "If your revenues are going to be more than your out-of-pocket costs, you should keep the flight on."

(continued on page 250)

APPLYING THE THEORY

(continued from page 249)

By "out-of-pocket costs" Whelan means just that: the actual dollars that Continental has to pay out to run a flight. He gets the figure not by applying hypothetical equations but by circulating a proposed schedule to every operating department concerned and finding out just what extra expenses it will entail. If a ground crew already on duty can service the plane, the flight isn't charged a penny of their salary expense. There may even be some costs eliminated in running the flight; they won't need men to roll the plane to a hangar, for instance, if it flies on to another stop.

Most of these extra flights, of course, are run at off-beat hours, mainly late at night. At times, though, Continental discovers that the hours aren't so unpopular after all. A pair of night coach flights on the Houston–San Antonio–El Paso–Phoenix–Los Angeles leg, added on a marginal basis, have turned out to be so successful that they are now more than covering fully allocated costs.

Alternative

Whelan uses an alternative cost analysis closely allied with the marginal concept in drawing up schedules. For instance, on his 11:11 P.M. flight from Colorado Springs to Denver and a 5:20 A.M. flight the other way, Continental uses Viscounts that, though they carry some cargo, often go without a single passenger. But the net cost of these flights is less than would be the rent for overnight hangar space for the Viscount at Colorado Springs.

And there's more than one absolute-loss flight scheduled solely to bring passengers to a connecting Continental long-haul flight; even when the loss on the feeder service is considered a cost on the long-haul service, the line makes a net profit on the trip.

Continental's data handling system produces weekly reports on each flight, with revenues measured against both out-of-pocket and fully allocated costs. Whelan uses these to give each flight a careful analysis at least once a quarter. But those added on a marginal basis get the fine-tooth-comb treatment monthly.

The business on these flights tends to be useful as a leading indicator, Whelan finds, since the off-peak traffic is more than normally sensitive to economic trends and will fall off sooner than that on the popular-hour flights. When he sees the night coach flights turning in consistently poor showings, it's a clue to lower his projections for the rest of the schedule.

Unorthodox

There are times, though, when the decisions dictated by the most expert marginal analysis seem silly at best, and downright costly at worst. For example, Continental will have two planes converging at the same time on Municipal Airport in Kansas City, when the new schedules take effect.

This is expensive because, normally, Continental doesn't have the facilities in K.C. to service two planes at once; the line will have to lease an extra fuel truck and hire three new hands—at a total monthly cost of $1,800.

But, when Whelan started pushing around proposed departure times in other cities to avoid the double landing, it began to look as though passengers switching to competitive flights leaving at choicer hours, would lose Continental $10,000 worth of business each month. The two flights will be on the ground in K.C. at the same time.

Full Work Week

This kind of scheduling takes some 35 percent of Whelan's time. The rest of his average work week breaks down this way: 25 percent for developing near-term, point-to-point traffic forecasts on which schedules are based; 20 percent in analyzing rates—Whelan expects to turn into a quasi-lawyer to plead Continental's viewpoint before the Civil Aeronautics Board; 20 percent on long-range forecasts and the where-should-we-go kind of planning that determines both which routes the line goes after and which it tries to shed. (Whelan's odd jobs in promotion, public relations, and general management don't fit into that time allotment; he says they "get stuck on around the side.")

The same recent week he was working on the data for his Kansas City double-landing problem, for instance, he was completing projections for the rest of 1963 so that other departments could use them for budget making, and was scrutinizing actions by Trans World Airlines, Inc., and Braniff Airways, Inc. TWA had asked CAB approval for special excursion fares from Eastern cities to Pacific Coast terminals; Whelan decided the plan worked out much the same as the economy fare on Continental's three-class service, so will neither oppose nor match the excursion deal. Braniff had just doubled its order—to 12—for British Aircraft Corp.'s 111 jets. Whelan was trying to figure out where they were likely to use the small planes, and what effect they would have on Continental's share of competing routes in Texas and Oklahoma.

At the same time, Whelan was meeting with officials of Frontier Airlines and Trans-Texas, coordinating the CAB-ordered takeover by the feeder lines of 14 stops Continental is now serving with leased DC-3s.

And he was struggling, too, with a knotty problem in consumer economics: He was trying to sell his home on Denver's Cherry Vale Drive and buy one in Los Angeles, where Continental will move its headquarters this summer.

Question

Once you have understood what Continental's economist, Chris Whelan, is doing in the actions described in this article, you should be able to answer the following similar (but hypothetical) decision problem correctly.

1. Suppose Ferguson Airlines flies between Tacoma and Portland. They lease their planes on a year-long contract, at a cost which averages out to $405 per flight. Other costs such as fuel, stewardesses, etc. amount to $595 per flight. The flight averages 15 passengers per flight at a ticket price of

(continued on page 252)

(continued from page 251)
$50. All prices and costs are expected to continue at their present levels. Which of the following is the profit-maximizing course for Ferguson to follow:

  a. Ferguson should drop this flight immediately?
  b. Ferguson should continue the flight indefinitely?
  c. Ferguson should continue flying until the lease expires and then drop the run?

Solution

1. The correct course of action is (c). The revenue per flight will be $50 × 15 or $750. The variable cost of the flight is $595. Since the additional revenue from running the flight exceeds the additional cost, the flight should be run as long as the lease is still in effect. (The lease is a fixed cost which must be paid regardless of whether the flight is undertaken. As such it has no bearing on the short-run decision.) However, in the long run—when the lease has expired—this flight should not be continued because at that point the additional revenue will not cover the additional cost ($405 + $595), since Ferguson does not have to renew the lease.

Source: Reproduced from *Business Week*, April 20, 1963, pp. 111–112, 114 by special permission. Copyright 1963 by McGraw-Hill, Inc.

Marginal Analysis in a Nutshell

Problem:	Shall Continental run an extra daily flight from City X to City Y?	
The facts:	Fully-allocated costs of this flight	$4,500
	Out-of-pocket costs of this flight	$2,000
	Flight should gross	$3,100
Decision:	Run the flight. It will add $1,100 to net profit—because it will add $3,100 to revenues and only $2,000 to costs. Overhead and other costs, totaling $2,500 [$4,500 minus $2,000], would be incurred whether the flight is run or not. Therefore, fully-allocated or "average" costs of $4,500 are not relevant to this business decision. It's the out-of-pocket or "marginal" costs that count.	

INTRODUCTION
9.1

"Perfect competition" is an exacting concept forming the basis of the most important model of business behavior. The essence of the concept, to be defined more fully below, is that the market is entirely *impersonal*. There is no "rivalry" among suppliers in the market, and buyers do not recognize their competitiveness vis-à-vis one another. Thus, in a sense, perfect competition describes a market in which there is a complete absence of direct competition among economic agents.

In ordinary conversation, the market for automobiles, say, or for razor blades would be described as highly competitive; each firm competes vigorously with its rivals, who are few in number. A major area of competition is in advertising. The advertisement of one firm will state that its product is superior to that of its rivals, which it will sometimes name. Firms also strive to attract customers by means of style features, method of packaging, claims of durability, and such. More generally, there is active, if sometimes spurious, quality competition.

The type of market just described, however, is not what the economist means when speaking of perfect competition. When this austere concept is used, no traces of personal rivalry can appear. All relevant economic magnitudes are determined by impersonal market forces.

Still, even this most abstract notion of competition is not inconsistent with what some managers think of as competition. Farmers selling wheat do so in what is close to a perfectly competitive market. Although no farmer sees any other particular farmer as a personal rival, each recognizes the discipline of the marketplace. If a farm is not able to produce as cheaply as others in the market, then it will not be able to compete successfully. In this sense, the most formal definition of perfect competition has its representation in common usage. Competition implies that relative performance is important. Even if one producer cannot identify his or her rival personally, rivalry with the market nonetheless exists.

PERFECT COMPETITION
9.2

An understanding of concepts of perfect competition and equilibrium in a perfectly competitive market is facilitated by the following scenario or parable. Consider the market for a given commodity and suppose that participants in this market are divided into two groups: one group consists of producers or suppliers of the commodity; the other group consists of consumers or demanders of the commodity. Exchange between these groups is accomplished through an auctioneer, in the following manner. The auctioneer announces a price for the commodity, and each consumer decides how much of the commodity to purchase at that price. Similarly, each producer decides how much of the commodity to supply at the announced price. The auctioneer adds up the demands of all the consumers and also adds up the supply offers of all the producers. If the aggregate demand equals the aggregate supply, the announced price is said to be the equilibrium price, and transactions are consummated at this price. If, at the currently announced price, the quantity that consumers wish to purchase is not the same as the quantity that producers wish to supply, a new price is announced by the auctioneer. This process is repeated until an equilibrium price is found.

Three important conditions are used by economists to define perfect competition. We will discuss these conditions and how each is related to the "auctioneer" parable.

Price-Taking Demanders and Suppliers
9.2.a

In the above parable, every market participant, whether demander or supplier, regards price as given. While it is true that the aggregate behavior of demanders and suppliers affects the price, no economic agent takes the effect of its behavior on price into account when making a consumption or production decision. Frequently, economists try to capture the essence of the price-taker assumption by stipulating that in a competitive market, every economic agent is so small, relative to the market as a whole, that it cannot exert a perceptible influence on price. The critical ingredient, however, is not the assumption of a large number of small economic agents but rather the assumption that each economic agent acts as if prices are given. In the wheat market, no one farm can affect price because its output is so small relative to the rest of the market. As such, each farm believes (rationally) that from its point of view, price is given and will not be affected by its sales of wheat. Similarly, the shopper who buys a loaf of bread (correctly) assumes that this single purchase will not drive up the price of bread. Because the buyer's demand is so small relative to the rest of the market, the effect of the purchase on price is trivial.

Homogeneous Product
9.2.b

A closely related provision is that the product of any one seller in a perfectly competitive market must be identical with the product of any other seller. This ensures that buyers are indifferent as to the firm from which they purchase.

The relationship of this assumption to the auctioneer parable is obvious: in that parable, consumers make no distinctions among the outputs of different producers.

Free Entry of Resources
9.2.c

A third condition for perfect competition is that resources can move in and out of the relevant industry in response to pecuniary signals.

Free entry means that new firms (or new capital) can enter and leave an industry without extraordinary difficulty. If patents or copyrights are required, entry is not free. Similarly, if average cost declines over an appreciable range of output, established producers will have cost advantages that make entry difficult.

In terms of the earlier parable, the assumption of free entry of resources means that during the auction process, individual producers can decide to offer no output if they so desire and also that new producers can enter and make supply offers when they wish.

Perfect Information about Prices
9.2.d

Consumers and producers must possess perfect information about prices if a market is to be perfectly competitive. If consumers are not fully cognizant of prices, they might buy at higher prices when lower ones are available. There will not be a uniform price in the market and consumers will search for the lowest price, while producers search for the highest. Such search behavior is an important topic, but it is not part of what is usually thought of as perfect competition.

The discussion to this point can be summarized by the following definition.

Perfect Competition: Perfect competition is an economic model of a market possessing the following characteristics: each economic agent acts as if prices are given, that is, each acts as a price taker; the product is homogeneous; there is free entry; and all economic agents in the market possess complete and perfect knowledge about the relevant prices.

These assumptions seem unrealistic for most markets, so why bother with such a model? The answer can be given in as much or as little detail as desired. For our present purposes, it is brief. First, generality can be achieved only by means of abstraction. Hence no theory can be perfectly descriptive of real-world phenomena. Further, the more accurately a theory describes one specific real-world case, the less accurately it describes all others. In any area of thought a theoretician does not select his assumptions on the basis of their realism; the conclusions, not the asumptions, are tested against reality.

This leads to a point of great, if pragmatic, importance. The conclusions derived from the model of perfect competition have, by and large, permitted accurate explanation and prediction of real-world phenomena. That is, perfect competition frequently *works* as a theoretical model of economic processes. The most persuasive evidence supporting this assertion is the fact that despite the proliferation of more "sophisticated" models of economic behavior, economists today probably use the model of perfect competition in their research more than ever before.

SHORT-RUN EQUILIBRIUM OF A FIRM IN A PERFECTLY COMPETITIVE MARKET
9.3

In the short run, the rate of output per period of time can be increased or decreased by increasing or decreasing the use of variable inputs. The individual firm can adjust its rate of output over a wide range, subject only to the limitations imposed by its fixed inputs (generally, plant and equipment). Since each firm adjusts until it reaches a profit-maximizing rate of output, the market or industry also adjusts until it reaches a point of short-run equilibrium.

Short-Run Profit Maximization, Total Revenue–Total Cost Approach
9.3.a

As noted, we assume that each firm adjusts its rate of output so as to maximize the profit obtainable from its business operation. Since profit is the difference between the total revenue from sales and the total cost of operation, profit is a maximum for the rate of output that maximizes the excess of revenue over cost (or minimizes the excess of cost over revenue).

Consider the example contained in Table 9.3.1 and shown graphically in Figure 9.3.1. The first two columns of the table give the demand curve for the perfectly competitive producer. Market price is $5 per unit; the firm can sell as many units as it wishes at this price. The product of columns 1 and 2 gives total revenue, the entries appearing in column 3. The straight line in Figure 9.3.1 is a graphical representation. Notice that the total revenue curve is always a straight line in the case of perfect competition because unit price does not change when quantity sold changes.

Columns 4, 5, and 6 give total fixed, total variable, and total cost, respectively. Total cost is graphed as the curved line in Figure 9.3.1. Profit—the difference between total revenue and total cost—is shown in the last column of Table 9.3.1, and it is represented by the positive or negative distance between the total revenue and total cost curves in Figure 9.3.1. Profit is first negative, becomes positive, and is ultimately negative again. In Figure 9.3.1, the shaded areas denote the range of output over which profit is negative (a loss is incurred). It is clear from either the table or the figure that maximum profit is $7.50, achieved with an output of either seven or eight units.[1]

The total revenue-total cost approach is a useful one from some standpoints; however, it does not lead to an analytical interpretation of business behavior. To get at this, the familiar marginal approach must be adopted.

Short-Run Profit Maximization, the Marginal Approach
9.3.b

The definitions of marginal revenue and marginal cost are familiar from Chapters 5 and 8, respectively. Similarly, the method of calculating each has been learned. Applying these methods to the data in Table 9.3.1, we obtain the information in Table 9.3.2.

---

[1]The seeming indeterminacy of the rate of output is attributable to the discrete data used in this hypothetical example. If continuous data were used, it would be obvious that the profit-maximizing output is eight units per period of time. This is because the maximum distance separating the two curves occurs at the point where the tangents to the curves have the same slope. From the two tangents constructed in Figure 9.3.1, it is easily seen that the slopes are equal only at the output of eight units per period of time.

Table 9.3.1 Revenue, cost, and profit for a hypothetical firm

(1) Market price	(2) Rate of output and sales	(3) Total revenue	(4) Total fixed cost	(5) Total variable cost	(6) Total cost	(7) Profit
$5.00	1	$ 5.00	$15.00	$ 2.00	$17.00	−$12.00
5.00	2	10.00	15.00	3.50	18.50	− 8.50
5.00	3	15.00	15.00	4.50	19.50	− 4.50
5.00	4	20.00	15.00	5.75	20.75	− 0.75
5.00	5	25.00	15.00	7.25	22.25	+ 2.75
5.00	6	30.00	15.00	9.25	24.25	+ 5.75
5.00	7	35.00	15.00	12.50	27.50	+ 7.50
5.00	8	40.00	15.00	17.50	32.50	+ 7.50
5.00	9	45.00	15.00	25.50	40.50	+ 4.50
5.00	10	50.00	15.00	37.50	52.50	− 2.50

Figure 9.3.1 Profit maximization by the total revenue–total cost approach

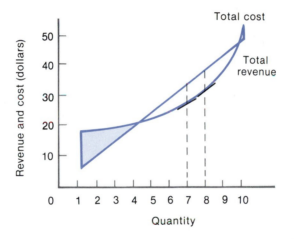

Columns 1 and 2 show the demand or marginal revenue curve, identical figures for the firm in a perfectly competitive market (as explained in Chapter 5). Column 3 contains the marginal cost figures, while average total or unit cost has been computed from column 6, Table 9.3.1, and entered in column 4. Unit profit, the difference between price and average total cost, is shown in column 5. Finally, total profit, the difference between total revenue and total cost, is contained in column 6.

As in the previous case, maximum profit corresponds to either seven or eight units of output and sales per period of time. Unit profit is a maximum at seven units of output, but this is immaterial inasmuch as the entrepreneur is concerned with total profit.

Table 9.3.2 Marginal revenue, marginal cost, and profit

(1) Output and sales	(2) Marginal revenue or price	(3) Marginal cost	(4) Average total cost	(5) Unit profit	(6) Total profit
1	$5.00	$ 2.00	$17.00	−$12.00	−$12.00
2	5.00	1.50	9.25	− 4.25	− 8.50
3	5.00	1.00	6.50	− 1.50	− 4.50
4	5.00	1.25	5.19	− 0.19	− 0.75
5	5.00	1.50	4.45	+ 0.55	+ 2.75
6	5.00	2.00	4.04	+ 0.96	+ 5.75
7	5.00	3.25	3.93	+ 1.07	+ 7.50
8	5.00	5.00	4.06	+ 0.94	+ 7.50
9	5.00	8.00	4.50	+ 0.50	+ 4.50
10	5.00	12.00	5.25	− 0.25	− 2.50

The data in Table 9.3.2 are plotted in Figure 9.3.2. The short-run equilibrium of the firm is clearly attained at point E, where marginal cost equals marginal revenue. Alternatively stated, since marginal revenue equals price for a perfectly competitive producer, short-run equilibrium occurs at the output point for which marginal cost equals price.

Proof of the Short-Run Equilibrium
9.3.c

To prove the proposition that a firm in perfect competition attains its profit-maximizing equilibrium at the rate of output for which marginal cost equals price, the hypothetical example of Figure 9.3.2 has been converted to the general representation in Figure 9.3.3. The theorem follows immediately from the definitions of marginal revenue and marginal cost.[2]

---

[2]Let $p = f(q)$ represent the inverse demand function. Hence $qf(q)$ is total revenue. Further, let $C = A + g(q)$ be the total cost function. Profit (π) is thus $\pi = qf(q) - A - g(q)$. Profit is a maximum when $d\pi/dq = 0$ and $d^2\pi/dq^2 < 0$. Taking the first derivative and equating with zero,

$$d\pi/dq = f(q) - g'(q) = 0 \qquad (9.3.1)$$

or

$$f(q) = g'(q), \qquad (9.3.2)$$

because $p = f(q)$ is a given constant. Marginal cost is $g'(q)$; see Chapter 8. Marginal revenue and price are both given by $f(q)$. Hence, equation (9.3.2) states that marginal revenue or price must equal marginal cost. This is the necessary condition for profit maximization. From equation (9.3.1) the second-order condition is that $d^2\pi/dq^2 = -g''(q) < 0$, or

$$g''(q) > 0. \qquad (9.3.3)$$

Hence, stability of equilibrium, by inequality (9.3.3), requires a *positively sloped* marginal cost curve.

Figure 9.3.2 Profit maximization by the marginal approach

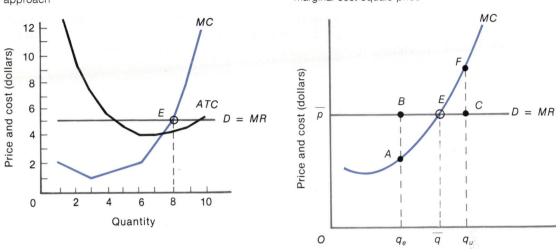

Figure 9.3.3 Short-run equilibrium at point where marginal cost equals price

Marginal revenue is the addition to total revenue attributable to the addition of one unit of sales, while marginal cost is the addition to total cost resulting from the addition of one unit to output. Thus it should be evident that profit increases when marginal revenue exceeds marginal cost and diminishes when marginal cost exceeds marginal revenue. Profit must, therefore, attain its maximum when marginal revenue and marginal cost are equal.

Consider Figure 9.3.3. The fundamental proposition is that at market price $O\overline{p}$, the firm attains a profit-maximizing equilibrium at point E, corresponding to the output of $O\overline{q}$ units per period of time. If the rate of output were less than $O\overline{q}$, say Oq_e, marginal revenue q_eB would exceed marginal cost q_eA. Adding a unit to output and sales would increase total revenue by more than total cost. Profit would accordingly increase, and it would continue to increase so long as marginal revenue exceeds marginal cost.

On the other hand, suppose the rate of output exceeded $O\overline{q}$ — say Oq_u. At this point, marginal cost q_uF exceeds marginal revenue q_uC. This unit of output causes total cost to increase by more than total revenue, thereby reducing profit (or increasing loss). As is evident from the graph, profit must be reduced by adding a unit of output and sales whenever marginal cost exceeds marginal revenue.

Therefore, since profit increases when marginal revenue exceeds marginal cost and declines when marginal revenue is less than marginal cost, it must be a maximum when the two are equal. Furthermore, since price equals marginal revenue for a firm in perfect competition, the following theorem has been proved.

Proposition: A firm in a perfectly competitive industry attains its short-run, profit-maximizing equilibrium by producing the rate of output for which marginal cost equals the given, fixed market price of the commodity.

Profit or Loss?
9.3.d

The equality of price and marginal cost guarantees either that profit is a maximum or that loss is a minimum. Whether a profit is made or a loss is incurred can be determined only by comparing total revenue to total cost. Since

$$\text{Profit} = \text{Total revenue} - \text{Total cost},$$

a loss is incurred whenever

$$\text{Total revenue} < \text{Total cost}.$$

Now,

$$TR = (p)(q)$$

and

$$AC = TC/q.$$

So profit is positive if

$$TR > TC$$

or if

$$(p)(q) > (AC)(q)$$

or if

$$p > AC.$$

So, if price exceeds unit cost, the firm will enjoy a profit in the short run. On the other hand, if unit cost exceeds price, a loss must be incurred.

Figure 9.3.4 illustrates this. MC and ATC represent marginal cost and average total cost, respectively. First, suppose short-run market equilibrium establishes the price Op_1 per unit. The demand and marginal revenue curves for the firm are, therefore, given by the horizontal line labeled $D_1 = MR_1$. Short-run equilibrium is attained when output is Oq_1 units per period of time. At this rate of output, total revenue (price times quantity) is given by the area of the rectangle $Oq_1 Cp_1$. Similarly, total cost (unit cost times quantity) is the area of $Oq_1 EF$. Total revenue exceeds total cost, and profit is represented by the area of the rectangle $CEFp_1$.

On the other hand, suppose the market price–quantity equilibrium established the price Op_2. In that case the optimum rate of output would be Oq_2 units per period of time. Total revenue is the area of $Oq_2 Bp_2$, while total cost is $Oq_2 AG$. Since total cost exceeds total revenue, a loss is incurred in the amount represented by the area of $p_2 BAG$.

When demand is $D_2 = MR_2$ there is no way the firm can earn a profit. If output were either smaller or greater than Oq_2 units per period of time, the loss would simply be greater. One might therefore ask why the firm does not go out of business since a loss is incurred at any rate of output.

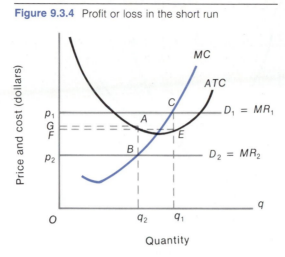

Figure 9.3.4 Profit or loss in the short run

Short-Run Supply Curve of a Firm in a Perfectly Competitive Industry 9.3.e

The basic answer to this question is that a firm incurring a loss will continue to produce in the short run if, and only if, it loses less by producing than by closing the plant entirely. As you will recall from Chapter 8, there are two types of costs in the short run: fixed costs and variable costs. The fixed costs cannot be changed and are incurred whether the plant is operated or not. Fixed costs, that is, are the same at zero output as at any other. These costs are already sunk. For example, once the lease on a plant has been signed, there is little that can be done about the rent until the lease is up. As such, the rent is a sunk cost and must be borne, independent of output.

So long as total revenue exceeds the total variable cost of producing the equilibrium output, a smaller loss is suffered when production takes place. Figure 9.3.5 is a graphical demonstration of this.

As previously explained, the business decision regarding production in the short run is not affected by fixed costs. Therefore, only the average total cost, average variable cost, and marginal cost curves are shown in Figure 9.3.5. Since our discussion involves only a loss situation, the price lines are constructed so as to lie entirely beneath the average total cost curve. First, suppose market price is Op_1, so the firm's demand–marginal revenue curve is given by $D_1 = MR_1$. Profit maximization (or loss minimization) leads to producing the output for which marginal cost equals price — production occurs at point B, or at the rate of Oq_1 units per period of time. At this rate of output the firm loses AB dollars per unit produced. However, at the price Op_1 average variable cost is not only covered but there is an excess of BC dollars per unit. The average cost of the variable inputs is $q_1 C$ dollars per unit of output. The price obtained per unit is $q_1 B$. The excess of price over average variable cost, BC, can be applied to the fixed costs. Thus

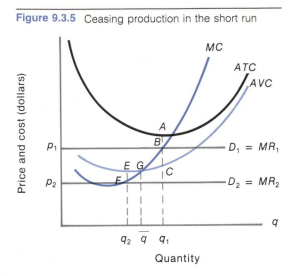

Figure 9.3.5 Ceasing production in the short run

not all of the fixed costs are lost, as would be the case if production were discontinued. Although a loss is sustained, it is smaller than the loss associated with zero output.

This is not always the case, however. Suppose market price were as low as Op_2, so that demand is given by $D_2 = MR_2$. If the firm produced at all, its equilibrium output would be Oq_2 units per period of time. Here, however, the average variable cost of production exceeds price. The firm producing at this point would not only lose its fixed costs, it would lose EF dollars per unit on its variable costs as well. Thus when price is below average variable cost, the short-run equilibrium output is zero.

As shown in Chapter 8, average variable cost reaches its minimum at the point where marginal cost and average variable cost intersect—point G in Figure 9.3.5. If price is less than $\overline{q}G$ dollars per unit, equilibrium output is determined by the intersection of marginal cost and the price line.

Using the proposition just discussed, it is possible to derive the short-run supply curve of an individual firm in a perfectly competitive market.[3] The process is illustrated in Figure 9.3.6. Panel A of the figure shows the marginal cost curve of a firm for rates of output greater than that associated with minimum average variable cost. Suppose market price is Op_1. The corresponding equilibrium rate of output is Oq_1. Now on Panel B find the point associated with the coordinates Op_1, Oq_1. Label this point S_1; it represents the quantity supplied at price Op_1.

Next, suppose price is Op_2. The equilibrium output is Oq_2. Plot the point associated with the coordinates Op_2, Oq_2 on Panel B—it is labeled S_2. Similarly, other equilibrium quantities supplied can be determined by postulating other

---

[3]An application of this principle is given in the article, "Airline Takes the Marginal Route" in the "Applying the Theory" section at the beginning of this chapter. Refer to its questions to test your understanding.

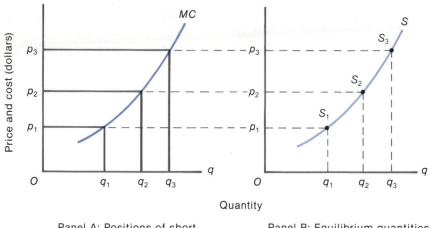

Figure 9.3.6 Derivation of the short-run supply curve of an individual producer in perfect competition

Panel A: Positions of short-run equilibria of firm

Panel B: Equilibrium quantities supplied by the firm

market prices (for example, price Op_3 leads to output Oq_3 and point S_3 on Panel B). Connecting all of the S points so generated, one obtains the short-run supply curve of the firm, the curve labeled S in Panel B. But by construction, the S curve is precisely the same as the MC curve. The following is therefore established:

Proposition: The short-run supply curve of a firm in perfect competition is precisely its marginal cost curve for all rates of output equal to or greater than the rate of output associated with minimum average variable cost. For market prices lower than minimum average variable cost, equilibrium quantity supplied is zero.

SHORT-RUN EQUILIBRIUM IN A PERFECTLY COMPETITIVE INDUSTRY
9.4

At this point it is useful to understand how individual firms' supply curves aggregate in the short run to produce an industry supply curve.

The Short-Run Industry Supply Curve
9.4.a

To make matters simple, let us suppose that there exist 100 identical firms in the industry, each with cost curves as shown in Figure 9.4.1, Panel A.

Recall that the supply curve for each of the 100 firms is merely the part of the marginal cost curve that lies above the (minimum of the) average variable cost

NUMERICAL EXERCISE

A perfectly competitive firm is faced with the following total cost schedule:

Q	0	1	2	3	4	5	6	7	8	9	10
TC	9	20	30	39	47	54	60	67	77	90	109

Questions

1. If the market price is $13, what output will the firm choose to produce to maximize profits? What is the maximum profit?
2. Suppose the market price falls to $6. How much will the firm choose to produce now and what will be its profit?
3. Graph the firm's MC and AVC curves. Show the firm's supply curve in the short run. How did you derive it?

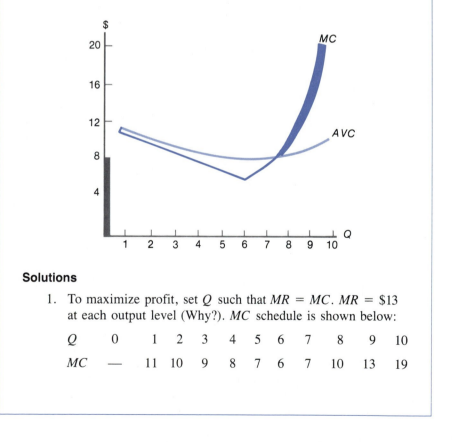

Solutions

1. To maximize profit, set Q such that $MR = MC$. $MR = $13 at each output level (Why?). MC schedule is shown below:

Q	0	1	2	3	4	5	6	7	8	9	10
MC	—	11	10	9	8	7	6	7	10	13	19

Profit is maximized at Q such that $MR = MC$. Since $MR = \$13$ everywhere, MC will produce 9 units.

$$\pi = TR - TC = (13 \times 9) - 90 = 117 - 90 = 27.$$

Maximum profit is $27.

2. Again, since the firm is in a perfectly competitive industry, $MR = P = 6$. Setting $MR = MC$, we find that profit is maximized where $MC = \$6$, or at an output of 6 units. However, when we calculate profit, we find:

$$\pi = TR - TC = (P \times Q) - TC = (6 \times 6) - 60$$
$$= 36 - 60 = -24.$$

That is, the firm suffers a loss of $24. However, if the firm shuts down and produces nothing, it will incur a total cost of $9 and earn no revenue, and thus suffer a loss of $9. Therefore, the firm will choose to produce nothing and lose $9 (rather than produce 6 units and lose $24.)

3. The darkly shaded curves are the firm's supply curve. For any P, a competitive firm has $MR = P$, so $MR = MC$ is satisfied for P, Q combinations represented by the rising portion of the MC curve. However, if $P < AVC$, the firm's revenues (TR) do not cover variable costs: as a result, the firm would lose more than its fixed costs by producing where $P < AVC$. It therefore will produce no output where $P < AVC$, or where $MC[=P] < AVC$, (which is the same thing). Thus, the supply curve is the same as the MC curve above the AVC curve, and $Q = 0$ for any lower price.

curve. For example, if the price were 2, each firm would supply 10 units; if it were 4, each would supply 15 units.

It follows immediately that the amount supplied by the entire industry at a price of 2 is 1,000 units (10 per firm × 100 firms) and that the amount supplied at a price of 4 is 1,500 units. This is shown in Panel B by points on the ΣMC curve. (The Σ is used to denote the summation across all of the 100 firms.)

Given that industry supply curve, it is a simple matter to calculate industry price and quantity. If the demand for the good by the entire market is given by D in Panel B, then the equilibrium price and quantity are derived as always: Equilibrium is at the intersection of market supply and market demand. This occurs at point A, where the quantity is 1,500 and the price is 4.

Figure 9 4.1 Output choice

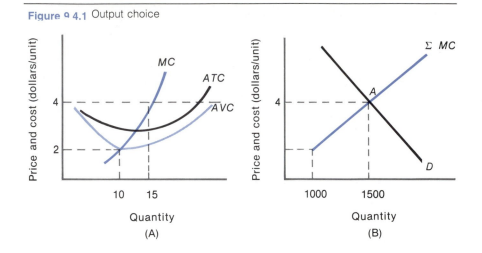

Obviously, this equilibrium must be consistent with the individual firms' supply curves, because the market supply curve was derived from those curves. Specifically, if the market price is 4, consumers demand 1,500 units. At a price of 4, each of the 100 firms would like to produce 15 units so that market supply is 1,500. Supply equals demand and a short-run equilibrium has been found.

Firms need not be identical. The analysis is the same when they are not; we sum the individual firms' managerial cost curves to obtain the industry supply curve.

LONG-RUN EQUILIBRIUM IN A PERFECTLY COMPETITIVE MARKET
9.5

Since all inputs are variable in the long run, an entrepreneur has the option of adjusting plant size, as well as output, to achieve maximum profit. In the limit, the business can be liquidated entirely by transferring its resources into a more profitable investment alternative. But just as established firms may leave the industry, new firms may enter the industry if profit prospects are brighter there than elsewhere. Indeed, adjustment of the number of firms in the industry in response to profit motivation is the key element in establishing long-run equilibrium.

Entry and Exit of Firms from the Industry
9.5.a

For the moment, let us ignore the possibility of different plant sizes. Assume instead that there is only one possible technology represented by the cost curves shown in Figure 9.5.1, Panel A.

Part Three   Theory of the Firm and Market Organization

Figure 9.5.1 Equilibrium price

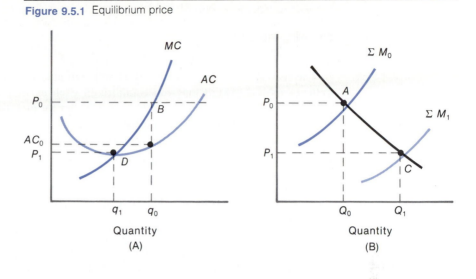

Again, suppose that at the outset there are 100 identical firms. This implies that the industry supply curve is 100 times the supply curve of each firm, shown as ΣMC_0 in Panel B. The market equilibrium is at Q_0 (= $100 \times q_0$) shown by point A.

Although this is a short-run equilibrium, it cannot be a long-run equilibrium. The reason is that profits are being made by each of the firms in the industry. We can see this directly in Panel A because P_0 lies above AC_0, so total revenue exceeds total cost.

This profit induces other firms to enter the industry. Each time a new firm enters with the same cost curve, the industry supply curve shifts rightward. This is because now we have to sum over, say, 101 individual firm supply curves rather than only over the initial 100. Firms continue to enter the industry until the ΣMC curve shifts to ΣMC_1. At that point, the equilibrium point has fallen to P_1 and the equilibrium market quantity is Q_1 shown at point C.

Each firm in the industry now elects to supply q_1 of output and locates at point D in Panel A. There are a number of interesting features that warrant discussion.

First, this is a long-run equilibrium because the level of economic profit in the industry is zero. (Recall that zero economic profit does not imply that the entrepreneur and capital do not earn their return. It merely requires that they earn no more here than would be available elsewhere.) No firms have an incentive to enter and none has an incentive to leave. Each is content to produce q_1 units and the total for the industry is Q_1, so supply equals demand. The difference between the long-run equilibrium and the short-run equilibrium is that although supply equals demand in both cases, long-run equilibrium is defined as that situation when supply equals demand and economic profits are exactly zero.

Long-Run Equilibrium: An industry is said to be in long-run equilibrium when two conditions hold: market supply equals market demand and all firms which are using the lowest cost technology earn zero economic profits.

The second interesting feature is that although industry output went up as the industry moved toward long-run equilibrium, each existing firm's output fell. (That is, $Q_1 > Q_0$, but $q_1 < q_0$.) This comes about for two reasons: First, industry output rises because more firms have entered the industry. But the reduction in price brought about by the additional supply makes each of the firms less willing to supply large quantities. So each firm cuts back somewhat, but the total output expands. How do we know that the expansion effect swamps the per-firm contraction? It is clear because the contrary results in a contradiction. If the cutback per firm were more important than the increase in the number of firms, then the total supply to the industry would fall. But if that were true, price would have to rise, because the demand curve has negative slope. However, if price rises, no firm wants to cut back output at all. With each firm expanding output and the number of firms increasing, total industry supply must rise, which implies a fall in price. This contradiction implies that the reverse must be true, namely that each firm reduces output, but that industry output rises.

Exercise: Suppose that the short-run equilibrium had firms taking losses. Trace the movement to a new long-run equilibrium and discuss changes in price, quantities, profits, and the number of firms in the industry.

Choice of Optimal Plant Size in the Long Run
9.5.b

In the long run, an entrepreneur adjusts plant size and rate of output to attain maximum profit. The adjustment process is illustrated in Figure 9.5.2.

Let market price be $O\overline{P}$ and suppose the firm has a plant whose costs are represented by SAC_1 and SMC_1 (short-run average total cost and marginal cost, respectively). With this plant, short-run equilibrium is reached at point A, corresponding to output of Oq_1 units per period of time. At this point the firm sustains a small loss on each unit of output produced and sold.

In looking to the long run, or the planning horizon, the entrepreneur has two options: go out of business or construct a plant of more suitable size. For example, the entrepreneur could decide upon the plant size represented by SAC_2 and SMC_2. At price $O\overline{P}$, the firm would produce Oq_2 units per period of time and make a pure profit of BC dollars per unit. However, with perfect knowledge, the plant represented by SAC_4 and SMC_4 would be constructed.

Although this adjustment occurs, point E cannot represent a long-run equilibrium because positive profits are being made ($\overline{P} > SAC_4$ at q_4). In the long run, it must be true that optimal plant size is selected and that profit equals zero.

Figure 9.5.2 Long-run adjustment of plant size

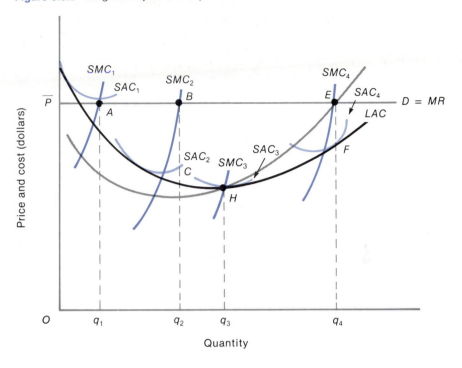

The equilibrium must be such that each firm selects the plant that corresponds to SAC_3 and produces at point H. There zero profit is attained and no change in plant structure can increase profitability.[4]

The process of *long-run equilibrium adjustment* is illustrated by Figure 9.5.3. Suppose each firm in the industry is identical. The original size is represented by SAC_1 and SMC_1 in Panel A. The market demand curve is given by DD' in Panel B, and the market supply is $S_1 S_1'$. Market equilibrium establishes the price of OP_1 dollars per unit and total output and sales of OQ_1 units per period of time. At price OP_1 each firm attains a point of short-run equilibrium where SMC_1 equals price. Each firm produces Oq_1 units per period of time and reaps a pure economic profit of AB dollars per unit. As Panel A is constructed, this position could be one of long-run equilibrium inasmuch as marginal cost equals price at this point.

From the standpoint of the market as a whole, however, the present situation is not stable. Each firm in the industry enjoys a pure economic profit — a rate of return on invested resources greater than could be earned in any alternative

---

[4]This assumes that q_3 is small relative to the total quantity sold on the market. If it is not, then the situation becomes more complex. In most competitive industries, q_3 is small relative to market supply.

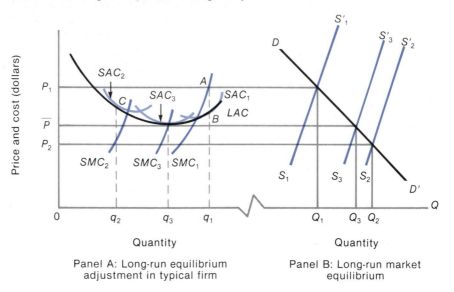

Figure 9.5.3 Long-run equilibrium through entry and exit

Panel A: Long-run equilibrium
adjustment in typical firm

Panel B: Long-run market
equilibrium

employment. Therefore, in the long run some firms in less profitable industries will switch to the industry in question because a greater profit can be earned there.

The process of new entry might be very slow, or it might be very fast; this depends primarily upon the liquid assets in other industries. In any event, as time elapses, new firms will enter the industry, thereby shifting the industry supply curve to the right. Suppose, indeed, the profit attraction is so strong that a substantial number of new firms enters the industry, shifting the industry supply curve to $S_2 S_2'$ in Panel B. In this situation equilibrium quantity will expand to OQ_2.

The long-run equilibrium of a firm in a perfectly competitive industry is explained by means of Figure 9.5.3. If price is above the level $O\overline{P}$, each established firm in the industry earns a pure profit. New firms are attracted into the industry, shifting the market supply curve to the right. Market equilibrium price declines, and the horizontal demand curve confronting each firm falls to a lower level. On the other hand, if price is below $O\overline{P}$, each firm in the industry incurs a pure economic loss. As their plants and equipment depreciate, some firms will leave the industry, thereby causing the market supply curve to shift to the left. Market price, and, accordingly, the horizontal individual demand curves rise.

The point of long-run equilibrium occurs at point H in Figure 9.5.2. There firms in the industry receive neither pure profit nor pure loss.

The position of long-run equilibrium is actually determined by the horizontal demand curve confronting each firm. Since the industry is perfectly competitive by assumption, firms will enter or leave the industry if there is either pure profit or pure loss. Therefore, since the position of long-run equilibrium must be consistent with *zero* profit (and zero loss), it is necessary that price equal average total cost. For a firm to attain its individual equilibrium, price must be equal to marginal cost. Therefore, price must equal both marginal and average total cost. This can only occur at the point where average total cost and marginal cost are equal, or at the point of minimum average total cost.

The statement, so far, could conceivably apply to any SAC and SMC. However, unless it applies *only* to the short-run plant that coincides with minimum long-run average cost, a change in the plant size would lead to the appearance of pure profit, and the wheels of adjustment would be set in motion again. These arguments establish the following:

Proposition: Long-run equilibrium for a firm in perfect competition occurs at the point where price equals minimum long-run average cost. At this point minimum short-run average total cost equals minimum long-run average total cost, and the short- and long-run marginal costs are equal. The position of long-run equilibrium is characterized by a "no profit" situation — the firms have neither a pure profit nor a pure loss, only an accounting profit equal to the rate of return obtainable in other perfectly competitive industries.

Input Prices
9.5.c

The previous analysis was based upon the tacit assumption of constant input prices, in the sense that expanded resource usage does not entail an increase in resource prices. To see the implications of this assumption, consider Figure 9.5.4.

Panel A shows the long- and short-run conditions of a typical firm in the industry, while Panel B depicts the market as a whole. $D_1 D_1'$ and $S_1 S_1'$ are the original market demand and supply curves, establishing a market equilibrium price of $\overline{OP}$ dollars per unit. Assume that the industry has attained a position of long-run equilibrium, so the position of each firm in the industry is depicted by Panel A — the price line is tangent to the long- and short-run average total cost curves at their minimum points.

Now suppose demand increases to $D_2 D_2'$. With the number of firms fixed, the price will rise to OP' and each firm will move to equilibrium at point A. However, at point A each firm earns a pure economic profit, thereby attracting new entrants into the industry and shifting the industry supply curve to the right. In this case we assume that all resources used in the industry are *unspecialized*; so increased usage does not affect the market price of the resources. As a consequence, the entrance of new firms does not increase the costs of existing firms; the *LAC* curve of established firms does not shift and new firms can operate with an identical *LAC* curve. Long-run equilibrium adjustment to the shift in demand is accomplished when the number of firms expands to the point at which $S_2 S_2'$ is the industry supply curve.

In other words, since output can be expanded by *expanding the number of firms* producing $\overline{Oq}$ units per period of time at average cost $\overline{OP}$, the industry has a *constant long-run supply price* equal to $\overline{OP}$ dollars per unit. If price were above

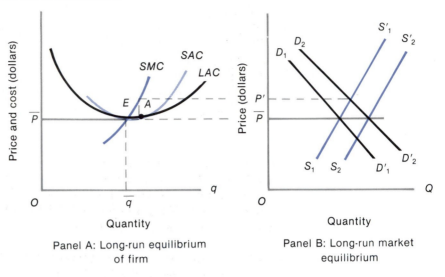

Figure 9.5.4 Long-run equilibrium and supply price in a perfectly competitive industry subject to constant cost

Panel A: Long-run equilibrium of firm

Panel B: Long-run market equilibrium

this level, firms of size represented by *SAC* would continue to enter the industry in order to reap the pure profit obtainable. If price were less than $O\overline{P}$, some firms would ultimately leave the industry to avoid the pure economic loss. Hence in the special case in which an expansion of resource usage does not lead to an increase in resource price, the long-run industry supply price is constant.

Let us now summarize and emphasize. First, we need the following:

Long-Run Supply Price: The long-run industry supply price shows for each level of output the *minimum* price required to induce this industry output after (a) each firm in the industry has made the optimal internal adjustment and (b) the number of firms in the industry has, by entry or exit, been optimally adjusted.

Exercise: What are the precise relations and analogies between long-run supply price for a perfectly competitive industry and long-run average cost for a perfectly competitive firm?

Long-run industry supply price will be constant if, and only if, the industry output can be expanded or contracted by expanding and contracting the number of firms without affecting minimum long-run average cost. This condition, in turn, will exist if, and only if, all resources used by the industry are unspecialized — which means that the prices the firms must pay for all resources do not change with the level of resource use. To put it another way, the supply curve of each resource used in the industry must be perfectly elastic so far as the firms in *that* industry are concerned. This means that the industry *as a whole* must be a perfect competitor in each resource market — the industry must have a position vis-à-vis each resource market that is exactly like the position of a consumer vis-à-vis each commodity market.

In Chapters 6 and 7 there was a discussion of "returns to scale," and in Chapter 8 this was related to the shape of a firm's long-run average cost curve. The relations merit further comment. First, suppose all resource prices are constant. If the firm's production function first shows increasing and then decreasing returns to scale, its long-run average cost curve will have a ∪ shape; *but* the long-run industry supply price will be constant because resource prices are constant (the number of firms producing at minimum *LAC* can be changed without affecting the *LAC* of any firm). On the other hand, if the production function exhibits constant returns to scale, the long-run average cost curve will rise if resource prices vary directly with resource usage. As we will now see, industry supply price also rises in this case. Before reading further, however, think through the *important* exercise that follows.[5]

Exercise: Suppose all resource prices are constant and that the production function of each firm in an industry exhibits constant returns to scale. Samuelson (*Foundations*, pp. 79–80) refers to this as the "indeterminacy of purest competition." Explain the meaning of this phrase.

Industries with Increasing Input Prices
9.5.d

Increasing cost or increasing industry supply price is depicted by Figure 9.5.5. The original situation is the same as in Figure 9.5.4. The industry is in a position of long-run equilibrium. $D_1 D_1'$ and $S_1 S_1'$ are the market demand and supply curves, respectively. Equilibrium price is OP_1. Each firm operates at point E_1, where price equals minimum average cost, both long- and short-run cost. Thus each firm is also in a position of long-run equilibrium.

---

[5]The text discusses changes in input prices resulting from changes in industry-wide demand for factors of production. Because this is a pecuniary (price) phenomenon and results from the external impact of the combined effect of all firms, it is often called a *pecuniary externality*. It is also possible that changes in the level of industry output can change the production technology available to individual firms. When this happens, it is called a technological externality. For example, if all clothiers locate on the same street, congestion results, which increases the cost of delivering products to consumers.

The general term *constant cost industry* is used to describe an industry which has neither pecuniary nor technological externalities. This means that the cost curves of individual firms are unaffected by the level of industry output. If the cost curves of individual firms shift upward as a result of an expansion of the total output of the industry (i.e., there are either pecuniary or technological externalities), the industry is said to be an *increasing cost industry*. Sometimes the externalities can be positive; that is, the cost curves of firms shift down as a result of increased industry output. This is called a *decreasing cost industry*.

Note that these terms refer to externalities and are not the same as constant, increasing or decreasing, returns to scale discussed in Chapter 8.

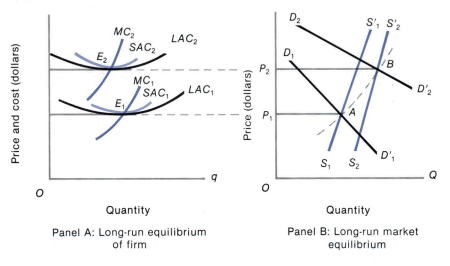

Panel A: Long-run equilibrium
of firm

Panel B: Long-run market
equilibrium

Let demand shift to $D_2 D_2'$, so price instantaneously rises to a much higher level. The higher price is accompanied by pure economic profit; new firms are consequently attracted into the industry. The usages of resources expands and now, we assume, resource prices expand with resource usage. The cost of inputs therefore increases for the established firms as well as for the new entrants. As a result the entire set of cost curves shifts upward, say to a position represented by LAC_2 in Panel A.

Naturally, the process of equilibrium adjustment is not instantaneous. The *LAC* curve gradually shifts upward as new entrants gradually join the industry. The marginal cost curve of each firm shifts to the left, thereby tending to shift the industry supply curve to the left. However, more firms are producing and this tends to shift industry supply to the right. The latter tendency must dominate, for otherwise new firms would have obtained resources *only* by bidding them away from established firms in the industry. Total output could not expand as dictated by the increase in market price. New resource units must have entered the industry, so the supply curve shifts to the right, though not by as much as it would in a constant–input price industry.

The process of adjustment must continue until a position of full long-run equilibrium is attained. In Figure 9.5.5 this is depicted by the intersection of $D_2 D_2'$ and $S_2 S_2'$, establishing an equilibrium price of OP_2 dollars per unit. Each firm produces at point E_2, where price equals minimum average total cost. The important point to emphasize is that for industries subject to increasing long-run supply price, new firms enter until minimum long-run average cost shifts upward to equal the new price. The number of firms and the industry output increase. However, there is no way to predict what will happen to the equilibrium output per firm. It may decrease, as shown in Figure 9.5.5, or it may remain constant or increase. But these items are certain: industry output, the number of firms, and long-run supply price will all increase.

Relations: The long-run supply curve for an industry with constant input prices is a horizontal line at the level of the constant long-run supply price (i.e., the minimum of the long-run average cost curve). The long-run supply curve for an industry with increasing input prices is positively sloped, and the long-run supply price increases as the long-run equilibrium quantity supplied expands.

THE COMPETITIVE MODEL IN PRACTICE: DEMAND-SUPPLY ANALYSIS
9.6

The analysis of market equilibrium is simple, but it is not simple-minded. Indeed, this type of analysis offers significant qualitative, if not quantitative, insight into the function of real-world markets. Let us consider an example.

Suppose that the demand for coal at the retail level is elastic over the relevant price range. Further, suppose the government feels that the price of coal is too high. It therefore places a price ceiling or maximum on coal at the mine. What will happen to the price of coal at the retail level? Will total receipts of retailers increase or decrease?

As a first step consider what happens at the mine (or mining area). Assume for analytical purposes that coal mining is a perfectly competitive industry, with increasing input prices. Assume also that before the imposition of the ceiling price, the industry was in equilibrium; each firm produced the quantity at which $P = LAC$ and therefore enjoyed no pure profit. Figure 9.6.1 shows the market demand and supply for coal at the mine. Demand $(D_m D_m')$ is the demand curve of retailers for coal at the mine. It is derived holding the demand for coal from retailers and other factors constant (we assume that individual consumers cannot purchase coal directly from the mine).

The long-run industry supply curve is $S_m S_m'$ It is the locus of long-run equilibria for the mining industry. Since we assume increasing input prices, $S_m S_m'$ is upward sloping. The equilibrium price at the mine is OW_c and equilibrium quantity is OQ_C.

Figure 9.6.2 shows demand and supply conditions at the retail level. $D_r D_r'$ is the consumers' demand for coal. $S_r S_r'$, based upon a given cost of coal at the mines to retailers (OW_c) the retailers' supply curve. Since coal is an input for the retailers, the supply curve for coal at retail should shift when the price of coal at the mine changes, just as a change in the price of any factor of production changes the supply of the product produced. Specifically, when the price at the mine falls, other things remaining the same, the retail supply curve should shift to the right. That is, if retailers can buy coal cheaper, they would be willing and able to supply more retail coal at every retail price. Equilibrium in the retail market occurs at

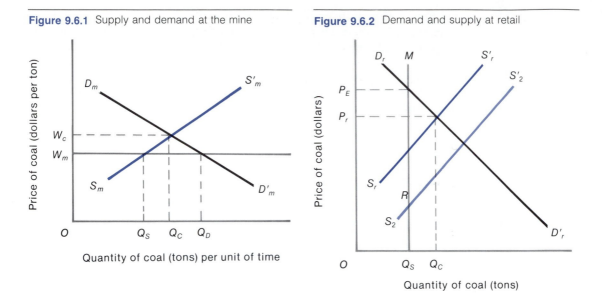

Figure 9.6.1 Supply and demand at the mine

Price of coal (dollars per ton)

D_m, S'_m, W_c, W_m, S_m, D'_m

O Q_S Q_C Q_D

Quantity of coal (tons) per unit of time

Figure 9.6.2 Demand and supply at retail

Price of coal (dollars)

D_r, M, S'_r, S'_2, P_E, P_r, S_r, R, S_2, D'_r

O Q_S Q_C

Quantity of coal (tons)

a price of OP_r (given a price at the mine of OW_c) and a quantity sold of OQ_c, obviously the same as OQ_C in Figure 9.6.1, because the retailers sell all that they buy.

Returning to Figure 9.6.1, assume that the government sets the ceiling price OW_m. Quantity demanded by retailers at the new price is OQ_D. The new price is below OW_c (the price at which neither profit nor loss occurs); thus firms begin to make losses and some leave the industry. Since we assume that mining faces increasing input prices, the exit of firms and the decrease in quantity produced lowers factor prices and hence lowers the long-run average and marginal cost curves of the remaining firms in the industry. Figure 9.6.3 shows the process. Long-run average and marginal costs fall from LAC_1 and MC_1 to LAC_2 and MC_2. The minimum point on LAC_2 equals the ceiling price OW_m. Each remaining firm now produces Oq_m (the new equilibrium output) rather than Oq_c, but there are fewer firms, none of which makes pure profit. The new quantity supplied by the industry, indicated in Figure 9.6.1, is OQ_S. Thus a shortage (excess demand) of $Q_S Q_D$ occurs at the mines, since retailers now wish to purchase OQ_D but the mines are only willing to sell OQ_S. The mining industry must find some method of allocation (rationing, first come–first served, favoritism, and so on) in order to determine which retailers get the available supply. In any case, only OQ_S is available to the retailers.

Now, according to our analysis the lower price of coal at the mine should cause supply at the retail to shift to $S_2 S'_2$ (Figure 9.6.2). Retail price should fall, and the quantity of coal sold should increase as determined by the intersection of $D_r D'_r$ and $S_2 S'_2$. But remember that only OQ_S is produced, so only OQ_S can be sold. The curve $S_2 S'_2$ specifies the quantities that retailers are *willing* to sell at the mine price of OW_m; the vertical line MQ_S indicates the maximum amount retailers

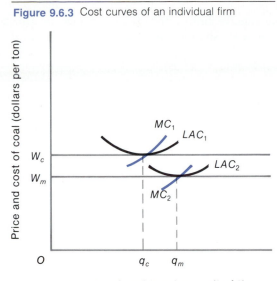

Figure 9.6.3 Cost curves of an individual firm

Price and cost of coal (dollars per ton)

W_c

W_m

MC_1

LAC_1

LAC_2

MC_2

O q_c q_m

Quantity of coal (tons) per unit of time

are *able* to sell at that price. Therefore, the curve $S_2 RM$ shows the quantities that retailers are *willing and able* to sell at each retail price when the mine price is fixed at OW_m.

The intersection of supply and demand now occurs at the price OP_E, clearly higher than the old price. The quantity sold is OQ_S. After the ceiling price at the mine is imposed, consumers pay a higher price for less coal. Since demand was assumed to be elastic, retailers receive less total revenue.

We noted above that despite the abstract and apparently unrealistic assumptions underlying the model of perfect competition, this model has proved very useful in predicting and explaining real world phenomena. For example, according to the theory, policies that restrict entry into industries can be expected to lead to persistent economic profits for those firms that are lucky enough to be in the industry. Taxicabs are licensed in many cities such as Chicago and New York. The number of taxicabs licensed tends to remain constant for long periods of time, and it is possible to enter the industry only by purchasing a license or "medallion" from someone who currently owns one. It follows that the price of the medallion should represent the value of the economic profits arising from restricted entry. The price of a medallion in Chicago was about $30,000 in 1978.[6]

In Chapter 11 we consider in some detail the effects of taxes, price ceilings, and other government policies using the apparatus developed in this chapter and in Chapter 10. In the "Applying the Theory" section which follows, we ask you

---

[6]When the price of the medallion is included in costs, the taxis earn only a competitive rate of return. The gain accrues solely to those people who were lucky enough to be given a medallion in the initial distribution of medallions.

to use graphs similar to those in this chapter to analyze how the mink industry (and representative firm) responds to a change in demand to changing input prices, both in the short run and long run.

CONCLUSION
9.7

Up to this point the salient feature of perfect competition is that in long-run market equilibrium, market price equals minimum average total cost. This means that each unit of output is produced at the lowest possible cost, either from the standpoint of money cost or of resource usage. The product sells for its average (long-run) cost of production; each firm accordingly earns the "going" rate of return in competitive industries, nothing more or less.

But so far we have seen only one side of perfect competition — the operation of firms within a perfectly competitive industry. The pricing of productive services under conditions of perfect competition is also an important feature, as is the question of general economic welfare in a perfectly competitive economy. While all of these studies are based upon a highly stylized set of assumptions, they ultimately provide criteria by which to evaluate actual market operation and practice.

SYNOPSIS
9.8

- *Perfect competition* is the term used by economists to describe a market situation where: (*a*) demanders and suppliers each treat price as given — they act as price takers in the market; (*b*) products of sellers are homogeneous, so that the product of one seller is identical with that of any other seller; (*c*) all resources are perfectly mobile and can readily move in or out of the market in response to pecuniary signals; and (*d*) consumers, producers, and resource owners possess complete and perfect knowledge. These assumptions are obviously unrealistic and no market ever has been observed to meet every one of the above conditions. Nonetheless, the model is often used by economists because the conclusions derived from the model have, by and large, permitted accurate explanation and prediction of real-world phenomena.
- When the firm operates in the short run in a competitive industry, it takes price as given and chooses output to equate price and marginal cost. At this output short-run profits are maximized (or losses minimized). If, at the output where price equals marginal cost, total revenue is less than total variable cost, the firm would produce nothing and experience a (minimum) short-run loss equal to fixed costs.

Mink Farming Is Growing More Scarce as Costs Rise and Fur Demand Declines

By Michael L. Geczi
Staff Reporter of *The Wall Street Journal*

NEW YORK—Mink farms could well be on the endangered-species list.

The animals themselves never have reached an endangered status, but the number of U.S. farms raising the small mammals for their pelts has decreased sharply in recent years. In the industry's peak year, 1966, about 6,000 mink farms were operating in the United States. Today, there are 1,221 according to the U.S. Agriculture Department.

Despite slight increases the past two years, total pelt production last year was 3.1 million, or half of the record 6.2 million pelts produced in 1966. Annual sales at the auction level, where most pelts are sold, were about $54 million in 1974, according to one estimate, down from more than $120 million in the mid-1960s.

The smaller operations have been the hardest hit. "The mom and pop outfits and the part-timers were the ones that folded," says an Agriculture Department official. "The bigger farms have kept operating."

Some industry officials say a profitable mink farm of any size is rare. "We've been in dire straits for the past four or five years," says Robert Langenfeld, president of Associated Fur Farms Inc., New Holstein, Wis., one of the nation's largest mink farms.

[A]

The industry's descent has been as rapid as its rise in the 1950s and 1960s, during which time mink grew in popularity as a fashionable status symbol. Growth was aided by the development of new colors (there are currently 13). As producers' feed and labor costs remained relatively stable in the face of strong demand, more people entered the industry.

Unsold Inventories

Growth proved to be too rapid, however; large unsold inventories from the record 1966 crop caused a price bust in 1967, and

[B]

the situation has worsened since. Feed and labor costs have climbed rapidly. Competition from less-expensive foreign pelts has heightened.

Perhaps most important, mink has lost much of its prestige. Industry officials say the desire to wear a mink coat has in many instances given way to ecological concerns. Cries from conservationists "caused a mass reaction for the 'poor animal,'" says Louis Henry, president of Hudson Bay Fur Sales

(continued on page 280)

(continued from page 279)
Inc., The Hudson's Bay Co. unit that handles about two thirds of the pelts sold at auction in the United States annually.

Mr. Henry recalls that in 1966 pelts sold at auction for an average of $24 each. The going price today for a mutation (colored) skin is about $14. Dark furs bring a slightly higher price.

[C]

In the 1960s, a mink producer would net about $5 on a mutation pelt, says Mr. Langenfeld. "Now," he says, "we're losing about $3 a pelt on our mutations." He says it costs the company $17 to raise a kit, or young mink, and bring its pelt to auction.

Mink farmers breed their animals in March. The kits — usually four to a litter — are born in early May. They're raised for six months before being killed — humanely, producers say — by gas or electrocution. The skins then are removed and readied for sale.

Finicky Animal

In most cases they are sent to one of four main U.S. auction centers, in New York City, Seattle, Minneapolis, and Milwaukee. Fees received by one of the two associations that offer the pelts for sale and by the company conducting the auction can take up to 7.75 percent of the pelt's selling price.

The price the producers get for their pelts is their reward for raising a finicky animal that prefers only the freshest meat, poultry, and fish. Most mink farms have expensive refrigeration, grinding and

mixing machines, and also must hire extra help to thaw and feed daily rations to the animals. All this causes the mink's diet to represent more than half of the total cost of raising a mink to pelt-producing size.

Mink researchers have been working to develop a dry diet that would be more economical and still satisfy the taste and nutritional requirements of the animal. Some farmers are using the dry diets, but they are far from gaining industry-wide acceptance.

U.S. producers are said to produce a high-quality pelt much prized by those who don't mind paying handsomely for a coat or stole. But about half of the six million or so pelts used annually in the United States are less-expensive foreign ones produced mainly in Scandinavia. Some industry officials say an increasing number of garments made from these pelts are being sold to people who formerly would have bought the more expensive item made from U.S.-produced pelts.

Mr. Henry says the worst may be over, however. "I think it (sales) will stabilize just about where it is," he says. Some observers expect a pickup in business as the recession eases.

Will business ever return to the good old days? "I don't know any mink farmers who ever had any good old days," says Mr. Langenfeld.

Questions

1. Consider passage A: Illustrate (graphically the effect of the increased demand on price, output, and profit in the short run and long run, both for the individual firm and the mink industry.

Assume the mink industry is a *constant cost* industry in your answer.

2. Consider passage B: starting with your graphs at the conclusion of question 1, show the effect of each of the following, both in the short run and the long run:

   a. "Mink has lost most of its prestige."

   b. "Feed and labor costs have climbed rapidly."

3. The results at the beginning of the article indicate that industry output has declined and the number of firms has fallen. Combine the effects of (*a*) and (*b*) above and show why industry output *Must* decline. Must it be true that the number of firms has fallen? Explain carefully.

4. Now consider passage C: Has the mink industry reached a new long-run competitive equilibrium? Explain.

5. Explain on a diagram why a mink producer might continue to produce even if this person observed that "We're losing about $3 a pelt on our mutations."

Solutions

(Throughout this solution, it is assumed that there is only one plant size, as in section 9.5.a.)

1. Start from a situation of long-run equilibrium. In the short run, the increase in demand bids up the price of mink. The individual firm, facing a higher price, chooses to produce more and earns positive profits. (See Figure A.)

Positive profits induce additional firms to enter the industry. By the assumption that factor prices are constant, in long-run equilibrium the price of mink will be back to its original level. The long-run equilibrium position for the individual firm is identical to the initial position. (See Figure B.)

(continued on page 282)

Figure A

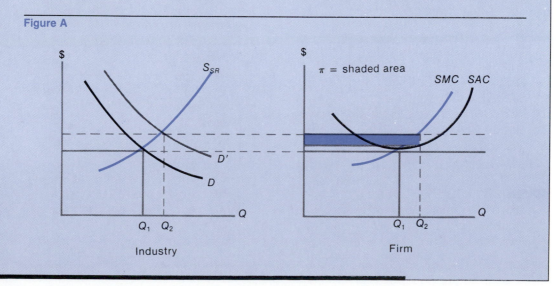

Industry

Firm

APPLYING THE THEORY

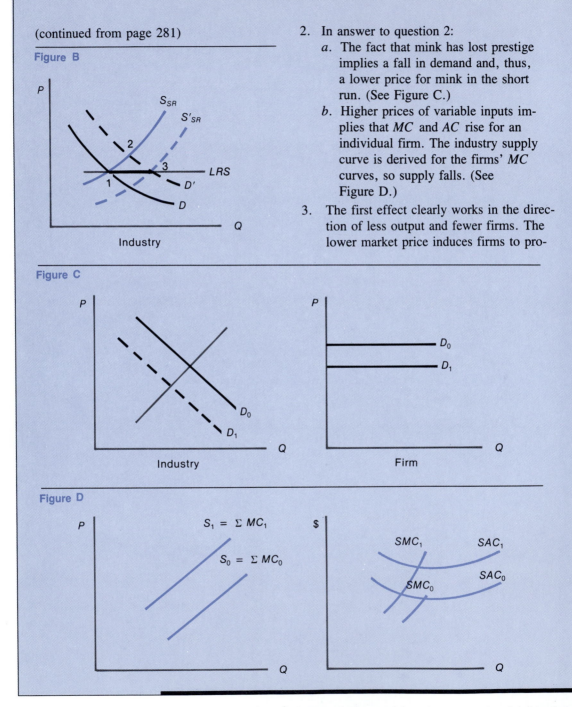

(continued from page 281)

Figure B

Industry

2. In answer to question 2:
   a. The fact that mink has lost prestige implies a fall in demand and, thus, a lower price for mink in the short run. (See Figure C.)
   b. Higher prices of variable inputs implies that MC and AC rise for an individual firm. The industry supply curve is derived for the firms' MC curves, so supply falls. (See Figure D.)
3. The first effect clearly works in the direction of less output and fewer firms. The lower market price induces firms to pro-

Figure C

Industry

Firm

Figure D

duce less output and incur losses. The second effect also leads to less output by shifting the supply curve to the left, but has an ambiguous effect on the number of firms. The higher costs suggest losses for the firms, but the short-run industry supply curve shifts left, resulting in a higher price in the short run, and having a positive effect on profits. The effects in the direction of losses will probably dominate, leading to the exit of firms from the industry. (See Figure E.)

4. The industry has not reached a new long-run equilibrium because there are still losses.

5. The mink producer will continue to produce if the losses while producing are less than the fixed costs that would be lost if the firm shut down (i.e., produce if $TR > TVC$). (See Figure F.)

Source: Reprinted by permission of *The Wall Street Journal*, © Dow Jones & Company, Inc., October 27, 1975. All rights reserved.

Figure E

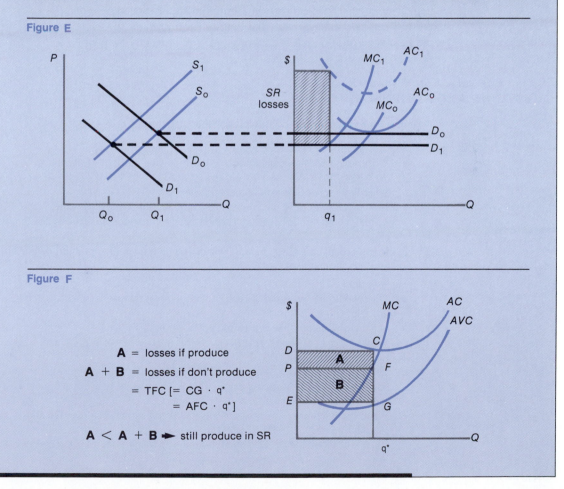

Figure F

A = losses if produce

A + B = losses if don't produce

= TFC [= CG · q*

= AFC · q*]

A < A + B ➤ still produce in SR

- When factor prices do *not* change in response to a change in industry factor usage, the short-run supply curve of a competitive industry will be simply the horizontal summation of the marginal cost schedules of the firms in the industry. (Note, however, that if price is below the average variable cost of every firm, industry output will be zero.) When factor prices change as industry factor usage rises, the supply curve will not be the horizontal summation of all firms' marginal cost curves. In this case, it is necessary to account for the shifts in each firm's marginal cost schedule as industry output rises when determining the industry supply schedule.

- Long-run adjustments in a competitive industry allow for full mobility of resources both into and out of the industry. The long-run equilibrium will occur at a price equal to the minimum of the typical firm's long-run average cost schedule. If the industry faces constant input prices, the equilibrium long-run price will always be minimum long-run average cost, and the long-run supply schedule will be a horizontal line. In an increasing-inputs price industry the long-run supply schedule will be upward-sloping. In each case, the long-run equilibrium *economic* profit of the firm is zero (although accounting profit will usually be positive).

QUESTIONS AND EXERCISES

(Use the output–cost data computed for the first question in Chapter 8.)

1. Suppose the price of the commodity is $1.75 per unit.
   a. What would net profit be at each of the following outputs? (*i*) 1,314; (*ii*) 1,384; (*iii*) 1,444; (*iv*) 1,494; and (*v*) 1,534.
   b. What is the greatest profit output?
   c. How much more revenue is obtained by selling this number of units than by selling one fewer? What is the relation between marginal revenue and selling price?
   d. If you are given selling price, how can you determine the optimum output by reference to marginal cost?

2. Suppose price is 70 cents.
   a. What would net profit be at each of the following outputs? (*i*) 410, (*ii*) 560, (*iii*) 700; (*iv*) 830; (*v*) 945; (*vi*) 1,234; (*vii*) 1,444.
   b. Is there any output that will earn a net profit at this price?
   c. When price is 70 cents, what is the crucial relation between price and average variable cost?
   d. Consider any price for which the corresponding marginal cost is equal to or less than 70 cents. At such a price, what is the relation between marginal cost and average variable cost?
   e. When the relation in (*d*) exists, what is the relation between average and marginal product?
   f. What will the producer do if faced with a permanent price of 70 cents?
   g. Why is it not socially desirable to have a producer operating when price is 70 cents.

Part Three   Theory of the Firm and Market Organization

3. Suppose price is 80 cents.
   a. What will the optimum output be?
   b. Can a profit be made at this price?
   c. Will the producer operate at all at this price?
   d. How long?

4. Determine the supply schedule of this individual producer, listing the quantity supplied at the following prices: $0.60, 0.70, 0.80, 0.90, 1.00, 1.10, 1.20, 1.30, 1.40, 1.50, 1.60, 1.70, 1.80, 1.90, and 2.00.

5. The following report appeared in *The Wall Street Journal:*

   > The world's first plant for the manufacture of gasoline from natural gas will be shut down as uneconomical, it was announced today by the Amoco Chemical Corp.
   >
   > The plant, at Brownsville, Tex., will be closed within the next few months, with a reduction of the work force to begin October 1.
   >
   > J. A. Forrester, president of Amoco, a subsidiary of the Standard Oil Co. (Indiana) said: "We have determined that the Brownsville plant cannot make gasoline and chemicals from natural gas at present market prices as cheaply as they can be made by other processes . . . ."
   >
   > Mr. Forrester declared: "We have proved the technical soundness of the process. However, results indicate that the units are more costly to operate and maintain than we had anticipated."

   Consider whether it was wasteful to close down the plant (*a*) from the point of view of the firm, and (*b*) from the point of view of society.

6. New York City licenses taxicabs in two classes: for operation by companies with fleets and for operation by independent driver-owners, each having only one cab. The city also fixes the rates the taxis may charge. For many years now, no new licenses have been issued in either class. There is an unofficial market for the "medallions" that signify the possession of a license. A medallion for an independent cab sold in 1987 for about $125,000.
   a. Discuss the factors determining the price of a medallion.
   b. What factors would determine whether a change in the fare fixed by the city would raise or lower the price of a medallion?
   c. Cab drivers, whether hired by companies or owners of their own cabs, seem unanimous in opposing any increase in the number of cabs licensed. They argue that an increase in the number of cabs, by increasing competition for customers, would drive down what they consider as an already unduly low return to drivers. Is their economics correct? Who would benefit and who would lose from an expansion in the number of licenses issued at a nominal fee?

7. Comment on the following quotation:

   > The orthodox tools of supply and demand assume that sellers and buyers are free to buy or sell any quantity they wish at the prices determined by the market. This assumption cannot validly be made when price controls or rationing are imposed by the government. It follows that these tools are useless in analyzing the effects of such government action. Economists should free themselves from slavish

adherence to outmoded concepts and fashion new tools of analysis for the new problems raised by the modern Leviathan.

8. Assume that the demand for shoes at the retail level is elastic. Further assume that a ceiling price below the current market price is placed on shoes at the factory (that is, a maximum price the shoe manufacturer can charge the retail dealer). The total revenue received from the sale of shoes at the retail level will increase because of the imposition of the ceiling price at the factory level. *Problem:* Decide whether the conclusion above is true, false, or uncertain, and defend your answer.

9. Suppose a frost kills a large portion of the orange crop, with a resulting higher price of oranges. It has been said that such an increase in the price benefits no one since it cannot elicit a supply response; the higher price, it is said, simply "lines the pockets of profiteers." Analyze this position. (Hint: Be sure to focus on the rationing function of market price.)

10. Assume that crab packing is a perfectly competitive industry on a national scale, or at least along the Eastern seaboard and Gulf Coast. The North Carolina crab packers have insisted that if the minimum wage is increased to $1.60 an hour, they will have to close their plants. Assume that they are correct. State the assumptions that must (implicitly) underlie their analysis and explain the situation graphically.

SUGGESTED READINGS

Henderson, James M., and **Quandt, Richard E.** *Microeconomic Theory: A Mathematical Approach,* 2nd ed. New York: McGraw-Hill, 1971, pp. 103–18.

Knight, Frank H. *Risk, Uncertainty and Profit.* London School Reprints of Scarce Works, No. 16, 1933, chaps. 1, 5, 6.

Machlup, Fritz. *Economics of Sellers' Competition.* Baltimore: Johns Hopkins University Press, 1952, pp. 79–125, esp. pp. 79–85 and pp. 116–25.

Stigler, George J. "Perfect Competition, Historically Contemplated." *Journal of Political Economy* 65 (1957), pp. 1–17.

CHAPTER

10 Theory of Price under Pure Monopoly

Students receiving financial aid end up paying less tuition than others to attend the same college. Is this practice of charging different buyers different prices for the same good (known formally as "price discrimination") consistent with profit-maximizing behavior? In this chapter we will explore "price discrimination" as one of several special topics in the theory of monopoly. We will also discover (refer to "Applying the Theory" section) that for two decades officials from 23 select Eastern colleges have met privately to ensure that a student seeking financial aid was offered roughly the same amount by each school. Apparently, the potential gains from averting price competition are such that attempting to collude, and behave like a monopoly, is not confined to business firms alone. ■

23 Colleges in East Adjust Aid to Avert Bidding for Students

By Fox Butterfield
Special to *The New York Times*

WELLESLEY, Mass, April 15 — For two decades officials representing a group of select Eastern colleges have met privately to ensure that a student seeking financial aid was offered roughly the same amount by each school.

"Some people tease us and say it's price fixing, but it's not," said Amy Nychis, director of financial aid Wellesley, where officials of 23 schools met last week. The basic purpose is to give students and their parents the freedom of choice to go to the school they really want and not to pick because one school offers them more aid than another."

Another purpose, some college officials acknowledge, is to help the schools stretch their financial aid budgets and avoid possible bidding wars over the most attractive students.

In some cases college officials may raise or lower their financial aid offers to a student after seeing what other schools have offered.

The meetings, which are not widely known about by students and parents, grew out of the shift in the late 1950s and early 1960s from scholarships based on academic or athletic ability toward aid based entirely on need.

But some officials at this year's meeting were surprised when two of the participating schools, Smith and Mount Holyoke, disclosed that they were introducing a new program to attract top students by offering cash grants regardless of need.

Although administrators at Smith and Mount Holyoke insisted the new awards were not merit aid because the amounts were relatively small, only $300 or $400 apiece, officials at several schools said they were concerned that the action might put pressure on other colleges to offer their own financial inducements as the number of college-age students declines.

"I think all of us would prefer Smith and Mount Holyoke not do it," a financial aid officer at another small New England college said. "It's a crack in the dike. The question arises, if they don't get the students with that amount of money, how much more will they offer, and won't other schools follow?"

Several colleges outside the 23-member group, including Northwestern and Duke, have recently begun offering some merit-based scholarships to attract top students as part of what some university officials said might be the beginning of a national trend.

Discrepancies Resolved

The annual meeting at Wellesley came after the colleges made their final selection of high school seniors and a week before today's mailing of acceptance notices to students.

The participating colleges were the eight members of the Ivy League (Brown, Columbia, Cornell, Dartmouth, Harvard, the University of Pennsylvania, Princeton and Yale), Barnard, Bryn Mawr, Mount Holyoke, Smith, Vassar, and Wellesley, the Massachusetts Institute of Technology, and a group called the Pentagonials, consisting of Amherst, Williams, Wesleyan and Bowdoin, Colby, Tufts, Middlebury, and Trinity.

Seamus Malin, director of financial aid at Harvard, said that in most cases the school officials were "fairly much in agreement" on how much aid a student would need and how much the parents should contribute.

But in about a third of the cases there are "wide discrepancies," which Mr. Malin described as $2,000 to $3,000. That, he noted, is still a small amount of the total cost of a year's education at an Ivy League school, which will range up from the $13,200 charged at Cornell this year, with all fees included.

It is these larger variations in proposed aid that the officials try to resolve in their annual conferences by either raising or lowering their offers to students.

Nothing Sneaky Going On

There is no rule requiring the schools to agree on the amount of parental contribution for a student who has been accepted at several colleges, Mr. Malin explained, but the officers generally narrow their differences to within $100 or so.

"It is a delicate issue in a sense," he conceded. "But there is nothing sneaky going on. It is not the Ivies getting together and dividing the talent."

School officials are normally close in their assessments of each student's needs, Mr. Malin said, because they work with standardized information and methods.

Every applicant for financial aid must first submit a form disclosing his parents' income and assets to the College Scholarship Service in Princeton, N.J., a division of the Educational Testing Service. The service analyzes this form by computer and sends the results to each school to which the student has applied.

The colleges then make their own analyses, Mr. Malin said, and it is at this stage that the variations in aid arise. A particular school may request more data from the parents, or an applicant may have a brother or sister at one of the colleges, which provides that school with additional financial information.

'Bidding' on Aid Denied

Financial aid officers at several of the colleges strongly denied that any member of their group would increase an aid offer after the meeting to entice a student coveted by the school, such as a bright young scientist or football player.

"There is a lot of pressure not to do that," said Jacqueline Foster, director of the undergraduate financial aid office at Yale. She added that "it would get back

(continued on page 290)

(continued from page 289) to you very quickly" because the parents might go to another college to see if they could get a higher offer there, too.

Nevertheless, an official at Brown said, some colleges might try to make their offer more attractive by raising the amount of grant assistance. Each aid package is made up of three parts; a grant, a loan, and self-help work provided by the school.

More controversial are the new grants based on a student's ability rather than need. A spokesman for Smith, Ann Shanahan, said the school had decided to award 36 achievement awards of $300 each to "the students we most want to have come to Smith."

"We don't think of them as merit aid because the amounts are so small," she said, adding that the money for the grants came from special funds designated by the administration and not out of regular aid allocations.

Pat Waters, director of financial aid at Mount Holyoke, said her school would provide 30 students with grants of $400 each regardless of financial need. She described them as "prizes" rather than aid, because, she said, "The amount isn't large enough to make anyone change their mind."

Questions

1. This article reports that for several decades officials representing a group of 23 select Eastern colleges have met privately to ensure that a student seeking financial aid was offered roughly the same amount by each school. What obstacles must be overcome by any group of sellers attempting to "collude" and "fix" prices?

2. Are there any indications in the article that these 23 colleges are having trouble overcoming these obstacles? Explain.

3. We've said price discrimination occurs when different prices are charged for the same commodity to different groups of buyers. In what sense do the scholarships here represent a form of price discrimination?

INTRODUCTION
10.1

"Perfect competition" provides the economist with a very useful analytical model, even though the exacting conditions of the model never exist in the real world. The same statement almost applies to the model of pure monopoly, to which we now turn. The conditions of the model are exacting; and it is difficult, if not impossible, to pinpoint a pure monopolist in real-world markets. On the other hand, many markets closely approximate monopoly organization, and monopoly analysis often explains observed business behavior quite well.

4. For profit maximization, we've shown that the more elastic the submarket demand, the lower the price that should be charged in that submarket. Is the practice of giving more scholarship aid to "needier" students consistent with this basic profit-maximizing rule? What about "achievement awards" from Smith, and Mt. Holyoke?

Solutions

1. The obstacles are many and difficult to overcome. They include the following: (*a*) Can the sellers prevent "cheating" and keep "chiseling" to a minimum? (*b*) Can the sellers agree on the price to charge? (*c*) Are all the potential sellers included in the colluding agreement? (*d*) Can non-price methods of competition be controlled?

2. Smith and Mt. Holyoke, according to the article, are "a crack in the dike"; they are offering slightly more aid and thus "cheating" on the agreement. Not all of the colleges' competitors are included. Duke and Northwestern are cited in the article. Stanford, too, is not included. In addition, there are many forms of non-price competition available to colleges. Even the aid package itself has various "mixes"—a grant, a loan, and work–study opportunities can be varied, even if the total award is the same.

3. Scholarships result in some students effectively paying less for tuition than other students. The product (in this case, the college education) is the same regardless of the tuition paid.

4. If needier students have a more elastic demand for college attendance, then this policy will be consistent with profit maximization. If the "achievement awards" (merit aid) being introduced by Smith and Mount Holyoke go to those with more elastic demand for these colleges, then they too are consistent with the profit-maximizing behavior.

Source: "23 Colleges in East Adjust Aid to Avert Bidding for Students," *The New York Times*, April 16, 1983.

Definition
10.1.a

A pure monopoly is said to exist if there is one, and only one, seller in a well-defined market. Thus, from the sales or revenue side, pure monopoly and perfect competition are polar opposites. The perfectly competitive firm has so many "rivals" in the market that competition becomes impersonal. Personal rivalry does not exist in the case of pure monopoly either, for the simple reason that there are no rivals.

Yet this may overstate the case somewhat, for two types of *indirect competition* and one source of *potential competition* tend to moderate the price–output policies of pure or near-pure monopolies. The first source of indirect competition is the general struggle for the consumer's dollar. *All* commodities compete for a place in the consumer's budget — the products of monopolists as well as the products of perfectly competitive firms. Unless a monopolist can secure a market for a product, monopoly position is worthless. For example, the files of the U.S. Patent Office would reveal many patents (and therefore output monopoly) for products that were never produced or were produced for only a short period of time. Monopoly does not guarantee success; it only guarantees that the monopolist can make the most of whatever demand conditions exist.

A second source of indirect competition lies in the existence of substitute goods. Needless to say, there are no *perfect* substitutes for a monopoly product; otherwise a monopoly would not exist. However, imperfect substitutes exist; and the true market power of a monopolist depends upon the extent to which other commodities may be used as substitutes in consumption. For example, whale oil lamps and gaslights, candles and Coleman lanterns are very poor substitutes for electricity in residential and commercial lighting. Therefore, electricity for lighting purposes closely approximates pure monopoly. On the other hand, there are quite good substitutes for electrical heating. Fuel oil and natural gas are strong competitors in the residential heating market; coal-fired steam heat, in addition to oil and gas, competes in the commercial market. As a consequence, the "monopoly" position of electrical power companies is very weak in these markets.

As has been said, the presence of indirect competition tends to moderate the price–output policies of monopolists. The threat of potential competition does so as well. In many cases potential competitors will be attracted into the market if profit prospects are bright. This is particularly true when the price–output policy of the existing monopolist is such that potential competitors feel they can readily capture a substantial portion of the market. While this situation is especially applicable to local or regional markets served by only one firm, it applies in broader situations as well. Whenever entry is possible, the position of an existing monopoly is perilous. To protect it, the monopolist must serve the market well; otherwise new entrants will be attracted and the monopoly broken.

To summarize:

Pure Monopoly: A pure monopoly exists when there is only one producer in a market. There are not direct competitors or rivals. However, the policies of a monopolist may be constrained by the indirect competition of all commodities for the consumer's dollar and of reasonably adequate substitute goods, and by the threat of potential competition if market entry is possible.

Bases of Monopoly
10.1.b

Since the business of entrepreneurs is profit, one might wonder why a monopoly ever arises, that is, why other firms do not enter the industry in an attempt to capture a part of the monopoly profit. Many different factors may lead to the establishment of a monopoly or near monopoly. For example, on a local level the personal characteristics of the owner-monopolist may bring all the trade to him. Other seemingly trivial reasons may explain monopoly; but monopolies so established are destined for a short life. Permanent monopoly must rest on firmer ground.

One of the most important bases for monopoly lies in the control of raw material supplies. Suppose input X is required to produce output Y. If one firm has exclusive control over or ownership of X it can easily establish a monopoly over Y by refusing to sell X to any potential competitors.[1] An interesting example of input-control monopoly can be taken from the economic history of the United States. Bauxite is a necessary ingredient in the production of aluminum. For many years the Aluminum Company of America (Alcoa) owned almost every source of bauxite in the United States. The control of resource supply, coupled with certain patent rights, provided Alcoa with an absolute monopoly in aluminum; it was only after World War II that the federal courts effectively broke Alcoa's monopoly of the aluminum market.

The discussion of Alcoa brings to light another important source of monopoly. The patent laws of the United States make it possible for a person to apply for and obtain the exclusive right to produce a certain commodity or to produce a commodity by means of a specified process. The patent lasts for 17 years, and it may be renewed after that time. Obviously, such exclusive rights can easily lead to monopoly. Alcoa is an example of a monopoly based upon both resource control and patent rights. E. I. du Pont de Nemours & Co. has enjoyed patent monopolies over many commodities, cellophane being perhaps the most notable. The Eastman Kodak Company enjoyed a similar position (by lease from a German company); the Minnesota Mining and Manufacturing Company (3M) had enjoyed patent monopoly or near monopoly with products such as their Scotch tape.

Despite these notable examples, patent monopoly may not be quite what it seems in many instances. A patent gives one the exclusive right to produce a particular, meticulously specified commodity or to use a particular, meticulously specified process to produce a commodity others can produce. But a patent does not preclude the development of closely related substitute goods or closely allied production processes. International Business Machines has the exclusive right to produce IBM machines; but other computers are available and there is keen competition in the computer market. The same is true of production processes. Thus, while patents may sometimes establish pure monopolies, at other times they are merely permits to enter highly — but not perfectly — competitive markets.

A third source of monopoly lies in the cost of establishing an efficient production plant, especially in relation to the size of the market. The situation we are now discussing is frequently called "natural" monopoly. It comes into existence

---

[1]Under some circumstances, all monopoly profits from Y can be captured by the owner of X even without extending the monopoly.

when the minimum average cost of production occurs at a rate of output more than sufficient to supply the entire market at a price covering full cost.

Suppose a situation such as this exists but two firms are in the market. If the market is split between the two, each must necessarily produce at a relatively high average cost. Each has an incentive to lower price and increase output because average cost will also decline. But if both act in this fashion, price will surely fall more rapidly than average cost. Economic warfare ensues, and the ultimate result is likely to be the emergence of only one firm in a monopoly position.[2] The term "natural" monopoly simply implies that the "natural" result of market forces is the development of a monopoly organization.

Figure 10.1.1 illustrates this point. Suppose that each firm's average cost curve and marginal cost curve is as shown. Specifically, the point of maximum efficiency, the minimum of the average costs curve, is associated with an output that is large relative to market demand for the product.

We know from the previous chapter that long-run equilibrium in a competitive industry occurs when price is at the minimum of the long-run average cost curve. In this case, that means that price is OP_0. Suppose there were two firms in the industry. At that price each would want to produce OQ_1 of output. But at price OP_0, only OQ_0 is demanded. Since $OQ_1 > OQ_0$, surely $2(OQ_1) > OQ_0$. Thus, a surplus exists. In order to eliminate the surplus, price must fall. But if price falls, no firm can break even; each of the two firms suffers losses. (Price below average cost implies total cost exceeds total revenue.) Thus, both firms go out of business! Evidently, it is impossible to have two or more firms that behave competitively in this industry. The reason is that there is not enough demand to justify the existence of two firms at efficent levels of output.

Examples of natural monopoly are not hard to come by. Virtually all public utilities are natural monopolies, and vice versa. Municipal waterworks, electrical power companies, sewage disposal systems, telephone companies, and many transportation services are examples of natural monopolies on either local or national levels.

The final source of monopoly to be discussed here is the market franchise. Use of a market franchise is frequently associated with natural monopolies and public utilities, but it need not be. A market franchise is actually a contract entered into by some governmental body (for instance, a city government) and a business concern. The governmental unit gives a business firm the exclusive right to market a good or service within its jurisdiction. The business firm, in turn, agrees to permit the governmental unit to control certain aspects of its market conduct. For example, the governmental unit may limit, or attempt to limit, the firm to a "fair return on fair market value of assets." In other cases the governmental unit may establish the price and permit the firm to earn whatever it can at that price. There are many other ways in which the governmental unit can exercise control

---

[2]For the classical treatment of this situation, see F. Zeuthen, *Problems of Monopoly and Economic Warfare* (London: Routledge & Kegan Paul, 1930).

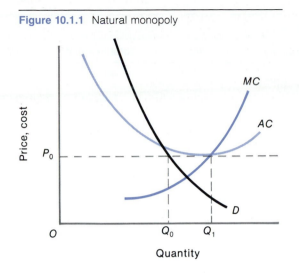

Figure 10.1.1 Natural monopoly

over the firm. The essential feature, however, is that a governmental unit establishes the firm as a monopoly in return for various types of control over the price and output policies of the business.

DEMAND UNDER MONOPOLY
10.2

The most important object of Part 1 was to show that market demand curves are negatively sloped (except for the truly insignificant case of the Giffen Paradox). Now, since a monopoly constitutes a one-firm market, the market demand curve *is* the monopoly demand curve. As explained in section 5.4 of Chapter 5, when demand is negatively sloped, average and marginal revenue are different, and for marginal profit calculations the latter is the relevant concept.[3]

Consider a hypothetical situation given by the data in Table 10.2.1. Market demand is indicated by the first two columns and is plotted graphically in Figure 10.2.1. Total revenue—the product of price and quantity—is given in column 3 and depicted graphically in Figure 10.2.1. (*Note:* The right-hand ordinate refers to total revenue while the customary left-hand ordinate refers to price and marginal revenue.) Finally, marginal revenue is shown in column 4.

As you will recall, marginal revenue is the addition to total revenue attributable to the addition of 1 unit of output (or sales). In this example, quantity

---

[3]The remainder of this section is a brief review of section 5.4 in Chapter 5. Students thoroughly familiar with the content of this section may proceed immediately to section 10.3.

Table 10.2.1 Demand and marginal revenue under monopoly

Quantity	Price	Total revenue	Marginal revenue
5	$2.00	$10.00	—
13	1.10	14.30	$0.54
23	0.85	19.55	0.52
38	0.69	26.22	0.44
50	0.615	30.75	0.35
60	0.55	33.00	0.23
68	0.50	34.00	0.13
75	0.45	33.75	−0.03
81	0.40	32.40	−0.23
86	0.35	30.10	−0.46

Figure 10.2.1 Demand and revenue under monopoly

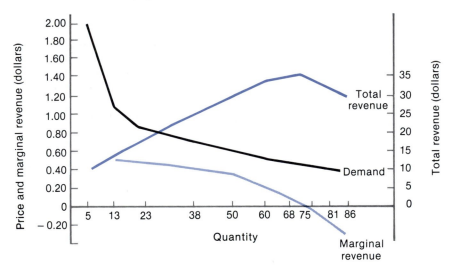

does not increase by single units. Thus marginal revenue must be calculated as the *average* marginal revenue over the corresponding quantity range. Thus[4]

$$MR = \frac{\Delta TR}{\Delta q} = \text{(for example)} \ \frac{\$14.30 - \$10.00}{13 - 5} = \$0.54 .$$

The corresponding plot is shown in Figure 10.2.1.

The highly discrete case in Figure 10.2.1 is generalized in Figure 10.2.2. The important relations, already discussed, are immediately apparent from the figure.

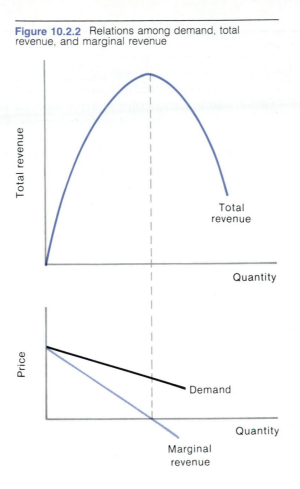

Figure 10.2.2 Relations among demand, total revenue, and marginal revenue

Relations: When demand is negatively sloped, marginal revenue is negatively sloped as well. Furthermore, marginal revenue is less than price at all relevant points. The difference between marginal revenue and price depends upon the price elasticity of demand, as shown by the formula $MR = p(1 - 1/\eta)$.

Total revenue at first increases, reaches a maximum, and declines thereafter. The maximum point on the total revenue curve is attained at precisely that rate of output and sales (quantity) for which marginal revenue is zero.

Remember that the elasticity of demand varies as one moves along the demand curve. Thus, the formula $MR = P(1 - 1/\eta)$ implies that when η is infinite, i.e., on the vertical intercept of the demand curve, $MR = P$, so demand and marginal revenue are the same. As η decreases, marginal revenue diverges from the demand curve.

COST AND SUPPLY UNDER MONOPOLY
10.3

The short-run cost conditions confronting a monopolist may be, for all practical purposes, identical with those faced by a perfectly competitive firm. In particular, an entrepreneur who is a monopolist in his product market may be a perfect (buying) competitor in the market for productive inputs. This would tend to be true if the monopolist required only unspecialized inputs, such as unskilled labor. In this event, the analysis of Chapter 7 would apply directly to cost under monopoly. In many instances, however, the monopolist requires certain *specialized* inputs for which there is no broad general market. There are only a few buyers of the specialized input (in the limit, only one). Thus the commodity-market monopolist may be a monopolist or near monopolist in various input markets as well.[5]

SHORT-RUN EQUILIBRIUM UNDER MONOPOLY
10.4

The analysis of perfect competition was based upon two important assumptions: each entrepreneur attempts to maximize profit; and the firm operates in an environment not subject to outside control. Monopoly analysis rests upon the same two assumptions; accordingly, the results must be modified when applied to franchise monopoly or to monopolies subject to some form of government regulation and control.

---

[4]For continuous cases, the demand function in the inverse form may be written

$$p = f(q), \quad f'(q) < 0, \tag{10.2.1}$$

where p and q denote price and quantity, respectively. Thus total revenue is

$$pq = qf(q), \tag{10.2.2}$$

and marginal revenue is

$$MR = \frac{d(pq)}{dq} = f(q) + qf'(q). \tag{10.2.3}$$

As you will recall from section 4.4 in Chapter 4, price elasticity of demand is

$$\eta = -\frac{dq}{dp}\frac{p}{q} = -\frac{1}{f'(q)}\frac{p}{q} = -\frac{p}{qf'(q)}. \tag{10.2.4}$$

Now, factor $p = f(q)$ from the right-hand side of expression (10.2.3), obtaining

$$MR = p\left[1 + \frac{qf'(q)}{p}\right]. \tag{10.2.5}$$

Thus from expression (10.2.4),

$$MR = p\left[1 - \frac{1}{\eta}\right]. \tag{10.2.6}$$

[5]In this case the monopolist is called a monopsonist or an oligopsonist. The use of this terminology is deferred until Chapter 15, where the present case is analyzed more intensely.

Total Revenue–Total Cost Approach
10.4.a

The monopolist, just as the perfect competitor, attains maximum profit by producing and selling at that rate of output for which the positive difference between total revenue and total cost is greatest. (Or, minimizes loss when the negative difference is least.) To illustrate the total revenue–total cost approach, the hypothetical revenue and cost data are presented in Table 10.4.1. The data are illustrated graphically in Figure 10.4.1.

The table and graph are almost self-explanatory. One should note that maximum profit ($4.50) is attained at 50 units of output and sales. By reference to the average cost column, this rate of output is less than that associated with minimum unit cost. Similarly, it is less than the maximum revenue output, and it is also less than the rate of output (somewhat greater than 60) for which price equals marginal cost. The latter condition is the "rule" for profit maximization under perfect competition. But it does not hold for monopoly, as the *marginal* approach makes clear.

Marginal Revenue–Marginal Cost Approach
10.4.b

Since all underlying concepts have been introduced, this section begins with a continuation of the example previously used. Table 10.4.2 provides the relevant data, shown graphically in Figure 10.4.2.

Under monopoly, maximum profit is attained at the rate of output and sales for which marginal cost equals marginal revenue. The hypothetical data in Table 10.4.2 clearly illustrate this proposition. For a proof, however, the continuous case represented by Figure 10.4.3 is used.

In that figure, marginal cost and marginal revenue are given by curves of customary shape, intersecting at point E. We wish to prove that producing output $O\overline{Q}$ associated with this intersection leads to maximum profit or minimum loss. The method of attack is "proof by contradiction." Suppose $O\overline{Q}$ were not the profit-maximizing output. First, assume that it is less than $O\overline{Q}$ — say OQ_l. At that point marginal cost is OA and marginal revenue is $OB > OA$. Hence adding a unit to output and sales will increase total revenue by more than it increases total cost. Therefore profit can be expanded, or loss reduced, by expanding output from the rate OQ_l. And this statement must hold for *any* output less than $O\overline{Q}$ since $MR > MC$ over the entire range from O to $\overline{Q}$.

Next, suppose the profit-maximizing output were greater than $O\overline{Q}$ — say, OQ_h. At this point marginal revenue is OC and marginal cost is $OD > OC$. At this rate of output an additional unit of output and sales adds more to total cost than to total revenue. Profit is accordingly diminished or loss augmented. Further, this must hold for *any* output greater than $O\overline{Q}$ because $MC > MR$ over that entire range of output.

Table 10.4.1 Profit maximization by the total revenue–total cost approach

Output and sales	Price	Total revenue	Total cost	Profit	Average cost	Marginal cost
5	$2.00	$10.00	$12.25	$−2.25	2.45	.45
13	1.10	14.30	15.00	−0.70	1.15	.34
23	0.85	19.55	18.25	+1.30	.80	.33
38	0.69	26.22	22.00	+4.22	.55	.25
50	0.615	30.75	26.25	+4.50	.53	.35
60	0.55	33.00	31.00	+2.00	.52	.48
68	0.50	34.00	36.25	−2.25	.53	.66
75	0.45	33.75	42.00	−8.25	.56	.42
81	0.40	32.40	48.25	−15.85	.60	1.04
86	0.35	30.10	55.00	−24.90	.64	1.35

Figure 10.4.1 Profit maximization by the total revenue–total cost approach

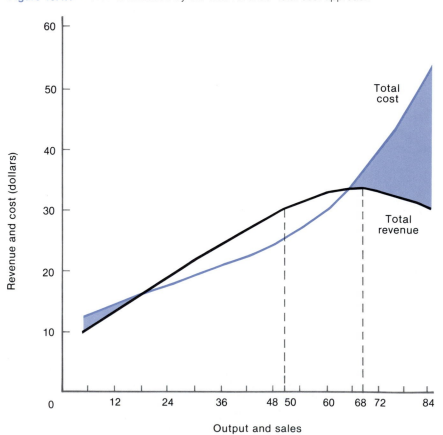

Part Three   Theory of the Firm and Market Organization

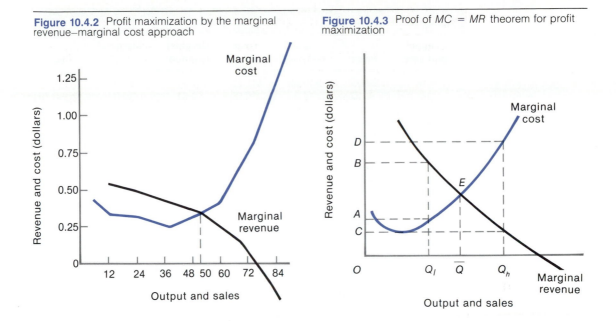

Figure 10.4.2 Profit maximization by the marginal revenue–marginal cost approach

Figure 10.4.3 Proof of $MC = MR$ theorem for profit maximization

Since the profit-maximizing output can neither exceed nor be less than $O\overline{Q}$, the following proposition is established.[6]

Proposition: A monopolist will maximize profit or minimize loss by producing and marketing that output for which marginal cost equals marginal revenue. Whether a profit or loss is made depends upon the relation between price and average total cost.

---

[6]Let the monopolist's demand function in inverse form be $p = f(q)$ and let the cost be $C = C(q)$. Thus profit (π) is

$$\pi = qf(q) - C(q). \qquad (10.4.1)$$

The first-order condition for profit maximization requires that the first derivative of expression (10.4.1) equal zero, or

$$d\pi/dq = f(q) + qf'(q) - C'(q) = 0. \qquad (10.4.2)$$

Marginal revenue is $d[qf(q)]/dq = f(q) + qf'(q)$. Similarly, marginal cost is $dC/dq = C'(q)$. Hence expression (10.4.2) gives the profit-maximization rule stated in the text.

For a true local maximum, the second derivative of expression (10.4.1) must be less than zero. That is, the second-order condition requires that

$$d^2\pi/dq^2 = 2f'(q) + qf''(q) - C''(q) < 0. \qquad (10.4.3)$$

The first two terms give the slope of the marginal revenue curve, while $C''(q)$ is the slope of the marginal cost curve. The second-order condition requires that the slope of the marginal revenue curve be less than the slope of the marginal cost curve (with respect to the quantity axis). Given a negatively sloped marginal revenue curve, the condition is obviously satisfied when marginal cost is positively sloped. However, monopoly differs from perfect competition in that the marginal cost curve may be negatively sloped at the profit-maximizing point, provided its slope is less steep (absolute value of slope is less) than that of marginal revenue.

Table 10.4.2 Marginal revenue–marginal cost approach to profit maximization

Output and sales	Price	Total revenue	Total cost	Marginal revenue	Marginal cost	Profit
5	$2.00	$10.00	$12.25	—	$0.45	$ −2.25
13	1.10	14.30	15.00	$0.54	0.34	−0.70
23	0.85	19.55	18.25	0.52	0.33	+1.30
38	0.69	26.22	22.00	0.44	0.25	+4.22
50	0.615	30.75	26.25	0.35	0.35	+4.50
60	0.55	33.00	31.00	0.23	0.48	+2.00
68	0.50	34.00	36.25	0.13	0.66	−2.25
75	0.45	33.75	42.00	−0.03	0.82	−8.25
81	0.40	32.40	48.25	−0.23	1.04	−15.85
86	0.35	30.10	55.00	−0.46	1.35	−24.90

Short-Run Equilibrium
10.4.c

Using the proposition just established, the position of short-run equilibrium under monopoly is easily described. Figure 10.4.4 is a graphical representation. The revenue side is given by the demand and marginal revenue curves, D and MR, respectively. Costs are depicted by the average total cost and marginal cost curves, ATC and MC, respectively.

The profit-maximization "rule" states that short-run equilibrium occurs at point E where marginal cost equals marginal revenue. The associated price and output are $O\overline{P}$ and $O\overline{Q}$. At the rate of output $O\overline{Q}$, average total or unit cost is $O\overline{C}$ ($= \overline{Q}B$). Profit per unit is $O\overline{P} - O\overline{C} = \overline{P}\,\overline{C}$. Thus short-run monopoly profit is $\overline{P}\,\overline{C} \times O\overline{Q} = \overline{P}AB\overline{C}$. It is thus represented by the area of the shaded rectangle in Figure 10.4.4.

In the example of Figure 10.4.4, the monopolist earns a pure profit in the short run, just as a perfect competitor may. If demand is sufficiently low relative to cost, the monopolist may also incur a loss, just as a perfect competitor may. In the short run the primary difference between monopoly and perfect competition lies in the slope of the demand curve. Either may earn a pure economic profit; either may incur a loss. Other comparisons are difficult. About the best that can be said is that a monopolistic firm is more likely to earn a pure profit in the short run because it can effectively exercise some market control.

Monopoly Supply in the Short Run
10.4.d

In perfect competition, one can define a unique "supply price" for each quantity: q units will be supplied for $\$x$ per unit. In monopoly, supply price is not unique. A given quantity would be supplied at different prices, depending on market

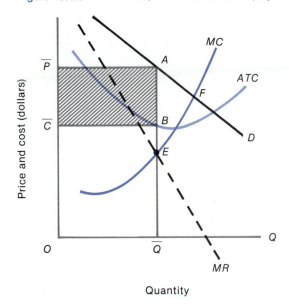

Figure 10.4.4 Short-run equilibrium under monopoly

Quantity

demand and marginal revenue. This is illustrated in Figure 10.4.5. This shows that the price a monopolist will charge depends on the demand curve, given the marginal cost curve MC. When demand is D_1 and marginal revenue is MR_1, the quantity $O\overline{Q}$ would be sold at a price of OP_1 per unit. If, however, the demand curve is D_2 and the marginal revenue curve is MR_2, the same quantity, $O\overline{Q}$, would be sold at OP_2.

Relations: Monopoly supply depends on the shape and location of the demand curve and does not have the clear and exact meaning that competitive supply has. It is meaningless to ask in general what price a monopolist will charge for a given output since the answer is not unique.

Stated alternatively, the output that a competitor produces depends only on cost conditions and price. The same statement cannot be true of a monopolist because a monopolist chooses his price simultaneously with the choice of output level. The competitor can only choose output.

Multiplant Monopoly in the Short Run
10.4.e

The discussion has so far been based upon the implicit assumption that a monopolist owns and produces by means of only one plant. This, however, is not necessarily the case. The monopolist may operate more than one plant, and cost conditions may differ from one plant to another. A hypothethical two-plant example is given in Table 10.4.3 and illustrated graphically in Figure 10.4.6.

Figure 10.4.5 Short-run monopoly supply for different
demand curves

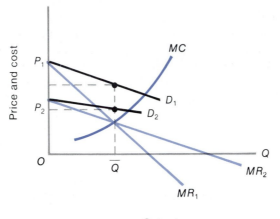

Table 10.4.3 Profit maximization in a mulitplant monopoly

Output and sales	Price	Marginal revenue	Marginal cost (Plant 1)	Marginal cost (Plant 2)	Multiplant Marginal cost
1	$5.00	—	$1.92	$2.04	$1.92
2	4.50	$4.00	2.00	2.14	2.00
3	4.10	3.30	2.08	2.24	2.04
4	3.80	2.90	2.16	2.34	2.08
5	3.55	2.55	2.24	2.44	2.14
6	3.35	2.35	2.32	2.54	2.16
7	3.20	2.30	2.40	2.64	2.24
8	3.08	2.24	2.48	2.74	2.24
9	2.98	2.18	2.56	2.84	2.32
10	2.89	2.08	2.64	2.94	2.34

The first three columns of Table 10.4.3 provide the revenue data, while the last three contain the relevant cost data. The marginal costs of plants 1 and 2 are shown in columns 4 and 5, and they are plotted in Panel A, Figure 10.4.6. Similarly, demand and marginal revenue are plotted in Panel B. The final column, "Multiplant marginal cost," is derived from the marginal cost curves of the individual plants.

If output is expanded from zero to one, the one unit should clearly be produced in plant 1, whose marginal cost is $1.92 (<$2.04 in plant 2). Hence, marginal cost for the multiplant monopoly is $1.92. If output is to be two units, both should

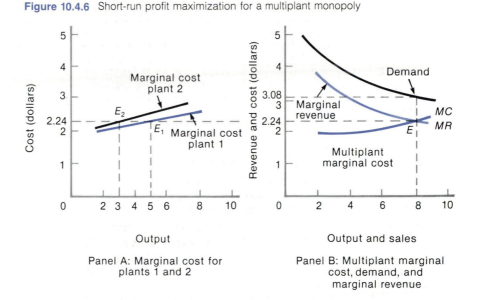

Figure 10.4.6 Short-run profit maximization for a multiplant monopoly

Panel A: Marginal cost for plants 1 and 2

Panel B: Multiplant marginal cost, demand, and marginal revenue

be produced in plant 1 because its marginal cost for the second unit ($2) is less than the marginal cost of producing one unit in plant 2. Hence monopoly marginal cost for two units is $2. If three units of output are to be produced, however, plant 2 should enter production because its marginal cost for the first unit ($2.04) is less than the marginal cost of the third unit in plant 1. By producing two units in plant 1 and one unit in plant 2, the multiplant monopoly has a marginal cost of $2.04 for the third unit. Column 6, "Multiplant marginal cost," is derived by continuing this line of reasoning for each successive unit of output.

Multiplant marginal cost is plotted in Panel B, Figure 10.4.6. It intersects marginal revenue at point E, corresponding to eight units of output and market price of $3.08. By the $MC = MR$ rule, this price–output combination is the one for which monopoly profit is a maximum. The problem faced by the monopolist is the allocation of production between plants 1 and 2.

First, observe that $MC = MR = \$2.24$ at the equilibrium point. A horizontal dashed line at the $2.24 level has been extended from Panel B to Panel A. The line intersects the plant marginal cost curves at E_1 and E_2, the points at which $MC_1 = MC_2 = MC = MR$. The associated outputs are five units for plant 1 and three units for plant 2; their combined quantity is precisely eight units, the profit-maximizing output. Thus the monopolist allocates production to the plants by equating plant marginal cost with the common value of multiplant marginal cost and marginal revenue at the equilibrium output.

Generalizing, we obtain the following:

Proposition: A multiplant monopolist maximizes profit by producing that output for which multiplant marginal cost equals marginal revenue. Optimal allocation of production among the various plants requires each plant to produce that rate of output for which the plant marginal cost is equal to the common value of multiplant marginal cost and marginal revenue at the monopoly equilibrium output.

LONG-RUN EQUILIBRIUM UNDER MONOPOLY
10.5

In a pure monopoly, *entrance* into the market by potential competitors is not possible. Thus whether or not a monopolist earns a pure profit in the short run, no other producer can enter the market in the hope of sharing whatever pure profit exists. Therefore, pure economic profit is not eliminated in the long run, as it is in the case of perfect competition. Certain economists prefer to say that in the long run pure profit does not exist irrespective of the type of market organization (whether perfectly competitive, monopolistic, etc.). They contend that the monopoly position or the monopoly-causing "ingredient" should be capitalized, thereby increasing total cost by the amount of the pure profit that would otherwise exist (in the absence of capitalization). This is a perfectly defensible argument; however, the interpretation used above is retained to facilitate comparisons among long-run equilibria under various types of market organization. If the no-profit approach is preferred, long-run equilibria can be compared in terms of differential returns to the same inputs.

The following example may clarify the point. Suppose that the monopolist in question produces mineral water that can be obtained only at one particular spring. The source of the monopoly rests in ownership of the land on which the spring flows. The monopolist's choice of price and output is shown as OP^*, OQ^* on Figure 10.5.1. If AC is the traditional average cost curve, then profit is given by rectangle P^*ABC. (That is, profit is total revenue − total cost. Rectangle P^*AQ^*O is total revenue, and rectangle CBQ^*O is total cost.) Since the source of this profit is the uniqueness of the property, the value of that property should include the profit that can be generated from it. Stated alternatively, if the monopolist wanted to sell the land, the price that he would receive would reflect the profit P^*ABC. In fact, competitive buyers of the land would be willing to pay a high enough price such that profit, after taking into account the price of the land, falls to zero. Since this is a fixed cost, it would shift the average cost to a new buyer to AC'. Any price of land that resulted in an average cost curve less than AC' results in positive profits. This causes buyers of the land to compete with one another until the land price is driven exactly high enough to eliminate profit.

This may be true for new buyers, but what of the existing owner of the land? Since the owner has the option of selling the land at the (high) price, the cost of retaining the land is the forgone opportunity of selling it. In a sense, the owner rents it to himself at the price the market will pay so he can regard his average cost curve as AC' also. The profit is capitalized into the value of the land.

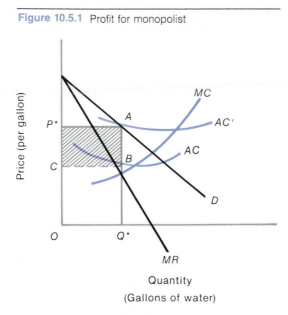

Figure 10.5.1 Profit for monopolist

Price (per gallon)

MC

A

P**

AC'

AC

B

C

D

O

Q**

MR

Quantity
(Gallons of water)

Long-Run Equilibrium in a Single-Plant Monopoly
10.5.a

Long-run equilibrium adjustment in a single-plant monopoly must take one of two possible courses. First, if the monopolist incurs a short-run loss and if there is no plant size that will result in pure profit (or at least, no loss), the monopolist goes out of business. Second, if the firm earns a short-run profit with its original plant, it must determine whether a plant of different size (and thus a different price and output) will earn a larger profit.

The first situation requires no comment. The second calls for the introduction of a new concept, long-run marginal cost.

Long-run marginal cost can be thought of most easily as the change in total cost that is associated with a change in output in the long run, that is, when all factors are permitted to adjust. Thus, long-run marginal cost can reflect expansion within one plant, and/or a change to a different plant altogether.

The example of Table 10.5.1 illustrates the point. In this simple case, a firm has the choice of using plant of type 1 or plant of type 2. If it wants to produce only one unit, then the best choice in the long run is to use plant of type 1 at a total cost of production of $15. If the firm wants to produce two units, its best choice remains plant 1 since $24 < $26. The *MC*1 column tells what marginal cost would be if plant 1 were used throughout, and the *MC*2 column tells what marginal cost would be if plant 2 were used throughout. *LMC* is the long-run marginal cost.

Table 10.5.1 Derivation of long-run marginal costs

Output	AC1	AC2	TO1	TO2	MC1	MC2	LMC
1	15	20	15˙	20	—	—	—
2	12	13	24˙	26	9	13	9
3	11	10	33	30˙	9	4	6
4	12	11	48	33˙	15	3	3

The marginal cost of the second unit in the long run is 9, because no change in plant is required and because the marginal cost of producing the second unit in plant 1 is 9.

Now consider production of the third unit. Three units are produced more cheaply in plant 2 than in plant 1 ($30 < $33). Thus, if the firm wishes to produce three in the long run, it switches to plant 2. What is the long-run marginal cost of producing the third unit? It is the difference between the total cost of producing three units optimally and the total cost of producing two units optimally. Thus, long-run marginal cost of the third unit is $30 - 24 = 6$. Note that this is higher than the marginal cost in plant 2. If the firm had used plant 2 to produce two units, it would be cheaper to move from 2 to 3. But this is irrelevant. Minimization of total cost, not marginal cost, is the goal in the long run. A switch in technology at three units is warranted irrespective of its effect on marginal cost.

This leads to the following definition:

Definition: Long-run marginal cost is the change in the total cost associated with a change in output when all factors, including the scale of plant, can vary. It may reflect the cost of increasing output without changing the plant or it may reflect the cost associated with changing the plant itself and producing an additional unit of output.

We can now examine how the monopolist adjusts to increase his profits in the long run. This is illustrated by Figure 10.5.2. DD' and MR show the market demand and marginal revenue confronting a monopolistic firm. LAC is the long-run envelope cost curve (see Chapter 8) and SMC is the short-run marginal cost curve.

Suppose in the initial period the firm builds the plant represented by SAC_1 and SMC_1. Equality of short-run marginal cost and marginal revenue leads to the sale of $O\overline{Q}_{SR}$ units at the price OA. At this rate of output, unit cost is $OD = \overline{Q}_{SR}C$; short-run monopoly profit is represented by the area of the shaded rectangle $ABCD$.

Since a pure economic profit can be reaped, the firm would not consider going out of business. However, it would search for a more profitable long-run organization. By an argument analogous to the one used in subsection 10.4.b to establish the $MC = MR$ rule, the profit-maximum *maximorum* is attained when

Part Three   Theory of the Firm and Market Organization

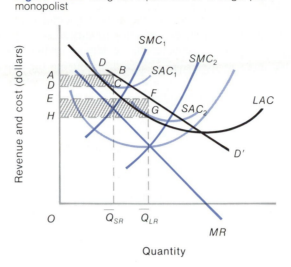

Figure 10.5.2 Long-run equilibrium for a single-plant monopolist

long-run marginal cost equals marginal revenue. The associated rate of output is $O\overline{Q}_{LR}$, and price is OE.

By reference to LAC, the plant capable of producing $O\overline{Q}_{LR}$ units per period at the least unit cost is the one represented by SAC_2 and SMC_2. Unit cost is accordingly OH, and long-run maximum monopoly profit is given by the area of the shaded rectangle $EFGH$. This profit is obviously (visually) greater than the profit obtainable from the original plant.

Generalizing, we have the following:

Proposition: A monopolist maximizes profit in the long run by producing and marketing that rate of output for which long-run marginal cost equals marginal revenue. The optimal plant is the one whose short-run average total cost curve is tangent to the long-run average cost curve at the point corresponding to long-run equilibrium output.

Comparison with Perfect Competition
10.5.b

The long-run equilibrium positions of a monopolist and a perfect competitor are somewhat more comparable than their short-run equilibria.

In perfect competition, price is determined in the long run by the minimum of the average cost curve. In the case of monopoly, the producer selects an output such that marginal cost equals marginal revenue and prices at the corresponding level on the demand curve.

Indeed, the perfect competitor produces at the point where marginal cost and price are equal. For the monopolist, price may exceed marginal cost by a substantial amount. Under certain conditions,[7] demand represents the marginal *social* valuation of a commodity by the members of the society. Similarly, long-run marginal cost usually represents the marginal *social* cost of production. Under monopoly, the marginal *value* of a commodity to society exceeds the marginal cost of its production to society. The society as a whole would therefore benefit by having more of its resources used in producing the commodity in question. The profit-maximizing monopolist will not do so, however, for producing at the point where price equals marginal cost would eliminate all, or almost all, profit. Indeed, there might be a loss. Therefore, all other things equal, social welfare tends to be promoted more by competitive than by monopolistic market organization.

This is easily seen in Figure 10.5.3. The monpolist chooses price OP^* and produces output OQ^*. But the efficient amount of output from society's point of view is OQ_c, which requires price OP_c. That OQ^* is inefficient can be understood by considering an increase in output from OQ^* to OQ_1. The cost of producing that additional unit is MC_1, shown at point B on the marginal cost curve. The value to the consumer who will buy the good is OP_1, shown at point A on the demand curve. Since the value exceeds the cost, the good should be produced from society's point of view. Of course, neither the monopolist nor the competitor is concerned much about society. Since profits are higher at OP^*, OQ^*, this is where the monopolist produces. The competitive firm would do likewise if it possessed sufficient market power.

Long-Run Equilibrium in a Multiplant Monopoly
10.5.c

In the long run a multiplant monopolist adjusts the number of plants to attain equilibrium. The process is illustrated in Figure 10.5.4.

The adjustment of each individual plant is shown in Panel A. Irrespective of original plant size, in the long run the monopolist can construct *each* plant of such size that short-run average cost coincides with long-run average cost at the minimum point on the latter curve. In other words, the firm can construct each plant of such size that the desired rate of output per plant can be produced at the irreducible minimum unit cost. But as the firm expands output by expanding the number of plants operating at minimum long-run average cost, the cost curves for each plant shift upward. This must be true because input prices increase with input usage (that is, one must presume that if *all* resources used were unspecialized, there would be a competitive market organization).

In Chapter 9 this type of situation was discussed. In that case we said the competitive industry faced increasing prices of inputs, and we showed how to construct the long-run supply curve (or curve showing the long-run supply price). A similar curve can be constructed for the multiplant monopolist; but it does *not* relate to long-run supply or long-run supply price (long-run supply, as well as

---

[7]The exceptions are noted in Chapter 17.

Figure 10.5.3 Difference in welfare under monopoly and perfect competition

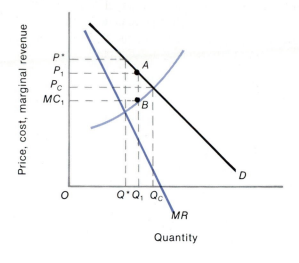

Figure 10.5.4 Long-run equilibrium in a multiplant monopoly

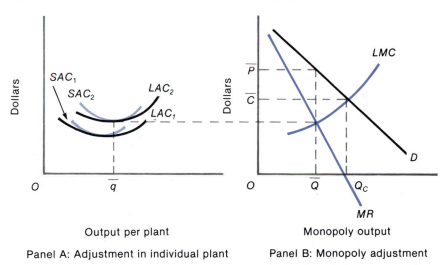

Panel A: Adjustment in individual plant

Panel B: Monopoly adjustment

short-run supply, is not well defined in the case of monopoly). To the monopolist this curve is the long-run marginal cost curve because it shows the *minimum increase in cost* attributable to an expansion of output by expanding the number of optimally adjusted plants (that is, plants operating at minimum long-run average cost).

The long-run marginal cost curve thus derived is labeled LMC in Panel B. The revenue conditions are shown by D and MR. Invoking the $LMC = MR$ rule, long-run profit maximizing equilibrium is attained at an output of $O\overline{Q}$ units per period and a price of $O\overline{P}$. The optimum output per plant is $O\overline{q}$. The number of plants n_m the monopolist constructs and utilizes is $n_m = O\overline{Q}/O\overline{q}$.

Comparison with Perfect Competition
10.5.d

In the long run both perfectly competitive firms and multiplant monopolists operate their plants at minimum long- and short-run unit cost. In this respect they are alike. Their differences will become clear by considering a hypothetical case.

Suppose each firm in a perfectly competitive industry is represented by Panel A, Figure 10.5.5. Then long-run industry equilibrium would occur at OQ_C in Panel B, where demand equals short-run supply. The associated market price is $O\overline{C}$, and the equilibrium number of firms n_c is presumably greater than n_m, the number of plants operated by the multiplant monopolist.

Next, suppose all firms are bought by the same individual, who creates an effective monopoly. As shown before, the monopolist will produce $O\overline{Q}$ units and sell them at $O\overline{P}$ each.[8] The monopolist would require only $n_m < n_c$ plants and would accordingly scrap the superfluous plants (in number, $n_c - n_m$). Thus, while either organization would be characterized by minimum-cost production, in comparison with the perfectly competitive industry, the multiplant monopolist would sell fewer units, charge a higher price, and operate fewer plants. In this case, as in the case of a single-plant monopoly, social welfare tends to be promoted to a greater extent by competition than by monopoly.

SPECIAL TOPICS IN MONOPOLY THEORY
10.6

Sections 10.1 through 10.5 described the theory of price under conditions of monopoly. In this concluding section two special types of monopoly organization are discussed.

Price Discrimination
10.6.a

Certain commodities are purchased by two or more distinct types of buyers. For example, commercial and residential purchasers of electric power usually can be sharply divided on the basis of demand elasticity. Similarly, tourists and business executives constitute two different types of markets for motel accommodations.

---

[8] The line $\overline{C}A$ is the long-run marginal cost because we assume that there LAC represents the most efficient plant and that it can be replicated at the same cost condition. To produce more output, indivisibilities aside, the monopolist increases the number of plants to keep unit cost at $O\overline{C}$.

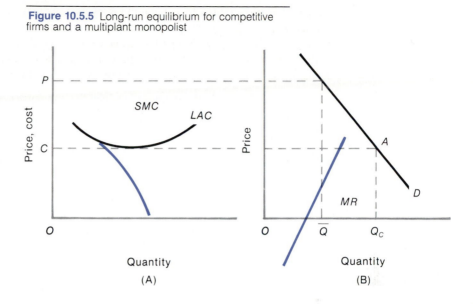

Figure 10.5.5 Long-run equilibrium for competitive firms and a multiplant monopolist

Monopolists may be able to augment monopoly profit in situations like these by a practice called *price discrimination* or *multipart pricing*. Price discrimination occurs when different prices are charged for the same commodity in different markets.

For simplicity, consider the case in which a general market can be divided into two distinct submarkets.[9] Suppose, first, that the monopolist has a fixed quantity of the product, say 100 units, to be sold in one or both of the two submarkets. How should the 100 units be allocated between the submarkets to maximize the monopolist's total revenue?[10] Suppose initially that the monopolist simply sold 50 units in each market. Also assume that with this allocation, marginal revenue in market 1 (MR_1) is \$5 and marginal revenue in market 2 (MR_2) is \$3. In this case, the monopolist could increase total revenue by reducing the number of units sold in market 2 and increasing the number of units sold in market 1. Hence, if one less unit is sold in market 2, total revenue declines by \$3 (= MR_2). But by selling this unit in market 1, total revenue increases by \$5 (= MR_1). Thus, by reallocating so that 51 units are sold in market 1 and 49 units are sold in market 2, there is a *net* increase in total revenue of \$2 (\$5 − \$3, or MR_1 − MR_2). Obviously this kind of revenue-increasing reallocation is possible

---

[9]In principle, the submarkets must be completely separate in the sense that when a different price is established in each, there is no reselling or arbitrage between the markets that would eliminate the demand in the higher-priced market. This leads to the implication that price discrimination is more common for services than for goods.

[10]For the present we are ignoring any production decisions, so maximization of total revenue is the appropriate criterion. Later, we will bring the production decision into the analysis.

whenever there is a difference in marginal revenue in the two submarkets. We can thus conclude that *to maximize the total revenue received from the sale of a given total quantity of a commodity, a price-discriminating monopolist will allocate the quantity sold between the submarkets so as to equate marginal revenue in each submarket.* Two qualifications to this general rule should be noted:

1. If the allocation of the output between the submarkets results in equal but *negative* marginal revenue in each submarket, the monopolist can increase total revenue by reducing sales in each submarket to the point where $MR_1 = MR_2 = 0$ and disposing of the excess output. In other words, the monopolist will not sell an output so large as to be in the inelastic portion of the demand curve in any submarket.

2. Let $MR_1(q_1)$ and $MR_2(q_2)$ be marginal revenue in market 1 and market 2, respectively, when q_1 units are sold in market 1 and q_2 units are sold in market 2. Suppose that $MR_1(q_1 + q_2) > MR_2(0)$. That is, suppose that when all the units are sold in market 1, marginal revenue in that market exceeds the marginal revenue in market 2 when nothing is sold in market 2. Then the monopolist will disregard market 2 and sell everything in market 1 as a nondiscriminating monopolist.

The principle that output be allocated among submarkets so as to obtain equal marginal revenue in each submarket can be illustrated in graphical form. Panel A of Figure 10.6.1 is the demand curve and marginal revenue curve for submarket 1. Panel B of this figure shows demand and marginal revenue for submarket 2. Finally, Panel C of this figure is constructed by *horizontally summing* the marginal revenue curves of submarkets 1 and 2 to get the kinked line designated $MR_1 + MR_2$.[11] Note that, in this case, MR_1 is greater than MR_2 when quantity is zero in each submarket (that is, the distance OU in Panel A is greater than OV in Panel B). This means that for an initial range of quantity, the horizontal sum in Panel C is identical with MR_1. Once quantity is large enough, both MR_1 and MR_2 enter the horizontal sum. This occurs at the "kink" designated V in Panel C, where V is the same distance above the quantity axis in Panel C as is the intercept (also V) of the MR_2 curve in Panel B.

The usefulness of Figure 10.6.1 as a graphical means of solving the above allocation problem can now be demonstrated. Suppose the monopolist has total output OB. Starting with Panel C, we locate this total quantity along the horizontal axis. Then, reading from the $MR_1 + MR_2$ in Panel C, we find that this total output is associated with marginal revenue OA. Next, reading Panel B and Panel A at marginal revenue OA, we find that the allocation of OB between the submarkets is OB_1 in submarket 1 and OB_2 in submarket 2 (where, by construction, $OB_1 + OB_2 = OB$). By our earlier argument, we know that this allocation between the submarkets yields the maximum total revenue that can be obtained

---

[11]The reader should be cautioned that the horizontal sum $MR_1 + MR_2$ in Panel C is *not* the marginal revenue curve that would be found by first horizontally summing the two demand curves and then constructing the marginal revenue curve for that aggregate demand.

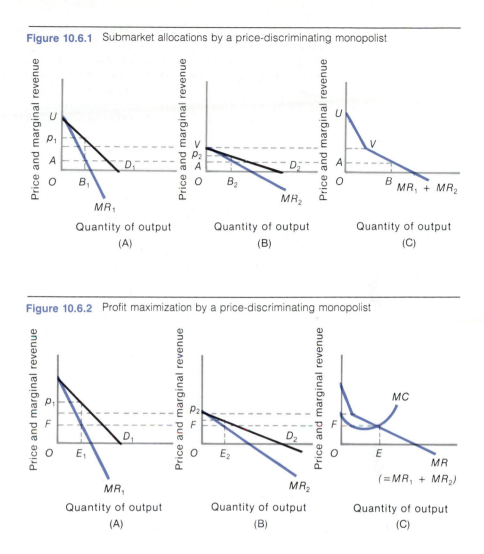

Figure 10.6.1 Submarket allocations by a price-discriminating monopolist

Quantity of output
(A)

Quantity of output
(B)

Quantity of output
(C)

Figure 10.6.2 Profit maximization by a price-discriminating monopolist

Quantity of output
(A)

Quantity of output
(B)

Quantity of output
(C)

from the sale of OB units of output. The demand curves in Panel A and Panel B can be used to ascertain the price in each market. Thus, when total quantity is OB, OB_1 is sold in submarket 1 at price Op_1 and OB_2 is sold in submarket 2 at price Op_2.

It is now a relatively easy step to complete the analysis by introducing the monopolist's marginal cost schedule so as to determine the profit-maximizing level of output. This marginal cost curve is designated MC in Panel C of Figure 10.6.2. (The demand curves and marginal revenue curves in Figure 10.6.2 are the same as in Figure 10.6.1.) The profit-maximizing level of output is determined by the intersection of MC and MR in Panel C (where $MR = MR_1 + MR_2$). The reason for this is straightforward. By construction, MR in Panel C of Figure 10.6.2 tells us the addition to total revenue arising from an additional increment of output when *output is optimally allocated to the submarkets*. As usual, the marginal cost schedule tells us the increase in total cost of an increment in output. Thus, by equating *MC* to *MR* in Panel C, we locate the total output which satisfies the familiar first-order condition for profit maximization.

In Figure 10.6.2 the profit-maximizing output is *OE*. Referring to Panel A and Panel B, we see that OE_1 units are sold in submarket 1 at price Op_1 and OE_2 units are sold in submarket 2 at price Op_2, where $OE_1 + OE_2 = OE$. It should be mentioned that this output represents the long-run profit-maximizing solution only if, at this output, total cost is no greater than total revenue. It is the short-run profit-maximizing output only if, at this output, total revenue exceeds total variable cost: otherwise, losses could be minimized by producing nothing.[12]

At any given positive output, it is visually apparent that demand is more elastic in market 2 than in market 1. Using this information in conjunction with the results above brings out an interesting, albeit rather obvious, point: the more elastic the submarket demand, the lower the equilibrium price in the submarket.[13] Among other things, this principle accounts for price differentials favoring commercial, as against residential, users of electrical power.

---

[12]The mathematical conditions are easy to derive. Let $TR_1(q_1)$ be total revenue in submarket 1 when q_1 units are sold there; let $TR_2(q_2)$ be total revenue in submarket 2 when q_2 units are sold there; and let $TC(q_1 + q_2)$ be the total cost of producing $q_1 + q_2$ units of output. The monopolist then chooses q_1 and q_2 to maximize the expression

$$TR_1(q_1) + TR_2(q_2) - TC(q_1 + q_2). \tag{10.6.1}$$

The first-order conditions are

$$MR_1(q_1) = MC(q_1 + q_2) \tag{10.6.2}$$

and

$$MR_2(q_2) = MC(q_1 + q_2) \tag{10.6.3}$$

or $MR_1(q_1) = MR_2(q_2) = MC(q_1 + q_2)$, where $MR_i(q_i)$ is the marginal revenue in market i ($i = 1, 2$) and $MC(q_1 + q_2)$ is marginal cost.

[13]This proposition is easily proved. First, recall that marginal revenue may also be written as

$$MR = p\left[1 - \frac{1}{\eta}\right]. \tag{10.6.4}$$

Next, since marginal revenue must be equal in both markets, we have

$$MR_1 = MR_2, \tag{10.6.5}$$

where subscripts denote the market. Using expression (10.6.4) in expression (10.6.5) we obtain

$$p_1\left[1 - \frac{1}{\eta_1}\right] = p_2\left[1 - \frac{1}{\eta_2}\right]. \tag{10.6.6}$$

Let market 1 be characterized by the higher price elasticity of demand. Hence,

$$\eta_1 > \eta_2,$$

and thus

$$\left[1 - \frac{1}{\eta_1}\right] > \left[1 - \frac{1}{\eta_2}\right].$$

Using the latter inequality in expression (10.6.6), equality between the left- and right-hand sides requires $p_2 > p_1$.

Part Three   Theory of the Firm and Market Organization

These results are summarized as follows:

Proposition: If the aggregate market for a monopolist's product can be divided into submarkets with different price elasticities, the monopolist can profitably practice price discrimination. Total output is determined by equating marginal cost with aggregate monopoly marginal revenue. The output is allocated among the submarkets so as to equate marginal revenue in each submarket with aggregate marginal revenue at the $MR = MC$ point. Finally, price in each submarket is determined directly from the submarket demand curve, given the submarket allocation of sales.

Block Pricing and Perfect Price Discrimination
10.6.b

Section 10.6.a dealt with monopoly price discrimination across submarkets. It was assumed there that only one price is charged in each submarket. A closely related but slightly different form of price discrimination arises when a monopolist sets different prices for the same market or consumer. This type of price discrimination often takes the form of volume discounts or block pricing. For example, the monopolist may charge the consumer a higher unit price for the first 10 units of a good than for the next 100 units. To explain this phenomenon we must first examine the concept of *consumer surplus*.

Refer to the demand curve AC in Panel A of Figure 10.6.3 and consider the following conceptual experiment. Suppose initially that the consumer would be willing to pay Op_1 for the first unit of the good rather than go without it. Thus, the area of the rectangle below the demand curve with base equal to 1 (that is, 1 unit) and height equal to Op_1 is a measure of the value of the first unit of the good to the consumer (that is, $Op_1 \cdot 1 = Op_1$). Having obtained one unit of the good, the demand curve tells us that the consumer would be willing to pay as much as Op_2 for the second unit.[14] Thus, the area of the rectangle beneath the demand curve with base 1 and height Op_2 (that is, $Op_2 \cdot 1 = Op_2$) measures the value to the consumer of the second unit of the good. Each additional unit can be valued in the same manner. By adding up the areas of such rectangles, the total value to the consumer of any given quantity of the good can be measured. For example, in Figure 10.6.3, Panel A, the value to the consumer of four units of the good is the sum of the areas of the four rectangles beneath the demand curve. These rectangles are constructed so that each has a unit base. Thus, the total area is simply the sum $Op_1 + Op_2 + Op_3 + Op_4$.

If we apply the same technique when the base of each rectangle is very small, the measure of the value to the consumer of any given quantity of the good is approximated by the area beneath the demand curve corresponding to the quantity

---

[14]This is not quite precise because the payment of p_1 for the first unit would reduce the consumer's income, so the demand curve would shift down (assuming the good is normal or superior). Thus, the above estimate of consumer surplus is not precise unless the good in question has a zero-income elasticity.

NUMERICAL EXERCISE

A profit-maximizing monopolist produces its output with a total cost (in dollars) function given by

$$TC = 5Q + 20 \quad \text{(note: } MC = 5\text{)}$$

and sells its output in two market segments which are completely separated from each other. The demand for the product in market segment 1 is:

$$Q_1 = 55 - P_1 \quad (MR_1 = 55 - 2Q_1)$$

while demand in market segment 2 is:

$$Q_2 = 70 - 2P_2 \quad (MR_2 = 35 - Q_2)$$

Questions

What quantities should the monopolist sell in each market segment? What prices should be charged in each market segment? Finally, explain the result in terms of the price elasticity of demand in the two market segments.

Solutions

$$TR_1 = 55Q_1 - Q_1^2 \qquad MR = 55 - 2Q_1 \qquad MC = 5$$

Thus, set

$$55 - 2Q_1 = 5 \ldots\ldots \qquad Q_1 = 25$$
$$MR_2 = 35 - Q_2; \ldots\ldots\ldots \qquad Q_2 = 30$$
$$P_1 = 55 - Q_1; \qquad P_1 = 30.$$
$$P_2 = 35 - Q_2/2 = 20.$$

The price is lower in the market with the more elastic demand. If the price is the same, the market with the more elastic demand has a greater MR than the market with the less elastic demand. To expand output in the market with the greater MR, you would want to lower price . . . vice versa in the market with the lower MR.

(Please refer to "Applying the Theory" section at beginning of the chapter for an application of this material to the price of college tuition.)

Figure 10.6.3 Measurements of value to the consumer

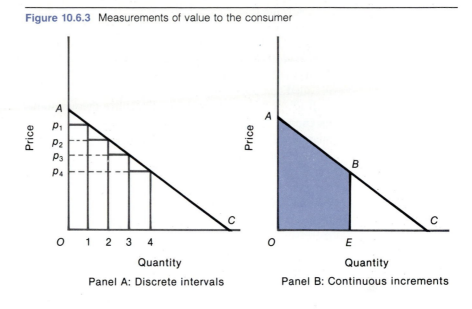

Panel A: Discrete intervals

Panel B: Continuous increments

Figure 10.6.4 Block pricing and monopoly total revenue

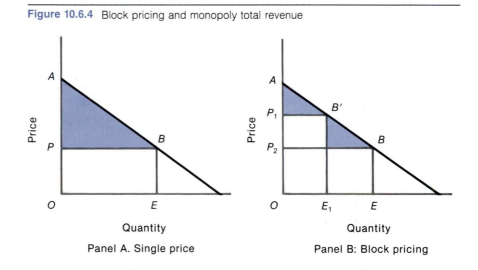

Panel A. Single price

Panel B: Block pricing

in question. [15] Thus, in Panel B of Figure 10.6.3, the value to the consumer of OE units of the good is the area of the trapezoid $OABE$ (shaded in the figure).

---

[15]Let the demand curve be given in inverse form by the expression $p = D(x)$. Then the total value to the consumer of q units of the good is measured by

$$V(q) = \int_0^q D(x)dx .$$

Note that, given this interpretation, the *marginal value* of an additional unit is the derivative of $V(q)$, which is simply $p = D(q)$.

Returning to our earlier discussion, suppose the monopolist sets price OP as in Panel A of Figure 10.6.4. At this price, the consumer purchases OE units of the good, which have a total value to the consumer given by the area of the trapezoid $OABE$. However, the consumer pays $OPBE$ for this quantity of the good, so the *net* value to the consumer is the shaded triangle PAB. This net value is called *consumer surplus*.

It is obvious from the discussion above that consumer surplus represents the maximum additional amount a consumer would be willing to pay for a given quantity of a good rather than do without it. If it is possible for a monopolist to know (or at least to make a reasonable estimate of) a consumer's demand curve, a multipart pricing strategy can be employed to capture more of this surplus for the monopolist. For example, in Panel B of Figure 10.6.4, the monopolist charges OP_1 per unit for the first E_1 units and OP_2 per unit for all units greater than E_1. This reduces consumer surplus to the area of the two shaded triangles and increases the total revenue of the monopolist by an amount equal to the reduction in consumer surplus. If the monopolist could *perfectly discriminate,* then each and every increment of the good would be priced separately so as to capture all the consumer surplus. Total revenue to the monopolist would then be the area beneath the demand curve up to the quantity sold, as in Panel B of Figure 10.6.3. This is called perfect price discrimination.

It is clearly difficult for a monopolist to know exactly each consumer's demand curve and, even if this were possible, it would be prohibitively complicated to establish a different price policy for each and every individual consumer. Nonetheless, a monopolist may be able to devise some scheme of block pricing or volume discounting which will increase total revenue above that associated with the best single-price policy. Block pricing and volume discounts are often used by public utilities and telephone companies. These price policies may be explained in part by the presence of lumpy costs associated with providing service to individual consumers, but there is good reason to suspect that some sort of price discrimination is also taking place.

SYNOPSIS
10.7

- A pure monopoly exists if there is exactly one seller in a market. The market demand curve is thus the monopolist's demand curve. This means that to increase the quantity sold, given the demand curve, the monopolist must reduce the price of the product.

- Because the monopolist faces a negatively sloped demand curve, marginal revenue is less than price at all relevant outputs. The monopolist will take into account the effect on price (and, hence, total revenue) of changes in output when determining the profit-maximizing quantity to produce and sell. The monopolist will choose output in the short run at the point where marginal cost equals marginal revenue so long as total revenue at this output exceeds total variable cost. If the latter condition is not satisfied, the monopolist will produce nothing.

■ In the long run, the monopolist will produce and sell the quantity at which long-run marginal cost equals marginal revenue (assuming that at this output total revenue is not less than total cost). The optimal plant in the long run is the one whose short-run average cost curve is tangent to the long-run average cost curve at the equilibrium level of output.

■ If a monopolist can successfully separate the general market into submarkets that have different demand curves, it will generally be profitable to engage in price discrimination by setting different prices in each submarket. The profit-maximizing output will be divided among the submarkets so as to equate marginal revenue in each submarket. Total output will be where marginal cost is equal to the horizontal sum of the marginal revenue curves of the submarkets.

■ By using block pricing or volume discounts instead of a single-price policy, a monopolist may capture additional consumer surplus relative to a single-price policy and therefore raise the total revenue obtained from the sale of any given quantity of output.

QUESTIONS AND EXERCISES

1. Federal milk marketing orders, covering most metropolitan areas, impose a specified price to be paid dairy farmers for milk used for industrial purposes (for example, in making cheese, ice cream, etc.) and a higher price for milk used for direct consumption (that is, drinking).
   a. Does such an arrangement affect the returns to the dairy farming industry?
   b. How do the marketing orders affect the allocation of resources and economic welfare of the community?

2. In a consent decree signed in the mid-1950s, IBM agreed to sell, as well as rent, various business machines. IBM also agreed to dispose of the facilities used to produce punch cards that were required to operate the machines and agreed further that IBM would no longer sell punch cards. Firms renting IBM machines formerly had to buy their punch cards from IBM. At this time IBM owned 90 percent of all machines in its field. What effect would prohibiting the producing and selling of punch cards have on IBM's pricing policy for machines?

3. On its leased duplicating machines, Xerox has used a pricing policy that involves a lower charge per copy the larger the number of copies of a given original. In other words, one copy of each of five separate originals costs more than five copies of a single original. What similarities does this pricing policy have with the IBM policy in question 2?

4. In a number of university towns, college professors receive discounts from the local bookstores, usually about 10 percent. Students are generally not given similar discounts. Assuming that this practice constitutes price discrimination, what conditions make it feasible and desirable for the stores?

5. Some time ago, most of the major airlines issued student travel cards at a nominal price. These cards permitted college students to fly "space available" (that is, no reservations allowed) at substantial discounts. When this practice was in effect, some older nonstudents were using the cards, and some students were ensuring themselves available space by reserving seats for fictitious passengers who then do not show up for the flight.

   a. Did the discounts represent price discrimination?

   b. Did the conditions necessary for successful discrimination exist?

6. From 1923 to 1945, Du Pont was virtually the sole American producer of "moisture-proof Cellophane," a product for which it held the key patents. In its opinion, which exonerated Du Pont of possessing any economically meaningful monopoly, the Supreme Court held "an appraisal of the 'cross-elasticity' of demand in the trade" to be of considerable importance to the decision. Why?

SUGGESTED READINGS

Allen, R. G. D. *Mathematical Analysis for Economists.* London: Macmillan, 1956, chap. 18.

Hicks, J. R. "Annual Survey of Economic Theory: The Theory of Monopoly." *Econometrica* 3 (1936), pp. 1–20.

Machlup, Fritz. *The Political Economy of Monopoly.* Baltimore: Johns Hopkins University Press, 1952.

_____. *The Economics of Sellers' Competition.* Baltimore: Johns Hopkins University Press, 1952, pp. 543–66.

Robinson, Joan. *The Economics of Imperfect Competition.* London: Macmillan, 1933, pp. 47–82.

Samuelson, Paul A. *Foundations of Economic Analysis.* Cambridge, Mass.: Harvard University Press, 1947, pp. 57–89.

Simkin, C. G. F. "Some Aspects and Generalizations of the Theory of Discrimination," *Review of Economic Studies* 15 (1948–1949), pp. 1–13.

11 Competition and Monopoly: Some Analytical Exercises

Will rent control laws decrease or increase the quantity of rental housing? The answer may vary, depending upon whether the rental housing suppliers behave more like perfect competitors or like a pure monopoly. This chapter explains this answer, as it applies the two basic models of monopoly and perfect competition to a variety of circumstances. In addition to considering the effects of price ceilings and various taxes, this chapter also considers the special case of producers who are monopolists in their domestic country, but perfect competitors when exporting to the rest of the world. Such a model is one possible explanation for the fairly common practice of charging a different price to domestic buyers from that charged to buyers in export markets. An explicit example of just such a practice is taken up in detail in the "Applying the Theory" section at the beginning of this chapter. ■

Pistachio Growers Applaud Tariff

By Bruce Keppel
Times Staff Writer

California's pistachio growers who claimed to have lost 40 percent of last year's domestic sales to cheap pistachios from Iran, predicted a boom in 1986 sales after the federal government last week slapped tariffs totaling 236 percent on the Iranian imports.

"Everybody is on quite an upbeat note," Ronald Khachigian, chairman of the California Pistachio Commission, said Friday. "We feel that we can sell any amount of pistachios we can grow."

The whopping 236 percent tariff — actually a combination of penalties — means that importers of Iranian pistachios will now have to post a $2.36 customs bond for every $1 worth of nuts that they bring into this country, commission lobbyist Robert I. Schramm said.

The International Trade Administration acted after California growers produced evidence that Iranian-grown pistachios that sold wholesale for $3.50 a pound in Tehran were selling wholesale on the East Coast for $1.30 a pound, Schramm said.

Khachigian said grower optimism stems in part from the timing of the decision. Pistachio trees alternate between producing huge crops and small crops, he explained, and "we're going into our 'up' year."

"We won't have the pressure of cheap pistachios hanging over our head, depressing prices," he said. "This is what happened to us two years ago."

Prices on the 1984 crop, sold last year, plunged up to 60 cents a pound as Iranian nuts augmented an already swollen California crop, flooding the market, Khachigian said.

Series of Decisions

Schramm said the 236 percent total in penalties reflects a series of decisions, some final, some subject to modification.

In a preliminary finding last December, the government imposed a 56.8 percent tariff on Iranian pistachios in response to evidence of unfair trade practices. In the final ruling this month, it replaced that with a 99.5 percent penalty and made the levy retroactive to last December 30.

The government also ordered a preliminary "anti-dumping" levy of 192.5 percent, effective last December 5. ("Dumping" — selling abroad at prices lower than production costs — is a violation of the international General Agreement on Tariffs and Trade.)

A final determination on that penalty is due by July 3.

Because of some overlap, the net result, fully effective last week, totaled 236 percent, Schramm said.

Schramm and Khachigian estimated that 4 million to 6 million pounds of Iranian nuts have been imported since the effective dates of the tariffs. Unless these are removed

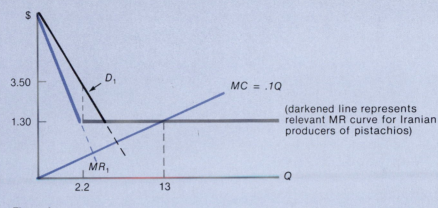

$

3.50 — D_1 $MC = .1Q$

                              (darkened line represents
1.30 —   relevant MR curve for Iranian
                              producers of pistachios)

            MR_1 Q

      2.2   13

Figure A

from sale, the penalties could net the government up to $10 million, Schramm said.

Due to an earlier customs ruling, upheld by the U.S. Court of International Trade, pistachio importers must now clearly label their packages to show the country of origin.

One importer was selling Iranian nuts under a "Pride of California" label; another labeled the nuts "Sun Ranch," listing a California address. (Virtually all U.S. pistachios are grown in California.)

Many retailers opposed the disclosure, Schramm said, not wishing to advertise their pistachios as "produce of Iran."

Questions

1. Assume the pistachio producers in Iran behave like the price-discriminating monopolist in section 11.6. In particular, assume they behave like a monopoly in Iran due to, say, protection from foreign competition by tariffs and import restrictions. In addition, suppose they could export pistachios on the world market where perfect competition prevails.

a. If the domestic demand for pistachios in Iran is

$$P(\text{in } \$) = 5.70 - Q$$
$$(MR = 5.70 - 2Q)$$

and the world price of pistachios is currently $1.30 per unit, and in addition, the marginal cost of producing pistachios in Iran is

$$MC = .1Q$$

(continued on page 326)

(continued from page 325)
find the equilibrium quantity of
pistachios produced.

b. How much of the quantity produced
in (a) is sold domestically? At what
price? Demonstrate your solution
graphically.

c. How much is exported? At what
price?

d. Compare the price and demand
elasticity in the domestic versus
world market (at the market prices
and quantities above). Is the result
consistent with a profit-maximizing,
price-discrimination monopolist?

e. Compare your prices in parts 1(b)
and 1(c) above with those reported
in the article. Can the behavior of
the Iranian pistachio producers be
explained by this model of an
international price-discriminating
monopoly?

2. Suppose that the government of Iran
decides to promote exports to the rest
of the world by providing an export
subsidy, s, of 40¢ per unit of pistachios
exported to the rest of the world. How
would this export subsidy change the
results in question 1 above? Are the
results consistent with the predictions
at the end of section 11.6?

3. In the article from the *Los Angeles
Times*, dumping is defined as "selling
abroad at prices lower than production
costs." How does this definition of
dumping differ from the one used in
this text? Can you think of any reason
why a firm would ever want to "sell
abroad at prices lower than production
costs"? Explain your answer.

Solutions

1. a, b, c.
Refer to Figure 11.6.1 in text for a
situation exactly analogous to this
problem.
For overall quantity, set
$MC = MR = 1.30$ $.1Q = 1.30$, or
$Q = 13$.
To determine domestic output, set
$MR_I = 5.70 - 2Q = MR_{ROW} =$
1.30.
Thus, $5.70 - 2Q_I = 1.30$, or
$Q_I = 2.20$, where I = Iran and
ROW = rest of world. The price in
Iran is given by demand curve, sub-
stituting 2.2 for Q:

$$P_I = 5.70 - 2.2 = \$3.50.$$

As Figure A illustrates, the domestic output is then 2.2 and the
amount sold in the rest of the world
is $13 - 2.2 = 10.8$ units.

d. The elasticity of demand in the export market (rest of the world) is infinite. At $P_I = \$3.50$, $Q_I = 2.2$, the

elasticity in Iran $= dQ/dP \times P/Q = 1 \times 3.5/2.2 = 1.59$.
Thus, $MR_{ROW} = \$1.30 + 40¢ = MC$.
Thus, $.1Q = 1.70$, or total $Q = 17$.
Hence, the market with the more elastic demand (rest of world) will face a lower price, and the sub-market with the less elastic demand (Iran) will face a higher price.

e. They are the same as indicated in the article. Yes.

2. The export subsidy raises the effective MR from selling exports to the rest of the world by s, the amount of the subsidy per unit.
   In Iran, set
   $$MR_I = 5.70 - 2Q = MR_{ROW} = 1.70.$$
   Thus, $Q_I = 2$. Amount exported now equals 15 ($17 - 2$). The price in Iran $= 5.70 - (2) = \$3.70$.
   The result of the export subsidy is to: (a) increase total output from 13 to 17; (b) increase the amount exported to the rest of the world from 10.8 to 15 ($17 - 2$); (c) increase the domestic price from $3.50 to $3.70 (and reduce domestic output from 2.2 to 2).

   The qualitative changes here are exactly those predicted at end of section 11.6 in the text.

3. In the text, "dumping" refers to the practice of selling in world markets at a price below the domestic price.

Given the conditions necessary for international price-discrimination, this practice is consistent with profit-maximization. However, note that the price in the world market will just equal marginal cost. Thus, if the "production costs" mentioned in the article refer to marginal cost, the definition in the article is different. We would not expect a price-discriminating monopolist to sell goods in the world market at a price below marginal cost.

The only exception to this rule might be the following: if the practice of "selling below production costs" resulted in a change in the structure of the industry, then such a practice might be consistent with long-run profit maximization. That is, by charging below cost in the short run, the firm might drive competitors out of business. At this point, they could conceivably raise the export price to the monopoly level.

This practice is sometimes referred to as "predatory pricing." While economists do not deny this possibility, they generally cast doubt on the efficacy of such a policy. This topic is left to more advanced courses.

Source: *Los Angeles Times*, April 15, 1986.

The models of Chapters 9 and 10 have played a central role in the economists' tool bag for many years. This is not because they always appear "realistic" on a priori grounds, but because they are capable of providing interesting hypotheses that have held up rather well in empirical tests.

The aim of this chapter is to illustrate the use of these models as hypothesis "generators." We will use the competitive industry model and the model of pure monopoly to analyze the impact of certain governmental and industrial policies such as taxes and price controls. The specific analyses presented are meant to be illustrative, not definitive. What we wish to do is show how the models can be used as analytical tools, and we have chosen some relatively simple examples and assumptions for this purpose. A more complete analysis would include a refinement of the assumptions, a more detailed consideration of secondary and tertiary effects, and at least some recognition of the general equilibrium aspects of the problem. Despite these simplifications, however, the discussion ought to help the reader develop a deeper understanding of how the models work.

The analysis is important not only because it is interesting to understand how taxes and subsidies affect an economy, but because almost all possible changes can be reinterpreted as a tax of one type or another. Thus, the effects of increases on variable input prices are completely analogous to those of a unit tax. Similarly, the effects of an increase in a fixed cost such as rent on the factory are analogous to those of a lump-sum tax. By understanding the analysis of this chapter, the economist has much of what he needs to describe the effects of any kind of cost change in the real world.

EXCISE TAXES IN A COMPETITIVE INDUSTRY
11.2

We begin with an analysis of the impact of a governmentally imposed excise tax in a competitive industry. We assume that the tax is imposed on a per unit basis; that is, for each unit sold a tax of, say, 10 cents must be paid.[1] The tax is paid to the government by the producer rather than the buyer, but this has no effect on the conclusions so long as we assume that collection costs are essentially the same for producers and buyers. We also assume that changes in total industry output do not affect technology or factor prices. The objective of the analysis is to determine what will happen to prices, industry output, firm output, and the number of firms in the industry when the tax is imposed. We will consider the effect on these magnitudes first in the short run and then in the long run.

---

[1]Such taxes apply to cigarettes, for example. A more familiar tax is an ad valorem tax where the tax is stated as a given *percentage* of the selling price. The ad valorem tax is analyzed in a manner similar to the unit tax, but the analysis differs in certain details.

Short-run Effects on Cost, Price, and Output
11.2.a

To facilitate the discussion, assume that all firms in the industry are identical and that there are n_0 such firms before the tax is imposed. The initial equilibrium is shown in Figure 11.2.1. Panel A shows the short-run average total cost and the associated marginal cost curve for a typical firm. The firm is in equilibrium at a price of p_0 and an output of q_0. Panel B in Figure 11.2.1 shows the industry supply curve and the demand curve. Given the constant-cost industry assumption, the supply curve is simply the horizontal summation of the marginal cost curves of the firms. Because we assume there are n_0 firms (all the same as the "typical" firm), the total quantity supplied and demanded is $n_0 q_0$.

When the tax is imposed on producers, marginal cost increases by the amount of the tax because the tax is paid on each unit sold. Hence, the marginal cost curve shifts up vertically by the amount of the tax. For the same reason the average cost curve also shifts up vertically by the amount of the tax.[2] Notice that this means the posttax minimum average cost occurs at the same output as the pretax minimum average cost. The new cost curves are shown in MC_1 and ATC_1 in Panel A of Figure 11.2.2.

Recall that short-run profits will be maximized (or losses minimized) by a competitive firm if output is chosen so as to equate price and marginal cost (given that this price is above average variable cost). The tax shifts the marginal cost curve so when firms equate price to marginal cost the posttax output of the firm will be lower at each price than pretax output at that price. This means the industry supply curve will shift. In particular, for a per-unit tax the industry supply curve shifts up vertically by the amount of the tax. This is shown by the posttax supply curve S_1 in Panel B of Figure 11.2.2.

The short-run equilibrium (that is, market-clearing price) will obtain where the short-run posttax supply curve intersects the demand curve. If the demand curve were completely inelastic, the new price would have to be greater than the old price by exactly the same amount of the tax. However, when the demand curve is not perfectly inelastic, the new price will be above the old price but by *less* than the amount of the tax. This is because increases in price reduce the quantity demanded and the market will not clear at a new price equal to the old price plus the tax because at that price producers would be willing to supply the *old* quantity but consumers would demand less than the old quantity. Thus, the new market price shown by p_1 in Figure 11.2.2 is above the old but by less than the tax.[3]

At p_1 each firm reduces its output from q_0 to q_1 and short-run industry output is $n_0 q_1$. It was noted above that the minimum of the average cost curve including

---

[2]If the total cost of the firm is $C(q)$ before the tax, then before-tax marginal cost is $C'(x)$ and before-tax average cost is $C(q)/q$. After the tax is imposed, total cost is $C(q) + tq$ where t is the tax. After-tax marginal cost is $C'(q) + t$, and after-tax average cost is $[C(q)/q] + t$. Observe that the minimum pretax average cost occurs at the same output as posttax average cost because these two functions differ only by the constant per-unit tax.

[3]We assume that the new price, p_1, is above the average variable cost including the tax.

Figure 11.2.1 Initial equilibrium in a competitive industry

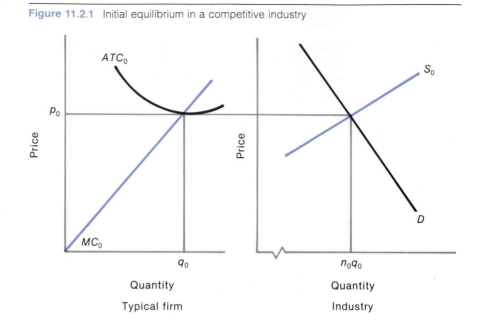

Typical firm / Industry

Figure 11.2.2 Short-run equilibrium with a unit tax

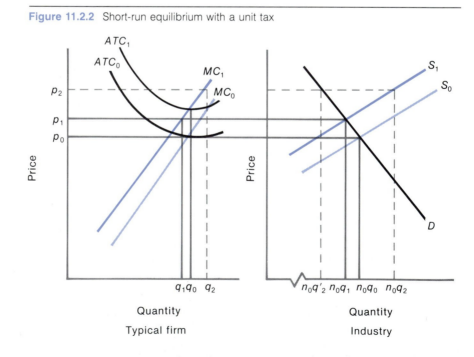

Typical firm / Industry

Part Three *Theory of the Firm and Market Organization*

Long-Run Effects of the Tax
11.2.b

The short-run losses that result from the tax cause firms to leave the industry.[4] The actual process by which this occurs is a dynamic question not answered by the comparative static models of Chapter 9. Thus we are not able to tell precisely which firms will leave or how fast this will happen. We know, however, that firms will exit so long as losses exist.

Of course the losses will not continue indefinitely as firms leave. Remember that the supply curve is the *sum* of the marginal cost curves of the firms. As firms leave, this sum will involve a smaller number of firms and thus the industry supply curve shifts upward and to the left. This is shown as the shift from S_0 to S_1 to S_2 in Figure 11.2.3. The shift will stop when economic profits are back to zero, which is, of course, at the price which exceeds the initial price by exactly the amount of the tax. (This is because the new average cost curve has a minimum that is equal to the minimum of the old average cost curve plus the tax.) At this point, firms are induced neither to enter nor to leave the industry. Thus, equilibrium is reached at p_2, with each firm producing q_0, but the total is only $n_2 q_0$. n_2 is smaller than n_0 because some firms have left the industry (see Table 11.2.1). the tax is at the same output, namely q_0, as the minimum of the pretax average cost curve. This means that p_1 is below the minimum average total cost and that firms are suffering short-run economic losses. The presence of losses in the short run sets in motion the forces that lead to the new long-run equilibrium.

From the way that Figure 11.2.2 is drawn, it is clear that price shifts up by less than the full amount of the tax. It is this proposition that leads to a reduction in the amount produced by each firm. But how do we know that price could not have shifted up by more than the tax? This is easily proved by contradiction. Reference to Figure 11.2.2 is useful.

Suppose that price has shifted up by more than the tax, say, to p_2 instead of p_1. This necessarily implies that each of the n_0 firms would like to produce q_2, which exceeds q_0. The total supply for the market would be $n_0 q_2$. But at a price of p_2, consumers are only willing to buy $n_0 q_2'$, which falls short of $n_0 q_0$, and certainly of $n_0 q_2$. Thus, the price p_2 cannot be an equilibrium.

In fact, this is the logic behind the rise in price. A price increase must reduce the amount sold because the demand curve is downward sloping. This implies that a short-run equilibrium can be reached only when each of the n_0 firms reduces output. The long run is somewhat different, however.

Ad Valorem Taxes
11.2.c

Ad valorem taxes, sometimes called "sales taxes," are imposed as a fixed percentage of the price of a commodity. The analysis is quite similar to that of the unit tax, but is somewhat easier to explain by assuming that the tax is collected

---

[4]This analysis assumes that the tax is not applied to all other industries. If it were, the alternative costs would be affected and the cost curves of the industry would be shifted.

Figure 11.2.3 Long-run equilibrium with a unit tax

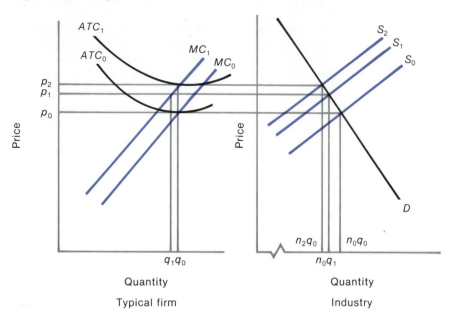

Typical firm   Industry

Table 11.2.1 The effects of a unit tax on a constant-cost competitive industry

Effect on	Short run	Long run
Price	Increased but less than tax	Increased by amount of tax
Firm output	Decreased	Unchanged
Industry output	Decreased	Decreased (by more than short-run decrease)
Number of firms	Unchanged	Decreased

from consumers rather than suppliers.[5] In view of these strong similarities, we will refer only to the industry curves in the graphs.

When an ad valorem tax is imposed, a fraction of the price paid by consumers is taken by the government and the price net of tax is received by producers. In Figure 11.2.4, the curve labeled D is the demand curve. This curve represents the gross amount consumers are willing to pay per unit for any given output. Before the tax is imposed, producers receive all that consumers pay and, assuming a supply curve S_0, the equilibrium price and quantity are p_0 and n_0q_0.

After the tax is imposed, producers do not receive all that consumers pay because some fixed fraction of the price goes to the government. Accordingly, we add an auxiliary curve, labeled D_T in Figure 11.2.4, which shows the price net

---

[5]The same analysis could be applied in the case of a unit tax with no change in the conclusions.

Figure 11.2.4 Ad valorem taxes

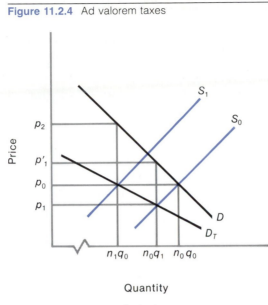

Quantity

Industry

of taxes received by producers.[6] For each quantity, the associated price on the demand curve D is reduced by the fixed tax percent and the resulting "net of tax" price is the point on D_T associated with that quantity. The D_T curve is the relevant one for determining the quantity at which the market clears. The height of D_T is a constant proportion of the height of D, because the producer receives, say, 96 percent of the total amount paid by consumers (if the tax were 4 percent).

In Figure 11.2.4 the short-run market-clearing quantity after the tax is n_0q_1 where the price received by producers is p_1 and the price paid by consumers is p_1'. The difference $p_1' - p_1$ is the tax per unit. Since the minimum average cost before the tax was equal to p_0 (remember there are zero economic profits in competitive equilibrium), the after-tax price p_1 is below this minimum average cost.[7] This means there are economic losses in the industry and, as in the unit tax case, firms begin to leave.

The reduction in the number of firms drives the supply curve up and to the left because we are summing over fewer firms to get this curve. When the supply curve finally shifts to S_1, the net-of-tax price is p_0, so firms are again making zero economic profit. In this posttax long-run equilibrium, each firm produces q_0, the

---

[6] It is inappropriate to add the tax to D since the demand curve depends only on the gross price paid for the good. Consumers decide how much to demand given the gross price; they are unconcerned about what the tax authority or the producer receives.

[7] We are accounting for the tax by the auxiliary curve D_T so the cost curves of the firm are not affected.

output before the tax, but there are fewer firms, so industry output, n_1q_0, is less than both initial output and short-run output. Price has risen so that the new equilibrium price exceeds the old by the amount of the tax.[8]

LUMP-SUM TAXES
11.3

Lump-sum taxes differ from unit taxes or ad valorum taxes in that they do not vary with output or price. The lump-sum tax, as its name suggests, is simply a fixed dollar tax obligation, that is, a fixed cost rather than a variable cost. It is a "long-run" fixed cost in the sense that it cannot be avoided except by going out of business. Annual operating license fees for retail stores are examples of lump-sum taxes.

Short-Run Effects of a Lump-Sum Tax in a Competitive Industry
11.3.a

Using the assumptions of section 11.2 we can analyze the effect of a lump-sum tax on a competitive industry. We note first that lump-sum taxes do not affect either marginal cost or average variable cost because they do not vary with output. They do affect average total cost just as any fixed cost would. Figure 11.3.1, like the figures in section 11.2, shows the cost curves for the typical firm and the supply and demand curves for the industry. Before the tax is imposed, the industry is in equilibrium at a price of p_0 and an industry output of n_0q_0. Each of the n_0 firms produces an output of q_0.

The imposition of the lump-sum tax raises the average total cost curve of each firm but does not affect marginal cost. After the tax is imposed the average cost curve shifts from ATC_0 to ATC_1. The marginal cost curve does not change, and this means that it must intersect ATC_0 at its minimum point *and* ATC_1 at its minimum point. The minimum of ATC_1 must be above and to the right of the minimum of ATC_0.[9]

The marginal cost curve determines the industry supply function in the constant-cost industry case, and because there is no change in the marginal cost function, the lump-sum tax does not affect the short-run supply schedule. This

---

[8]We have treated the tax as if it were deducted from the price paid by the consumer. Let λ be the tax; then $p_T = p - \lambda p$ is the price received by the producer where p is the price paid by the consumer. This tax is equivalent to a tax of $\lambda/(1 - \lambda)$ *added* to the price received by the producer. Hence a 5 percent sales tax added to the producer's price can be treated as a 4.76 percent tax deducted from the price paid by the consumer for analytical purposes.

[9]Let T be the lump-sum tax. Then, if $C(q)$ is the total cost function before the tax, $C(q) + T$ is total cost after the tax. Marginal cost is unchanged, but average total cost goes from $C(q)/q$ to $C(q)/q + T/q$.

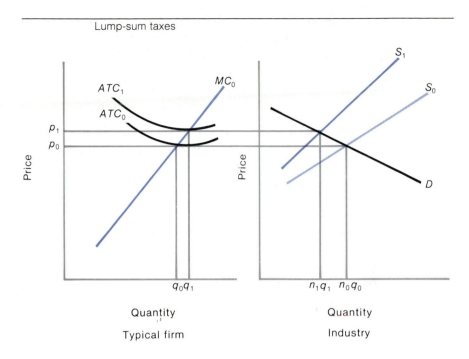

Lump-sum taxes

means that in the short run there is no change in price, firm output, or industry output.[10] The short-run situation will not persist indefinitely, however, because all firms are experiencing economic losses equal to the amount of the lump-sum tax.

Long-Run Effects of a Lump-Sum Tax
11.3.b

The economic losses caused by a lump-sum tax in the short run result in an exodus of firms from the industry. As firms leave, the supply curve shifts up and to the left because we are summing over a smaller number of firms. This causes price to rise (and industry output to fall) until the firms remaining in the industry return to zero economic profits. As shown in Figure 11.3.1, the new equilibrium obtains at a price of p_1 equal to the minimum of the posttax average cost curve. At the new equilibrium firms remaining in the industry are producing a larger output than before the tax. Posttax industry output is smaller. These results are summarized in Table 11.3.1.

---

[10]Students sometimes find this result puzzling and they tend to think the firms will want to increase price to cover fixed costs. It must be remembered, however, that in a competitive industry firms are *price takers* not price setters. Given price, the firms will continue to produce along their marginal cost curve because this decision maximizes profits (or minimizes losses). Hence, since the industry supply schedule is unchanged in the short run, the market-clearing price remains unchanged.

Table 11.3.1 Effects of a lump-sum tax in a constant-cost competitive industry

	Short run	Long run
Price	Unchanged	Increased
Firm output	Unchanged	Increased
Industry output	Unchanged	Decreased
Number of firms	Unchanged	Decreased

The only counterintuitive result is that each firm produces more, while total output is less. The reason behind this is that the lump sum tax has increased the efficient scale of operation, as all increases in fixed costs do. This means that if a firm is to produce, it must do so at a larger level of output. But this means that the industry can support fewer firms. Further, since price rises, total output sold must contract because consumers are unwilling to buy the old amount at the higher price. We elaborate in the next section.

Lump-Sum Taxes and the Size Distribution of Firms
11.3.c

The analysis of subsection 11.3.b suggests that lump-sum taxes tend to have the long-run effect of decreasing the number of firms in an industry and increasing their size. In other words, lump-sum taxes tend to concentrate output among a smaller number of larger firms, and the bigger the tax the more pronounced will be this effect.

This is not to say that lump-sum taxes necessarily favor firms that are relatively larger before the tax is imposed. To illustrate this, suppose that an industry contains firms of two sizes. Smaller-sized firms achieve minimum average total cost at three units of output, and larger firms achieve minimum average total cost at five units of output. The two sizes of firms can coexist in the industry so long as both have the same minimum average cost. Table 11.3.2 presents the relevant data for a lump-sum tax of $10. Column 1 of the table is output, column 2 is the average lump-sum tax, column 3 is pretax average total cost for a typical small firm, column 4 is posttax *ATC* for a small firm, column 5 is pretax *ATC* for a typical large firm, and column 6 is posttax *ATC* for a large firm. Before the tax small and large firms each have a minimum *ATC* of $100. After the tax the minimum *ATC* for small firms is $101.70, and for large firms $101.91. Hence the large firms cannot exist in the industry after the tax is imposed, and those firms which were small before the tax survive. It is true, of course, that the pretax small firms produce a larger output after the tax than the firms did before the tax, so our earlier conclusion that lump-sum taxes increase the average firm size is still true.[11]

---

[11]This increase in the size of the firm always holds when small and large firms have the same pretax minimum cost.

Table 11.3.2 Examples of the effect of lump-sum taxes in an industry with firms of different sizes

Output (units)	Average cost of lump-sum tax ($10/q)	Average cost for small firm		Average cost for large firm	
		Before tax	After tax	Before tax	After tax
1	$10.00	$100.20	$110.20	$101.00	$111.00
2	5.00	100.10	105.10	100.75	105.75
3	3.33	100.00	103.33	100.50	103.83
4	2.50	100.10	102.60	100.25	102.75
5	2.00	100.20	102.20	100.00	102.00
6	1.66	100.30	101.96	100.25	101.91
7	1.42	100.40	101.82	100.50	101.92
8	1.25	100.50	101.75	100.75	102.00
9	1.11	100.60	101.71	101.00	102.11
10	1.00	100.70	101.70	101.25	102.25
11	0.909	100.80	101.709	101.50	102.40
12	0.83	100.90	101.73	101.75	102.58
13	0.76	101.00	101.76	102.00	102.76
14	0.71	101.10	101.81	102.25	102.96
15	0.66	101.20	101.86	102.50	103.16

The disadvantage of the pretax large firms in these examples arises because the *ATC* of large firms rises much more rapidly than that of small firms, as output deviates from the output associated with minimum *ATC*. It is easy to construct alternative examples in which the large firms survive the lump-sum tax, and the small firms leave. The examples are intended to show that this depends on the shape as well as the location of the *ATC* curve.

PRICE CONTROLS
11.4

Efforts by the government to put ceilings (and in some cases floors) on prices are fairly common. Major efforts of this kind were made during World War II, and more recently in the Phase I and Phase IV policies of the Nixon administration. Other examples such as rent controls in New York City and in foreign cities have been around for many years. In this section we examine the effect of price ceilings in competitive and monopolistic industries.

Price Controls in a Competitive Industry
11.4.a

Figure 11.4.1 shows the industry supply curve S_0 and the industry demand curve *D* for a competitive constant-cost industry of the kind discussed in sections 11.2

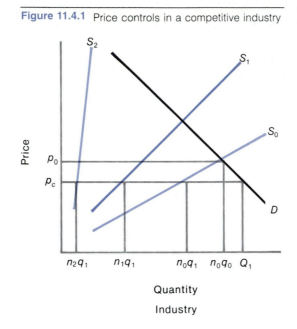

Figure 11.4.1 Price controls in a competitive industry

and 11.3. Before controls are imposed the market clears at a price of p_0 and an industry output of n_0q_0. (There are n_0 firms, each producing q_0.)

Now suppose the government imposes a price ceiling of p_c (where $p_c < p_0$). At this lower price consumers demand Q_1 units but firms each cut back their output to n_0q_1. The shortage created by the ceiling price is thus $Q_1 - n_0q_1$ initially. Because p_c is below the minimum ATC $(= p_0)$ of firms, there is an exodus of firms from the industry. This causes a shift of the supply curve, say to S_1. The shortage grows to $Q_1 - n_1q_1$ because there are fewer firms in the industry. The reduction in the number of firms does not affect the controlled price, so the exodus continues. As time goes on and more firms leave, the supply curve shifts to S_2 and the shortage grows to $Q_1 - n_2q_1$. Ultimately all firms will leave the industry.

As simple as this analysis is, it captures two interesting features of price control programs that are frequently observed in the real world:

a. Shortages appear to become greater the longer the controls are in effect. A big part of the explanation has to do with dwindling supply, as the above analysis suggests.

b. The longer the controls are in effect the greater will be the rise in price needed to clear the market in the short run. This is so because fewer firms are present, and industry supply will lie further to the left. In the long run the price will return to its precontrol level.[12]

---

[12]In the comparative static analysis used here we assume that no dynamic shifts in supply or demand conditions occur during the period of controls.

Part Three   Theory of the Firm and Market Organization

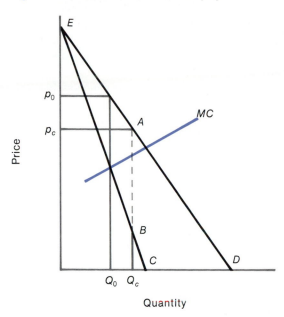

Figure 11.4.2 Price controls in a monopoly

Price Controls in a Monopoly
11.4.b

An interesting difference between the effect of price controls on a monopoly as compared with the competitive industry case is that in a monopoly the controls need not lead to a shortage. Consider Figure 11.4.2 where the line *EAD* is the demand curve, *EBC* is the marginal revenue curve, and *MC* is marginal cost. Before a price ceiling is imposed, the monopolist chooses the output Q_0 where marginal revenue equals marginal cost. The output is sold at price p_0.

Now suppose a price ceiling of p_c is imposed on the monopolist. Given the demand curve, the most that can be sold at this price is output Q_c. If more are to be sold than Q_c, the price must be reduced below p_c. This means that for outputs up to Q_c the monopolist has marginal revenue equal to p_c. Marginal revenue drops to B when output is increased slightly beyond Q_c. This is because the reduction in price needed to sell additional output must also be applied to the output Q_c which was previously sold at the ceiling price p_c. For further output increases the marginal revenue is given by the segment *BC* of the original marginal revenue curve.

The effect of the ceiling price is thus to change marginal revenue from *EBC* to the broken line $p_c ABC$. The segment *AB* is actually a discontinuity in the postcontrol marginal revenue curve. Marginal cost, as drawn in Figure 11.4.2, passes through the discontinuous segment *AB* of the new marginal revenue curve. Hence, for outputs less than Q_c, marginal revenue ($= p_c$) is greater than marginal cost and the monopolist increases profit by increasing output over this region. For outputs greater than Q_c, marginal cost is greater than marginal revenue so profits are increased by reducing output over this range. It follows that after the price ceiling is imposed the profit-maximizing output is Q_c which is sold at the ceiling price p_c. The price ceiling has led the monopolist to increase output, and no shortage occurs—at least for the particular price ceiling shown in Figure 11.4.2.[13]

Price ceilings *can* cause shortages in a monopoly (as shown in Figure 11.4.3). When the price ceiling is pushed down far enough, the marginal revenue curve becomes $p_c A Q_D$. The marginal cost curve intersects this marginal revenue curve at the point B in the horizontal segment $p_c A$. The monopolist produces Q_c after the ceiling is imposed because this is the point at which marginal revenue $(= p_c)$ equals marginal cost. At the ceiling price p_c, consumers demand Q_D and a shortage of $Q_D - Q_c$ obtains.

PRICE SUPPORTS AND OUTPUT RESTRICTIONS
11.5

Governments put floors under some prices just as they put ceilings on others. Agricultural price supports are a well-known example in the United States. For many years political pressures have led Congress and the Executive to provide legislation that keeps farm prices above market-clearing levels. In this section we examine two common ways in which this is done.

Price Floors
11.5.a

Figure 11.5.1 is the supply and demand curve for a competitive industry. Before price supports are introduced, the market clears at price p_0 and quantity Q_0. If the government supports the price at p_s (where $p_s > p_0$) supply will increase to Q_2 and demand will decrease to Q_1. The government buys and stores the surplus $Q_2 - Q_1$. The monetary cost to the government is $p_s \times (Q_2 - Q_1)$. The cost to society would be measured by the inefficient shift of resources to the farm sector and the loss of consumer welfare arising from the increased price.[14] The price support programs in the United States have led the government to hold substantial stocks of farm products. For the period 1961–65 annual carryover stocks of wheat averaged 1,104 million bushels, and for 1966–70 the annual average carryover stock was 600 million bushels of wheat. The figure decreased somewhat in the early 70s, averaging 334 million bushels from 1971 to 1975, but increased back to an average of almost 500 million bushels of wheat for the period 1976–81. Farm income support programs in 1980–81 cost the government over $4.4 billion and represented more than 17 percent of net farm income.

---

[13]This phenomenon is often used to justify regulation of monopolists' prices. In reality, it is hard to pick the right price, and errors can be made that do lead to shortages, as we shall soon see.

[14]The surplus and associated costs could be even larger if we account for entry into the industry (or the failure of inefficient firms to exit) that arises because of the price supports.

Figure 11.4.3 Shortages in a monopoly Figure 11.5.1 Price supports

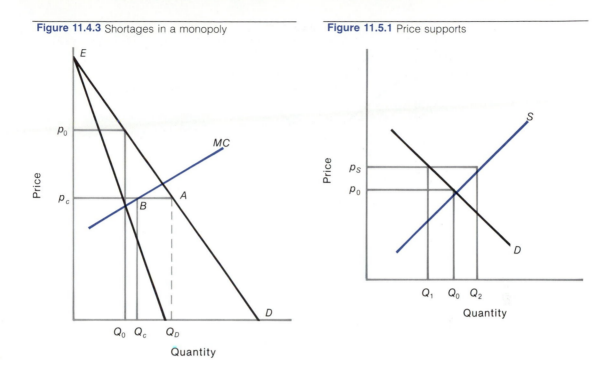

Output Restrictions
11.5.b

Another way of sustaining farm prices at greater than competitive levels is to use output restrictions. The "soil bank" programs which limit the amount of acreage that farmers plant are an example of such policies. Assume the government restricts the amount of land that farmers can use to grow crops. The short-run effect is illustrated in Figure 11.5.2 where the acreage restriction reduces output to Q_1 and results in an increase in price from p_0 to p_s.

A major difficulty with acreage restriction programs is that farmers are encouraged to increase other inputs to get more output. For example, they may use more fertilizer, plant crops closer together, and so on. This is an inefficient alternative to using more land and it leads to an increase in costs. Because of these cost increases, the supply curve shifts upward to S' in Figure 11.5.2. Farmers are able to expand output along this curve because they are meeting the government's acreage restriction while substituting other inputs for land. The result is a reduction in market price to p_s' and a greater cost of producing the corresponding output (namely, Q_2) than would obtain in the absence of the acreage restrictions.

This difficulty can be circumvented by a restriction on output, rather than input. Instead of the government limiting the amount of an input, land, that can be used, the government can place a restriction on the amount of output that a

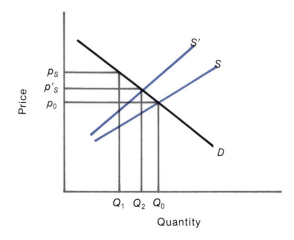

Figure 11.5.2 Output restrictions

farmer can sell. This provides the farmer with the right incentives to produce that output as efficiently as possible. The total revenue he receives is at most $(p_s)(Q_1)$, so profit, equal to $(p_s)(Q_1)$ − cost, is maximized by minimizing cost.

Even this solution is not without its shortcomings. Since the amount of output that is produced is somewhat random (weather, disease, insects, etc., affecting the yield), it is possible that the farmer might end up producing an amount greater than this quota. Under the restricted output plan, he would be forced to throw the extra crop away, which is clearly inefficient from society's point of view. The restriction on input does not suffer from the same difficulty since the farmer is allowed to sell everything he grows on the given amount of land.

Attempts to limit the amount produced or to support the price directly invariably lead to inefficiencies of some sort. Most economists oppose such measures on the grounds that there are better ways to transfer income to groups that are labeled deserving for one reason or another.

AN INTERNATIONAL MONOPOLIST—DUMPING AND PRICE DISCRIMINATION
11.6

Consider a firm that is a monopolist in its home country and which is protected from foreign competition by tariffs and other import restrictions. Suppose that there are no export restrictions, so the firm could, if it wished, also sell the good in the world market where there is a perfectly competitive market for the good in question. The firm's situation is shown in Figure 11.6.1. The firm's domestic monopoly is represented in Panel A by the downward-sloping demand curve AD with marginal revenue curve MR_1. The world market as seen by this firm is shown

Figure 11.6.1 Price discrimination and dumping

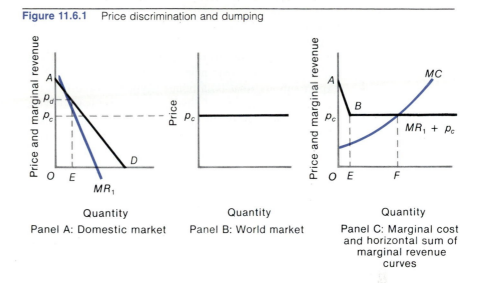

Panel A: Domestic market

Panel B: World market

Panel C: Marginal cost and horizontal sum of marginal revenue curves

in Panel B where the competitive price is p_c. The firm is a price taker in the world market, so the horizontal line p_c is also the firm's marginal revenue schedule for exported output.

Even though the firm is a monopolist only in the domestic market, the analytical techniques of subsection 10.6.a in Chapter 10 apply. The firm will allocate any given level of total output between the domestic and foreign markets so as to have equal marginal revenue in each. The horizontal sum of MR_1 and p_c is shown in Panel C of Figure 11.6.1. The downward-sloping segment AB in Panel C corresponds to the segment of MR_1 that lies above the world price. Thus, if output is OE or less, all of it will be sold domestically and the firms will not enter the world market. For outputs larger than OE, the relevant marginal revenue is the foreign price, p_c. This is shown by the horizontal segment of $MR_1 + p_c$ in Panel C. The explanation of this horizontal segment is intuitively clear; for outputs above OE, the marginal revenue in the domestic market is less than the world price. Thus, the firm never has to settle for *less* than p_c for any unit it sells.

To find the profit-maximizing total output, we locate the point where the firm's marginal cost schedule (MC in Panel C) intersects the horizontal sum of the marginal revenue curves. This happens at output OF in Panel C. This output is larger than OE, so we know that some output will be sold in the world market. In fact, we know from the above discussion that no more than OE units will be sold in the domestic market. Thus, it is easy to see that OE units will be sold domestically and the remaining EF units will be exported. The domestic sales occur at price p_d (see Panel A), and the foreign sales are made at the competitive world price p_c.

Domestic price is above the world price because the firm is a price-discriminating monopolist. In international trade it is more common to describe the above situation as "dumping." Sometimes a government will wish to encourage exports as a means of improving the balance of trade or to acquire larger holdings of foreign currencies. To stimulate exports the government may offer an export subsidy (that is, a bonus payment to the firm for each unit it exports).

If an export subsidy of s per unit of output is paid to the firm described above, the effect will be to increase p_c to $p_c + s$. The reader can trace through the analysis to show that the effect of such an export subsidy is to:

1. Increase total output of the firm above OF.
2. Increase the quantity of the good exported, both in absolute and relative terms.
3. Increase domestic price.

An example demonstrating dumping and price discrimination by an international monopolist is presented in the "Applying the Theory" section at the beginning of this chapter.

SUPPRESSION OF INVENTIONS IN A MONOPOLY[15]
11.7

It is frequently asserted, especially in popular discussion, that monopolists will suppress inventions and decrease the durability of a good in order to increase sales. To analyze this question we consider the following problem: Suppose a monopolist can produce two different qualities of a good with the same total cost function for each. The better-quality good provides a greater flow of services per unit of time than the lower quality good.[16] Which quality will the monopolist produce?

The interesting answer to this question is that the monopolist will always produce the better-quality good. To show why, we begin by looking at the consumer's behavior. Let K be the amount of the good the consumer purchases, and let p_k be the price of the good. The service flow per unit of the good will be given by a constant u. Thus the consumer who has K units of the good has a total service flow of uK. The consumer also consumes another good X which has price p_x. If the consumer's money income is M then the utility maximization problem is

maximize $U(X, uK)$

subject to $M = p_x X + p_k K$.

---

[15]This section is somewhat more technical than the rest of the chapter and can be skipped without loss of continuity.

[16]The approach taken here is the same as that given by Jack Hirschleifer, "Suppression of Inventions," *Journal of Political Economy* 79 (1971), pp. 382–83. By using a more complicated model, Professor P. L. Swan has established analogous results for the problem of product durability. See P. L. Swan, "Durability of Consumption Goods," *American Economic Review* 60 (1970), pp. 884–94.

Denote the total service flow by $Y = uK$ and rewrite the maximization problem as

$$\text{maximize } U(X, Y)$$

$$\text{subject to } M = p_x X + \frac{p_k}{u} Y.$$

Let X^* and Y^* be the values of X and Y that solve this problem. Next suppose that the service flow per unit of K is increased by λ where $\lambda > 1$. If the price of K were simultaneously increased by λ, the new maximization problem would be

$$\text{maximize } U(X, Y)$$

$$\text{subject to } M = p_x X + \frac{\lambda p_k}{\lambda u} Y.$$

In the new problem the λ cancels in the numerator and denominator of the fraction in the budget constraint so the new problem is *identical* with the old. This means that if X^*, Y^* solved the initial problem then X^*, Y^* also solve the new problem. It is important to note however, that the optimal K for the old problem is $K^* = Y^*/u$ and the optimal K for the new problem is the smaller quantity $K^{**} = Y^*/\lambda u$ because $Y = \lambda u K$ in the new problem.

This result says that the demand curve for K shifts when u is increased. The specific shift can be determined as follows: pick a K on the old demand curve, increase the associated price by a factor of λ, then K/λ is the quantity associated with this price on the new demand curve.[17] The shift is illustrated in Figure 11.7.1 for the case of a linear demand curve with $\lambda = 2$. The old demand curve is D_1, and the new curve (after u is doubled) is D_2. Because $\lambda = 2$ the distance OA is one half of OB and the distance OE is twice OC.

It is now easy to answer the original question. If the monopolist can offer two goods, one with a service flow per unit of u and the other with a service flow of λu (where $\lambda > 1$), the latter will be offered if production costs are the same. This is because, given the demand curve shift, the monopolist could raise the price from p_k to λp_k and get the same revenue, since consumers will then demand $1/\lambda$ of their original quantity of K. The monopolist's costs are reduced, however, since the quantity of output has dropped. Thus profits are increased. Of course, the actual change in price need not be an increase by a factor of λ, but the preceding argument shows that the profits at the optimum price with the new demand curve must be greater than the optimum profits for the old demand curve since we have shown at least one way to increase profits over the old optimum.

The intuition is straightforward. If the high-quality good increases value to consumers by more than it increases cost to producers, then the monopolist will do better by producing the high-quality good. Since consumers are willing to pay proportionately more for the high-quality good, and since cost rises less than proportionately, more profit can be had by shifting toward high quality.

---

[17]If the old demand curve is $p_k = h(K)$, the new one is $p_k = \lambda h(\lambda K)$.

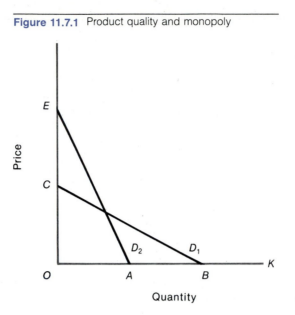

Figure 11.7.1 Product quality and monopoly

QUESTIONS AND EXERCISES

1. Using the format of Table 11.2.1, show the effects of a unit tax on price, firm output, industry output, and the number of firms, both in the short run and the long run, for an industry that faces increasing input prices.

2. Using the format of Table 11.3.1, show the effects of a lump-sum tax on price, firm output, industry output, and the number of firms, both in the short run and the long run, for an industry that faces increasing input prices.

3. Discuss the effects of price controls in a competitive industry that faces increasing input prices.

4. What are the short-run and long-run effects of a lump-sum subsidy (in a constant-cost industry) on price, firm output, industry output, and the number of firms when:
   a. The subsidy is given to all firms in the industry, including those that decide to enter after the subsidy program is established.
   b. The subsidy is given only to firms in the industry at the time the subsidy is established and not to any new entrants to the industry.

5. What are the short-run and long-run effects of a unit tax on a monopolist?

6. What are the short-run and long-run effects of an ad valorem tax on a monopolist?

Part Three   Theory of the Firm and Market Organization

12 Theory of Price Under Monopolistic Competition

Many goods are produced in markets where there are numerous firms, but each firm's product is slightly different from that of others. Examples of such goods might include soap, grocery stores, and motels. This chapter deals with the economic theory (historically and recently) developed to analyze these markets. This theory is applied to the market for "luxury hotels in downtown Atlanta" in the "Applying the Theory" section at the beginning of the chapter. ■

Dog Days for Atlanta's Dazzling New Hotels

When the Hyatt Regency Hotel opened for business in 1967, its dramatically soaring 20-story interior not only set a new approach to hotel design but also helped turn Atlanta into a booming convention city. The 1,000-room Regency, designed by architect John C. Portman, consistently ran upward of 90 percent occupancy and turned away guests in droves. Today, things have changed. Atlanta is distinctly over-hoteled, with far more first-class rooms than travelers to fill them. The Regency's occupancy rate has slipped to around 65 percent. "For a number of years we were the only ball game in town," says General Manager Darryl W. Hartley-Leonard. "We sure know we aren't now."

Hartley-Leonard is hardly overstating the case. Six major luxury hotels are now fighting for business in Atlanta, four of them operated by national chains and five of them neighbors in a six-block area downtown. In the past year, Hilton Hotels Corp. and Western International Hotels Co. opened new hotels — the Atlanta Hilton and the Peachtree Plaza. During the same period, Hyatt Corp. spent $5 million to refurbish the Regency. And Marriott Corp., one of the first national chains to enter the Atlanta market, spent $2.5 million to redo its 799-room motor hotel downtown. In addition, during the past year the Omni International, part of a major development that includes a sports arena and a big amusement park, all under one roof, opened its doors downtown, and two years ago another luxury hotel, the Fairmont, operated by the Fairmont Hotel Co. of San Francisco, opened on Peachtree Street north of downtown. In all, these hotels added some 5,000 new or redecorated hotel rooms over the past two years.

Breakeven Efforts

Of these six, only the oldest — the Marriott — reports occupancy at a healthy rate — 78 percent — though even that is off 7 percent from its high level during its first eight years of operation. Occupancy is suffering at the other five, and some of them are struggling just to break even.

The Atlanta Hilton, for example, whose 1,250 rooms make it the city's largest hotel, expects to finish the year with an occupancy rate of 56 percent to 58 percent, below its 59 percent to 61 percent break-even level. The Omni, part of a locally based chain of three hotels, figures to end 1976 with an occupancy rate four points below its 59 percent breakeven point. And the Fairmont, located in the Colony Square office-residential complex that has filed for protection under the bankruptcy laws, has lost money since it opened two years ago. Finally, there is Peachtree Plaza, another Portman hotel that is operated by Western International and boasts 1,100 rooms, a lake in the lobby, and a 70-story circular glass tower. It is operating at 7 percent below the pre-opening projections and will wind up the year $2 million short of its gross-revenue goal of $27 million. "It's the fierce competition," says General Manager Joseph D. Guilbault. And Harry Mullikin, Western International president, says it may take three years before the growth of Atlanta catches up with the new hotel rooms.

With each hotel trying to gain an edge, together they are spending $2 million dollars to beef up sales staffs and advertising budgets to go after markets that, they say, have been neglected in the past. Geared to trade conventions and large corporate meetings, they have until now felt little need to be aggressive in luring the overnight guest and the small corporate meeting, which might involve just 15 or 20 rooms a night. "We are going to pay a lot more attention to the heavy travelers and to the small business-meeting planners," says Guilbault. Thus, Peachtree Plaza is committing $150,000 of its $536,000 advertising budget this year to reaching customers through national radio and print.

Spending More

Another big spender is the Hyatt, whose advertising budget went up 122 percent this year over last year. "The phone used to ring right off the hook, but now we have to go out to look for business," says Hartley-Leonard.

The Omni is spending 60 percent of its $250,000 advertising budget locally in an attempt to win over Atlantans, not only for its restaurant and bar business but also for its lodging business. " You must have the local businessman to be successful because when people come to town they ask him, 'Where do you think we should stay?'" explained Bruce Lucker, Omni's vice-president for sales and marketing. "If it's a corporate meeting, it's the local sponsorship that is always taking the responsibility, and he is concerned that he better look good."

Lesson Learned

It is a failure in precisely this area that has hurt the Fairmont so much. Since last year, occupancy has stumbled along at 53 percent to 55 percent and is expected to be about the same next year. By opening in September 1974—a year before any of the other new hotels—the Fairmont had the advantage of a head start, but it lost it through a combination of poor service and arrogant managers.

"Sometimes I think about getting together with our advertising people and running a full-page ad in the paper that says, 'Atlanta, we goofed and we're sorry. Please give us another chance,'" says Albert Rapuano, who took over as the Fairmont manager a year ago. But he has decided against that and says he will try to get the thought over more subtly. He plans to present top-name entertainment, as do the other three Fairmont Hotels. This has been attempted in Atlanta before, but it was discontinued because Atlantans balked at paying $5 and $10 cover charges. This time, Rapuano thinks that the new competition may help the Fairmont. "With all the new hotels, people will see that the Fairmont is not all that expensive," he says. "The idea is to increase our exposure to the
(continued on page 350)

(continued from page 349)
local community—to make it the community hotel, so the local people will say "The Fairmont's a good place.' "

III What the hotel managers really think is going to pull them through, however, is the new state-financed trade center, called the Georgia World Congress Center, which just opened. With 350,000 sq. ft., the center enables Atlanta to handle large trade shows, those involving 25,000 to 30,000 people. Prior to this, the largest facility available was the 70,000 sq. ft. Atlanta Civic Center, which could handle 10,000 people.

The Outlook

Though the city's Convention & Visitors Bureau says it may take up to five years before the new center reaches its full annual potential of 30 to 40 meetings of 15,000 to 20,000 delegates each, the bureau says it has already signed up 20 meetings for next year. But the average attendance for each is only 7,000. The reason that big-ger meetings could not be enticed, explains James W. Hurst, executive vice-president of the bureau, was that "we met strong resis-tance" from trade associations that were afraid that "we might not open on time."

But with the center opening on schedule, most Atlanta hotel executives are ecstatic. "It's pretty much our belief that Atlanta is going to be a city with a bright future in conventions," says the Hilton's general

manager, William J. Utnik. "The large national conventions would not consider Atlanta before."

On a more somber note, Hyatt's Hartley-Leonard concludes: "Without the Congress Center, we would have been in a dire condition."

Questions

1. Suppose "luxury hotels in Atlanta" can best be described as models of monopolistic competition (developed in this chapter) and can therefore be viewed as a relevant "product group." If this is true, what would you expect the size of the cross-price elasticity of demand to be between "luxury hotels in Atlanta" and "inexpensive hotels in Atlanta"? Between "luxury hotels in Atlanta" and "luxury hotels in Florida (and other areas of the Southeast United States)"? Explain.

2. Refer to passage I in the article.
   a. Show graphically the short-run equilibrium position of the Hyatt Regency in 1967. What does the model of monopolistic competition predict should happen in the long run?
   b. At the time the article was written (1976), do you think the industry was in long-run equilibrium? Why? If not, what do you predict should happen in the long run?
   c. Show graphically the situation of the representative firm once long-

run equilibrium has been achieved. What are economic profits at this point for this firm?

d. Use your diagram in 2(c) to explain why some economists argue that monopolistic competition results in "excess capacity." What would be Chamberlin's response to such a charge in this case?

3. Refer to passage II of the article: Is the existence of large advertising budgets by these hotels consistent with the model of perfect competition? Is it consistent with the model of monopolistic competition?

4. Refer to passage III: How will the new state-financed trade center affect the situation in questions 2(b) and 2(c)?

Solutions

1. It should be quite low. As discussed in Chapter 3, the greater the cross-price elasticity of demand, the greater the degree of substitutability. If this elasticity were high, then the relevant product group should probably be "hotels in Atlanta" rather than "luxury hotels in Atlanta." Similarly, in geographic space, if luxury hotels in Florida (and other areas of the Southeast United States) are good substitutes for luxury hotels in Atlanta, then the relevant product group should probably be "luxury hotels in the Southeast," and the cross-price elasticity between lux-

ury hotels in Atlanta and luxury hotels in Florida would be high.

2. a. The graph would be exactly analogous to Figure 12.3.2. Note that there are presumably short-run economic profits, so that price exceeds AC at Hyatt's profit-maximizing P, Q. In the long run, these profits should attract entry of similar luxury hotels.

b. To the extent that the firms in the article were experiencing losses, the industry (product group) was not in long-run equilibrium. In monopolistic competition, the long-run equilibrium position will have firms making zero economic profits. Perhaps there has been "over-entry" since 1967. If there were no further changes in industry demand, we would predict that some firms would exit in the long run.

c. The graph would be exactly analogous to Figure 12.4.1. Note that economic profits here are zero ($P = AC$ for the representative firm).

d. At q_e, the firm is not operating at the bottom of the LAC curve. See figure 12.5.1 for more details. Chamberlin would respond that as long as there is price competition in this product group, then this "excess capacity" is really just the cost for product differentiation.

(continued on page 352)

APPLYING THE THEORY

(continued from page 351)

3. No. In perfect competition, the firm is assumed to sell a homogeneous product and can already sell all it wants at the market price. There is therefore no incentive for an individual firm to advertise. (Note, however, that the industry as a whole still might try to shift the **industry** demand curve out through advertising. An example of this would be milk producers getting together with ad slogans like the recent, "milk does a body good.") This is not the case in monopolistic competition, as advertising could further differentiate the individual firm's product and increase profits.

4. It should increase the market demand and indirectly alter the representative firm's demand curve. As such, it might allow the product group to reach a long-run equilibrium without the exit of firms referred to in 2(b).

Source: *Business Week*, September 27, 1976.

INTRODUCTION
12.1

Chapters 9 and 10 dealt with the "pure" and "extreme" cases of perfect competition and monopoly. The two models are pure in that the analytical results are completely independent of personal influences, especially entrepreneurial expectations and speculation concerning the behavior of rivals. They are "extremes"—from the standpoint of numbers and profit. In perfect competition the number of firms in an industry is indefinitely large, while at the opposite end of the "numbers" spectrum, monopoly is a one-firm industry. Similarly, zero economic profit per firm is the central characteristic of long-run equilibrium in perfect competition. In contrast, monopolization of a market guarantees the single firm a greater long-run pure profit than it could earn under any other organization of the market (that is, than if there were one or more rival firms in the market).

Historical Perspective
12.1.a

With the exception of a few "naive" duopoly theories, discussed in Chapter 13, the theories of perfect competition and monopoly constituted "classical" microeconomic theory from Marshall to Knight. In point of fact, the theory of perfect competition was not thoroughly developed until the publication of Knight's *Risk,*

Uncertainty, and Profit.[1] Stigler even argued that Knight's meticulous discussion of perfect competition, clearly pointing out the austere nature of the rigorously defined concept, caused a widespread reaction against the use of perfect competition as a model of economic behavior.[2] This is probably true; but whatever the cause, in the late 1920s and early 1930s there was definitely a reaction against the use both of perfect competition and of pure monopoly as analytical models of business firms and market behavior.

A Cambridge economist, Piero Sraffa, was among the first to point out the limitations of "competition–or–monopoly" analysis;[3] he was soon followed by others. Hotelling emphasized that "the difference between the Standard Oil Company in its prime and the little corner grocery store is quantitative rather than qualitative. Between the perfect competition and monopoly of theory lie the actual cases."[4] Similarly, Zeuthen argued that "neither monopoly nor competition are ever absolute, and the theories about them deal only with the outer margins of reality, which is always to be sought between them."[5]

In the late 1920s and early 1930s economists began turning their attention to the middle ground between monopoly and perfect competition. Two of the most notable achievements were attributable to an English economist, Joan Robinson,[6] and to an American, Edward Chamberlin.[7] Initial attention in this chapter is directed toward Chamberlin's unique achievement. The later sections deal with more modern interpretations.

Product Differentiation
12.1.b

Chamberlin based his theory of "monopolistic competition" on a solid, empirical fact: there are very few monopolists because there are very few commodities for which close substitutes do not exist; similarly, there are very few commodities that are entirely homogeneous among producers. Instead, there is a wide range of commodities, some of which have relatively few good substitutes and some of which have many good, but not perfect, substitutes.

Let us begin with an example. The American Tobacco Company has an absolute monopoly in the manufacture and sale of Lucky Strike cigarettes. To be

---

[1]Knight, *Risk, Uncertainty, and Profit* (Chicago: University of Chicago Press, 1971).

[2]George J. Stigler, "Perfect Competition, Historically Contemplated," *Journal of Political Economy* 65 (1957), pp. 1–17.

[3]Piero Sraffa, "The Laws of Returns under Competitive Conditions," *Economic Journal* 36 (1926), pp. 535–50.

[4]Harold Hotelling, "Stability in Competition," *Economic Journal* 29 (1929), pp. 41–57; citation from p. 44.

[5]F. Zeuthen, *Problems of Monopoly and Economic Warfare* (London: Routledge & Kegan Paul, 1930), p. 62.

[6]Joan Robinson, *The Economics of Imperfect Competition* (London: Macmillan, 1933).

[7]E. H. Chamberlin, *The Theory of Monopolistic Competition,* 6th ed. (Cambridge, Mass.: Harvard University Press, 1950).

sure, another concern could manufacture identically the same cigarette; but it could *not* label the cigarette Lucky Strike. However, other concerns can manufacture cigarettes and call them Chesterfield, Camel, and so forth. Just as American Tobacco has an absolute monopoly of Lucky Strikes, Liggett & Myers has an absolute monopoly of Chesterfields, and Reynolds Tobacco has an absolute monopoly of Camels. Each concern has a monopoly over its own product; but the various brands are closely related goods and there is intense, *personal* competition among the firms.

Two important points are to be gleaned from the example. First, the products are *heterogeneous* rather than homogeneous; hence perfect, and *impersonal,* competition cannot exist. Second, although heterogeneous, the products are only slightly differentiated. Each is a very close substitute for the other; hence competition exists but it is a *personal* competition among rivals who are well aware of each other.

This general type of market is characterized by product differentiation; and product differentiation, in turn, characterizes most American markets. There is not one homogeneous type of automobile; nor, for that matter, are there homogeneous types of soap, men's suits, television sets, grocery stores, magazines, or motels. Each producer tries to differentiate his product so as to make it unique; yet to be in the market at all, particular products must be closely related to the general product in question.

There are many ways of differentiating products, some quite real and others very spurious. In case of real product differentiation one can usually catalog the differences in terms of chemical composition, services offered by the sellers, horsepower, cost of input , and so on. In other cases — which many regard as spurious — product differentiation is based upon advertising outlays, difference in packaging material or design, brand name only (consider the aspirin market), and others.

In any event, when products are differentiated each product is unique and its producer has some degree of monopoly power. But usually it is very little, because other producers can market a closely related commodity. It is not by change that the selling price of cigarettes is almost uniform from brand to brand.

**Industries and Product Groups
12.1.c**

In Chapter 9, an industry was defined as a collection of firms producing a homogeneous good. For example, by specifying clip, denier, and other characteristics of raw apparel wool, we can define the "raw apparel wool" industry. But when products are differentiated one cannot define an industry in this narrow sense. There is no "automobile" industry or "furniture" industry. Each firm having a distinct product is, in a sense, an industry in itself, exactly as a monopoly was described in Chapter 10. Nonetheless, we can usefully lump together firms producing very closely related commodities and refer to them as a *product group*. Thus hand soap, ready-to-eat cereal, or automobiles, for example, comprise instantly recognizable product groups, even though in our terminology they cannot be called industries.

Naturally enough, combining firms to make product groups is somewhat arbitrary. It is not possible to state precisely how "good" the substitutes must be. Chewing gum is a substitute for cigarettes, at least to people who are trying to quit smoking. But it is doubtful that anyone would place the Wrigley Company in the "cigarette" product group. On the other hand, although decaffeinated coffee is not a substitute for regular coffee for many people, few would not place Sanka in the "coffee" product group.

It is the difficulty of defining the group that has led most economists away from the monopolistic competition paradigm. More recently, a more rigorous way of thinking of monopolistic competition has been developed and more is said about it below.

PERFECT COMPETITION

At our initial level of abstraction, we ignore the difficulty of precise definition. When "industry" is used, perfect competition or monopoly is implied. When product differentiation is an important feature of the market, "product group" is used to denote the collection of firms, however combined, that produce some variety of the "product."

To set the stage for the exposition of monopolistic competition, it is helpful to review the model of perfect competition from a slightly different viewpoint. Suppose there are n identical firms in the industry and also suppose that consumers distribute their purchases so that each firm sells $1/n$ of total market demand when all firms charge the same price. Given these assumptions, we can analyze the behavior of the industry, using Figure 12.2.1. In this figure the curves LAC and MC are the average total cost and the marginal cost curves, respectively, for a representative or typical firm. The curve D is the amount of demand going to a typical firm when all firms are charging the same price. This curve is constructed by taking $1/n$ of total market quantity demanded at each price. We will refer to this curve as the *proportional* demand curve.

Assume first that the market price is p and each firm is getting $1/n$ of the total market (equal to q_1 in Figure 12.2.1). In perfect competition each firm thinks it can sell all it wishes at the market price, and thus the demand curve perceived by the *individual* firm is the horizontal line d. Each firm will therefore wish to sell q_2 units of output, since at this output marginal cost is equal to price. Thus at price p the market supply ($= nq_2$) will exceed market demand ($= nq_1$) and the market is not in equilibrium.[8]

The efforts of all firms to sell more output than the market demands at the price p causes the price to be driven down. Equilibrium occurs only when the price is such that the horizontal demand curve perceived by each firm intersects MC at exactly the point where the proportional demand curve D intersects the curve MC. In Figure 12.2.1 equilibrium is at the price p'. This is the equilibrium

---

[8]Recall that market equilibrium requires supply to equal demand at the market price.

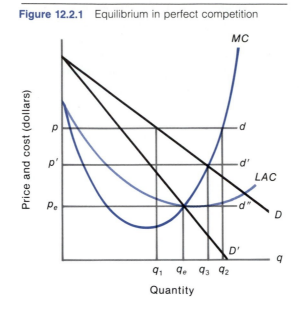

Figure 12.2.1 Equilibrium in perfect competition

because each firm has precisely the sales quantity q_3 it desires, given its perceived demand curve d'; and since D intersects d' at this price, market supply equals market demand.

This equilibrium is only short run, however, because at p' each firm is making a positive economic profit. As more firms are attracted to the industry by this profit, the market demand is divided among a larger number of competing firms. The larger number of firms causes D to move down and to the left because at each price the representative firm has a smaller proportion of the market. Long-run equilibrium exists when D has shifted to D' and the price is p_e.[9] At p_e the horizontal demand curve d'' perceived by the individual firm is tangent to the minimum point of LAC and economic profits are zero. The proportional demand curve D' intersects LAC at its minimum so each firm is able to sell q_e, which is exactly the output it wishes.[10]

SHORT-RUN EQUILIBRIUM IN MONOPOLISTIC COMPETITION
12.3

It is an easy step from the discussion of perfect competition in section 12.2 to Chamberlin's model of monopolistic competition. The proportional demand curve D has the same meaning as in section 12.2, and it is also assumed that all

---

[9]We assume a constant input–price industry. Long-run equilibrium could also be obtained if factor prices, and hence the ATC and MC curves, rose as entry occurs.

[10]At prices below p_e firms would produce less output than is required to meet market demand, so price would rise.

Part Three   Theory of the Firm and Market Organization

firms have identical costs.[11] The key difference is that each firm perceives its own demand curve (that is, the one that would obtain if it changed its price while all other firms left their price unchanged) to be less than perfectly elastic because its output is not a perfect substitute for the output of other firms. This is illustrated in Figure 12.3.1 where the demand curve perceived by the representative firm, d, is downward sloping instead of horizontal as in Figure 12.2.1. If every firm charged p, each would sell q_1 units of output. As in section 12.2 the typical firm, acting on the assumption that the other firms will keep price at p, finds it profitable to reduce price to p' and sell an output of q_2. (Note that p' and q_2 are on the perceived demand curve d.) The important difference between this case and that in section 12.2 is that the downward slope of d means that the firm perceives that it must reduce price to get more customers. Accordingly, the curve mr, which is the marginal revenue curve for d, will be equated with the marginal cost curve MC to find the profit-maximizing output and price p' and q_2, respectively. This is the "monopolistic" aspect of monopolistic competition.

Just as in section 12.2, the assumption that all firms are identical means that what looks good to one looks good to all. When every firm cuts its price, a new d curve is established for every firm. The new d curve intersects D at a lower price than the former d curve, and the firm's attempt to get to output q_2 is frustrated. Such price cutting will continue so long as each firm finds it advantageous to expand output by reducing its price below the current market price.

In strict analogy to section 12.2 the short-run equilibrium must have the characteristic that at the current market price no firm has an incentive to change its own price.[12] This means that in equilibrium the mr curve of each firm must equal marginal cost at an output such that the market price at that output is on D. This is illustrated in Figure 12.3.2. When firms equate mr with MC, the output q_e is exactly that required for a market price of p_e, as indicated by the intersection of d and D at p_e. *In summary, short-run equilibrium in monopolistic competition has two characteristics: (a) each firm picks output to equate* mr *and* MC, *and (b)* d *intersects* D *at the output chosen by the firm.*

LONG-RUN EQUILIBRIUM IN MONOPOLISTIC COMPETITION
12.4

The equilibrium in Figure 12.3.2 showed that each firm was making positive economic profits because price was above average cost at output q_e. Monopolistic competition assumes that entry of new firms to the product group is uninhibited.

---

[11]Chamberlin clearly intended this definition of D at least for expositional purposes. In his words, "Such a curve will, in fact, be a fractional part of the demand curve for the general class of product, and will be of the same elasticity. If there were 100 sellers, it would show a demand at each price which will be exactly 1/100 of the total demand at that price (since we have assumed all markets to be of equal size)" (*Theory of Monopolistic Competition*, 8th ed., p. 90).

[12]If the market price were too low, each firm would be motivated to raise its price to equate mr and MC. When all firms do this, there is an upward movement of d along D until the short-run equilibrium defined in the text is reached.

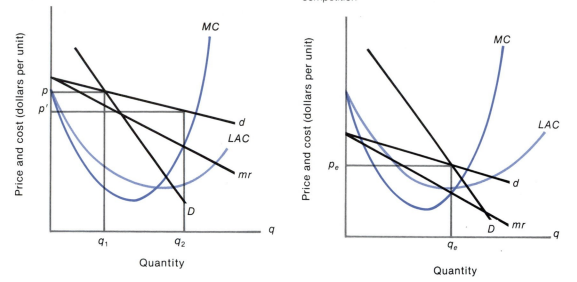

Figure 12.3.1 The firm in monopolistic competition

Figure 12.3.2 Short-run equilibrium in monopolistic competition

As firms enter, the proportional demand curve *D* will move to the left until economic profits are driven to zero. A typical long-run equilibrium (zero economic profit) is shown in Figure 12.4.1. This equilibrium has the short-run characteristic that no firm has an incentive to alter its price or output, since *mr = MC* at q_e. Moreover, at the market price p_e, the proportional demand curve *D* intersects the average cost curve so no economic profits are being made and no firm has a motivation to enter or leave the product group.

Long-run equilibrium is defined by the two conditions: (a) d *must be tangent to the average total cost curve, and* (b) *the proportional demand curve* D *must intersect both* d *and average cost at the point of tangency. The conditions are the same as for short-run equilibrium with the additional requirement that* d *be tangent to* ATC *at the equilibrium output.*

CHARACTERISTICS OF MONOPOLISTIC COMPETITION
12.5

In this section we examine some of the characteristics of the model of monopolistic competition that have attracted the attention of a number of economists.

"Ideal Output" and Excess Capacity
12.5.a

The concept of ideal output and the associated concept of excess capacity refer only to the long run. In the short run, under any type of market organization, there can be all sorts of departures from the ideal, reflecting incomplete adjustment to existing market conditions.

Part Three   Theory of the Firm and Market Organization

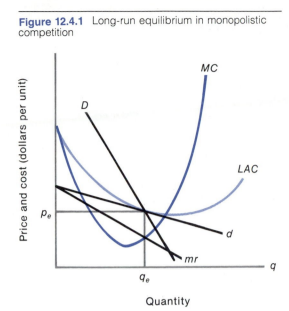

Figure 12.4.1 Long-run equilibrium in monopolistic competition

From Marshall to such later writers as Kahn, Harrod, and Cassels,[13] the ideal output of a firm was generally regarded as that output associated with minimum long-run average cost, the output corresponding to the points labeled E_c in Figure 12.5.1. Consequently, the ideal plant size is the one giving rise to the short-run average cost curve that is tangent to the long-run average cost curve at the latter's minimum point. Excess capacity, therefore, is the difference between ideal output and the output actually attained in long-run equilibrium. In Figure 12.4.1 excess capacity is measured by the distance between the output associated with the minimum point on *LAC* and q_e.

Following Cassels, excess capacity is composed of two parts, as illustrated in Figure 12.5.1. Suppose that in a monopolistically competitive market a typical firm attains long-run equilibrium at the point E_p, with output OQ_E. From the standpoint of the *firm,* long-run optimal plant size is given by SAC_p. According to the present view of ideal output, the socially optimal plant size is represented by SAC_c, and excess capacity (negative, notice) is measured as $Q_E Q_C$ units of output.

The measure of excess capacity may be divided in two parts. First, given the plant SAC_p, the firm operates at point E_p rather than at the point of minimum unit cost M. From a social point of view, the resources used by the firm would be more efficiently utilized if OQ_E', rather than OQ_E, units were produced. Thus a portion of excess capacity, represented by $Q_E Q_E'$, is attributable to socially inefficient utilization of the resources actually used. The second portion of excess capacity,

[13]R. F. Kahn, "Some Notes on Ideal Output," *Economic Journal* 45 (1935), pp. 1–35; R. F. Harrod, "Doctrines of Imperfect Competition," *Quarterly Journal of Economics* 49 (1934–35), pp. 442–70; and J. M. Cassels, "Excess Capacity and Monopolistic Competition," *Quarterly Journal of Economics* 51 (1936–37), pp. 426–43.

Figure 12.5.1 Ideal output and excess capacity

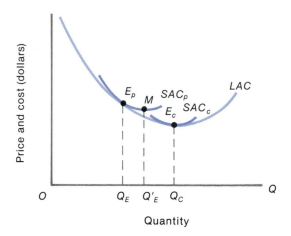

$Q'_E Q_C$, arises because socially and individually optimal sizes differ. The monopolistically competitive firm does not employ enough of society's resources to attain minimum unit (dollar and resource) cost.

The view of ideal output just expounded rests, fundamentally, upon the horizontal demand curve faced by a perfect competitor. But if individual demand curves are negatively sloped, if active price competition characterizes the market, and if entry is free into the product group, Chamberlin argues that E_c does not correspond to ideal output. Product heterogeneity is desired per se; and, according to Chamberlin, it inevitably gives rise to negatively sloped individual demand curves.

"Differentness" is considered a quality of the product and entails a cost just as any other quality. The cost of differentness is represented by production to the left of minimum average cost. The difference between actual (long-run equilibrium) output and output at minimum cost is, then, a measure of the "cost" of producing "differentness" rather than a measure of excess capacity. But this is true only so long as there is effective price competition in the market. The presence of price competition guarantees that buyers can select the "amount" of differentness they wish to purchase. In the case of price competition, Chamberlin regards E_p as a "sort of ideal" for a market in which there is product differentiation.[14]

Nonprice Competition and Excess Capacity
12.5.b

According to Chamberlin, long-run excess equilibrium under monopolistic competition does not give rise to excess capacity so long as the market is characterized by active price competition. In his view, excess capacity arises when free entry

---

[14]Chamberlin, *Theory of Monopolistic Competition*, p. 94.

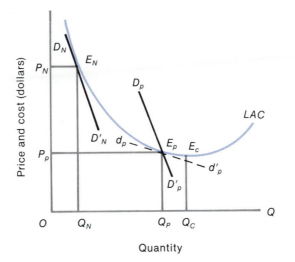

Figure 12.5.2 Long-run equilibrium with nonprice competition and excess capacity

is coupled with the absence of price competition. This brand of excess capacity is illustrated by Figure 12.5.2.

LAC, as usual, represents long-run average cost. If there is free entry and price competition, long-run equilibrium is attained at E_p, where the perceived demand curve $d_p d_p'$ is tangent to *LAC*. As noted, E_p must lie to the left of the competitive equilibrium E_c; but with active price competition it will tend to lie rather close to the competitive point.

For many reasons, active price competition may not characterize certain markets. A "live and let live" outlook on the part of sellers, tacit agreements, open price associations, price maintenance, customary prices, and professional ethics are a few causes of nonaggressive price policies. If price competition is, in fact, lacking, individual entrepreneurs will have no regard for the existence of curves such as $d_p d_p'$. They will be concerned only with the effects of a general price rise or decline, or with the $D_p D_p'$ curve.

With free entry in the absence of price competition, long-run equilibrium is attained (pure profit eliminated) only when enough firms have entered the industry to push the demand curve to $D_N D_N'$. Equilibrium is attained at E_N, with output OQ_N and price OP_N per unit. In Chamberlin's opinion, $Q_N Q_P$ represents excess capacity: it is the difference in output attributable to the absence of effective price competition. If the latter prevails, the firm attains a "sort of ideal" output.

Chamberlin then concludes that by nonaggressive price policies sellers

> protect, over short periods, their profits, but over longer periods,
> their numbers, since when prices do not fall costs rise, the two
> being equated by the development of excess productive
> capacity . . . for which there is no automatic corrective. . . . It may

develop over long periods with impunity, prices always covering costs, and may . . . become permanent and normal through a failure of price competition to function. The result is high prices and waste . . . [attributable to] the monopoly element in monopolistic competition.[15]

COMPARISONS OF LONG-RUN EQUILIBRIA
12.6

A comparison of long-run equilibria is rather difficult inasmuch as it must rest essentially upon statements pertaining to cost curves. Conditions giving rise to monopoly probably lead to noncomparable differences between competitive and monopolistic costs; for similar reasons, noncomparability is also likely between either of these two and monopolistic competition. However, a few generalizations are possible if one bears in mind that the statements are relative, not absolute. The relevant points follow immediately from a comparison of Figures 9.5.4, 10.5.2, and 12.4.1.

Equilibrium in the Firm
12.6.a

For emphasis, it may be well to note the "competitive" and "monopolistic" aspects of monopolistic competition. A monopolistically competitive firm is like a monopoly in that it faces negatively sloped demand and marginal revenue curves; it therefore determines its price–output policy by equating marginal cost with marginal revenue rather than with price, as in perfect competition. At the same time, the monopolistically competitive firm is like a perfectly competitive one in that it faces direct market competition. The long-run result is the absence of pure profit, just as in the competitive case. While all three types may enjoy economic profit in the short run, freedom of entry eliminates it in the long run, except under conditions of pure monopoly. The qualitative nature of rivalry is also different. In perfect competition rivalry is completely impersonal. At the opposite extreme, there is no direct (only indirect and potential) rivalry under monopoly. The case of monopolistic competition is somewhat different, but it lies closer to perfect competition. The monopolistic competitor, at least in abstract, is aware of the slightly differentiated, highly substitutable products of other firms. There would be personal rivalry except for the condition of large numbers — so large that each entrepreneur believes his actions will go unnoticed by his competitors (because they are so numerous that his actions will not have a readily perceptible effect upon any *one* of them).

---

[15]Ibid., pp. 107, 109.

Long-Run Equilibria in Industries and Product Groups
12.6.b

In long-run competitive equilibrium, total industry output is produced in a group of plants each of which operates at (long-run) minimum average cost. The product is sold at a price equal to minimum average cost, and it is significant to note that long-run marginal cost equals both price and average cost at this point.

Under monopoly the long-run equilibrium situation is substantially different. The industry output is produced by one firm which may operate one or more plants. If the monopolist operates one plant, it is very unlikely to be of such size as to produce at (long-run) minimum average cost; if multiple plants are used, however, each will operate at minimum cost. In neither case will price equal minimum average cost or marginal cost. Indeed, price will exceed both, so that in long-run equilibrium the marginal social valuation of the commodity exceeds the marginal cost of its production.

In the competitive case, each firm operates a plant of ideal size and the industry produces the ideal output. Thus, according to the Marshall–Kahn–Cassels version, there is no excess capacity in long-run competitive equilibrium. In a multiple monopoly each plant is of ideal size; however, there are not enough plants to produce the ideal industry output. As a consequence there is long-run (negative) excess capacity under monopoly market organization.

Monopolistic competition is somewhat more difficult to analyze in these terms. In large-group equilibrium with active price competition, price is above marginal cost, although it equals average cost. The latter is not minimum average cost; but Chamberlin argues that the difference between cost at E_p and E_c is itself the "cost" of product differentiation. Since product heterogeneity is apparently desired per se, the cost of differentiation is a valid social cost. Hence, according to Chamberlin's argument, E_p actually represents the minimum attainable average cost when *all* relevant social costs are included. Each firm, and the product group as a whole, produces the "sort of ideal" output, and excess productive capacity does not appear in long-run equilibrium.

If Chamberlin's argument is accepted (and it is *not,* universally), one difficulty remains. Suppose E_p does represent minimum attainable unit cost, including the "cost" attributable to the "ideal" amount of product differentiation. Even then, long-run price exceeds short-run marginal cost for the plant in question. The marginal social valuation of the product exceeds its marginal cost for the established level of differentiation. Socially, output should be expanded and price reduced until $P = MC$. Given the plant size, plant MC intersects $D_p D_p'$ somewhere below both SAC and LAC. Hence the socially desirable output would cause each firm to sustain a long-run pure loss, a situation incompatible with private enterprise.

In short, the social welfare aspects of monopolistic competition are ambiguous. From a very microscopic standpoint, each firm produces less than the socially optimal output. On the other hand, if each firm were somehow forced to produce this seemingly desirable level of output at marginal cost price, private enterprise would no longer represent a viable economic system. Finally, the abolition of private enterprise would violate a macroscopic welfare criterion that apparently transcends microscopic considerations, at least in the United States and most industrially advanced Western nations. Thus while the theoretical analysis of monopolistic competition is quite clear, the welfare implications of this analysis are not. Micro- and macroeconomic welfare criteria are not consistent and/or reconcilable. The economist qua economist can only indicate the dilemma; establishing definitive social goals and welfare standards is beyond his professional capacity.

AN APPRAISAL OF CHAMBERLIN'S MONOPOLISTIC COMPETITION
12.7

Economists have been aware of the model of monopolistic competition since the early 1930s, but the model has not played a very central role in economic analysis. In part, this is because many situations that economists wish to analyze are explained quite well by the models of perfect competition or pure monopoly. Those situations that do not seem to fit these models well often fall into the broad class of oligopoly models (small numbers of sellers) discussed in Chapter 13.

The model of monopolistic competition also has met with some strong challenges on theoretical grounds. Professor George Stigler has criticized Chamberlin's definition of the product group. Stigler noted that every product has many "close" substitutes that do not fit easily into any systematic definition of a product group. Stigler gives the example of housing of people who live in New York City. He observes that housing facilities range from incredible estates to unbelievable slums. The housing facilities are geographically diverse, extending directly to several states and ultimately to the whole world. It is perfectly possible that the product group contains only one firm or, on the contrary, all the firms of the economy. This makes it likely that the products of the group are heterogeneous from the technological viewpoint. The problem in defining the product group makes it difficult to provide any rigorous explanation for the downward-sloping d curve in monopolistic competition.[16]

R. F. Harrod has criticized the excess capacity findings of the monopolistically competitive model. He finds it inconsistent that the firm equates a long-run marginal cost curve and a short-run marginal revenue curve to determine output. If the long-run marginal revenue curve were used, the output of the firm would be greater because long-run demand is assumed to be more elastic.[17]

Cohen and Cyert have raised an important objection to the behavioral assumptions underlying Chamberlin's model.[18] They find it puzzling that firms do not eventually learn that their actions induce predictable reactions from other firms.

---

[16]George J. Stigler, *Five Lectures on Economic Problems* (London: Longmans, Green, 1949).

[17]R. F. Harrod, *Economic Essays* (New York: Harcourt Brace, 1952).

[18]K. J. Cohen and R. M. Cyert, *Theory of the Firm,* 2nd ed. (Englewood Cliffs, N.J.: Prentice-Hall, 1975).

Firms cannot continue to believe that their perceived *d* curve provides real price–output opportunities when they find themselves continually frustrated in their efforts to move along this curve. If the firms do learn from experience, then the market is appropriately analyzed using a model of monopoly, oligopoly, or perfect competition according to the conditions of entry.

Perhaps it is for these reasons that economists rarely use the Chamberlin model of monopolistic competition to analyze markets. Although initially appealing because of the apparent realism of its assumptions, it is a theory that leaves too many loose ends to be of much practical use. This leads to more modern concepts of monopolistic competition.

EX ANTE COMPETITION AND EX POST MONOPOLY
12.8

One way to define monopolistic competition is that firms compete with each other for customers, but once customers arrive at firms, the firms behave monopolistically. The following example[19] illustrates the point.

Consider a motorist driving through the countryside on a warm summer day. As he drives, he encounters a number of fruit stands, located at the side of the road. The fruit stands may look identical to the traveler and all may advertise the same products on their road signs. It is unlikely that a complete price list is advertised, however, because the driver does not have time to read the list as he passes. Instead, one or two items are usually featured. For simplicity, suppose that all stands put up signs that say, "Artichokes, 5 for $1." The stands are surely competitive in that they look alike, sell identical products, and are in the same basic location. Yet there is potential for monopoly pricing.

The motorist arbitrarily selects one of the stands to stop at and after doing so, decides that some tomatoes would be nice as well. The seller realizes that this is the case and in anticipation of the event faces the demand curve shown in Figure 12.8.1 as *DD'*. At a price greater than $2 per pound, the customer decides not to buy, but instead to look at the prices at some other fruit stand. At a price equal to $2 per pound the customer buys 3 pounds, and at lower prices he demands greater quantities. The marginal revenue schedule is shown by *MR*.

What price should the farmer charge for his tomatoes? To make things simple, suppose that this is the last customer of the day and that the tomatoes will not keep until tomorrow. Suppose further that he has 100 pounds of tomatoes on hand. This means that the marginal cost of selling a tomato is zero; it has no other use and the seller could satisfy the consumer's entire demand, even if the good were free. But the seller instead selects a price of $1.43 and sells only 5 pounds of tomatoes, throwing all the rest out.

This reflects the classic monopolistic inefficiency: the consumer would take another 5 pounds of tomatoes, but they are thrown away in the interest of

---

[19]This analysis is drawn from Edward P. Lazear, "Retail Pricing and Clearance Sales," *American Economic Review,* October 1986.

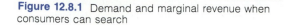

Figure 12.8.1 Demand and marginal revenue when consumers can search

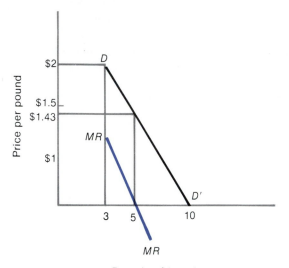

Pounds of tomatoes

increasing the farmer's profit. Yet the fruit-stand industry is competitive; all fruit stands produce identical goods. As fundamental is the fact that the farmer does not make supercompetitive profits on his stand. If he did, other farmers would open stands until each one's profits were driven to zero.

The conundrum reflects the distinction between ex ante and ex post when information is not freely available. A farmer who is thinking of opening a fruit stand knows that he will have some monopoly power once the car pulls into his driveway. But he also knows that because he must compete with other stands before the car pulls in, the number of stands will adjust until each, exercising ex post monopoly power, earns zero profit. Ex ante, he competes with other stands for the attention of passing motorists. Ex post, he behaves as a monopolist, knowing that it is not costless for the driver to investigate the prices at another stand.

MONOPOLISTIC COMPETITION AND SPATIAL EQUILIBRIUM
12.9

Another way to think of monopolistic competition is in geographic space. This helps make rigorous the notion of the group, although the assumptions made do affect the outcome.

The original specification comes from Harold Hotelling,[20] who thought of the problem of competition between monopolists as one that could be described in geographical space.

---

[20]See Harold Hotelling, "Stability in Competition," *Economic Journal* 39 (1929), pp. 41–57.

Figure 12.9.1 Hot-dog stands on a beach

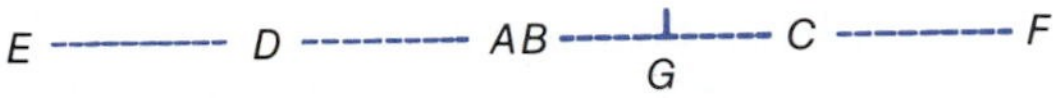

E ————— D ——————— AB ————|———— C ——————— F
                                    G

Imagine a beach scene during the summer. The beach is one mile long and people are spread evenly over this one-mile stretch. This is illustrated by the line in Figure 12.9.1. An entrepreneur wants to open a hot-dog stand on the currently empty beach. Suppose that every individual will buy one and only one hot dog at a price of $1. The stand is most effectively located a point A, right at the half-mile mark. This minimizes the average distance that individuals must walk to get their hot dogs.

Now suppose that a second entrepreneur wants to open a stand. Suppose, further, that customers go to the stand that is closest to their position on the beach. Given that the first stand is located at A, the second stand's best strategy is to locate right next to the first, say, at B. Then all customers between F and B go to the second stand, whereas all customers between E and A go to the first stand. The average distance traveled is 1/4 mile.

The problem is that this is not optimal from a social point of view. For example, customers would be better served if stands relocated at C and D. Then, those between B and F would go to C, whereas those between E and A would go to D. No one would walk more than 1/4 mile and the average distance traveled would be $\frac{1}{8}$ mile.

Timing, and lack of cooperation is important, because if the two stands were opened simultaneously by the same owner, he would have an incentive to locate them at C and D, instead of A and B. Since it reduces the amount of travel time, it is likely to result in the sale of more hot dogs. The point is that a monopolistically competitive market does not necessarily create an environment where products are differentiated to the appropriate degree. In this case, the products are too similar; they are sold at A and B rather than at C and D.

This example does not only pertain to locational problems. Other examples fit as well. Suppose we were talking about wine, which can be from very sweet to very dry. We can think of very sweet as being at F and very dry at E. Consumers line up along this "line" in terms of their preferences for sweet or dry wine. The first wine producer locates in the middle; so does the second. Both produce the same item, even though society's interests would be better served if there were one sweet wine at C and a dry one at D.

This analysis is useful, but does not tell the entire story. Perhaps the most important problem is that quality differences cannot always be represented on a line. A circle is sometimes a better description of the quality spectrum. When a circle, rather than a line is used, results become more complicated.[21] An example

---

[21]See A. P. Lerner and H. W. Singer, "Some Notes on Duopoly and Spatial Competition," *Journal of Political Economy* 45 (1937), and more recently, E. C. Prescott and M. Visscher, "Sequential Location Decisions among Firms with Foresight," *Bell Journal of Economics* 8 (1977), and Steven Salop, "Monopolistic Competition with Outside Goods," *Bell Journal of Economics* 10 (Spring 1979), pp. 141–56.

of product choices that fit a circle rather than a line is the choice of an airline schedule. A flight at 7 A.M. is a closer substitute to a flight at 8 A.M. than is a flight at midnight, but is the midnight flight or noon flight "closer" to a 6 A.M. flight? A line is less natural than a circle in this situation.

What is also true is that the definition of equilibrium is important. The previous analysis hinged on the idea that one hot dog stand set up first, and then could not be bribed to move. The second stand, however, could pay the first seller something to move his stand down the beach toward D. This creates a different set of solutions. Additionally, once demand curves are allowed to have their characteristic downward slope, the Hotelling solution is not always correct.

For example, suppose that consumers will pay \$1 for the hot dog if their walk is less than 1/4 mile, but only \$.25 if they must walk over 1/2 mile. Given that the first stand locates at A, the second stand makes more money by locating at C. If he locates at B, he makes \$1 on everyone between B and C, and \$.25 on everyone between C and F. If there are N people on the beach, he earns $N(1/4)(1) + N(1/4)(1/4) = 5/16(N)$. If instead, he chose C, he would get all customers from G to F and earn \$1 on each. Thus, he would realize $N(3/8)$ from locating at C. Since $3/8 > 5/16$, he is better off at C than at B. Table 12.9.1 shows the revenue associated with locating at each point between A and F, with location of 0 corresponding to F, .25 corresponding to C, and .5 corresponding to A (i.e., it is the distance from the right endpoint). The revenue that the seller receives at each point is also given. As the table reveals, the maximum is at point C, with revenues of 3/8. If the first seller can move his stand, after the second seller has made his choice, things get more complicated. Game-theoretic maneuvering of this sort is discussed in the following chapter.

These ideas formalize the notion of the group that Chamberlin had in mind. They also make specific the nature of substitution between products.

SYNOPSIS 12.10

- Chamberlin developed his theory of monopolistic competition in response to rising concern in the 1920s and 1930s that models of pure competition and pure monopoly were too extreme to serve as analytical models of business firms and market behavior. Chamberlin used the somewhat nebulous concept of a "product group" in an effort to capture the idea that many goods have close, but not perfect, substitutes.

- Short-run equilibrium in monopolistic competition occurs when: (*a*) each firm chooses output to equate marginal revenue (from its perceived demand curve) with marginal cost; and (*b*) the firm's perceived demand curve intersects the proportional demand curve at the output chosen by the firm. The same general framework can be used to explain the concept of equilibrium in purely competitive markets. The key difference is that in the purely competitive case the firm's perceived demand curve is horizontal, whereas it has a negative slope in the case of monopolistic competition. In this sense, the difference

Table 12.9.1	
Location	**Revenue**
0.00000	$0.25000
0.03125	0.26563
0.06250	0.28125
0.09375	0.29688
0.12500	0.31250
0.15625	0.32813
0.18750	0.34375
0.21875	0.35938
0.25000	0.37500
0.28125	0.36719
0.31250	0.35938
0.34375	0.35156
0.37500	0.34375
0.40625	0.33594
0.43750	0.32813
0.46875	0.32031
0.50000	0.31250

between monopolistic competition and pure competition is a matter of degree. If the perceived demand curve is negatively sloped but has a very high price elasticity, the monopolistically competitive equilibrium will differ from pure competition only trivially. At the other extreme, if the firm's perceived demand curve is nearly coincident with the proportional demand curve, the monopolistically competitive solution will differ only trivially from a purely monopolistic equilibrium. It has not been shown empirically that the model of monopolistic competition provides a significantly more accurate explanation of firm behavior, particularly with respect to price and output behavior, than either of these other models.

■ Long-run equilibrium in monopolistic competition has the characteristics of short-run equilibrium with the additional condition that entry and exit of firms to the "product group" leads each firm in the group to have zero economic profit.

■ In the absence of price competition, Chamberlin argued that the industry would come into equilibrium at a point where prices are high and substantial excess capacity prevails. The reasons provided for lack of price competition (which may be covert through the use of premiums and other devices) are not especially convincing in this context, however.

■ Chamberlin's model has been the subject of various criticisms. One of the most important of these is that the firm's behavior persistently fails to account for the reaction of rival firms. One might reasonably expect that firms would learn about rivals' responses through experience. But, in that case, the market is more appropriately analyzed using the models of pure competition, pure monopoly, or one of the models of oligopoly discussed in Chapter 13.

- More modern theories of monopolistic competition take two forms: The first results from imperfect information so that firms are competitors before the customer walks in the door, but monopolists thereafter. The second category includes models of spatial equilibria. These models attempt to predict where firms will locate on some quality spectrum. Their results are somewhat specific to the assumptions made about the nature of substitution between the goods.

QUESTIONS AND EXERCISES

1. Explain the difference between short-run equilibrium and long-run equilibrium in monopolistic competition.

2. Given the market demand curve $Q = 100 - 1/2p$, what is the proportional demand curve when there are 20 firms in the industry? Show that the proportional demand curve has the same elasticity at any price as the market demand curve.

3. Show that the model of monopolistic competition is the same as the model of pure monopoly when there is only one firm in the industry and entry is prohibited.

4. Given the long-run equilibrium proportional demand curve $p = 51 - 2q$ and the ATC curve $ATC(q) = q^2 - 16q + 100$ for a firm in monopolistic competition:
   a. What is the long-run equilibrium price and quantity?
   b. What is the slope of the perceived demand curve d at the equilibrium quantity?
   c. What is the marginal revenue perceived by the firm at the equilibrium output?

5. Consider a street lined with identical stands that sell leather purses. No advertising of prices on the outside is permitted. The demand for purses at any one stand is given by $P = 10 - Q$ where P is price and Q is quantity. This demand curve takes into account the ability of a customer to shop at another stand. A purse costs $2 to produce. A stand costs $80 to build and there are 100 potential customers. Solve for the equilibrium price of a purse and the equilibrium number of stands.

SUGGESTED READINGS

Chamberlin, E. H. *The Theory of Monopolistic Competition,* 8th ed. Cambridge, Mass.: Harvard University Press, 1962, esp. chap. 5, pp. 77–116.

Ferguson, C. E. "A Social Concept of Excess Capacity," *Metroeconomica,* 8 (1956), pp. 84–93.

Machlup, Fritz. *The Economics of Sellers' Competition.* Baltimore: Johns Hopkins University Press, 1952, pp. 135–241.

Robinson, Joan. *The Economics of Imperfect Competition.* London: Macmillan, 1933, pp. 133–76.

Smithies, Arthur. "Equilibrium in Monopolistic Competition." *Quarterly Journal of Economics* 55 (1940), pp. 95 ff.

Triffin, Robert. *Monopolistic Competition and General Equilibrium Theory.* Cambridge, Mass.: Harvard University Press, 1949, pp. 17–96.

13 Theories of Price in Oligopoly Markets

What obstacles do cartels face? Is OPEC past its prime as a successful international cartel? Such questions stem directly from the material in this chapter, which examines the situation when sellers are few and each is acutely conscious of the actions and potential reactions of its rivals. In addition to analyzing the formal "classical" and "market" solutions to oligopoly, the chapter also presents a glimpse at the notorious electrical equipment cartel. In the "Applying the Theory" section at the beginning of the chapter, we examine the difficulties the 11 bauxite-producing nations are encountering as they struggle to establish an international cartel, the International Bauxite Association. ■

Bauxite-Producing Nations' Price Push
Eases Some in Wake of Aluminum Slump

By Gay Sands Miller
Staff Reporter of *The Wall Street Journal*

Cracks are appearing in the cartel-like campaign by some bauxite-producing nations to get more money for ore mined in their countries.

As a result, North American aluminum companies, which use bauxite to make aluminum, are growing less nervous about their bauxite supplies. "We don't expect rapid increases in bauxite prices" in the foreseeable future, says one major U.S. producer.

Such talk hardly resembles the tense mood of 1974, when Jamaica led six producers' independent moves to boost their revenues from bauxite up to 600 percent, and the International Bauxite Association was formed. At that time, aluminum companies "were more worried about the security of their supplies and what the future held," a State Department official recalls.

Yet the 11-nation IBA, stung by the steep 1975 slump in aluminum demand, so far hasn't succeeded in fulfilling some members' hopes of "organizing" world prices for the red, clay-like ore. With oil-price rises and rampant inflationary pressures of earlier years abating, several nations have begun going their own ways in taxing the commodity.

"The evidence is mounting that the major companies have largely made their peace with the countries," says C. Fred Bergsten, senior fellow with the Brookings Institution, a Washington-based research

organization. He does, however, see bauxite prices rising "moderately" once world demand recovers from the recession.

Formula Status Uncertain

So far, the would-be cartel hasn't even agreed on a common-pricing formula, a device IBA backers have said is necessary to keep aluminum companies from playing off one producing country against another. The fact that a still-secret common-price formula was only "recommended" — not "approved" — by IBA's top ministers last fall means it won a two thirds majority, but wasn't unanimously backed.

The naysayers are understood to have included Australia, the world's largest bauxite producer. While that nation's support is viewed as crucial to any effective IBA move to common pricing, it's far from guaranteed. The government that brought the country into the association was replaced by a more conservative one last fall. And Australia hasn't a federal bauxite levy, though the state of Queensland does.

The IBA members, of course, continue to cooperate in "long-term" pricing studies. "The honeymoon is over, but we still have a marriage," says Henri Guda, IBA's secretary general. One source describes the tone of the IBA executive board's first 1976 session held in Kingston, Jamaica, last month as "low-key . . . much less action-oriented on the question of pricing."

No one seems anxious to predict that a common-price strategy might emerge by November, when the top IBA ministers gather in Sierra Leone for their third annual meeting. (Members include Jamaica, Surinam, Guyana, the Dominican Republic, Haiti, Ghana, Guinea, Sierra Leone, Yugoslavia, Indonesia and Australia.)

Threat of New Sources

For one thing, new sources of ore could undermine the IBA members. Brazil plans to expand its bauxite production greatly, but to date has refused to join the group. And industry sources argue that projected costs to use alternate (nonbauxite) ores set a "ceiling" on how far bauxite prices can rise.

Meanwhile, the bauxite countries are just recovering from the effects of last year's severe decline in demand for aluminum. Bureau of Mines figures show that U.S. imports of dried bauxite last year tumbled 25 percent from 1974 to 10.7 million long tons.

This decline "had a significant effect on the revenues of major exporters" of bauxite to the United States, according to the IBA's third quarterly review issued recently. But the association does contend that revenues were supported to some degree by improved aluminum ingot prices and the so-called "Jamaican formula," which first tied bauxite levies to ingot quotes.

And the outlook for bauxite revenues naturally is expected to improve as world economies strengthen. Guyana Bauxite Co., or Guybau, formed five years ago to operate the former holdings of Alcan Aluminium Ltd., expects 1976 sales to rise about $20 million, or 18 percent, from last year's $109.1 million, Patterson Thompson, chairman, says.

But the 1975 slump has prompted several concessions from the bauxite nations. For instance, Jamaica, the feisty price leader, has given ground on its "minimum production" requirements initiated two years ago when it boosted ore levies sharply. (These set minimum ore tonnages on which companies would be taxed, regardless of how much they actually mined.) Reynolds Metals Co., for example, last year got a 27 percent reduction from the 3,128,000-ton production minimum originally set for 1975.

And the size of the levies is inching upward more slowly these days. Jamaica, which originally had planned to raise its levy to 8.5 percent of the "realized" U.S. price of primary aluminum ingot by this year, has since negotiated to keep it at 7.5 percent at least through 1977.

A three-year pact valued at about $68 million recently signed between Surinam and an Aluminum Co. of America unit, negotiated against the background of the recession, calls for that country's levy to remain at the present 6 percent level through 1978. "We've been realistic," says

(continued on page 374)

(continued from page 373)

John deVries, Surinam's consul general. In the United States "if you ask for an increase (in levy) but as a result you get a drop in production, then where are you?" he asks.

It isn't clear how fast the countries can move toward their longer-range goal of more control over bauxite facilities. Jamaica has reached preliminary agreements to take a 51 percent stake in bauxite mining and shipping operations of such companies as Richmond, Va.–based Reynolds and Oakland, Calif.–based Kaiser Aluminum & Chemical Corp. (38 percent owned by Kaiser Industries Corp.).

Pittsburgh-based Alcoa, which expects to conclude its agreement within a month, isn't denying reports from Kingston that Jamaica is seeking far less of a share in its $150 million alumina refinery than in its $30 million bauxite operation. Alumina is the intermediate product in the processing of raw bauxite ore into aluminum metal.

Questions

1. Based upon your reading in section 13.3a, b, and c, as well as this article, what obstacles must any successful cartel overcome?

2. Are there any indications in this article that the hoped-for bauxite cartel is experiencing any difficulties overcoming these potential obstacles? Be specific.

3. Assuming the countries can get together and set price much like a pure mo-nopolist would, show how a "slump in aluminum demand" affects the price of bauxite.

4. If this were an "ideal" cartel represented by Figure 13.3.1, how should the cartel determine each nation's production quota?

Solutions

1,2. Obstacles to overcome:
   a. Can you agree on a common price? This is a major difficulty according to the article. Australia, for one, seems to be at odds with the suggested pricing formula. And the "common-pricing formula" has not yet been agreed to. It has only been "recommended" by IBA's top ministers. While it received a two thirds majority, it did not receive unanimous backing.
   b. Can you prevent "cheating"? As section 13.3 indicates, an enforcement mechanism is often necessary here. The article doesn't seem to indicate that there is an obvious one.
   c. Are the major competitors (producer nations in this case) included? In this article, it is noted that Australia and Brazil may not join. A cartel will provide an umbrella under which excluded producers can grow. ("Competitors" in this context also should include pro-

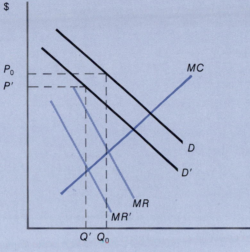

$

P_0
P'

MC

D

D'

MR

MR'

Q' Q_0

Q bauxite

ducers of close substitutes for the product.) Brazil, according to the article, is planning to expand its bauxite production greatly, but to date has refused to join the cartel.

d. What about non-price methods of competition? This may not be a particularly important problem when the product is fairly homogeneous as appears to be the case for bauxite. However, for goods such as air travel, or doctor visits, once price is eliminated as an arena for competition, firms (physicians) can still compete on product quality.

(Please refer to the "Applying the Theory" section in Chapter 10 for more discussion of the difficulties encountered by cartels.)

3. Since bauxite is an important input for aluminum, a decrease in the demand for aluminum would be expected to decrease the demand for bauxite (more on this in the next chapter). Assuming the demand for bauxite decreases, then the cartel should produce where the new MR curve intersects MC. This quantity is shown as Q' below. Price will be set according to the height of the new demand curve at Q'. There is not enough information to determine whether the new price (P') will be above or below the original price (P_0).

(continued on page 376)

(continued from page 375)

4. Quotas that "minimize total cartel cost" would be the ideal here. As the material in section 13.3.b indicates, this is identical to the short-run problem of allocating monopoly output among plants in a multiplant monopoly. (See Figure 10.4.6.) Minimum cartel cost is achieved when each firm produces the rate of output for which its marginal cost equals the common value of cartel marginal cost and marginal revenue. Thus, in Figure 13.3.1, each firm (or nation in this case) would produce the amount for which its marginal cost equals OA. As noted in section 13.3.b, to make this method acceptable to all cartel nations, a profit-sharing system more or less independent of sales quotas must be devised.

Source: Reprinted with permission of *The Wall Street Journal.* ©Dow Jones & Company, 1976. All rights reserved. (June 14, 1976).

INTRODUCTION
13.1

Oligopoly, or its limiting form duopoly, is a market situation intermediate between the cases previously studied. In monopoly only one seller is in the market; there competition, in either the technical or the popular sense, does not exist. Perfect competition and large-group monopolistic competition represent the opposite. So many firms are in the market that the actions of each are expected to be imperceptible to the others. There is competition in the technical sense, but little or none in the popular sense. The reverse tends to be true in oligopoly; technically, competition is lacking, but sometimes there is intense rivalry or competition in the popular sense.

Oligopoly is said to exist when more than one seller is in the market but when the number is not so large as to render negligible the contribution of each. If only two sellers are in the market, the special case of duopoly exists. For simplicity the duopoly market organization will be discussed rather than the more general oligopoly; since the fundamental problem is the same in most cases, generality is not sacrificed.

The Oligopoly Problem
13.1.a

The discussion so far may seem to indicate that there is primarily a quantitative difference among the various types of market organizations. In monopoly there is one seller; in duopoly two; and so on. To be sure, a quantitative difference does exist, and it is convenient to classify markets according to this difference. Yet there is a qualitative difference of transcending importance. Briefly, when numbers are few, each seller must be acutely conscious of the actions and potential reactions of rival firms.

Consider a duopoly market. Each firm must almost surely recognize that its actions affect the rival firm, which will react accordingly. Since the market is divided between the two, most courses of action benefiting one firm will be harmful to the other; hence action by one rival will have its counterpart in a maneuver by the other. Thus many different courses of action may result.

The rivals may spend their lives trying to "second guess" each other; they may tacitly agree to compete by advertising but not by price changes; or, by recognizing their monopoly potential, they may form a coalition and cooperate rather than compete. In fact, there are just about as many different results as there are oligopolies; to examine each would carry taxonomy too far. Thus we concentrate our attention on two sets of oligopoly theories. First, a few "classical" solutions to the duopoly problem are analyzed. Next, some theoretical "market" solutions are examined. But our investigation cannot be complete, for that would require one or more volumes in itself. Nonetheless, the principal feature of oligopoly markets should be clear. The firms are interdependent; the policies of one directly and perceptibly affect the others. Hence competition cannot be impersonal.

Some Concepts and Assumptions
13.1.b

First, for analytical convenience we assume that the products within an oligopoly market are homogeneous. As a practical matter, most oligopolies are characterized by product differentiation; yet the distinction is not of paramount importance because the firms are interdependent whether they produce identical commodities or not. Second, we assume that oligopolistic firms purchase inputs in perfectly competitive markets. This may or may not be true; it may hold for some inputs but not for others. However, when the assumption does great violence to reality, a small modification of the cost curves is all that is required. Finally, for the present, we assume that the firms behave independently even though they are interdependent in the market. That is, the case of collusive oligopoly is ruled out even though to the firms concerned it is a highly desirable and sometimes realized solution. Since the Sherman Antitrust Act, this is more a legal than an economic matter.

Formal speculation about the duopoly problem is sometimes dated from the work of a French economist, A. A. Cournot. Beginning with his famous "mineral springs" case, some of the outstanding theories of oligopoly behavior will be analyzed. Except for game-theory models and the Hotelling case, little credence is today accorded these solutions. However, as Machlup put it, "Familiarity with the classical models has become a kind of hallmark of the education of an economic theorist, even if it helps him more in the comprehension of the traditional lingo than in the analysis of current economic problems."[1]

The Cournot Case[2]
13.2.a

Assume, with Cournot, that two mineral springs, furnishing identical mineral water, are situated side by side. One is owned by A, the other by B. The springs are actually artesian wells to which purchasers must bring their own containers. Consequently the only costs are the fixed costs of sinking the wells; in particular, marginal cost is zero for each producer. The duopoly market so constructed is illustrated in Figure 13.2.1. DQ is the market demand for mineral water, and MR is the marginal revenue curve.

Suppose A is initially the only seller in the market. To maximize profit A sells OQ_1 units of mineral water, so that marginal revenue equals the zero marginal cost. Price is OP_1 per unit, and profit is OQ_1CP_1. Now B enters the market and Cournot's crucial assumption comes into the picture.

To get at an analytical solution of a duopoly situation one must make a behavioral assumption concerning each entrepreneur's expectations of the rival's policies. Cournot's assumption is that each entrepreneur expects that the other will *never* change output. Thus B enters the market expecting A always to market OQ_1 units of mineral water. In other words, B views the segment CQ as the proportion of total demand left after A sells OQ_1 units and the relevant marginal cost curve as MR_2. Taking this segment as the relevant demand curve, B maxi-

---

[1] Fritz Machlup, *The Economics of Sellers' Competition* (Baltimore: Johns Hopkins University Press, 1952), p. 369.

[2] Augustin Cournot, *Recherches sur les principes mathématiques de la théorie des richesses* (Paris, 1838). English translation by Nathaniel T. Bacon entitled *Researches into the Mathematical Principles of the Theory of Wealth* (New York: Macmillan, 1897; reprinted 1927).

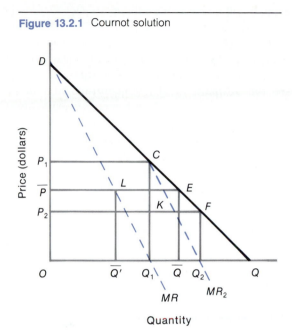

Figure 13.2.1 Cournot solution

mizes profit by selling $Q_1 Q_2$ units at price OP_2.[3] At this point, B's anticipated profit is $Q_1 Q_2 FK$ and A's anticipated profit falls to $OQ_1 KP_2$.[4]

Now A, in turn, expects B always to market $Q_1 Q_2 = Q_2 Q$ units of mineral water. According to this belief, OQ_2 represents the total market available to A. With straight-line demand and marginal revenue curves, the best A can do is to market $OQ_2/2$ units. Thus, A reduces output somewhat and market price rises accordingly. B views the situation anew and sees more of the market now available, specifically $OQ - OQ_2/2$. Consequently, B increases output to $1/2(OQ - OQ_2/2)$, price falls somewhat, and A must reappraise the situation.

---

[3]Recall the method of deriving marginal revenue from demand and the fact that marginal cost equals zero.

[4]The dynamics of transition from an initial monopoly position to an ultimate duopoly equilibrium can be explained in various ways, none of which is particularly satisfactory. The presentation in the text is adopted because it is the one most frequently found in the literature and because if one ignores certain minor points, it is the most easily understood. But the "minor points" may cause the serious student some concern. For example, upon entering the market, B charges a price of OP_2 per unit. Price for both A and B is accordingly OP_2, and total sales are OQ_2. But since the products of A and B are homogeneous, OQ_2 would be evenly divided between A and B, not divided two thirds for A and one third for B as the analysis in the text assumes. With some considerable graphical difficulty, the analysis can be revised to allow for market sharing subsequent to price changes. The same conclusion, however, ultimately emerges. Mathematical treatment of the Cournot case is not encumbered by this difficulty.

Believing B will forevermore sell $(OQ - OQ_2/2)/2$ units, the available market for A appears to be $OQ - (OQ - OQ_2/2)/2$. A's profit-maximizing output is thus $[OQ - (OQ - OQ_2/2)/2]/2$, somewhat less than previously. And so the process continues, A gradually decreasing sales and B increasing sales. But there is a limit; the adjustment mechanism converges.

To see the ultimate result, concentrate first on B. B initially sells $Q_1Q_2 = Q_2Q = OQ/4$ units. Then B increases output to $(OQ - OQ_2/2)/2 = (OQ - 3OQ/8)/2 = OQ(1/2 - 3/16) = 5OQ/16$. B thus expands by $5/16 - 1/4 = 1/16$. The next expansion is by $1/64$; the next by $1/256$; and so on. B's final output is $OQ(1/4 + 1/16 + 1/64 + \ldots) = OQ/3$.

A, on the other hand, initially had one half of the market, $OQ_1 = 1/2OQ$. A's ouput first falls to $OQ_2/2 = (3OQ/4)/2 = 3OQ/8$. This is a loss of one eight of the market in the first round. Next, A's output falls to $[OQ - (OQ - 3OQ/8)/2]/2 = 11OQ/32$. In this round A loses $1/32$ of the market; in the next, A loses $1/128$, and so on. A's final output is $OQ(1/2 - 1/8 - 1/32 - 1/128 - \ldots) = OQ/3$.

Graphically, A produces $O\overline{Q}'$ units, B produces $\overline{Q}'\overline{Q}$ units, and market price is $O\overline{P}$. A's profit is $O\overline{Q}'L\overline{P}$. B's is $\overline{Q}'\overline{Q}EL$, and the total profit is $O\overline{Q}E\overline{P}$. If price were set equal to (zero) marginal cost, OQ units would be sold, and profit would be zero. This is the perfectly competitive solution. Under monopoly, output would be $OQ/2$ and profit would be OQ_1CP_1. Thus duopoly output $2OQ/3$ is smaller than the competitive output but somewhat larger than monopoly output. The duopoly price (OP) is two thirds of the monopoly price; total duopoly profit is two thirds of potential monopoly profit.

The Cournot case is one possible solution to the duopoly problem. However, it is based upon an extraordinarily naive assumption: each entrepreneur believes the other will never change output, even after repeatedly observing such changes. The next duopoly model is based upon a similarly naive assumption.[5]

The Edgeworth Case
13.2.b

Although written in 1838, Cournot's work received little attention until a much later date. Indeed, it was 1883 before a review of his book appeared. This review was written by a French mathematician, Joseph Bertrand, who criticized Cournot for having his entrepreneurs assume that quantity is held constant. Instead, said Bertrand, a solution should be based on the assumption that entrepreneurs believe

---

[5]The mathematically trained reader may wish to show that when the market demand curve is given by $p = a - bQ$, where Q is total output of all producers, then, when there are n firms, each acting as a Cournot oligopolist, the output of each firm in equilibrium is $a/[2b + b(n - 1)]$. If $n = 2$, $q = a/3b$ and $Q = 2a/3b$. If $n = 1$, the monopoly solution obtains, and as n approaches infinity, output per firm approaches zero and total industry output approaches the competitive solution $Q = a/b$. This tendency toward the competitive solution as $n \to \infty$ could not hold unless there are no scale economies in production as shown by Roy J. Ruffin, "Cournot Oligopoly and Competitive Behavior," *Review of Economic Studies* 38 (1971), pp. 493–502.

their rivals will maintain a constant price.[6] This suggestion was developed by Edgeworth into the duopoly solution that bears his name.[7]

As in the Cournot situation, suppose two firms are selling a homogeneous product at zero marginal cost. Edgeworth assumes that each seller has a capacity limitation and that every consumer has an identical demand curve for the product. Suppose one of the sellers sets a price, say p_1. The other seller can do one of two things: (a) set a slightly lower price than p_1, taking most of the market from the first seller, or (b) set a monopoly price for those customers who could not purchase from the first seller because of the first seller's capacity limit. The situation can be illustrated best with a numerical example. Suppose there are 1,000 consumers, each with a demand curve $q = 1 - p$ where p is price and q is quantity. Each seller has a capacity of 400 units.

Consider, first, seller A's pricing decision. In the absence of any competition from B, the best price to charge is .6. This can be seen in Table 13.3.1. Any price below .6, demand exceeds 400, but the seller can only supply 400. Revenue increases with price up to $p_{A_1} = .6$. At price greater than .6, demand falls below capacity and revenue falls because the increased price does not offset the decreased quantity sold.

Now B has the two options listed above. Recall that B assumes that A does not alter price. Thus, choosing $P_{B_1} = .6$ is clearly inferior to choosing $P_{B_1} = .59$, because with the former, B sells 200 at .6 and with the latter, B sells 400 at .59. (Consumers go first to the lowest-priced firm.)

Firm A has lost virtually all sales to firm B and therefore will undercut P_{B_1} of .59, say, by charging $P_{A_2} = .58$. This undercutting process proceeds for a while, but not forever.

For example, suppose that $P_{A_t} = .28$. If B undercuts to .27, then B receives (.27)(400) or \$108. But a better strategy is available. At $P_{A_t} = .28$, the demand for the good $= (1 - .28)1000$ or 720. But A can only supply 400. Each of the first 555 customers can buy their full .72 before A runs out. The next customer gets only a fraction of what he wants and there is none left for anyone else. This means that the remaining 444 consumers are forced to go to B, who recognizes that he is in a monopoly position now with respect to these consumers. The best price to charge each of them is .5. He sells $(1 - .5)(444^+) = 222^+$ of the items at a price of .5 and so has a revenue of \$111.11. This exceeds \$108 and so is a preferred strategy.

The market has a low-priced seller, A, with a price of .28 and a high-priced seller, B, with a price of .5. All go to A first, but when A runs out they are forced to go to B. But this is not the end of it.

---

[6]Joseph Bertrand, "Theorie mathématiques de la richesse sociale," *Journal des savants* (Paris, 1883), pp. 499–508.

[7]F. Y. Edgeworth, "La Teoria ura del monopolio," *Giornale degli economistic* 15 (1897), pp. 13–31. The article was reprinted in English as "The Pure Theory of Monopoly," in Edgeworth, *Papers Relating to Political Economy* (London: Macmillan, 1925) 1, pp. 111–42.

Table 13.3.1		
A's first price	A's first quantity	A's revenue
0	400	0
0.1	400	40
0.2	400	80
0.3	400	120
0.4	400	160
0.5	400	200
0.6	400	240
0.7	300	210
0.8	200	160
0.9	100	90
1	0	0

Given that B charges $P = .5$, A is better off raising price. At $P_A = .49$, A can attract all customers from B and earn $.49(400) = \$196$. So A raises price. But now B does better by slightly undercutting A.

And so it goes, price continually moving between $0.50 and $0.2785. The duopoly situation, according to Edgeworth, is unstable and indeterminate (in the same sense that the solution to the bilateral monopoly problem is indeterminate).[8]

Stability in Oligopoly Markets: Chamberlin Solution
13.2.c

Chamberlin proposed a stable duopoly solution that depends upon mutual recognition of market interdependence.[9] Chamberlin's case is exactly that of Cournot except for the final result (see Figure 13.2.2). DQ is the linear demand for mineral water. A first enters the market and sells OQ_1 units at price OP_1, thereby reaping monopoly profit. B next enters the market. Seeing that A produces OQ_1 units, B regards CQ as the demand function. The best B can do is to market $Q_1 Q_2$ units. Price falls to OP_2, and total profit for both entrepreneurs is $OQ_2 FP_2$.

The difference between Cournot and Chamberlin now arises. According to the latter, A will survey the market situation after B's entry, recognize their mutual interdependence, and recognize also that sharing monopoly profit $OQ_1 CP_1$ is the best either of them can do. A consequently reduces output to $OQ_2' = OQ_1/2$.

---

[8]Edgeworth implicitly assumes that price differentials will not lead to arbitrage among consumers who buy at different prices. This is a highly questionable assumption, and it does not obtain in the Cournot model where the prices of the two firms are always the same. It is also worth noting that the oscillatory prices in Edgeworth's model depend on the assumption of fixed capacity. If capacities were unlimited, the assumption by each firm that the rival will not cut price would lead to a bidding down of the price to zero.

[9]E. H. Chamberlin, *The Theory of Monopolistic Competition* (Cambridge, Mass.: Harvard University Press, 1933), pp. 46–51. An earlier model of stability in oligopolistic markets was provided by Harold Hotelling, "Stability in Competition," *Economic Journal* 39 (1929), pp. 41–57.

Figure 13.2.2   Chamberlin solution

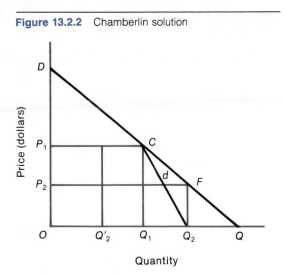

B also recognizes the best solution, and therefore maintains output at $Q_1Q_2 = Q_2'Q_1 = OQ_1/2$. Hence, total output is OQ_1, price is OP_1, and A and B share equally the monopoly profit OQ_1CP_1.

This simply says that the best solution for all firms is to behave as if there were only one firm, charge the monopoly price, and split the proceeds among the rivals.

There are two difficulties with this solution. The first is that in the absence of some form of collusion, each rival has an incentive to undercut price OP_1 and then to declare that he didn't really mean it. In the meanwhile, he earns a larger share of the profits. Second, this strategy leaves existing firms open to blackmail. For example, if a potential entrant recognizes that existing firms will be forced to share profits with it upon entry, it can threaten to enter unless the incumbents pay ransom. If they do not pay, the entrant receives 1/3 of the profits. If this were to continue, eventually no profit would be left for the original firm.

Stability in Oligopoly Markets: Sweezy Solution 13.2.d

Another model of stable oligopoly price that was at one time popular is the "kinked demand-curve hypothesis" of Sweezy,[10] illustrated in Figure 13.2.3. Suppose the demand curve confronting an oligopolist is given by the "kinked"

---

[10]Paul Sweezy, "Demand under Conditions of Oligopoly," *Journal of Political Economy* 47 (1939), pp. 568–73. George Stigler has argued that the popularity of this model has dropped to zero among professional economists, and that it is therefore puzzling that the model continues to show up in current textbooks. Those readers who agree with Stigler (and Gould and Lazear are among them) can skip this section with no real loss, except possibly in the grade in the course they are taking. See G. J. Stigler, "The Literature of Economics: The Case of the Kinked Oligopoly Demand Curve," *Economic Inquiry* 16, no. 2 (April 1978), pp. 185–204.

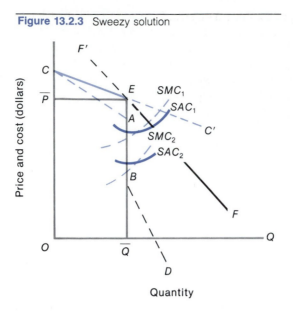

Figure 13.2.3 Sweezy solution

curve *CEF*. The slope of the curve changes drastically at the point *E*, corresponding to price $O\overline{P}$. The kink in the demand curve causes a finite discontinuity in the marginal revenue curve, which is given by the dashed line *CABD*. *CA* is the segment corresponding to the *CE* portion of the demand curve; *BD* corresponds to the less elastic *EF* segment. At point *E*, however, there is a finite discontinuity represented by the segment *AB*.

The principal feature is the absolutely vertical section *AB*. Marginal cost can intersect marginal revenue at any point from A to B and nonetheless result in the same market price $O\overline{P}$ and sales $O\overline{Q}$. For example, suppose initial cost conditions give rise to the plant represented by SAC_2 and SMC_2. SMC_2 intersects marginal revenue in the vertical segment *AB*, so price is $O\overline{P}$. If costs rise appreciably, so that SAC_1 and SMC_1 now represent the plant operating costs, price does not change. Or going the other way around, cost could fall from SMC_1 to SMC_2 without affecting market equilibrium price and quantity. Thus, according to Sweezy, oligopoly price tends to be very sticky, changing only infrequently and as the result of very significant changes in cost.[11]

The question on which the Sweezy thesis falls is *why* the kink occurs at a specific point *E* and remains there. One approach assumes that each entrepreneur believes (*a*) competitors will not match a price increase, so *CE* is

---

[11]For a variety of views concerning oligopoly price, consult the papers by Ackley, Alderson, Bailey, Baumol, Lanzillotti, Lerner, and Weston, in *The Relationship of Prices to Economic Stability and Growth, Compendium of Papers Submitted by Panelists Appearing before the Joint Economic Committee* (Washington, D.C.: Government Printing Office, 1958). For some recent research on related topics see the papers in *Industrial Concentration: The New Learning,* ed. H. Goldschmid, H. Mann, and F. Weston (Boston: Little, Brown, 1974).

relevant for price increases, but (*b*) they will match any price decreases, so the proportional market demand curve *EF* is relevant for price declines. This analysis explains *how* a kink occurs but it does not explain *where*. If one knows the equilibrium price ($\overline{OP}$) one can rationalize it by means of the Sweezy hypothesis. But the purpose of price theory is to explain how the interaction of demand and cost establishes a unique price–quantity equilibrium. The kinked demand theory does not do this because market equilibrium is consistent with a wide variety of cost situations. The Sweezy thesis, accordingly, must be regarded as an ex post rationalization rather than as an ex ante explanation of market equilibrium.

George Stigler challenged Sweezy's theory on both theoretical and empirical grounds.[12] Stigler found in several industries with a small number of sellers (cigarettes, automobiles, anthracite, steel, dynamite, gasoline, and potash) that price *increases* by one firm were often followed by rival's increases and that in potash a price decrease was not followed. In Stigler's words:

> This indicates only that not every oligopoly has reason to believe
> that it has a kinky demand curve and most adherents of the theory
> would readily concede this. On the other hand, there are seven
> industries in which the existence of the kinky demand curve is
> questionable — a list which is longer by seven than the list of
> industries for which a prima facie case has been made for the
> existence of the kink.[13]

Reaction Function and Stackelberg Leaders
13.2.e

The Cournot model was criticized for its level of naivete. There, both firms were assumed to behave as if they took the other firm's output level as given, not recognizing that the second firm would react to the first firm's choices. There are some situations in which this assumption is valid. For example, as the number of firms in an industry increases, the amount by which they respond to the actions of any one firm may be trivial. But in other cases, it is useful to have a more sophisticated description of the behavioral process.

To do this, it is useful to introduce the notion of "reaction functions." Recall that in Figure 13.2.1, if firm A chose output Q_1, then on the assumption that firm A would not change its output in response to firm B's output, firm B would choose to produce $Q_1 Q_2$.

Had A chosen to produce more than Q_1, say $\overline{Q}$, then B would have chosen to produce some amount smaller than $Q_1 Q_2$; in this case, $(\overline{Q}Q)/2$. The optimal output of B, given any output of A, can be graphed. Figure 13.2.4 presents that as curve *BB'*. It is read as follows: If A chooses to produce a_1 of output, then B will choose to produce b_1 of output if B is a Cournot duopolist.

---

[12]George J. Stigler, "The Kinky Oligopoly Demand Curve and Rigid Prices," *Journal of Political Economy* 55 (1947), pp. 432–49.

[13]Ibid., p. 441.

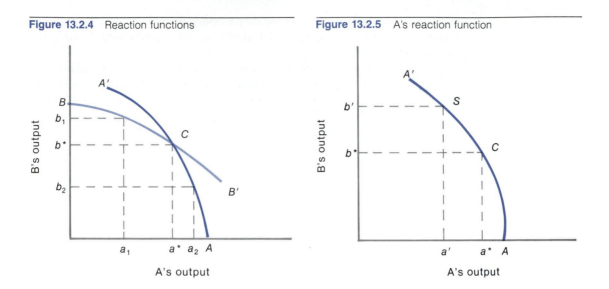

Figure 13.2.4 Reaction functions

Figure 13.2.5 A's reaction function

A similar curve reaction function can be drawn for firm A. A, acting as a Cournot duopolist, would take firm B's output as given and choose to produce the amount that maximized A's profits, subject to B's chosen level of output. For example, if B had chosen to produce b_2 of output, then A would choose to produce a_2 of output, assuming that B will not react to that choice. Thus, AA' is firm A's reaction function.

The intersection of AA' and BB' describes the outcome of a Cournot equilibrium. (This is sometimes called a Cournot-Nash equilibrium after John Nash, who formalized these concepts.) It is the only point at which both A's and B's optimizing behavior is consistent. At point C, firm A chooses to produce a^* of output. Firm B's reaction function tells us that B would produce b^* under those circumstances. Similarly, if B produces b^* of output, then firm A chooses to produce a^* of output, so choices are consistent.

The reaction function construct makes it easy to consider more sophisticated behavior by firms. For example, suppose that firm B anticipates that A will react to B's choices in exactly the way described by curve AA'. Then B can do better than behaving in the mechanical way described by BB'. By choosing an output level that B knows will induce A to produce at a level that B desires, B can increase profits. This can be shown diagrammatically.

Figure 13.2.5 portrays this situation. Note that BB' has been deleted from the picture, because it is now irrelevant. B can do better than to move along BB' because B now recognizes that B's action induces a reaction by A. Point C is the old Cournot-Nash equilibrium.

Since B knows that A will react according to schedule AA', B can simply examine that function and select the point on it that yields the highest profit to B. For example, B's profit might be higher at point S than at point C. In order

Part Three   Theory of the Firm and Market Organization

to induce A to produce a', which is necessary to end up at S, B need only announce that it will produce b'. Given that A behaves according to AA', a' is chosen rather than a^*.

Firm B is said to be a "Stackelberg leader," after Stackelberg (1952). Firm B leads because it recognizes that A follows in a particular pattern. As such, firm A is said to be a Stackelberg follower. Although B recognizes A's reaction, A does not recognize B's. This asymmetry may be disturbing, but before discussing it, let us consider a numerical example.

Example 13.2.1:

Suppose that the industry demand is as depicted in Figure 13.2.1 and that its algebraic representation is given by

$$P = 100 - Q$$

where P is price and Q is industry output. Q is the sum of output by firm A and firm B so

$$Q = A + B$$

If A and B are Cournot-Nash duopolists, their reaction functions can be derived algebraically.[14] They are

$$A = 50 - B/2 \text{ for A}$$

and

$$B = 50 - A/2 \text{ for B.}$$

The logic is that B takes A's output as given, so B's demand curve is the residual after A has chosen output. For example, in Figure 13.2.1, if A chooses Q_1, B's demand curve is CQ. Output $(Q_1Q/2)$ maximizes B's revenue. The equation $B = 50 - A/2$ is equivalent to producing $1/2(100 - A)$, which is the same as splitting Q_1Q in two.

---

[14]A's problem is to choose A so as to maximize revenue:

$$\text{Rev}_A = PA$$
$$= (100 - A - B)A$$
$$= 100A - A^2 - BA.$$

Differentiating with respect to A yields

$$\partial/\partial A = 100 - 2A - B = 0$$

or

$$A = 50 - B/2.$$

This is A's reaction function since it gives the optimal output for A for any given choice by B. Similarly, B's reaction function is

$$B = 50 - A/2.$$

The reaction functions are drawn below (Figure 13.2.E.1). They intersect at point C and both A and B produce 33.33 units. Each has revenue of $P(33.33)$ or of $(100 - 66.67)33.33 = (33.33)^2 = \$1,111.11$.

If B recognizes that AA' is A's reaction function, then B can do better than point C. Table 13.2.E.1 shows all possibilities.

As the table shows, B maximizes profit by selecting $B = 50$. This induces A to produce 25 and the situation is represented by S in Figure 13.2.E.1. Profits to B are $\$1,250$.

If A and B both behave as followers, then they end up at C and B only earns $\$1,111.11$.

The concept of a "leader" is an important one because it gives economists a simple way to model that agents take other's reactions into account before making a decision. This is surely at the heart of many business decision processes. But the Stackelberg leader is a somewhat primitive version of more sophisticated concepts of reaction analysis. One major drawback is that one firm is assumed to be a leader and the other a follower. This kind of asymmetry is troublesome, although it is not without its application. For example, a new entrant may have more freedom of behavior than a firm that is already in the industry. It can enter with a scale of plant that best suits its needs, knowing that the other firm must adapt, given its current plant structure. Still, such examples may be rare. Game theory explores other behavior that does not require asymmetries. It is explored in more detail in the next section.

Theory of Games and Oligopoly Behavior
13.2.f

For a time, one of the most exciting new developments in economic theory was John von Neumann and Oskar Morgenstern's *Theory of Games and Economic Behavior.*[15] It represents a unique approach to the analysis of business decisions; and these decisions make up the ultimate raw material with which economic theorists must work.

The general object of game theory is to determine standards of rational behavior in situations in which the outcomes depend upon the actions of interdependent "players." Indeed, von Neumann and Morgenstern had, as their purpose, " . . . to find the mathematically complete principles which define 'rational behavior' for the participants in a social economy, and to derive from them the general characteristics of that behavior. . . . The immediate concept of a solution is plausibly a set of rules for each participant which tells him how to behave in every situation which may conceivably arise."[16]

---

[15]John von Neumann and Oskar Morgenstern, *Theory of Games and Economic Behavior* (Princeton, N.J.: Princeton University Press, 1953). Even the nonmathematical student can read with profit pp. 1–45.

[16]Ibid., p. 31.

Figure 13.2.E.1 More reaction functions

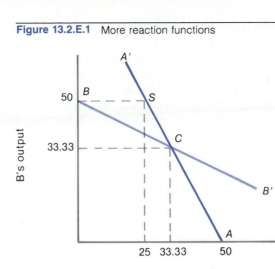

Table 13.2.E.1					
B	A	Profit for B	B	A	Profit for B
0	50	$ 0	50	25	$1,250
2	49	98	52	24	1,248
4	48	192	54	23	1,242
6	47	282	56	22	1,232
8	46	368	58	21	1,218
10	45	450	60	20	1,200
12	44	528	62	19	1,178
14	43	602	64	18	1,152
16	42	672	66	17	1,122
18	41	738	68	16	1,088
20	40	800	70	15	1,050
22	39	858	72	14	1,008
24	38	912	74	13	962
26	37	962	76	12	912
28	36	1,008	78	11	858
30	35	1,050	80	10	800
32	34	1,088	82	9	738
34	33	1,122	84	8	672
36	32	1,152	86	7	602
38	31	1,178	88	6	528
40	30	1,200	90	5	450
42	29	1,218	92	4	368
44	28	1,232	94	3	282
46	27	1,242	96	2	192
48	26	1,248	98	1	98
			100	0	0

Initially, it will be helpful not to restrict ourselves to an economic context. A "game" is any situation in which two or more people compete. Tennis and poker are good examples, but so also are Russian roulette and duopoly markets. For simplicity, we restrict our discussion to games in which there are two participants, called "players." Whatever data are initially available make up the "rules of the game," such as the dimensions of a tennis court, the ranking of poker hands, exact specification of commodities, and so forth. In a game one assumes that all possible courses of action for each player are known. Each particular course of action is called a "strategy" which, by definition, is a complete specification of the action to be taken by a player under every possible contingency in the playing of the game. Obviously, this information requirement is satisfied in few, if any, real world situations because each player must know the full set of strategies available to every participant, including all opponents in the game.

In certain cases the information required is even greater. In a wide variety of games (games of chance), the outcome is not known with certainty; it depends upon a chance variable. When chance enters the picture it is useful to assume perfect knowledge of the probability of each possible outcome corresponding to every possible combination of strategies by the players. The necessary information is readily available for the game of matching pennies; but in more interesting games such as bridge or duopoly the likelihood that the probabilities are known is negligible. Failing that, it generally suffices to assume that players know each others' assessments of the relevant probabilities, even if those probabilities are inaccurate.

The simplest class of games, and the only class to be discussed here, are "strictly adversary" games in which the possible outcomes are ranked in opposite order by the players. Among the games of this class the most prevalent are "constant-sum" games, which means that the sum of the winnings of the players is the same regardless of its distribution among participants. A market in which demand is completely inelastic is illustrative of constant-sum games. Finally, a special case of constant-sum games is the "zero-sum" game, perhaps best illustrated by the game of matching pennies. Briefly, in a zero-sum game the winnings of one player are matched exactly by the losses of another. The constant to which the winnings sum, in other words, is zero.

With these preliminaries out of the way let us turn to a constant-sum strictly adversary, "strictly determined" game. In this case the von Neumann–Morgenstern "minimax" solution is most readily explicable. Assume that player A can choose among three strategies (a, b, c) while player B has four possible strategies (a', b', c', d'). Any two-person, constant-sum game of this nature can be completely described by a payoff matrix, as represented in Table 13.2.2.

A's alternative strategies are listed in the stub column and B's in the row stub. A's payoff for each possible combination of strategies is given by an element in the matrix. For example, if A chooses strategy c and B chooses strategy a', A wins six. B wins the constant value of the game minus A's winnings. If the constant value is 20, B wins 14. In summary, each element e_{ij} in the matrix represents the amount obtained by A if he chooses the strategy corresponding to the ith row and B chooses the strategy corresponding to the jth column.

Table 13.2.2 Payoff matrix for a two-person, constant-sum game

A's strategies	B's strategies				Row minima
	a'	b'	c'	d'	
a	10	9	14	13	9
b	11	8	4	15	4
c	6	7	15	17	6
Column maxima	11	9	15	17	9 = 9

Initially, assume A is allowed to select first and chooses c. B, who selects next, would immediately choose a' to maximize winnings, given the strategy adopted by A. On the other hand, suppose B chooses first and selects c'. A would choose strategy c to obtain maximum winnings for B's chosen strategy. In actuality, with full knowledge assumed (each player knows the precise entries in the payoff matrix), the choices indicated above would never be made.

A realizes that for any strategy (row) selected, B will select the strategy (column) which minimizes A's winnings (or maximizes B's return). Thus A is really interested in the row minima, shown in the last column of Table 13.2.2. A chooses strategy a because it guarantees the largest return. In all cases, A adopts the strategy that corresponds to the maximum of the row minima, the "maximin." Similarly, B is only interested in the column maxima, or more precisely, in the constant sum minus the column maxima. B knows, for example, when selecting strategy a', that A will choose strategy b. Hence, B's return would be 20 − 11, or 9. Consequently, to assure the maximum payoff B selects the strategy corresponding to the minimum of the column maxima: the minimax.

The strategy pair a, b' is determined: A wins 9 and B wins 20 − 9, or 11. This game is strictly determined because each player selects and pursues a unique, pure strategy; when these two strategies are adopted, the maximum of the row minima equals the minimum of the column maxima. Neither player could possibly accomplish more.

The case of unique or "pure" strategies is an interesting one from the standpoint of economic theory. The more sophisticated treatments of duopoly using the older tools of analysis stress the importance of recognizing mutual interdependence. But in a strictly determined game this is irrelevant so long as each participant behaves rationally. So long as one of the rivals pursues a minimax strategy the other will also find that a minimax strategy is optimal. Furthermore, advanced knowledge of the opponent's strategy does not aid in determining one's own plan of action. Thus the Chamberlin duopolist sets monopoly price.

Unfortunately, both the more common games of chance and more general game theoretic models of economic behavior are not strictly determined. In essence this means that if pure strategies are selected by the participants, the

Figure 13.2.6 A nonstrictly determined game

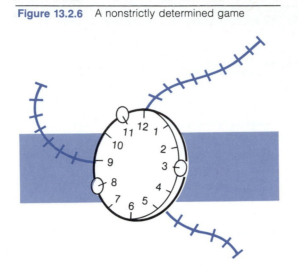

Table 13.2.3 Payoff matrix for a nonstrictly determined game

A's location	B's location			Row minima
	3	8	11	
3	19	23	11	11
8	15	19	20	15
11	27	18	19	18
Column maxima	27	23	20	20 ≠ 18

maximum value of the row minima is less than the minimum value of the column maxima. Such a game is illustrated by Figure 13.2.6 and Table 13.2.3.[17]

The diagram in Figure 13.2.6 represents a market in which demand is completely inelastic. Twelve customers are located in the circular portion of the market and are numbered like hours on a clock. Additionally, at 5, 9, and 12 o'clock there are branch markets containing 5, 9, and 12 buyers each. Each buyer purchases one unit of commodity per unit of time. There are two sellers, A and B, of a homogeneous commodity; they can choose among three different locations: 3, 8, and 11 o'clock. Both may situate at the same location. Since the commodities are identical and we now assume zero transportation cost, price must be the same for each seller. Buyers purchase from the nearer seller.

---

[17]This example is due to William Vickrey, "Theoretical Economics," Part III-A (mimeograph manuscript).

Table 13.2.4 A nonstrictly determined game: matching pennies

A's strategy	B's strategy		Row minima
	Heads	**Tails**	
Heads	1	−1	−1
Tails	−1	1	−1
Column maxima	1	1	1 ≠ −1

This market game is represented by the payoff matrix in Table 13.2.3. The entries show A's sales per unit of time as a function of the locations (strategies) selected by A and B. The game has a constant value of 38 [= 12 + (5 + 9 + 12)]. B's sale for any pair of strategies is found by subtracting A's sales from the constant value of the game.

Let us suppose A locates first and selects 11 o'clock. B will then locate at 8 o'clock. With B established at 8 o'clock, A can increase sales from 18 to 23 by relocating at 3 o'clock. But when A does so, B moves to 11 o'clock, captures the two larger branch markets, and A's sales decline to 11 units. But with B at 11 o'clock, A moves to 8 o'clock, expanding sales to 20 units. Then B moves to 3 o'clock, A moves to 11 o'clock, and we are right back where we started. The process of continuous relocation goes on because there is no unique minimax: the minimum of the column maxima exceeds the maximum of the row minima. As this game is constructed there is no unique stable solution.

There is a way out of the impasse in many games, however. To illustrate, consider the game of matching pennies, represented by the payoff matrix in Table 13.2.4. A tries to match B; if so, A wins 1 cent, losing 1 cent otherwise. As in the market game, the minimum of the column maxima exceeds the maximum of the row minima. To this stage there is no formal equilibrium solution. Von Neumann and Morgenstern provided a solution, however, by introducing the concept of mixed strategies, defined as " . . . an assignment of probabilities to the feasible pure strategies in such manner that the sum of the probabilities is unity for each participant."[18]

Since probability elements are now present in the analysis of a game, the object of each participant can no longer be stated as the maximization or minimization of a particular value. One must look to the *expected value* of the game, which is determined by performing two simple operations on the payoff matrix: (*a*) multiply each element in the matrix by the compound probability that it is selected and (*b*) sum these products for all elements in the payoff matrix.

To illustrate further, let p_i be the probability that A selects the strategy corresponding to the *i*th row. Similarly, q_j is the probability that B chooses the strategy corresponding to the *j*th column. Thus $p_i q_j$ is the compound probability that the

---

[18]Von Neumann and Morgenstern, *Theory of Games and Economic Behavior*, p. 145.

strategy pair i, j is selected. If a_{ij} is the associated element in the payoff matrix, step (a) above involves computing $p_i q_j a_{ij}$ for all i and j. Step (b) simply requires summing, so the expected value of the game $(\bar{v})$ is

$$\bar{v} = \sum_i \sum_j p_i q_j a_{ij},$$

where, by requirement,

$$p_i \geq 0, \quad q_j \geq 0, \quad \sum_i p_i = 1, \quad \text{and} \quad \sum_j q_j = 1.$$

In the game of matching pennies, suppose each player chooses heads with probability one half. Thus each must also choose tails with probability one half. Consequently, the expected value of the game is

$$\bar{v} = (1/2)(1/2)(1) + (1/2)(1/2)(-1) + (1/2)(1/2)(-1)$$
$$+ (1/2)(1/2)(1) = 0.$$

Von Neumann and Morgenstern showed that if mixed strategies are allowed, every constant-sum game has a unique minimax solution. That such a minimax strategy actually exists for the game of matching pennies can easily be shown. Compute the expected value of the game from A's standpoint for all possible probability assignments by A, assuming B always selects the most advantageous probability combination, given A's selection. As an example, try the following probabilities for A: one third heads, two thirds tails. Then B can set probabilities as nine tenths heads, one tenth tails. The expected value of the game is minus four fifteenths to A.[19] Assuming B always selects the best strategy, given A's selection, the maximum expected value of the game for A is zero, obtained when A sets probabilities one half heads, one half tails. Thus the *optimal mixed strategy* for A is $p_H = p_T = 1/2$. When A plays this strategy, the best B can do is set $q_H = q_T = 1/2$; the expected value of the game to B is also zero.

In contrast to strictly determined games, advanced knowledge of the opponent's plans is very important in games requiring mixed strategies for a minimax solution. As von Neumann and Morgenstern wrote:

> It constitutes a definite disadvantage for each player to have his intentions found out by his opponent. Thus one important consideration for a player in such a game is to protect himself against having his intentions found out by his opponent. Playing several different strategies at random, so that only their probabilities are determined, is a very effective way to achieve a degree of such protection: By this device, the opponent cannot possibly find out what the player's strategy is going to be, since the player does not know it himself. Ignorance is obviously a very good safeguard against disclosing information directly or indirectly.

---

[19]The probabilities for B were limited to small numbers. B can gain more by setting the probabilities of heads closer to unity. In the limit, given A's choice of one third heads, two thirds tails, B can gain one third (that is, the expected value of the game to A is minus one third). More generally, if A sets probability $p_H < p_T$, B always wins by setting probabilities $q_H = 1$, $q_T = 0$. If A sets probabilities $p_H > p_T$, B always wins by setting $q_H = 0$, $q_T = 1$.

In other words, the best way of deciding whether to show heads or tails is to flip a coin and let the toss decide.

Having sketched the outlines of game theory, we can now turn to some more general considerations. The heart of game theory is the minimax principle; and there are numerous criticisms of applying this principle to decision making in economics and business. Essentially, the minimax principle requires the player to choose a strategy under the assumption that the rival player always takes the least desirable course of action from the former's standpoint. Slightly less precisely, the minimax principle requires the player (or entrepreneur) to adopt the plan of action that will make the best of the worst possible situation. But this plan of action will not be the best if the worst possible situation does not arise. It does not allow the entrepreneur to exploit favorable changes in the market or, in any sense, to be "dynamic."

Many economists believe the minimax principle is an unnecessarily conservative standard. Furthermore, it is frequently asserted that minimax strategy is not compatible with the dominant entrepreneurial psychology. The object of most entrepreneurs is not to make the best of a bad situation. Indeed, it appears that many entrepreneurs attempt to maximize their objective under the assumption that very favorable conditions will prevail. And, of course, they generally expend considerable effort to influence the market so as to make the assumption correct.

Most economic situations are not well illustrated by constant-sum games. In fact, it is the essence of economics that there are gains from trade. The seller's gain is not the buyer's loss. In order to analyze these situations, nonzero-sum games must be introduced. One simple nonzero-sum game, called the "prisoner's dilemma," is often used to describe the problem of duopoly.

The prisoner's dilemma comes from the following, somewhat gruesome tale. Two prisoners, A and B, are confronted with a decision: Each must declare innocence or guilt, but the payoff matrix in Table 13.2.5 is relevant. It is interpreted as follows: If A pleads quilty and B pleads guilty, then both receive sentences of three years imprisonment (northwest corner). If both A and B declare innocence, both are executed (southeast corner). If A declares innocence and B admits guilt, A goes free and B is executed. If B declares innocence and A admits guilt, B goes free and A is executed.

The dilemma is that although both would like to agree to admit guilt, that is not an equilibrium strategy. In fact there is no way to avoid the execution of both prisoners. Here is why:

Mr. A sits in his cell with the paper on which he must write the word "innocent" or "guilty." He thinks to himself: "I do not know what B wrote. Suppose that B wrote guilty. Then my choice is clear. If I declare innocence, I go free. If B wrote innocent, then I will be executed in either case. Therefore, I might as well declare innocence on the (slim) hope that B wrote guilty." Of course, Mr. B goes through the same process and also declares his innocence. The equilibrium is the southeast corner, where both prisoners are executed.

There is a way around this, but it requires an outside enforcer. If, for example, A and B can pay the jailer in advance to shoot either one at the instance that he starts to write the word "innocent" on paper, then the structure is changed. Now,

Table 13.2.5 The prisoner's dilemma

A's strategies	B's strategies	
	Guilty	**Innocent**
Guilty	3 years for both	A executed B free
Innocent	B executed A free	Both executed

neither party has any incentive to declare innocence and the equilibrium, with the assistance of the jailer, is the northwest corner.

Examples of using third parties to eliminate opportunistic behavior exist in the antitrust literature and are discussed below. A more colorful example involves a crew of boatsmen who collectively hired a taskmaster, paying him to whip any shirkers. In the absence of the outside enforcement, each rower had an incentive to slack off, letting someone else do the rowing. If all thought that way, the boat would have moved much more slowly and the boatsmen could not collect as large a fee. The taskmaster prevents that situation from arising.

SOME "MARKET" SOLUTIONS TO THE DUOPOLY PROBLEM
13.3

The classical treatments of duopoly, with the possible exception of Chamberlin's, are based upon the assumption that entrepreneurs act independently of one another even though they are interdependent in the market. We turn now to some theories based upon explicit or implicit collusion among firms.

Cartels and Profit Maximization
13.3.a

A *cartel* is a combination of firms whose object is to limit the scope of competitive forces within a market. It may take the form of open collusion, the member firms entering into an enforceable contract pertaining to price and possibly other market variables. This is perhaps best illustrated by the German *Kartelle;* but the NRA codes of our Great Depression years fall into this category as well. On the other hand, a cartel may be formed by secret collusion among sellers; many examples of this exist in American economic history. Most tend to date to the early years of the 20th century.[20]

The cases of open and secret collusion offer the best examples of cartels. However, in a broad sense, trade associations, professional organizations, and the like perform many functions usually associated with a cartel.

Of the wide variety of services a cartel may perform for its members, two are of central importance: price fixing and market sharing. In this section, we will examine price fixing in an "ideal" cartel.

Suppose a group of firms producing a homogeneous commodity forms a cartel. A central management body is appointed, its function being to determine the uniform cartel price. The task, in theory, is relatively simple, as illustrated by Figure 13.3.1. Market demand for the homogeneous commodity is given by DD', so marginal revenue is given by the dashed line MR. The cartel marginal cost curve must be determined by the management body. If all firms in the cartel purchase all inputs in perfectly competitive markets, the cartel marginal cost curve (MC_c) is simply the horizontal sum of the component marginal cost curves of the member firms. Otherwise, allowance must be made for the increase in input price accompanying an increase in input usage; MC_c will stand further to the left than it would if all input markets were perfectly competitive.

In either case the management group determines cartel marginal cost, MC_c. The problem is the simple one of determining the price that maximizes cartel profit—the monopoly price. From Figure 13.3.1 marginal cost and marginal revenue intersect at the level OA; thus the market price $O\overline{P}$ is the one the cartel management will establish. Given the demand curve DD', buyers will purchase $O\overline{Q}$ units from the members of the cartel. The second important problem confronting the cartel management is *how* to distribute the total sales of $O\overline{Q}$ units among the member firms.

Cartels and Market Sharing
13.3.b

Fundamentally there are two methods of sales allocation: non-price competition and quotas. The former is usually associated with "loose" cartels. A uniform price is fixed, and each firm is allowed to sell all it can at that price. The only

---

[20]As a matter of fact, government prosecution of collusive price-fixing activities in violation of Section 1 of the Sherman Antitrust Act are filed regularly.

In fiscal 1970, the Antitrust Division filed 19 price-fixing cases and 23 in the preceding fiscal year. It should be noted that vertical price-fixing agreements, that is, those agreements not exempt from prosecution under Fair Trade exemptions, constituted about 75 percent of those cases filed in 1970 and roughly 40 percent of those filed in 1969.

The Federal Trade Commission, under Section 5 of the Federal Trade Commission Act, may file civil suits against price-fixing conspirators. However, this would be rare since under present liaison arrangements with the Antitrust Division all hard-core price-fixing cases, of the type discussed in this subsection are prosecuted by the Antitrust Division.

Mr. William J. Curran provided helpful advice regarding this point.

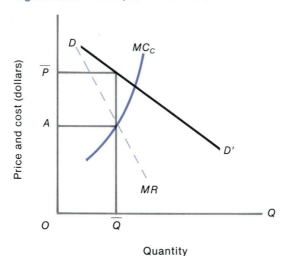

Figure 13.3.1 Cartel profit maximization

requirement is that firms do not reduce price below the cartel price. There are many examples of this type of cartel organization in the United States today. For instance, in most localities both medical doctors and lawyers have associations whose code of ethics is frequently the basis of price agreement. All doctors, for example, will charge the same rate for office and house calls. The patient market is divided among the various doctors by non-price competition: each patient selects the doctor of his or her choice. Similarly, the generally uniform prices of haircuts, major brands of gasoline, and movie tickets do not result from perfect competition within the market. Rather, they result from tacit, and sometimes open, agreement upon a price; the sellers compete with one another but *not* by price variations.

The so-called fair-trade laws of many states establish loose, but very legal, cartels. Under these laws the manufacturer of a commodity may set its retail price. The retail sellers of the commodity (the sometimes reluctant members of the cartel) are forbidden by law to charge a lower price. The various retailers compete for sales by advertising, customer credit policies, repair and maintenance services, delivery, and such.

The second method of market sharing is the *quota* system, of which there are several variants. Indeed, there is no uniform principle by which quotas can be determined. In practice, the bargaining ability of a firm's representative and the importance of the firm to the cartel are likely to be the most important elements in determining a quota. Beyond this there are two popular methods. The first of these has a statistical base, either the relative sales of the firm in some precartel base period or the "productive capacity" of the firm. As a practical matter, the choice of the base period or of the measure of capacity is a matter of bargaining among the members. Thus, as said above, the most skillful bargainer is likely to come out best.

Part Three   Theory of the Firm and Market Organization

The second popular basis for the quota system is geographical division of the market. Some of the more dramatic illustrations involve international markets. For example, an agreement between Du Pont and Imperial Chemicals divided the market for certain products so that the former had exclusive sales rights in North and Central America (except for British possessions) and the latter had exclusive rights in the British Empire and Egypt. Another example is an agreement between the American company Rohm and Haas and its German counterpart Roehm und Haas. The former was given exclusive rights in North, Central and South America, and in Australia, New Zealand, and Japan; the latter was given Europe and Asia, except for Japan. The illustrations can be multiplied many times over, but these should serve to indicate the quota by geographical division.

While quota agreement is quite difficult in practice, in theory some guidelines can be laid down. Consider the "ideal" cartel represented by Figure 13.3.1. A reasonable criterion for the management group would be "minimize total cartel cost." This is identical with the short-run problem of allocating monopoly output among plants in a multiplant monopoly (see Figure 10.4.6). Minimum cartel cost is achieved when each firm produces the rate of output for which its marginal cost equals the common value of cartel marginal cost and marginal revenue. Thus each firm would produce the amount for which its marginal cost equals OA (Figure 13.3.1); by the summing process to obtain MC_c, total cartel output will be $O\overline{Q}$. The difficulty involved with this method is that the lower-cost firm obtains the bulk of the market and the bulk of profits. To make this method of allocation acceptable to all members, a profit-sharing system more or less independent of sales quotas must be devised.

In certain cases the member firms may be able to agree upon the share of the market each is to have. This is illustrated in Figure 13.3.2 for an "ideal" situation. Suppose only two firms are in the market and they decide to divide the market evenly. The market demand curve is DD', so the half-share curve for each firm is Dd. The curve marginal to Dd is the dashed line MR, the half-share marginal revenue for each firm. Suppose each firm has identical costs, represented by SAC and SMC. Each will decide to produce $O\overline{Q}$ units with price $O\overline{P}$, corresponding to the intersection of marginal revenue and marginal cost. A uniform price of $O\overline{P}$ is established and $OQ_c = 2O\overline{Q}$ units are supplied. This happens, in our special case, to be a tenable solution because the market demand curve is consistent with the sale of OQ_c units at the price $O\overline{P}$.

To see this, let us go the other way around. Suppose a cartel management group is formed and given the task of maximizing cartel profit. With the demand curve DD', the management group views Dd as marginal revenue. Next, summing the identical SMC curves it obtains cartel marginal cost MC_c.[21] The intersection of cartel marginal cost and cartel marginal revenue occurs at the level OF, corresponding to output OQ_c and price $O\overline{P}$. The same is true for the individual

---

[21]The problem, of course, will be more complicated if input prices vary with input usage. In this case, the cartel marginal cost cannot be directly obtained by summing the members' marginal cost curves.

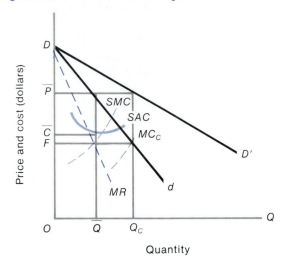

Figure 13.3.2 Ideal market sharing in a cartel

firms, so the firms' decision to share the market equally is consistent with the objective market conditions. But this is a rare condition; cost differences between the firms would have created a situation inconsistent with market conditions and the voluntary market-sharing agreement would have collapsed. That, as we shall see, is what is most likely to happen to cartels anyhow.

Short and Turbulent Life of Cartels — The Great Electrical Conspiracy 13.3.c

Unless backed by strong legal provisions, cartels are very likely to collapse from internal pressure (before being found out by the Antitrust Division of the Department of Justice). A few large, geographically concentrated firms producing a homogeneous commodity may form a very successful cartel and maintain it. But the greater the number of firms, the greater the scope for product differentiation, and the greater the geographical dispersion of firms, the easier it is to "cheat" on the cartel's policy. Enterprising entrepreneurs will discover what they believe to be ingenious methods of cheating.

The typical cartel as a functioning organization is characterized by high (perhaps monopoly) price, relatively low output, and a distribution of sales among firms such that each firm operates at an output less than that at which unit cost is minimized. In this situation any one firm can profit greatly from secret price concessions. Indeed, with homogeneous products, a firm offering price concessions can capture as much of the market as it desires, providing the other members adhere to the cartel's price policy. Thus secret price concessions do not have to be extensive before the obedient members experience a marked decline in sales. Recognizing that one or more members are cheating, the formerly obedient members must themselves reduce price in order to remain viable. The cartel accordingly collapses. Without effective *legal* sanctions, the life of a cartel is likely to be brief.

One of the most notorious examples of a market-sharing cartel occurred in the electrical equipment industry between 1950 and the early 1960s when it was finally broken up by the federal government. During the days of the Office of Price Administration, major suppliers of electrical switchgear began to get together to decide pricing strategies. After the abolishment of the OPA, the electrical equipment suppliers continued to meet regularly, if secretly, at the Penn-Sheraton Hotel in Pittsburgh. Between 1951 and 1958 the cartel split $75 million of annual sales in electrical switchgear by agreeing in advance which company would be the "low" bidder on upcoming contracts. In 1951 the market was split as follows: General Electric, 45 percent; Westinghouse, 35 percent; Allis-Chalmers, 10 percent; and Federal Pacific, 10 percent. There was constant chiseling among the cartel members especially on sealed bid business where policing was difficult. In 1954–55 there was a severe breakdown of the cartel known as the "white sale" when prices were discounted by 40 to 45 percent in a very short period of time. The cartel was reconstituted in 1956; but within about a year, Westinghouse gave one customer, Florida Power and Light Company, a price break on circuit breakers by hiding the discount in its transformer order. This triggered another breakdown of the cartel, and between 1957 and 1958 prices dropped by 60 percent. When the cartel was reformed in 1958, the entry of ITE resulted in a new sharing agreement: General Electric, 40.3 percent; Westinghouse, 31.3 percent; Allis-Chalmers, 8.8 percent; Federal Pacific, 15.6 percent; and ITE, 4 percent. The fascinating history of this cartel is strewn with episodes of breakdowns in its agreements and devious schemes of cartel members to capture business in violation of the cartel rules.[22]

The breakdown of cartels results because the payoff structure to the game of collusion is that of a prisoner's dilemma. If A and B are two firms that are attempting to collude, then the payoff structure might be represented by Table 13.3.1.

Table 13.3.1 Pricing Strategies

A's strategies	B's strategies	
	Maintain price	Cut price
Maintain price	A = 5 B = 5	A = 0 B = 9
Cut price	A = 9 B = 0	A = 0 B = 0

---

[22]Richard Austin Smith has detailed the history of this cartel in "The Incredible Electrical Conspiracy," *Fortune* 63 (April and May 1961), pp. 132 ff. (April) and pp. 161 ff. (May).

The table is read as before. If both A and B hold price at its monopoly level, then each receives profits of 5. If both cut price, then competition prevails and no profits are made by either. If B cuts price while A maintains the agreed-upon price, all buyers go to B and A sells nothing. There B receives 9 (not 10, because of the price cut) and A receives 0. Conversely, if A cuts and B holds, A receives 9 and B receives 0.

This payoff matrix has the same structure as that of Table 13.2.5. As such, each player has an incentive to cut price. The equilibrium is the southeast corner, which illustrates why cartels tend to break down.

What is required is an outside enforcer. If there were a way that these firms could penalize one another for price cutting, then the equilibrium would move to the northwest corner and both would be better off.

Many have argued that the Interstate Commerce Commission of the federal government used to perform this function for the trucking industry. Trucking is inherently competitive. In order to maintain a monopoly price, the industry saw to it that their prices were regulated by the government, preventing any firm from acting as a price cutter. Rather than keeping prices low for consumers, the price was kept artificially high by the government. The government acted as outside enforcer. Deregulation has borne the argument out, at least for some segments of the trucking industry.

Price Leadership in Oligopoly
13.3.d

Another type of market solution of the oligopoly problem is *price leadership* by one or a few firms. This solution does not require open collusion but the firms must tacitly agree to the solution. Price leadership has in fact been quite common in certain industries. For example, Clair Wilcox lists, among others, the following industries as characterized by price leadership: nonferrous alloys, steel, agricultural implements, and newsprint.[23] Similarly, in their interview study, Kaplan, Dirlam, and Lanzillotti found that Goodyear Tire and Rubber, National Steel, Gulf Oil, and Kroger Grocery follow the price leadership of other firms in the market.[24]

To introduce the price-leadership model, consider the simple illustration in Figure 13.3.3 an extension of the market-sharing cartel model of Figure 13.3.2. Two firms produce a homogeneous commodity whose market demand is given by *DD'*. By either explicit collusion or tacit agreement the firms decide to split the market evenly. Thus each views *dd'* as its demand curve and *MR* as its marginal

---

[23]Clair Wilcox, *Competition and Monopoly in American Industry,* Temporary National Economic Committee, Monograph No. 21 (Washington, D.C.: Government Printing Office, 1940), pp. 121–32.

[24]A. D. H. Kaplan, Joel B. Dirlam, and Robert F. Lanzillotti, *Pricing in Big Business* (Washington, D.C.: Brookings Institution, 1958), pp. 201–7.

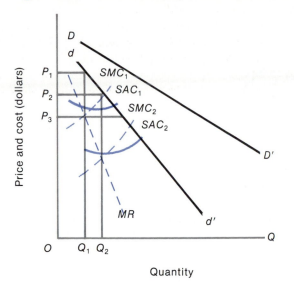

Figure 13.3.3 Price leadership by the lower-cost firm

revenue curve. In this case, however, the costs of the two producers are different; firm 1 has substantially higher costs than firm 2, as shown by $SAC_1 - SMC_1$ and $SAC_2 - SMC_2$, respectively.

Other things equal, firm 1 would like to charge OP_1 per unit, selling OQ_1 units. This price–output constellation would lead to maximum profit for firm 1; but firm 2 can do much better since its marginal cost is substantially below its marginal revenue at this point. In this situation, firm 2 has an effective control. Being a lower-cost producer, firm 2 can set the lower price OP_2 that maximizes its profit. Firm 1 has no choice but to follow; if it tries to retain OP_1 its sales will be zero. Hence, the higher-cost firm must be content to accept the price decision of the lower-cost firm.

The particular solution shown here is not a very likely one. If this situation existed in a market, firm 2 would hardly agree, tacitly or otherwise, to split the market evenly. But given the antitrust laws in the United States, it would not drive

The particular solution shown here is not a very likely one. If this situation existed in a market, firm 2 would hardly agree, tacitly or otherwise, to split the market evenly. But given the antitrust laws in the United States, it would not drive firm 1 out of the market. Firm 2 has the power to do so. By setting a price such as OP_3, it can earn a pure profit and ultimately drive firm 1 out of the market. But then it would face the legal problems of monopoly. A better solution, from the viewpoint of the lower-cost firm, is to tolerate a "competitor." Thus, while not sharing the market equally, as in this illustration, firm 2 would nevertheless set a price high enough for firm 1 to remain in the market.

A much more typical example of price leadership is illustrated by Figure 13.3.4. The model is a somewhat exaggerated representation of a situation

Figure 13.3.4 Price leadership by the dominant firm

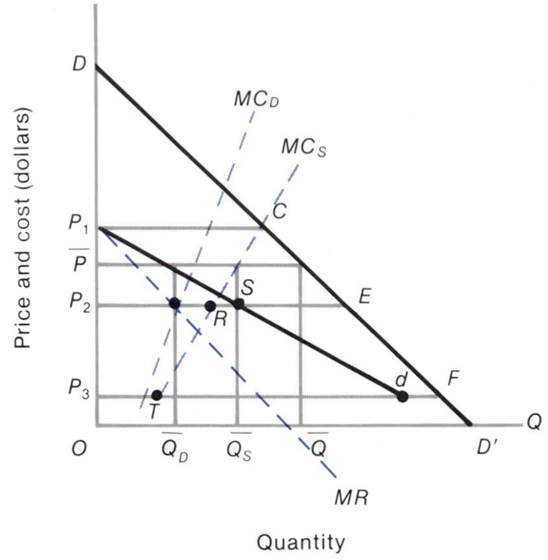

which, some say, exists in several American industries. There is one (or a small number of) dominant firm(s) and numerous small ones. As shown by the marginal cost curves in Figure 13.3.4, the dominant firm is almost as large as all the small firms combined.

The dominant firm could possibly eliminate all its rivals by a price war. But this would establish a monopoly with its attendant legal problems. A more desirable course of action for the dominant firm is to establish the market price and let the small firms sell all they wish at that price. The small firms, recognizing their position, will behave just as perfectly competitive firms. That is, they will regard their demand curve as a horizontal line at the prevailing price and sell that amount for which marginal cost equals price. Notice, this does not entail the long-run zero profit solution because price may be set far above (minimum) unit cost.

The problem confronting the dominant firm is to determine the price that will maximize its profit while allowing the small firms to sell all they wish at that price. To do this it is necessary to find the demand curve for the dominant firm. Suppose DD' is the market demand curve and MC_S is the horizontal summation of the marginal cost curves of the small firms. Since the small firms equate marginal cost and price, MC_S is also the collective supply curve of the small firms.[25]

First, suppose the dominant firm sets the price OP_1. The small firms would sell P_1C units, exactly the market quantity demanded. Hence, sales by the dominant

---

[25]Again, for simplicity, we ignore the problem created by rising input prices. In principle, the solution is determinate if input prices rise as input usage increases; however, the case cannot be analyzed graphically.

firm would be zero, and P_1 would be a point on its demand curve. If price OP_2 were set by the dominant firm, the small firms would sell P_2R units and the dominant firm would sell $RE = P_2S$ units; thus S is also a point on its demand curve. Finally, suppose the price were set at OP_3. The small firms would sell P_3T units and the dominant firm $TF = P_3d$ units. For a price below OP_3, only the dominant firm would sell. Hence, its demand curve is P_1dFD', and its marginal revenue is given by the dashed line MR.

Equating marginal revenue and marginal cost (MC_D), the dominant firm sets the price $\overline{OP}$ and sells $\overline{OQ}_D$ units. At this price the small firms sell $\overline{OQ}_S$ units; and by construction of the demand curve P_1dFD', $\overline{OQ}_D + \overline{OQ}_S$ must equal $\overline{OQ}$, the total quantity sold at price $\overline{OP}$.

Many variations of this basic price-leadership model can be constructed by changing the assumptions. One may allow for two or more dominant firms, for product differentiation, for geographically separated sellers and transportation cost, and so on. Nonetheless, the basic results are much the same; and they may help to explain price–output policies in a variety of oligopoly markets.

COMPETITION IN OLIGOPOLY MARKETS
13.4

Non-price competition is an essential feature of oligopolistic markets. Perhaps the most important technique of non-price competition is advertising. In the United States, and increasingly in European countries, advertising is the uniformly most accepted and acceptable method of attracting customers, at least to entrepreneurs if not to economists. The "pros and cons" of advertising expenditure have been argued at length; the argument is likely to continue because the question at stake is a moot one. But for good or not, advertising is an established practice that is presumably considered worthwhile by entrepreneurs; otherwise they would not continue to spend billions of dollars annually on this type of non-price competition.[26]

The major plus for advertising is that it informs consumers of a product's existence and uses. More information is generally (although not always) a good thing. The minus is that much of advertising may go merely to move a buyer from one seller to another. If all sellers advertised equally effectively, there would be no net movement, but society would have wasted valuable resources in the effort to attract other firms' customers.

Another important type of non-price competition consists in creating bona fide (but sometimes spurious) quality differentials among products. The general effect of quality differentiation is to divide a broad market into a group of submarkets among which there is usually a relatively large price differential. The automobile

---

[26]The reader should be careful not to fall into the trap of assuming that advertising implies oligopolistic structure of the industry. Advertising can be viewed as consistent with competition in many respects. See L. G. Telser, "Advertising and Competition," *Journal of Political Economy* 72 (December 1964), pp. 537–62; and P. Nelson, "Information and Consumer Behavior," *Journal of Political Economy* 78 (March–April 1970), pp. 311–29.

market offers a good example. There are definite, physically specifiable differences between a Ford Escort and the Ford Motor Company's Continental. There is also a substantial price difference; no one buyer is likely to be a potential customer in both markets, except perhaps for automobiles to perform two fundamentally different services (family car and business runabout).

Ford is not alone in creating quality differentials, however. General Motors and Chrysler do the same; and they engage in active non-price competition within each of the submarkets. Further, the automobile market example brings to light a social criticism of quality competition. Too many quality differentials may be created so that items supposedly in one class overlap with items in another. Thus within the broad market not only is there competition to create new quality classes and gain the competitive edge of being the first in the market; there is also competition within quality classes.

Finally, a third major technique of non-price competition is design differences. This type could also be illustrated by the automobile market; but the market for golf clubs serves just as well. MacGregor, Wilson, Spaulding, and other producers now "change models" annually, just as do the automobile manufacturers. They also create (possibly spurious) quality differentials between sporting-goods stores and pro shops. But within, say the pro-shop market, the competition among companies is strictly a matter of club design.

These three types of non-price competition far from exhaust the possible methods, but they do illustrate the ways in which entrepreneurs can spend resources in an effort to attract customers to their particular "brands."

WELFARE EFFECTS OF OLIGOPOLY
13.5

Since there are many models of oligopoly behavior, each predicting somewhat different results, it is impossible to be precise about the welfare effects of oligopolistic market organization. Furthermore, any set of static welfare criteria one applies to the situation may be relatively insignificant in a dynamic context. Nonetheless, a few things may be said.

First, whatever the model, two characteristics common to all oligopoly markets can be isolated. Firms in an oligopoly presumably produce their output at the minimum attainable unit cost. But there is no reason to believe their output uniquely corresponds to minimum long-run unit cost. Hence oligopoly organization requires more units of resources per unit of commodity produced than absolutely necessary. Furthermore, since pure economic profit normally accompanies oligopolistic market organization, price is higher than both unit and marginal cost. In whatever equilibrium is reached, the marginal valuation of buyers is greater than the marginal cost of output. If the commodity were priced at either marginal or average cost, buyers would like to purchase more than producers would be willing to sell.

A second consideration is also important. Already mentioned is that vast amounts of resources are devoted to advertising and to creating quality and design differentials. The allocation of some resources for these purposes is doubtless justifiable. For example, to the extent that advertising merely reports price and seller location, it helps keep buyers better informed. Similarly, certain quality and design differentials may be socially desirable. Nonetheless, there is a strong presumption (based upon purely empirical grounds) that oligopolists push all forms of non-price competition beyond the socially desirable limits. In absence of evidence to the contrary, it is reasonable to conclude that buyers in oligopoly markets would be better off if there were more active price competition and less non-price competition.

STATIC AND DYNAMIC EFFICIENCY
13.6

The welfare criteria discussed in the last section are inherently static. But there is another issue that is dynamic, that is, it relates to the way that industry and cost conditions change over time.

Some have argued that monopolistic firms have more incentive to innovate, to invest in R&D technology than competitive firms. The argument goes like this:

Suppose that a firm is considering undertaking an investment that produces some new product, say a light bulb that never burns out. Once that light bulb is invented, it pays to have it marketed competitively. Any monopolistic restriction of output results in inefficiency because consumers are willing to pay more than the cost of producing an additional bulb.

The problem arises because if the firm knows that the good will be sold competitively, it also knows that price will fall such that all other firms selling the bulb earn zero profits. This means that the firm that invented the bulb will never recoup the cost of the investment. Anticipating this development, the firm is reluctant to invest in the first place.

If the investing firm knows that it will face monopolistic conditions, say because of the granting of a patent, then it has an incentive to spend resources inventing the new bulb. It will bear the costs, but capture the returns to the R&D activity.[27]

To the extent that oligopoly is closer to monopoly than is competition, oligopoly provides more incentive to innovate than a perfectly competitive environment. Some have even gone so far as to argue that oligopoly, because of its constant implicit rivalry, encourages more investment in R&D than monopoly. The logic is that the oligopolistic firm that succeeds in inventing a better mousetrap may monopolize the industry as its prize. Still, it is difficult to understand why this would ever yield larger incentives to innovate than pure monopoly.

---

[27]As it turns out, even a pure monopolist does not invest enough in R&D. The ability to price discriminate perfectly would correct this situation. Otherwise, there are untapped rents that would justify additional expenditures on research, that cannot be captured.

- *Oligopoly* refers to a form of market organization typically characterized by a small number of sellers, each of whom consciously takes into consideration the actions and reactions of rival sellers when making price and output decisions. Duopoly is a special case involving exactly two sellers. Classical theories of duopoly, especially those of Cournot and Edgeworth, are primarily of historical interest. These early models are flawed by the assumption that each seller persistently fails to anticipate the rival seller's behavior, even after observing this behavior over long periods of time.

- A more recent approach to oligopoly theory, *the theory of games,* was developed by von Neumann and Morgenstern in the late 1940s. In this theory, each participant in the game chooses a maximizing strategy while specifically recognizing that the other participant(s) will also behave in an optimal manner. Solutions to such games involve "minimax" strategies in which each participant, in effect, tries to get the largest payoff that is possible, given the rational behavior of opposing players. In many cases, this requires players to choose a probabilistic strategy that maximizes the expected payoff from playing the game. This approach has many advantages over the classical theories but has not as yet provided the basis for a definitive, widely accepted theory of oligopolistic behavior.

- Formal agreements, or *cartels,* are one way in which sellers have dealt with the oligopoly problem. Cartels typically involve market-sharing arrangements taking the form of non-price competition and/or cartel member output and sales quotas. The historical record indicates that, in the absence of strong legal provisions, cartels tend to break apart because of secret price chiseling by the firms in the cartel. This chiseling behavior is predicted by economic theory, because each firm in the cartel stands to gain by secretly cutting price while the other cartel members maintain the agreed-upon price.

- Another type of market solution of the oligopoly problem is *price leadership* by one or a few firms. In the dominant-firm model, one firm sets price and all other firms take this price in making their output decisions. Thus, the dominant firm faces a "residual" demand curve, which is the total market demand less the quantity supplied by the other firms at each price. The dominant firm sets the industry price by choosing its output to maximize its profits, using its marginal cost curve and the marginal revenue curve from the "residual" demand curve. There are many variations on this basic model. In the version known as the "barometric firm" model, the price-setting firm need not be dominant in terms of its relative size—it may simply be a firm that is traditionally accepted as the price leader by all firms in the industry.

QUESTIONS AND EXERCISES

1. Assume that the skilled laborers in a competitive industry are represented by a strong union that is able to fix the wage at its monopoly level. Also assume that the firms are effectively prevented from colluding by strong antitrust laws, but unions are free to collude.

   a. Is it in the interest of the firms to have the union enforce an output restriction on behalf of the employers, assuming that the union would not change the wage rate for skilled labor or otherwise make new demands on the firms?

   b. Would the above output restriction be in the union's interest?

   c. If your answer to (a) is yes and to (b) is no, could the firms make the output restriction attractive both to themselves and the union by offering a higher wage?

   d. If your answer to (c) is no, is there any arrangement that would make output restriction mutually beneficial?

2. Explain the nature of the harm, if any, done to the efficiency of the economy when the firms in an industry:

   a. Organize to prevent other firms from entering the industry.

   b. Agree to charge a uniform price.

   c. Restrict the output of the firms so as to increase the total profit earned by all firms together.

   d. Sell all their output through a cooperative selling agency.

   e. Establish different selling prices for two different markets.

3. Discuss the following statement: "In oligopoly there is a tendency toward the maximization of aggregate industry profits. . . . But this tendency is counteracted by other forces" (Fellner, *Competition among the Few,* p. 142).

4. "The problem of bilateral monopoly is obviously one of negotiating and bargaining in order to reach an agreement between certain limits of feasibility. . . . [it] is useful to consider the oligopoly problem as being 'essentially' of this character" (Fellner, *Competition among the Few,* p. 23).

   a. What are the aspects of oligopoly behavior that Fellner views as equivalent to "negotiating and bargaining"?

   b. Why is such behavior to be expected in an oligopoly situation?

5. Assume that the bituminous coal industry is a competitive industry and that it is in long-run equilibrium. Now assume that the firms in the industry form a cartel.

   a. What will happen to the equilibrium output and price of coal, and why?

   b. How should the output be distributed among the individual firms?

   c. After the cartel is operating, are there incentives for the individual firms to cheat? Why?

   d. Does the possibility of entry by other firms make a difference in the behavior of the cartel?

SUGGESTED READINGS

Chamberlin, E. H. *The Theory of Monopolistic Competition.* Cambridge, Mass.: Harvard University Press, 1933, 8th ed., 1962, pp. 30–55, 221–29.

Fellner, William. *Competition among the Few: Oligopoly and Similar Market Structures.* New York: Alfred A. Knopf, 1949.

Hicks, J. R. "Annual Survey of Economic Theory: The Theory of Monopoly." *Econometrica* 3 (1935), pp. 1–20.

Hotelling, Harold. "Stability in Competition." *Economic Journal* 39 (1929), pp. 41–57.

Machlup, Fritz. *The Economics of Sellers' Competition.* Baltimore: Johns Hopkins University Press, 1952, pp. 347–514, esp. pp. 368–413.

Malinvaud, E. *Lectures on Microeconomic Theory.* New York: American-Elsevier Co., 1972, pp. 144–62.

Rothchild, K. W. "Price Theory and Oligopoly." *Economic Journal* 57 (1947), pp. 299–320.

Stackelberg, Heinrich, Freiherr von. *The Theory of the Market Economy.* Trans. Alan Peacock. London: William Hodge and Company, 1952.

4 Theory of Distribution

Parts 1 and 3, together with the tools developed in Part 2, present the modern or neoclassical theory of value — a theory explaining the origin of demand, supply, and market price. It is hoped that the market price so determined represents the marginal social valuation of the commodity. If so, some theoretical statements concerning economic welfare can be made (Part 5).

A central part of this theory of value is the marginal cost of production and its possible reflection in the supply curve. Costs and supply, in turn, depend on the technological conditions of production and the cost of productive services. So far we have assumed that both are given; and we will continue to assume that the physical conditions of production are technologically given and do not change over the time period relevant to our analysis. But now we must determine the prices of productive services, the distribution half of "Value and Distribution," or modern microeconomic theory. The theories of value and distribution are then brought together in Part 5, first to discuss the general economic equilibrium and second to analyze economic welfare in a competitive society.

Broadly speaking, the theory of input pricing does not differ from the theory of pricing goods. Both are fundamentally based on the interaction of demand and supply. In the present case, demand arises from business firms (rather than consumers) and supply, at least the supply of labor services, arises from individuals who are not only sellers of labor time but also consumers. Furthermore, for the most interesting cases of capital and labor, one determines the price of using the resource for a stipulated period of time, not the price of purchasing the resource. In other respects, however, the theory of distribution is the theory of value of productive services.

The previous level of abstraction is maintained throughout Part 4. This is certainly to be expected in Chapter 14, which presents the marginal productivity theory of distribution in perfectly competitive input and output markets. When imperfections appear in either market, however, the situation changes appreciably. This is especially true when large employers bargain directly with representatives of powerful labor organizations. When market imperfections arise, labor unions tend to arise as well. The theoretical discussion in Chapter 15 may seem far removed from the dramatic world of GM versus UAW. Indeed it is, in a certain sense. Yet the theoretical results obtained do set limits within which collective bargaining agreements are likely to occur.

Our point of view is that collective bargaining between management and union representatives constitutes bilateral monopoly, an indeterminate economic situation. Our analysis sets broad limits within which the solution lies. To push further requires one or more *courses*, not chapters. For example, there is a substantial body of theory concerning the collective bargaining process,[1] but an understanding of labor markets also requires an extensive knowledge of the institutional framework within which labor unions and business management operate.[2] This type of knowledge must be acquired in "applied" courses or contexts, just as "applied" courses supplement the other portions of microeconomic theory. ∎

---

[1] For a taste of this body of theory, see Allan M. Cartter, *Theory of Wages and Employment* (Homewood, Ill.: Richard D. Irwin, 1959), pp. 77–133.

[2] For institutional setting, see John T. Dunlop and James J. Healy, *Collective Bargaining: Principles and Cases,* rev. ed. (Homewood, Ill.: Richard D. Irwin, 1953).

14 Marginal Productivity Theory of Distribution in Perfectly Competitive Markets

The Immigration Reform and Control Act was recently enacted. Its major provisions include an amnesty program for illegal aliens who have been U.S. residents since 1982, and civil and criminal penalties for employers who hire illegal aliens in the future, will undoubtedly result in profound changes in the U.S. economy and labor market. But can economic theory help us predict exactly what these profound changes will be? The material in this chapter, which deals with the determination of input prices, is designed to be used to help analyze just such changes. By acknowledging explicitly the forces behind the demand and supply of labor (and other inputs), you should be able to answer a variety of questions currently being asked about the effects of the new immigration law: Will U.S. citizens now replace former illegal aliens in unskilled jobs? Will employers of unskilled labor in the United States benefit? How about U.S. consumers? What about Americans taken as a whole? In the "Applying the Theory" section you will be asked to use the material in this chapter to answer just such questions. ■

Aliens Law to Change Nation, Experts Say

The United States will undergo profound changes — ranging from population and industry shifts to serious financial burdens on local governments with high immigrant populations — in coming years as the new immigration law gradually takes effect, according to specialists on immigration and population issues.

The major provisions of the law, signed Nov. 6 by President Reagan, include an amnesty program for illegal aliens who have been U.S. residents continuously since Jan. 1, 1982, and civil and criminal penalties for employers who hire illegal aliens in the future. There also is an amnesty provision for alien farm workers who can prove they worked in U.S. agriculture for 90 days in the year ended May 1, 1986.

Population and immigration specialists said it is much too early to be sure how the new law will affect the country, especially since no one is certain how many illegal aliens are here. The estimates range from 2 million to more than 20 million.

But many agreed on a number of likely trends, which are expected to occur gradually:

■ Unless the government allows a new underclass of illegal aliens to take the place of the newly legalized aliens, the country will lose an entire segment of the work force that has been cheap, docile and willing to work in undesirable jobs.

■ Many of the industries where the illegal aliens worked will not be competitive if they are forced to pay higher wages. They may have to mechanize or move abroad in order to survive.

■ The newly legalized aliens will suddenly find themselves with new options. Instead of remaining in low-profile jobs to evade the Immigration and Naturalization Service, they are expected to compete for better jobs. Some will join unions.

■ Some specialists worry about a backlash from low-income citizens against the newly legalized aliens. Illegal aliens have competed for jobs with poor Americans in the past, and will be seen as moving virtually overnight from the status of lawbreaker to legal resident. The specialists added that some citizens already resent the growing prevalence of the Spanish language in some areas of the country.

■ Since the majority of the illegal immigrants are Hispanic, a migration back toward the southern United States is expected — both because of the warmer climate and because the aliens will want to be closer to relatives — once they do not have to worry about the possibility of being apprehended by the INS.

■ All the specialists agree that most of the illegal alien population is concentrated in small areas of the country and that local governments in those areas will face staggering financial problems that may not have been anticipated. The law provides $4 billion in reimbursement costs over four years, but some specialists said the local cost may be many times that.

One of the most striking aspects of the new law, at least in the short run, is that it will have such disproportionate impacts on different parts of the country. "Most of the country won't be affected, but certain parts are in deep trouble," said Patrick Burns, director of the William Vogt Center for U.S. Population Studies.

A recent study by Burns' group found that nearly half of the illegal aliens in the country live in California, most of them in the Los Angeles–San Diego region. He found that other high-impact states are New York, Texas, Illinois, and Florida. Burns added that the Washington, D.C., metropolitan area also will be heavily affected.

While a large majority of the illegal immigrants is believed to be Hispanic, there are other groups. Burns said that Detroit, for example, has a high concentration of illegal Arab aliens while Washington, D.C., is home to a number of illegal Nigerians, Ethiopians, Iranians, and Filipinos.

While the law prohibits the newly legalized aliens from collecting federal welfare for five years, there is nothing to make them ineligible for local assistance programs.

A study published last year by the Urban Institute on legal and illegal Hispanic immigrants in southern California found that they tended to be less educated than black or white Americans and paid less in taxes. The study also found that the Hispanic families had a substantially higher birth rate and sent more children to the local public school districts, driving up local costs.

David North, an immigration scholar at the New TransCentury foundation said that California law would allow the newly legalized aliens to collect welfare payments, a policy that will hit Los Angeles County especially hard. He added that the county

passed by a Democratic-dominated state legislature which does not contribute to the funding.

The Urban Institute study also found that illegal workers have taken jobs away from Americans and have had a tendency to force down wages in industries in which they are concentrated.

Michael S. Teitelbaum of the Alfred P. Sloan foundation has found that the Americans who most often lose jobs because of illegal immigration are "citizens with characteristics most similar to the illegal workers, the working poor: disadvantaged American minorities, young people, and recent legal immigrants and refugees."

Although most Americans have a stereotype of illegal immigrants picking fruit and vegetables in the fields in the Southwest, experts said that they have moved into many businesses and farm work all over the country.

University of Delaware Prof. Mark Miller describes the movement of illegal workers into the southern Pennsylvania mushroom industry: "Once certain employers began to hire illegal Mexican workers at low wages, they created an incentive for the others to do that to compete." Now, he said most of the mushroom work is done by illegals.

The INS has estimated that illegal aliens make up 25 percent of the workers in the high-tech Silicon Valley near San Francisco, where they work on assembly lines soldering circuit boards.

In Los Angeles, illegal immigrants are heavily employed in the foundry and gar-

(continued on page 416)

(continued from page 415)
ment industries, and in the Southwest they make up a large portion of the construction industry.

In Houston, for example, Prof. Don Huddle of Rice University found in a study that 37 percent of the city's construction industry was made up of illegal workers, some of them making up to $12 an hour and taking jobs that unemployed Americans would have competed for.

Huddle has found companies that virtually excluded Americans because they preferred the cheap, docile workers who are readily available in the area.

In Houston, he said, "They congregate at a certain spot like an army of the unemployed. At the refineries, they wait at the gates every morning for whatever may be available," he said.

All over the country, they work as maids and babysitters, taxi drivers, dishwashers and busboys in restaurants, and in low-level jobs in the hotel industry.

Many immigration scholars agreed that the biggest unanswered questions involving the new law concern how many of the illegal aliens will come forward for amnesty and whether the INS will have adequate personnel to monitor the amnesty program and force employers to comply with the new law. If the law is not enforced adequately, they said that the number of newly legalized aliens will grow and employers will probably continue to import illegal labor across the border.

There was widespread resistance to the idea of civil and criminal penalties for employers who hire illegal aliens in the future. The penalties range from fines of $200 to $10,000 for each illegal alien employed to a six-month prison sentence for an employer convicted of "pattern and practice" violations.

Teitelbaum argued that if INS—which has under 12,000 employees across the country—is not staffed or funded adequately, employer sanctions will not work. And if the Justice Department gives priority to the immigration issue and prosecutes the cases, they will be ignored.

"If people believe in this . . . it may work. But if they view it like the sale of drugs on the street in New York City, with the profits high, the police on the take and a revolving door in the courts, that will just breed cynicism, and they will fail," Teitelbaum said.

Miller, who has studied employer sanctions in European countries, said that they have had an impact on illegal immigration in those countries and are seen there as an extension of labor laws because of the exploitation of the illegal workers and the unfair business competition by employers who use them.

North added that if the law is enforced, "I have a strong impression that the employer sanctions' obligation in the 1980s will be comparable to the 1930s and 1940s when we imposed the minimum wage, the mandatory Social Security pension and tax withholding. They were all considered radical and drastic at the time. But all eventually became part of our culture."

He said industry will adapt if it is forced to: "You can grow a labor-intensive crop and rely on docile, inexpensive labor, or you can grow for the cannery . . . and harvest mechanically. It doesn't mean the grower is moving toward bankruptcy. . . . Restaurants who pay $2.50

per hour may. . . . have to pay a little more or maybe they'll put in an automatic dish-washing machine . . . It may be painful, but it creates a more equitable society."

No one is certain how many aliens are eligible for amnesty or how many will come forward. Conservative estimates have placed the figure at 1 million. But some experts believe the figure may be higher.

Burns said he believes 2 million will come forward, but he said that if the INS is forced to "rubber stamp" amnesty requests because of manpower shortages, fraudulent document sales will soar and many more aliens may come forward. "The potential is monumental," he said.

Huddle's most conservative projection is that 3.5 million will come forward and that they will soon be followed by 3 million to 10 million family members, mostly wives and children. In his studies in the Houston barrios, Huddle found that 70 percent said they were ready to come forward, whether they met the eligibility requirements or not.

Huddle also found that two out of every three illegal aliens had already obtained fraudulent identification cards that would allow them to get around the employer sanctions provisions in the law. The documents are readily available in Houston, he said, for as little as $10 to $20.

Questions

1. The new immigration law imposes civil and criminal penalties for employers who hire illegal aliens in the future. In addition, because of the amnesty provisions, the newly legalized aliens will have new options and will no longer be confined to jobs for unskilled workers.

Suppose these provisions eliminate the supply of illegal aliens in the unskilled labor market. Using a supply and demand diagram for unskilled labor, analyze the effects of such a change on the following groups in the United States:

a. Unskilled U.S. citizens (do not worry about the previous illegal aliens who are now made legal as a result of the new law).

b. Consumers in the United States.

c. Employers of unskilled labor in the United States.

d. Americans other than illegal aliens (assume that capital and other non-labor factors are owned entirely by Americans other than illegal aliens).

In your analysis for (c) and (d), also make use of the results in subsection 14.4.c and Figure 14.4.3.

2. According to the article, the Urban Institute found that illegal workers have taken jobs away from Americans and have had a tendency to force down wages in industries in which they are concentrated.

a. Are these results consistent with your analysis in question 1?

b. Does it follow that if, say, x number of illegal aliens are no longer employed as a result of the new immigration law, the number of unemployed U.S. citizens who will now be employed will be x? Explain carefully.

3. Some argue that illegals perform jobs that no American citizen would do. Use the analysis from question 1 to show why this is a bit naive.

(continued on page 418)

(continued from page 417)

4. The article also indicates that experts predict that many of the industries where the illegal aliens worked may now have to mechanize. As one official is quoted as saying: "You can grow a labor intensive crop and rely on . . . inexpensive labor, or you can . . . harvest mechanically." Explain this prediction by distinguishing between the substitution, output, and profit-maximizing effects of an increase in the price of unskilled labor, using the analysis in subsection 14.2.b.

Solutions

1. a. We will analyze the market for "unskilled labor" before the imposition of the new immigration law and then show the effects after its imposition. Before the imposition, the market wage is W_2, and quantity L_2 workers are employed—L_3 Americans and $(L_2 - L_3)$ illegal aliens. If illegal aliens are no longer part of the market supply of unskilled workers, the wage rate will rise to W_1 and L_1 Americans will now be employed as unskilled workers. (We ignore in this diagram any previous illegal aliens who are now made legal. To the extent that some of these individuals continue to supply labor in the unskilled labor market, the "domestic supply" curve in the graph would be slightly farther to the right.) As a result, American unskilled workers gain, as their total wages rise from OW_2vL_3 to OW_1yL_1. $L_2 - L_3$ illegal

aliens have lost their jobs, and $L_1 - L_3$ Americans have gained jobs as a result. There is no reason for $L_2 - L_3$ to equal $L_1 - L_3$. The numbers of workers in these groups will depend on the slopes of the supply and demand curves.

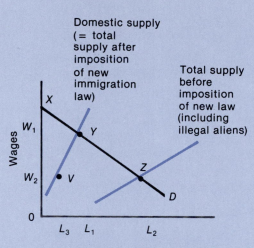

Unskilled Labor Market

Domestic supply (= total supply after imposition of new immigration law)

Total supply before imposition of new law (including illegal aliens)

Wages

W_1 Y

W_2 V

X

Z

D

0

L_3 L_1 L_2

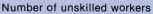

Number of unskilled workers

b. Consumers in the United States would be hurt as a result of the new law. Wages for unskilled workers rise, and hence prices for products that are produced with unskilled labor rise.

c. Employers of unskilled labor will be hurt by the new law as well. The return to capital (profits) are reduced from W_2xz to W_1xy. See subsection 14.4.c and Figure 14.4.3 for this argument.

(All of the above assumes that the reduction of immigrants will have no effect on the aggregate demand curve. If the reduction in earnings for illegal aliens reduces overall demand, then workers who are not close substitutes for illegal aliens may be losers as well.)

d. Americans other than illegal aliens as a whole lose as a result of the new law. As long as illegal aliens were earning a wage equal to the *VMP* of the last worker employed, the earnings of native Americans must decrease. The only exception would be if immigrants were previously obtaining government services or payments in excess of the payroll, income, sales, and property taxes they paid.

2. a. The conclusions of the Urban Institute study are consistent with the analysis above. Illegal aliens have resulted in a reduction in the wage of unskilled workers, and they have reduced the jobs of unskilled native Americans by $(L_1 - L_3)$.

b. However, there is no reason for there to be a one-to-one expansion of native American workers' jobs from illegal aliens, as demonstrated in the solution to question 1. In general, the number of individuals in each category depends on the shapes of the demand and supply curves.

3. At wage rate W_2, only L_3 Americans want unskilled jobs. However, at the higher wage that will result from the new immigration law, L_1 Americans want unskilled jobs. In short, the domestic supply curve of unskilled workers indicates that the number of

Americans who desire to work in unskilled jobs is not independent of the wage rate.

4. If the wage rate of unskilled workers rises, the analysis in Chapter 14 predicts that the quantity of workers hired will fall for two key reasons, labeled as the substitution effect and the output effect. The substitution effect refers to the movement along a given isoquant as the slope of the isocost line changes. At any Q, the least-cost rule predicts just such a reduction in labor demanded. It is this effect that can account for the predictions in the article. In addition, as the wage rate rises, the quantity produced will decrease *for a given expenditure on resources,* resulting in a decrease in both the quantity of labor and capital hired. This latter effect is what is referred to as the "scale effect" or output effect. Figure 14.2.4 shows these two effects for a wage decrease. However, it only includes the result for a given expenditure on resources; it does not show the profit-maximizing amounts of inputs hired. When the wage rate rises, the marginal cost of production rises for every level of output, and thus the profit-maximizing output for a competitive firm falls. This is an additional effect referred to in Chapter 14 as the profit-maximizing effect. This also reduces the quantity of labor hired (as well as capital). The substitution effect is responsible for the change in the factor proportions cited in the article, however.

Source: "Aliens Law to Change Nation, Experts Say," the *Washington Post,* November 28, 1986, pp. A16–A17.

As indicated in the introduction to Part 4, this section is not intended to be a practical guide to wage determination. Yet the marginal productivity theory constitutes a framework in which practical problems can be analyzed; thus it is a useful analytical tool for economic theorists.

The origin of marginal productivity theory is more or less dim.[1] Perhaps John Bates Clark is most widely associated with its development;[2] however, earlier hints appeared in Von Thünen's *Der isolierte Staat* (1826), Longfield's *Lectures on Political Economy* (1834), and Henry George's *Progress and Poverty* (1879). Indeed, George presented a "universal law of wages" that clearly indicates marginal productivity analysis:

> Wages depend upon the margin of production, or upon the produce which labor can obtain at the highest point of natural productiveness open to it without the payment of rent. . . . Thus the wages which an employer must pay will be measured by the lowest point of natural productiveness to which production extends, and wages will rise or fall as the point rises or falls.[3]

In the preface to his important work, Clark acknowledged his indebtedness to George and summarized his theory simultaneously:

> It was the claim advanced by Mr. Henry George, that wages are fixed by the product which a man can create by tilling rentless land, that just led me to seek a method by which the product of labor everywhere may be disentangled from the product of cooperating agents and separately identified; and it was this quest which led to the attainment of the law that is here presented, according to which the wages of all labor tend, under perfectly free competition, to equal the product that is separately attributable to labor.[4]

But in the 1880s and 1890s, Clark was not alone in developing the marginal productivity concept. Jevons, Wicksteed, Marshall, Wood, Walras, Barone, and others made important contributions.[5] Indeed, during this period an important distinction between views of marginal productivity theory arose.

---

[1] For a survey of its development, see Allan M. Cartter, *Theory of Wages and Employment* (Homewood, Ill.: Richard D. Irwin, 1959), pp. 11–32.

[2] John Bates Clark, *The Distribution of Wealth* (New York: Macmillan, 1902).

[3] Henry George, *Progress and Poverty* (1879), p. 213.

[4] Clark, *Distribution of Wealth,* p. viii.

[5] W. Stanley Jevons, *The Theory of Political Economy;* Philip Wicksteed, *An Essay on the Coordination of the Theory of Distribution;* Alfred Marshall, *Principles of Economics;* Stuart Wood, "The Theory of Wages," American Economic Association Publications, no. 4 (1889); Leon Walras, *Elements d'économie politique pure;* Enrico Barone, "Studi sulla distribuzione," *Giornale degli economisti* 12 (1896).

First, to state the *marginal productivity principle* (developed in subsection 14.2.a): there is a direct functional relation between wages and the level of employment; each profit-maximizing entrepreneur will attempt to adjust employment so that the marginal product of labor equals the wage rate.

From Clark's point of view, this principle, slightly embellished, constituted the theory of wages. Marshall strongly disagreed:

> This doctrine [the marginal productivity principle] has sometimes been put forward as a theory of wages. But there is no valid ground for any such pretension. . . . Demand and supply exert equally important influences on wages; neither has a claim to predominance; any more than has either blade of a scissors, or either pier of an arch . . . [but] the doctrine throws into clear light the action of one of the causes that govern wages.[6]

According to Clark, the marginal productivity principle determines wages. Marshall, and later Hicks, and most other theorists, regard the principle as determining only the *demand* for labor. The supply of labor, or any other productive service, must enter before a full theory of wage determination is developed. This modern, or neoclassical, view is adopted here.

DEMAND FOR A PRODUCTIVE SERVICE[7]
14.2

Following the Marshall-Hicks approach, one must pay heed both to the demand for and supply of a productive service. In this section the theory of input demand, based on the marginal productivity principle, is developed. The theory is applicable to any productive service although the most natural application, and the bulk of literary treatments, refers to the demand for labor. Thus we shall usually speak of "the demand for labor," but "the demand for a productive service of any sort" is implied.

Demand of a Firm for One Variable Productive Service
14.2.a

Before embarking on a formal analysis, it may be useful to point out the direct analogy between the behavior of the firm in determining its profit-maximizing output and its profit-maximizing combination of resources. In the former study, we assumed that market demand and supply determine market equilibrium price, without first explaining the origin of market supply. Next, since each firm is too small to affect price by changes in its output, the demand curve confronting each producer is a perfectly elastic horizontal line at the level of market price. Our

---

[6]Marshall, *Principles of Economics,* pp. 518, 538.

[7]The analysis of sections 14.2 and 14.4 relies heavily on the tools developed in Chapters 5 and 6. The reader may wish to review these chapters as a background for the material presented here.

problem in that case was to determine marginal cost, and thus supply, given the state of technology and input prices. The analysis was completed by obtaining market supply from the individual supply curves.

The procedure in the present case is completely analogous, but reversed. First, we assume that the market demand for and supply of labor determine the market equilibrium wage rate, without initially explaining the origin of the demand for labor curve.[8] Next, since each firm is too small to affect the wage rate by changes in its labor input, the supply of labor curve confronting each producer is a perfectly elastic horizontal line at the level of the market wage rate. Our problem now is to determine the individual demand for labor curve, given the state of technology and the market price of the output produced. The analysis is then completed by obtaining market demand from the individual demand curves.

Let us begin with an example, given in Table 14.2.1 and graphically illustrated in panels A and B, Figure 14.2.1. We consider a production process involving fixed inputs, and thus fixed costs, but only *one* variable input, labor. Thus total labor cost equals total variable cost. The product sells for $5 per unit, and labor costs $20 per unit. The production function is specified by the first three columns. Column 5 shows total revenue (total product multiplied by commodity price), and column 8 lists total variable cost (units of labor input multiplied by the price per unit). Finally, the last column shows total revenue minus total variable cost, a proxy for profit inasmuch as it (profit) differs from column 9 only by the constant fixed cost.[9] The difference between total revenue and total variable cost is greatest when seven units of labor are used; this solution accordingly corresponds to the profit-maximizing organization of production. The total revenue–total variable cost approach is illustrated in panel A, Figure 14.2.1. The maximum distance between the two curves occurs when their slopes are equal, or when marginal revenue per unit of labor equals marginal cost per unit of labor.

From the standpoint of input analysis it is more useful to approach the profit-maximizing problem in a different way. First, note that the supply of labor curve (panel B) is given by the entries in column 7, Table 14.2.1. It is a horizontal line at the $20 level, indicating the addition to total cost attributable to the addition of one unit of labor. The marginal product of successive additional units of labor is shown in column 3. Multiplying these entries by commodity price, one obtains the value of the marginal product shown in column 6.

Value of Marginal Product: The value of the marginal product of a variable productive service is equal to its marginal product multiplied by the market price of the commodity in question.

---

[8]The supply curve, in this instance, has not been explained either. It is analyzed in section 14.3.

[9]For example, if total fixed cost is $50, profit is column 9 minus $50. Thus maximum profit corresponds to the maximum entry in column 9.

Table 14.2.1 Value of the Marginal Product and Individual Demand for Labor

Units of Labor Input	Total Product	Marginal Product	Product Price	Total Revenue	Value of Marginal Product	Wage per Unit of Labor	Total Variable Cost	TR Minus TVC
0	0	—	$5.00	$ 0	—	$20	$ 0	$ 0
1	10	10	5.00	50	$50	20	20	30
2	19	9	5.00	95	45	20	40	55
3	27	8	5.00	135	40	20	60	75
4	34	7	5.00	170	35	20	80	90
5	40	6	5.00	200	30	20	100	100
6	45	5	5.00	225	25	20	120	105
7	49	4	5.00	245	20	20	140	105
8	52	3	5.00	260	15	20	160	100
9	54	2	5.00	270	10	20	180	90
10	55	1	5.00	275	5	20	200	75

Figure 14.2.1 Graphical Illustration of Profit Maximization by Two Approaches

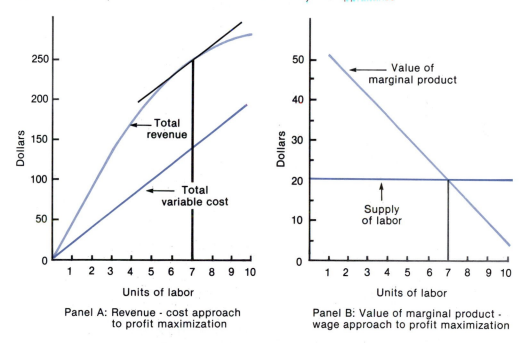

Panel A: Revenue - cost approach to profit maximization

Panel B: Value of marginal product - wage approach to profit maximization

From panel B, Figure 14.2.1, it is easily seen that the value of the marginal product curve intersects the supply of labor curve at a point corresponding to seven units of labor input. As we have previously seen, this is precisely the profit-maximizing labor input.

To get more directly to the proposition we seek, consider the generalization of panel B shown in Figure 14.2.2. Suppose the value of the marginal product is given by the curve labeled *VMP* in Figure 14.2.2. The market wage rate is $O\overline{w}$, so the supply of labor to the firm is the horizontal line S_L. First, suppose the firm employed only OL_1 units of labor. At that rate of employment, the value of the marginal product is $L_1 C = Ow_1 > O\overline{w}$, the wage rate. At this point of operation an additional unit of labor adds more to total revenue than to total cost (inasmuch as it adds the value of its marginal product to total revenue and its unit wage rate to cost). Hence a profit-maximizing entrepreneur would add additional units of labor; and indeed, would continue to add units so long as the value of the marginal product exceeds the wage rate.

Next, suppose OL_2 units of labor were employed. At this point the value of the marginal product $L_2 F = Ow_2$ is less than the wage rate. Each unit of labor adds more to total cost than to total revenue. Hence a profit-maximizing entrepreneur would not employ OL_2 units, or any number for which the wage rate exceeds the value of the marginal product. These arguments show that neither more nor fewer than $O\overline{L}$ units of labor would be employed and that to employ $O\overline{L}$ units leads to profit maximization. The statements are summarized as follows:

Proposition: A profit-maximizing entrepreneur will employ units of a variable productive service until the point is reached at which the value of the marginal product of the input is exactly equal to the input price.

In other words, given the market wage rate or the supply of labor curve to the firm, a perfectly competitive producer determines the quantity of labor to hire by equating the value of the marginal product to the wage rate. If the wage rate were Ow_1 (Figure 14.2.2), the firm would employ OL_1 units of labor to equate the value of the marginal product to the given wage rate. Similarly, if the wage rate were Ow_2, the firm would employ OL_2 units of labor. By definition of a demand curve, therefore, the value of the marginal product curve is established as the individual demand for labor curve.[10]

---

[10]The results of this section can be developed mathematically. Let the production function be

$$q = f(x), \tag{14.10.1}$$

where x is the single variable productive service. Marginal product is accordingly given by $f'(x)$. Under the assumptions of this chapter, the producer is a perfect competitor in both commodity and factor markets. Hence the market price of the commodity *(p)* and the market price of the input *(w)* are given.

The profit function is

$$\pi = pq - wx - F = pf(x) - wx - F. \tag{14.10.2}$$

where F represents fixed cost and *wx* is the variable cost. The entrepreneur adjusts input usage so as to maximize profit. Mathematically, this is represented by

$$\frac{d\pi}{dx} = pf'(x) - w = 0, \tag{14.10.3}$$

or

$$pf'(x) = w, \tag{14.10.4}$$

the theorem stated in the text.

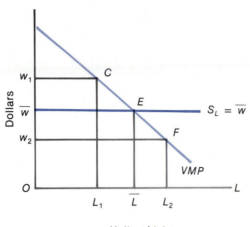

Figure 14.2.2 Proof of $VMP = w$ Theorem

Units of labor

Individual Demand for a Productive Service: The individual demand curve for a single variable productive service is given by the value of the marginal product curve of the productive service in question.

Individual Demand Curves When Several Variable Inputs Are Used 14.2.b

When a production process involves more than one variable productive service, the value of the marginal product curve of an input is not its demand curve. The reason lies in the fact that the various inputs are interdependent in the production process, so that a change in the price of one input leads to changes in the rates of utilization of the others. The latter, in turn, shifts the marginal product curve of the input whose price initially changed.[11]

Consider Figure 14.2.3. Suppose an equilibrium initially exists at point A. The market wage rate is Ow_1, the value of the marginal product curve for labor is VMP_1 when labor is the only input varied, and OL_1 units of labor are employed. Now let the equilibrium wage rate fall to Ow_2, so that the perfectly elastic supply curve of labor to the firm is S_{L_2}.

The change in the wage rate *in general* has three effects that are admittedly difficult to explain because they do not lend themselves conveniently to graphical analysis. Two effects—the substitution effect and the output effect—can be explained by means of Figure 14.2.4. For convenience, assume that there are only two variable inputs, capital (K) and labor (L). Q_1 and Q_2 are production isoquants, and the initial input price ratio (when the wage rate is Ow_1 in Figure 14.2.3) is given by the slope of EF. As explained in Chapter 7, equi-

---

[11]For a review, see Chapter 6.

Figure 14.2.3 Individual Input Demand When Several Variable Inputs Are Used

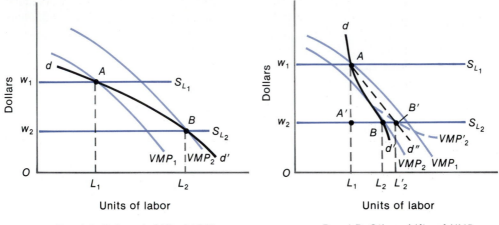

Panel A: Outward shift of *VMP*

Panel B: Other shifts of *VMP*

Figure 14.2.4 Substitution and Output Effects of a Change in Input Price

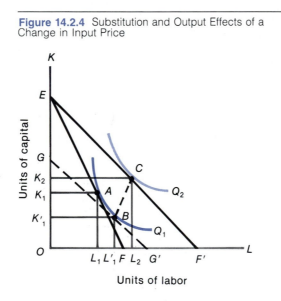

Units of labor

librium is attained at point A, with inputs of OL_1 units of labor and OK_1 units of capital. Now let the wage rate fall to Ow_2, the cost of capital remaining constant. The new input price ratio is represented by the slope of the new isocost curve EF'. Equilibrium is ultimately attained at point C on the higher isoquant Q_2, with OL_2 units of labor and OK_2 units of capital employed.

The movement from A to C can be decomposed into two separate "effects." The first is a *substitution effect*, represented by the movement along the original isoquant from A to B. To understand this movement, construct the fictional isocost curve GG' with the following characteristics: (*a*) it is parallel to EF', thus representing the new input price ratio, but (*b*) it is tangent to Q_1, thus restricting output to the initial level. The movement from A to B is a pure substitution of labor for capital as a result of the decrease in the relative price of labor. The movement *would* occur if the entrepreneur were restricted to the original level of output at the new input price ratio.

The movement from B to C represents the *output effect*. First, recall that Figure 14.2.4 depicts the maximization of output for a *given* expenditure on resources. When the price of labor falls, more labor, more capital, or more of both may be bought at the given, constant expenditure. The movement from B to C represents this, and position C indicates the ratio in which the inputs will be combined if expenditure on resources remains unchanged.[12]

In summary, the substitution effect resulting from a reduction in the wage rate causes a substitution of labor for capital. This effect alone, therefore, shifts labor's marginal product curve to the left because there is less of the cooperating factor (capital) with which to work. The output effect generally[13] results in an increased usage of both inputs. Thus the output effect alone tends to shift labor's marginal product curve to the right because there is usually more of the cooperating factor with which to work.

It is important to emphasize that point C, Figure 14.2.4, indicates the optimal input *ratio* for the given expenditure on resources; but it does not show the profit-maximizing *amounts* of the inputs. When the wage rate falls, the marginal cost of production is reduced for every level of output unless labor is an inferior factor. The marginal cost curve shifts to the right, and the profit-maximizing output of the perfectly competitive firm increases. This is a separate effect that may be called the *profit-maximizing effect*. In terms of Figure 14.2.4, the isocost curve EF' shifts outward and to the right, remaining parallel to itself, as it were. The profit-maximizing effect normally leads, via an expansion of output, to an increase in the usage of both inputs. Hence this effect also shifts labor's marginal product curve to the right.

Now return to Figure 14.2.3. When the wage rate falls from Ow_1 to Ow_2, the usage of labor expands. However, the expansion does not take place along VMP_1. When the quantity of labor used and the level of output change, the usage of other inputs changes as well. The substitution effect of the change causes a leftward shift of labor's marginal product curve. But the output and profit-maximizing effects cause a reverse shift to the right unless labor is an inferior factor.

Panels A and B, Figure 14.2.3, illustrate the ways in which the VMP curve may shift. In panel A, the value of the marginal product curve shifts uniformly

---

[12]The analysis is not affected if either of the inputs is "inferior" (see Chapter 7).

[13]There can be exceptions, but they are unusual. See the references in footnote 14.

outward to the right, from VMP_1 to VMP_2. The equilibrium usage of labor at wage rates Ow_1 and Ow_2 correspond to the points A and B respectively. Generating a series of points such as A and B by varying the wage rate also generates the labor demand curve dd'. Panel B illustrates that the value of the marginal product curve may shift uniformly inward to the left (VMP_2) or that it may "twist" (VMP_2'). In either case, connecting points such as A and B or A and B' generates factor demand functions such as dd' or dd'', respectively. The only requirement is that the new VMP curve intersect S_{L_2} at a point to the right of A in panel B. The factor demand curve, that is, *must* be negatively sloped.[14]

Thus the input demand curve, while more difficult to derive, is just as determinate in the multiple-input case as in the single-input situation. The results of this section may be summarized in the following:

Proposition: An entrepreneur's demand curve for a variable productive agent can be derived when more than one variable input is used. The demand curve must be negatively sloped because, on balance, the three effects of an input price change *must* cause quantity demanded to vary inversely with price.

Determinants of the Demand for a Productive Service 14.2.c

The determinants of the demand for a variable productive service by an individual firm, while embodied in our derivation of the demand curve, have not been stated explicitly. It may serve well to enumerate them now.

First, the greater the quantity of cooperating services employed, the greater the demand for a given quantity of the variable service in question. This proposition follows immediately from the facts that (*a*) the product price is fixed for our analysis and (*b*) the greater the quantity of cooperating inputs, the greater the marginal product of the input in question.

Second, the demand price for a variable productive service will be greater the higher the selling price of the commodity it is used to produce. Fixing marginal product, the greater the commodity price, the greater the value of the marginal product.

Third, the demand price for a variable productive service will be lower the greater the quantity of the service currently in use. For a given commodity price, this proposition follows immediately from the law of diminishing marginal physical returns.

---

[14]Unfortunately this assertion, which is essential for the results of this section, cannot be proved graphically and the mathematical proof is long and tedious. For detailed treatments of the general case, see C. E. Ferguson, "Production, Prices, and the Theory of Jointly Derived Input Demand Functions," *Economica*, N.S. 33 (1966), pp. 454–61; C. E. Ferguson, "'Inferior Factors' and the Theories of Production and Input Demand," *Economica*, N.S. 35 (1968), pp. 140–50; C. E. Ferguson, *The Neoclassical Theory of Production and Distribution* (London and New York: Cambridge University Press, 1969), Chapters 6 and 9; and C. E. Ferguson and Thomas R. Saving, "Long-Run Scale Adjustments of a Perfectly Competitive Firm and Industry," *American Economic Review* 59 (1969), pp. 774–83.

Finally, the demand for a variable productive service depends on "the state of the art," or technology. Given the production function, marginal product and the value of the marginal product for each commodity price are known and do not change except for the first point above. However, technology does change; and it should be apparent that technological progress changes the marginal productivity of all inputs. Thus a technological change that makes a variable input more productive also makes the demand for any given quantity of it greater, and vice versa.[15]

Market Demand for a Variable Productive Service
14.2.d

The market demand for a variable productive service, like the market demand for a commodity, is the total of the constituent individual demands. However, in the case of productive services, the process of addition is considerably more complicated than simple horizontal summation of individual demand curves, because when all firms expand or contract simultaneously, the market price of the commodity changes.[16] Nonetheless, the market demand curve can be obtained, as illustrated in Figure 14.2.5.

A typical employing firm is depicted in panel A. For the going market price of the commodity produced, $d_1 d_1'$ is the firm's demand curve for the variable productive service, as derived in Figure 14.2.3. If the market price of the resource is Ow_1, the firm uses Ov_1 units. Aggregating over all employing firms, OV_1 units of the service are used. Thus point A in panel B is one point on the market demand curve for the variable productive service.

Next, suppose the price of the service declines to Ow_2 (because, for example, the supply curve of the variable service shifts to the right). Other things being equal, the firm would move along $d_1 d_1'$ to point b', employing Ov_2' units of the service. But other things are not equal.[17] When all firms expand their usage of the input, total output expands. Or stated differently, the market supply curve for the commodity produced shifts to the right because of the decline in the input's price. For a given commodity demand, commodity price must fall; and when it does, the individual demand curves for the variable productive service also fall.[18]

In panel A, the decline in individual input demand attributable to the decline in commodity price is represented by the shift leftward from $d_1 d_1'$ to $d_2 d_2'$. At input price Ow_2, b is the equilibrium point, with Ov_2 units employed. Aggregating for all employers, OV_2 units of the productive service are used and point B is

---

[15] For more explanation, see Alfred Marshall, *Principles of Economics*, 8th ed. (New York: Macmillan, 1920), pp. 381-93.

[16] An algebraic analysis of the derivation of market demand is simple but lengthy. For one version, see George J. Stigler, *The Theory of Price* (New York: Macmillan, 1949), pp. 184–86.

[17] Compare the following to the derivation of market commodity supply by summing individual supply curves.

[18] Let p_1 and p_2 be the original and the new commodity prices, respectively. Thus $VMP_1 = p_1 MP$, $VMP_2 = p_2 MP$, and $VMP_1 > VMP_2$, since $p_1 > p_2$.

Figure 14.2.5 Derivation of the Market Demand for a Variable Productive Service

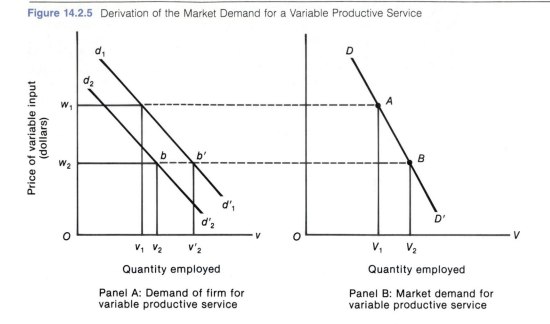

Panel A: Demand of firm for variable productive service

Panel B: Market demand for variable productive service

obtained in panel B. Any number of points such as *A* and *B* can be generated by varying the market price of the productive service. Connecting these points by a line, one obtains *DD'*, the market demand for the variable productive service.

SUPPLY OF A VARIABLE PRODUCTIVE SERVICE
14.3

All variable productive services may be broadly classified into three groups: natural resources, intermediate goods, and labor. Intermediate goods are those produced by one entrepreneur and sold to another who, in turn, utilizes them in the productive process. For example, cotton is produced by a farmer and (after middlemen) sold as an intermediate good to a manufacturer of damask; the damask, in turn, becomes an intermediate good in the manufacture of upholstered furniture. The supply curves of intermediate goods are positively sloped because they are the *commodity outputs* of manufacturers, even if they are variable inputs to others; and, as shown in Part 3, commodity supply curves are positively sloped.

Natural resources may be regarded as the commodity outputs of (usually) mining operations. As such, they also have positively sloped supply curves.[19] Thus our attention can be restricted to the final, and most important, category: labor.

---

[19]There is some difficulty involving the optimal time for marketing natural resources; but this generally does not affect the slope of their supply curves. For an elegant treatment, see Harold Hotelling, "The Economics of Exhaustible Resources," *Journal of Political Economy* 39 (1931), pp. 137–75.

General Considerations
14.3.a

As population increases and its age composition changes, as people migrate from one area to another, and as education and reeducation enable people to shift occupations, rather dramatic changes can occur in the supply curves of various types of labor at various locations throughout the nation. These changes represent *shifts* in the supply curve and are quite independent of its slope. To get at the supply curve for a well-defined market, assume that the following are constants: the size of the population, the labor force participation rate, and the occupational and geographic distribution of the labor force. Thus one first asks, what induces a person to forgo leisure for work?

Indifference Curve Analysis of Labor Supply
14.3.b

The supply of labor offered by one individual can, in principle, be determined by indifference curve analysis, as shown in Figure 14.3.1. Hours of leisure are measured along the horizontal axis, OM representing the maximum, or the total number of potential work hours in the week. The total money income from work is measured along the vertical axis. The slope of a line connecting M and any point on the vertical axis represents a wage per hour. For example, if OY_1 is the money income that would be received for OM hours of work, the hourly wage rate is OY_1/OM, or the slope of MY_1. Finally, curves I, II, and III represent indifference curves between income and leisure. For example, along the lowest shown level of indifference curve I, an individual (who works CM hours) is indifferent between OC hours of leisure and income CF, and OG hours of leisure (GM hours of work) and income GH.

When the wage rate is given by the slope of MY_1, the tangency condition for maximization[20] establishes equilibrium at point F on curve I. The individual works CM hours for income CF. Leisure, therefore, is OC. Let the wage rate increase, as given by the slope of MY_2. The new equilibrium is E on curve II. Hours of work expand from CM to BM as a result of the increase in the wage rate; they would further expand to AM if the wage line changed to MY_3. The equilibrium points F, E, D, . . . can be connected by the dashed line S, showing the supply of labor offered by one individual. In this case the supply curve is positively sloped because an increase in the wage rate results in an increase in the number of hours worked.

Figure 14.3.2 illustrates the opposite case. Individual labor supply curves can behave in a variety of ways; the crucial question is how their *sum* behaves — what is the shape of the market supply curve of any specified type of labor?

---

[20]Utility is regarded as a function of income and leisure. The problem is to maximize utility for a given hourly wage rate.

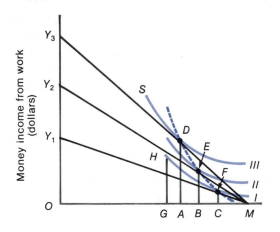

Figure 14.3.1 Indifference Curve Analysis of Labor Supply

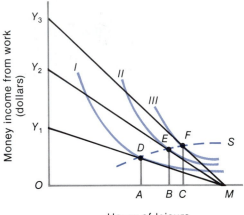

Figure 14.3.2 Indifference Curve Analysis of Labor Supply, Negatively Sloped Curve

The Market Supply of Labor
14.3.c

In fact, considerably more can be said about the *sum* than about the constituent parts. First, consider the situation in which one industry uses exclusively a specialized type of labor (obviously, technically skilled). In the short run nothing can be said about the slope or shape of the labor supply curve. It may be positive, it may be negative, or it may have segments of positive and negative slope. But now let us relax our assumption concerning occupational immobility; and in the long run, one must. The master baker can become an apprentice candlestick maker if the financial inducement is sufficient. But more to the point, young people planning their education and career must surely be affected by current returns, and even more by expected future returns, in various professions. Thus in the long run the supply of specialized labor is likely to have a positive slope.

The other case, in which labor is not specialized to one particular industry, is even more clear. In particular, if more than one industry uses a particular type of labor, the labor supply curve to any one industry must be positively sloped. Suppose any one industry increases its employment; the wage rate must rise for two reasons. First, to expand employment, workers must be obtained from the other industries, thereby increasing the demand price of labor. Second, the industries that lose labor must reduce output; hence commodity prices in these industries will tend to rise, causing an additional upward pressure on the demand

Part Four   Theory of Distribution

price of labor. Thus the industry attempting to expand employment must face a positively sloped supply of labor curve.[21]

In summary, we have the following:

Relation: The supply curves of raw materials and intermediate goods are positively sloped, as are the supply curves of nonspecialized types of labor. In the very short run the supply of specialized labor may take any shape or slope; but in the long run it, too, tends to be positively sloped.

MARGINAL PRODUCTIVITY THEORY OF INPUT RETURNS
14.4

The currently accepted version of marginal productivity theory follows immediately from the tools developed above. Indeed, it is merely another application of demand and supply analysis.

Market Equilibrium and the Returns to Variable Productive Services
14.4.a

The demand for and supply of a variable productive service jointly determine its market equilibrium price; this is precisely marginal productivity theory. In Figure 14.4.1, DD' and SS' are the demand and supply curves. Their intersection at point E determines the stable[22] market equilibrium price $O\overline{W}$ and quantity demanded and supplied $O\overline{V}$. The only features unique to this analysis are the methods of determining the demand for variable productive services and the supply of labor services. The fact that input demand is based on the value of the marginal product of the input gives rise to the label "marginal productivity theory."

Short Run and Quasi Rents
14.4.b

Up to this point we have not been very specific about the short run and the long. Indeed it has not been necessary, because marginal productivity theory is concerned with the price of *variable* productive services. In the long run all inputs

---

[21]There are two possible exceptions, each of which leads to a horizontal industry supply of labor curve. First, if the industry is exceedingly small or if it uses only very small quantities of labor, its effect on the market may be negligible. That is, the industry may stand to the market as a perfectly competitive firm does to the industry. Second, if there is unemployment of the particular type of labor under consideration, the supply of labor to all industries may be perfectly elastic up to the point of full employment. Thereafter the supply curve would rise.

[22]**EXERCISE:** Prove graphically that this is a stable equilibrium. Next, let the SS' curve bend back on itself. Can you generate an unstable case?

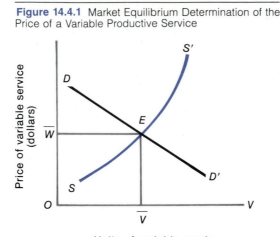

Figure 14.4.1 Market Equilibrium Determination of the Price of a Variable Productive Service

are variable; so marginal productivity theory covers all resources in the long run. However, in the short run certain inputs are *fixed;* they cannot be varied and hence a "marginal product" cannot readily be generated. The return to short-run fixed inputs therefore requires another explanation. Following Marshall, this return is denoted "quasi rent." [23]

The explanation of quasi rents requires the customary cost curve graph, illustrated in Figure 14.4.2. In that figure, ATC, AVC, and MC denote average total cost, average variable cost, and marginal cost, respectively. Suppose market price is $O\overline{P}$. The profit-maximizing firm produces $O\overline{Q}$ units of output and incurs variable costs that, on average, amount to $OA = \overline{Q}D$ dollars per unit of output. Thus the total expenditure required to sustain the necessary employment of variable productive services is represented by $OAD\overline{Q}$. Total revenue is $O\overline{P}E\overline{Q}$; thus the difference between total revenue and total variable cost is $A\overline{P}ED$. Similarly, if market price were OA per unit, the difference between total revenue and total variable cost would be $HAFG$.

This difference is quasi rent, which must always be nonnegative (if price fell to OJ, total revenue and total variable cost would be equal; if price fell below OJ, production would cease and total revenue and total variable cost would both equal

---

[23]In classical usage, "rent" is the return to a resource whose supply is absolutely fixed and nonaugmentable (that is, whose supply curve is a line perpendicular to the quantity axis). The return to short-run fixed inputs is called quasi rent because their quantities are variable in the long run.

The definition of quasi rent used in the text, which is the customary modern definition, differs slightly from Marshall's original definition (see his *Principles of Economics*, 8th ed. [London: Macmillan, 1920], footnote on pp. 426–27). Marshall defined quasi rent as the return to a temporarily fixed input *minus* the cost of maintenance and replacement. Quasi rent as defined by Marshall cannot be illustrated by means of conventional cost diagrams. In particular, Marshall's definition is *not* equivalent to the text definition minus the area *ABCD* in Figure 14.4.2.

Part Four   Theory of Distribution

Figure 14.4.2 Determination of Quasi Rent

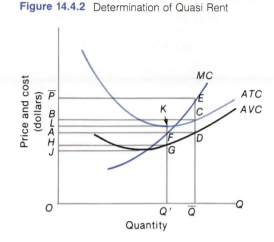

zero). Notice that quasi rent is the total return ascribable to the fixed inputs. If price is $O\overline{P}$, quasi rent can be divided into two components: the amount $ABCD$, representing their opportunity cost; and the amount $\overline{BP}EC$, representing the pure economic profit attributable to their use in this industry rather than in their best alternative use. Similarly, if market price is OA, quasi rent ($HAFG$) has two components: the amount $HLKG$, the opportunity cost of using the fixed inputs in this industry; and the (negative) amount $ALKF$, representing the pure economic loss incurred as a penalty for using the resources in their current employment.

Finally, a rather obvious point should be noted: the sum of (total) variable cost and quasi rent as imputed above precisely equals the dollar value of the total product. This is simply a matter of definition and arithmetic; but it has a logical foundation, as we shall now see.

Clark-Wicksteed Product-Exhaustion Theorem 14.4.c

In short-run equilibrium the sum of total variable cost and quasi rent definitionally equals the dollar value of output. As has been said, this is a simple and obvious matter of arithmetic. It is not obvious, however, that in long-run competitive equilibrium the total physical product will be exactly sufficient to pay each input its marginal product. This is an important theorem attributable to Clark, Wicksteed, and other pioneers of marginal productivity theory.

To repeat:

Proposition: In long-run competitive equilibrium, rewarding each input according to its marginal physical product precisely exhausts the total physical product.

A mathematical proof of the Clark-Wicksteed theorem is in the appendix to this chapter; in this section a graphical demonstration attributable to Chapman is presented.[24]

Consider an economy composed of n identical farms, each worked by an identical number of laborers. In Figure 14.4.3 the horizontal axis represents the number of workers per farm and the curve MP is the marginal product of labor. Suppose OL workers are employed per farm and that each is paid his or her marginal physical product. The real wage is $OA = LE$, and total wages are $OAEL$. The total physical product per farm is $OMEL$, so rent per farm is AME. Rent so computed is merely a residual; our problem is to prove that AME is also the marginal product of land.

First, observe that the total product of the economy is $n \times OMEL$. Next, suppose another farm is added to the economy, the number of workers remaining unchanged. If we can determine total output with $n + 1$ farms, the difference in total output when there are $n + 1$ and n farms is the marginal product of land.

When the $(n + 1)$-st farm is added, each existing farm must supply its proportional share of workers to the new farm. There are $n \times OL$ workers available; each farm now employs a number of workers, say OL', such that $(n + 1) \times OL' = n \times OL$. When each farm employs OL' workers, output per farm is $OMCL'$ and the total output of the economy is

$$(n + 1) \times OMCL' = n \times OMCL' + OMCL'.$$

The total product with n farms is

$$n \times OMEL = n \times OMCL' + n \times L'CEL.$$

The marginal product of land, therefore, is the difference, or

$$n \times OMCL' + OMCL' -$$
$$n \times OMCL' -$$
$$n \times L'CEL = OMCL' - n \times L'CEL$$
$$= BMC + OBCL' - n \times L'CEL.$$

Now consider the last term above:

$$n \times L'CEL = n \times L'CDL - n \times CDE.$$

Since $n \times L'L = OL'$ by the equal division of workers, it follows than $n \times L'CDL = OBCL'$, the total return to labor per farm when OL' workers are employed on each farm. Therefore, the marginal product of the $(n + 1)$-st farm is

$$BMC + OBCL' - OBCL' + n \times CDE = BMC + n \times CDE.$$

---

[24]S. J. Chapman, "The Remuneration of Employers," *Economic Journal* 16 (1906), pp. 523–28. This is a problem in long-run analysis. In terms of Figure 14.4.3, in the short run there is an excess rent or profit equal to the area of triangle CDE. In the long run the number of farms must adjust so that area CDE approaches zero.

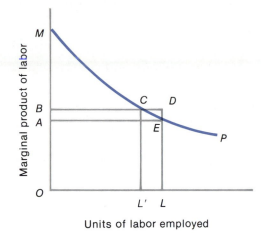

Figure 14.4.3 Product-Exhaustion Theorem

Marginal product of labor (vertical axis)

Units of labor employed (horizontal axis)

The last term, $n \times CDE$, approaches zero as n increases without bound—that is, as the size of each farm decreases. Thus for an infinitesimally small increase in land, the marginal product of land is BMC. But BMC is also the rent per farm computed by the residual method when OL' workers are on each farm. Consequently, the marginal product of land is the same as the residual, proving the Clark-Wicksteed theorem.

DISTRIBUTION AND RELATIVE FACTOR SHARES
14.5

The basic elements of marginal productivity theory have been known since the time of Marshall, Clark, and Wicksteed. However a fully systematic exposition, together with a theory of relative factor shares, was not presented until Hicks published his important *Theory of Wages*. [25] This may be regarded as the foundation of the modern neoclassical theory of distribution and relative factor shares. Before we get into concepts, however, a bit of review is in order.

Least-Cost Combination of Inputs, Linearly Homogeneous Production Functions, and Homothetic Production Functions
14.5.a

The present section is a brief review of the topics developed in Chapter 7, especially subsections 7.3.c and 7.4.c. First recall that the least-cost combination of inputs is obtained when the marginal rate of technical substitution equals the input-price ratio. This proposition is illustrated in Figure 14.5.1, in which Q_0 is

---

[25]John R. Hicks, *The Theory of Wages,* 2nd ed. (London: Macmillan, 1932, 1963).

Figure 14.5.1 Least-Cost Combination of Inputs

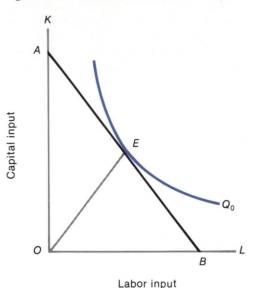

Labor input

an isoquant and the slope of AB represents the wage-rent ratio. The slope of the isoquant at any point is the ratio of the marginal product of labor to that of capital. Least-cost input proportions are attained only when the ratio of marginal products (the marginal rate of technical substitution) equals the input-price ratio. This occurs at point E, and the slope of the ray OE defines the optimal input (capital-labor) ratio.

The capital-labor ratio is important in any circumstance; but when the production function is homogeneous of degree one it plays an even more vital role. To say a production function is linearly homogeneous implies that the marginal product of each input, and hence the marginal rate of technical substitution, is a function of the input ratio exclusively. Or, in terms of Figure 14.5.1, the marginal rate of technical substitution of capital for labor is a function of the capital-labor ratio only. In particular, the marginal rate of technical substitution is *not* a function of the scale of output.[26]

---

[26] Let the production function be

$$Q = F(K,L),$$ (14.26.1)

where $F(K,L)$ is homogeneous of degree one in K and L. By its homogeneity property, equation (14.26.1) may be written

$$q = f(k),$$ (14.26.2)

where $q = Q/L$ and $k = K/L$. It is a simple matter to show that the marginal products $\partial Q/\partial K$ and $\partial Q/\partial L$ are given by

$$\frac{\partial Q}{\partial K} = f'(k)$$ (14.26.3)

An isoquant map for a linearly homogeneous production function is shown in Figure 14.5.2. Consider any ray from the origin, say OR, which specifies a capital-labor ratio. This ray intersects all isoquants in points (such as $E_1, \dots, E_4$) such that the slopes of the isoquants are identical; in other words, the marginal rate of technical substitution is the same at E_1, E_2, E_3, and E_4. This is true not only of the ray OR but of *any* other ray as well. Hence a single isoquant fully describes the isoquant map when the production function is homogeneous of degree one.

Whenever a production function has the property described in the last paragraph, namely, that the marginal rate of substitution is the same along any ray through the origin, it is said to be *homothetic*. Using the terminology of Chapter 6, a homothetic production function is one for which every isocline is a straight line through the origin. We have seen that linearly homogeneous production functions are homothetic. The converse is not true; there are homothetic production functions that are not linearly homogeneous.[27]

The Elasticity of Substitution
14.5.b

We noted in subsection 14.5.a that when a production function is linearly homogeneous, or more generally when it is homothetic, the *MRTS* is a function of the capital-labor ratio only. We also know from the "*VMP* rule" that the *MRTS* will be equal to the ratio of the price of labor to the price of capital. That is, by slightly rearranging the *VMP* rule we have

$$MRTS = \frac{MP_L}{MP_K} = \frac{(w/p)}{(r/p)} = \frac{w}{r}$$

where MP_L is the marginal product of labor, MP_K is the marginal product of capital, w is the price of labor, r is the price of capital, and p is the price of output. Combining this information we see that the capital-labor ratio can be thought of as a function of the ratio of the price of labor, w, to the price of capital, r. For convenience, we will write this function as

$$\frac{K}{L} = h\left(\frac{w}{r}\right). \tag{14.5.1}$$

---

and

$$\frac{\partial Q}{\partial L} = f(k) - kf'(k). \tag{14.26.4}$$

These last two equations show that the marginal products are functions of the capital-labor ratio only.

[27] For example, the production function $Q = F(K,L) = 100K^{.6}L^{.8}$ is homogeneous of degree $1.4 (= .6 + .8)$. Note that $F_K = 60K^{-.4}L^{.8}$ and $F_L = 80K^{.6}L^{-.2}$. The marginal rate of technical substitution is thus

$$MRTS = \frac{F_L}{F_K} = \frac{80K}{60L} = \frac{4}{3}\frac{K}{L},$$

which is a function of the capital-labor ratio only. Thus, $F(K,L)$ is homothetic but not linearly homogeneous.

Figure 14.5.2 Isoquant Map for Homogeneous
Production Function

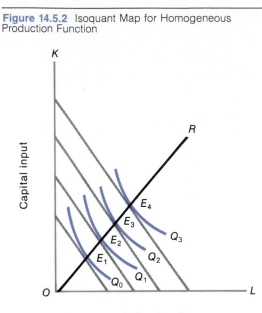

Labor input

Example: Let $Q = F(K, L) = 300K^{1/3}L^{2/3}$. For this production function

$$MP_K = \frac{\partial F}{\partial K} = 100K^{-2/3}L^{2/3}$$

and

$$MP_L = \frac{\partial F}{\partial L} = 200K^{1/3}L^{-1/3}.$$

Thus, in equilibrium we have

$$\frac{MP_L}{MP_K} = 2\frac{K}{L} = \frac{w}{r}$$

or

$$\frac{K}{L} = \frac{1}{2}\frac{w}{r}.$$

In this case, K/L is simply ½ times the ratio of w to r. In other words,

$$h\left(\frac{w}{r}\right) = \frac{1}{2}\frac{w}{r} \text{ for this example.}$$

We are now ready to discuss the *elasticity of substitution,* a concept at the heart of neoclassical theory that was introduced by Hicks in 1932.[28] Just as every elasticity, it measures the relative responsiveness of one variable to proportional changes in another.

Elasticity of Substitution: The elasticity of substitution measures the relative responsiveness of the capital-labor ratio to given proportional changes in the marginal rate of technical substitution of capital for labor.

This definition clearly indicates that the capital-labor ratio is understood to be a well-defined function of the *MRTS.* That will be true, as we have just seen, when the production function is homothetic.

By formula, the elasticity of substitution (σ) is

$$\sigma = \frac{\Delta\left(\dfrac{K}{L}\right)}{\left(\dfrac{K}{L}\right)} \div \frac{\Delta(MRTS)}{MRTS} = \frac{\Delta\left(\dfrac{K}{L}\right)}{\Delta(MRTS)} \times \frac{MRTS}{\left(\dfrac{K}{L}\right)}. \tag{14.5.2}$$

The above expression defines σ directly in terms of the production function. In equilibrium, however, *MRTS* will be equal to w/r. Thus, σ can also be defined as the elasticity of K/L with respect to w/r (where K/L is related to w/r as indicated by [14.5.1]). Hence, in equilibrium, the elasticity of substitution may be written as:

$$\sigma = \frac{\Delta\left(\dfrac{K}{L}\right)}{\Delta\left(\dfrac{w}{r}\right)} \times \frac{\left(\dfrac{w}{r}\right)}{\left(\dfrac{K}{L}\right)} = \frac{\Delta\left(\dfrac{K}{L}\right)}{\left(\dfrac{K}{L}\right)} \div \frac{\Delta\left(\dfrac{w}{r}\right)}{\left(\dfrac{w}{r}\right)}. \tag{14.5.3}$$

The elasticity of substitution can also be written in terms of the expression (14.5.1). To simplify the notation, let $k = K/L$ and let $u = w/r$; then, using (14.5.1) we have

$$\sigma = \frac{dk}{du}\frac{u}{k} = h'(u)\frac{u}{k}. \tag{14.5.4}$$

In (14.5.3) and (14.5.4), the elasticity of substitution shows the proportional change in the capital-labor ratio induced by a given proportional change in the factor-price ratio.

Exercise: Show that the production function in the example following equation (14.5.1) has $\sigma = 1$.

---

[28] Hicks, *Theory of Wages,* p. 117.

Elasticity of Substitution and Changes in Relative Factor Shares 14.5.c

In the notation introduced just above, the relative share of labor in output — that is, the total payment to labor divided by the total value of output — is

$$\frac{wL}{pQ}.$$

Similarly, the relative share of capital is

$$\frac{rK}{pQ};$$

thus the ratio of relative shares is

$$\frac{wL}{rK}.^{29}$$

Now consider the right-most expression in (14.5.3). Suppose the wage-rent ratio increases by 10 percent. An increase in the relative price of labor will, of course, lead to a substitution of capital for labor and, thereby, to an increase in the capital-labor ratio. Suppose it increases by 5 percent. Then the elasticity of substitution is less than one. Knowing this allows us to infer the behavior of relative factor shares. In the case above, w/r increases by 10 percent and K/L increases by only 5 percent. It therefore follows that wL/rK increases.

Let us look briefly at the cause. By assumption, the wage-rent ratio increases — because, perhaps, the supply of capital increases proportionately more than the supply of labor. As labor becomes relatively more expensive, entrepreneurs substitute capital for labor to the extent permitted by the production function. Now if the production function is characterized by inelastic substitutability, entrepreneurs cannot substitute capital for labor in the same proportion as the wage rate has risen relative to capital rent. Thus the relative share of labor must rise.

The same sort of reasoning applies when the elasticity of substitution is equal to or greater than unity. Hence we may summarize the relation between the elasticity of substitution and the behavior of relative factor shares in the following:

Proposition: Consider a two-factor model in which the absolute return to one factor increases relative to the absolute return to the other; the relative share of the former will increase, remain unchanged, or decrease according as the elasticity of substitution is less than, equal to, or greater than unity.[30]

---

[29] Consider the expression for labor's relative share. The real marginal product of labor is w/p, and L/Q is the reciprocal of labor's average product. Hence,

$$\text{labor's relative share} = \frac{MP_L}{AP_L} = \epsilon_L,$$

the output elasticity of labor (see the appendix to this chapter). This is always true when labor is paid its real marginal product. Thus we may state the following:

Relation: The relative share of an input is equal to its output elasticity.

Whether the elasticity of substitution is greater than, less than, or equal to unity is an empirical question; but it is one of great importance to various socioeconomic groups. For the American economy and for the manufacturing sector as a whole, there is strong evidence that the elasticity of substitution is substantially less than unity.[31] This is in keeping with the increases in the relative wage rate and in the relative share of labor. On the other hand, however, many specific industries and product groups apparently have production functions whose elasticities of substitution exceed unity.[32] In such industries the share of capital increases even though its relative return diminishes.

Classification of Technological Progress
14.5.d

So far we have operated under the tacit assumption that a production function is both given and unchanging over the period of analysis; our case has been strictly static. Technological progress does occur; and it is of some interest to classify the nature of technological change.

Many years ago Hicks defined technological progress as capital-using, neutral, or labor-using, according as the marginal rate of technical substitution of capital for labor diminishes, remains unchanged, or increases at the originally prevailing capital-labor ratio. In other words, if technological change increases the marginal product of capital more than the marginal product of labor (at a given capital-labor ratio), progress is capital-using because a producer now has an incentive to use more capital relative to labor — its (capital's) marginal product has increased relative to that of labor. The same type of statement holds, *mutatis mutandis*, for neutral and for labor-using technological progress.

Basically, technological progress consists of any change (graphically, shift) of the production function that either permits the same level of output to be produced with less input or enables the former level of inputs to produce a greater output.

Technological progress is shown graphically in Figures 14.5.3 and 14.5.4. The figures are constructed with uniform notation. The level of output is I, and

---

[30] This proposition can be demonstrated mathematically as follows. Using the notation above where $k = K/L$ and $u = w/r$, we see that the relative share ratio wL/rK can be written u/k. Differentiating,

$$\frac{d\left(\dfrac{u}{k}\right)}{du} = \frac{k - u\dfrac{dk}{du}}{k^2} = \frac{k\left(1 - \dfrac{u}{k}\dfrac{dk}{du}\right)}{k^2} = \frac{1 - \sigma}{k}.$$

It follows that if $\sigma < 1$, then wL/rK will increase; if $\sigma = 1$, this ratio is unchanged; and if $\sigma > 1$, this ratio decreases.

[31] As only one example, see J. W. Kendrick and Ryuzo Sato, "Factor Prices, Productivity, and Growth," *American Economic Review* 53 (1963), pp. 974–1003.

[32] See C. E. Ferguson, "Cross-Section Production Functions and the Elasticity of Substitution in American Manufacturing Industry," *Review of Economics and Statistics* 45 (1963), pp. 305–13; and C. E. Ferguson, "Time-Series Production Functions and Technological Progress in American Manufacturing Industry," *Journal of Political Economy* 73 (1965), pp. 135–47.

Figure 14.5.3 Neutral Technological Progress

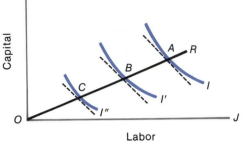

Figure 14.5.4 Biased Technological Progress

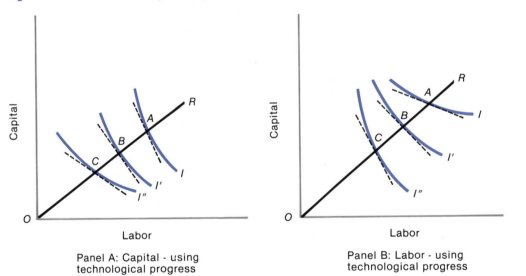

Panel A: Capital - using
technological progress

Panel B: Labor - using
technological progress

the various isoquants (I, I', and I'') show the combinations of inputs capable of producing this given level of output. OR is the ray whose slope gives a constant capital-labor ratio. The points A, B, and C show the points of production at the given capital-labor ratio as technological progress occurs.

Technological progress is shown graphically by a shift of an isoquant in the direction of the origin. In Figure 14.5.3, the three isoquants—I, I', and I''—all represent the same level of output. As technological progress takes place, I' shows that the given level of output can be produced by smaller quantities of inputs than at I. Similarly, as technological progress continues, I'' shows that still smaller input combinations can produce the same level of output.

Figure 14.5.3 illustrates neutral technological progress. Recalling the definition, technological progress is neutral if at a constant capital-labor ratio the marginal rate of technical substitution of capital for labor is unchanged. The constant capital-labor ratio ray *OR* intersects the three isoquants at points *A*, *B*, and *C*, respectively. At these points, the slope of the isoquants — or the marginal rate of technical substitution of capital for labor — is the same. Hence it represents a shifting production function characterized by neutral technological progress.

Panels A and B, Figure 14.5.4, illustrate capital-using and labor-using technological progress, respectively. Capital-using technological progress occurs when, at a constant capital-labor ratio, the marginal product of capital increases relative to the marginal product of labor. In other words, since the marginal rate of technical substitution of capital for labor is the ratio of the marginal product of labor to that of capital, capital-using technological progress occurs when the marginal rate of technical substitution declines along a constant capital-labor ray. As one moves from *A* to *B* to *C* in panel A, the slope of the isoquant diminishes, representing a decline in the marginal rate of technical substitution. Hence this panel depicts a shifting production function characterized by capital-using technological progress.

By the same line of reasoning, panel B illustrates labor-using technological progress because the marginal rate of technical substitution increases as one moves from *A* to *B* to *C*.

Biased Technological Progress and Relative Factor Shares
14.5.e

Observed changes in relative shares depend on changes in relative input prices and in the responsiveness of input proportions to these changes. Over time, changes in relative shares depend on the nature of technological progress as well. Indeed, this is evident from the definition of biased technological progress introduced in the subsection above.[33]

First, consider neutral technological progress. By definition, the capital-labor ratio and the marginal rate of technical substitution of capital for labor remain unchanged. Next, recall that in equilibrium, the marginal rate of technical substitution of capital for labor must equal the input-price ratio. Therefore the wage-rent ratio also remains unchanged. That is, both (K/L) and (w/r) are unchanged

---

[33]The relations among relative shares, changes in relative factor supplies, the elasticity of substitution, and the nature of technological progress can readily be developed mathematically. However, a mathematical treatment requires more space than is here available. For details, see C. E. Ferguson, "Neoclassical Theory of Technical Progress and Relative Factor Shares," *Southern Economic Journal* 34 (1968), pp. 490–504; and C. E. Ferguson, *The Neoclassical Theory of Production and Distribution*, Chapters 12 and 13.

by neutral technological progress. Consequently, relative shares are not affected by technological progress when the latter is neutral.

Now suppose technological progress is capital-using. This implies that at a constant capital-labor ratio the marginal rate of technical substitution, and hence the wage-rent ratio, declines. This is tantamount to saying that r increases relative to w while K/L is constant. The relative share of capital accordingly increases and that of labor declines.

By a similar line of reasoning, one may show that labor-using technological progress causes a decrease in the relative share of capital with a corresponding increase in the relative share of labor. Summarizing, we have the following:

Relations: The relative share of labor increases, remains unchanged, or decreases according as technological progress is labor-using, neutral, or capital-using; the opposite relation holds for the relative share of capital.

As a final empirical note, there is some evidence that the American economy has been characterized by labor-using technological progress over the postwar years.[34]

SYNOPSIS 14.6

■ The demand by a firm for one variable productive service (for example, labor) is given by the value of the marginal product of that factor to the firm. If the factor is labor (L) with marginal product MP_L, and if the firm sells output at price p, then the value of the marginal product of labor is $VMP_L = pMP_L$. If labor is the only variable input (short run), then labor will be demanded by the firm so as to satisfy the condition $VMP_L = w$, where w is the price of a unit of labor.

■ When more than one variable factor is involved, the demand for any one of them by an individual firm will be affected by substitution opportunities among the variable factors and also by changes in the level of output of the firm. Taking all these effects into account, it can be shown that the firm's demand for each variable factor is negatively sloped, as it is in the case of demand for one variable factor.

■ The supply of labor may, in principle, be derived using indifference curve analysis if we assume the individual's utility function depends both on money income and leisure. The analysis is ambiguous as to the shape of the individual's labor supply curve; however, in the long run, the *market* supply curve of labor and other factors is likely to be positively sloped.

---

[34]See Murray Brown and John S. de Cani, "Technological Changes in the United States, 1950–1960," *Productivity Measurement Review*, no. 29 (May 1962), pp. 26–39; and C. E. Ferguson, "Substitution, Technical Progress, and Returns to Scale," *American Economic Review, Papers and Proceedings* 55 (1965), pp. 296–305.

- Quasi rents are the return to short-run fixed inputs. In long-run competitive equilibrium, the Clark-Wicksteed theorem shows that when each factor is paid its marginal physical product (for example, the wage paid to labor is MP_L in output units), then the sum of the factor payments is exactly equal to total physical product; that is, factor payments precisely exhaust total product.

- When the production function is homothetic (a linearly homogeneous production function is a special case of a homothetic production function), there is a well-defined functional relationship between the marginal rate of technical substitution and the capital-labor ratio. Using this relationship one can define the *elasticity of substitution*. The numerical magnitude of the elasticity of substitution determines how relative factor *shares* will change in response to changes in relative factor prices.

- Technological change also can affect relative factor shares. Hicks classified technological change as capital-using, neutral, or labor-using. A capital-using technological change is one that increases the marginal product of capital relative to the marginal product of labor at a given capital-labor ratio. Neutral and labor-saving technological changes are defined accordingly. To illustrate, it can be shown that capital-using technological change will increase the relative share of capital.

APPENDIX

I. THE CLARK–WICKSTEED THEOREM

The proof of the theorem used here is attributable to Erich Schneider in his *Theorie der Produktion* (New York: Springer-Verlag, 1935), pp. 19–21. Let the production function be

$$q = f(x_1, x_2, \ldots, x_n) \tag{1}$$

where q is physical output and x_i is the input of the ith productive service. Denote $\partial f/\partial x_i$ by f_i. Then from (1) we have

$$dq = \sum_i f_i \, dx_i. \tag{2}$$

Increase all inputs by the constant proportion λ. Thus

$$\lambda = \frac{dx_1}{x_1} = \frac{dx_2}{x_2} = \cdots = \frac{dx_n}{x_n}. \tag{3}$$

Substitute (3) into (2), multiply by q, and divide by λq, obtaining

$$q\frac{dq}{\lambda q} = \sum_i f_i x_i. \tag{4}$$

Consider the term $dq/\lambda q$, which shows the relative change in output attributable to the same relative change in all inputs. This term may be called the *function coefficient* or the *elasticity of the production function*. (Schneider's term [*Theorie der Produktion,* p. 10] is *ergiebigkeitsgrad.*) The term *elasticity of production* is attributable to W. E. Johnson, "The Pure Theory of Utility Curves," *Economic Journal* 23 [1913], p. 507. The term *function coefficient* is used by Sune Carlson, *A Study on the Pure Theory of Production,* Stockholm Economic Studies, no. 9, 1939, p. 17.) Denote the function coefficient by ϵ. Thus from (4) we have:

$$q\epsilon = \sum f_i x_i . \tag{5}$$

Thus competitive imputations (paying each input its marginal product) precisely exhaust the total product if, and only if, $\epsilon = 1$. If there are constant returns to scale, $\epsilon = 1$; in this case average cost is also constant. But this is precisely the condition of long-run competitive equilibrium, in which output is expanded or contracted by the exit and entry of firms, each producing at the point of minimum long-run average cost. Thus, the Clark-Wicksteed theorem holds at the point of long-run competitive equilibrium — that is,

$$q = \sum_i f_i x_i \tag{6}$$

is an equation holding only for the precise set of equilibrium inputs, not an identity holding for any set of values of the variables.

II. THE OUTPUT ELASTICITY OF PRODUCTIVE SERVICES

Using the production function (1), the output elasticity of the ith productive service is defined as:

$$\epsilon_i = \frac{\partial q}{\partial x_i} \cdot \frac{x_i}{q} = f_i \frac{x_i}{q} . \tag{7}$$

The marginal product of x_i is f_i, and its average product is q/x_i; hence, from (7)

$$\epsilon_i = \frac{MP_i}{AP_i}$$

or, in words, the output elasticity of a productive service is the ratio of its marginal product to its average product.

QUESTIONS AND EXERCISES

1. The United States has a law that requires equal pay for women who perform the same job as men in a given plant. What is the effect of this law on the wage and employment of men and women?

2. "An increase in the income tax rate will induce laborers to work more since their net incomes will decline." Discuss.

3. "The completion of the marginal productivity theory of distribution was achieved only with the development of the proof that if all productive agents are rewarded in accord with their marginal products, then the total product will be exhausted." Explain.

4. Consider a model that rationalizes a person's choice between income and leisure. If leisure is a normal good, the resulting supply of labor curve may be negatively sloped. Derive such a labor-supply function. How would the analysis be affected if we were to introduce a progressive income tax? If the wage rate for overtime work is 150 percent of the basic wage rate?

5. How do the elasticity of substitution and the change in relative factor supply relate to changes in relative factor shares?

6. "If the production function in a particular industry exhibits constant returns to scale, a tax imposed on the employment of one factor will in the short run increase that factor's marginal product and in the long run will have no effect." Discuss.

7. "Inputs A and B are used in the production of the same product. An increase in the price of A (due to a shift in A's supply curve) will result in a decline in the price of B." Discuss.

8. "A is a product used in the production of B. Price control is imposed on the production of A but not B. The ceiling price imposed on A is less than the equilibrium price. This will result in a fall in the price of B." Discuss.

9. "Increasing the minimum wage to $4.65 per hour would have no effect outside the South if all workers earning less than $4.65 are located in the South." Discuss.

10. Part of the following statement follows directly from price theory, part not. Separate into the components: "Southern wages are lower than wages in the North (even in the same industry) because southern workers have less education and the southern climate causes everybody to work at a slower pace. Southern plants typically employ less capital per man. So, all in all, southern workers are less efficient. They get paid less because they deserve less."

SUGGESTED READINGS

Cartter, Allan M. *Theory of Wages and Employment.* Homewood, Ill.: Richard D. Irwin, 1959, pp. 11–74.

Douglas, Paul H. *The Theory of Wages.* New York: Macmillan, 1934.

Ferguson, C. E. "'Inferior Factors' and the Theories of Production and Input Demand." *Economica,* N. S. 35 (1968), pp. 140–50.

————. *The Neoclassical Theory of Production and Distribution.* London and New York: Cambridge University Press, 1969, Chapters 6 and 9.

————. "Production, Prices, and the Theory of Jointly-Derived Input Demand Functions." *Economica,* N. S. 33 (1966), pp. 454–61.

Ferguson, C. E., and **Thomas R. Saving.** "Long-Run Scale Adjustments of a Perfectly Competitive Firm and Industry." *American Economic Review* 59 (1969), pp. 774–83.

Hicks, John R. *The Theory of Wages.* New York: Macmillan, 1932.

————. *Value and Capital.* 2nd. ed. Oxford: Clarendon Press, 1946, pp. 78–111.

Samuelson, Paul A. *Foundations of Economic Analysis.* Cambridge, Mass.: Harvard University Press, 1947, pp. 57–89.

Stigler, George J. *Production and Distribution Theories.* New York: Macmillan, 1941, pp. 296–387.

15 Theory of Employment in Imperfectly Competitive Markets

Was Reggie Jackson worth his 1982 California Angels salary of $975,000, or Fernando Valenzuela the $1 million he was paid by the Los Angeles Dodgers? We already know from the last chapter that the maximum amount employers in competitive markets are willing to pay for any factor—be it a pitcher or a ton of steel—is the factor's *MRP*, or as George Steinbrenner, owner of the New York Yankees, puts it, the increased revenue resulting from the additional "number of fannies he puts in the seats." In this chapter we extend the previous analysis of input prices to conditions of imperfect competition, which many economists believe exists in professional sports. In baseball, for example, owners may be monopolists in the product market; that is, they might be the only baseball team in town. In addition, until the late 1970s, due to something called the reserve clause, a player was owned by his team. The team could sell or trade him, but the player was not free to offer his services to other teams. Under these conditions the owner can be viewed as the only demander of baseball players in the relevant input market. When there is a single buyer of an input, a "monopsony" is said to exist.

What can we expect to happen to factor prices under such conditions? Are baseball players like Reggie Jackson and Fernando Valenzuela paid their *MRP*? The answer to the first question comprises the core of the theoretical material of this chapter. An explicit answer to the second has also been attempted by a number of economists. In the "Applying the Theory" section ("Are Professional Athletes Worth the Price?")—which deals with the application of imperfect competition in factor markets to athletes' salaries—these economists' answers are considered in detail. ■

Are Professional Athletes Worth the Price?

Is Reggie Jackson worth $975,000 per year? Or, for that matter, is Wayne Gretsky worth $825,000? Is John Elway, with his 1983 B.A. in economics from Stanford, worth $900,000 to the Denver Broncos?

In one sense, the answer is obviously yes. Those salaries are, after all, agreed to voluntarily. But what determines how much someone is willing to pay for a player's services?

A firm will pay any factor of production—be it a ton of coal or a cornerback—up to the marginal revenue product of the factor. That marginal revenue product is simply the extra revenue attributable to hiring an additional unit of the factor.

George Steinbrenner, owner of the New York Yankees, puts the point somewhat more colorfully: "You measure the value of a ballplayer by how many fannies he puts in the seats."

Howard University economist John Leonard estimates that Reggie Jackson put as much as $1.5 million worth of fannies in the seats in 1982—his first year with the California Angels, and their second year in the playoffs.

The technique most commonly used to estimate the marginal revenue product of a player was developed by George Scully, an economist at Southern Methodist University. Writing in the December 1974 American Economic Review, Mr. Scully estimated the factors that determined a baseball team's total revenue in the 1968 and 1969 seasons.

Mr. Scully found, not surprisingly, that a major determinant of team revenues was the percentage of games won. He estimated the relationship between winning and the batting and pitching skills of a team's roster. By measuring an individual player's contribution to the team averages that determined winning, and then translating that contribution to an increase in the percentage of games won, Mr. Scully was able to measure the career marginal revenue products of players.

The results were startling. Players did not earn their marginal revenue products. They earned far less.

Table 15A gives Mr. Scully's findings.

Table 15A Career Marginal Revenue Products and Salaries

Hitters	Net MRP	Salary
Mediocre	−$ 124,300	$ 60,800
Average	906,700	196,200
Star	3,139,100	477,200
Pitchers		
Mediocre	−$ 53,600	$ 54,800
Average	1,119,200	222,500
Star	3,969,600	612,500

He grouped hitters and pitchers into performance categories. His measure of net marginal revenue product subtracts costs such as training and transportation associated with a single player from the marginal revenue product estimate. Mr. Scully assumed career lengths of 4, 7, and 10 years for mediocre, average, and star players, respectively.

Star pitchers and hitters were handsomely paid; their annual salaries were about $50,000 per year (remember this was the '60s). But, in terms of their contributions to team revenues, they were grossly underpaid, receiving only about 15 percent of their net marginal revenue products.

Mr. Scully suggests the explanation of salaries so far below marginal revenue product lies in the theory of monopsony. Under the "reserve clause" in effect then, a player was owned by his team. The team could sell or trade him, but the player was not free to offer his services to other teams. A player who wanted a baseball career could deal with only one team; that team thus had monopsony power over the player's services.

A monopsony team faces an upward-sloping supply curve for players of a particular category. That means that each extra player of a given type requires more money. That, in turn, is likely to drive up the wages paid to the players of that category the team already has. The result is that the extra cost of an extra player is higher than that player's actual salary.

Figure 15A shows the result, using Mr. Scully's estimate of marginal revenue products and salaries of star hitters. The supply curve facing a team for these hitters

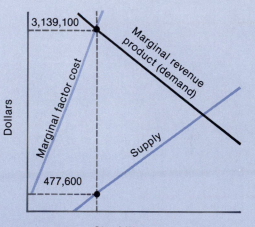

Figure 15A Monopsony Exploitation of Star Hitters

has the usual shape; the marginal factor cost curve shows the increase in salary costs associated with hiring each additional player. The demand curve, with star hitters as the only variable factor, is the marginal revenue product curve for these players.

Players, understandably, were unhappy with this arrangement. The reserve clause was challenged successfully by Andy Messersmith in 1975. The first group of "free agents," players now able to negotiate with other teams, was available for the 1977 season.

With competitive bidding for their services, the monopsony power of teams was weakened. Salaries should have moved closer to marginal revenue products.

(continued on page 454)

(continued from page 453)

They did. Paul Sommers and Noel Quinton, of Middlebury College, reported their estimates of the marginal revenue products of 14 of these free agents in the Summer 1982 issue of the Journal of Human Resources [Table 15B]. Using

Table 15B The 1977 Free Agents		
Hitters	**MRP**	**1977 Contract Cost**
Jackson	$1,132,093	$580,000
Rudi	286,044	440,000
Matthews	577,978	312,500
Baylor	579,310	274,167
Grich	169,424	330,000
Tenace	422,634	265,000
Cash	557,257	256,667
Bando	538,864	281,200
Campaneris	433,702	202,000
Pitchers		
Garland	282,091	230,000
Gullett	340,846	349,333
Fingers	303,511	332,000
Campbell	205,639	210,000
Alexander	166,203	166,677

Mr. Scully's approach, they found that the salaries of hitters had increased to about half of marginal revenue products; pitcher salaries were about equal to estimated marginal contributions to team revenue.

Professors Sommers and Quinton used the contributions of hitters to a team's slugging average and of pitchers to the team's strikeout to walk ratio to estimate individual contributions to revenues. A slugging average is the number of total bases divided by the number of times at bat.

The poorer than expected performances of Bobby Grich and Joe Rudi were due to injuries, which caused them to miss part of the 1977 season. Sommers and Quinton were unable to say why pitcher salaries came so close to marginal revenue product, while hitter salaries continued to fall short.

Monopsony power still exists in baseball. Players are allowed to become free agents only after six years in the game. But the opportunity to be a free agent has clearly had a powerful effect on salaries.

In a study reported at the Western Economic Association meeting last summer, Mr. Leonard estimated the same relationships for the 1982 season. He calculates that the monopsony gap has been closed still further; hitters had salaries averaging 75 percent of estimated marginal revenue product.

According to Mr. Leonard, one of the most spectacular examples of monopsony exploitation of athletes is in college football. He argues that NCAA rules against paying players a salary can be viewed as a monopsony price-fixing scheme to keep player costs down.

If that is its goal, it certainly succeeds. Mr. Leonard estimates that a star college football player, defined as an athlete that leads the national rankings in a category such as yards rushing or is named to an All-American team, has a marginal revenue product to his school of $100,000 per year. He is paid scholarship revenues of only about $5,000 per year.

Mr. Leonard's analysis of the monopsony problem in college football is presented in the October-December issue of the Eastern Economic Journal.

Mr. Leonard has tested for monopsony power in other sports as well. A professional football player is, for example, eligible to become a free agent after five years. But, if another team hires him, it must offer compensation, in the form of players or draft choices, to the player's present team.

The result, Mr. Leonard says, is that almost no one changes teams until he is traded or released by his own team. Mr. Leonard's calculations suggest, for example, that running backs earn salaries equal to only a third of their marginal revenue products. On the other hand, he estimates that quarterbacks are overpaid.

Mr. Leonard admits, however, that it is much harder to estimate an individual's contribution in a sport like football than it is in baseball.

That has not stopped him from trying. Mr. Leonard estimates that basketball players also earn much less than their marginal revenue products; he finds that centers are the worse victims.

The only sport in which Mr. Leonard finds players earning more than their estimated marginal revenue product is professional hockey — although he thinks Wayne Gretsky's marginal revenue product is considerably greater than the $825,000 that Sport magazine estimated he earned last year.

Estimates of marginal revenue products are, necessarily, somewhat arbitrary. There is more to a hitter's appeal than his slugging average, more to a quarterback than the number of touchdown passes relative to interceptions. But the work of economists studying sports salaries suggests quite clearly that the salaries paid professional athletes are not as outrageous as they may seem. To the extent that players are still subject to monopsony power, their salaries are still much lower than would prevail in a competitive market.

Even management is beginning to admit the worth of top players. Detroit Tigers Manager Sparky Anderson, asked to comment on pitcher Bruce Sutter's $900,000 salary, said "I don't think anybody's worth that kind of money. But if anybody is, he is."

Questions

1. Suppose the *MRP* curve in Figure 15A is drawn under the assumption that baseball owners are monopolists in the product market; that is, there is only one supplier of baseball games in the relevant city. Draw the new *MRP* schedule that would result if instead, there were many suppliers of a product called "entertainment," in which baseball games were just one of many alternatives.

2. Use your altered Figure 15A diagram (from question 1) to demonstrate the monopolistic exploitation by baseball owners. Also show the monopsonistic exploitation by baseball owners. (See Figure 15.3.3 in the text for reference.)

3. After 1975, a labor-relations ruling allowed certain players the right to become "free agents," which meant that these players could sell their services to any team. Owners, who

(continued on page 456)

APPLYING THE THEORY

(continued from page 455)
objected to the free-agent system, argued that it would harm the competitive balance among the teams by enabling the best and richest teams to grab up all the star players.

a. If one team progressively loses star hitters to a competitor, what happens to the *MRP* of star hitters on each of the two teams involved?

b. How does your answer to part (*a*) relate to the claim that "the best teams will grab up all the star players"?

4. This question refers to the relationship derived in footnote 7 in the text of this chapter, namely that $MEI = W(1 + 1/e)$ where e = elasticity of labor supply curve. According to the estimates of Mr. Scully reported in the article, star pitchers and hitters received a salary equal to only 15 percent of their (net) marginal revenue product. Assuming the owners were profit-maximizing monopsonists in the hiring of star pitchers and hitters, what does this imply about the elasticity of labor supply to such monopsonists? (Hint: start with the assumption that profit-maximizing monopsonists will hire a given factor up to the point where the $MRP = MEI$.)

5. This article has largely ignored the fact that baseball players have become unionized, and might actually bargain as a single group with baseball owners. Show that the following statement is correct:

Unions in monopsonistic markets can eliminate the portion of total monopsonistic exploitation that is uniquely attributable to monopsony in the labor market; however, the portion attributable to monopoly can in no way be eliminated by trade union activity.

(Refer to the discussion in subsection 15.3.3 and Figure 15.3.5 of the text for further help here.)

Solutions

1. *MRP* represents the net addition to total revenue attributable to the addition of one unit of the variable productive factor, or marginal revenue multiplied by the marginal physical product of the variable productive factor. Under conditions of perfect competition in the product market, *MRP* and *VMP* (*MPP* × market price) are equivalent since *for a perfect competitor,* the market price of the commodity equals marginal revenue. However, under conditions of monopoly in the product market, *MRP* is less than *VMP*, since for a monopolist, market price exceeds marginal revenue.

If there were competition in the "entertainment" market instead of a monopoly, the actual *MRP* schedule (which would be equivalent to the *VMP* schedule under such conditions) would lie above the schedule displayed in Figure 15A of the article. The difference would be exactly the same as that shown in Figure 15.3.3 in the text. The value of marginal product curve shown in Figure 15.3.3 would be the actual *MRP* schedule under such conditions.

The *MRP* schedule shown in Figure 15A of the article (drawn assuming baseball owners are monopolists in the product market) would correspond to the curve labeled marginal revenue product in Figure 15.3.3.

2. See the discussion in subsection 15.3.d ("Monopsonistic Exploitation") which refers to Figure 15.3.3. This discussion contrasts monopolistic exploitation (represented by distance *RM* in Figure 15.3.3) with monopsonistic exploitation (represented by distance *RW* in Figure 15.3.3).

3. *a.* A player's marginal product (or increase in the number of fans that attend as a result of having him on the team) is not independent of the quality of other inputs being used. In the case of star baseball hitters, a given star's *MRP* (*MP* × *MR*) depends on the number of other star players already on the team. Thus, the *MRP* of the remaining star hitters on the team that is losing them will rise. The *MRP* of the star hitters on the "competitor team" that is gaining them will fall. (If Valenzuela were on a team that had more excellent pitchers than the Dodgers, then attendance might not increase the 5,000 plus it has been estimated to increase on weeknights when he pitches. His *MRP* would be lower under these circumstances.)

   b. This claim by owners is dubious. The above analysis suggests that *MRP*'s of free agents will tend to be higher on teams with poor

records or who are located in areas with large potential markets. This prediction seems to be consistent with some of the initial evidence under "free agency." In their text, *Modern Labor Economics,* Ehrenberg and Smith report (2nd ed. Glenview, Ill.: Scott, Foresman and Co., 1985, pp. 56–57) that 31 of the first 46 "star quality" free agents signed with teams that had poorer records than the team they were on. Of the remaining 15, 7 signed with teams located in larger markets.

4. Since profit-maximizing monopsonists hire units of labor such that *MRP* = *MEI*, we can substitute *MRP* for *MEI* in the equation given in the question. Further, the wage is given as 15 percent of *MRP*. Substituting these values into equation (15.7.7) in footnote 7 yields the following:

$$(MRP) = (.15\ MRP) \times (1 + 1/e)$$

If we solve this equation for *e*, the elasticity of the labor supply, it turns out to equal .15/.85, or .176.

5. See the analysis in section 15.3.e (and Figure 15.3.5) of the text. The quote in the question comes from this section of the text.

Source: Timothy Tregarthen, "Are Athletes Worth the Price?" *The Margin,* November 1985, pp. 6–8.

The analytical principles underlying the theory of resource price and employment are the same for perfectly and imperfectly competitive markets. Demand and supply determine market-equilibrium resource price and resource employment; and marginal productivity considerations are the fundamental determinants of demand. To be sure, some adjustments must be made to allow for the fact that commodity price and marginal revenue are different in imperfectly competitive markets. Thus the value of the marginal product of a variable service is not the relevant guide. Furthermore, imperfect competition in the resource buying market must be introduced. Hence two additions to marginal productivity theory are presented in this chapter.

MONOPOLY IN THE COMMODITY MARKET
15.2

The first situation is that of a monopolist in the commodity market, or more generally an oligopolist or a monopolistic competitor, purchasing variable productive services in perfectly competitive input markets. Since the principle is precisely the same for all types of imperfect competition in the selling market, our attention is restricted to monopoly, except for subsection 15.2.d.

Marginal Revenue Product
15.2.a

When a perfectly competitive firm employs an additional unit of, say, labor, output is augmented by the marginal product of that unit. In like manner, total revenue is augmented by the value of its marginal product inasmuch as market (selling) price remains unchanged. When a monopolist employs an additional unit of labor, output is also increased by the marginal product of the worker. However, to sell this larger output, market price must be reduced for all units sold; hence total revenue is not augmented by the value of the marginal product of the additional worker. A numerical example is given in Table 15.2.1.

The first three columns of the table give the production function. Column 4 shows the price at which the total product can be sold; hence columns 2 and 4 give the demand function. Columns 5 and 6 contain the figures for total and marginal revenue, respectively. Finally, column 7 shows marginal revenue product, whose meaning and derivation must be explained.

Suppose the monopolist is producing and selling 27 units of the commodity at $8.45 per unit. This rate of output and sales requires three units of the variable productive service. Now consider what happens if a fourth unit of the variable service is used. Output increases to 34, or the marginal physical product of the fourth unit is 7. To sell 34 units per period of time, the monopolist must decrease price to $7.94 per unit. Total revenue expands, but *not* by 7 × $8.45 or

Table 15.2.1 Marginal Revenue Product for a Monopolistic Seller

Units of Variable Service	Total Product	Marginal Product	Selling Price per Unit	Total Revenue*	Marginal Revenue	Marginal Revenue Product
0	0	—	—	—	—	—
1	10	10	$10.00	$100	$10	$100
2	19	9	9.05	172	8	72
3	27	8	8.45	228	7	56
4	34	7	7.94	270	6	42
5	40	6	7.50	300	5	30
6	45	5	7.11	320	4	20
7	49	4	6.78	332	3	12
8	52	3	6.44	335	1	3
9	54	2	6.20	335	0	0
10	55	1	6.05	333	−2	−2

*Rounded to nearest dollar.

$7 \times \$7.94$. Total revenue expands by only $42; so on average, marginal revenue is $6. The addition of a unit of the variable service expands revenue, therefore, by the product of marginal revenue and marginal product, or by the increase in total revenue attributable to the addition of the marginal product (not one unit) to output and sales. This magnitude is called the *marginal revenue product* of the variable service.

An alternative arithmetic derivation of marginal revenue product may be helpful. When labor input expands from 3 to 4 units, output and sales expand by 7 units (from 27 to 34). Consequently, one might say that the *gross* increase in revenue attributable to the fourth unit of labor is $7 \times \$7.94$ which, rounded, equals $56. That is, the gross increase equals the increase in output multiplied by the new market price per unit of output. However, when output expands, market price falls by 51 cents, from $8.45 to $7.94. Therefore, the 27 units that had been selling at $8.45 must now be sold at $7.95; thus 27×51 cents, or, rounded, $14 must be deducted from the gross increase in revenue. As a result the *net* increase in revenue, or the marginal revenue product of the fourth unit of labor, is $\$56 - \$14$, or $42.[1]

---

[1]A simple algebraic demonstration that marginal revenue product equals marginal revenue multiplied by marginal physical product is also revealing. Let MRP, TR, TP, MPP, and L denote marginal revenue product, total revenue, total product, marginal physical product, and labor input, respectively. Also, as customary, let Δ denote "the change in."

By definition (in the text)

$$MRP = \frac{\Delta TR}{\Delta L}. \tag{15.1.1}$$

From the definition of marginal revenue ($MR = \Delta TR / \Delta TP$), one may write

$$\Delta TR = MR \times \Delta TP. \tag{15.1.2}$$

(continued on page 460)

Marginal Revenue Product: Marginal revenue product equals marginal revenue multiplied by the marginal physical product of the variable productive service; or, marginal revenue product is the net addition to total revenue attributable to the addition of one unit of the variable productive service.

Before utilizing marginal revenue product to determine the monopolist's demand for a variable productive service, it may be well to show a graphical derivation of marginal revenue product. Panel A, Figure 15.2.1, shows a smooth

---

(continued from page 459)

Similarly, from the definition of marginal physical product ($MPP = \Delta TP/\Delta L$), the change in labor input may be expressed as

$$\Delta L = \frac{\Delta TP}{MPP}. \tag{15.1.3}$$

Substituting expressions (15.1.2) and (15.1.3) in (15.1.1), the definition of marginal revenue product is obtained:

$$MRP = \frac{MR \times \Delta TP}{\dfrac{\Delta TP}{MPP}} = MR \times MPP. \tag{15.1.4}$$

A more directly mathematical derivation may be given. Let the demand function in inverse form be

$$p = h(q), \qquad h' < 0. \tag{15.1.5}$$

Thus total revenue is

$$TR = qh(q), \tag{15.1.6}$$

and marginal revenue is

$$MR = h(q) + qh'(q). \tag{15.1.7}$$

The production function, assuming only one variable input x, is

$$q = f(x), \qquad f' > 0. \tag{15.1.8}$$

By definition, marginal revenue product is the change in total revenue attributable to a small (say, unit) change in input. Thus

$$MRP = \frac{d(TR)}{dx}. \tag{15.1.9}$$

From (15.1.6), we find

$$MRP = h(q)\frac{dq}{dx} + qh'(q)\frac{dq}{dx}. \tag{15.1.10}$$

From (15.1.8), $dq/dx = f'(x)$. Hence we have

$$MRP = [h(q) + qh'(q)]f'(x). \tag{15.1.11}$$

By (15.1.7) and (15.1.8),

$$MRP = MR \cdot MP. \tag{15.1.12}$$

If there is a multi-input production function, $f'(x)$ is replaced by $\partial f/\partial x_i$ for the ith input. Equation (15.1.10) becomes

$$MRP_i = [h(q) + qh'(q)]\frac{\partial f}{\partial x_i} \tag{15.1.13}$$

or

$$MRP_i = MR \times MP_i. \tag{15.1.14}$$

Part Four   Theory of Distribution

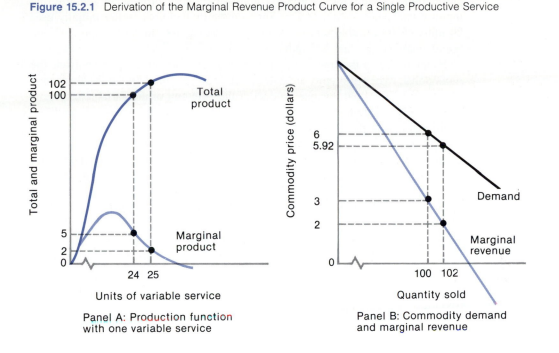

Panel A: Production function
with one variable service

Panel B: Commodity demand
and marginal revenue

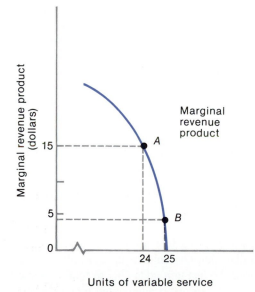

Panel C: Marginal revenue
product of variable
productive service

production function for a certain commodity whose production requires the input of only one variable service. Suppose the monopolistic seller initially uses 24 units of the variable service, thereby producing 100 units of output. At that point, marginal product is 5 units.

Panel B shows the demand and marginal revenue curves that confront the monopolist. When 100 units are sold, price is $6 per unit and marginal revenue is $3. Hence marginal revenue product of the 24th unit of the variable service is $5 \times \$3$ or $15, plotted as point A in panel C. Now let the monopolist add an additional unit of the variable service. Output increases to 102 units per period, and the marginal physical product of the 25th unit of variable service is 2. When output expands to 102 units per period, the monopolist must reduce the selling price to $5.92 per unit to clear the market. Hence marginal revenue declines to $2 per unit. As a consequence, when 25 units of the variable service are employed, marginal revenue product becomes $2 \times \$2$, or $4, plotted as point B in panel C.

Performing this operation for all feasible levels of employment generates the marginal revenue product curve. It obviously slopes downward to the right because two forces are working to cause marginal revenue product to diminish as the level of employment increases: (*a*) the marginal physical product declines (over the relevant range of production) as additional units of the variable service are added, and (*b*) marginal revenue declines as output expands and market price falls.

Monopoly Demand for a Single Variable Service
15.2.b

Under the present assumption the monopolist purchases the variable service in a perfectly competitive input market. Hence, just as a perfectly competitive producer, the monopolist sees the supply (of variable service) curve as a horizontal line at the level of the prevailing market price. Such a supply curve is illustrated by S_v in Figure 15.2.2, where the market price of the output is $O\overline{w}$.

The marginal revenue product curve is also shown in the figure; our task is to prove the following:

Proposition: An imperfectly competitive producer who purchases a variable productive service in a perfectly competitive input market will employ that amount of the service for which marginal revenue product equals market price. Consequently, the marginal revenue product curve is the monopolist's demand curve for the variable service when only one variable input is used.

Given the market price $O\overline{w}$, our task is to prove that equilibrium employment is $O\overline{v}$. Suppose the contrary; in particular, that Ov_1 units of the variable service are used. At the Ov_1 level of utilization, the last unit adds Ow_1 to total revenue but only $O\overline{w}$ to total cost. Since $Ow_1 > O\overline{w}$, profit is augmented by employing that unit. Furthermore, profit increases when additional units are employed so long as marginal revenue product exceeds the market equilibrium price of the

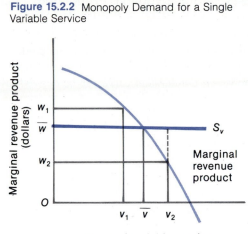

Figure 15.2.2 Monopoly Demand for a Single Variable Service

input. Thus a profit-maximizing monopolist would never employ fewer than $O\overline{v}$ units of the variable service. The opposite argument holds when more than $O\overline{v}$ units are employed, for then an additional unit of the variable service adds more to total cost than to total revenue. Therefore, a profit-maximizing monopolist will adjust employment so that marginal revenue product equals market equilibrium input price. If only one variable productive service is used, the marginal revenue product curve is the monopolist's demand curve for the variable service in question.[2]

---

[2]In the notation of footnote 1, let the demand and production functions be given, respectively, by

$$p = h(q), \qquad h' < 0; \qquad q = f(x), \qquad f' > 0. \tag{15.2.1}$$

Let the competitively given price of the input be w. Thus total profit (π) may be written

$$\pi = pq - wx - F, \tag{15.2.2}$$

where F is fixed cost. Using (15.2.1), we may rewrite (15.2.2) as

$$\pi = h[f(x)]f(x) - wx - F. \tag{15.2.3}$$

Maximizing profit, one obtains

$$\frac{d\pi}{dx} = f(x)\frac{dp}{dq}\frac{dq}{dx} + p\frac{dq}{dx} - w = 0, \tag{15.2.4}$$

or

$$\left(q\frac{dp}{dq} + p\right)\frac{dq}{dx} - w = 0. \tag{15.2.5}$$

This may be written as

$$[h(q) + qh'(q)]f'(x) = w. \tag{15.2.6}$$

This establishes the relation in the text, that is, $MRP = w$. It is further interesting to note that using the expression for marginal revenue developed in Part 3, we may write

$$p\left(1 - \frac{1}{\eta}\right)f'(x) = w, \tag{15.2.7}$$

showing the relations among commodity price, factor price, elasticity of demand, and the production function.

Monopoly Demand for a Variable Production Service When Several Variable Inputs Are Used
15.2.c

When more than one variable input is used in the production process, the marginal revenue product curve is not the demand curve for the reasons discussed in Chapter 14. However, the demand curve can be derived just as it was derived in that chapter.

Suppose, as in Figure 15.2.3, that at a given moment the market input price of a particular variable service is Ow_2 and that its marginal revenue product is given by MRP_1. The monopolist attains equilibrium employment at point A, using Ov_1 units of the variable service. Next, let the price of the service fall to Ow_1 (because, for example, the market supply curve for the input shifts to the right). Other things being equal, the monopolist would expand along MRP_1 to A' in panel A. But other things are not equal.

Substitution, output, and profit-maximizing effects exist, as explained in Chapter 14. Exactly the same analysis applies to a monopolist or set of oligopolists as applies to a set of perfectly competitive producers. The substitution, output, and profit-maximizing effects, on balance, cause a shift of the marginal revenue product curve, which may be outward, inward, or twisted. Panel A, Figure 15.2.3, illustrates the first mentioned; panel B illustrates the last mentioned. In any event, as in Chapter 14, the fall in marginal revenue cannot completely offset the expansive forces. The factor demand function must be negatively sloped.[3]

The results of this section may be clearly summarized in the following:

Proposition: Input demand curves are negatively sloped regardless of the market organization in the product market.

Market Demand for a Variable Productive Service
15.2.d

If a group of monopolists uses a variable productive service, the market demand for the service is simply the sum of the individual demands of the various monopolists. There are no *external* effects of expanded output on price; the effect of expansion is internal to each monopolist and has already been considered in obtaining his or her individual demand curve. Similarly, if all sorts of producers use the variable service, the market demand curve is the sum of the various

---

[3]For proofs, see C. E. Ferguson, "Production, Prices, and the Theory of Jointly Derived Input Demand Functions," *Economica,* N.S. 33 (1966), pp. 454–61; C. E. Ferguson, " 'Inferior Factors' and the Theories of Production and Input Demand," *Economica,* N.S. 35 (1968), pp. 140–50; C. E. Ferguson and Thomas R. Saving, "Long-Run Scale Adjustments of a Perfectly Competitive Firm and Industry," *American Economic Review* 59 (1969), pp. 774–83. The mathematical analysis contained in these papers is presented in greater detail in C. E. Ferguson, *The Neoclassical Theory of Production and Distribution* (London and New York: Cambridge University Press, 1969), Chapters 6 and 9.

Figure 15.2.3 Monopoly Demand for a Variable Productive Service When Several Variable Services Are Used

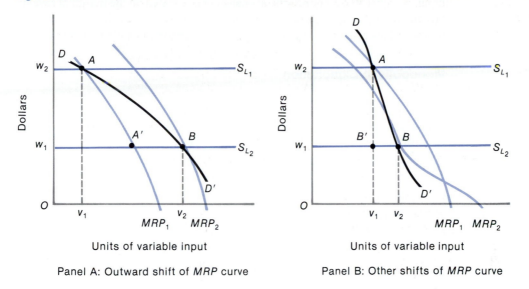

Panel A: Outward shift of *MRP* curve

Panel B: Other shifts of *MRP* curve

component *industry* demand curves, where the industries may be composed of any number of firms. However, a minor qualification is required in cases of oligopoly and monopolistic competition. Since the situation is the same in both cases, only monopolistic competition is considered.

The demand curve for a variable service on the part of any one monopolistically competitive producer is derived in the same way as a monopolist's demand curve. But when all sellers in the product group expand output, market price diminishes (along Chamberlin's *DD'* curve), just as in a perfectly competitive industry. Thus to obtain the market demand from individual demand curves one must allow for the decrease in market price and marginal revenue. Graphically, the derivation is exactly like that in Figure 14.2.5, except that the individual demand curves are based on marginal revenue product rather than the value of the marginal product.

Equilibrium Price and Employment
15.2.e

The analysis of market equilibrium price and employment of a variable agent is no different whether the employers are monopolists or perfectly competitive producers. The determination of quasi rents is also the same; thus the discussion of Chapter 14, subsections 14.4.a and 14.4.b, applies equally well in the present context.

While the *analysis* does not change, there is one important difference to bear in mind: in cases of monopoly the demand curve is based on the marginal revenue product of the variable productive service rather than on the value of its marginal product. This gives rise to what is sometimes called monopolistic exploitation.[4]

Monopolistic Exploitation
15.2.f

According to Robinson's definition, a productive service is exploited if it is employed at a price that is less than the value of its marginal product.[5] As we have seen in Chapter 14 and in the foregoing portion of this chapter, it is to the advantage of any individual producer (whether monopolist or competitor) to hire a variable service until the point is reached at which an additional unit adds precisely the same amount to total cost and total revenue. This is simply the input market implication of profit maximization.

When a perfectly competitive producer follows this rule, a variable service receives the value of its marginal product because price and marginal revenue are the same. This is not true, however, when the commodity market is imperfect. Marginal revenue is less than price, and marginal revenue product is correspondingly less than the value of the marginal product. Profit-maximizing behavior of imperfectly competitive producers causes the market price of a productive service to be less than the value of its marginal product.

If the market price of the commodity reflects its social value, the productive service receives less than its contribution to social value. Raising the input price is not a remedy, however, because producers would merely reduce the level of employment until marginal revenue product equaled the higher input price. The trouble initially lies in the fact that imperfectly competitive producers do not use as much of the resource as is socially desirable and do not attain the correspondingly desirable level of output. The fundamental difficulty rests in the difference between price (marginal social valuation) and marginal (social) cost at the profit-maximizing output. Thus, so long as imperfectly competitive producers exist there must be some "monopolistic exploitation" of productive agents.

The significance of this "exploitation" can easily be exaggerated. Following Chamberlin, product differentation is desired per se; and whenever there is differentiation, price and marginal revenue diverge so that exploitation is inevitable. Furthermore, the alternatives to exploitation are not attractive. Either there must be state ownership and operation of all nonperfectly competitive industries or else there must be rigid price control by the state. For a variety of reasons, either alternative is likely to raise more problems than it solves.[6]

---

[4]This term is apparently attributable to Joan Robinson. See her *Economics of Imperfect Competition* (New York: Macmillan, 1933), pp. 281–91.

[5]Ibid., p. 281.

[6]Cf. C. E. Ferguson, *A Macroeconomic Theory of Workable Competition* (Durham, N.C.: Duke University Press, 1964).

The analysis of pricing and employment of productive services has so far rested on the assumption that each producer (buyer of the service in question) cannot affect the market price of the service by changes in his or her utilization of it. This assumption obviously does not hold in all situations. There are sometimes only a few, and in the limit one, purchasers of a productive service. Where there is a single buyer of an input, a *monopsony* is said to exist; if there are several buyers, *oligopsony* is the proper designation.

A wide variety of categories can be classified. Broadly speaking, commodity markets may be perfectly competitive, monopolistically competitive, oligopolistic, or monopolistic. For each of these four types of commodity market organizations, the input market can be either a monopsony or an oligopsony. However, the analytical principle is the same irrespective of the organization of the commodity and input markets (so long as there is not perfect competition in the input market). Thus we restrict our attention to the case in which there is monopoly in the commodity market combined with monopsony in the input market.

Marginal Expense of Input
15.3.a

The supply curve for most productive services or production agents is positively sloped. A buyer in a perfectly competitive input market views the supply of input curve as a horizontal line because such a buyer's purchases are so small, relative to the market, that they do not perceptibly affect market price. A monopsonist, however, being the only buyer in the market, faces a positively sloped market supply of input curve. As a result, changes in the volume of purchases do affect input price; as input usage expands, input price increases. The monopsonist, therefore, must consider the *marginal expense* of purchasing an additional unit of a variable productive agent.

Computation of the marginal expense of input is shown in Table 15.3.1, and the supply and marginal expense of input curves are illustrated in Figure 15.3.1. Columns 1 and 2 show the supply curve, plotted as the right-most curve in Figure 15.3.1. When only one unit of the variable agent is employed, its cost is $2; thus the total cost of the input, and total variable cost when only one agent is used, is also $2. If two units are used, the supply price per unit is $2.50; total cost of the input $5, an increase of $3 over the previous total cost, even though the price per unit increased by only 50 cents. In other words, hiring an additional unit of input increases total cost by more than the price of the unit because all units employed receive the new, higher price.

The marginal expense of input, the left-most curve in Figure 15.3.1, is calculated by successive subtraction in the "total cost of input" column. Since the price unit rises as employment increases, the marginal expense of input exceeds its

Table 15.3.1 Monopsony and the Marginal Expense of Input

Units of Variable Input	Price per Unit	Total Cost of Input	Marginal Expense of Input
1	$2.00	$ 2.00	—
2	2.50	5.00	$ 3.00
3	3.00	9.00	4.00
4	3.50	14.00	5.00
5	4.00	20.00	6.00
6	4.50	27.00	7.00
7	5.00	35.00	8.00
8	5.50	44.00	9.00
9	6.00	54.00	10.00
10	6.50	65.00	11.00

Figure 15.3.1 Marginal Expense of Input

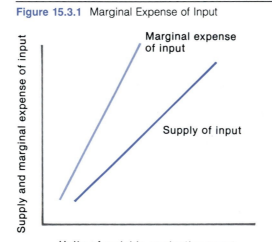

price at all employment levels; and the marginal expense of input curve is positively sloped, lies to the left of the supply of input curve, and typically rises more rapidly than the latter.[7]

---

[7]These statements can easily be proven. Let the input-supply function in inverse form be

$$w = g(x),$$ (15.7.1)

where w is input price, x is the quantity of the input supplied, and $g'(x) = dw/dx > 0$ by assumption (that is, the input supply curve is positively sloped). Total variable cost is

$$C(x) = wx = xg(x).$$ (15.7.2)

Marginal Expense of Input: The marginal expense of input is the increase in total cost (and in total variable cost and in total cost of input) attributable to the addition of one unit of the variable productive agent.

Price and Employment under Monopsony When One Variable Input Is Used
15.3.b

The market demand curve for a productive service is the demand curve of the single buyer under monopsony conditions. Furthermore, if only one variable input is used in the production process, the demand curve is the monopsonist's marginal revenue product curve. Confronting the monopsonist is the positively sloped supply of input curve and the higher marginal expense of input curve. The situation is illustrated in Figure 15.3.2. Using this graph we will prove the following:

Proposition: A profit-maximizing monopsonist will employ a variable productive service until the point is reached at which the marginal expense of input equals its marginal revenue product. The price of the input is determined by the corresponding point on its supply curve.

By definition, the marginal expense of input is

$$MEI = \frac{dC(x)}{dx} = g(x) + xg'(x) = w + x\frac{dw}{dx}. \tag{15.7.3}$$

Since $g'(x) > 0$ by assumption, a comparison of (15.7.1) and (15.7.3) shows that the marginal expense of input curve must lie above the input supply curve for each quantity supplied. Usually, the *MEI* curve is positive and rises more rapidly than the input supply curve. The slope of the latter is $g'(x)$, while the slope of the former is given by

$$\frac{dMEI}{dx} = 2g'(x) + xg''(x). \tag{15.7.4}$$

Thus *MEI* must be positive and have the steeper slope unless the input supply curve is *very* concave (that is, $g'' < 0$ and large in absolute value).

Finally, we may relate the *MEI* to input price and input-supply elasticity in the same way that marginal revenue is related to commodity price and the elasticity of commodity demand. By definition, the elasticity of input supply is

$$\theta = \frac{dx}{dw}\frac{w}{x}. \tag{15.7.5}$$

Now write (15.7.3) as

$$MEI = w + x\frac{dw}{dx} = w\left(1 + \frac{x\,dw}{w\,dx}\right). \tag{15.7.6}$$

Using (15.7.5) in (15.7.6), one obtains

$$MEI = w\left(1 + \frac{1}{\theta}\right). \tag{15.7.7}$$

When the input-supply curve is perfectly elastic, $\theta \to \infty$ and $MEI = w$, that is, monopsony does not exist.

Exercise: State and explain all of the relations between $MR = (1 - 1/\eta)$ and

$$MEI = w\left(1 + \frac{1}{\theta}\right).$$

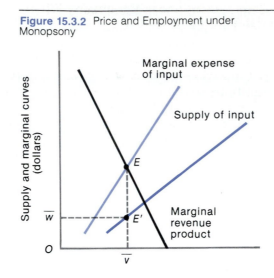

Figure 15.3.2 Price and Employment under Monopsony

Marginal expense of input

Supply of input

Supply and marginal curves (dollars)

E

$\overline{w}$

E'

Marginal revenue product

O

$\overline{v}$

Units of variable input per unit of time

The proof of this proposition follows immediately from the definitions of marginal revenue product and marginal expense of input. Marginal revenue product is the addition to total revenue attributable to the addition of one unit of the variable input; the marginal expense of input is the addition to total cost resulting from the employment of an additional unit. Therefore, so long as marginal revenue product exceeds the marginal expense of input, profit can be augmented by expanding input usage. On the other hand, if the marginal expense of input exceeds its marginal revenue product, profit is less or loss greater than if fewer units of the input were employed. Consequently, profit is maximized by employing that quantity of the variable service for which marginal expense of input equals marginal revenue product.

This equality occurs at point E in Figure 15.3.2; $O\overline{v}$ units of the service are accordingly employed. At this point the supply of input curve becomes particularly relevant. $O\overline{v}$ units of the variable productive agent are associated with point E' on the supply of input curve. Thus, $O\overline{v}$ units will be offered at $O\overline{w}$ per unit. Hence, $O\overline{w}$ is the market equilibrium input price corresponding to market equilibrium employment $O\overline{v}$.[8]

---

[8]This proposition may easily be proved by using footnotes 1 and 7. Summarizing,

$$p = h(q), \qquad q = f(x), \quad \text{and} \quad w = g(x) \tag{15.8.1}$$

are the commodity demand function, the production function, and the input-supply function, respectively. Ignoring fixed cost, the profit function is

$$\pi = pq - wx = qh(q) - xg(x) = f(x)h[f(x)] - xg(x). \tag{15.8.2}$$

Price and Employment under Monopsony When Several Variable Inputs Are Used
15.3.c

To secure the least-cost combination of variable inputs, an entrepreneur must employ productive services in such proportion that the marginal rate of technical substitution equals the input-price ratio. But this proposition holds if, and only if, the inputs are purchased in perfectly competitive markets. Otherwise, a change in input composition entails a change in relative input prices.

Let us illustrate this algebraically. Suppose there are two variable inputs, capital (K) and labor (L). Denote the marginal physical products by MP_K and MP_L and their market prices by r and w respectively. If the input markets are perfectly competitive, the least-cost combination rule requires that

$$\frac{MP_K}{MP_L} = \frac{r}{w}. \tag{15.3.1}$$

Stated alternatively,

$$\frac{MP_K}{r} = \frac{MP_L}{w}. \tag{15.3.2}$$

Equation (15.3.2) implies that the marginal product per dollar spent on each input must be the same. The *reason* for this rule is that marginal physical product represents the additional revenue, and input price the additional cost attributable to the input. This holds for both competitive and monopolistic commodity markets; price changes as output changes in monopoly markets, but the price change is the same whether output is expanded by increasing the employment of capital, the employment of labor, or both.

The proposition stated in equation (15.3.2) is fairly obvious, but it might be well to discuss it some more. Suppose

$$\frac{MP_K}{r} > \frac{MP_L}{w}. \tag{15.3.3}$$

The entrepreneur determines the amount of the variable input so as to maximize profit:

$$\frac{d\pi}{dx} = h[f(x)]f'(x) + \frac{dh(q)}{dq}f'(x)f(x) - g(x) - xg'(x) = 0, \tag{15.8.3}$$

or

$$\left[h(q) + q\frac{dh}{dq} \right]f'(x) = [g(x) + xg'(x)]. \tag{15.8.4}$$

By footnote 1, the left-hand side of (15.8.4) is marginal revenue product. By footnote 7, the right-hand side is the marginal expense of input. Thus the theorem is proved.

Also using footnotes 1 and 7, we may write this relation as

$$p\left(1 - \frac{1}{\eta}\right)f'(x) = w\left(1 + \frac{1}{\theta}\right). \tag{15.8.5}$$

Exercise: State and explain the interesting relations implicit in equation (15.8.5).

By inequality (15.3.3), a dollar's worth of capital contributes more to output than a dollar's worth of labor, at the *present* capital-labor ratio. If the input markets are perfectly competitive, rates of employment can be changed without affecting input prices. Therefore the entrepreneur would substitute capital for labor so as to obtain the same output for less cost. Because of this substitution, the marginal product of capital declines and the marginal product of labor increases. With market determined r and w, the entrepreneur will continue the substitution until equality (15.3.2) is established.

If the input markets are monopsonistic, changes in the volume of employment cause corresponding changes in input prices. In particular, the entrepreneur must look to the marginal expense of input (MEI) rather than its market price when making employment decisions. Consider labor only, for the moment. An additional unit adds its marginal product to output, but it does not add w to total cost; instead, with a positively sloped input supply curve, it adds its marginal expense MEI_L.

Suppose the capital-labor ratio in production at a given moment is such that

$$\frac{MP_K}{MEI_K} > \frac{MP_L}{MEI_L}. \tag{15.3.4}$$

Inequality (15.3.4) has the following meaning: at the prevailing input combination, an entrepreneur can obtain a greater increase in output per additional dollar of cost by employing capital rather than labor. Consequently, the entrepreneur can maintain the same output but reduce cost by substituting capital for labor. As a result of this substitution, two forces work to bring about an equality: as the employment of capital expands and that of labor declines (*a*) the marginal product of capital declines and that of labor increases and (*b*) the marginal expense of input of capital rises and that of labor declines. Since the entrepreneur can reduce cost so long as the inequality in expression (15.3.4) prevails, capital will be substituted for labor until

$$\frac{MP_K}{MEI_K} = \frac{MP_L}{MEI_L}. \tag{15.3.5}$$

When equality (15.3.5) obtains, no change in input composition will reduce cost. Consequently, we have demonstrated the following:[9]

---

[9]The proof of this proposition is accomplished by an easy extension of footnote 8. Let

$$p = h(q), \qquad q = f(K,L), \qquad r = g(K), \qquad w = m(L) \tag{15.9.1}$$

be the commodity demand function, the production function, the supply of capital function, and the labor-supply function, respectively. The profit function is, accordingly,

$$\pi = qh(q) - Kg(K) - Lm(L). \tag{15.9.2}$$

The entrepreneur adjusts both inputs so as to maximize profit:

$$\frac{\partial \pi}{\partial K} = q\frac{dh}{dq}\frac{\partial f}{\partial K} + h(q)\frac{\partial f}{\partial K} - g(K) - Kg'(K) = 0, \tag{15.9.3}$$

$$\frac{\partial \pi}{\partial L} = q\frac{dh}{dq}\frac{\partial f}{\partial L} + h(q)\frac{\partial f}{\partial L} - m(L) - Lm'(L) = 0, \tag{15.9.4}$$

Proposition: A monopsonist who uses several variable productive inputs will adjust input composition until the ratio of marginal product to marginal expense of input is the same for all variable inputs used. The least-cost combination is accordingly obtained when the marginal rate of technical substitution equals the marginal expense of input ratio.

In the two-input situation, we have

$$\frac{MP_L}{MP_K} = \frac{MEI_L}{MEI_K} \tag{15.3.6}$$

Thus one sees that rule (15.3.1) for perfectly competitive input markets is a special case of rule (15.3.6); rule (15.3.1) is valid because in perfectly competitive input markets, the marginal expense of input is precisely equal to its market price.[10]

---

or

$$[qh'(q) + h(q)]\frac{\partial f}{\partial K} = g(K) + Kg'(K), \tag{15.9.5}$$

$$[qh'(q) + h(q)]\frac{\partial f}{\partial L} = m(L) + Lm'(L). \tag{15.9.6}$$

The two equations just above state that the marginal revenue product of each input must equal its marginal expense of input. Taking the ratio of the two equations and canceling the marginal revenue term yields

$$\frac{MP_K}{MP_L} = \frac{MEI_K}{MEI_L}. \tag{15.9.7}$$

Transforming (15.9.7) yields the relation stated in the text.

[10]An important matter is here relegated to a footnote because even a graphical exposition requires some mathematics. *But note:* The student, whether mathematically trained or not, should read this footnote.

The relation in equation (15.3.6) in the text states that the marginal rate of technical substitution of capital for labor equals the ratio of their marginal expenses of input. This is the "rule" for optimum input proportions. As explained in the text and in footnote 9, the rule is based on profit maximization. It can, of course, be so based. But the important point is that this rule can be established on the much weaker assumption that entrepreneurs minimize the cost of producing a given output or maximize the output obtainable from a given expenditure on resources.

Just as in Chapter 7, this may be shown graphically by use of isoquants and isocost curves. The mathematics enters in showing that the isocost curve is not a straight line. Everything else follows from the definitions introduced above.

Exercise: For mathematically trained students only. Suppose $\overline{C}$ is spent on resources. Thus the isocost curve is $Kg(K) + Lm(L) = \overline{C}$. Show the following relations: (a) the isocost curve is "usually" concave, but may be convex if an input supply function is negatively sloped; (b) the "rule" stated in equation (15.3.6) mathematically; (c) if an input-supply function is negatively sloped, *economically* efficient operation may require the entrepreneur to produce in the *technologically* inefficient region (that is, the region in which one marginal product is negative).

Exercise: Give an economically rational explanation of (c) above.

Reference for exercises: Ferguson, *Neoclassical Theory of Production,* Chapters 8 and 9.

Monopsonistic Exploitation
15.3.d

In subsection 15.2.f it was shown that monopoly in the commodity market leads to "monopolistic exploitation" in the input market. Monopolistic exploitation exists in the sense that each productive service is paid its marginal revenue product, which, because of the negatively sloped commodity demand curve, is less than the value of its marginal product. Each unit of resource receives the amount that, on average, it contributes to the firm's total receipts; but the units of resources do not receive the values of their marginal products.

Monopsonistic exploitation is something in addition to this, as illustrated by Figure 15.3.3. The figure is constructed to cover a variety of cases; the curves would doubtlessly change as the type of market organization changes. However, allowing for this, Figure 15.3.3 is a schematic device for illustrating monopolistic and monopsonistic exploitation.

First, suppose both the commodity and input markets are perfectly competitive. The value of the marginal product curve is the industry demand for input curve.[11] As you will recall, it is not the *direct* sum of the individual curves; however, it does represent the value of the input's marginal product to the industry as a whole. Demand and supply intersect at point A, each unit of input receiving the market value of its marginal product.

Next, let the commodity market be monopolistic, while the input market is perfectly competitive. The marginal revenue product curve represents the collection of monopoly demand curves (just as the value of the marginal product curve represents the collection of individual demand curves). Equilibrium is attained at point B. The difference between the wage rates corresponding to points A and B ($OR - OM = RM$) is the "monopolistic exploitation" of the input. Because of monopolistic exploitation, fewer units of the input are employed and the unit price of each is less. Nonetheless, each unit of input receives an amount equal to what its employment adds to total receipts.

Finally, suppose there is monopoly in the commodity market and monopsony in the input market. Equilibrium is attained at C, at a still lower price and employment level. Monopsonistic exploitation is represented by the difference between points A and C, or by the difference in input prices between the competitive and monopsonistic equilibria ($OR - OW = RW$). The portion RM is attributable to monopoly in the commodity market; it is not unique to monopsony. The additional portion MW, however, is uniquely attributable to monopsony (or more generally, to oligopsony). The existence of the differential MW is caused by the fact that each unit of input contributes OM to total receipts but

---

[11]The concept of a *VMP* curve for an industry is somewhat ambiguous. For a firm it is clear: it is the input's marginal product multiplied by the *constant* (to the firm) commodity price. For an industry it is somewhat different. For each level of employment and output, industry *VMP* is the marginal product of the input (efficient operation of firms assures equality among firms) multiplied by the market price associated with that level of output. Of course, market price decreases as output increases; and the various marginal products are multiplied by the relevant, *but changing*, market price.

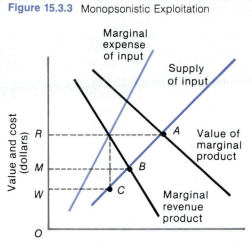

Figure 15.3.3 Monopsonistic Exploitation

Marginal expense of input

Supply of input

Value and cost (dollars)

R — — — — — — — — — A   Value of marginal product

M — — — — — — B

W — — — — C

Marginal revenue product

O

Units of variable input

receives only *OW* in return. Thus the chief feature of monopsonistic exploitation is that each unit of input does not receive in pay an amount equal to its contribution to total receipts.

In subsection 15.2.f, it was indicated that while monopolistic exploitation could be removed, the "cure" might be worse than the "disease." Indeed, within a free enterprise economic system, monopolistic exploitation is bound to arise. Even bona fide product differentiation causes this type of "exploitation." The same is not true of monopsonistic exploitation. Countermeasures exist, and they are not fundamentally destructive to a free enterprise system.

Monopsony and the Economic Effects of Labor Unions 15.3.e

A study of labor unions and of the collective-bargaining process, even on a purely theoretical level, is beyond the scope of this work.[12] However, the issue of monopsonistic exploitation allows one briefly to indicate the economic effects of labor unions. Consider any typical labor market with some kind of supply-of-labor curve; for simplicity, assume that it is positively sloped. If the workers in this market are unionized, the union fundamentally has one power to exert: it can make the effective supply-of-labor curve a horizontal line at any wage level it wishes, at least until the horizontal line reaches the existing supply curve. Thus the marginal expense of input is the same as the supply price of labor over the horizontal stretch of the union supply curve. That is to say, the union can name a wage rate and guarantee the availability of workers at this price.[13]

---

[12]For an excellent theoretical treatment, see Allan M. Cartter, *Theory of Wages and Employment* (Homewood, Ill.: Richard D. Irwin, 1959), pp. 77–133.

[13]This is, of course, an heroic oversimplification, but it is a useful one for analytical purposes.

To introduce this topic, let us suppose the labor market in question is perfectly competitive (large number of purchasers of this type of labor) and unorganized. The situation is depicted in panel A, Figure 15.3.4, where D_L and S_L are the demand for and supply of labor, respectively. The market equilibrium wage rate is $O\overline{W}$, and $O\overline{Q}$ units of labor are employed. Each individual firm (panel B) accordingly employs $O\overline{q}$ units. Next, suppose the labor market is unionized. If the union does not attempt to raise wages, the situation might remain as it is. However, scoring wage increases is the raison d'être of unions. Thus, suppose the bargaining agency sets OW_u as the wage rate; in other words, the union supply-of-labor curve $W_u S_u S_L$ is established. OQ_u units of labor are employed, each firm taking Oq_u units. The result is a rise in wages and a decline in employment. In perfectly competitive input markets, this is *all* unions can do.

This does not necessarily mean a union cannot benefit its members. If the demand for labor is inelastic, an increase in the wage rate will result in an increase in total wages paid to the workers, even though the number of workers employed is less. If the union can somehow equitably divide the proceeds of OQ_u employed workers among the $O\overline{Q}$ potential workers, all will benefit. Such a division is easy to achieve. Suppose $OQ_u = \frac{1}{2} O\overline{Q}$ and that a 40-hour week characterizes the market. Then OQ_u units of labor can be furnished by having $O\overline{Q}$ units work a 20-hour week.

The other side of the coin is worth noting, however. If the demand for labor is elastic, total wage receipts will decline and the union cannot compensate the $Q_u \overline{Q}$ workers who are unemployed because of the increase in wage rates. Thus, in perfectly competitive labor markets, labor unions are not an unmitigated blessing.[14]

In monopsonistic or oligopsonistic markets, however, unions *must* benefit their members if they employ rational policies. Consider the monopsony labor market represented by Figure 15.3.5. If the labor force is not organized, equilibrium is attained at point c, where marginal revenue product equals the marginal expense of input (based on the positively sloped supply of input curve S_L). The equilibrium wage is $O\overline{W}$, and equilibrium employment is $O\overline{L}$. Now suppose the workers establish a union that bargains collectively with the monopsonist.

At one extreme the union may attempt to achieve maximum employment for its members. To this end, it establishes the supply of labor curve $W'aS_L$. The associated marginal expense of input curve accordingly becomes $W'abMEI_L$. Marginal revenue product equals the marginal expense of input at point a; OL_m units of labor are therefore employed at the wage OW'. Consequently, as one alternative, the union can achieve a small increase in wages accompanied by an increase in the number of workers employed. Each unit of labor receives its contribution to the firm's total receipts; the exploitation uniquely attributable to monopsony is eliminated.

---

[14]**Exercise:** Suppose panel A, Figure 15.3.4, represents the market for unskilled labor in the absence of a minimum-wage law. What are the market effects of the establishment of a minimum wage by some government agency? Is there any empirical evidence that the analytical result you obtain is descriptive of the real world?

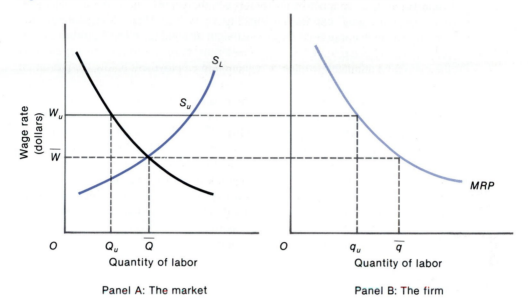

Panel A: The market

Panel B: The firm

Figure 15.3.5 Economic Effects of a Labor Union in a Monopsonistic Labor Market

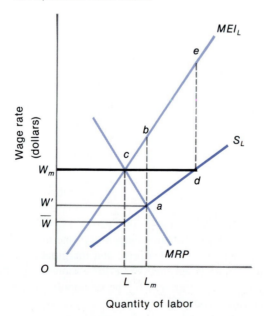

Quantity of labor

At another extreme, suppose the union decides to maintain the initial level of employment $\overline{OL}$. It accordingly establishes the supply curve $W_m dS_L$. The corresponding marginal expense of input curve is $W_m deMEI_L$. Marginal revenue product equals the marginal expense of input at point c; hence equilibrium employment is $\overline{OL}$ and the associated equilibrium wage is OW_m. This wage rate is the maximum attainable without a reduction in employment below the pre-union level. At the wage OW_m, however, the union can achieve a substantial wage increase without affecting employment. Again, the unique portion of monopsonistic exploitation is removed.

We have considered only two extremes. The union can, in fact, select intermediate policies, scoring increases in both employment and the wage rate. The union can harm its members only if the demand for labor is elastic, and it sets the supply-of-labor curve so that the equilibrium wage exceeds OW_m. But even then the unique portion of monopsonistic exploitation would be eliminated. Thus we have a general principle that broadly describes the economic effects of labor unions: labor unions can eliminate the portion of total monopsonistic exploitation that is uniquely attributable to monopsony in the labor market; however, the portion attributable to monopoly can in no way be eliminated by trade union activity.

SYNOPSIS 15.4

- Marginal revenue product of a variable input is marginal revenue multiplied by the marginal physical product of the input. A monopolist purchasing the input in a competitive market at price S_v will purchase the input at that quantity for which $S_v = MRP_v$, where MRP_v is the marginal revenue product of the variable input.

- When several variable inputs are used, the monopolist's demand for any one of them must take into account substitution, output, and profit-maximizing effects (as in Chapter 14), because these effects will usually cause shifts in the marginal revenue product curve of each factor as quantities are adjusted.

- Market demand for a variable factor by a monopolist is analyzed in exactly the same way as in the case of competitive producers (see subsections 14.4.a and 14.4.b of Chapter 14). When the producers are oligopolists or monopolistic competitors, one must allow for the effect of changes in output on market price and marginal revenue. Because marginal revenue is less than price for a monopolist, the market price of a productive service employed by the monopolist will be less than the value of its marginal product.

■ When there is only a single buyer of an input (a monopsonist), that buyer will take into account the effects in changes on the quantity purchased of the input on the price of the input. This effect is measured by the *marginal expense of input,* which is the increase in total cost attributable to the addition of one unit of the variable productive agent. A profit-maximizing monopsonist will employ a variable input to the point where the marginal expense of input equals the input's marginal revenue product. A profit-maximizing monopsonist using several variable inputs will choose that input composition for which the ratio of the marginal product to marginal expense of input is the same for all variable inputs used.

QUESTIONS AND EXERCISES

1. Since monopolists do not pay factors of production the value of their marginal products, how do monopolists retain factors when perfect competitors use the same kind of resources in producing their output?

2. Provide an economic analysis of the U.S. minimum wage law. Do the same thing for a *state* (or county, or city) minimum wage law.

3. The government imposes a ceiling price on commodity A but not on the competing commodity B. *C*, *D*, and *E* are factors used in producing A, while *D*, *E*, and *F* are factors used in producing B. *C* is used in the production of A only and not in the production of any other commodity in the economy. Discuss the effects of this ceiling price on the product and factor markets.

4. "Without collective bargaining, the workers' market disadvantage would enable the owners of other productive agents to appropriate income that would otherwise go to labor." Discuss.

5. Assume that an industrial union's primary purpose is to raise the wages of its members above the competitive level. (*a*) Explain on a theoretical level how this increase might be accomplished. (*b*) What conditions would make the union's job easier?

6. Consider a trade union that is strong enough to prevent nonmembers from working at the trade in question. For simplicity, assume that membership is not affected by the level of returns to members. Finally, assume that there is immigration into the country of unskilled workers. What will be the effect of the immigration on the incomes of the union members? What factors tend to increase income? What factors tend to cause it to decline? Is there a clear balance in favor of either increase or decline?

7. "If a union succeeds in raising wages, it will cause the ratio of the cost of union labor to total cost to rise." Discuss.

SUGGESTED READINGS

Cartter, Allan M. *Theory of Wages and Employment*. Homewood, Ill.: Richard D. Irwin, 1959, pp. 77–133.

Hicks, John R. *The Theory of Wages*. 2nd ed. New York: Macmillan, 1964.

Robinson, Joan. *The Economics of Imperfect Competition*. New York: Macmillan, 1933, pp. 218–28, 281–304.

5 Theory of General Equilibrium and Economic Welfare

Well over 100 years ago, Frederic Bastiat, a noted French economist, wrote about the Paris of his day. Hundreds of thousands of people then lived in Paris, each consuming a wide variety of commodities, especially food products not produced in the city. The survival of the city required the constant influx of goods and services. No single agency planned the daily inflow of commodities; but each day goods did arrive in approximately correct quantities: Paris survived. "Imagination is baffled when it tries to appreciate the vast multiplicity of commodities which must enter tomorrow in order to preserve the inhabitants from falling prey to the convulsions of famine, rebellion, and pillage," Bastiat wrote. "Yet all sleep, and their slumbers are not disturbed for a single minute by the prospect of such a frightful catastrophe."

Paris survived because of the unplanned cooperation of many people, most of whom competed against each other. Not for altruistic motives, to be sure, but for the profit to be gained from selling in the Paris market. Even before the days of Bastiat, Adam Smith had observed the effects of cooperation in production. Smith visited a small pin factory, one doubtless primitive by modern standards. Yet Smith was so struck by the gain in productivity resulting from cooperation and the specialization of labor that he wrote an account now classic in economic literature:

> One man draws out the wire, another straights it, a third cuts it, a fourth points it, a fifth grinds it at the top for receiving the head; to make the head requires two or three distinct operations; to put it on is a peculiar business; to whiten it is another; it is even a trade by itself to put them into paper. . . . I have seen a small factory of this kind where ten men only were employed and where some of them consequently performed two or three distinct operations. But though they were very poor and therefore but indifferently accommodated with the necessary machinery, they could, when they exerted themselves, make among them about twelve pounds of pins in a day. There are in a pound upwards of 4,000 pins of

Figure V.1 Circular Flow of Economic Activity

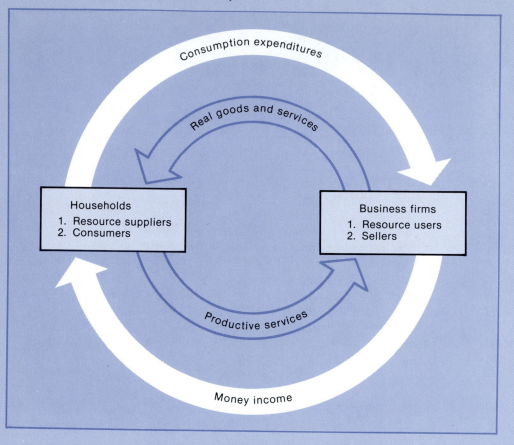

Consumption expenditures

Real goods and services

Households	Business firms
1. Resource suppliers	1. Resource users
2. Consumers	2. Sellers

Productive services

Money income

middling size. Those ten persons, therefore, could make among them upwards of 48,000 pins a day.... But if they had all wrought separately and independently ... they could certainly not each of them make twenty, perhaps not one pin in a day....

Specialization and division of labor make possible a larger output than if each person worked alone and were self-sufficient. But self-sufficiency does guarantee that the consumer gets what he wants, or what he wants most and what is within his ability to achieve. When each person is not self-sufficient, the economy either must be *planned* by some central agency or there must be some mechanism that accomplishes the same goal. Adam Smith chose to call this mechanism the "invisible hand"; in the terminology of today it might better be called a "great computer in the sky." But whatever the terminology, a free enterprise price system generally functions so as to achieve the goals of state planning, usually much more efficiently than planned economies achieve them. Economic welfare under a free enterprise system is the topic of Chapter 17. It is preceded by the analysis of general economic equilibrium in Chapter 16.

To this point, our discussion has focused only upon the economic behavior of single economic agents or of single industries or product groups. But there are millions of economic agents in the economy, and we have not yet seen how the behavior of each is coordinated to achieve a general equilibrium.

Looked at differently, the familiar graph shown in this introduction illustrates the problem. On the one hand, households function both as consumers and resource suppliers. On the other hand, business firms use the resources, organize production, and sell the products of the process. There is a flow of *real* productive services from households to businesses and a return flow of *real* goods and services from business firms to households. If a barter system were feasible in an advanced industrial nation, we should have to go no further. But it is not; money must be introduced.

Rather than trading output for input, business firms pay to households a money income for the productive services supplied. In their roles as consumers, households create a counterflow of consumption expenditures to business firms, exchanging their money income for the real goods and services supplied to them. Thus there is a monetary flow in one direction to offset each real flow in the opposite direction. The problem of general equilibrium analysis is to determine the process by which the various flows balance. ■

16 Theory of General Economic Equilibrium

Many might believe that the best way to deal with a severe drought is to divide up the available water evenly among individuals or households. According to the article in the "Applying the Theory" section, that is exactly how officials in Marin County decided to ration water during the drought in the winter of 1977. Yet, the principles to be developed in this chapter lead directly to the conclusion that a better rationing scheme exists, to the extent that no one will be made worse off than under the Marin County scheme and many will be made better off.

By illustrating how the price system coordinates the activities and decisions of diverse economic agents in producing a general equilibrium, this chapter develops some key principles that will ultimately lead to the conclusion that a competitive price system maximizes social welfare. You will be asked in the "Applying the Theory" section to show precisely why the Marin County scheme of water rationing is not the best (Pareto optimal) one, and why the proposed alternative method (which uses a price system) is superior. ■

How to Ration Water

By Milton Friedman

While the East has been freezing and buried in snow, the Far West has been suffering from drought. In northern California, this is the second straight winter of drought. Water reservoirs are at a record low, and one community after another has begun to ration water.

Although the individual schemes vary, the one adopted in Marin County is fairly representative. Marin County, just north of San Francisco over the Golden Gate Bridge, is one of the wealthiest counties in the United States — the bedroom for many of the top executives in San Francisco. Over the years, it has resisted extensions of water systems in an attempt to limit the inflow of additional residents. In ordinary years, however, water has been ample and charges for water, which is metered to all residents, have been moderate.

The rationing scheme adopted in Marin County assigns to each household a flat maximum number of gallons per day — 37 gallons per person per day for a household of four. Any household that exceeds its ration is subject to a steep fine and, if it persists, to having its supply reduced to a trickle.

There Is a Better Way

This scheme provides no incentive for persons to use less than the permitted maximum (other than saving the usual charge on water used), and it provides no flexibility for special cases requiring more than the maximum. Suppose for example, some family were to use less than its allowance. Would there be any objection to its selling the water saved to someone who wished to use more?

Such voluntary transactions can readily be provided for by a simple modification of the Marin scheme. Let the water authorities set a supplemental price per gallon of water; let them charge this price for all gallons used in excess of the present limit; and let them pay this price to families using less than their limit. If the price is set so that the amount some families save is equal to the excess amount other families use, total water use would remain the same; the revenues to water authorities would be the same; and every separate family would be better off — those saving water, because their actions reveal that they prefer the money to the water;

(continued on page 488)

(continued from page 487) those using extra water, because their actions reveal the reverse.

This alternative plan seems clearly preferable to the plan actually adopted. It is certainly simple enough to have occurred to many of the able people who inhabit Marin. Why, then, has it not been adopted—and is not likely to be? That seems to me to be the most interesting question raised by the Marin experience.

Why It Won't Be Tried

One possible answer is the difficulty of determining an appropriate price—given that the emergency is expected to be brief. But this seems highly implausible. There are dozens of market-research experts in Marin. In any event, water can be bought and trucked in, in tank cars, at a well-defined market price, which surely should give an upper limit to the supplemental price.

A more plausible answer is the general aversion to using a price system in any form, for any purpose—even by the executives in Marin who owe their affluence to the effective operation of a price system. They, too, have become corrupted by the collectivist sentiment of our time, which reveals by its actions that it prefers orders by bureaucrats to voluntary exchanges by free individuals.

A more appealing variant of this explanation is that the Marin scheme reflects a feeling of membership in a family, induced by a common shock. Would a mother permit one of her children to sell the food she provides him to a sibling? Similarly, it is OK to truck in water from outside the community, but it is morally wrong for some of "us" to be permitted to "bribe" others of "us" to give up some of their assigned water. There is real psychological satisfaction in a community effort, and in "suffering" jointly—satisfaction that is not diminished by a level of water use that is affluent compared to the amount available to the bulk of the world's population.

If none of these explanations seems to you adequate to explain why Marin County uses so rigid and unsatisfactory a method of rationing water, when a preferable method is readily available, I share your puzzlement. But community masochism aside, can you offer a better one?

Questions

1. Explain why the plan adopted for the allocation of water in Marin County during the drought is not "Pareto Optimal." Illustrate your answer, using a diagram similar to Figure 16.2.3 (General Equilibrium of Exchange).
2. Explain how Friedman's proposal makes no one worse off and some better off. Illustrate your answer, using a diagram similar to Figure 16.2.4 (Competitive Equilibrium).

Solutions

1. The plan adopted in Marin County assigns each household a flat maximum number of gallons per day — 37 gallons per person for a household of four. (Any household that exceeds its ration is subject to a steep fine.) Since each household is basically restricted to a given amount of water there is no guarantee of fulfilling the condition that "the MRS of different consumers must be equal" under this allocation.

   We know that if consumers may freely exchange water for other goods they will reach an equilibrium where each consumer's MRS of water for all other goods (*aog*) will equal the ratio of the relative prices of these two goods, e.g., *P water /P aog*. As long as all individuals face the same prices for these two goods, all must have the same MRS in equilibrium (even though they may have different tastes for water) because they will buy varying quantities so as to equate their MRS of water for all other goods equal to the price ratio. Under the Marin County scheme, however, they are not allowed to buy or sell water, so that if households have different tastes they will have differing MRSs, given their ration (endowment) of water.

   In terms of Figure 16.2.3, take two households in Marin County, Oa and Ob, and have them consuming two goods, water (X) and all other goods

(Y). The Marin County scheme places the households in a position like point *D*, but with initial endowment *Xa* equal to initial endowment *Xb* (since the allocation is the same for all households). At point *D* (the initial allocation) the MRS of Oa exceeds the MRS of Ob, so we must not be on the contract curve, and we are not at a Pareto optimal organization. Both households can reach a higher level of utility through exchange of X and Y at any rate between their respective MRSs.

2. Friedman suggests that the Marin authorities should basically play the role of the "auctioneer" in section 16.2.c. They could set a supplemental price per gallon of water, charge this price for all gallons used in excess of the present limit, and pay this price per gallon to all households using less than their limit. (Households are free to consume as much or as little water as they want at the announced supplemental price, and the announced price is to be set such that the amount some families save is equal to the excess amount other families use, so that total water use remains the same.)

   As Friedman indicates, every separate family must be better off — those saving water, because their actions reveal that they prefer the money (*aog*) to the water; those using extra water, because

(continued on page 490)

APPLYING THE THEORY

(continued from page 489)
their actions reveal their opposite choice.

In terms of Figure 16.2.4, Friedman's solution allows a movement from initial allocation (point D), to a point on the contract curve, T. The authorities announce a price of water resulting in price line $R_3 R_3'$. Given this announced price of supplemental water, and their initial endowment at point D, household Oa buys the exact amount of water that household Ob wants to sell, and they end up at point T in the diagram. Both have reached a higher level of utility,

and at T both purchase quantities of both goods such that their MRSs equal the ratio of the price of water to the price of all other goods. Thus, at T it is impossible for household Oa to reach a higher indifference curve without household Ob reaching a lower indifference curve, and vice versa. In short, the allocation at T represents a Pareto optimal organization and the MRS of household Oa equals the MRS of household Ob.

Source: *Newsweek,* March 21, 1977. © Newsweek. Reprinted by permission.

INTRODUCTION
16.1

According to the principle of maximization adhered to throughout the book, each economic agent attains an equilibrium position when *something* is maximized. A consumer maximizes satisfaction subject to a budget constraint; an entrepreneur maximizes profit, possibly subject to the constraint imposed by the production function; workers may determine their labor supply curves by maximizing satisfaction derived from leisure, subject to given wage rates. In terms of an old cliché, we have studied the trees fairly intensely but we have not yet seen the forest.

The problem of forests arises, however. Millions of economic agents pursue their own goals and strive for their own equilibrium without particular regard for others. The problem is to determine whether the more or less independent behavior of economic agents is consistent with each agent's attaining equilibrium. All economic agents, whether consumer, producer, or resource supplier, are *inter-*

dependent; will *independent* action by each lead to a position in which equilibrium is achieved by all? This is the problem of general (static or stationary) economic equilibrium.

Quesnay's "Tableau Économique"
16.1.a

At this point a digression to history may be useful. Perhaps the earliest notion of stationary general equilibrium is in the work of a group of French economists called the "physiocrats." Foremost among them was an economist named Quesnay who, as early as 1758, presented a picture of general equilibrium by means of his "Tableau économique." [1] Quesnay divided the economic agents of a society into three classes: the productive or agricultural class, the proprietary class, and the nonproductive class. He then suggested that the riches of a nation must be distributed among the three classes so as to attain a stationary (or flowing) equilibrium.

Quesnay's concept may be explained by an example taken from his book. Suppose there is a country with 130 million acres of land and 30 million people. The land properly tilled will produce 4 million units of food and 1 million units of raw material. Quesnay suggested that the "riches" must be distributed in the following manner. The productive class will retain 2 million units of food, which comprise the "avances annuelles" to sustain it during the next year. The productive class will pay 2 million units of food to the proprietary class as rent for the land, and trade the 1 million units of raw material to the nonproductive class (manufacturers) for 2 million units of manufactured goods. The proprietary class will retain 1 million units of food and subsistence and trade 1 million units to the nonproductive class for manufactured goods. Finally, the nonproductive class receives 1 million units of raw material from the productive class, transforms it into 3 million units of manufactured products, and exchanges 2 million units for 1 million units of raw materials from the productive class and 1 million units of food from the proprietary class.

Now we are back where we started; the system can continue to function in the same way year after year. It is a very simple model; perhaps it may seem trivial. Yet it represents a beginning point for general equilibrium theory. To quote Fossati:

> It is against a background like this, which in essence is the idea of
> the stationary state, that the concept of the equilibrium of the
> economic system has been defined. . . . The stationary state is one
> in which every year the same processes are repeated, and the same
> distribution of goods takes place through the same channels. The

---

[1]F. Quesnay, *Tableau économique et maximes générales du gouvernement économique* (Paris, 1758). For a later contribution, see J. Turgot, *Reflections sur la formation et la distribution des richesses* (Paris, 1776).

stationary state of the "Tableau économique" is a model showing the conditions required for certain processes to function steadily and maintain each other in being on an unchanging scale indefinitely, like fountain-jets ever in movement yet always rising to the same height. It may not seem to offer a great contribution to the analysis of equilibrium, yet in view of the time of its formulation, it is a landmark in our science.[2]

Walras, Pareto, and Leontief
16.1.b

The theory of general equilibrium was developed much more thoroughly by the "Lausanne School," especially by Leon Walras and Vilfredo Pareto.[3] Concerned as it is with the individual equilibrium of millions of economic agents and the overall equilibrium of the system, the theory of general economic equilibrium has always been essentially mathematical in nature. In the 20th century, major efforts toward empirical quantification of general economic equilibrium have been made by Leontief and others through the use of "input-output" analysis.[4]

A Simple Two-Person Economy
16.1.c

To get a handle on the concept of general economic equilibrium we will examine a variety of relatively simple cases. The concepts and propositions that hold in these simple cases also apply to more complex economies albeit with a good deal of additional mathematical notation.

Consider an economy consisting of two individuals, say two farmers. Each farmer owns a fixed amount of land which can be used to produce a homogeneous output. The output of each farm depends on the amount of labor put to work on the farm. We will think of each farmer in two separate roles. On the one hand each farmer is an entrepreneur who hires labor to work on the farm. The farmer pays labor the market wage, which is denominated in terms of the output of the farm, and keeps the remaining output as a rent on the farm land. On the other hand each farmer can be viewed as a household which consumes farm output and supplies labor. The rental income earned by the farmer as entrepreneur is part of the income the farmer spends as a consumer. In subsection 16.1.d, we examine

---

[2]Eraldo Fossati, *The Theory of General Static Equilibrium* (Oxford: Basil Blackwell, 1957), pp. 37–38.

[3]Leon Walras, *Elements d'économie politique pure* (Lausanne: F. Rouge, 1874); for translation, see Suggested Readings at end of chapter. Vilfredo Pareto, *Cours d'économie politique* (Lausanne: F. Rouge, 1897).

[4]W. W. Leontief, *The Structure of the American Economy, 1919–1939* (New York: Oxford University Press, 1951).

the farmers in their role as entrepreneurs making output decisions and deciding how much labor to hire. In subsection 16.1.e, we examine the farmers in their role as householders deciding how much to consume and how much labor to supply. Finally, we bring both sides of the market together to show how a general equilibrium is achieved — as in the diagram showing the circular flow of economic activity in the introduction to this part.

The Farmer as Entrepreneur
16.1.d

The explanation of the farmer as an entrepreneur is based on the following assumptions:

$e1$: Output of the farm is an increasing function of the amount of labor used on the farm, and since the amount of land is assumed to be constant, the law of diminishing returns applies to labor. This is the situation described in Chapter 6.

$e2$: Each farmer acts as a price taker both with respect to sales of output and the hiring of labor. We use the output of the farm as *numéraire,* or unit of account, and hence set its price equal to one. The wage rate is given by w. Instead of saying that an hour of labor costs $20, we say that an hour of labor costs w units of good. Obviously, one unit of food costs one unit of food, so its price is 1.[5]

$e3$: Each farmer, when acting as entrepreneur, chooses output and employment, given the wage rate, to maximize the rental income of the land. The rental income will be the amount of output left after wages have been paid.

To see how the farmer behaves in the role of entrepreneur, given these assumptions, we consider the case of the first farmer, called Farmer 1. Farmer 1 has a production function that relates labor input to farm output as shown by the curved line $Q_1 = f_1(L_1)$ in Figure 16.1.1. Q_1 refers to the output of Farmer 1, L_1 is the amount of labor used by Farmer 1, and $f_1(L_1)$ is the production function of the first farmer. f_1 is written as a function of labor only because land is assumed fixed. The function $f_1(L_1)$ is concave in accordance with the assumption $e1$ that the law of diminishing returns applies to labor.

Now suppose the wage rate is w. The total wage bill for Farmer 1 will be wL_1, depending on the amount of labor he employs. This is shown in Figure 16.1.1 as a straight line with slope w. At any given use of labor on the farm (along the horizontal axis) output is given by the line $Q_1 = f_1(L_1)$, total wages are the corresponding point on the line wL_1 and the difference between $f_1(L_1)$ and wL_1 is

---

[5]The reader will recall from earlier discussion that we are dealing with *relative* prices in this book. Thus, if p is the output price and w the wage rate, the equilibrium determines only w/p (or p/w), not p and w separately. Thus, we are justified in setting $p = 1$ for expositional purposes. Note that w is the *real* wage when this convention is used.

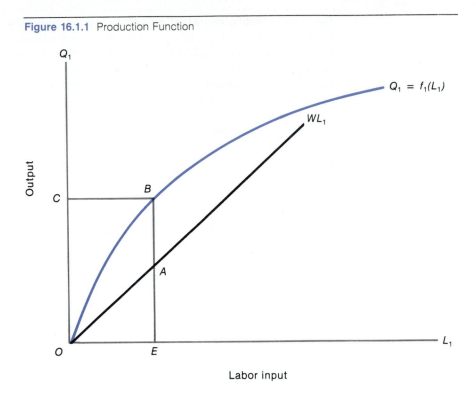

Figure 16.1.1 Production Function

Labor input

the output left for the entrepreneur after wages have been paid (that is, the rent on the land). We know from Chapter 14 that rent on land will be maximized when the value of the marginal product of labor equals the wage rate. Since the price of output is set at 1, this means that the distance between $f_1(L_1)$ and wL_1 is maximized when L_1 is chosen, so that the slope of $f_1(L_1)$ is equal to the wage rate.[6] In Figure 16.1.1, when the wage rate is w the farmer hires OE units of labor, produces EB ($= OC$) units of output, pays EA in wages and keeps BA ($= EB - EA$) as rent on land. Since the slope of $f_1(L_1)$ is decreasing as more labor is used, it follows that to maximize rental income the farmer will hire more labor as the wage rate decreases and less labor as the wage rate increases. Hence, we get a demand for labor function that is inversely related to the wage rate as shown by the line L_{D_1} in Figure 16.1.2.

By similar arguments we can derive Farmer 2's demand for labor. This is shown by L_{D_2} in Figure 16.1.2. The total demand for labor at any given wage rate

---

[6]The rent on the land is the residual $f_1(L_1) - wL_1$, and this is maximized when $f'_1(L_1) = w$. The slope, $f'_1(L_1)$, is the marginal product of labor.

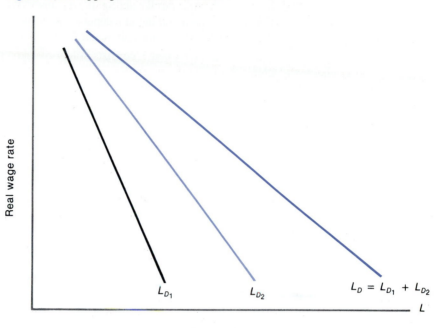

Figure 16.1.2 Aggregate Demand for Labor

Real wage rate

L_{D_1} L_{D_2} $L_D = L_{D_1} + L_{D_2}$

L

Labor demanded

is the sum of the demands for labor by Farmer 1 and Farmer 2. In Figure 16.1.2, this is shown by the line L_D, which is the horizontal sum of L_{D_1} and L_{D_2} at each wage rate.

The Farmer as Consumer–Laborer
16.1.e

The explanation of the farmer as a consumer–laborer is based on the following assumptions.

$c1$: Farmer 1 chooses consumption and the amount of labor supplied so as to maximize a utility function $U_1(Q_{D_1}, L_{S_1})$. Q_{D_1} is the amount of consumption of Farmer 1 and L_{S_1} is the amount of labor supplied by Farmer 1. The utility function U_1 is increasing in Q_{D_1} and decreasing in L_{S_1}. In other words, the farmer gains utility from more consumption and loses utility from more labor (that is, less leisure). Similarly, Farmer 2 acts to maximize $U_2(Q_{D_2}, L_{S_2})$ where Q_{D_2} is the amount of output demanded and L_{S_2} is the amount of labor supplied by Farmer 2.

$c2$: Rental income obtained by the farmer acting as an entrepreneur is treated as income by the farmer acting as consumer. We have seen in subsection 16.1.d that rental income depends on the wage rate and hence can be denoted by $R_1(w)$ for Farmer 1 and $R_2(w)$ for Farmer 2.[7]

$c3$: The income of Farmer i consists solely of labor income and rental income. Accordingly, when the wage rate is w, the farmer chooses Q_{D_i} and L_{S_i} to maximize utility subject to the budget constraint

$$Q_{D_i} = wL_{S_i} + R_i(w).$$

$c4$: Each farmer can be self-employed or can work for the other farmer. A farmer can be self-employed part of the time and work for the other farmer part of the time.

To see how the farmer acts in his role as consumer–laborer, consider Figure 16.1.3. First, the farmer now has two sources of income. He can use his farm to produce goods and then receive rent on the land. The amount of rent that he receives depends on the wage rate. For example, if the wage rate were w, then there is some rent $R_1(w)$ that is the most that he can receive, given that wage rate is w. This would be obtained when the farmer hired labor such that the distance between line wL_1 and curve $f_1(L_1)$ in Figure 16.1.1 was maximized. That vertical distance is his rent. (Of course, if the wage rate were lower, so that the wage line was flatter, he would hire more labor and end up with more rent).

For the given w, the most rent he can receive is $R_1(w)$. This is his rental income and is plotted as the vertical distance $OR_1(w)$ in Figure 16.1.3. But in addition to that rental income, the farmer has the option of supplying his own labor, either to his own farm or to a neighbor. If he supplies his own labor, he receives w per unit of labor. That means that at zero hours of labor supplied, he only has income of $R_1(w)$, but if he supplies L of labor, his income is $R_1(w) + wL$. That is the equation of the line $R_1(w)$ A in Figure 16.1.3. Any point on that line is obtainable. Note that if the farmer works for a neighbor, he receives an actual payment of wL goods. If he works for himself, he avoids paying other laborers wL and consequently takes home wL more than he would have had he merely rented the land.

The indifference curves from the utility function $U_1(Q_{D_1}, L_{S_1})$ are shown by the curves marked I, II, and III in Figure 16.1.3. These indifference curves are upward sloping because labor is considered a bad (that is, more labor is less leisure, or a reduction in a good).[8] To maximize utility the farmer finds the

---

[7]For Farmer i ($i = 1,2$), let $L_{D_i}^*(w)$ be the amount of labor demanded at wage rate w when the optimal output decision is made. Then, $R_i(w) = Q_{S_i}^* - wL_{D_i}^*(w)$, where $Q_{S_i}^*$ is the rent-maximizing output for wage rate w.

[8]See Question 5 of Chapter 2.

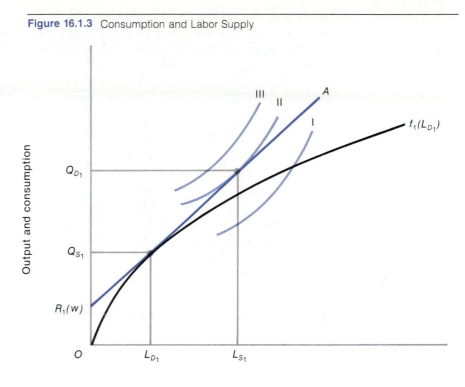

Figure 16.1.3 Consumption and Labor Supply

Labor demanded and supplied

indifference curve which is tangent to the budget line.[9] This tangency occurs at L_{S_1} in Figure 16.1.3. Hence, when the wage rate is w the farmer supplies L_{S_1} units of labor and consumes Q_{D_1} units of output.

Also shown on Figure 16.1.3 is the curve $f_1(L_{D_1})$, i.e., the farmer's production function on his own farm. It is drawn such that it is tangent to the line $R_1(w)$ at labor L_{D_1}. That is not an accident. Recall that the farmer hires labor up to the point that maximizes his rent. Recall also that at that point, the slope of the production function, that is, the marginal product of labor, must equal w. (At any other point, rent can be increased by moving to L_{D_1} of labor.) Since the slope of $R_1(w)$ is w, it must be the case that labor is hired when the slope of the production function is equal to the slope of $R_1(w)$. But a tangency requires not only that slopes are

---

[9]Given w, the farmer's problem is max $U_1(Q_{D_1}, L_{S_1})$, subject to $Q_{D_1} = wL_{S_1} + R_1(w)$. The first-order condition is given by $-(\partial U_1/\partial L_{S_1})/(\partial U_1/\partial Q_{D_1}) = w$, which is the tangency indicated in Figure 16.1.3.

equal, but also that the line and the curve are touching. In order for them to touch, the height of the line at L_{D_1} must equal the height of the production function at L_{D_1}. This means that $R_1(w) + wL_{D_1} = f_1(L_{D_1})$. But that merely says that rent on the land plus wages paid to labor must equal total output. In fact, that was how rent was derived. It was defined as the difference between total output and wages paid or $R_1(w) = f_1(L_{D_1}) - wL_{D_1}$. Thus, the typical farmer produces Q_{D_1} on his farm, hires L_{D_1} of labor, supplies L_{S_1} of labor himself, and consumes Q_{S_1}. As we shall soon see, w must change so that all of these quantities are consistent across the entire economy.

Changing the wage rate has two effects. An increase in the wage rate lowers the rent that the farmer receives on his own land. The more labor costs, the less that the farmer can extract for himself as rentier. This lowers the intercept of $R_1(w)$. It by itself is likely to result in more labor supplied by the farmer since poorer individuals consume less leisure (which is a normal good) and therefore work more hours. At the same time, an increase in wage rate steepens the slope of the line $R_1(w)$ A because at higher wages, the marginal value of working is higher. This, too, usually increases the amount of labor supplied because the price of leisure is higher; the farmer-as-worker gives up more for each hour that he keeps out of the labor market and uses for leisure.

The tangency of an indifference curve with a new, higher wage, budget constraint is likely to lie to the right of the old tangency. This means that at a higher wage rate, the individual supplies more labor. Farmer 1's supply of labor is shown as L_{S_1} in Figure 16.1.4, derived as above. A similar curve is derived for Farmer 2 and the sum is the labor supply of the entire economy, shown as L_S.

The equilibrium wage rate, that is, the wage rate that equates the supply and demand for labor, can be found by combining Figure 16.1.2 and Figure 16.1.4. This is done in Figure 16.1.5. The equilibrium wage rate w^* is where L_S and L_D intersect. At this point Farmer 1 supplies $L_{S_1}^*$ units of labor and demands $L_{D_1}^*$. Farmer 2 demands $L_{D_2}^*$ units of labor and supplies $L_{S_2}^*$. Farmer 1 is a net demander of labor (since $L_{D_1}^* > L_{S_1}^*$) and Farmer 2 is a net supplier of labor (since $L_{D_2}^* < L_{S_2}^*$). Obviously $L_{D_1}^* - L_{S_2}^* = L_{S_1}^* - L_{D_2}^*$.[10]

It remains to show that the product market is in equilibrium when the labor market is in equilibrium. Let w^* be the equilibrium wage. Then we have the following equations:

$$\begin{aligned}
R_1(w^*) &= Q_{S_1}^* - w^*L_{D_1}^* \\
R_2(w^*) &= Q_{S_2}^* - w^*L_{D_2}^* \\
Q_{D_1}^* &= w^*L_{S_1}^* + R_1(w^*) \\
Q_{D_2}^* &= w^*L_{S_2}^* + R_2(w^*)
\end{aligned} \tag{16.1.1}$$

---

[10] $L_S^* = L_{S_1}^* + L_{S_2}^*$ and $L_D^* = L_{D_1}^* + L_{D_2}^*$. Since in equilibrium $L_S^* = L_D^*$, it follows that $L_{D_1}^* - L_{S_2}^* = L_{S_1}^* - L_{D_2}^*$.

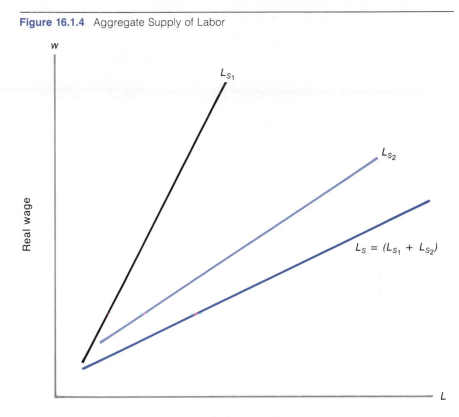

Figure 16.1.4 Aggregate Supply of Labor

w

Real wage

L_{S_1}

L_{S_2}

$L_S = (L_{S_1} + L_{S_2})$

L

Labor supply

where the asterisks indicate the values of the variables at w^*. Solving the last two equations for $R_1(w^*)$ and $R_2(w^*)$ and substituting in the first two equations

$$
\begin{aligned}
Q_{D_1}^* - w^*L_{S_1}^* &= Q_{S_1}^* - w^*L_{D_1}^* \\
Q_{D_2}^* - w^*L_{S_2}^* &= Q_{S_2}^* - w^*L_{D_2}^*.
\end{aligned}
\tag{16.1.2}
$$

Adding these two equations

$$
Q_{D_1}^* + Q_{D_2}^* - w^*(L_{S_1}^* + L_{S_2}^*) = Q_{S_1}^* + Q_{S_2}^* - w^*(L_{D_1}^* + L_{D_2}^*).
\tag{16.1.3}
$$

We know that w^* is such that the labor market is in equilibrium so $L_{S_1}^* + L_{S_2}^* = L_{D_1}^* + L_{D_2}^*$. Hence, (equation 16.1.3) becomes

$$
Q_{D_1}^* + Q_{D_2}^* = Q_{S_1}^* + Q_{S_2}^*
$$

Figure 16.1.5 Equilibrium in the Labor Market

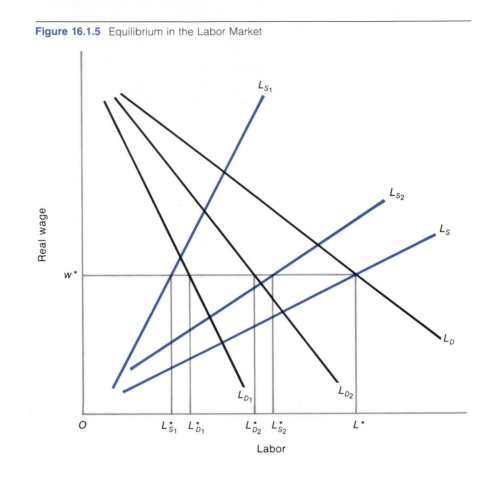

which says that aggregate demand of output equals aggregate supply of output. Thus, the product market is in equilibrium when the labor market is in equilibrium.

This result is known as **Walras's Law.** That law states that in an economy with n markets, equilibrium in $n - 1$ of those markets assures that equilibrium must hold in the nth market also.[11]

This simple model illustrates how the price system coordinates the activities and decisions of diverse economic agents in producing a general equilibrium. The entrepreneur acting to maximize profits (in this example, the rent on land) ends up making a set of decisions that mesh perfectly with the consumption–labor

---

[11]Walras, *Elements d'économie politique pure.*

choices of the household. The same kind of coordination of demand and supply occurs in more complex economies through virtually the same kind of price mechanisms. That the price system can achieve such coordination of the mind-boggling assortment of markets that we see in real world economies is truly astonishing. It is even more interesting, as we shall see in Chapter 17, that a competitive price system also maximizes social welfare.

GENERAL EQUILIBRIUM OF EXCHANGE
16.2

The model of section 16.1 is useful in showing how general equilibrium is achieved in an economy with one consumption good. In this section we develop a method for the analysis of equilibrium when there are two or more goods in the economy. In the next section we will see how the same apparatus can be applied in the analysis of allocating productive factors to the production of two or more goods.

Edgeworth Box Diagram
16.2.a

The Edgeworth box diagram is a graphical technique for illustrating the inter-action between two economic activities when their inputs are fixed in quantity. It is thus an ideal instrument for analyzing general equilibrium and economic welfare.

(Two basic Edgeworth box diagrams are illustrated in Figure 16.2.2. Panel a shows the construction for a consumption problem whose inputs are types of, say food; Panel b refers to production activities whose inputs are factors of production.)

First consider Panel A in 16.2.1. There are two consumption goods, X and Y; these goods are available in absolutely fixed amounts. In addition, there are only two individuals in the society, A and B; they initially possess an endowment of X and Y, but the endowment ratio is not the one either would choose if given the opportunity to specify it. This general equilibrium problem is graphically illus-trated by constructing an *origin* for A, labeled O_A, and plotting quantities of the two goods along the abscissa and ordinate. Thus from the origin O_A, the quantity X held by A (X_A) is plotted on the abscissa and the quantity of Y (Y_A) on the ordinate. A similar graph for individual B, with origin O_B, may be constructed beside the graph for individual A. These two basic graphs are illustrated in Panel a, Figure 16.2.1.

Next, rotate B's graph 180°, so that it appears to be "upside down" (Shown in Panel b of Figure 16.2.1). The Edgeworth box diagram is formed by bringing the two graphs in Panel b together. There could conceivably be a problem involving

Figure 16.2.1 Constructing the Edgeworth Box Diagram for a Consumption Problem

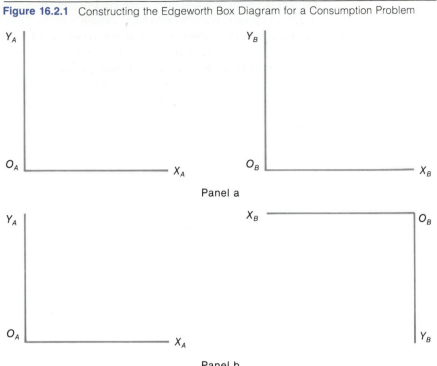

Panel a

Panel b

Figure 16.2.2 Edgeworth Box Diagrams

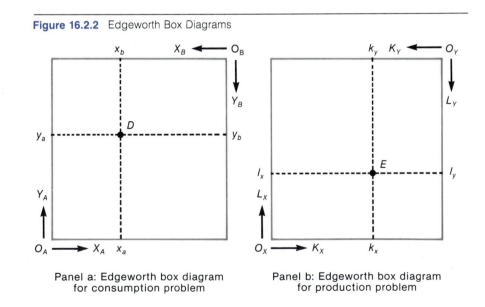

Panel a: Edgeworth box diagram
for consumption problem

Panel b: Edgeworth box diagram
for production problem

the lengths of the axes; if the X axes meshed, the Y axes might not. The problem does not in fact exist, however, because $X_A + X_B$ must equal X, and $Y_A + Y_B$ must equal Y. The length of each axis measures the fixed quantity of the good it represents; when the two "halves" in Panel b are brought together, both axes mesh. One thus obtains Panel a, Figure 16.2.2.

The point D in Panel a of Figure 16.2.2 indicates the initial endowment of X and Y possessed by A and B. A begins with $O_A x_A$ units of X and $O_A y_A$ units of Y. Since the aggregates are fixed, B must originally hold $O_B x_B = X - O_A x_A$ units of X and $O_B y_B = Y - O_A y_A$ units of Y.

In a similar fashion, not illustrated in detail, one may construct an Edgeworth diagram for a production problem. The finished product is shown in Panel b, Figure 16.2.2. Two goods, X and Y, are produced by means of two inputs, K and L. The two inputs are fixed in aggregate quantity. The origin of coordinates for good X is O_X, for good Y is O_Y. The inputs of K and L used in producing X and Y are plotted along the axes. Accordingly, any point in the box represents a particular allocation of the two inputs between the two production processes. At point E, for example, $O_X k_X$ units of K and $O_X l_X$ units of L are used in producing X. As a consequence, $O_Y k_Y = K - O_X k_X$ units of K and $O_Y l_Y = L - O_X l_X$ units of L are allocated to the production of Y.

Equilibrium of Exchange
16.2.b

Consider an economy in which exchange of initial endowments takes place. For the moment, production is ignored. If you like, you may think of the problem in the following context. There exists a small country with two inhabitants, A and B, each of whom owns one half the land area. These individuals truly resemble the lilies of the field, for they neither toil nor do they reap. They merely gather and exchange manna which, providentially enough, falls nightly on their land. Manna of two different types, X and Y, falls nightly; but the two types do not fall uniformly. There is a relatively heavy concentration of Y manna on A's property and, consequently, a relatively heavy concentration of X manna on B's land.

The problem of exchange is analyzed by means of the Edgeworth box diagram in Figure 16.2.3. To the basic box diagram, whose dimensions represent the nightly precipitation of manna, we add indifference curves for A and B. For example, the curve I_A shows combinations of X and Y that yield A the same level of satisfaction. In ordinary fashion, II_A represents a greater level of satisfaction than I_A; III_A than II_A; and so on. Quite generally, A's well-being is enhanced by moving toward the B origin. Because B's situation is depicted upside down, the highest indifference curve in the diagram, I_B, yields B lower utility than the curve below it, II_B. Although what A gains in X is necessarily lost by B, and what B gains in Y is necessarily lost by A, trade can make both parties better off.

Suppose the initial endowment (the nightly fall of manna) is point D; A has $O_A x_A$ units of X and $O_A y_A$ units of Y. Similarly, B has $O_B x_B$ and $O_B y_B$ units of

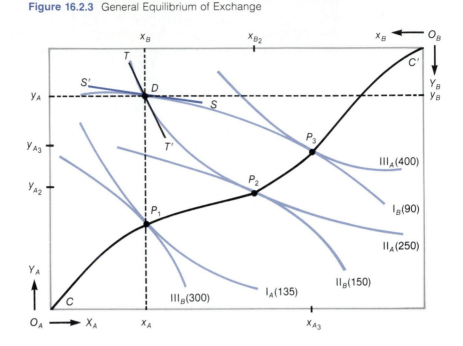

Figure 16.2.3 General Equilibrium of Exchange

X and Y, respectively. The initial endowment places A on indifference curve II_A and B on curve I_B. At point D, A's marginal rate of substitution of X for Y, given by the slope of TT', is relatively high; A would be willing to sacrifice, say, three units of Y in order to obtain one additional unit of X. At the same point, B has a relatively low marginal rate of substitution, as shown by the slope of SS'. Or turning it around, B has a relatively high marginal rate of substitution of Y for X. B may, for example, be willing to forgo four units of X to obtain one unit of Y.

Situations such as this will always lead to exchange if the parties concerned are free to trade. From the point D, A will trade some Y to B, receiving X in exchange. The exact bargain reached by the two traders cannot be determined. If B is the more skillful negotiator, B may induce A to move along II_A to the point P_2. All the benefit of trade goes to B, who jumps from I_B to II_B. Just opposite, A might steer the bargain to point P_3, thereby increasing satisfaction from II_A to III_A, B's real income remaining I_B. Starting from point D, the ultimate exchange is very likely to lead to some point between P_2 and P_3; but the skill of the bargainers and their initial endowments determine the exact location.

One important thing can be said, however. Exchange will take place until the marginal rate of substitution of X for Y is the same for both traders. If the two marginal rates are different, one or both parties can benefit from exchange; neither party need lose. In other words, the exchange equilibrium can occur only at points such as P_1, P_2, and P_3 in Figure 16.2.3. The locus CC', called the **contract curve**, is a curve joining all points of tangency between one of A's indifference curves and one of B's. It is thus the locus along which the marginal rates of substitution are equal for both traders. We accordingly have the following:

Proposition: The general equilibrium of exchange occurs at a point where the marginal rate of substitution between every pair of goods is the same for all parties consuming both goods. The exchange equilibrium is not unique; it may occur at any point along the contract curve (for multiple traders, it is more properly called the **contract hypersurface**).

The contract curve is an optimal locus in the sense that if the trading parties are located at some point not on the curve, one or both can benefit, and neither suffer a loss, by exchanging goods so as to move to a point on the curve. To be sure, each trader views some points not on the curve as preferable to some points on the curve. But for any point not on the curve, one or more attainable points on the curve are preferable.

The chief characteristic of each point on the contract curve is that a movement away from the point must benefit one party and harm the other. Every organization that leads to a point on the contract curve is said to be a **Pareto-optimal organization**.

Pareto Optimality: A Pareto-optimal organization is one in which any change that makes some people better off makes some others worse off. That is, an organization is Pareto optimal if, and only if, there is no change that will make one or more better off without making anyone worse off. Thus, every point on the contract curve is Pareto optimal, and the contract curve is a locus of Pareto optimality.

Competitive Equilibrium in an Exchange Economy 16.2.c

Recall Figure 16.2.3. There, any point on the contract curve between indifference curves I_B and II_A was fair game. We said that the actual allocation depended upon the bargaining strength of A and B, but conjectured the allocation should be one that is on the contract curve. The reason was that a move from a point off the contract to one on it can make both parties better off.

This statement is not quite correct because individuals may, in their attempt to outmaneuver their opponent, take actions that prevent them from reaching a point on the contract curve. For example, suppose that A and B start at point D in Figure 16.2.3. Consider an extreme situation, where they agree that one and only one take-it-or-leave-it offer will be made by each, A and B. A, in his greedy attempt to end up at point P_3, says that he will give up as much as $O_A y_A - O_A y_{A_3}$ of Y, but he must be given at least $O_A x_{A_3}$ in return. He will not trade any Y unless he gets at least $(O_A x_{A_3} - O_A x_A)/(O_A y_A - O_A y_{A_3})$ per unit of Y. Conversely, B says that he will give up at most $O_B x_B - O_B x_{B_2}$ of X, but he will pay no more than $(O_B x_B - O_B x_{B_2})/(O_A y_A - O_A y_{A_2})$ in X per unit of Y that he receives. Since $O_A x_{A_3} - O_A x_A > O_B x_B - O_B x_{B_2}$ and since $O_A y_A - O_A y_{A_3} < O_A y_A - O_A y_{A_2}$, A is demanding more X per unit of Y than B is willing to give. Thus, no trade takes place because each is trying to outbargain the other. And so the economy starts and ends at D.[12]

There is a way out of this situation that generally leads to a point that is on the contract curve. That is to think of an impersonal "auctioneer" who calls out prices and asks both A and B how much they would like to trade at the various prices. This is illustrated by Figure 16.2.4. That figure duplicates the situation of Figure 16.2.3, but adds the dimenson of prices. Suppose that the auctioneer announced that the price line was $R_1 R_1'$. A would then like to trade to leave himself at a tangency, or at point Q. B would like to trade to the tangency at point V. But this means that A wants to buy more X at this price than B is willing to supply. Similarly, B wants to buy less Y than A is willing to supply at these prices. Since demand for X exceeds supply and since supply of Y exceeds demand, the price of X should rise and the price of Y should fall. Suppose, then, that the auctioneer announced prices consistent with price line $R_2 R_2'$. A would want to trade to S and B would want to trade to U. This means that A would want to buy less X than B wanted to supply and that B would want to buy more Y than A was willing to supply. We have gone too far. But consider $R_3 R_3'$. With that price line, both A and B want to move to point T. At T, A wants to buy exactly the amount of X that B wants to sell. Moreover, B wants to buy exactly the amount of Y that A wants to sell. A **competitive equilibrium** has been reached.

Definition: A competitive equilibrium is a set of prices and associated quantities such that, given the individual's endowments, voluntary trade results in supply equal to demand in each and every market.

A competitive equilibrium always exists, given the situation as depicted by the endowment at D and corresponding indifference curves. It is possible, however, that there are more than one competitive equilibria. For most of our purposes, this is unimportant.

Note that the competitive equilibrium must be on the contract curve. This follows from the fact that at the competitive equilibrium, indifference curves are tangent to the same price line at the same point. This implies that the indifference curves are tangent to each other, which defines a point on the contract curve.

---

[12]Whether the one-time take-it-or-leave-it offer is enforceable is another matter. In fact, if both A and B know that after the game fails another round will follow, the strategies of each player may be different. Nor is it obvious that the offers described above are the ones that will be made. That depends on players' beliefs about their opponent and on information that each possesses.

Figure 16.2.4 Competitive Equilibrium

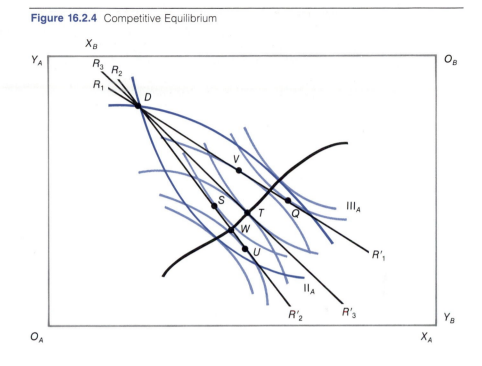

As must be obvious, although the competitive equilibrium is a point on the contract curve, the converse does not hold: Not all points on the contract curve are competitive equilibria. For example, point W in Figure 16.2.4 is on the contract curve, but is not a competitive equilibrium because neither A nor B would voluntarily choose to move to that point.

Deriving the Utility-Possibility Frontier
16.2.d

The contract curve is a Pareto-optimal locus in **commodity space**; it shows all pairs of allocations of X and Y to A and B such that the marginal rate of substitution is equal for both parties. This exchange equilibrium locus can be transformed from commodity space to **utility space**, obtaining what is called the **utility-possibility frontier** relative to the particular endowment aggregate in Figure 16.2.3. The process of derivation is illustrated in Figure 16.2.5.

First consider the point P_1 in Figure 16.2.3. In A's scale of utility measurement, all points on I_A are valued at 135; thus P_1 is associated with a utility value of 135. Similarly, in B's utility scale, all points along III_B have the value 300. Now construct a graph, as in Figure 16.2.5, whose coordinate axes are A's and B's utility scales. The point P_1, with coordinates 135 and 300, can be plotted on this graph. Similarly, all other points along the contract curve in commodity

Figure 16.2.5 Deriving the Utility-Possibility Frontier from the Contract Curve

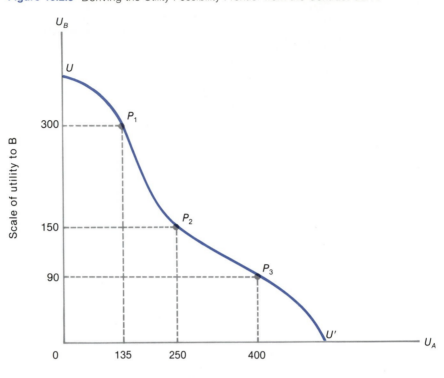

Scale of utility to A

space can be plotted in utility space by noting the pair of utility values associated with each point of tangency. Connect all such points by a curve, labeled UU' in Figure 16.2.5. This curve is the utility-possibility frontier.

Utility-Possibility Frontier: The utility-possibility frontier is the locus showing the maximum level of satisfaction attainable by one trading party for every given level of satisfaction of the other. The curve so generated depends upon the absolute endowment of each commodity and upon the aggregate commodity endowment ratio — that is, upon X, Y, and Y/X.[13]

The Core of the Economy
16.2.e

When there are more than two traders, things get more complicated. For example, suppose there are four traders: two are of type A and two are of type B. Their endowments are given at point E in Figure 16.2.6. The dimensions of the

---

[13]Remember that the utility numbers are purely arbitrary so far as interpersonal utility comparisons are concerned. In particular, 300 for B is not necessarily greater than 135 for A, although to A, 136 is greater than 135.

Part Five   Theory of General Equilibrium and Economic Welfare

Figure 16.2.6 The Core of the Economy

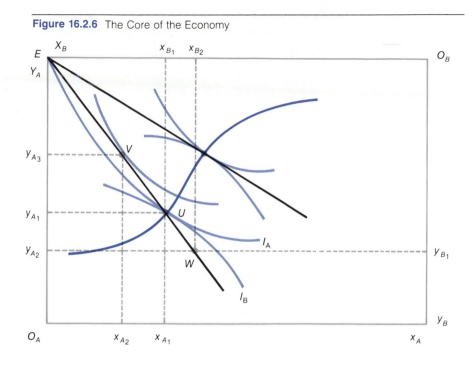

box reflect the endowments to each individual. That is, each A has $O_A y_A$ of Y and zero X and each B has $O_B x_B$ of X and zero Y.

One way to think of the economy is to imagine splitting it up into two A-B pairs. Let A_1 trade with B_1, and A_2 trade with B_2. Then, there are two Edgeworth boxes and the situation is identical to the one already considered. But unfortunately, things are not that easy. The ability of A_2 to trade with B_1 renders certain allocations on the contract curve "blockable." A point is blockable if some coalition of traders can get together and, by trading with one another, make everyone in that coalition better off than they were at the original point.

Consider, for example, the point U in Figure 16.2.6. Suppose that each pair traded to point U. That point is blockable because there is a coalition of two As and one B that can, by trading among themselves, make all three better off. To see this, suppose that the two As get together and each offers to give up $O_A y_A - O_A y_{A_3}$ in return for $O_A x_{A_2}$. This would leave each A at point V. Now B would have received $2(O_A y_A - O_A y_{A_3}) = O_B y_{B_1}$. In return, he would have given up $O_B x_B - O_B x_{B_2}$, which leaves him at point W. The X is split between the two As so that each receives $O_A x_{A_2} = (O_B x_B - O_A x_{B_2})/2$ so that the trade is complete. B gets twice the Y that any one A gave up and A gets half of the X that B gave up. This makes all three parties better off. The As are better off because V is on a higher indifference curve than I_A. Thus, point U is blockable.

What of the second B? He has no one to trade with and necessarily ends up at point E, worse off than he would have been at U. This may lead him to offer better terms to the two As, but that is irrelevant. The point to remember is that the allocation cannot be sustained because better terms can be offered to all members of some coalition. *A point that is blockable is said to be outside the "core" of the economy.*

Definition: The core of the economy consists of those points on the contract curve that cannot be blocked. Thus, the core refers to allocations that cannot be improved upon by a reorganization of resources among members of some coalition.

It is always true that the *competitive equilibrium, if one exists, is in the core of the economy.* (The student should show this by attempting to block point T, the competitive equilibrium in Figure 16.2.4.) That point is never blockable. But not all situations have a competitive equilibrium. For example, consider a game where \$1 is to be given to any team of two persons who can agree on a way to allocate it. Suppose that there are three individuals: A, B, and C. A and B get together and opt to split the dollar evenly. But now C gets nothing. In response, he offers to give A \$.51 and take \$.49. A prefers this, but now B is left out. B then offers \$.50 to C, which dominates, as far as C is concerned. This goes on forever, since the left-out party can always block any conjectured equilibrium.

A more important proposition that comes out of the theory of the core is that as the number of traders increases, the core shrinks to the competitive equilibrium. This means that all points on the contract curve, other than point T, can be ruled out if there is a large number of traders. This is an important result because it implies that in modern economies, most situations can be analyzed with the simple tools of supply and demand since they are designed to determine the competitive equilibrium. Bargaining problems, and other points on the contract curve, can generally be neglected. Of course, in situations where there are a small number of traders, bargaining may be at the heart of the problem and neglecting it may lead to inaccurate predictions.

GENERAL EQUILIBRIUM OF PRODUCTION AND EXCHANGE
16.3

In the model of section 16.2, production does not occur; consumers simply exchange existing stocks or endowments of commodities. We shall now expand by adding a production side to the model. There are still only two consuming units in the society, A and B; there are also only two *producible* commodities, X and Y. But now they must be produced by means of two inputs, K and L. The production functions for X and Y are assumed to be given, and there are fixed, nonaugmentable quantities of the inputs K and L. In other words, the initial endowments in the present model are the fixed input supplies rather than fixed quantities of the two consumption goods.[14]

---

[14]Note that in contrast to section 16.1 we do not assume a variable labor supply. Both K and L are assumed fixed for purposes of this discussion. By using more mathematics we can account for variable supplies as well as variable outputs.

General Equilibrium of Production
16.3.a

The analysis of the general equilibrium of production is precisely the same as that of the general equilibrium of exchange. The only difference is terminology (economic jargon). The fixed endowments of inputs K and L determine the dimensions of the Edgeworth box diagram in Figure 16.3.1. Next, the given and unchanging production functions for goods X and Y enable us to construct the isoquant maps for each, illustrated by curves such as II_X and III_Y.

Suppose inputs are originally allocated between production of X and Y so that $O_X k_X$ units of K and $O_X l_X$ units of L are used in making X; the remainder, $O_Y k_Y$ and $O_Y l_Y$ units of K and L, respectively, is used to produce Y. This allocation is represented by point D in the Edgeworth box — the point at which II_X intersects II_Y. At the allocation D, the marginal rate of technical substitution of K for L in producing X, given by the slope of SS', is relatively low. The marginal product of K in producing X is high relative to the marginal product of L. The II_X level of production can be maintained by substituting a relatively small amount of K for a relatively larger amount of L. The opposite situation prevails in Y production, as shown by the slope of TT'. The marginal rate of technical substitution of K for L in producing Y is relatively high; thus a comparatively large amount of K can be released by substituting a relatively small amount of L while maintaining the II_Y level of output.

Suppose the producer of X at point D can substitute one unit of K and thereby release two units of L. The producer of Y, by employing the two units of L released from X production, can maintain output and release, let us suppose, four units of K. Thus, from a point such as D, input substitution by producers will enable the society to move to P_2, P_3, or any point in between. At P_2, the output of X is the same as at D but the output of Y has been increased to the III_Y level. If the movement is to P_3, the output of X increases with no change in the volume of Y production.

The foregoing discussion establishes a pervasive principle. Whenever the marginal rate of technical substitution between two inputs is different for two producers, one or both outputs may be increased, and neither decreased, by making the appropriate input substitutions. In the example in Figure 16.3.1, the X producer would substitute K for L, decreasing the marginal product of K, increasing that of L, and thereby raising the marginal rate of technical substitution. The producer of Y, on the other hand, could substitute L for K, with the opposite results. Production of one or both goods can always be increased without an aggregate increase in inputs unless the marginal rates of technical substitution between the inputs are the same for both producers.

The locus CC', again called the *contract curve,* is a curve showing all input allocations that equalize the marginal rates of technical substitution — that is, the locus of tangencies between an X isoquant and a Y isoquant. Accordingly, we can state the following:

Proposition: The general equilibrium of production occurs at a point where the marginal rate of technical substitution between every pair of inputs is the

Figure 16.3.1 General Equilibrium of Production

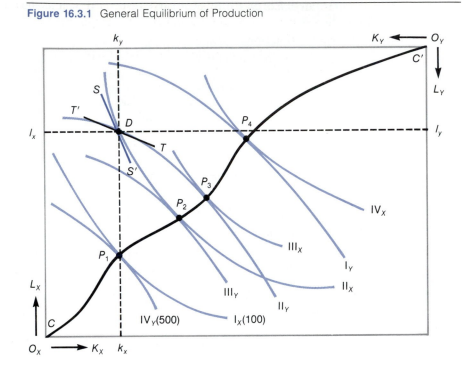

same for all producers who use both inputs. The production equilibrium is not unique; it may occur at any point along the contract curve, but each point represents a Pareto-optimal equilibrium organization.

The contract curve is an optimal locus in the sense that if the producers are located at a point not on the curve, the output of one or both commodities can be increased, and the output of neither decreased, by making input substitutions so as to move to a point on the curve. For any point not on the curve there are one or more attainable points on the curve associated with a greater output of each good.

General Equilibrium of Production and Exchange 16.3.b

For any input endowment there are an infinite number of potential production equilibria that are Pareto optimal, that is, any point on the contract curve in Figure 16.3.1. Each point represents a particular volume of output of X and Y, and thereby dictates the dimensions of an Edgeworth box diagram for exchange (such as Figure 16.2.3). Furthermore, each consumption-exchange box leads to an infinite number of potential exchange equilibria that are Pareto optimal, that is, any point on the contract curve associated with the box in question. Accordingly, there are a multiple infinity of potential general equilibria of production and exchange.

The object of any society is to attain that particular general equilibrium which maximizes the economic welfare of its inhabitants. As we shall see in Chapter 17, there are ways by which either a free enterprise system or a planned economy may attain the optimum. A major difference between the two is the informational requirement of the various economic agents.

Deriving the Production-Possibility Frontier, or Transformation Curve 16.3.c

The contract curve associated with the general equilibrium of production is a locus of points in *input space;* the curve shows the optimal output of each commodity corresponding to every possible allocation of K and L between X and Y. With the allocation of inputs indicated by point P_1 in Figure 16.3.1, 500 units of Y and 100 units of X are the maximum attainable production. By constructing a graph whose coordinate axes show the quantities of X and Y produced, and plotting the output pairs corresponding to each isoquant tangency in Figure 16.3.1, one may generate the curve labeled TT' in Figure 16.3.2. The curve so obtained is called the **production-possibility frontier** or the **transformation curve**. Only the tangencies are relevant because any point that is not a tangency in input space is dominated by a point on the contract curve. That is, more of each commodity can be had so these nontangencies correspond to points that are inside the production-possibility frontier. For example, point D in Figure 16.3.1 corresponds to D in Figure 16.3.2. By moving from D to P_2 in 16.3.1, X is unchanged, but Y is increased. This is shown as the vertical move from D to P_2 in 16.3.2. Similarly by moving from D to P_3 in 16.3.1, Y is unchanged, but X is increased. This is shown as the horizontal move from D to P_3 in Figure 16.3.2.

The transformation curve is obtained by mapping the contract curve from input space into output space. Fundamentally, this locus depicts the choices a society can make. It shows, in other words, the various (maximum) combinations of X and Y that are attainable from the given resource base (input endowment). No output combination represented by a point lying outside the production-possibility frontier (such as S) can be attained; such a level of output would require a greater resource base. On the other hand, a point lying inside the locus (such as D) is neither necessary nor desirable; it would entail a needless sacrifice of goods attributable to unemployment of available resources. Thus one object of a society is to attain an equilibrium position **on** its production-possibility frontier—not below.

Production-Possibility Frontier: The production-possibility frontier or transformation curve is a locus showing the maximum attainable output of one commodity for every possible volume of output of the other commodity, given

Figure 16.3.2 Deriving Production-Possibility Frontier from the Contract Curve

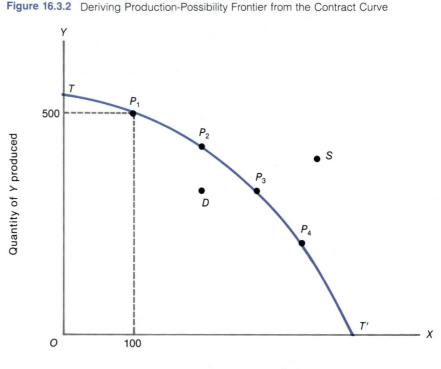

Quantity of X produced

the fixed resource base. The curve so generated depends upon the absolute endowment of each resource, upon the aggregate input endowment ratio, and upon the "state of the art" (the production functions for both goods).

GENERAL COMPETITIVE EQUILIBRIUM IN A TWO-GOOD ECONOMY
16.4

We have already discussed competitive equilibrium in an exchange economy and presented a graphical description in Figure 16.2.4. In this section, we generalize that to an economy with *production as well as exchange* and we look at the system algebraically. For simplicity, we restrict attention to the case of a fixed coefficient production model where there is no substitution of factors of production. A more general model that includes substitution of factors in production would parallel the analysis presented here.[15]

---

[15]For a discussion of the more general model, the reader may wish to consult Murray C. Kemp, *The Pure Theory of International Trade and Investment* (Englewood Cliffs, N.J.: Prentice-Hall, 1969), chap. 1.

Part Five   Theory of General Equilibrium and Economic Welfare

Production in a Two-Good Economy
16.4.a

We will denote the output of good 1 by Q_1 and the output of good 2 by Q_2. The labor requirements for good 1 and a_{L_1} per unit of output, and the capital requirements per unit of output of good 1 are a_{K_1}. Similarly, a_{L_2} and a_{K_2} are, respectively, the labor and capital requirements per unit of output of good 2. The coefficients a_{L_1}, a_{K_1}, a_{L_2}, and a_{K_2} are fixed constants. Total labor and capital requirements for good 1 when Q_1 units are produced are

$$L_1 = a_{L_1} Q_1$$
$$K_1 = a_{K_1} Q_1 . \qquad (16.4.1)$$

Total labor and capital requirements for an output Q_2 of good 2 are

$$L_2 = a_{L_2} Q_2$$
$$K_2 = a_{K_2} Q_2 . \qquad (16.4.2)$$

The total amount of labor and capital available in the economy are assumed fixed at the level L and K, respectively. Hence,

$$L_1 + L_2 \leq L$$
$$K_1 + K_2 \leq K . \qquad (16.4.3)$$

Combining equations (16.4.1), (16.4.2), and the inequalities in (16.4.3), we get the inequalities

$$Q_1 \leq \frac{K}{a_{K_1}} - \frac{a_{K_2}}{a_{K_1}} Q_2 \qquad (16.4.4)$$

and

$$Q_1 \leq \frac{L}{a_{L_1}} - \frac{a_{L_2}}{a_{L_1}} Q_2 \qquad (16.4.5)$$

where equation (16.4.4) represents the capital constraint on output of good 1 when Q_2 units of good 2 are produced and equation (16.4.5) is the labor constraint on output of good 1 when Q_2 units of good 2 are produced. Hence the production-possibility frontier is given by

$$Q_1 = \min \left\{ \frac{K}{a_{K_1}} - S_K Q_2 , \frac{L}{a_{L_1}} - S_L Q_2 \right\} \qquad (16.4.6)$$

where $S_K = a_{K_2}/a_{K_1}$ and $S_L = a_{L_2}/a_{L_1}$.[16] The production frontier is shown in Figure 16.4.1. The line DEA is the capital constraint (16.4.4) and shows the maximum Q_1 that can be produced for each output of Q_2, given the fixed capital stock K

---

[16]The reader may wish to show that this production-possibility frontier can be derived from an Edgeworth box as in section 16.3. The fixed coefficient model production function for Q_1 is $Q_1 = \min\{L_1/a_{L_1}, K_1/a_{K_1}\}$ and for Q_2 is $Q_2 = \min\{L_2/a_{L_2}, K_2/a_{K_2}\}$. The isoquants are right angles for the fixed coefficient production function. Note that the production functions are linear homogeneous.

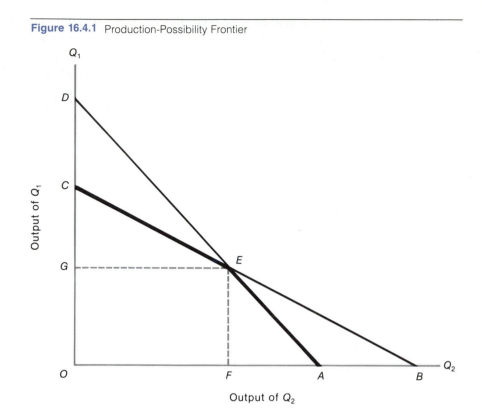

Figure 16.4.1 Production-Possibility Frontier

in the economy. Similarly, the line CEB is the maximum output of Q_1 for each output of Q_2, given the labor constraint. The set of achievable outputs (that is, combinations of Q_1 and Q_2 that do not violate either the labor or capital constraint) is the area $OCEA$. The production frontier is CEA.

From this description of Figure 164.1 we see that the point D is K/a_{K_1} and the slope of DEA is $-S_K$. The point C is L/a_{L_1}, and the slope of CEB is $-S_L$. As drawn, $S_K > S_L$ and the lines intersect at E.[17] Over the range of output of Q_2 from O to F in Figure 16.4.1, production of Q_1 occurs along CE. Hence, capital is a redundant factor (less than K is needed for production in this range), and accordingly, its price is zero for these outputs. Since an additional unit of capital is worth nothing in this range, producers will pay nothing for it. Only when more labor is employed can they use up the capital that they already have. Similarly, over the range from F to A of output of Q_2 (that is, output of Q_1 along EA), labor is redundant and its price is zero for these outputs. Only at output F of Q_2 (or output G of Q_1) are both labor and capital fully employed.

---

[17]Other possibilities exist, of course, but for concreteness in the discussion we will stick with this case. Production-possibility frontiers consisting of straight-line segments like the one shown in Figure 16.4.1 are said to be "piecewise linear."

Part Five   Theory of General Equilibrium and Economic Welfare

In the general equilibrium to be discussed we will be interested in determining the prices of goods 1 and 2, the wage rate, and the interest rate or rental rate on capital. As in section 16.1, we recognize that only relative prices can be determined, so we pick a *numéraire* commodity and set its price equal to 1. Suppose Q_2 is the *numéraire*; then we need to determine p_1 (the relative price of good 1), the relative wage w, and the relative rental rate on capital r. In a competitive equilibrium, economic profits in Industry 1 (which produces good 1) and Industry 2 (which produces good 2) will be zero. These zero economic profit requirements can be stated as

$$p_1 Q_1 = wL_1 + rK_1$$
$$Q_2 = wL_2 + rK_2$$
(16.4.7)

where the first equation says that total revenue equals total cost in Industry 1 and the second equation says the same for Industry 2. Dividing the first equation by Q_1 and the second by Q_2, we get the following conditions.[18]

$$p_1 = w\frac{L_1}{Q_1} + r\frac{K_1}{Q_1} = wa_{L_1} + ra_{K_1}$$
(16.4.8)

$$1 = w\frac{L_2}{Q_2} + r\frac{K_2}{Q_2} = wa_{L_2} + ra_{K_2}$$
(16.4.9)

Now suppose output of Q_2 is in the range F to A in Figure 16.4.1. In this range, output of Q_1 is in the range O to G; and since labor is redundant, the wage rate is zero. Setting $w = 0$ in (16.4.8) and (16.4.9) and solving these equations simultaneously, we find $p_1 = a_{K_1}/a_{K_2} = 1/S_K$ and $r = 1/a_{K_2}$ over this range of outputs. When output of Q_2 is in the range O to F in Figure 16.4.1, output of Q_1 is in the range G to C and capital is redundant. This means the rental rate for capital, r, is zero. Setting $r = 0$ in (16.4.8) and (16.4.9) and solving, we see that over this range of output $p_1 = a_{L_1}/a_{L_2} = 1/S_L$ and $w = 1/a_{L_2}$.

Combining these results we derive the supply curve of good 1 in Figure 16.4.2. Over the range of output O to G, the price of good 1 is $1/S_K$ as represented by the horizontal segment $1/S_K A$ in Figure 16.4.2. Similarly, over the output range G to C the price is $1/S_L$, represented by the horizontal segment BE in this figure. The supply function Q_1 is thus an increasing step function.[19]

Equilibrium in a Two-Good Economy
16.4.b

To complete the analysis of equilibrium in this economy, we must introduce demand curves for good 1 and good 2. Once commodity prices are known we know factor payments. Given factor payments and the distribution of the community's assets, both total income and its distribution are known. From this informa-

---

[18]Since the production functions are homogeneous of degree one, these conditions also say that marginal cost equals price because marginal cost and average cost are equal.

[19]A similar supply function for Q_2 can be derived in terms of its *relative* price $1/p_1$.

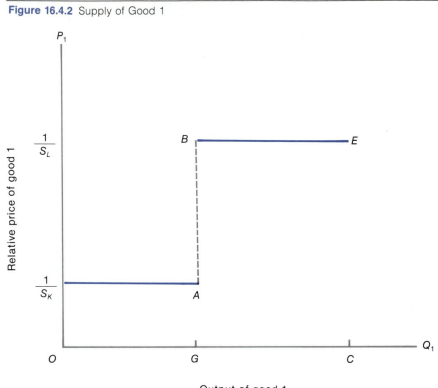

Figure 16.4.2 Supply of Good 1

Output of good 1

tion we can in principle calculate the determinants of individual, and hence total, commodity demands. We can thus introduce aggregate demand curves specified as $d_1(p_1, 1)$ and $d_2(p_1, 1)$ for commodities 1 and 2, respectively. We also note that by Walras's Law we can ignore one of these demand functions — say the second — since this market will be in equilibrium if the rest of the markets in the economy are in equilibrium.[20]

If the demand curve for product 1 intersects the supply curve of Figure 16.4.3 in the segment $1/S_K A$, then, as we have seen, the price of good 1 is $1/S_K$, $w = 0$, and $r = 1/a_{K_2}$. The output of industry 1 is in the interval OG at the point that d_1 intersects the supply curve. If d_1 intersects the segment BE of the supply curve,

---

[20]Recall our use of Walras's Law in a related context in section 16.1. Since total income of the economy is given by equations (16.4.7), the consumer budget requirement that total demand equal total income yields

$$p_1 d_1 + d_2 = p_1 Q_1 + Q_2.$$

Hence, if $p_1 d_1 = p_1 Q_1$, it follows that $d_2 = Q_2$. Equilibrium in market 2 is assured by equilibrium in market 1.

Part Five   Theory of General Equilibrium and Economic Welfare

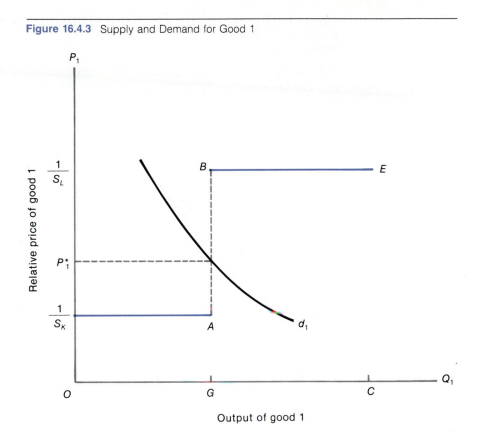

Figure 16.4.3 Supply and Demand for Good 1

then output, Q_1, is in the interval GC at the point of intersection of supply and demand. In this case $p_1 = 1/S_L$, $w = 1/a_{L_2}$, and $r = 0$.

When d_1 passes between points A and B as in Figure 16.4.3, output of good 1 will be OG and price can be determined along d_1 at this output. In Figure 16.4.3 this price is given by p_1^*. Given this price, equations (16.4.8) and (16.4.9) can be solved for the equilibrium values of r and w. The results are

$$r^* = \frac{S_L p_1^* - 1}{a_{K_2}\left(\dfrac{S_L}{S_K} - 1\right)}$$

$$w^* = \frac{S_K p_1^* - 1}{a_{L_2}\left(\dfrac{S_K}{S_L} - 1\right)}, \quad \text{for } \frac{1}{S_K} \le p_1^* \le \frac{1}{S_L}. \tag{16.4.10}$$

In our graphical example $S_K > S_L$ and, from equations (16.4.10), this means that an increase in p^* decreases the interest rate and increases the wage rate.

Factor Intensities and the Relationship between Factory Prices and Commodity Prices
16.4.c

When output in Industry 1 is Q_1, demand for labor and capital in that industry are $L_1 = a_{L_1} Q_1$ and $K_1 = a_{K_1} Q_1$. The capital-labor ratio in Industry 1 is thus

$$\frac{K_1}{L_1} = \frac{a_{K_1}}{a_{L_1}} \tag{16.4.11}$$

$$\frac{K_2}{L_2} = \frac{a_{K_2}}{a_{L_2}} \tag{16.4.12}$$

If $a_{K_1}/a_{L_1} > a_{K_2}/a_{L_2}$, Industry 1 is said to be relatively capital-intensive (and Industry 2 is relatively labor-intensive). If $a_{K_1}/a_{L_1} < a_{K_2}/a_{L_2}$, then Industry 2 is said to be relatively capital-intensive (and Industry 1 is relatively labor-intensive). Using equations (16.4.10), we see that r^* will increase as p_1^* does if $S_L/S_K - 1 > 0$ and w^* will increase as p_1^* does if $S_K/S_L - 1 > 0$. Observe, however, that $S_L/S_K - 1 > 0$ means that $a_{K_1}/a_{L_1} > a_{K_2}/a_{L_2}$, so as p_1^* increases r^* will increase if Industry 1 is relatively capital-intensive. Since $S_L/S_K - 1 > 0$ means $S_K/S_L - 1 < 0$, an increase in the price of Q_1 decreases w^*. The reverse would hold if Industry 1 were labor-intensive. This illustrates what is known as the Stolper-Samuelson Theorem. This theorem says that an increase in the price of a commodity gives rise to an increase in the real reward of the factor used relatively intensively in the production of that commodity, and to a decline in the real reward of the other factor.[21]

SYNOPSIS
16.5

■ Having dealt with consumers, entrepreneurs, and other individual economic agents in the earlier chapters, we now turn our attention to how the actions of all these more or less independent economic agents fit together in an economic *system*. This line of inquiry, known as the theory of general economic equilibrium, has a history going back to the work of F. Quesnay in the 18th century.

■ By examining simple economies in which each individual may act in two or more different roles (such as entrepreneur/land owner on one hand and consumer/labor supplier on the other hand), it can be seen how the analytical techniques in the first four parts of this book can be put together to describe a stationary general equilibrium. A new concept that emerges from this exercise is Walras's Law, which states that in an economy with

---

[21]For further detail see Wolfgang F. Stolper and Paul A. Samuelson, "Protection and Real Wages," *Review of Economic Studies,* IX, no. 1 (November 1941), pp. 53–73. Reprinted in *Readings in the Theory of International Trade,* ed. Howard S. Ellis and Lloyd A. Metzler (Philadelphia: Blakiston Co., 1949), pp. 333–57.

n markets, equilibrium in any $n - 1$ of them assures equilibrium in the remaining market. By using general equilibrium analysis we are able to see how relative prices and outputs are determined in the aggregate economy.

■ The analysis of a simple exchange economy shows how individuals can gain by trading until the allocation of goods is such that the marginal rate of substitution between every pair of goods is the same for all parties consuming the goods. The set of all allocations that satisfy the equilibrium condition is known as the contract curve. Points on the contract curve are Pareto optimal; that is, given any point not on the contract curve, it is possible to find at least one point on the curve that is preferred in the sense that it makes one or more parties better off and no party worse off. Using the contract curve, one can derive the utility-possibility frontier showing the maximum satisfaction attainable by one of two parties for each given level of satisfaction of the other.

■ A competitive equilibrium is a particular point on the contract curve. When prices are set at the levels that correspond to the competitive equilibrium, individuals voluntarily trade until that point is reached. The competitive equilibrium in an economy depends on the initial endowments of the economic agents.

■ The core of an economy refers to those points on the contract curve that cannot be blocked. A point can be blocked if there is some coalition that can get together and make all of its members better off than they would have been at the original point. As the number of traders increases, the core shrinks to the competitive equilibrium so that we can confine our attention to that one (or those few) points on the contract curve.

■ The general equilibrium of production occurs when the marginal rate of technical substitution between every pair of inputs is the same for all producers using both inputs. This point is not unique; the collection of all such equilibrium points is again called the contract curve. This contract curve is optimal in the sense that, if producers are not on the curve, the output of one or both of the commodities can be increased and the output of neither decreased. This contract curve can be used to derive the production-possibility frontier showing the maximum attainable output of one commodity given each possible level of output of the other.

■ In an economy with two inputs (each fixed in supply), two outputs (Q_1 and Q_2), and fixed coefficient production functions, the production-possibility frontier usually will be piecewise linear like the one shown in Figure 16.5.1.

■ In this simple economy, it is easy to see the equilibrium *relative* prices of inputs and outputs. The relative prices of the inputs depend on the relative prices of the outputs and the capital-labor ratios in each industry. The relationship between changes in input prices and output prices in this kind of economy illustrates the Stolper-Samuelson Theorem, which states that

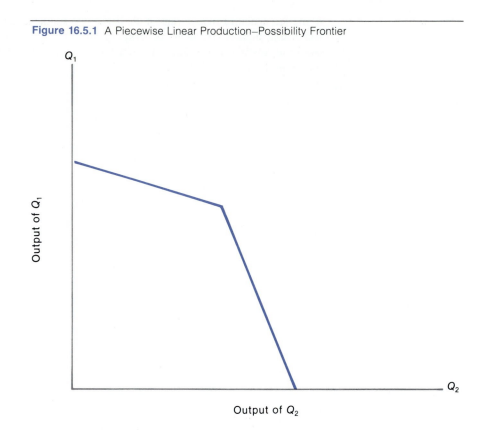

Figure 16.5.1 A Piecewise Linear Production–Possibility Frontier

an increase in the price of a commodity gives rise to an increase in the relative price of the input used relatively intensively in the production of that commodity.

QUESTIONS AND EXERCISES

1. Using the model of section 16.1, describe the general equilibrium of an economy consisting of a single farmer.

2. Using the model of section 16.1, describe the general equilibrium when one farmer owns all the land (but never works) and the other farmer works but does not own any land.

3. Consider a pure exchange economy consisting of two goods, X and Y, and two individuals, A and B. Both A and B regard goods X and Y as *strict* complements. If individual A has utility U_A, the strict complementarity requires that A have the following quantities of X and Y:

$$X_A = 3U_A$$
$$Y_A = 10U_A.$$

Part Five   Theory of General Equilibrium and Economic Welfare

(These are minimum requirements in the sense that additional units of X above the indicated amount do not add utility if no additional units of Y are given to A, and vice versa.) Similarly, if B has utility U_B, the strict complementarity requires that B have the following quantities of X and Y:

$$X_B = 10U_B$$
$$Y_B = 3U_B.$$

There is a total of 300 units of X in the economy and a total of 540 units of Y in the economy. Find the utility-possibility frontier for this economy.

4. How does the supply curve in Figure 16.4.2 change:
   a. When the total capital stock K is increased?
   b. When the total labor force L is increased?
   c. When both a_{K_1} and a_{L_1} double?
   d. When both a_{K_1} and a_{K_2} double?

SUGGESTED READINGS

The first two sources listed provide thorough but mathematically rigorous statements of modern general equilibrium theory.

Arrow, Kenneth J., and **Hahn, F. H.** *General Competitive Analysis.* San Francisco: Holden-Day, Inc., 1971.

Debreu, Gerard. *Theory of Value: An Axiomatic Analysis of Economic Equilibrium.* New Haven, Conn.: Yale University Press, 1959.

Fossati, Eraldo. *The Theory of General Static Equilibrium.* Oxford: Basil Blackwell, 1957, pp. 79–183.

Henderson, James M., and **Quandt, Richard E.** *Microeconomic Theory,* 2nd ed. New York: McGraw-Hill, 1971, pp. 153–71.

Kuenne, Robert E. *The Theory of General Economic Equilibrium.* Princeton, N.J.: Princeton University Press, 1963. Chapter 1 (pp. 3–39) is an excellent statement concerning methodology; there little, if any, mathematics is required of the reader. Especially relevant are pp. 43–195.

Leontief, Wassily. *The Structure of the American Economy, 1919–1939.* New York: Oxford University Press, 1951.

Quirk, James, and **Saposnik, Rubin.** *Introduction to General Equilibrium Theory and Welfare Economics.* New York: McGraw-Hill, 1968.

Telser, Lester. *Economic Theory and the Core.* Chicago: University of Chicago Press, 1978.

Walras, Leon. *Elements of Pure Economics,* trans. W. Jaffe. London: Allen & Unwin, 1954.

17 Theory of Welfare Economics

Should local phone companies be allowed to charge for directory assistance calls? What are the consequences of the current minimum wage law for economic efficiency? How about retail sales taxes? The material in this chapter demonstrates that as long as the strict conditions of the perfectly competitive model are met, an unregulated price system will perform the function of fulfilling the marginal conditions necessary for Pareto optimality. Mastery of this material provides the framework for the analysis of the efficiency effects of myriad forms of government intervention in the economy, including the policies associated with each of the questions just posed. This chapter also considers what happens when the strict conditions of the perfectly competitive model are not met—for example, when "external diseconomies" or "external economies" are present in the form of pollution or "public goods" such as national defense. ■

Directory Assistance Telephone Pricing

Cincinnati (UPI)—Pam Sanders is one of 370 telephone operators here who do nothing but handle the monthly load of more than 2.25 million "directory assistance" calls.

"Almost all the calls I get are for numbers in the phone book," says Pam, who estimates she talks to 600 callers each three hour work split. "I try to be diplomatic and say, 'the number is listed as . . . ,' but what I really mean is, 'next time look in your book.'"

Callers may start looking in the book because soon it's going to cost 20 cents to get the number from Pam or another information operator here.

Beginning Sunday, the Cincinnati Bell Telephone Co. will allow its customers only three free information calls a month within the large Southwestern Ohio area code of 513, and then charge 20 cents for all subsequent requests.

And if you dial "0" for the regular operator and request a phone number, it will cost you 40 cents because two operators will be involved.

Cincinnati Bell, which serves about a half-million customers, is believed to be the first phone company in the nation to charge such a fee. It could be the start of a national trend since other phone companies across the country have filed similar requests with their state utility commissions.

But the move by Cincinnati Bell has not been without opposition.

A citizens protest is being led by Jim Howard Witt, a suburban Fairfield Radio News Director, who believes his "Citizens for Fair Telephone Rates" group is the only stopgap in what he calls the "telephone domino theory."

Questions

1. If the goal is to obtain Pareto optimality, which of the two pricing policies below would you favor for directory assistance calls:

   Policy 1. Charging only directory assistance callers a given price per directory assistance call (as Cincinnati Bell just instituted).

   Policy 2. Putting the average cost of all the directory assistance calls into every customer's basic monthly service charge, whether or not the customer actually made any directory assistance calls. (This is the policy currently followed by most phone companies, according to the article.)

2. How does your answer relate to the three marginal conditions for social welfare explained at the beginning of the chapter? Which condition would be violated if the pricing policy you chose not to use were in place?

Solutions

1. The policy of putting the average cost of all the directory assistance calls into every customer's basic monthly service charge (policy 2) is *inefficient* and will not lead to a pareto maximum. To see this, first note that this policy results in

(continued on page 526)

(continued from page 525)
a zero effective price for directory assistance calls by any one person — such person's call(s) will have a negligible effect on total cost, and therefore average total cost. As a result of this policy, we would expect quantity Q_d calls to be made (see following figure), for directory assistance

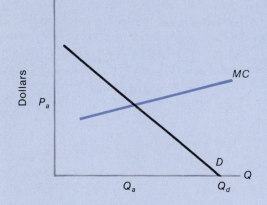

Directory assistance calls

calls can be expected to be made as long as the "marginal value" (or MRS in terms of money) is the smallest bit above zero.

This will lead to "overuse" (overproduction) of directory assistance calls as long as the marginal cost (at Q_d) is above zero. Thus, instead of producing directory assistance calls until the price (marginal value) equals marginal cost, or equivalently, where the marginal benefit equals the marginal cost, this second pricing policy results in too many calls (and too few all other goods.)

The first policy of charging directly for directory assistance calls will be efficient (and result in a Pareto maximum) as long as this price is set equal to the height of the demand curve at the point where the demand curve intersects the marginal cost curve. (This would occur at price P_a in Figure 17A.) The resulting output level (Q_a) is the one where the benefit of the "marginal call" (measured by the height of the demand curve) just equals the cost of the "marginal call."

2. In terms of the marginal conditions for social welfare presented at the beginning of the chapter, the "marginal condition for product substitution" is violated. Note that the current pricing policy (policy 2) results in the effective price for directory assistance to be zero, while the marginal cost is greater than zero. As a result of this price not reflecting marginal cost, the MRS of directory assistance calls for all other goods (AOG) will be less than the MRT of directory assistance calls for AOG. The latter is equal to

$$MC_{\text{directory assistance}}/MC_{AOG},$$

while the former equals

$$P_{\text{directory assistance}}/P_{AOG}.$$

As explained in the discussion accompanying Figure 17.1.1 in the text, this implies that production should be shifted away from directory assistance calls toward more all other goods (AOG).

Source: Excerpts from UPI dispatch concerning directory assistance telephone calls

The general equilibrium conditions of production and exchange, analyzed in Chapter 16, can be used to develop the "marginal" conditions for maximum social welfare and to assess the efficiency of a perfectly competitive economy. It might also help explain why there is usually only one unique general equilibrium of relevance among the multiple infinity of possible general equilibria that are Pareto optimal.

Marginal Conditions for Social Welfare
17.1.a

First return to Figure 16.2.3, which illustrates the general equilibrium of exchange. As you will recall, we proved that a position of equilibrium must occur on the contract curve because if some other distribution momentarily existed, one or both trading parties could benefit, and neither be harmed, by moving to a point on the contract curve. Any point on the contract curve satisfies the *optimum conditions of exchange* and gives rise to the first marginal condition for a Pareto-welfare maximum.

Marginal Condition for Exchange: To attain a Pareto maximum, the marginal rate of substitution between any pair of consumer goods must be the same for all individuals who consume both goods.

If this does not hold, one or more individuals would benefit from exchange (without injuring others), as shown by Figure 16.2.3.

The second marginal condition is based on Figure 16.3.1, which illustrates the general equilibrium of production. With the aid of that figure, we proved that equilibrium must be attained on the contract curve because if a different allocation of inputs momentarily prevailed, the output of one or both commodities could be increased, and the output of neither decreased, by moving to a point on the curve. All points on the production contract curve satisfy the *optimum conditions of factor substitution* and lead to the second marginal condition for a Pareto-welfare maximum.

Marginal Condition for Factor Substitution: To attain a Pareto maximum, the marginal rate of technical substitution between any pair of inputs must be the same for all producers who use both inputs.

Otherwise, a reallocation of resources would result in a greater aggregate output, without a reduction in the output of any commodity.

The final marginal condition for a welfare maximum is based on the *optimum conditions of product substitution*. It is actually a combination of the two previous sets of conditions and may be stated as follows:

Marginal Condition for Product Substitution: To attain a Pareto maximum, the marginal rate of transformation in production must equal the marginal rate of substitution in consumption for every pair of commodities and for every individual who consumes both.

This final proposition is established with the aid of Figure 17.1.1.

The curve labeled *TT'* is the production-possibility frontier, or transformation curve, as derived in Figure 16.3.2. Given full resource utilization, it shows the maximum producible amount of either commodity for every given level of output of the other. The slope of the transformation curve at any point shows the number of units of good Y that must be sacrificed in order to free enough resources to produce one additional unit of good X. With full employment of all resources, more of one good necessarily entails less of another.

Marginal Rate of Transformation: The negative of the slope of the transformation curve is called the marginal rate of transformation of X into Y. It shows the number of units by which the production of Y must be decreased in order to expand the output of X by one unit.

Now suppose a pair of consumers has attained an exchange equilibrium, which means that their marginal rates of substitution in consumption are equal. Further, suppose the common marginal rate of substitution is such that both consumers are willing to exchange two units of Y for three units of X. Next, suppose a producer (or producers) has attained an equilibrium of production, in which the marginal rate of technical substitution between each pair of inputs is the same in the production of X as in the production of Y. Finally, suppose this organization of production leads to the point *P* on the transformation curve *TT'* in Figure 17.1.1, at which the marginal rate of transformation is ½—that is, by curtailing the output of Y by ½ unit, one additional unit of X may be produced.

Clearly a general equilibrium has not been obtained. By reducing the output of Y, the output of X can be expanded *by more than enough* to keep each consumer on his or her original indifference curve. Since consumers are willing to give up 2Y for 3X, and since producers can turn 2Y into 4X, there is room for improvement. Producers can reduce their output of Y by four units and sell the eight units of X to the two consumers. Since each consumer views three units of X as a substitute for two units of Y, each would be willing to pay more for four units of X than for the two units of Y. If producers shift their resources from Y production to X production, both consumers may be made better off. Consequently, the initial position could not have been one of Pareto optimality.

Thus, if the marginal rate of transformation is less than the common marginal rate of substitution in consumption, a point of Pareto optimality cannot exist. A similar line of reasoning will show that if the marginal rate of transformation

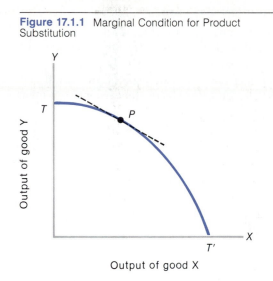

Figure 17.1.1 Marginal Condition for Product Substitution

exceeds the common marginal rate of substitution in consumption, producers should shift some resources from X production to Y production. Therefore, since an organization cannot be Pareto optimal if the marginal rate of transformation is not equal to the common marginal rate of substitution in consumption, the marginal condition for product substitution is established: a Pareto-optimal organization is achieved only if the marginal rate of transformation is equal to the common marginal rate of substitution in consumption for all pairs of consumer goods.

Welfare Maximization and Perfect Competition
17.1.b

The three sets of marginal conditions developed above state the necessary conditions for welfare maximization in any type of society, that is, for the attainment of a Pareto-optimal equilibrium. We now wish to show, subject to the reservations in section 17.3, that a perfectly competitive free enterprise system guarantees the attainment of Pareto optimality. The proof rests on the *maximizing* behavior of producers and consumers. To recall the dictum of Adam Smith, each individual, in pursuing his own self-interest, is led as if by an "invisible hand" to a course of action that promotes the general welfare of all.

Look just at the marginal condition for exchange, which requires equality of the marginal rates of substitution between every pair of goods for all consumers. As shown in Chapter 2, to maximize satisfaction subject to limited income, each consumer arranges purchases so that the marginal rate of substitution is equal to the price ratio for every pair of goods. Under perfect competition, prices, and therefore price ratios, are uniform for all buyers. Hence each consumer purchases goods in such quantity that *his or her* marginal rate of substitution equals the *common* price ratio faced by all consumers. Therefore, the marginal rate of substitution between every pair of goods must be the same for all consumers; the marginal conditions for exchange are a consequence of the price system under perfect competition.

Next, consider the marginal condition for factor substitution: The marginal rate of technical substitution between every pair of inputs must be the same for all producers who utilize them. As shown in Chapter 14, each perfectly competitive producer employs inputs in such proportions that the marginal rate of technical substitution (the ratio of marginal products) equals the input-price ratio. Entrepreneurs do this to maximize profit (obtain the least-cost combination of inputs). In a perfectly competitive market, input prices are the same to all producers; hence each equates the firm's marginal rate of technical substitution to a common input-price ratio. The marginal rates of technical substitution are equated accordingly across firms; and the marginal condition of factor substitution is also a consequence of the price system under perfect competition.

Finally, we come to the marginal condition for product substitution: The marginal rate of transformation in production must equal the marginal rate of substitution in consumption for each pair of goods. The proof in this case requires a slight digression.

As previously said, the marginal rate of transformation shows the number of units by which the production of Y must be curtailed in order to free enough resources to produce an additional unit of X. If the output of X is increased by one unit, the marginal cost of producing X shows how much each additional unit of X costs. But if the output of X is increased, the output of Y must be diminished; hence the marginal cost of producing Y shows how much is saved by reducing Y output one unit. Hence, dividing the marginal cost of producing X by the marginal cost of producing Y, one finds the number of units of Y that must be sacrificed to obtain an additional unit of X.[1] Accordingly, the marginal rate of transformation of X into Y equals the ratio of the marginal cost of X to the marginal cost of Y.

Under perfect competition profit maximization is achieved by producing that volume of output for which marginal cost equals price. Thus under perfect competition the marginal rate of transformation of X into Y must equal the ratio of the price of X to that of Y (because both must equal the marginal cost ratio). By previous argument, the marginal rate of substitution of X for Y must equal the ratio of the price of X to the price of Y. As in the two previous cases, the marginal condition for product substitution is a consequence of the price system under perfect competition.[2]

---

[1]Consider point P in Figure 17.1.1. With the output of Y large relative to the output of X, the marginal cost of Y will be large relative to that of X. Suppose the marginal cost of Y is $10 and the marginal cost of X is $5. Their ratio is $5/$10 or ½. Thus one half of a unit of Y must be sacrificed to produce one additional unit of X.

[2]If X is increased by ΔX then the increase in cost is $MC_X \Delta X$ where MC_X is the marginal cost of X. The reduction in Y, ΔY, must reduce cost by the same amount, otherwise the point would not be on the transformation curve and producers could do better. Thus, $MC_X \Delta X = -MC_Y \Delta Y$, or

(continued on page 531)

EXERCISE 1

In 1977 the U.S. Postal Service was considering a new pricing scheme for first-class postage stamps. Buyers were either categorized as businesses or nonbusinesses; businesses were to be charged 16 cents for first-class stamps, while nonbusinesses were to be charged 13 cents. Assuming the Post Office could distinguish the two groups, would this result in a Pareto maximum? If not, explain which of the marginal conditions in subsection 17.1.a is violated and why.

Solution

This pricing scheme would not result in a Pareto maximum, since it results in a violation of the marginal condition for exchange, whereby the *MRS* between any pair of consumer goods must be the same for all individuals who consume both goods. Each consumer will maximize her utility by setting her *MRS* equal to the ratio of the commodity prices. But since businesses face a different price for stamps than nonbusinesses, the two groups end up with different *MRS*s in equilibrium. In equilibrium (using AOG to represent the other good),

$$MRS_{\text{stamps/AOG}} \text{ of business will equal } P_{\text{stamps}}/P_{\text{AOG}} = 16/P_{\text{AOG}}.$$

This will exceed $MRS_{\text{stamps/AOG}}$ of nonbusinesses, which will equal $P_{\text{stamps}}/P_{\text{AOG}} = 13/P_{\text{AOG}}$. As a result, there can be further exchange between businesses and nonbusinesses that will enable both to be better off. Businesses could purchase stamps from nonbusinesses at any price between the ratios above. For example, if we think of the other good as dollars (with $P_{\text{AOG}} = 1$), businesses could gain by buying stamps for 15 cents, since they were willing to give up 16 cents for another stamp and remain indifferent. Similarly, nonbusinesses would gain from *selling* stamps for 15 cents since they would be indifferent to giving up a stamp if they received 13 cents. The key here is that unlike the case under perfect competition, all consumers don't face the same price for stamps.

(continued from page 530)

$$\frac{MC_X}{MC_Y} = -\frac{\Delta Y}{\Delta X} = MRT_{X \text{ into } Y}.$$

When the price of X and the price of Y equal their respective marginal costs,

$$\frac{P_X}{P_Y} = \frac{MC_X}{MC_Y} = MRT_{X \text{ into } Y}.$$

EXERCISE 2

Consider the current U.S. minimum wage law, which is sometimes referred to as a "selective" minimum wage law; that is, the statutory minimum wage (currently $3.35 per hour) applies to some, but not all workers. For example, workers in the manufacturing sector are covered, but not those in agriculture. (Incidentally, this feature of the law makes the situation exactly analogous to the situation analyzed in the "Applying the Theory" section in Chapter 7, where shrimp peelers in Texas were covered by the minimum wage law, but similar workers just across the border in Mexico were not.)

Show that the current U.S. minimum wage law violates the marginal condition for factor substitution (in subsection 17.1.a) that leads to a Pareto-welfare maximum. Also explain carefully how it would be possible to produce more manufacturing goods or agricultural goods or both (while the output of neither is reduced) by rearranging factors of production between these two sectors. (Note: the efficiency implications of a *general* minimum wage law—one that applies to all workers—is considered in subsection 17.2.j of this chapter.)

Solutions

The marginal condition for factor substitution says that to obtain a Pareto maximum, the marginal rate of technical substitution between any pair of inputs must be the same for all producers who use both inputs. Producers in manufacturing who use both unskilled workers and machinery will hire inputs such that

$$MP_l/MP_k = P_l/P_k,$$

where

MP_l = marginal product of (unskilled) labor;

P_l = price of labor;

MP_k = marginal product of machinery;

P_k = price of machinery.

Producers in agriculture who use both unskilled workers and machinery will do the same thing. In the absence of the minimum wage law, all producers using both inputs would (presumably) face the same factor prices, and therefore,

$$[MP_l/MP_k]^M = [MP_l/MP_k]^A.$$

Thus, the marginal condition for factor substitution would be fulfilled. However, as a result of the minimum wage law, producers who use unskilled workers in manufacturing will face a *higher* price for (unskilled) labor than producers who use the same labor in agriculture (where the minimum wage doesn't apply). As a result,

$$[MP_l/MP_k]^M = (P_l/P_k)^M, \text{ which exceeds } P_l/P_k^A$$
$$= [MP_l/MP_k]^A.$$

Therefore, $[MP_l/MP_k]^M$ will exceed $[MP_l/MP_k]^A$, and the marginal condition for factor substitution will be violated.

The situation as a result of the minimum wage law is exactly equivalent to that at point D in Figure 16.3.1. Let agricultural goods be represented by x and manufactured goods by y. By rearranging factors of production between these two types of producers, it is possible to get more of one good without producing any less of the other. (It is also possible to produce more of both goods.) If producers of y (manufactured goods) gave up some machinery (k) but received more workers (l) to move to a point like P_2, then the output of manufactured goods would increase — they would be on isoquant IIIy instead of IIy. If the producers of agricultural goods (x) received the machinery given up from the y producers and provided the labor for the change above, they would find their output level unchanged along isoquant IIx. Any exchange of factors at a rate between the ratios of marginal products above (or equivalently, the ratio of the input prices) would result in a greater aggregate output without a reduction in the output of either manufacturing or agricultural goods.

The result of this section may be summarized by the following:

Proposition: If the political organization of a society is such as to accord paramount importance to its individual members, social welfare will be maximized if every consumer, every firm, every industry, and every input market is perfectly competitive.

An interesting extension of this proposition applies to a planned economy. In the introduction to Part 5 it was said that the "invisible hand" might more appropriately be called the "invisible computer." Neither designation gives much hint of the underlying principle: each individual maximizes in light of *market-*

determined (parametric) prices. The functioning of the price system in perfectly competitive markets leads to the social welfare maximum; stated alternatively, when each individual implicitly solves his or her constrained maximization problem, the result is a set of prices that, given the individual behavior, leads to maximum social welfare. Speaking mathematically, these prices are nothing more than Lagrange multipliers, perhaps ground out by the "invisible computer" in the process of solving the welfare-maximization problem.

This invisible computer is not available to a planned society; however a visible, tangible one (or its equivalent) is. The state planning agency (given knowledge of individual preference patterns and production functions) could use the visible machine to solve the now explicit constrained maximization problem. The resulting Lagrange multipliers are "shadow" prices, the equivalent of market-determined prices under perfect competition. Maximum social welfare in this type of society can be attained by following the so-called Lange-Lerner rule.

Proposition (Lange-Lerner Rule): To attain maximum social welfare in a decentralized socialist society, the state planning agency should solve the constrained-maximization problem and obtain the shadow prices of all inputs and outputs; publish this price list and distribute it to all members of the society; and instruct all consumers and all plant managers to behave as though they were satisfaction or profit maximizers operating in perfectly competitive markets.

Of course, things are not that simple. For the actual computer to grind out the correct shadow prices, it must have the correct data. That means that every consumer's utility function must be programmed into the computer. Furthermore, every firm's production function must reside in that computer's memory. A major virtue of a market economy is that each consumer and producer need only possess the information relevant to him- or herself; he or she must only know his or her own utility or production function. The market ensures that the knowledge of individual agents is coordinated in the appropriate fashion.[3] But the problem is more than one of mere programming. Although that task is obviously enormous, there are additional incentive difficulties.

Telling consumers and producers to behave as though they were satisfaction or profit maximizers and getting them to do so are two different matters. If a manager's compensation does not depend on behaving appropriately, he or she has little incentive to do so. If the manager is compensated only for maximizing profits, if workers are paid for their labor, and consumers must use this income to buy goods and services, then there is little distinction between the computer shadow price economy and the one where the computer is invisible, but actual prices are used.

---

[3]See F. V. Hayek, "Economics and Knowledge," *Economica* 4 (1937), pp. 33–54.

We now examine the problem of welfare maximization in greater detail.[4]

General Assumptions
17.2.a

The model employed here is identical with that used in the general equilibrium analysis of production and exchange, except that one additional assumption (4) is required. Our original assumptions are now recounted and the additional one supplied.

(1) There exist fixed, nonaugmentable endowments of two homogeneous and perfectly divisible inputs, labor (L) and capital (K). Alternatively, one may assume that these inputs are inelastically supplied and the period of analysis is not sufficiently long to permit a change in the given supplies.

(2) Only two homogeneous goods are produced in the economy, fish (F) and cabbage (C). The production function for each is given and does not change during the analysis. Each production function is smooth (continuous), and each exhibits constant returns to scale and diminishing marginal rates of technical substitution along any isoquant.

(3) There are two individuals in society, A and B. Each has a well-defined ordinal preference function yielding indifference curves of normal shape. For convenience, an arbitrary numerical index is adopted for each function, denoted U_A and U_B.

(4) There exists a *social welfare function* that depends exclusively on the positions of A and B in their own preference scales [for example, $W = W(U_A, U_B)$]. The social welfare function permits a unique preference ordering of all possible situations (hereafter called *states*).[5]

With these assumptions, our problem is to determine the welfare-maximizing value of the following variables: the input of labor into fish and cabbage production (L_F, L_C); the input of capital into fish and cabbage production (K_F, K_C); the total amount of fish (F) and cabbage (C) produced; and the distribution of F and C between A and B (F_A, F_B, C_A, C_B).

---

[4]This section is based on Francis M. Bator, "The Simple Analytics of Welfare Maximization," *American Economic Review* 47 (1957), pp. 22–59, especially pp. 23–31.

[5]Assumption 4 is heroic and involves some controversy. Clearly, it includes some ethical valuations concerning the relative positions of A and B. On this thorny problem, see Kenneth J. Arrow, *Social Choice and Individual Values* (New York: John Wiley & Sons, 1951); Paul A. Samuelson, *Foundations of Economic Analysis* (Cambridge, Mass.: Harvard University Press, 1947), pp. 203–53; and Paul A. Samuelson, "Social Indifference Curves," *Quarterly Journal of Economics* 70 (1956), pp. 1–22.

Retracing Some Steps: From Production Functions to the Production-Possibility Frontier
17.2.b

By assumption 1, there are fixed endowments of two homogeneous inputs; suppose the amounts are $\overline{K}$ and $\overline{L}$ of capital and labor, respectively. The magnitudes of these endowments determine the dimensions of the Edgeworth box diagram shown in Figure 17.2.1. Next, by assumption 2, the production function for each commodity is given and characterized by smooth isoquants that exhibit constant returns to scale and diminishing marginal rates of technical substitution. These isoquants are plotted as $I_F, \ldots, IV_F$ and $I_C, \ldots, V_C$ in Figure 17.2.1. Satisfying the optimum conditions of factor substitution (equal marginal rates of technical substitution) leads to the contract curve in input space, labeled EE'. As we have already shown in Chapter 16, subsection 16.3.c, the contract curve may be mapped from input space into output space, thereby becoming the production-possibility frontier, or transformation curve.

The particular transformation curve associated with the contract curve EE', and therefore directly associated with the fixed input endowments, is plotted as TT' in Figure 17.2.2. As you will recall, the slope of this curve indicates the marginal rate of transformation of fish into cabbage. It indicates exactly how many cabbages can be produced by a marginal transfer of capital and labor from fish production to cabbage production, under the assumption that inputs are optimally reallocated in each production process after the transfer (so as to maintain the optimal condition of factor substitution). Consequently, the marginal rate of transformation is the marginal cabbage cost of an additional fish, or the inverse of the marginal fish cost of an additional cabbage.

Production Possibilities and the Optimum Conditions of Exchange
17.2.c

Select any point on the transformation curve TT' in Figure 17.2.2. Let the point be S, so that the total output of fish and cabbage are $O\overline{F}$ and $O\overline{C}$ respectively. the corresponding point in input space (and the associated allocation of K and L to F and C production) is labeled S'' in Figure 17.2.1.

The outputs $O\overline{F}$ and $O\overline{C}$ determine a particular volume of goods available to A and B; these outputs accordingly determine the dimensions of an Edgeworth box diagram for exchange. This diagram is constructed in Figure 17.2.2 by dropping perpendiculars to the axes from the point S. The original origin O becomes the origin for A, O_A, and the point S becomes B's origin, O_B. By assumption 3, each individual has a well-defined preference function. Thus in the usual way, indifference curves for A and B are constructed in the exchange box. Curves $U_{A1}, \ldots, U_{A4}$ illustrate A's preference field and $U_{B1}, \ldots, U_{B4}$ show B's. The locus of tangencies, or the *feasible* points of exchange, is the contract curve $G_S G_S'$. The points on this contract curve are feasible because (a) an increase in the level of satisfaction of one trading party can be achieved only at the expense of the other, and (b) consumption at any point on the curve precisely exhausts the

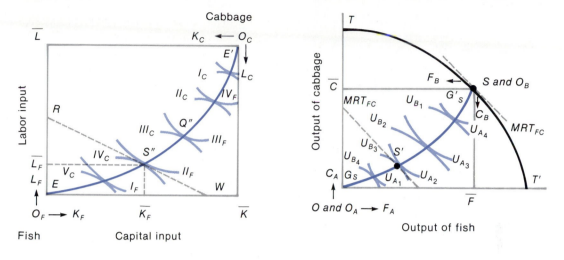

entire output of fish and cabbage. Thus the contract curve is labeled $G_S G_S'$ to denote that it is the curve relative to the point S on the transformation curve; and, as you will recall, it is the locus of exchange possibilities satisfying the optimum conditions of exchange (that is, it is a locus of Pareto-optimal points).

Retracing Some Steps: From the Contract Curve to the Utility-Possibility Frontier
17.2.d

By observing the utility levels of A and B at each point along the contract curve in Figure 17.2.2, one may generate the utility-possibility curve relative to the output point S, as shown in Chapter 16, subsection 16.2.d. The utility-possibility curve relative to S is plotted as $G_S G_S'$ in Figure 17.2.3. This curve alone does not help us much because it shows an infinite number of Pareto-optimal utility pairs corresponding to each of an infinite number of Pareto-optimal production pairs. We are just where we were at the end of Chapter 16; a multiple infinity of possible equilibria exist. However, we can remove one "infinity" dimension.

The optimum conditions of product substitution require equality between the marginal rate of transformation in production and the marginal rate of substitution in consumption for all pairs of goods and for all individuals consuming these goods. For our particular model, the conditions require equality between the marginal rate of transformation of fish into cabbage and both A's and B's marginal rate of substitution of fish for cabbage. Recall that if this condition did not hold, there was a better way to organize production that would make all individuals better off.

Figure 17.2.3 Utility-Possibility Frontier: From Output to Utility Space

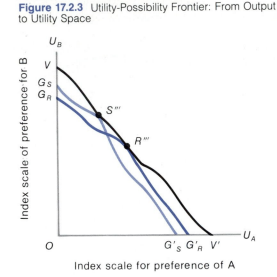

Index scale for preference of A

At the production point S in Figure 17.2.2, the marginal rate of transformation is indicated by the slope of the dashed line tangent to TT' at S, labeled MRT_{FC}. To satisfy the optimum conditions of product substitution, the marginal rate of substitution of both A and B must equal this particular value of the marginal rate of transformation. As indicated graphically, this condition is satisfied at the unique point S' in Figure 17.2.2. Consequently, while the locus G_SG_S' in Figure 17.2.3 is the utility-possibility frontier relative to S, only the single point S''', corresponding to S' in Figure 17.2.2, is relevant. Relative to the output combination S, S'' in Figure 17.2.1 is the only allocation of inputs that satisfies the optimum conditions of factor substitution. Furthermore, relative to the same output combination of S, S' is the only allocation of fish and cabbage between A and B that satisfies both the optimum conditions of exchange and the optimum conditions of substitution. As a consequence, S''' is the only relevant point on G_SG_S'. One dimension of "infinity" is removed: S' is the only efficient output allocation relative to S; but S can be anywhere on TT' in Figure 17.2.2. One dimension of "infinity" remains.

From a Utility-Possibility Point to the Grand Utility-Possibility Frontier
17.2.e

Still using Figures 17.2.2 and 17.2.3, we can generate the "grand" utility-possibility frontier, or the utility-possibility frontier relative to *any* point on the production-possibility frontier. Imagine S moving to a point further down TT'. At the new point there would be more fish and fewer cabbages; a new Edgeworth exchange diagram would be constructed and a new contract curve generated. When mapped into utility space, the new contract curve might look like $G_R G_R'$ in Figure 17.2.3.

Yet at the new output combination point on the production-possibility frontier TT', there would be a unique marginal rate of transformation. Again, the optimum conditions of product substitution would dictate a single relevant point on the contract curve or the utility curve $G_R G_R'$ in Figure 17.2.3. This single relevant point is indicated by R''' in Figure 17.2.3.[6]

As the output combination varies over all points on TT', new Edgeworth exchange boxes and new contract curves are generated. But at each output combination point there is a unique marginal rate of transformation. This unique rate, together with the optimum conditions of product substitution, dictates a unique output allocation between A and B relative to the output combination, and each of these unique points can be plotted in Figure 17.2.3 as a unique utility combination point. The overall utility-possibility frontier is obtained by connecting all these points (points such as S''' and R''' in Figure 17.2.3). This frontier is shown by the heavily shaded line VV'. Each point on this line shows: (a) a unique utility combination for A and B associated with (b) a unique output allocation between A and B corresponding to (c) equality between the marginal rate of transformation and marginal rate of substitution of F for C (d) at a particular $F - C$ output combination on the production-possibility frontier; furthermore, each $F - C$ output combination dictates (e) a unique allocation of the $K - L$ input endowments between the production of fish and cabbage. Quite a bit is embodied in VV'; but there is still a single infinity of possible solutions (any point on VV').[7]

From the Utility-Possibility Frontier to the Point of Constrained Bliss 17.2.f

Up to this point the analysis of social welfare has required only assumptions 1–3 in subsection 17.2.a. To reduce the single infinity of possible solutions to a unique solution requires the fourth assumption: there exists a *social welfare function* that depends exclusively on the positions of A and B in their own preference scales.

As previously indicated, this is a heroic assumption. It definitely requires ethical valuations regarding the "deservingness" of A and B; in this respect it is unquestionably an ascientific concept. Furthermore, even the construction of a

---

[6]For expositional purposes this example was chosen so that there is only one point (R''') in Figure 17.2.3 that satisfies the optimality criterion. In some cases it is possible that there are several points on the contract curve at which the marginal rate of substitution is equal to the marginal rate of transformation.

[7]The mathematically inclined reader will realize that VV' may be derived as the envelope of the utility-possibility curves associated with each point on the production-possibility frontier.

theoretical social welfare function is a difficult conceptual task, unless the society is ruled by a dictator. In that case the social welfare function is the dictator's individual preference function.

In the absence of a dictator (ironclad adherence to tradition, customs, mores, and such can be a "dictator" for social welfare purposes), how is a welfare function developed? By direct vote or by representative vote through a legislature would seem logical answers. But either method is likely to fail because of the famous "voting paraodox."[8]

The matter may be viewed somewhat differently. Suppose you are A. Your principle interest is U_A; and with given and fully employed resources, the greater U_A, the lower U_B. You wish to push as far down and to the right on VV' as possible. You probably want a social welfare function that dictates a position very close to V' (and distant from V). But not necessarily. You are interested in U_A as a *consumer*; you are interested in the social welfare function as a *citizen*. In the latter capacity, you may prefer somewhat less U_A in order for some U_B to exist. This is more or less the situation when a property owner whose child attends a private school votes for a bond issue (and increased property tax) to improve the public school system. Similarly, any contribution to charity is an act that reduces one's satisfaction as a consumer but increases one's satisfaction as a citizen.

Nonetheless, a social welfare function is difficult to construct. We merely assume that one exists. Its existence enables us to represent it by a family of social indifference curves, just as an individual's preference function can be represented by a family of consumption indifference curves. A portion of this family of curves is shown by the set $W_1 W_1', \ldots, W_4 W_4'$ in Figure 17.2.4.

The utility-possibility frontier VV' is also plotted in this figure. It shows all possible combinations of utilities to A and B, given the existing resource base, the production functions, and the individual preference orderings. In other words, it shows the utility combinations that are physically achievable. The social indifference curves show utility combinations that result in equal levels of social welfare. The higher the curve, the greater is aggregate social welfare.

For reasons that should now be thoroughly familiar, maximum social welfare is attained at Q, where a social indifference curve is just tangent to the utility-possibility frontier. The infinity of possible equilibria has been reduced to a unique equilibrium point by considering the welfare of the society as a whole. This unique equilibrium Q is called the point of "constrained bliss" because it represents the unique organization of production, exchange, and distribution that leads to the maximum *attainable* social welfare. The society, of course, would be more "blissful" on $W_4 W_4'$. But a state on this higher curve is not attainable. The resource endowment and the state of the arts "constrains" the society to a point on VV'. In view of the constraint, society reaches its point of "constrained bliss" at Q.

---

[8]The "voting paradox" is illustrated in exercise 7 of Chapter 2, where it is seen that orderings established by majority votes may be inconsistent (intransitive).

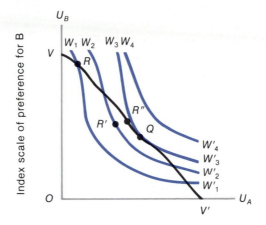

Figure 17.2.4 Maximization of Social Welfare: From Utility Possibilities to "Constrained Bliss"

Index scale for preference of A

It is useful to digress for a moment to consider how everyday notions translate into shapes of the welfare curves.

First consider that A and B have very different personalities, much like two of the Seven Dwarfs. Mr. A is a Happy-type individual so that little is required to achieve a given level of utility. Mr. B is a Grumpy-type. Almost nothing can be done to satisfy him. How should the welfare indifference curves look?

Two issues are involved. First, implicit in these statements, and indeed in any set of welfare functions, is interpersonal comparisons of utility. To say that it requires less to bring Happy to a given level of utility than Grumpy is a statement that requires comparisons of satisfaction levels across individuals. This is a radical departure from the ordinalist notions that are used throughout this book. As soon as welfare comparisons are made, it becomes necessary to think of the cardinal measures of utility as having some meaning.

The second issue is should society attempt to equalize happiness across individuals? If so, should it do this for total utility or for marginal utility? That is, if we believe that all individuals should achieve the same level of happiness, then at the extreme, the welfare curves in Figure 17.2.4 would be L-shaped lines with the kink right on the 45 degree line as shown in Figure 17.2.5. Additional utility to A does not contribute to social welfare in the absence of an equal augmentation of B's utility. Of course, since B is hard to please, this will require that much more fish and cabbage go to B than to A. Some might believe that this is a waste of society's resources.

Another notion of egalitarianism holds that marginal utilities per unit of expenditure should be equated. That is, society should always give the in-

Figure 17.2.5 Equalization of Total Utility

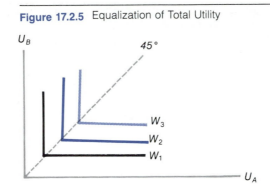

cremental dollar to the individual who derives the most pleasure from it. If all one cared about was total utility of a society, this rule would maximize it.[9]

Of course, this would cause almost all resources to go to A. He appreciates everything and B appreciates nothing. Under those circumstances, the welfare indifference curves would be straight lines with slopes of -1 as in Figure 17.2.6. Since it is cheaper to provide utility to A than B, we are likely to end up at a corner, giving all of society's wealth to A.

Recently, these ideas have been extended to deal with human emotions such as love, hate, and altruism. This has been pushed the furthest in considering behavior within a family unit.[10]

For example, suppose that A is the father and B is the son. Suppose further that A is the decision maker who controls the family's resources. A father who loved his son as much as himself would have indifference curves that were symmetric around the 45 degree line with a slope of -1 at that line as shown in Figure 17.2.7. At any point on the 45 degree line, the father is indifferent between giving an additional unit of utility to himself or to his son. The social welfare indifference curves would, in this case, be the father's indifference curves. This approach has been used to explain behavior within a family and to attempt to better define the distribution of welfare within a household unit.

---

[9]Recall that $C = C_A + C_B$ and $F = F_A + F_B$. All resources are allocated either to A or B. Maximization of total utility requires setting C_A, F_A so as to maximize $W = U_A + U_B$. (Once C_A is chosen, C_B is determined, and similarly for F_A and F_B.) The first-order conditions are

$$\frac{\partial W}{\partial C_A} = \frac{\partial U_A}{\partial C_A} + \frac{\partial U_B}{\partial C_B} \cdot \frac{\partial C_B}{\partial C_A} = 0$$

and

$$\frac{\partial W}{\partial F_A} = \frac{\partial U_A}{\partial F_A} + \frac{\partial U_B}{\partial F_B} \cdot \frac{\partial F_B}{\partial F_A} = 0.$$

[10]See G. S. Becker, "The Theory of Social Interactions," *Journal of Political Economy* 82 (November/December 1974), pp. 1063–94; and E. P. Lazear and R. Michael, *The Allocation of Income within the Household* (Chicago: University of Chicago Press, forthcoming), Chapter 3.

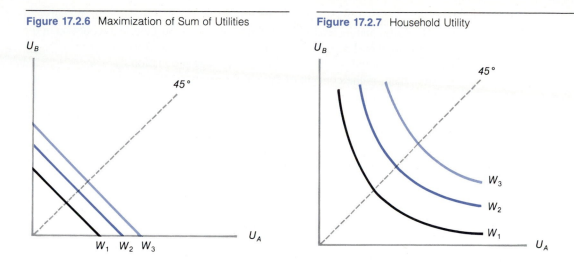

Constrained Bliss and Efficiency
17.2.g

This section begins with a digression to recount the meaning of Pareto optimality or efficiency.

Pareto Optimal Organization: Any organization (point) is said to be Pareto optimal or Pareto efficient when every reorganization that augments the utility of one individual necessarily reduces the utility of another.

Some examples should make this definition clear.

The contract curve for exchange is a Pareto-optimal locus. In deriving the locus in Chapter 16, Figure 16.2.3, the following argument was made.

Suppose the original distribution of the initial commodity endowment placed A and B at point D (not on the contract curve). At this point, A is willing to trade a relatively large amount of Y for a unit of X, and B is willing to trade a relatively large amount of X for a unit of Y. Both parties generally benefit from exchange; in the limit, B receives all the benefit, but A is no worse off, if trading moves the distribution to P_2. Similarly, A receives all the benefit, but B does not suffer, if the move is from D to P_3. At any point on CC' between P_2 and P_3, both parties benefit from exchange.

Clearly the point D is not Pareto optimal or efficient. A reorganization from D can benefit both traders (can augment the value of both utility variables). But *all* points on the contract curve are Pareto optimal. For example, a reorganization from P_2 to P_3 benefits A; but it simultaneously places B on a lower indifference curve.

The very same line of reasoning shows that the contract curve for production is a Pareto-optimal locus. If the allocation of inputs initially leads to a point not on the curve, the output of one or both goods can be increased, and the output of neither reduced, by moving to a point on the curve. But once on the curve, a reorganization that increases the output of one good must cause a reduction in the output of another. For example, in Figure 17.2.1, a reorganization from S'' to Q'' increases the output of fish but reduces cabbage production.

This, then, is the concept of Pareto optimality or efficiency: an organization such that a change that "helps" one must "hurt" another. As we have repeatedly seen, an infinite number of Pareto-optimal points (or organizations) are associated with each problem. One example is the utility-possibility frontier VV' in Figure 17.2.4. An infinite number of points such as R and Q are on this curve. A reorganization from, say, R to Q definitely benefits A because U_A is greater; but B suffers a loss because U_B declines. Thus each point on VV' is Pareto efficient and the entire curve is a Pareto-optimal locus.

Let us now examine a unique characteristic of the "constrained bliss" point Q in Figure 17.2.4. It is the only point of the infinitely many on the utility-possibility frontier that has unequivocal prescriptive significance. It is not only Pareto optimal, it is uniquely associated with maximum social welfare. Pareto optimality or efficiency is a *necessary,* but not *sufficient,* condition for a welfare maximum. The marginal conditions developed in section 17.1 only give the Pareto-efficiency requirements; alone they do not guarantee a welfare maximum. For this an explicit welfare function is required.

Furthermore, once a social welfare function is defined, the limited importance of "efficiency" becomes clear. The point of "constrained bliss" is Pareto optimal. But compare points R and R'. The former is Pareto efficient inasmuch as it lies on VV'. Yet a reorganization from R to R', a point that is Pareto inefficient, is clearly desirable because a higher level of social welfare is attained. Of course, starting from an "inefficient" point such as R', one or more points on VV' (such as R'' and Q) are socially preferable. But with the single exception of the "constrained-bliss" point Q, for any efficient point on VV', one or more inefficient points are socially more desirable.

Inputs, Outputs, Distribution, and Welfare
17.2.h

Using assumptions 1–4 in subsection 17.2.a, a unique constrained-bliss point has been determined by means of Figures 17.2.1–17.2.4. The process may now be reversed to find the *optimizing* values of the 10 variables listed in subsection 17.2.a: the inputs of labor and capital into the production of fish and cabbage (L_F, L_C, K_F, K_C); the total outputs of fish (F) and cabbage (C); and the distribution of fish and cabbage to A and B (F_A, F_B, C_A, C_B).

The constrained-bliss point Q in Figure 17.2.4 is a unique point on VV'. As shown in subsection 17.2.e, each point in VV' is associated with a unique point on the production-possibility frontier because the marginal conditions for product

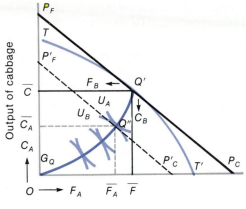

Output of cabbage (vertical axis)

Output of fish (horizontal axis)

substitution must be satisfied. Let the point on the production-possibility frontier corresponding to the constrained-bliss point Q be Q' in Figure 17.2.8, where TT' is the transformation curve. Locating the point Q' immediately determines two variables: the general equilibrium and maximum welfare outputs of fish and cabbage of $O\overline{F}$ and $O\overline{C}$, respectively.

Next, return to Figure 17.2.1. The total outputs of $O\overline{F}$ and $O\overline{C}$ associated with Q' can be produced efficiently in only one way, by producing at the point on the contract curve EE' corresponding to Q' on TT'. Let this point be S''. The organization of production is determined by this point, as are the values of four more variables. The input of capital into fish production (K_F) is $O\overline{K}_F$; labor input (L_F) is $O\overline{L}_F$. Thus the input of capital into cabbage production (K_C) is $O\overline{K} - O\overline{K}_F$, and labor input ($L_C$) is $O\overline{L} - O\overline{L}_F$.

The final four variables are determined by constructing the Edgeworth exchange diagram whose dimensions represent the optimizing values of fish and cabbage output. Dropping perpendiculars from Q' in Figure 17.2.8, the box is given by $O\overline{C}Q'\overline{F}$. The contract curve relative to Q', labeled $G_QG'_Q$, is constructed in the usual way. Finally, imposing the condition that the marginal rate of transformation (given by the slope of P_FP_C) must equal the common marginal rate of substitution (given by the slope of $P'_FP'_C$), one determines the unique point Q'' associated with Q'. Thus A gets $O\overline{F}_A$ units of fish and $O\overline{C}_A$ units of cabbage. B gets the rest: $O\overline{F} - O\overline{F}_A$ units of fish and $O\overline{C} - O\overline{C}_A$ units of cabbage.

In summary, a unique general equilibrium has been attained and this equilibrium point is uniquely associated with the maximum social welfare attainable by the society from the given resource base.

From Constrained Bliss to Prices, Wages, and Rent
17.2.i

Subsection 17.1.b contained an informal suggestion of the way the price system under perfect competition leads to the point of maximum social welfare. Our final step is to determine these prices for the two inputs and the two outputs,[11] denoted as p_F (price of fish), p_C (price of cabbage), w (wage rate), and r (capital rent).

Let us first concentrate our attention on wages and rent (see Figure 17.2.1). To attain the least-cost combination of resources, each producer must employ units in such proportions that their marginal rate of technical substitution equals the input-price ratio. Furthermore, the optimum conditions of factor substitution require equality of the marginal rate of technical substitution among all producers using the two inputs in question. This principle establishes the point S'' in Figure 17.2.1. The common marginal rate of technical substitution is indicated by the slope of the dashed line RW. Since this common marginal rate must equal the input-price ratio, we know that the rent-wage ratio (r/w) must be indicated by the slope of RW.

Next consider Figure 17.2.8. At the maximizing point Q', the marginal rate of transformation of fish into cabbage is given by the slope of $P_F P_C$. The optimum condition for product substitution requires that the marginal rate of transformation in production equal the common marginal rate of substitution in consumption. This principle determines the point Q'' and the marginal rate of substitution given by the slope of the dashed line $P_F' P_C'$. Finally, the optimum condition for exchange requires equality between the common marginal rate of substitution of fish for cabbage and the fish-cabbage price ratio. Hence p_F/p_C is given by the slope of $P_F' P_C'$ (which equals the slope of $P_F P_C$).[12]

---

[11] The social welfare maximum has been called the point of constrained bliss because constraints are imposed by input limitations and the production function. Let $K = \overline{L}$ and $L = \overline{L}$ represent the input endowments; and $K_F + K_C = \overline{K}$ and $L_F + L_C = \overline{L}$. Further, suppose the production functions for fish and cabbage are $F = F(K_F, L_F)$ and $C = C(K_C, L_C)$, respectively. Finally, let the social welfare function be given by $W = W(U_A, U_B)$, where $U_A = U_A(F_A, C_A)$ and $U_B = U_B(F_B, C_B)$, and where $F_A + F_B = F$ and $C_A + C_B = C$. The constrained maximization problem is represented by the following equations: maximize $W = W(U_A, U_B)$, subject to $K - \overline{K} = 0, L - \overline{L} = 0, F(K_F, L_F) - \overline{F} = 0$, and $C(K_C, L_C) - \overline{C} = 0$.
The corresponding Lagrange expression may be written

$$\Lambda = W(U_A, U_B) - r(K - \overline{K}) - w(L - \overline{L}) - p_F[F(K_F, L_F) - \overline{F}]$$
$$- p_C[C(K_C, L_C) - \overline{C}],$$

where r, w, p_F, and p_C are Lagrange multipliers. As already indicated, these multipliers are actually prices, so that the solution to the Lagrange problem gives (scale) solutions for the prices of fish and cabbage (p_F and p_C), the wage rate (w), and the rental on capital (r). The solution prices are the maximizing ones, whether the economic system is a free enterprise system with perfect competition or a decentralized socialist economy following the Lange-Lerner rule. Smith's "invisible hand" is the market mechanism that, if perfectly competitive, happens to establish w, r, p_F, and p_C. A computer (conceptually) can solve the Lagrange problem to obtain the "shadow prices" w, r, p_F, and p_C.

[12] Recall that from the theory of the household (Chapter 3, subsection 3.2.b), consumers will equate the ratio of marginal utilities to prices in a competitive market. This means

$$\frac{p_F}{p_C} = \frac{MU_F}{MU_C} = \frac{MC_F}{MC_C} = MRT_{F \text{ into } C} = MRS_{F \text{ for } C}.$$

Graphical analysis enables us to determine the optimizing input- and output-price *ratios*; absolute values, however, are so far unknown. Given the production functions and input allocation, one principle enables us to relate input prices to output prices: each profit-maximizing entrepreneur must employ units of each resource until the point is reached at which the value of its marginal produce equals its (input) price. Denoting the marginal product of input i in producing output j by MP_{ij}, we have

$$r = p_F MP_{KF} = p_C MP_{KC}, \qquad (17.2.1)$$

and

$$w = p_F MP_{LF} = p_C MP_{LC}. \qquad (17.2.2)$$

Now let us take stock. Denote the marginal rate of technical substitution by *MRTS* and the marginal rate of substitution by *MRS*. Equality of the marginal rate of technical substitution and the input-price ratio may be represented by

$$r = w(MRTS), \qquad (17.2.3)$$

Similarly, equality between the marginal rate of substitution and the output-price ratio implies

$$p_F = p_C(MRS). \qquad (17.2.4)$$

Substitute expression (17.2.4) in, say, the first part of expression (17.2.2), obtaining

$$w = p_C(MRS)(MP_{LF}). \qquad (17.2.5)$$

Next, substituting expression (17.2.5) into (17.2.3) yields

$$r = p_C(MRS)(MP_{LF})(MRTS). \qquad (17.2.6)$$

All terms in parentheses in equation (17.2.6) represent *known* values — values determined by the welfare-maximizing equilibrium solution. Hence r can be determined once p_C is known. If r is known, equation (17.2.3) can be solved for w. Finally, equation (17.2.4) will give the optimum value of p_F if p_C is known.[13] But there is no equation to determine p_C. Prices, wages, and rents are not unique (although the general equilibrium is). They are determined only as to scale or ratio. One of the prices must be designated as the numéraire of the system; then all other prices will be known. For example, one might specify that the price of one unit of cabbage is unity, $p_C = 1$. Then values of r, w, and p_F, corresponding to $p_C = 1$, can be found. The reason the price side of the system is determinate only as to scale lies in the fact that our discussion has involved only *real* (nonmonetary) variables.

Accordingly, when the economy is competitive, prices establish the indicated equality between the marginal rate of transformation in production and the common marginal rate of substitution in production.

[13]The entire manipulation can be turned around to express r, w, and p_C as a function of p_F.

Recall that the point of constrained bliss was Pareto optimal and maximized social welfare. It implied a set of prices, and consequently a set of endowments of factors of production that would allow A and B to trade to reach the point of constrained bliss. But it is not necessary that endowments of factors of production be consistent with constrained bliss to achieve Pareto optimality. Suppose that labor and capital were endowed exogenously in some arbitrary fashion. Fish and cabbage producers, and A and B as workers, owners of capital, and consumers, would trade to a point that was on the VV' curve in Figure 17.2.4. But that point would only by the greatest coincidence be point Q. However, there is always a way to redistribute the initial endowments of factors of production to induce the economy to end up at Q. That is what has led some economists to argue for redistribution of property rather than arbitrary price controls to achieve social goals. The next section illustrates the difference by examination of minimum wage laws.

Minimum Wages and Pareto Efficiency: A Digression[14]
17.2.j

The usefulness of the models in Chapters 16 and 17 lies in their power as analytical devices. To illustrate, in a simple case, how such analyses proceed, we consider the welfare effects of a minimum wage law.

In section 16.4 we developed a simple two-input, two-good general equilibrium model with fixed production coefficients. Suppose demand conditions in the economy are such that the equilibrium occurs at an output of Q_1^* such that the relative price of Q_1 is $p_1 = 1/S_K = a_{K_1}/a_{K_2}$. In other words, the demand curve intersects the supply curve in the range $1/S_K A$ of Figure 16.4.3. Given the assumptions of section 16.4, we know that over this range of output, labor is redundant and the wage rate is zero. The rental rate on capital is $r = 1/a_{K_2}$.

Now suppose a minimum wage law is enacted that sets the minimum wage rate at $\underline{w} > 0$. The zero-profit equations (16.4.8) and (16.4.9) are then two equations in two unknowns, p_1 and r, and can be solved for these values. That is:

$$p_1 = \underline{w}a_{L_1} + ra_{K_1}$$

$$1 = \underline{w}a_{L_2} + ra_{K_2}$$

can be solved for r and p_1 in terms of $\underline{w}$. The solution is

$$\underline{r} = \frac{1 - \underline{w}a_{L_2}}{a_{K_2}}$$

$$\underline{p_1} = \frac{a_{K_1}}{a_{K_2}} + \underline{w}\left(a_{L_1} - a_{L_2}\frac{a_{K_1}}{a_{K_2}}\right).$$

---

[14]We are indebted to Professor Roy J. Ruffin for suggesting this application.

In section 16.4, it was assumed that $a_{L_1} - a_{L_2} a_{K_1}/a_{K_2} > 0$; hence the relative price p_1 is increased by the introduction of the minimum wage and the rental rate is reduced. This means the demand for good 1 is lower at the new equilibrium price p_1 than it was before the minimum wage was introduced.[15] Moreover, since good 1 is assumed to be relatively labor-intensive, this reduction in demand for good 1 reduces the employment of labor.

Does the new equilibrium meet the conditions of Pareto optimality? The answer is clearly no. We note that consumers are faced with a relative price of p_1 that is equal to $a_{K_1}/a_{K_2} + \underline{w}(a_{L_1} - a_{L_2} a_{K_1}/a_{K_2})$. However, since the new equilibrium is still in the segment EA of the production-possibility frontier shown in Figure 16.4.1, the marginal rate of transformation is unchanged by the minimum wage law. Thus, after the minimum wage is introduced, the marginal rate of substitution is no longer equal to the marginal rate of transformation and one of the conditions for Pareto optimality is violated.[16]

Minimum wage legislation is ostensibly intended to benefit low-wage, low-income individuals. Some individuals no doubt do benefit from minimum wage legislation, but only at the cost of Pareto inefficiency in the economy. For this reason, many economists oppose minimum wage laws and would prefer to solve poverty problems by direct income transfers. Such direct transfers achieve the goal of reducing hardship, but do not violate conditions of Pareto optimality. An income transfer is very likely to cause a shift in the point of general equilibrium, but so long as prices are permitted to adjust, the new equilibrium will be another Pareto-efficient point.

It should be emphasized, however, that it is extremely difficult (some say impossible) to devise income distribution policies that do not involve some loss of Pareto efficiency or some "deadweight" costs. For example, an income redistribution policy financed through a sales tax will drive a wedge between the price paid for the taxed commodity (including the tax) and the marginal cost of the commodity. Because of the tax, there will be a difference between the marginal rate of substitution in consumption and the marginal rate of transformation and, hence, a violation of the condition of Pareto optimality. Similar losses of Pareto efficiency arise from wage or income taxes, which lead individuals to substitute leisure for income even though the marginal value of the forgone output exceeds the marginal value of the additional leisure. These considerations are at the heart of the difficult policy choice between "equity" and "efficiency" that appears to occupy much of the attention of political leaders.

---

[15]Strictly speaking, we must also account for possible shifts in the demand curve that arise from income changes after the minimum wage is introduced. In other words, there may be distributive effects of a minimum wage. Given reasonable assumptions about the utility functions of consumers, it can be shown that the minimum wage does indeed reduce the equilibrium demand for good 1 in our example when these distributive effects are taken into account.

[16]In terms of Figure 17.2.8, the effect of the minimum wage law is to cause the slope of $P_F'P_C'$ to differ from the slope of P_FP_C.

The perfectly competitive prices (or the Lange-Lerner Lagrange multipliers) may not be the right ones; or at the set of prices that would properly ration the constrained-bliss outputs, profit-maximizing entrepreneurs will not in fact produce the bliss configuration. If this happens, maximum welfare is not achieved, despite the existence of perfect competition in all markets.

To explain this market failure a third approach to welfare maximization is necessary.

Social Benefits and Costs
17.3.a

In several instances it has been stated that demand represents the marginal social valuation or the marginal social benefit derived from an additional unit of the commodity in question. The demand for each commodity, in other words, shows the price or marginal resource cost consumers are *willing* to pay for an additional unit. In perfect competition price equals marginal cost; it is hoped that marginal cost is the marginal resource cost society *must* incur to have an additional unit produced. Thus by the customary "marginal" argument social welfare is a maximum when marginal social cost equals marginal social benefit, or when the resource sacrifice that consumers are willing to make exactly equals the resource sacrifice that society must make to secure an additional unit of output.

In certain cases, however, the marginal cost that governs the behavior of profit-maximizing entrepreneurs is not the same as the marginal cost to society as a whole. With obvious definitions, marginal *private* cost does not equal marginal *social* cost. In perfect competition, profit maximization implies that price equals marginal private cost. Maximum social welfare is only attained, however, if marginal private cost also equals marginal social cost, for it is only then that marginal social benefit and marginal social cost are equal.

External Economies: An external economy (diseconomy) is said to exist when marginal social cost is less than (is greater than) marginal social benefit.

In this terminology perfect competition does not lead to maximum social welfare if external economies or diseconomies are present.

Ownership Externalities[17]
17.3.b

There are three sources of external economies and diseconomies, or three reasons for a divergence between marginal social cost and marginal social benefit. The

---

[17]Much of the remainder of this chapter is based upon Francis M. Bator, "The Anatomy of Market Failure," *Quarterly Journal of Economics* 72 (1958), pp. 351–79.

first is called "ownership externality." An explanation of this source of divergence may make the notion of "externality" somewhat clearer.

The classic example of an external diseconomy involves the poor widow who supports herself by hand laundry and the factory next door whose smoke blackens the laundry. A more recent and relevant example is smog. The private cost of smoke disposal is the cost incurred in building smokestacks, automobile exhausts, and the like; and the *marginal* private cost to which price is equated is virtually zero. However the social cost is definitely positive when smoke disposal by many factories and automobiles causes smog. Marginal social cost exceeds (the zero) marginal private cost and hence price; social welfare is not maximized.

The externality concept should become even clearer from the following example of an external economy (due to Meade). A beekeeper and an apple grower are situated side by side. The production of apples, we may assume, requires only labor; thus the apple production function may be written $A = A(L)$. Now in the course of growing, apple blossoms first appear on the trees; the apples come later. The bees feed on the essential apple nectar from the blossoms and subsequently produce honey. The labor of the beekeeper is naturally involved; but so is the availability of apple blossoms and, accordingly, the level of apple production. As a consequence, the honey production function is $H = H(L, A)$.[18]

The marginal private cost of increased apple production depends only on the (perfectly competitive) wage rate. If one additional unit of labor can produce one additional unit of apples, the marginal private cost of apples is the wage rate. But producing an additional unit of apples entails more apple blossoms and apple nectar; more bees can be fed and more honey produced. The marginal social cost of apples equals marginal private cost *minus* the value of the increment in honey production; the perfectly competitive output of apples is not as great as it "should" be for welfare maximization.

Where is the difficulty? Apple blossoms clearly enter into honey production; they have a positive marginal product and should, therefore, have a positive market price. But the grower cannot protect the equity in apple nectar; this scarce factor of production is divorced from effective ownership. Apple nectar has a zero market price; even a perfectly competitive market fails to impute the correct value to apple nectar. Profit-maximizing decisions therefore fail properly to allocate resources at the margin because scarcity is divorced from ownership. In this situation market failure is attributable to an ownership externality.

In a seminal article in 1960, Professor Ronald Coase pointed out that in many cases the assignment of property rights can lead private individuals to account for ownership externalities in their decisions.[19] Coase's analysis can be illustrated by a simple example. Suppose that a farmer, who grows tomatoes, and a rancher, who raises cattle, are situated right next to one another. The problem is that cows trample tomatoes, producing an external diseconomy. Now, one might think that if the law sided with the rancher and said that ranchers need not compensate

---

[18]We abstract from the bee service of cross-pollenization.

[19]Ronald Coase, "The Problem of Social Cost," *Journal of Law and Economics* 3 (October 1960), pp. 1–44.

farmers for trampled tomatoes, there would be too many cows and not enough tomatoes. Not so, says Coase. It does not matter who has the property rights, just so long as those rights are well defined.

For example, suppose that an additional cow is worth $100 to the rancher, but that it will trample $90 worth of tomatoes. If the rancher is not required to compensate the farmer, then the cow will be brought onto the ranch and it should be: $100 of value exceeds $90 of loss, so society is better off with the cow than with the tomatoes. Suppose the law said that the rancher had to pay the farmer for damaged tomatoes. The rancher would gain $100, but be forced to pay the farmer $90. Still, the rancher prefers this to not raising the additional cow so again, the cow is brought onto the ranch. The court's ruling does not affect the allocation between cows and tomatoes.

Turn the story around. Suppose that the cow is worth $90 and the tomatoes are worth $100. If the rancher is forced to pay, he clearly will not do so and he should not: From society's point of view, the $90 value of the cow is less than the $100 loss in damaged tomatoes. Now suppose that the rancher need not compensate the farmer. The cow will still not be brought onto the land! The reason is that the farmer would offer the rancher $91 to keep the cow off the land since $91 < $100. The rancher would accept because $91 > $90. So the cow is not raised, independent of the status of the law.

A crucial assumption in this analysis is that bargaining costs are zero. If the farmer had to hire an attorney to present the "bribe" to the rancher, the cost might outweigh any benefit in saved tomatoes. Under those circumstances, whether the rancher had to pay or not could make all the difference.

A second crucial assumption is that the original locations are fixed. If the rancher knew before he located his ranch that he would have to compensate the farmer for damages, he might locate elsewhere to avoid such charges. If the farmer were required to bribe the rancher, the rancher might locate next to the farmer simply to collect the bribes.

A related issue is that of blackmail. The law can change the "threat points" as it is called in game-theoretic terms. If the law says that farmers must bribe ranchers, then ranchers have incentives to threaten to bring cows onto the land even if they have no intention of doing so. This is analogous to hijackers threatening to blow up a plane, even though it is in no one's interest, including their own, to carry out the threat. These strategic considerations are ignored by the Coase analysis. Still, the point made by Coase is one of the most important ones in the analysis of the law and its interaction with economics.

A closely related means of taking external costs into account in the private sector is through vertical integration. In the earlier example of the honey producer and the apple grower, the positive externality can be captured if the honey producer buys out the grower and then produces both honey and apples. When both the orchard and the bees are owned by the same party, that party is able to maintain equity in the apple nectar and is, therefore, willing to increase apple production. Obviously, the same would be true if the grower bought out the beekeeper. Vertical integration may be a way to reduce bargaining costs, but it would be a mistake to assume that vertical integration is a panacea. The problems that arise in setting up contracts between grower and beekeeper are not automatically eliminated when they merge. It still is necessary to set some way to compensate the two individuals within the firm. Solving this problem in a way consistent with economic efficiency is generally no less difficult than trying to coordinate action of a separately owned apple orchard and apiary.

Price Externalities
17.3.c

Another class of externalities, sometimes called price externalities, does not pose problems for the allocation of resources. These externalities do not have anything to do with the technology of production or consumption, but merely relate to the fact that prices are interdependent.

For example, a blacksmith might have viewed the automobile as a negative externality. Its invention definitely reduced the demand for blacksmiths' services and thus caused a fall in their wealth levels. Carrying the logic of the previous section over, blacksmiths might have been willing to pay something to prevent automobiles from being invented. But these externalities are not inefficient. Any interaction that works directly through the market is appropriately internalized by the resulting set of market prices. Although there may be distributional consequences of such interactions, they do not result in any deviation from Pareto optimality.

Public Good Externalities
17.3.d

Let us return to the two-person, two-good model: A and B consume X and Y. Let X be available in amount $\overline{X}$. Then X is said to be a public good if both A *and* B can each consume $\overline{X}$ units of X (rather than having $X_A + X_B = \overline{X}$). For example, one person viewing a pyrotechnic display does not preclude another from viewing it as well; concerts may be attended by more than one person, and, to a point, so too may public schools.

Perfect competition establishes equality between the marginal rate of transformation of X into Y and A's and B's common marginal rate of substitution of X for Y. But in the public good case, since A's consumption of X does not restrict B's, the marginal rate of transformation should equal the *sum* of the two marginal rates of substitution. Perfect competition, and perfectly competitive prices, lead to underproduction and underconsumption of public goods.

It can be shown, however, that a monopolist who can price discriminate will produce an efficient amount of the public good. He or she will price each unit of the good separately to each individual such that the marginal revenue that he or she receives exactly equals the marginal cost of producing one more unit. This assumes that the producer knows each individual's demand schedule and that he or she can exclude nonpayers from enjoying the public good. (Cable TV is an example of a public good where producers can exclude nonpaying customers.)

DISTORTIONS AND THE SECOND BEST
17.4

The analysis of Pareto inefficiencies treats each such distortion in isolation. In real-world economies, however, numerous such distortions are often simultaneously present. Political and other institutional considerations may render it impossible to eliminate every such distortion. In such a situation, the usual conditions for Pareto efficiency may not apply even for those distortions where some policy action is feasible.

To illustrate, suppose that a firm creates a negative externality in the form of pollution. Viewed as an isolated situation in a purely competitive equilibrium, one might conclude that the firm should be induced to cut back its output to take into account the social cost of the negative externality. But suppose that the firm is a monopolist. We know that the distortion associated with monopoly per se is that the firm produces too little of the monopolized product. Thus, if it is not feasible to break up the monopoly and replace it with a competitive industry, efforts to reduce further the firm's output may, in fact, move the economy further away from Pareto efficiency. In other words, at least in this example, the problems of monopoly and pollution are offsetting to some degree.

The key point of this illustration is that, in assessing any given apparent real-world distortion, one can be misled by failing to consider the effect of other distortions that are too costly to eliminate and, hence, that must be treated as institutional facts of life.[20] The analysis of distortions in this kind of "imperfect" world framework is known as the economics of the second best.[21]

SYNOPSIS
17.5

■ The analysis in Chapter 16 established various necessary conditions for Pareto optimality. For example, the *marginal condition for exchange* says that, at a Pareto optimum, the marginal rate of substitution between any pair of consumer goods must be the same for all individuals who consume both goods. The other two conditions are the *marginal condition for factor substitution* and the *marginal condition for product substitution*. In an economy where every consumer, every firm, every industry, and every input market is perfectly competitive, it can be shown that these conditions are satisfied. In other words, the price system in an economy of perfectly competitive markets leads to a Pareto-optimal equilibrium. These

---

[20]If the cost of eliminating a "distortion" exceeds the benefits that would result from its elimination, it is perhaps more accurate to call it a technological constraint or simply a cost, rather than a distortion.

[21]R. G. Lipsey and K. Lancaster, "The General Theory of the Second Best," *Review of Economic Studies* 24 (1956–57), pp. 11–32.

same marginal conditions also apply in a decentralized socialist society containing a central planning agency that aims to maximize social welfare. The state planning agency would have to replace the price system with an explicit calculation of "shadow prices" based on detailed knowledge of individual preference patterns and production functions. According to the Lange-Lerner rule, the planning authority then publishes this price list and instructs all consumers and all plant managers to treat the published prices as given and to act as though they were satisfaction or profit maximizers operating in perfectly competitive markets.

■ The price system will not be able to perform the function of establishing the marginal conditions for Pareto optimality unless the strict conditions of the perfectly competitive model are met. If, for example, external diseconomies (for example, pollution) or external economies are present, the cost of any activity as reckoned by a private individual will differ from the cost to the society as a whole. In such a circumstance, either too much or too little of certain goods may be produced, as measured by the criterion of Pareto optimality. In some cases, an assignment of property rights can lead individuals to take into account these externalities (Coase theorem), but not when transactions costs are prohibitively high. The effect that one consumer or producer has on another is not inefficient if it operates only through the price system without any technological interaction. Public goods are not produced efficiently by a competitive industry, but under certain circumstances, a monopolist will produce the correct amount of the good. The Pareto-optimal criterion is not always applicable. When some distortions cannot be changed for institutional or other reasons, the attainment of maximum (constrained) social welfare will generally *not* involve the usual marginal conditions for Pareto optimality. The appropriate necessary conditions in this case come from the economic theory of the second best.

QUESTIONS AND EXERCISES

1. In 1965 the first hurricane in many years struck New Orleans, causing severe property damage. The government, in the form of aid to distressed areas, paid property owners for part, and sometimes all, of their losses. What considerations would be uppermost in your mind if you were asked to write a lengthy essay on the impact of these payments on the allocation of resources and the distribution of income?

2. Excise taxes are said to distort harmfully the allocation of resources in favor of untaxed commodities. Why?

3. Modern welfare economics frequently makes use of the concept of Pareto optimality. Define the concept and explain its role in the theory of welfare economics. Demonstrate the application of the above welfare criterion to a typical

welfare problem (for example, the distribution of income, resource allocation, etc.). Be sure to include in your discussion the problem of evaluating alternative positions from which society may choose.

4. If completely free trade implies maximum economic welfare, does it necessarily follow that any movement toward free trade would *improve* welfare?

5. Show the conditions that ensure efficient distribution of a given combination of products between two consumers. Would the same conditions ensure maximum *equity?*

6. "Resources are misallocated in the television industry since the cost is borne by advertisers rather than by viewers directly." Discuss.

7. It is often asserted that a monopolist generally operates inefficiently, that is, at some point on the average cost curve other than its minimum point, while competitive firms operate at their minimum average cost, and hence operate efficiently. Critically analyze this definition of economic efficiency, and if you find it unsatisfactory, suggest an alternative.

8. How might a community attempt to control a monopoly in the public interest?

9. "A society or firm that is capable of imputing appropriate prices to the factors of production has, in those prices, a tool that can be used to provide efficient direction to its production activities." Explain.

10. Assume that we now have a socially optimal distribution of factors of production among industries. The imposition of an income tax will not affect this distribution. True or false, and explain.

11. "The government's policies toward agriculture over the last 30 years or so have been basically defective because the policies fail to separate the 'economic' problem of resource allocation from the 'ethical' problem of income distribution." Discuss.

12. "Increasing returns to scale make the achievement of Pareto optimality easier for a society." Discuss.

13. Assume that resources are now allocated optimally within a community. How will the following affect this allocation: (*a*) the imposition of a progressive income tax, (*b*) the imposition of a proportional income tax, (*c*) an industry in the economy becomes monopolized, and (*d*) a new method of producing some product is introduced that has an undesirable by-product (for example, water pollution)?

SUGGESTED READINGS

Bator, Francis M. "The Anatomy of Market Failure." *Quarterly Journal of Economics* 72 (1958), pp. 351–79.

————. "The Simple Analytics of Welfare Maximization." *American Economic Review* 47 (1957), pp. 22–59.

Becker, Gary S. "A Theory of Social Interactions." *Journal of Political Economy* 82 (November/December 1974), pp. 1063–94.

Ferguson, C. E. "Transformation Curve in Production Theory: A Pedagogical Note." *Southern Economic Journal* 29 (1962), pp. 96–102.

Hayak, F. V. "Economics and Knowledge." *Economica* 4 (1937), pp. 33–54.

Henderson, James M., and **Richard E. Quandt.** *Microeconomic Theory,* 2nd
ed. New York: McGraw-Hill, 1971, pp. 254–92.

Kenen, Peter B. "On the Geometry of Welfare Economics." *Quarterly Journal
of Economics* 71 (1957), pp. 426–27.

Reder, Melvin W. *Studies in the Theory of Welfare Economics.* New York:
Columbia University Press, 1947.

Samuelson, Paul A. *Foundations of Economic Analysis.* Cambridge, Mass.:
Harvard University Press, 1947, pp. 203–53.

Scitovsky, Tibor. *Welfare and Competition.* Homewood, Ill.: Richard D. Irwin,
1971.

18 Capital, Interest, and Investment

A past issue of *Consumer Reports* magazine raised the question whether someone about to purchase a home might gain from financing the purchase of appliances by adding it to the mortgage. The alternatives considered were: (1) purchase of appliances from a retail store for $675, financed by a 2-year contract at 15 percent interest; (2) purchase of the same appliances for $450 from the homebuilder, financed by adding the $450 to the 27-year mortgage, with an interest rate of 7.75 percent. The material in this chapter — dealing with the theory of capital, interest, and investment — is directly relevant to determining which alternative is better.

The analysis develops the theory of interest in a manner formally equivalent to that of general equilibrium theory by introducing dated commodities and a time-dependent form of the utility function. Investment can be viewed as a process of physically transforming one endowment stream into another, and when individuals can trade claims to their endowment, the analysis shows that the investment decision can be separated from the consumption decision. By using the device of a contingent claim, the analysis is further extended to cases involving risk. The "Applying the Theory" section comes back to the choice of the home buyer above and asks you to evaluate the conclusion reached by *Consumer Reports*. ∎

Notes to Home Buyers—On Financing Future Schlock

Mortgage interest rates at last have descended part way out of the stratosphere, setting hammers to tap-tapping again in housing developments. The long blight on home construction is over, and house-hunters heading for new subdivisions and suburban tracts this spring will find that real estate developers are not only building houses again but are expanding into the appliance and furnishings business in a big way.

Builders now sell 25 or 30 percent of all major appliances, according to trade sources, doubling their share of those sales a decade ago. Only a range top and an oven used to come already installed in a new house. Now many large national construction companies are offering dishwashers, washing machines, dryers, garbage disposers, refrigerators and, most recently, trash compactors. The Census Bureau reports that half of all homes built in 1969 came equipped with dishwashers, 10 percent with refrigerators and 2 percent with washers and dryers. According to a study by Westinghouse Electric Corporation, the average new house in 1970 included 3.1 major appliances and, by 1980, will include 4.4 major appliances.

Wall-to-wall carpeting, usually with no finished wood flooring beneath it, is another standard feature in many tract houses. The Federal Housing Administration (FHA), which, together with the Veterans Administration, insures the mortgages of one third of new houses, permits builders to lay carpet directly over the sub-flooring, as long as the carpet meets FHA quality standards. Why require expensive hardwood floors, the reasoning goes, when almost every homeowner immediately carpets them over.

Lower Appliance Prices

Builders claim that appliances and carpeting help to sell houses. They also claim they can offer those items at much lower prices than you would pay for identical brands and models in retail stores, and there is some truth to that. Homebuilding has become a big business with big purchasing power. Kaufman and Broad, Inc., of Los Angeles, built 5,700 one-family houses last year and expects to put up more than 7,000 this year. The Larwin Group, a subsidiary of the giant CNA Financial conglomerate, built almost 8,000 dwelling units in 1971. The National Appliance and Radio-TV Dealers Association complains that big builders are able to negotiate special deals with manufacturers and to sell appliances to homebuyers for at least one third below store prices.

Along with low prices goes the convenience of moving into a fully equipped house without having to shop for appliances and carpets, and, more important, without having to put up much extra money. This convenience is not unadulterated. For one thing, while the builder may offer a choice of models, he usually sells only one manufacturer's brand, selected

(continued on page 560)

(continued from page 559)
less for its quality, perhaps, than for its negotiated wholesale price. The builder's brand may not be the one you would have picked. And as CU's brand Ratings and Frequency-of-Repair data often bring out, there can be significant differences in estimated overall quality and maintenance costs. Furthermore, builders in general have not won good reputations for honoring their warranties.

Economics of Financing

The economics of financing such things as washing machines and carpets with a mortgage should also be seriously weighed. Consider, for instance, that the average mortgage on a new house has a term of 27 years. Yet the average life of a washing machine is said to be 10 years, of a dryer 12 years, a dishwasher 10 years, and a refrigerator 15 years, including second-hand use. The life expectancy of carpeting is utterly unpredictable but may be considerably shorter than that of an appliance. This much is plain: A mortgaged appliance or carpet may have to be replaced before it has been anywhere near paid for.

In the simple arithmetic of interest costs, a mortgage appears to be a very expensive way to finance home furnishings. To illustrate, let's assume that the builder is offering a washing machine, clothes dryer, and automatic dishwasher. Their total price at an appliance store is $675. The builder's price is one third less, $450. Let's further assume a mortgage of average length, 27 years, at the national average interest rate (last December) of 7¾

percent. Finally, let's compare the mortgage finance charges with those for the same appliances purchased at the store's price and with the store's two-year, 15 percent installment contract. Here are the figures:

	Cost from Store	Cost from Builder
Purchase price	$675	$ 450
Finance charge	110	625
Total	$785	$1,075

At those terms, the appliances would cost $290 more from the builder than from the store.

Let's take a set of terms more favorable to the builder's case. In some parts of the country last winter, mortgage money was available at 7 percent. Some stores, meanwhile, were charging 18 percent interest on a two-year appliance contract. The consumer's arithmetic would look like this:

	Cost from Store	Cost from Builder
Purchase price	$675	$ 450
Finance charge	134	553
Total	$809	$1,003

At those terms, the appliances would cost an extra $194 from the builder.

It can be said in favor of the builder's deal that mortgage payments after a number of years will probably be made with inflation-cheapened dollars. Unfortunately, inflation won't stem the rapidly depreciating value of carpets and appliances, even though the value of the house may appreciate handsomely.

Turnover Rate

The fact is, houses change hands an average of once every seven or eight years, and so the average homeowner doesn't pay the full finance charges on his mortgage. He sells his house, uses some of the proceeds to pay off his mortgage and, more than likely, plunks down the rest as down payment on another house. His mortgage payments over the first eight years of ownership consisted mostly of interest. Hardly any principle was paid off: that is the nature of a long-term mortage. Thus the homeowner finds himself still owing the mortgage lender almost the whole purchase price of any carpets and appliances lumped into the mortgage. Now used and worn, they are hardly worth the price of moving them to his new house. The people buying his old house, however, may not want used carpets or appliances and certainly won't pay for them.

Moral: It is expensive to buy appliances, carpets and other home furnishings on credit, no matter where you finance them. Take advantage of the builder's low-priced furnishings if you wish—but only after making sure they are less expensive than from a store—and try to make a large enough cash down payment to cover their price.

A Modular Future?

The selling trend is going very much in the direction of lumping all sorts of short-lived furnishings into the mortgage. Build-

ers at the Houston home show last January told *Home Furnishings Daily* they will include in the mortgage package "anything and everything." They mentioned not only carpets and appliances but also draperies and hardware.

Two of the biggest developers, Levitt & Sons and the Larwin Group, already operate furniture stores on some of their building sites, although furniture is not yet being included in their mortgages. The FHA, for its part, seems to be loosening rather than tightening restrictions on items includable in the mortgages it insures.

The trend reaches its present zenith with mobile homes, many of which come completely furnished and financed. The future, as predicted by some students of the construction industry, will be dominated by factory-built modules—ready-made rooms with furniture, rugs and appliances already installed. Turn-key houses, they are called, because the buyer has only to turn the key and start living in them. And paying for them, as the English say, on the never-never.

Let's carefully consider the "costs" of buying the appliances from the builder, *according to the article*. This "cost" is equal to the purchase price of the appliances ($450) plus the interest cost over 27 years of 7.75 percent of the unpaid balance. According to the article this comes to an additional $625, for a *total cost of $1,075*. This amount is paid over 27 years, so that the yearly payment comes to $39.81 ($1,075/27) to be paid for 27 years. (This $39.81 payment is not explicitly mentioned in the article, but is the direct implication of the analysis.)

(continued on page 562)

(continued from page 561)

Let's further assume that if you buy the appliances from a "store," you pay nothing for two years, but then pay the purchase price of $675 plus a finance charge of 15 percent. According to the article, the *total cost* would come to $785 ($675 purchase price + $110 finance charge) which is due at the end of the two years.

The authors of the article then point out that although the purchase price is higher from the store, the total cost (including the interest payments) is less, and therefore, you should buy appliances from the store, not the builder.

Questions

1. What is wrong with this analysis?
2. How would you compare the true "cost" of buying the appliances from the store versus from the builder? (Show how you would set up the correct calculations that would need to be carried out.)
3. How does this example relate to the material presented in Chapter 18?
4. The article also makes a point of stressing the fact that most appliances don't last 27 years. Does this affect your analysis?

5. Similarly, the article emphasizes that the average turnover of a house is between 7 or 8 years. Does this alter your conclusion as to which offer is better?

Solutions

1. Payments made in different years (or endowments received in different years) cannot simply be added up. As the material in Chapter 18 stresses, the timing of consumption (or payment) is a key characteristic of any commodity. The correct comparison between two payment streams can only be made if both streams are converted to their *present value*. The article never makes this conversion, but implies that a dollar paid two years from now is equivalent to a dollar paid 27 years from now.

2. The present value of the $39.81 dollars paid in the second year equals $39.81/(1 + r)$, where r is the rate of interest. The present value of $39.81 paid in the third year is $39.81/(1 + r)^2$. The present value of $39.81 paid in the 27th year is $39.81/(1 + r)^{26}$. Thus, the *present value* of all the payments for the appliances purchased from the builder equals,

$39.81 + \$39.81/(1 + r) + $39.81/(1 + r)^2 + \ldots\ldots\ldots\ldots +$39.81/(1 + r)^{26}$

(The above assumes, for simplicity, that you pay the first-year payment immediately, and the second-year payment at the start of the second year, etc.) If you assumed instead that no payment was made until the end of the first year, then the first term above would be $[\$39.81/(1 + r)]$, and the last term would be $[\$39.81/(1 + r)^{27}]$. The *present value* of $785 paid in the second year would equal $785/$ $(1 + r)$, using the previous conventions. [If no payment was made until two full years had passed, the present value would be $785/(1 + r)^2$.] You will notice that if $r = 7.75$ percent, the *present value* of the payment stream from the builder is actually quite a bit less than the present value of the payment to the store. In short, the consumer should definitely purchase the appliances from the builder if the market interest rate is 7.75 percent!

3. The material in Chapter 18 starts (subsection 18.1.a) with the point that the timing of consumption is a key characteristic of a commodity. "The consumption of a banana today is not the same as the consumption of a banana one year from now." This applies equally to the timing of payments. A one-dollar payment today is not the same as a one-dollar payment one year from now (or 27 years from now). Future consumption/payments/endowments must be converted to their present values. The analysis above just extends equation 18.1.16 to payments made further into the future than one year (next period).

4,5 The fact that the appliances won't last 27 years or that you might sell your house (and appliances) before they are completely worn out has no bearing on the question of which alternative payment stream is cheaper. As long as the appliances purchased from the store are the same as the appliances purchased from the builder, the above analysis is the correct way to compare alternative payment schemes.

*Excerpts from this article were cited in J. Hirshleifer, *Price Theory and Applications,* 2nd ed., (Englewood Cliffs, N.J.: Prentice-Hall 1980).

Source: *Consumer Reports,* April 1972.

The theory of capital, interest, and investment has been one of the most fascinating and controversial topics in the history of economic thought.[1] Aristotle in his *Politics* looked upon interest as a social evil and for a period of 1500 years the clergy and, to a large extent, government leaders and legislators adamantly opposed the payment of interest on loans. In 1311 Pope Clement V at the Council of Vienna went so far as to threaten with excommunication those secular magistrates who passed laws allowing the payment of interest. Among the first to disagree with this widespread view were the theologian Calvin and the French jurist Dumoulin (Carolus Molinaeus) (1546). Despite such disagreements, the "theory" of interest was for many years primarily a topic of religious and philosophical concern.

According to Böhm-Bawerk, Turgot provided the first attempt to develop a scientific explanation of interest in his work *Reflexion sur la Formation et Distribution des Richesses* (1776). It was more than another 100 years, however, before the theory of interest, investment, and capital was fully integrated into the general framework of neoclassical price theory. The key contributors to this development were Eugen von Böhm-Bawerk in his book *The Positive Theory of Capital* (1891), John Rae, *The Sociological Theory of Capital* (1905) and, most importantly, Irving Fisher, whose influential treatise *The Theory of Interest* (1930) forms the basis for much of the material in this chapter.[2]

Karl Marx (*Das Kapital* [1894]) thought of interest as the return that capital received as a result of its exploitation of labor. Now it is recognized that interest is a way to express the price of future goods in terms of present consumption. Still, Soviet economists generally deny the existence of interest in the Soviet Union, where its recognition would have serious political overtones.

This chapter abstracts from political and theological ramifications of interest. It treats the topic at its purest level, recognizing interest as one of many kinds of prices in a complex economy.

A Simple Time-Preference Model
18.1.a

A key concept in the modern theory of interest is the notion that individuals regard *timing* of consumption as one of the characteristics of a commodity bundle. Hence, for the typical individual, the consumption of a banana today is not the same as the consumption of a banana one year from now. Children often

---

[1]For a detailed history of the theory of interest, upon which parts of this introduction are based, see Eugen von Böhm-Bawerk, *Capital and Interest*, trans. William Smart (London: Macmillan & Co., 1890; reprint ed., New York: Augustus M. Kelley, 1970).

[2]John Rae's book originally appeared in 1834 under the ponderous title *Statement of Some New Principles on the Subject of Political Economy, Exposing the Fallacies of the System of Free Trade, and Some Other Doctrines Maintained in* "The Wealth of Nations." The authors are indebted to Professor Don Patinkin for pointing out the existence of this earlier edition of Rae's work.

display an extreme form of "time preference." Telling a child that he can have 10 ice-cream cones three years from now if he will only part with the one that he currently holds is unlikely to persuade him to diet now.

This concept may be expressed formally by explicitly dating the commodities that enter the individual's utility function. To illustrate, suppose there is one good (say apples) and only two periods (today and next week). Apples consumed today are denoted C_0 and apples consumed next week are denoted C_1. The utility function of a typical individual is written

$$U(C_0, C_1).$$ (18.1.1)

The indifference map of this utility function has the usual properties; that is, the indifference curves are convex, downward sloping, and do not intersect. We also suppose that (1) each individual has an endowment of apples in each period (E_0, E_1) but these endowments are not necessarily the same for all individuals and (2) each individual faces a market price, ρ, which represents the number of apples that must be paid this period in return for one apple next period.

By selling all E_1 claims to next period's apples, the individual can have $E_0 + \rho E_1$ apples for consumption for this period. On the other hand, by selling all of this period's apples (E_0), the individual can have $E_1 + E_0/\rho$ apples for consumption next period. Any intermediate point between these extremes can also be achieved.

Just as before, the fact that an individual was endowed with less of X and more of Y than he wanted to consume did not prevent the consumption of X. Similarly, an individual who wants to consume more today can do so by trading with an individual who has some apples today in return for apples next period. Of course, total consumption cannot exceed this period's endowment of apples, but the identity of the consumer can be altered by trade.

We refer to the quantity $E_0 + \rho E_1$ as the *present value of the endowment stream*, or *wealth*. It represents the maximum current-period consumption available to the individual, given (E_0, E_1) and ρ. For individuals, consumption in each period need not equal endowment in that period. By trading apples for future apples (or vice versa) the individual can have a pattern of consumption that differs from the endowment pattern. If we denote current consumption by C_0 and future consumption by C_1, the "wealth" constraint has the form

$$C_0 + \rho C_1 \le E_0 + \rho E_1.$$ (18.1.2)

(The reader will notice the similarity of this model to the time-preference example in section 4.7. Later we shall discuss the relationship of ρ and the interest rate.)

The individual chooses C_0 and C_1 to maximize utility (18.1.1) subject to the constraint (18.1.2). We assume here that the utility function has positive first partial derivatives (more is better), so (18.1.2) will hold as an equality. The right-hand side of (18.1.2), which, as noted, is called wealth, or present value, will be denoted by V. Thus, the individual chooses C_0 and C_1 to solve

$$\max U(C_0, C_1),$$ (18.1.3)

subject to:

$$C_0 + \rho C_1 = V,$$

where:

$$V \equiv E_0 + \rho E_1.$$

For a given value of ρ, this is a straightforward maximization problem of the kind dealt with in Chapter 3.

Our primary concern here is how ρ, the price of future consumption claims, is determined. The answer involves general equilibrium analysis of the type used in Chapter 16. Suppose there are N individuals in the economy. Given any specific value for ρ, each of these individuals will solve a problem like (18.1.3) to determine C_0 and C_1. For individual i, we designate the solution to this problem as

$$C_{i0}(\rho), C_{i1}(\rho) \qquad i = 1, \ldots, N, \tag{18.1.4}$$

where the dependence of the solution on ρ is noted explicitly. First consider current-period consumption choices. We see that individual i will have a current-period *excess demand* of

$$C_{i0}(\rho) - E_{i0}. \tag{18.1.5}$$

Notice that the individual's excess demand can be positive, zero, or negative. A negative excess demand means that the individual has more apples this period than he or she wishes to consume this period and is thus a net supplier of current-period apples.

In a competitive general equilibrium, the equilibrium value of ρ is determined so as to have an *aggregate* excess demand of zero for the economy as a whole.[3] Thus, the equilibrium value of ρ (denoted ρ^e) is such that the sum of the excess demands is zero.[4] In other words, ρ^e satisfies

$$\sum_{i=1}^{N} [C_{i0}(\rho^e) - E_{i0}] = 0. \tag{18.1.6}$$

This merely says that supply of apples in period ϕ equals demand for apples in period zero. There is an equivalent expression for period 1.

It is important to know if ρ^e also provides an equilibrium in period 1. In this second period, aggregate excess demand is

$$\sum_{i=1}^{N} [C_{i1}(\rho^e) - E_{i1}]. \tag{18.1.7}$$

---

[3]The situation is similar to that in subsection 16.1.f, where the equilibrium wage is determined such that the aggregate excess demand for labor is zero.

[4]The existence and uniqueness of such an equilibrium is a nontrivial mathematical question which we do not take up here.

The budget constraint from (18.1.3) says that for individual i

$$C_{i0}(\rho^e) + \rho^e C_{i1}(\rho^e) = E_{i0} + \rho^e E_{i1}$$

or

$$C_{i0}(\rho^e) - E_{i0} = -\rho^e[C_{i1}(\rho^e) - E_{i1}] .$$

Summing over all N individuals, we obtain

$$\sum_{i=1}^{N}[C_{i0}(\rho^e) - E_{i0}] = -\rho^e \sum_{i=1}^{N}[C_{i1}(\rho^e) - E_{i1}] . \qquad (18.1.8)$$

The left side of (18.1.8) is (18.1.6) and is, therefore, equal to zero. It follows that when ρ^e is not equal to zero, the summation of the right side of (18.1.8) is zero. But this summation is simply (18.1.7), so we see that equilibrium also holds in the second period when $\rho = \rho^e$. This is another case of Walras's law, discussed in Chapter 16. Thus, the supply-equals-demand condition for period 1 that is equivalent to (18.1.7) for period zero need not be introduced explicitly. It holds automatically, given (18.1.7) and all individuals' budget constraints.

An Example of Equilibrium
18.1.b

Consider the case of two individuals ($i = 1, 2$) with identical utility functions but with different endowments. Suppose each individual has a utility function of the form

$$U(C_{i0}, C_{i1}) = C_{i0}^{\alpha} C_{i1}^{\beta} ,$$

where α and β are positive constants. The Lagrangian for the maximization problem (18.1.3) is

$$L(C_{i0}, C_{i1}, \lambda) = C_{i0}^{\alpha} C_{i1}^{\beta} + \lambda(V_i - C_{i0} - \rho C_{i1}) ,$$

where

$$V_i \equiv E_{i0} + \rho E_{i1} .$$

For individual i, the first-order conditions for a maximum are

$$\alpha C_{i0}^{\alpha-1} C_{i1}^{\beta} = \lambda ,$$
$$\beta C_{i0}^{\alpha} C_{i1}^{\beta-1} = \rho\lambda , \qquad (18.1.9)$$
$$V_i = C_{i0} + \rho C_{i1} .$$

Eliminating λ from the first two of these conditions, we get

$$\frac{\beta}{\alpha} \frac{C_{i0}}{C_{i1}} = \rho \qquad i = 1, 2 . \qquad (18.1.10)$$

From equation (18.1.10) we obtain

$$\frac{C_{10}}{C_{11}} = \frac{C_{20}}{C_{21}}.$$

It is easily checked that if (18.1.10) holds, then

$$\frac{C_{10}}{C_{11}} = \frac{C_{20}}{C_{21}} = \frac{C_{10} + C_{20}}{C_{11} + C_{21}}. \qquad (18.1.11)$$

Aggregate consumption will equal aggregate endowments in each period,[5] so

$$C_{10} + C_{20} = E_{10} + E_{20}$$

and

$$C_{11} + C_{21} = E_{11} + E_{21}.$$

Substituting these conditions in (18.1.11), we find

$$\frac{C_{i0}}{C_{i1}} = \frac{E_{10} + E_{20}}{E_{11} + E_{21}} \qquad i = 1, 2. \qquad (18.1.12)$$

Substituting from (18.1.12) into (18.1.10), we obtain an explicit equilibrium value of ρ for this simple economy:

$$\rho^e = \frac{\beta}{\alpha} \left[\frac{E_{10} + E_{20}}{E_{11} + E_{21}} \right]. \qquad (18.1.13)$$

Notice that α and β act like "weights" given to present and future consumption, respectively. Thus, intuitively, the ratio β/α is an index of time preference or impatience. The lower the value of β/α, the more impatient are the individuals. In this example, ρ^e decreases as the individuals become more impatient. Notice also that ρ^e increases as current endowments ($E_{10} + E_{20}$) increase relative to future endowments ($E_{11} + E_{21}$).

The Rate of Interest
18.1.c

Although it may not be immediately obvious, the relationship of the analysis of subsections 18.1.a and 18.1.b to the theory of interest is simply a matter of interpretation. When we speak of the simple interest on a money loan, we mean the amount that is paid back to the lender in excess of the principal. Thus, if a loan of $100 results in a return payment of $105 in one year, we say that the interest is $5 and that the annual interest *rate* is .05, or five percent ($= \frac{5}{100}$). In subsections 18.1.a and 18.1.b we saw that by giving up consumption of ρ apples this period the individual gets one more apple next period. For example, suppose

---

[5]It is implicitly assumed that endowments cannot be carried into the future period. In other words, the commodity is perishable. Inventories can be handled in a manner similar to investment, a topic we consider in section 18.2.

$\rho = 3/4$. Then the individual can get four apples next period by giving up three apples today. Thus, he earns one apple "interest" on his principal of three apples. The interest rate is thus 33 percent. In general, the interest (denominated in apples) is $1 - \rho$ and the interest *rate* is $(1 - \rho)/\rho$. If r denotes the interest rate, then we see that

$$\rho = \frac{1}{1 + r}.$$ (18.1.14)

Expressing (18.1.13) as an interest rate [that is, using the rule $r = (1 - \rho)/\rho$], we see that

$$r^e = \frac{\alpha}{\beta} \left[\frac{E_{11} + E_{21}}{E_{10} + E_{20}} \right] - 1 .$$ (18.1.15)

Thus, the equilibrium interest rate, r^e, increases when the current endowments decrease, when future endowments increase, or when α increases relative to β. This is plausible because these changes all have the effect of making current consumption more attractive than future consumption on the margin.

It is common to express V in terms of interest rates rather than prices of claims on future consumption. Thus, applying (18.1.14) to the definition of V, we obtain

$$V = E_0 + \frac{E_1}{1 + r}.$$ (18.1.16)

At this point, it is apparent that, at the level of the individual, this analysis of the determination of interest rates is equivalent to the discussion of time preference in Chapter 4 (section 4.7). Interpreting the theory of interest in terms of the price of claims on future goods has advantages, as we shall see in the remainder of this chapter.

INVESTMENT OPPORTUNITIES
18.2

Section 18.1 describes an economy with exogenous endowments. In such an economy, the interest rate (or equivalently, ρ) is determined solely by the exchange of claims of future endowments for current endowments. The analysis is somewhat limited because individuals have no direct control over the amount of their future and present endowments. It is much more interesting to assume that individuals have a range of choices regarding present and future endowments. For example, the owner of a piece of land may be able to use the land for several different (but usually mutually exclusive) economic activities; for example, the land could be used for farming, for building houses and apartment buildings, or perhaps for a private recreation area. Associated with each use of the land will be a different stream of current and future payments. Thus, if the land is used for farming, it may provide income of, say, $1,000 this year and $1,500 next year, whereas if it is used to build houses, it may return $500 this year and $2,000 next year.

When land or other assets can be used in different ways, the individual has a *choice* among various income streams. The act of making this choice is usually called *investment*.[6] In a perfectly certain world of the kind we are now considering, the investment decision will be affected primarily by the interest rate. The problem is, therefore, similar to that considered in section 18.1 except that, given ρ, the individual first chooses the investment plan that maximizes V (wealth) and then chooses current and future consumption by trading claims in the market. Thus, investment differs from pure trade in that investment changes the relationship between *aggregate* consumption in one period and *aggregate* consumption in another. Pure trade keeps aggregate consumption constant, even though the way it is distributed varied with trade. The distinction, and the process of investment, are described and illustrated in the next subsection. Subsection 18.2.b deals with the determination of the equilibrium rate of interest when investment opportunities exist.

The Individual's Investment Decision
18.2.a

For simplicity, we again consider the "two-period" model of subsection 18.1.a. The key difference here is that, instead of having a given endowment of present and future goods, each individual faces two or more mutually exclusive endowment alternatives. Such alternatives will be denoted (E_0, E_1) where E_0 is the current-period endowment of the good and E_1 is the second-(future) period endowment. We will call the set of all such endowment alternatives the *set of investment opportunities*. As before, the individual's ultimate objective is to choose C_0 and C_1 to maximize a utility function $U(C_0, C_1)$ subject to a wealth constraint like (18.1.3). The critical difference is that the individual now has some choice about E_0 and E_1 and, hence, V. Because the utility function is increasing in *both* C_0 and C_1, the individual always prefers a larger value of V to a smaller one. The investment decision thus amounts to choosing that endowment alternative (E_0, E_1) from the set of investment opportunities which *maximizes V*, given the value of ρ.

To give analytical substance to the model, we need a fuller description of the investment-opportunity set. It is a common practice in the economics literature to draw the two-period investment-opportunity set as a convex, negatively sloped line such as *ABCD* in Figure 18.2.1. If we represent this line as a function

---

[6]This interpretation of the concept of investment is the one used by Irving Fisher in *The Theory of Interest*. Another common interpretation is to regard investment as an addition to the stock of capital. Upon reflection it is obvious that the two interpretations amount to the same thing. The Fisherian concept is more useful for our current purposes.

Figure 18.2.1 Two-period Investment-Opportunity Set

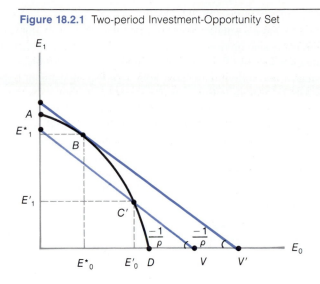

$E_1 = f(E_0)$ (with $df/dE_0 < 0$ and $d^2f/dE_0^2 < 0$), then the individual's investment decision is to choose E_0 (and hence E_1) to maximize $V \equiv E_0 + \rho E_1 \equiv E_0 + \rho f(E_0)$. The first-order condition for this problem is

$$\frac{dV}{dE_0} = 1 + \rho f'(E_0) = 0$$

or

$$f'(E_0) = -\frac{1}{\rho}.$$

(18.2.1)

Geometrically, equation (18.2.1) says that the optimum pair (E_0^*, E_1^*) is such that the slope of the investment-opportunity set (that is, $f'[E_0]$) is equal to $-1/\rho$. In Figure 18.2.1 the optimum pair is at the point B. The present value, or wealth, associated with any point (endowment) in the (E_0, E_1) space can be found by drawing a straight line with slope $-1/\rho$ through the point. The intercept of this line along the E_0 axis is the present value of the associated endowment.[7] As can

_____

[7] The straight line with slope $-1/\rho$ that passes through the point $(\hat{E}_0, \hat{E}_1)$ has the form

$$E_1 = \hat{E}_1 - \frac{1}{\rho}(E_0 - \hat{E}_0).$$

All points on this line have the same present value, since it is possible to achieve each such point by appropriate exchanges of E_0 and E_1. When $E_1 = 0$, E_0 is equal to this present value. Thus, solving the equation for E_0 with $E_1 = 0$, we see that

$$E_0 = \hat{E}_0 + \rho \hat{E}_1.$$

Thus, the E_0 intercept gives the present value of $(\hat{E}_0, \hat{E}_1)$ as stated above.

be seen from Figure 18.2.1, any point such as C on the investment-opportunity line will have a smaller present value than B (for example, $V < V'$).

What is also obvious from Figure 18.2.1 is that investment changes the aggregate endowment of the economy. Suppose, for example, that the economy consisted of two individuals, each with identical investment opportunities as shown by $ABCD$. If both individuals choose point B, then society would have 2 (E_0^*) in period zero and 2 (E_1^*) in period 1 to distribute. Alternatively, if both individuals choose point C, society would have 2 (E_0') in period zero and 2 (E_1') in period 1 to distribute. The aggregate amounts of consumption depend on the investment decision. If no investment possibilities were available and each individual's endowment were fixed at E_0', E_1', then trade could only redistribute; the aggregate amount of consumption would be fixed at E_0' in period zero and E_1' in period 1.

The Determination of Interest in the Presence of Investment Opportunities
18.2.b

The theory of investment of the last subsection can be combined with the analysis of section 18.1 to determine the equilibrium rate of investment in the economy. The discussion following equation (18.1.1) applies when investment opportunities exist except that the endowments in the wealth constraint in (18.1.3) will depend on the value of ρ. Thus, the wealth constraint becomes

$$C_0 + \rho C_1 = V(\rho),$$

where

$$V(\rho) \equiv E_0^* + \rho E_1^*,$$

and where (E_0^*, E_1^*) is the solution to the investment problem of subsection (18.2.a). Because E_0^* and E_1^* depend on ρ, it is more accurate to write the wealth variable V as

$$V(\rho) \equiv E_0^*(\rho) + \rho E_1^*(\rho).$$

The conditions for a competitive general equilibrium expressed in equations (18.1.6), (18.1.7), and (18.1.8) continue to hold except that E_{i0} and E_{i1} are now functions of ρ and are thus written $E_{i0}^*(\rho)$ and $E_{i1}^*(\rho)$. Once ρ^e is known from the equilibrium conditions, it is possible to calculate the equilibrium values of $E_{i0}^*(\rho^e)$, $E_{i1}^*(\rho^e)$, $V_i(\rho^e)$ $[\equiv E_{i0}^*(\rho^e) + \rho^e E_{i1}^*(\rho^e)]$, $C_{i0}(\rho^e)$ and $C_{i1}(\rho^e)$ for all $i = 1, \ldots, N$.

A Numerical Example
18.2.c

To illustrate this model of investment and interest, we consider a very simple two-period, two-individual case. Each individual ($i \equiv 1, 2$) has a utility function of the form

$$U(C_{i0}, C_{i1}) = C_{i0}^{.8} C_{i1}^{.6} \, i = 1, 2.$$

Each individual owns a piece of land that can be used in exactly one of two ways. Thus, in this example, the investment-opportunity set consists of exactly two points. The values of E_0, E_1 for each investment alternative and for each individual are in Table 18.2.1. We see, for example, that by choosing investment alternative 1, individual 1 will have an endowment of 100 apples this period and 125 apples next period. The investment alternatives are not the same for the individuals, and they need not choose the same alternative.

From subsection 18.2.a we know that, given ρ, individuals choose investments so as to maximize the present value of V. For individual 1, we see that for $\rho \leq 2/3$

$$100 + 125\rho \geq 90 + 140\rho ,$$

so individual 1 will choose investment 1 for $\rho \leq 2/3$ and investment 2 for $\rho \geq 2/3$.[8] By similar reasoning, individual 2 prefers investment 1 for $\rho \leq \frac{1}{2}$ and investment 2 for $\rho \geq \frac{1}{2}$. The results are summarized in Table 18.2.2: Using the data from the current-period total column and the next-period column in Table 18.2.2, one can calculate the value of the right-hand side of (18.1.13) as a function of ρ. The results, using $\beta/\alpha = .75$, are shown in Table 18.2.3.

We acknowledge the dependence on ρ of the ratio in the last column of this table by denoting it $R(\rho)$. The equilibrium value of ρ^e in this economy is such that $\rho^e = R(\rho^e)$. In other words ρ^e must be such that the investments made at ρ^e satisfy equation (18.1.13). This reflects the equilibrium condition that resources available in any period must equal consumption demands in that period. Thus, $\rho^e = R(\rho^e)$ is, in effect, the condition that supply equals demand in equilibrium. We see from Table 18.2.3 that when $\rho \leq \frac{1}{2}$, $R(\rho) = .6064$, so ρ^e cannot be less than $\frac{1}{2}$. Similarly for $\rho \geq 2/3$, $R(\rho) = .4722$, so ρ^e cannot be greater than $2/3$. When $\rho = .5294$, $R(\rho)$ also has this value (see the middle row of Table 18.2.3). Thus, $\rho^e = .5294$. Consulting Table 18.2.1 and 18.2.2, we see that for $\rho = .5294$, individual 1 chooses investment 1 and individual 2 chooses investment 2. Applying the present-value formula $V = E_0^* + \rho E_1^*$, we see that for individual 1, $V = 166.18$ and for individual 2, $V = 148.82$. In the current period, individual 1 consumes $C_{10} = 94.96$.[9] Thus, individual 1 lends 5.04 to

---

[8]When $\rho = 2/3$, the individual is indifferent between investment 1 and investment 2. Thus, $E_{10}^*(\rho)$ and $E_{11}^*(\rho)$ will be discontinuous at $\rho = 2/3$. When the investment frontier is concave and has continuous first derivatives, this discontinuity will not be present.

[9]From (18.1.10) we know that

$$C_{i1} = \frac{1}{\rho}\frac{\beta}{\alpha}C_{i0} \qquad i = 1, 2 .$$

Substituting this equilibrium value in the wealth constraint we find that

$$C_{i0} + \rho C_{i1} = C_{i0}\left(1 + \frac{\beta}{\alpha}\right) = E_{i0}^* + \rho E_{i1}^* .$$

(continued on page 574)

Table 18.2.1 Investment Opportunities for Each Individual

	Individual 1		Individual 2	
Investment Alternative	This Period 0	Next Period 1	This Period 0	Next Period 1
1	100	125	90	110
2	90	140	80	130

Table 18.2.2 Investment Choices as a Function of ρ

	Current-Period (0) Endowments			Next-Period (1) Endowments		
ρ	$E^*_{10}(\rho)$	$E^*_{20}(\rho)$	Total	$E^*_{11}(\rho)$	$E^*_{21}(\rho)$	Total
$0 \le \rho \le \frac{1}{2}$	100	90	190	125	110	235
$\frac{1}{2} \le \rho \le 2/3$	100	80	180	125	130	255
$2/3 \le \rho$	90	80	170	140	130	270

Table 18.2.3 The Right-Hand Side of Equation (18.1.13) as a Function of ρ

ρ	$E^*_{10} + E^*_{20}$	$E^*_{11} + E^*_{21}$	$\dfrac{\beta}{\alpha}\left(\dfrac{E^*_{10} + E^*_{20}}{E^*_{11} + E^*_{21}}\right) \equiv R(\rho)$
$0 \le \rho \le \frac{1}{2}$	190	235	.6064
$\frac{1}{2} \le \rho \le 2/3$	180	255	.5294
$2/3 \le \rho$	170	270	.4722

individual 2 in the current period. In the current period, individual 2 consumes 85.04 (80 of endowment plus 5.04 lent by individual 1). In the next period, individual 1 consumes 134.52 apples (125 endowment plus 9.52 from individual 2, representing the return of principal plus interest on the loan). In the next period, individual 2 consumes 120.48 (endowment less the 9.52 payment to individual 1).

(continued from page 573)

Thus, in equilibrium,

$$C_{i0} = \frac{\alpha}{\alpha + \beta}(E^*_{i0} + \rho E^*_{i1}) = \frac{\alpha}{\alpha + \beta}V_i$$

and

$$C_{i1} = \frac{\beta}{\rho(\alpha + \beta)}(E^*_{i0} + \rho E^*_{i1}) = \frac{\beta}{\rho(\alpha + \beta)}V_i.$$

The equilibrium rate of interest implicit in this example[10] is easily calculated to be

$$r^e = \frac{1 - \rho^e}{\rho^e} = .89 \,.$$

Exercise: Find ρ^e, E_{10}^*, E_{20}^*, E_{11}^*, E_{21}^*, C_{10}, C_{20}, C_{11}, C_{21}, and r^e when $\alpha = 1$ and $\beta = .92$.

The Separability of the Investment and Consumption Decision
18.2.d

The reader might have noticed that the optimal investment decisions of the last subsection were made without reference to any specific utility functions. In other words, we were able to ascertain the optimal investment by knowing only ρ; we did not need to know the individual's specific utility function. It is easy to see why we can so separate the investment and consumption choices. Suppose ρ is given and there are two investments: one with present value 1000 and the other with present value 2000. Obviously, any choice of C_0, C_1 that is feasible with wealth of 1000 is also feasible with wealth of 2000. Thus, given an optimal choice of C_0 and C_1 consistent with 1000 of wealth, it would be possible to have this amount of C_0 and C_1 plus more of either or both with a wealth of 2000. Because we assume that utility increases as C_0 and C_1 increase, the larger wealth is always preferred.

Separability of investment and consumption is analogous to separability of production and consumption of earlier chapters. It was not necessary to take the manager's preferences for consumption into account to determine the amount that he would produce. All that was necessary was that he maximize profit. Given that, he could trade for the consumption bundle that maximized his utility. Maximization of profits ensured that there he received the maximum possible utility after trade. The same principle holds here. An entrepreneur who makes his investment decision to maximize his wealth will place himself in the best possible position for trade. By doing that, he can always achieve the highest possible level of utility, consistent with his investment opportunities.

The separability property is a strong result. It means, for example, that an entrepreneur or manager can choose investments for a corporation without knowing the specific utility functions of the shareholders of the corporation. The specific pattern of the dividend stream is irrelevant to the stockholders if they can lend or borrow at the market interest rate r (or equivalently, ρ). All that is relevant is the present value of the dividend stream.

The separability property does not hold if there are restrictions on borrowing or lending, if the interest rate for borrowing is not the same as the lending rate,

---

[10] An interest rate of .89 may seem "high," but we cannot judge that without specifying how long a "period" is. If "next period" is 10 years later than "this period," the annual rate would be about 6.5 percent, because $(1.065)^{10} \approx 1.89$.

or if the individual is not a price taker with respect to the interest rate (or equivalently, ρ). In these cases, it will usually be necessary to consider simultaneously the investment and consumption decision.

INVESTMENT, INTEREST, AND RISK
18.3

In the last section, investments were endowment streams that had no uncertainty or risk associated with them. However, many investments do involve some sort of risk or uncertainty. Even bonds issued by the federal government, which are usually regarded as risk free (that is, the government is almost certain to repay the principal plus interest), are subject to the risk of inflation (or deflation), because the interest and principal payments are specified in nominal dollars.[11] Other forms of debt, such as corporate securities and personal debt, are subject to inflation risk and to uncertainty about the amount of payment (corporate securities) or default risk (such as the case of the Penn Central).

Interestingly, the formal models used in sections 18.1 and 18.2 can be used to deal with risky investments and loans. For that matter, they can be used to analyze the economics of insurance contracts, wagers on sporting events, and other similar kinds of transactions involving risky outcomes. These situations can be handled by introducing the concept of a *contingent claim*.

In sections 18.1 and 18.2 we saw that individuals bought and sold claims to current and future endowments. Claims on future endowments are, in effect, *contingent* claims where the "contingency" is simply the arrival of the day (or time period) when the promised endowment is to be delivered. By elaborating the conditions (or contingencies) involved in contingent claims, we have a natural way to introduce risk into the analysis. This is seen most easily in the case of a lottery. In several states, for example, New York and Illinois, people can purchase state lottery tickets. Such a ticket will pay a certain amount of money to the holder on a specific day if the number on the ticket matches a number randomly selected by the lottery officials. The lottery ticket is thus a contingent claim, where the "contingency" involves not only the time period but also the condition that the lottery ticket number match the randomly selected number.

Other kinds of contingent claims are also well known. Accident insurance policies for automobile drivers are contingent claims that, under certain conditions, pay the policyholder for some or all of the accidental damages during the period of the policy.[12] Earnings that accrue to the stockholders of a corporation often are complex contingent claims for which the amount paid depends on the performance of the company, the condition of the economy, changes in laws and other institutional changes, and the capital structure of the firm.

---

[11]From time to time, state and local governments default and national governments repudiate their debt. At the national level, repudiation of debt is a fairly unusual occurrence often associated with revolution or the loss of a major war.

[12]The contingencies for which the insurance contract will provide payment are usually described in detail in the contract.

There is a convenient way to conceptualize the notion of a contingent claim. At any point in time we can imagine several mutually exclusive "states of the world." These states of the world are *ex ante* possibilities, only one of which will actually be realized. To illustrate with a simple example, consider an individual who purchases a 12-month auto insurance policy. For the purpose of this insurance contract, we can identify two states of the world: in state 1 there is no accidental damage and in state 2 there is accidental damage to the insured automobile. If, during the 12-month period, state 2 obtains (that is, accidental damage occurs), the insurance company will make a payment to the insured individual. If state 1 obtains (no accident), then no payment is made.

In general, there will be a large number of states, and contingent claims may involve payments in one or more of these states at one or more points in time. The following table illustrates situations where there are S states and T time periods. The time/state combinations are represented by the $T \times S$ cells in the table. Thus, cell 2 represents state 2 in time period 1, cell $2S + 1$ represents state 1 in time period 3, and cell $(T - 1)S + 3$ is state 3 in time period T.[13] For purposes of exposition, we restrict our attention to situations involving a finite number of states and a finite number of time periods. Note, however, that finite does not mean small; S and T could be large integers, such as 10^{100}.

Time Period	State			
	1	2	...	S
1	1	2	...	S
2	$S + 1$	$S + 2$	...	$2S$
3	$2S + 1$	$2S + 2$	...	$3S$
4	.			
.	.			
.	.			
.	.			
T	$(T - 1)S + 1$	$(T - 1)S + 2$	...	TS

Using these ideas it is a straightforward matter to describe the economics of risky assets. A risky asset is a contingent claim and hence is equivalent to a payment in one or more of the time/state cells. Individuals derive satisfaction or utility from ownership of these contingent claims. The contingent claim for a payment of C in cell k of the time/state table will be denoted C_k. Using this notation, we can represent the individual's preference for different bundles of contingent claims by a utility function of the form

$$U(C_1, C_2, \ldots, C_{TS}).$$

---

[13]In general, state R in time period t is represented by cell $(t - 1)S + R$.

The indifference curves for any pair of contingent claims C_k and C_j will usually be negatively sloped and convex as in Figure 18.3.1, Panel A. The specification used here is quite general, however, and it is possible that for some C_i the indifference curves will not have this familiar shape. For example, one of the time/state cells may represent the event that a herd of dinosaurs tramples the corn fields in Iowa in the year 2003. Because this event is infeasible, individuals will not get an increase in utility from an increase in the contingent claims on this particular time/state cell. Suppose C_j represents claims on such an infeasible cell and let C_k be claims for some feasible cell. In this case, the indifference map would be a set of straight lines as in Panel B of Figure 18.3.1.

Exercise: Draw an indifference map for *two* infeasible states.

The Demand for Contingent Claims by an Individual
18.3.a

Individuals have an initial set of contingent endowments, that is, endowments that are available to the individual contingent upon the realization of some time/state cell. For example, a farmer who has planted a crop will have contingent endowments available at harvest time which depend upon weather conditions, demand for the crop, and other factors which influence the price of the commodity being grown. Another simple example would be a person who might lose personal property or income due to fire or some other accident during the next year or some other appropriate future interval of time. We represent these contingent endowments the same way we represented contingent claims. Thus, E_3 is the contingent endowment available to the individual in time/state cell 3 and E_i is the contingent endowment for time/state cell i. The individual faces a set of contingent claim prices $\rho_1, \rho_2, \rho_3, \ldots$, where ρ_i is the price of a contingent claim for time/state cell i. The individual is able to buy or sell contingent claims at these prices.[14]

It is probably obvious by now that the situation described here is formally equivalent to the riskless case described in section 18.1 and the familiar current-period theory of consumer demand described in Chapter 3. The algebraic representation of the consumer choice problem is given by the following maximization problem for the case where, for notational convenience, we replace TS with a single letter, K (that is, $K = TS$).

Consumer Choice Problem   Choose $C_0, C_1, C_2, \ldots, C_K$ to maximize

$U(C_0, C_1, \ldots, C_K)$

subject to the budget or wealth constraint:

$$C_0 + \rho_1 C_1 + \rho_2 C_2 + \ldots + \rho_K C_K = E_0 + \rho_1 E_1 + \rho_2 E_2 + \ldots + \rho_K E_K.$$

---

[14]If, for some reason, individuals cannot buy and sell claims for certain time/state cells, they would have to accept whatever contingent endowment they had for those states. The following analysis applies only to those time/state cells where buying and selling of contingent claims are possible.

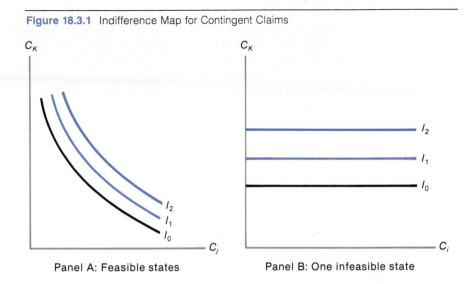

Figure 18.3.1 Indifference Map for Contingent Claims

Panel A: Feasible states

Panel B: One infeasible state

In these expressions E_0 and C_0 are, respectively, the endowment and consumption of the *numéraire* claim. By definition of the *numéraire*, $\rho_0 = 1$. It is common to use claims on the current period and the current state of the world as the *numéraire*. For these claims the "contingency" is really a certainty because the current time and current state have been realized. The wealth constraint reflects the fact that the value of the consumer's contingent claims will be equal to the value of the consumer's contingent endowment. The value of the contingent claims $C_0, C_1, \ldots, C_K$ held by the consumer in equilibrium cannot exceed the value of the consumer's endowments, just as in Chapter 3 expenditures cannot exceed income (or wealth). On the other hand, because contingent claims are "MIB" commodities, the consumer will not hold fewer contingent claims than is feasible.

The solution to this consumer choice problem will result in a set of demand functions for contingent claims that depend on the prices $\rho_1, \ldots, \rho_K$ and the consumer's endowments $E_0, E_1, \ldots, E_K$. This is like saying that the demand for commodities depends on prices and income (or wealth).

As formulated here, the consumer is given $E_0, E_1, \ldots, E_K$ by some exogenous means. In a more general treatment, it would be possible to introduce investment opportunities that allowed the consumer to transform one or more contingent endowments into one or more contingent endowments of some other type. This would correspond to an investment decision of the sort discussed in subsection 18.2.a.

Determination of Equilibrium Contingent Claim Prices 18.3.b

The determination of equilibrium contingent claim prices is a general equilibrium problem very similar to the kind discussed in subsections 18.1.a and 18.1.b. In the case considered here, there is only one state in the initial time period 0 (the present), and there are K possible next-period states (the future). Future states are numbered 1 to K. When there are N individuals, we can specify the current-period and contingent endowments of individuals by E_{ij} where the index i stands for the individual ($i = 1, \ldots, N$) and the index j stands for the state ($j = 0, \ldots, K$). Thus, E_{10} is the current-period endowment for individual 1, and E_{64} is the contingent endowment of individual 6 in state 4 (next period). Using a similar notation, we write C_{ij} for the state j contingent claims held by individual i.

We will assume that individuals have a utility function that is linear in the natural logarithms of contingent claims. Thus,[15]

$$U(C_{i0}, C_{i1}, \ldots, C_{ik}) = \ln C_{i0} + \alpha_1 \ln C_{i1} + \ldots + \alpha_K \ln C_{iK} \, .$$
(18.3.1)

Individual i will choose $C_{i0}, \ldots, C_{iK}$ to maximize this utility function subject to the budget constraint that

$$C_{i0} + \rho_1 C_{i1} + \ldots + \rho_K C_{iK} = E_{i0} + \rho_1 E_{i1} + \ldots + \rho_K E_{iK}$$

where $\rho_1, \ldots, \rho_K$ are the contingent claim prices. We know in general equilibrium models of this sort that only *relative* prices are determined. Thus, no generality is lost by setting $\rho_0 = 1$, as we have in this example. Using the standard Lagrangian technique (see subsection 18.1.b), we obtain the first-order conditions

$$\frac{1}{C_{i0}} = \lambda_i$$

and

$$\frac{\alpha_j}{C_{ij}} = \rho_j \lambda_i \qquad \begin{matrix} j = 1, \ldots, K \\ i = 1, \ldots, N \end{matrix} \, .$$

Eliminating λ_i by substitution, we get

$$C_{ij} = \frac{\alpha_j C_{i0}}{\rho_j} \qquad \begin{matrix} j = 1, \ldots, K \\ i = 1, \ldots, N \end{matrix} \, .$$
(18.3.2)

The first-order conditions (18.3.2) can be used to find C_{i0}. Substituting C_{ij} from (18.3.2) into the budget constraint and collecting terms, we obtain

$$C_{i0} = \theta(E_{i0} + \rho_1 E_{i1} + \ldots + \rho_K E_{iK})$$
(18.3.3)

where

$$\theta = [1 + \sum_j \alpha_j]^{-1} \, .$$

_____
[15]To simplify the algebra in the subsequent examples, it is assumed that all individuals have the same log-linear utility function. Also, α_0 is set equal to 1 with no loss of generality.

If the equilibrium values of $\rho_1, \ldots, \rho_K$ are known, it would be a simple matter to use (18.3.3) to find C_{i0} and then to use (18.3.2) to find C_{ij}. However, in order to find $\rho_j (j = 1, \ldots, K)$, we need to take into account the fact that in any time/state cell j the equilibrium value of ρ_j will be such as to equate the demand for claims and the supply of claims (that is, endowments) over the population of individuals. This equilibrium condition may be written

$$\sum_{i=1}^{N} C_{ij} = \sum_{i=1}^{N} E_{ij} \qquad i = 1, \ldots, K .$$

(18.3.4)

Combining (18.3.1) and (18.3.3), we get an expression that determines ρ_j; namely,

$$\rho_j = \frac{\alpha_j R_0}{R_j} \qquad j = 1, \ldots, K ,$$

(18.3.5)

where

$$R_j = \sum_{i=1}^{N} E_{ij} \qquad i = 0, 1, \ldots, K .$$

Examples of Equilibrium Contingent Claim Prices
18.3.c

In this subsection we provide two numerical examples of the equilibrium contingent claim price model of the last subsection. In each example there are two individuals $(i = 1, 2)$.

Example 1 In this example each of the two individuals has a current-period endowment of 1500. Next period each will again have 1500 unless an accident occurs. If an accident occurs, the individual in question suffers a loss of 1000. There are four possibilities (states): no accident occurs (state 1); individual 1 suffers an accident (state 2); individual 2 suffers an accident (state 3); both 1 and 2 suffer an accident (state 4). The utility function for each individual is log-linear with $\alpha_1 = .64$, $\alpha_2 = .16$, $\alpha_3 = .16$, and $\alpha_4 = .04$ (see [18.3.1]). The contingent endowments (E_{ij}) are given in Table 18.3.1. Applying (18.3.5), we find that

$$\rho_1 = \frac{.64(3000)}{3000} = .64$$

Similarly, $\rho_2 = .24$, $\rho_3 = .24$, and $\rho_4 = .12$. By convention, the current state is the *numéraire* state, so $\rho_0 = 1$. Using these values of $\rho_0, \rho_1, \rho_2, \rho_3,$ and ρ_4, we can determine the wealth of each individual. Individual 1 has a wealth of 3000, calculated from $E_{10} + \rho_1 E_{11} + \rho_2 E_{12} + \rho_3 E_{13} + \rho_4 E_{14} = 1500 + .64(1500) + .24(500) + .24(1500) + .12(500)$. Applying the same technique, individual 2 also has wealth of 3000. For this problem,

$$\theta = \frac{1}{1 + \alpha_1 + \alpha_2 + \alpha_3 + \alpha_5} = \frac{1}{2} .$$

Table 18.3.1 Contingent Endowments (*example 1*)

Individual (*i*)	State (*j*)				
	0	1	2	3	4
1	1500	1500	500	1500	500
2	1500	1500	1500	500	500
Total (R_j)	3000	3000	2000	2000	1000

Table 18.3.2 Equilibrium Contingent Claims and Prices (*example 1*)

Individual (*i*)	State (*j*)				
	0	1	2	3	4
1	1500	1500	1000	1000	500
2	1500	1500	1000	1000	500
Total (R_j)	3000	3000	2000	2000	1000
ρ_j	1	.64	.24	.24	.12

Using equation (18.3.3), we calculate,

$$C_{10} = 1500$$
$$C_{20} = 1500 .$$

Finally, applying equation (18.3.2), we find the remaining values of $C_{ij}(i = 1, 2,$ and $j = 1, \ldots, 4)$. The results are summarized in Table 18.3.2.

Comparing Tables 18.3.1 and 18.3.2 is instructive. We see that individuals trade contingent claims to "smooth" their consumption across states. Because the individuals have the same utility function and the same endowment in states 0, 1, and 4, no trading claim occurs for these states. In states 2 and 3, where initial endowments are different, because only one individual suffers an accident, there is a trading of claims. We see that individual 1 gets 500 of individual 2's state-2 endowment and, in exchange, gives 500 to individual 2 in state 3. This arrangement amounts to a simple mutual insurance company.

Example 2 In this example there is one current-period state (state 0) and two next-period states (states 1 and 2). State 2 can be thought of as a "boom" condition because each individual has a relatively large endowment in that state. State 1 is a "bust" condition, because endowments are relatively low. Contingent endowments are shown in Table 18.3.3. Given $\alpha_1 = \alpha_2 = .5$, we can apply equation (18.3.5) to find ρ_1 and ρ_2. These values can be used to find C_{10} and C_{20} from equation (18.3.3). Finally, equation (18.3.2) is used to calculate C_{11}, C_{21}, C_{12}, and C_{22}. The results are shown in Table 18.3.4.

Comparing these last two tables once again illustrates the willingness of individuals to make trade-offs between the level of contingent claims they hold

Table 18.3.3 Contingent Endowments (*example 2*)

Individual (i)	State (j)		
	0	**1**	**2**
1	800	400	2500
2	1000	800	1100
Total (R_j)	1800	1200	3600

Table 18.3.4 Equilibrium Contingent Claims and Prices (*example 2*)

Individual (i)	State (j)		
	0	**1**	**2**
1	862.50	575	1725
2	937.50	625	1875
Total (R_j)	1800	1200	3600
ρ_j	1	.75	.25

and the "smoothness" of these claim holdings across periods. In Table 18.3.3 of this example we see that individual 1 has a relatively "uneven" set of endowments. The state-2 endowment for individual 1 is more than 6 times as large as the state-1 endowment and more than 3 times the current-period endowment. Individual 2 has a relatively smoother set of endowments. At the equilibrium shown in Table 18.3.4, individual 1 has smoothed these endowments by trading state-2 endowments to individual 2 in exchange for more claims in state 1 and the current period. Individual 2 has a less smooth set of contingent claims than before trading with individual 1 but has received enough of an increase in state-2 endowments to compensate (in utility terms) for the relatively small reductions in the current-period and state-1 contingent claims.

The individual's willingness to trade depends not only on the endowments, but on the likelihood of particular events occurring. Recall that in the example of the dinosaurs trampling the Iowan corn field, no one wanted to buy claims that would restore some of the corn if such an event occurred. Similarly, even though individual 1's endowment is not very smooth, it is possible that individual 1 might want to trade for even more of consumption in state 2. But for individual 1 to be willing to pay a higher price for that consumption than individual 2, one of two conditions must hold. Either 1 must place a higher likelihood on state 2 occurring than individual 2. Or individual 1 must have different preferences than individual 2. The point is that assessments of the event's likelihood also affect the equilibrium prices of the contingent claims.

Debt, Equity, and the Value of a Firm
18.3.d

The contingent claims model is a useful device for analyzing the issues in the modern theory of finance. One such issue has to do with the relationship of debt and equity in a firm's capital structure to the value of the firm. For example, consider a firm in a three-person world where there are two possible states of the economy (boom or bust) in each period and all three periods are future periods. The cash flow, or profit, of the firm in each time/state cell is shown in Table 18.3.5. This table says, for example, that if there is a "bust" in time period 2, the firm's cash flow is $200 million in that time period.

The contingent claim prices for these time/state cells are shown in Table 18.3.6 (where the current period is treated as the *numéraire* state). Table 18.3.6 says that a claim that pays $1.00 in period 1, if there is a boom in period 1, can be bought or sold currently for $0.81. Because there are only two possible states of the economy in this example, a payment of $1.00 for certain in period 1 can be purchased for $0.90 (= .81 + .09) currently. In other words, by purchasing both a "boom" claim and a "bust" claim for period 1, an individual gets a certain payment or $1.00 in period 1. The reason that a certain dollar in period 1 only costs $.90 is that individuals have preference for income now over income in period 1. Thus, the implicit "riskless" interest rate is, from the inverse of equation (18.1.14),

$$\frac{1 - .9}{.9} = .111, \text{ or } 11.11\%.$$

Both debt (bonds) and equity (for example, common stock) represent claims on a firm's profits. The difference between debt and equity is essentially one of priority in rights to claim on the firm's profits. Bondholders' claims are satisfied first. Any profits that are left after the bondholders' claims are met go to the equity holders (stockholders). To simplify exposition, it will be assumed that all profits left after paying bondholders are distributed as dividends to stockholders. The *value of the firm* is the sum of the value of the debt and equity claims on the firm.

Suppose the firm of Table 18.3.5 issues bonds that promise to pay $100 million in each of the three time periods. Any remaining profits are then distributed to stockholders. We are interested in the following question: What is the value of the bonds, value of the equity, and the total value of the firm? It is understood that the answer is to be given in terms of current-period values (the *numéraire* state).

Table 18.3.5 The Firm's Cash Flow (*profits, in millions of dollars*)

Time Period	State of the Economy	
	Boom	Bust
1	200	100
2	500	200
3	650	250

Table 18.3.6 Contingent Claim Prices

Time Period	State of the Economy	
	Boom	Bust
1	.81	.09
2	.70	.11
3	.61	.12

This table gives the current-period prices of claims that pay $1 in the indicated time/state cell.

The answer to this question is found by using the time/state contingent claim prices of Table 18.3.6 and the cash-flow data from Table 18.3.5. Observe first that in all three time periods there will be at least $100 million to pay the bondholders no matter what state — boom or bust — obtains. Hence, there is no default risk associated with this bond issue. The bonds are thus equivalent to a *certain* payment of $100 million in each of the next three periods. By using the contingent claim prices in Table 18.3.6, we see that $1.00 for certain in period 1 has a current price of $0.90 (=.81 + .09); a $1.00 payment for certain in period 2 has a current period price of $0.81 (=.70 + .11); and a $1.00 payment for certain in period 3 has a current price of $0.73 (=.61 + .12). Therefore, the bonds are valued at $100,000,000 × (.90 + .81 + .73) = $244 million in the current period.[16]

By subtracting the $100 million payment from each of the cash flows in Table 18.3.5, we find the amount of remaining profits available for distribution to stockholders in each time/state cell. These are shown in Table 18.3.7. Because

---

[16]It is not necessary that the implicit interest rate that converts period-zero dollars into period-1 dollars equal the rate that converts period-1 dollars into period-2 dollars. In this example, the period-0 interest rate was 11.11%. The period-1 interest rate is

$$\frac{.9 - .81}{.81} = 11.11\%.$$

But the period-2 interest rate is $\dfrac{.81 - .73}{.73} = 10.96\%.$

Table 18.3.7 Firm's Cash Flows after Payments to Bondholders (*millions of dollars*)

Time Period	State of the Economy	
	Boom	Bust
1	100	0
2	400	100
3	550	150

the stockholders receive the payments shown in Table 18.3.7, we can find the value of the stock (equity) by multiplying each payment by the appropriate price from Table 18.3.6. Thus, the value of the stock is calculated as follows:

$$\begin{aligned} \text{Stock value (in \$millions)} &= (.81 \times 100) + (.09 \times 0) \\ &+ (.70 \times 400) + (.11 \times 100) \\ &+ (.61 \times 550) - (.12 \times 150) \\ &= \$725.5 \text{ million.} \end{aligned}$$

In other words, the value of the stock, which is simply a collection of contingent claims, is $725,500,000. The total value of the firm is the sum of the value of the bonds and the value of the stock (that is, the value of *all* the claims or the cash flows). The total value of the firm is $244 million plus $725.5 million, or $969.5 million. This could also be found directly by multiplying the contingent payments in Table 18.3.5 by the corresponding contingent claim prices in Table 18.3.6.

Now consider what happens when the bonds are issued with a promise to pay $100 million in period 1, $100 million in period 2, and $300 million in period 3. If there is a "bust" in period 3, there is only $250 million of profits. In this situation, the bonds go into default. Because of the possibility of default, the bonds are risky; bondholders are paid $100 for certain in the first two time periods but get either $300 or $250 in period 3, depending upon the state of the economy in period 3. The value of the bonds is calculated as follows:

$$\begin{aligned} \text{Bond value (in \$millions)} &= (100 \times .9) + (100 \times .81) \\ &+ (300 \times .61) + (250 \times .12) \\ &= \$384 \text{ million.} \end{aligned}$$

As before, the stockholders are paid whatever profits are left after payments to the bondholders are made. Note, however, that the stockholders never get charged personally for default losses; this is what is meant by the limited liability status of corporate stockholders. In other words, the stockholders get nothing in period 3 if there is a bust but they are not billed personally for the $50 million default on the bonds. The value of the stock is, therefore:

$$
\begin{aligned}
\text{Stock value (in \$millions)} = {} & (.81 \times 100) + (.09 \times 0) \\
& + (.70 \times 400) + (.11 \times 100) \\
& + (.61 \times 350) + (.12 \times 0) \\
= {} & \$585.5 \text{ million}.
\end{aligned}
$$

The value of the firm is the sum of these two values, or $969.5 million (= $384 + $585.5 million).

It is interesting to note that there is no effect from this change on the total value of the firm. This is because the reallocation of the claims between bondholders and stockholders does not affect the underlying cash flows of the firm; it only affects the distribution of these cash flows between the two groups. This is a very important result in the theory of financial economics. It was first shown by Professors Merton Miller and Franco Modigliani and is known as the Modigliani-Miller theorem.[17]

THE EXPECTED UTILITY HYPOTHESIS
18.4

Risk was discussed in section 18.3 in a very general fashion. Once the concept of a contingent claim was introduced, it was easy to specify that contingent claims are seen as goods by individuals, so that the utility function for contingent claims has the standard properties.

It is quite common in the current economics literature to use a separate, more specific theory of utility for choices involving risk. This theory, known as the expected utility hypothesis, was developed by John von Neumann and Oscar Morgenstern in their book *Theory of Games and Economic Behavior* (1943). The expected utility hypothesis is developed from a set of axioms describing how individuals will choose among a set of risky alternatives. Although the axiomatic development involves some rather sophisticated mathematical reasoning, the resulting expected utility theorems can be stated easily.

Consider a set of mutually exclusive outcomes of some experiment or "gamble." These outcomes are equivalent to the states (or time/state cells) described in the last section. Each outcome or state provides the individual with a specified payoff or wealth level, and each outcome also has a specific probability associated with it. Suppose there are K possible outcomes. The payoff for outcome j is C_j ($j = 1, \ldots, K$) and the probability of outcome j is π_j

---

[17]F. Modigliani and M. H. Miller. "The Cost of Capital, Corporation Finance and the Theory of Investment," *American Economic Review*, 48 (June 1958), pp. 261–97.

$(j = 1, \ldots, K)$. These probabilities have the usual property that $\pi_j \geq 0$ and $\sum_{j=1}^{K} \pi_j = 1$. Let the utility of a *certain payoff* of C_j be $U(C_j)$. The expected utility hypothesis says that the utility attached to a lottery with payoffs $C_1, \ldots, C_K$, having probabilities $\pi_1, \ldots, \pi_K$, respectively, is

$$\pi_1 U(C_1) + \pi_2 U(C_2) + \ldots + \pi_K U(C_K).$$

Readers familiar with the probabilistic concept of expected value will see that this utility theory assigns to a gamble the expected value of the utilities of the possible payoffs of the gamble. For example, suppose the individual has a utility function of the form $U(C) = \sqrt{C}$ and suppose this individual is offered a lottery ticket that pays 0 with the probability $\frac{1}{2}$ and 100 with probability $\frac{1}{2}$. The utility value associated with this lottery ticket is

$$\frac{1}{2}\sqrt{0} + \frac{1}{2}\sqrt{100} = 0 + 5 = 5.$$

The expected utility hypothesis is really just a special case of the more general contingent claims model described in section 18.3. The contingent claims model does not require the utility function to depend on outcome probabilities as does the expected utility model. In the contingent claims case, utility can be "state dependent." That is, the utility of an outcome may be affected by more than just the probability of the state and the payoff as is required by the von Neumann-Morgenstern axioms. In fact, as we have seen in section 18.3, the contingent claims model (sometimes known as the state-preference model) does not require explicit or even implicit use of the probability concept.

SYNOPSIS
18.5

■ The theory of interest can be developed in a manner formally equivalent to the neoclassical theory of general equilibrium by introducing dated commodities and a time-dependent form of the utility function. In this formulation, interest rates are, in effect, prices of dated commodities (or money).

■ Investmemt can be viewed as a process of physically transforming one endowment stream into another or as a choice among the various endowment streams provided by a capital asset such as a piece of land. This choice will depend on the time-prices of the endowment stream (denoted $\rho_1, \rho_2, \ldots$ in the chapter), or interest rates. The interest rate, r, is simply a transformation of a time-price, ρ, of the form

$$r = \frac{1 - \rho}{\rho}$$

or

$$\rho = \frac{1}{1 + r}.$$

- When individuals can trade claims to their current- and future-period endowments, the investment decision can be separated from the consumption decision. In this case, the investment decision amounts to choosing that endowment from the investment-opportunity set with the largest present value, or wealth, given the prices $\rho_1, \rho_2, \ldots$.

- By using the conceptual device of a contingent claim, it is possible to extend the analysis to cases involving risk. In this form of the model, the prices $\rho_1, \rho_2, \ldots$ are the price of a claim on a commodity that becomes available to the claim holder contingent upon the realization of one or more states of the world at one or more points in time.

QUESTIONS AND EXERCISES

1. Suppose, for the model described in subsection 18.1.b, that $E_{10} = E_{11} = 100$ and $E_{20} = E_{21} = 150$. Also suppose $\alpha = .45$ and $\beta = .5$. What is r^e? Why is r^e negative? Do individuals trade in this case?

2. How does the answer to question 1 change if it is possible for individuals to carry inventories of current endowment into the next period for consumption?

3. a. Suppose the two-period investment-opportunity set is linear with slope -1.05. That is, suppose individuals can choose any nonnegative values of E_0 and E_1 that satisfy

    $$E_1 = 100 - 1.05E_0.$$

    Assume there are two identical individuals, each with a utility function like that used in subsection 18.2.b. Show that the equilibrium value of the interest rate, r^e, is 0.5. What are E_0^* and and E_1^* for individual 1? What are C_0 and C_1 for individual 1?

    b. Suppose that the investment-opportunity set is linear for each individual but that the slopes and intercepts are not the same. In particular, suppose that individual 1 has an investment-opportunity set given by

    $$E_{11} = 99 - 1.1E_{10}$$

    and individual 2 has an investment-opportunity set given by

    $$E_{21} = 84 - 1.05E_{20}.$$

    Using the utility function of subsection 18.2.b (identical for both individuals) find ρ^e, r^e, E_{20}^*, E_{21}^*, C_{10}, C_{11}, C_{20}, and C_{21}.

4. Consider a model involving risk with one (certain) current period and two possible states next period. Suppose the individual has 1,000 units of endowment in the current period and no endowment in either state next period. If $\rho_1 = .675$ and $\rho_2 = .225$, how much will it cost the individual to have 450 units of consumption for certain next period? What is the riskless rate of interest for one-period loans?

SUGGESTED READINGS

Arrow, K. J. "The Role of Securities in the Optimal Allocation of Risk-Bearing," *Review of Economic Studies,* 31 (1964) pp. 91–96.

Debreu, G. *The Theory of Value: An Axiomatic Analysis of General Equilibrium Theory*. New York: John Wiley & Sons, 1959, chap. 7.

Fama, E., and **Miller, M.** *The Theory of Finance*. New York: Holt, Rinehart & Winston, 1972.

Fisher, I. *The Theory of Interest*. Reprint ed. New York: Augustus M. Kelley, 1965.

Hirshleifer, J. *Investment, Interest and Capital*. Englewood Cliffs, N.J.: Prentice-Hall, 1970.

Marx, Karl, *Das Kapital: Kritik der politischen Oekonomie, Book III: Der Gesammtprocess der kapitalistichen Produktion*. Hamburg: Verlag von Otto Meissner, 1894.

19 Imperfect Information

Why should the price of women's clothes be higher than men's, given we could rule out differences in costs of production? Why do we see firms announcing markdowns (or clearance sales), which are attempts to move merchandise at a price (significantly) below the original price? Why should employers care whether a job applicant has a college degree, when going to college will not improve the applicant's performance on that job? Why do some products come with guarantees?

The answers to all of these seemingly unrelated questions are related to the material in this chapter, which is concerned with circumstances where all information is not held by each and every economic agent. Throughout most of this book, it has been assumed that information is perfect, or that it takes a particular, deterministic form. While under most circumstances this unrealistic assumption greatly simplifies the analysis and still results in quite accurate predictions of behavior, this is not always true.

We will see that imperfect information gives *consumers* an incentive to spend resources searching for the best price. When there is uncertainty about demand, *firms* must "search" for the best price to charge. We will discover that in dealing with this uncertainty, firms will benefit from reducing their prices over time rather than keeping them at some constant level. We will also explore circumstances of adverse selection, where one party has more information than the other. If you have successfully mastered the material in this chapter, you should be able to provide the answers to the questions just posed in the opening paragraph of this chapter. The "Applying the Theory" section contains a newspaper advertisement announcing a fairly typical markdown sale of famous name brand men's shoes, which will be used to test your understanding of some of the material here. ■

Prices Slashed on 1,000's of Pairs of Men's Name Brand Shoes

Questions

1. Suppose that Michaels Shoes has some idea about the prices that consumers are willing to pay for a brand name shoe, but they do not have the demand curve pinned down exactly, especially with regard to particular new styles/colors. How does this assumption help explain their pricing behavior as represented in this advertisement?

2. Suppose it is the case that women's brand name shoes sell for more than men's brand name shoes, given cost conditions. How would you explain such a fact, based on the material in this chapter?

3. The ad indicates that the markdown is 25 percent for famous brand genuine leather casuals. The numerical examples presented in the text in section 19.3 (based on Table 19.3.1) always resulted in a second period price (P_2) that was exactly half that of the first period price (P_1). Is Michaels Shoes pricing strategy therefore inconsistent with the explanation given for markdown sales in this chapter? Explain.

4. The prices in the ad also make it clear that the markdown on some shoes is greater than the 25 percent markdown on genuine leather casuals. Suppose you ask Michaels Shoes the reason for this difference, and they respond that

the percentage of customers who are browsers (versus actual shoppers) is different for genuine leather casuals than for these other shoes with a greater markdown. For which type of shoe is the percentage of browsers greater? Explain.

Solutions

1. The analysis in section 19.3 indicates that markdowns or clearance sales can be interpreted as the direct result of the search by firms for the best price when there is uncertainty about the exact nature of the demand for their product. Uncertainty makes the ability to vary price over time valuable. Such a strategy enables them to learn from their "mistakes." Although the specific example introduced in section 19.3 is for a designer dress by Yves St. Laurent, the analysis is also applicable to selling a new product where there are many potential copies. It also applies when the seller may not know enough about which particular style or color is most in demand. (The small print in the ad states that "not all brands, colors, & styles available" at these "slashed" prices.)

2. The explanation for this difference lies in the fact that when demand is uncertain, there is a difference between the average price charged and the expected revenue per good. It may well be that women's shoes have a high average price *if* they sell, but a lower probability of selling. Men's shoes might have a lower average price at sale, but a higher probability of selling. The expected revenues of the two types of goods may well be the same. Thus, it is possible for the average price of men's name brand shoes to be lower than the average price of women's name brand shoes, even if it costs the same (or more) to produce men's brand name shoes.

3. The result in the text in section 19.3 that $P_2 = \frac{1}{2}P_1$ is a direct result of the assumption that the distribution of V is uniform (or equally likely) at all the intermediate prices between the highest and lowest values. Notice that this is the case in Table 19.3.1. Thus, the fact that there are 25 percent markdowns at Michaels Shoes is not necessarily inconsistent with the analysis in section 19.3.

4. The higher the percentage of browsers, the less that is learned from the fact that a given price is rejected. Thus, the rate of price decline is smaller, the larger the proportion of browsers to actual shoppers. We would therefore predict that there is a higher percentage of browsers for genuine leather shoes than for the shoes with a greater markdown.

Source: Advertisement, *The Los Angeles Times*, August 15, 1987.

INTRODUCTION
19.1

Throughout most of this book, it has been assumed that the relevant agents possessed all the necessary information. However, in the real world, it is rare that all is known by all parties. Consumers may not be aware of the price that every store charges for a particular good. Sellers may not know the exact demand curve for their products. The quality of the good may be uncertain. These considerations affect the interaction between buyers and sellers. This chapter takes a brief look at the effects of imperfect information on market organization. The analysis takes us to the frontiers, because the economics of information is a relatively new area of research.[1]

THE THEORY OF SEARCH
19.2

One of the most basic features of a market where uncertainty is prevalent is that not all firms charge the same price for a given commodity. If firms charge different prices for the same commodity, then some consumers may opt to look around or to search for the lowest prices. In this section, we consider how the existence of many prices, rather than one price, affects the behavior of consumers.

To make things simple, we consider a fanciful example. Imagine a town is endowed with 10 hot springs that have the effect of curing the aches and pains of all those who bathe in any of the springs. The springs are owned by 10 different individuals whose prices are not necessarily the same even though the springs are substitutes for one another. (In a later section, we will analyze how the prices are determined. For right now, simply take those prices as given.)

Tourists arrive at the train station in the center of town and then select some strategy for choosing a spring. Since the tourists do not know the prices of each of the springs before they get there, they must seek out the lowest price. The logic of what follows is that they continue to search until the expected decline in price associated with another inquiry is just equal to the "cost" of making the additional visit.

Search and the Distribution of Purchase Prices
19.2.a

Although consumers do not know where the lowest prices are to be found, they do have an idea as to what prices are likely to be. One way to justify this assumption is to assume that tourists have vacationed in other, similar towns, and

---

[1]The pioneering work in this area is by George Stigler, "Economics of Information," *The Journal of Political Economy* 69, no. 3 (June 1961), pp. 213–25.

through experience they have learned that prices are likely to be distributed as shown in Table 19.2.1:

Table 19.2.1 The Distribution of Hot Spring Prices	
Price	Number of Springs Charging That Price
$10	1
12	2
14	3
16	2
17	2
	10 firms total

The tourist knows that there is likely to be a $10 spring in the town, but she does not know which of the 10 springs to call on first.

Let us suppose that the consumer randomly chooses to visit spring A and finds that its price is $16. What is the value to looking at an additional spring? The value depends on which spring the individual encounters. If she gets lucky, and the next spring is the $10 spring, then she has saved $6 as a result of having searched. The chances of this happening are only one in nine, however, since there are nine firms left and only one has a price of $10. If she is less lucky, she may find a spring that charges $16 or $17. The value of finding those prices is zero, since there is no reason for her to choose to bathe there over the first spring visited, which offered a price of $16. Thus, there is a three in nine chance that the value of the search will be zero. There is also a three in nine chance that she will come across a firm that charges $14, in which case the return to her search will have been $2. Finally, there is a two in nine chance that she will visit a spring that charges $12, yielding a savings of $4. Thus, the individual's expected return from searching at one more spring, given that she has already found a price of $16, is

$$(1/9)\$6 + (2/9)\$4 + (3/9)\$2 + (3/9)\$0 = \$2.22 .$$

The expected return to search is $2.22, but this is conditional on having found the $16 price first. What if the tourist had been fortunate enough to find the $10 price on the first try? Then the return to an additional search would be zero, because nine of the nine other prices exceed the one that she has already found.

In a similar way, the expected return to an additional unit of search can be determined, conditional on each of the five possible prices. If there were a large number of tourists, and if each of the springs is equally likely to be paid a visit, then 1/10 of the consumers would encounter the $10 firm on their first call, 2/10 would encounter the $12 firms, 3/10 the $14 firms, 2/10 the $16 firms, and 2/10 the $17 firms. This, plus knowledge of the cost of search, tells us how many tourists make the second search and tells us the proportion of buyers at each price.

Table 19.2.2 gives the expected return to search, given the price encountered on the first search. The expected return is calculated for each initial price as described above.

Suppose that the only cost involved in visiting another spring is the gasoline used in travel. Suppose that the springs are spaced equally so that it always costs $.60 in gasoline to make one more visit. Table 19.2.2 tells us that all of those individuals who have encountered a first price that exceeds $12 will find it profitable to search, since the expected return exceeds the cost. Thus, 7/10 of the consumers canvass (at least) two firms, and 3/10 of the consumers buy from the first spring they encounter. Stated alternatively, 1/10 buy at $10, 2/10 buy at $12, and 7/10 search.

To find out exactly what each consumer pays, consider first those individuals who encountered a $17 spring on their first try. Of those, 1/9 will encounter the other $17 spring on their second try. They end up paying $17 for the bath. (We ignore additional searches.) Thus, 1/9 of the original .2 pay $17, or only 1/45 of the population ends up paying $17 for the bath. All other individuals pay less than that, either because they encountered a lower priced spring on the first try or because they searched again and found a lower priced spring on the second try. Only 1/45 had the misfortune to end up paying $17 even though 2/10 of the springs charge $45. This is an important point. The proportion of sales at $17 is far smaller than the proportion of springs that charge that price because consumers have the option of rejecting the high-priced springs.

Of the remaining 8/9 of those who encountered $17 on the first try, 2/9 end up paying $16, 3/9 end up paying $14, 2/9 pay $12, and 1/9 pay $10.

It is tedious to follow this through for all groups in the example, but after having done so, the final distribution of transaction prices is given in Table 19.2.3.

The expected selling price is

$$.1777(\$10) + .3555(\$12) + .3333(\$14) + .1111(\$16) + .0222(\$17)$$
$$= \$12.86.$$

In the absence of any search beyond the first inquiry, the expected selling price would have been

$$.1(\$10) + .2(\$12) + .3(\$14) + .2(\$16) + .2(\$17) = \$14.20.$$

Thus, search cuts the average price paid. This is logical since no one would search if he or she thought it would result in paying a higher price.

Again note from Table 19.2.3 that buyers are not distributed evenly among the firms. Even though only .1 of the springs charge a price of $10, .17 of the tourists take their baths there. Conversely, .2 of the springs charge a price of $17, but only .02 of the tourists bathe there. Search tends to concentrate sales at the lower priced firms.

Table 19.2.2 Expected Return to Search

Initial Price Encountered	Proportion of Buyers	Expected Return
$10	.1	$0
12	.2	.22
14	.3	.89
16	.2	2.22
17	.2	2.44

Table 19.2.3 The Distribution of Transaction Prices

Purchase Price	Proportion of Buyers	Proportion of Springs
$10	.1777	.1
12	.3555	.2
14	.3333	.3
16	.1111	.2
17	.0222	.2
	1.0	1.0

Equilibrium Price Distributions
19.2.b

The spirit of this example is correct, but something is incomplete. Examination of Table 19.2.3 reveals that the firm that charges $14 has the largest expected revenue. Since that spring gets .3333 of the sale, its expected revenue is

$$(.3333)(\$14)(N) = (\$4.66)N$$

where N is the number of tourists who visit the town. This exceeds the expected revenue of any other spring. At the opposite end, the firm that charges a price of $17 has the lowest expected revenue. It receives

$$(.0222)(\$17)(N) = (\$.38)N.$$

That suggests that the initial distribution of prices that was assumed is not stable. The spring that charges $17, for example, will find it profitable to change its price to $14. If it does so, it will change the number who search and the number of customers that each of the firms that charge $14 receives. An equilibrium is not reached until all firms are satisfied with the prices that they are charging; there is no way that any of them can make more money by changing their prices.

To examine the full equilibrium, it is useful to simplify the example somewhat by assuming that there are only two springs. In equilibrium, both springs must earn the same expected profit, or it will pay for one spring to change its strategy to that of the more profitable firm.

This is a game-theoretic problem and assumptions are important. The assumption that we make is that each spring, when changing its price, assumes that the other firm will hold its price constant. This assumption results in what is generally called a Bertrand equilibrium. It is somewhat unrealistic when there are only two springs, but as the number of springs increases, the assumption becomes much more plausible. In a town with 100 springs, it is not unreasonable that there will be little reaction to a change in price by one firm.

Additionally, it is assumed that the firm believes that its change in price does not alter the customers' search strategies. This assumption is important also and realistic when there are a large number of sellers. Under these circumstances, it is possible to achieve equilibrium.

We repeat the analysis of 19.2.a, but with a minor simplification: Let there be only two kinds of firms — a high-priced type and a low-priced type. Suppose that 60 percent of the firms charge the low price, whereas 40 percent charge the high price. Let the cost of the first and second search be zero, but the cost of the third search is $2. (This can be justified by allowing the value of the water to the customer to decline with delay to consumption.) Finally, suppose that customers buy no water at prices greater than $1.

To show that this is an equilibrium, it is sufficient to demonstrate two things: First, at the equilibrium prices, customers' search is consistent with the final distribution of purchases across firms. Second, no firm has an incentive to change price.

Let us conjecture that prices of $.19 and $1 are the equilibrium prices. Since 40 percent of the firms charge $1, 40 percent of customers encounter an initial price of $1. Since the cost of the next search is zero, all of them search. Approximately 60 percent of them encounter a low-priced firm, whereas 40 percent encounter a price of $1 again. (Assume a large number of customers and firms.) That leaves

$$.6 + .4 \times .6 = .84$$

customers at a firm with price of $.19 after two searches. Those who still have found only $1 firms do not search again because the cost of the third search is $2 and the value of the search is $.6(\$1 - .19) = \$.49$, which is less than $2. Thus, 84 percent buy from firms that charge $.19 and 16 percent buy from firms that charge $1.

The first part of the analysis is complete: 84 percent buy at the low price, 16 percent at the high price. Now we must show that all firms are content with their current prices.

This is straightforward. High-priced firms get .16 of the customers, so the expected revenue for any given high-priced firm is $(.16)(N/M)(\$1)$, where N is the total number of customers and M is the total number of firms. The expected revenue at the low-priced firm is similarly

$$(.84)(N/M)(\$.19) .$$

But

$$(.84)(N/M)(\$.19) = \$.16(N/M)$$

as well. So what the low-priced firms lose in price, they make up in volume. Both types of firms make the same profit.

Now ask, does a low-priced firm have any incentive to change price? If a low-priced firm raised its prices to, say, $.20, all of its customers would make the second search, since their cost of search is zero. But then those firms end up with only .16 of the customers and $(.16)(N/M)(\$.20) < (.84)(N/M)(\$.19)$. The same is true for all prices between $.19 and $1. A price of $1 results in the same profit as the $.19 price, so that is no better. At a price above $1, there are no sales since customers refuse to buy if the water costs more than $1. A price lower than $.19 does no good because it does not alter the number of customers. All who encounter the high price already make the second search and a lower price cannot induce them to make the third.

The same reasoning applies to high-priced firms. At any price greater than $1, no purchases are made. At prices below $1, the firm loses because it still gets $(.16)(N/M)$ of the customers and the selling price is lower. (It gets only $(.16)(N/M)$ of the customers because all make the second search and none make the third.) Thus, no firm wants to change price, so there is an equilibrium.

This example is somewhat unrealistic. The assumptions about the jumpy nature of search costs generates an equilibrium with more than one price. In the real world, differences in prices across stores are more likely to reflect subtle differences in products. For example, an individual interested in buying a new camera can go to an expensive store in a fancy shopping mall, or can choose to order the same camera through a mail-order outlet at a lower price. The prices are different in equilibrium, but so are the products. The expensive store probably has a more lenient policy on returns and is more likely to assist the customer if the camera turns out to be defective. Some individuals prefer the low price, low service mail-order outlet and some prefer the higher price, higher service mall store. Each individual has an incentive to search for the store that suits him or her best. But the search is for a combination of price and service, rather than for price alone.

The labor market is characterized by this kind of search. Workers and firms try each other out, as it were, to make sure that they are a good match. Some firms offer high pay, but demand long hours. Others offer lower pay, but have more relaxed working conditions. Workers search over firms to learn whether the combination of work conditions and pay is the one that suits them best. This generally occurs early in an individual's work life and explains why individuals change jobs frequently when they are young, but eventually settle into a permanent one (see Rosen, 1972; Jovanovic, 1979; and Hall, 1982 in the Suggested Reading list at the end of this chapter).

Note that the two different reasons for search have different implications for efficiency. If search is generated simply as a multiple-price equilibrium, then all search is socially wasteful. In the spring example, some individuals left the first spring and used gasoline and time to drive to the second spring, merely to obtain a lower price. But the product that they eventually received was assumed to be identical. If prices had been the same in the first place, then no search within the town would occur. No gasoline would be wasted and (at least) the same number of baths would be taken.

Search that helps an individual find his or her niche, either in the labor market or in the product market, is not necessarily wasteful. The customer who does not value his or her time highly and is willing to forgo good service is truly better off as a result of having driven around to find the low-priced, low-quality store. The better service costs society something to produce, and it may well be the case that the additional gas and time used cost less than providing the additional, and unwanted, service.[2]

LEARNING DEMAND OVER TIME
19.3

In the previous section, discussion was focused on search by consumers who recognize that all firms do not charge the same price (or offer exactly the same product). But when there is uncertainty about demand, firms must "search" for the best price to charge. Throughout this book, it has been assumed that the price-setting firm knows the demand curve that it faces with certainty. In reality, it has an idea about prices that consumers are willing to pay for a good, but it rarely has the demand curve pinned down exactly. Thus, sellers must select a pricing strategy that enables them to learn from their mistakes. Their ability to change the price over time in response to experience is an essential feature of price setting. Markdowns or clearance sales are a result of the search by firms for the best price. This process is at the heart of retail pricing.[3]

The point can be made best by considering a specific example. Imagine that the designer dress department of a large department store has just received Yves St. Laurent's latest creation, of which only one exists. The manager must decide how to price that dress, not knowing exactly what some woman may be willing to pay. To make matters simple, suppose that the price that the buyer who values it the most is willing to pay is V. The problem is that the seller does not know V, but may have an idea about its value. For example, suppose that from experience, the seller knows that some dresses sell for as much as $10,000 and that some must be given away. Suppose further that all intermediate prices are equally likely. Thus, the probability that the dress can command a price higher than $10,000 is zero, and the probability that it sells at a price higher than zero is one. Table 19.3.1 reports potential prices and the probability of a sale at each of those prices. Table 19.3.1 is also represented graphically in Figure 19.3.1. Here, the

---

[2]It is not obvious that even this kind of search is always efficient because firms may have an incentive to select services offered in a nonoptimal way.

[3]This analysis is taken from Edward P. Lazear, "Retail Pricing and Clearance Sales," *American Economic Review*, March 1986, pp. 14–32.

Table 19.3.1 Prices and the Probability of Sale

Price	Probability of Sale	Expected Revenue
$10,000	0	$ 0
8,000	.2	1,600
6,667	.3333	2,222
5,000	.5	2,500
3,333	.6667	2,222
2,000	.8	1,600
0	1.0	0

Figure 19.3.1 Uniform Prior on V

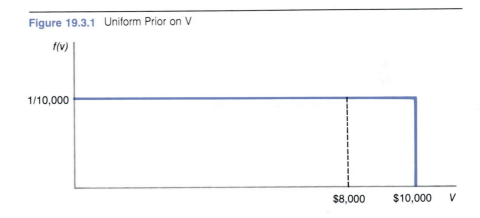

probability that a sale takes place at any given price is the area of the rectangle formed by the vertical line at that price and the vertical line at price $10,000. Thus, if the price were $8,000, the probability that $V \geq 8,000$ is

$$(10,000 - 8,000) \times (1/10,000) = .2.$$

It is easily seen that if the firm must select one price and stick to it, the price that maximizes expected revenue is $5,000. (We ignore the costs of acquiring the dress throughout.) Under those conditions, the store will sell the dress half of the time so that its expected revenue is $2,500. No other price yields as high an expected revenue. But this is too static a view of retailing. The firm has the option of changing its price after having been disappointed by the first price.

To see the importance of being able to change price, imagine that the firm can price at two separate times during the season. Think of this as two periods. The firm can charge one price during the first part of the season, called period 1, and a different price during the second part of the season, called period 2, if the good does not sell during the first.[4]

---
[4]We assume that the discount rate is zero so that we do not have to worry about a preference for selling during the first period.

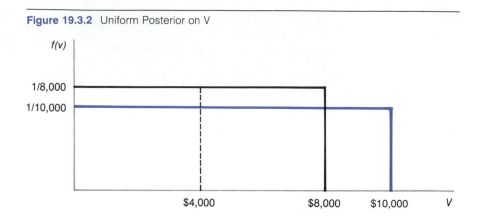

Figure 19.3.2 Uniform Posterior on V

The firm must select a price P_1 for period 1 and P_2 for the second period. What is crucial is that the choice of P_1 gives the firm information that is valuable for setting the price in period 2. This is why setting prices when demand is uncertain is somewhat different from setting price when demand is certain.

Let us derive P_2, contingent on P_1, first. Consider a firm that had selected some price P_1 in period 1, but found that the good did not sell. If it did not sell, then it must have been the case that $P_1 > V$. Women who came into the store rejected the chance to buy the dress because its price exceeded the value that they attached to it. Thus, suppose that the firm had selected a price of $8,000. If it remains unsold after the first period, then it must be the case that $V < \$8,000$. This is a valuable piece of information. Now, the distribution of potential purchase prices has changed. A statistical concept, known as Bayes' theorem, allows the firm to update its assessment of V. Since it knows that $V > \$8,000$ is impossible, it must now be the case that V lies between 0 and $8,000, with all values equally likely. Given that assessment, Figure 19.3.2 shows the relevant distribution. A firm facing those probabilities in period 2 maximizes expected revenue by choosing a price of $4,000, or by splitting the new distribution in half. This yields an expected revenue of $2,000 in period 2, which can be shown to dominate any other choice.

Thus, if the price in the first period was $8,000 and the good did not sell, then the price in the second period should be $4,000. If $P_1 = \$7,000$, then P_2 should be $3,500, with an expected revenue in period 2 of $1,750, and so forth.

The most important lesson so far is that the price in period 2 is lower than the price in period 1. The reason is obvious. If the good did not sell at P_1 in period 1, then it pays for the firm to try a lower price in period 2. A higher price in 2 does no good, because the firm has already ruled out the possibility of selling the dress even at P_1.

This is the logic behind markdowns and clearance sales. A disappointed seller reduces the price of the dress in the second period in hopes of selling it. The firm chooses a high price in period 1 knowing that if the good does not sell, it always has the option of trying a lower price next period.

It is immediately clear that the firm must take period 2 into account before choosing a price in period 1. Since period 2's price is $P_1/2$ (in this example), a higher price in period 1 increases the revenue available through sale in period 2. But a high price in period 1 has two adverse effects as well. First, the higher the period 1 price, the lower is the chance that the dress will sell at that price. Since $P_1 > P_2$, the firm would prefer to sell at the period 1 price. Second, if the price in period 1 is too high, it provides very little information to use in period 2. For example, if the firm set $P_1 = \$9,999$, the fact that the dress did not sell would not give the firm much useful information about the price to be chosen in period 2. Only a trivial part of the original possibilities could be ruled out.

In the current example, it turns out that the best price for period 1 is $\$6,667.$[5] If it does not sell at that price, then in period 2 the best price is $3,333. Under these circumstances, expected revenue is

$$(.3333)(\$6667) + (.3333)(\$3333) = \$3333.$$

Notice that when the firm could only select one price, the expected revenue was only $2,500. The ability to price twice, and to learn from experience, increases the expected revenue of the firm.

Sometimes the store will not be able to sell the dress before the end of the second period. Since $P_2 = 3,333$, if the maximum amount that any buyer would pay is 2,000, then the dress goes unsold. Retailers understand that this event is a possibility, but choose to price the dress at 3,333, because if it does sell, the firm makes higher profits. This means that the average price at which the good sells and expected revenue are not the same. If the good sells, half the time it will sell at P_1 and half the time it will sell at P_2. The average selling price is

---

[5]This can be seen more formally. Let $F(V)$ be the "prior" distribution function on V. Then the probability that $V > P_1$ is $1 - F(P_1)$. Given that the good was not sold in period 1, the firms can rule out that $V > P_1$. The new distribution function is $F_2(V)$. If V is distributed uniformly between 0 and 10,000, then $F_2(V)$ is uniform between 0 and P_1 (by Bayes' theorem). The probability that the good is sold in period 1 is $1 - F(P_1)$. The probability that it is sold in 2 at price P_2 is $F(P_1)[1 - F_2(P_2)]$. Thus, the firm chooses P_1 and P_2 to maximize

$$P_1[1 - F(P_1)] + P_2 F(P_1)[1 - F_2(P_2)]. \tag{19.3.1}$$

Given the uniformity of $F(V)$, (19.3.1) becomes

$$\text{Max}_{P_1,P_2} P_1(1 - P_1/10,000) + P_2(P_1/10,000)(1 - [P_2/P_1]) \tag{19.3.2}$$

or

$$\text{Max}_{P_1,P_2} P_1 - (P_1^2/10,000) + (P_2 P_1/10,000) - (P_2^2/10,000).$$

The first-order conditions are

a. $\dfrac{\partial}{\partial P_1} = 1 - \dfrac{2P_1}{10,000} + \dfrac{P_2}{10,000} = 0$ \hfill (19.3.3)

b. $\dfrac{\partial}{\partial P_2} = \dfrac{P_1}{10,000} - \dfrac{2P_2}{10,000} = 0.$

Equation (19.3.3b) implies that $P_2 = \frac{1}{2}P_1$. Substituting into (19.3.3a) yields

$$P_1 = 6,667$$

so

$$P_2 = 3,333.$$

therefore $5,000. But expected revenue was only $3,333 because it only sells 2/3 of the time.

The difference between expected revenue and average price received when the good sells is important. Some goods have very high average prices if they sell, but a low probability of selling. Some have lower average prices at sale, but a higher probability of selling. The expected revenues of the two types of goods may well be the same. It is possible, therefore, that the average price of men's clothes is lower than the average price of women's clothes, even if it costs more to produce men's clothes. If prices are such that retailers of men's clothing rarely find their clothes unsold, but that retailers of women's clothing throw away garments often (or sell them for scrap value), expected revenue on men's clothing could be higher than that on women's. But the prices that the consumer sees on the rack are higher for women's clothes than for men's.

The same kind of logic can be applied to pricing a new product of which there are many potential copies. For example, an established computer firm is trying to decide how to price a new model. It can raise the price if it finds that the price that it charged initially was too low, or can lower it if it finds that its first price was too high. This kind of learning affects not only the way it changes price, but also its choice of the initial price. Just as in the case of the designer dress, it generally pays to start with a high price. If expectations are disappointed, the price can be lowered. If the firm does better than expected, it generally pays to leave the price at its first-period level. This principle, which requires considerable algebra to derive, is based on the following logic: The price in the first period should always be set high enough so that learning that V equals or exceeds that price would not change the optimal pricing policy.

There are two points to this section: First, pricing when demand is uncertain is not the same as pricing when demand is known. Uncertainty makes the ability to vary price over time valuable. When demand is known (and stable), the price chosen for period 1 is also the optimal price for period 2. Generally, uncertainty about demand results in prices that fall the longer the good remains unsold.

Second, there is a difference between the average price charged and the expected revenue per good when demand is uncertain. The reason is that some goods go unsold when demand is uncertain. If demand were certain, firms would never produce more than could be sold. Under those circumstances, the average price and expected revenue would be the same. Since each good sells at price P, expected revenue is (revenue/quantity) = price.

OTHER ISSUES OF IMPERFECT INFORMATION
19.4

In the real world, all information is not held by each and every economic agent. Throughout most of this book, it has been assumed that information is perfect, or that it takes a particular, deterministic form. Under most circumstances, this unrealistic assumption greatly simplifies the analysis and is still quite an accurate predictor of behavior. That is not always true, however. In this section, we consider a few other areas where imperfect information makes a difference. It should be mentioned that this is a relatively new area of research and so what follows is a mere sketch of an investigation that is currently in its infancy.

Adverse Selection
19.4.a

Adverse selection arises when one party has more information than another. The less well-informed party knows that he or she is at a disadvantage and the equilibrium that results reflects that caution. As before, an example best illustrates the principles.[6]

When an individual decides to sell his car, he has more information about it than a prospective buyer. In fact, it may be exactly that information that induces him to sell the car. For example, subtle indications that the transmission is soon going to explode might make him decide to trade the car in. Thus, used car lots are filled with potential disaster. Of course, the prospective used car buyer knows this and takes it into account when making an offer. He recognizes that the selection of cars on the lot is an adverse one. It is not a random sample of cars of that type. Instead, it is overrepresented by cars with mechanical defects. Adverse selection affects the market price.

If all cars on used car lots had the identical problem of the transmission being ready to blow, then the equilibrium price of those cars would equal the value of that car with a new transmission, minus the cost of the transmission replacement. Consider the price on a used 1973 Ford. It might command a market price of $1,500 if it were in perfect running order. However, if it were known that owners only traded Fords that had faulty transmissions, then all used Fords would soon require transmission repairs. If the cost of repairing the transmission were $500, then the market price would be $1,000.

The determination of price is somewhat more complicated, however, because some of the 1973 Fords on the lot do not have transmission difficulties. In fact, some are there merely because their owners want to upgrade their level of transportation, perhaps to their newly acquired status. Thus, the population of used cars consists of some lemons and some good cars that are no longer best suited to their previous owners. In what follows, the market equilibrium is characterized.

Suppose that the demand for used Fords in good condition is perfectly elastic at $1,400. Thus, the value of a Ford that requires, say, $300 of repairs is $1,100. There are 10,000 Fords in existence. The owners of 8,000 of the 10,000 would not sell their cars for $1,400 or less, so those cars are irrelevant to the used Ford market. Of the 2,000 remaining, 1,000 are in perfect condition, but the owners

---

[6]The example derives from George Akerlof, "The Market for 'Lemons': Quality Uncertainty and the Market Mechanism," *Quarterly Journal of Economics* 84 (August 1970), pp. 488–500.

are anxious to buy a new car. They will sell for any price over $1,000. The other 1,000 need repairs that vary in cost from $0 to $500, uniformly. Thus, the average repair on those cars is $250.

Adverse selection means that the worst cars are the ones most likely to be up for sale. This can be introduced in the following simple way. If R is a "random variable" that represents the amount of expenditure necessary to repair the car, then R goes from $0 to $500. Those owners with the cars that are least costly to repair are least likely to sell. This can be represented by the following sell condition that pertains to the group that has cars in need of repair. (The other group sells at any price above $1,000.)

$$\text{Sell if} \quad P > \$1,500 - R \tag{19.4.1}$$

or if

$$R > \$1,500 - P,$$

where P is the market price. Owners of cars in need of repairs costing $400 will sell at any market price above $1,100. Those owning cars requiring only $200 repairs will not sell unless $P > \$1,300$.

Thus, at any price greater than $1,000, the used car market consists of two kinds of cars. One thousand cars are in perfect shape. Additionally, there will be some cars on the market that require repair. For example, if the price were $1,200, then only 2/5 of the 1,000 owners of defective cars would put theirs on the market. They would be the owners for whom $R \geq \$300$. The average repair bill on those cars would be $400. There would be 1,400 cars on the market, 400 of which needed average repairs of $400, 1,000 of which are in perfect shape. In general, if we define R^* as the minimum value of repair necessary to induce an individual to sell his car, then, using (19.4.1),

$$R^* = 1,500 - P. \tag{19.4.2}$$

In general, then, the proportion of owners of cars in need of repair who opt to sell is

$$1 - R^*/500, \tag{19.4.3}$$

for example, when $P = \$1,200, R^* = 300$, so 2/5 opt to sell. The average level of repair on those defective cars that are sold is therefore

$$\text{Average repair} = (\$500 + R^*)/2. \tag{19.4.4}$$

The value of a car to a buyer is $1,400 if it were in perfect shape, but only $1,400 - R$ if it needs repairs. Recall that because only the seller knows whether a car needs repair, and if so how much, the buyer who buys a car has a

$$1,000/[1,000 + (1 - R^*/500)1,000]$$

chance of getting a perfect car and a

$$(1 - R^*/500)1,000/[1,000 + (1 - R^*/500)1,000]$$

chance of getting a car in need of repairs. The denominator is the total number of cars available on the market. The expected value of cars on the market that are in need of repair is $\$1,400 - [(500 + R^*)/2]$ since the second term is the average repair bill on these cars.

If the buyer is risk neutral, then the value of a randomly selected car is

$$\text{Value} = \$1,400 \left(\frac{1,000}{1,000 + \left(1 - \dfrac{R^*}{500}\right)1,000} \right)$$
$$+ \left(\$1,400 - \left(\frac{\$500 + R^*}{2} \right) \right)$$
$$\cdot \left(\frac{\left(1 - \dfrac{R^*}{500}\right)1,000}{1,000 + \left(1 - \dfrac{R^*}{500}\right)(1,000)} \right) \qquad (19.4.5)$$

Since value must equal price for equilibrium (recall that demand is perfectly elastic), equilibrium is given by

$$P = \$1,400 \left(\frac{1,000}{1,000 + \left(1 - \dfrac{R^*}{500}\right)1,000} \right)$$
$$+ \left(\$1,400 - \left(\frac{\$500 + R^*}{2} \right) \right)$$
$$\cdot \left(\frac{\left(1 - \dfrac{R^*}{500}\right)1,000}{1,000 + \left(1 - \dfrac{R^*}{500}\right)(1,000)} \right) \qquad (19.4.6)$$

On the supply side, the condition that determines the seller who is just indifferent to putting his car on the market is equation (19.4.2). Substitution of it into (19.4.6) yields an equation in R^* alone that can be solved. Its solution yields

$$R^* = \$228.22$$

which, using (19.4.2), implies $P = \$1,271.78$.

Let us interpret this. Any owner of a defective car with needed repairs costing less than $\$228.22$ does not sell. All others do. Thus, $1 - 228/500$ of the owners of defective cars sell. This means that there are $1,000 + 544$ cars on the market. The $1,000$ are perfect, the 544 need repairs, the average of which cost $(\$500 + 228.22)/2$ or $\$364.11$. Substitution of these values into (19.4.5) tells us that the average value is $\$1,271.78$. That is also the price that induces exactly those owners with $R > 228.22$ to sell. Thus, all is consistent.

Some buyers get perfect cars, some get lemons. They know this in advance and the market price, which is below the value of a car in perfect condition, reflects the probability of buying a lemon. Adverse selection occurs because sellers have better information about their cars than buyers. Thus, on average, the worst cars get sold. But since the market is aware of this fact, the market price adjusts so that on average, buyers get exactly what they expect.[7]

Guarantees, Pooling, and Separating Equilibria
19.4.b

In the previous example, those individuals with the better cars to sell were hurt because their cars were pooled together with those that were of lower quality. Buyers could not be sure whether the 1973 Ford that they were buying was in need of $500 of repair, or no repair at all. The price that they were willing to offer fell short of $1,400 as a result. This meant that those with cars that were truly worth $1,400 lost out.

The equilibrium described in the previous section is called a *pooling equilibrium* because the good cars and bad cars are pooled in the same market. Sometimes it is possible to separate the good cars from the bad, even if buyers cannot observe the quality of the good when they buy it. If good cars can be separated from bad cars, then a *separating equilibrium* is said to exist.

One way to bring about a separating equilibrium is to offer guarantees. A guarantee is a form of contingent contract since it says that a payment from seller to buyer is made if a particular event occurs. The event in this case is breakdown of the automobile.

Suppose that the present owner of the Ford could promise to pay the repair bill on the car if it turned out that the car was in need of repair. Prospective buyers then would be willing to pay $1,400 for the car with guarantee, because they would be certain of obtaining a car in perfect running condition at that price. Owners of cars that required no repairs surely would offer the guarantee. If they do not, then they receive only $1,271 for their car. If they do, they receive $1,400 and since they know that the car will need no repair, the full $1,400 that they receive is kept.

Recall that in the last example, only owners of defective cars that required more than $228 of repairs put their cars up for sale. None of these owners would be willing to offer a guarantee if they could continue to receive $1,271 for their cars. The best car of that group, namely the one that needs only $228.22 of repair, sells for $1,400 with the guarantee. But the seller then ends up paying $228.22 and receives a net of only $1,171.78. Thus, he prefers to sell at $1,271.78 without the guarantee. All other sellers of defective cars are even more anxious to sell without guarantees.

---

[7]See Edward P. Lazear, "Salaries and Piece Rates," *The Journal of Business* 59, no. 3 (July 1986), pp. 405–31, for an example of adverse selection in the labor market.

The sellers of defective cars will find that the option of selling without guarantees is no longer available to them, once the sellers of good cars offer guarantees. Consumers know that the seller of a good car prefers the higher price with guarantee to the lower price without. Thus, the consumer automatically infers that the car is defective if it does not come with a guarantee. On average, the repair will cost $364.11, so the buyer would now pay only $1,400 - 364.11 = $1,035.89 for the car. But if that is the price, only those sellers with cars needing repairs that exceed $1,500 - 1,035.89 = $464.11 will sell their cars (see equation 19.4.1). Now, however, the average repair is $482.05, so consumers will only be willing to pay $1,400 - 482.05 = $917.95. But at that price, no defective cars are supplied. The lemons have been eliminated from the market completely. The reason is that not providing a guarantee allows consumers to infer that the car is defective. The equilibrium is a separating one because it has separated the market for good cars from that for lemons.

It is efficient that in this separating equilibrium, no defective cars are sold. Equation (19.4.1) tells us that the value of any defective car to its current owner is $1,500 - R$. For any value of R, the value to the current owner exceeds its value to a new owner. If the market operates efficiently, it must allocate resources to their highest valued use so the current owners of defective cars should retain possession. They behaved in a way that was socially inefficient because they could pass their cars off as the average vehicle. When no guarantees are permitted, the average quality of cars sold was higher than the average quality of defective cars because good cars were in the pool as well. Owners of lemons sold their cars because they could profit from having their cars pooled with good ones. Guarantees prevent pooling from occurring and rob lemon owners of the opportunity to hide behind the veil of the average car.

Moral Hazard and Enforceability
19.4.c

If all of this is true, why don't all cars come with comprehensive warranties? There are at least two major reasons.

First, "moral hazard" is a problem. Moral hazard results when one party insures another against some event over which the insured party has some control. In the previous example, a car that is sold to a new owner in perfect condition may break down because the new owner does not exercise proper maintenance. In fact, the fact that the car is guaranteed gives the new owner an incentive to spend less on the car's preventive maintenance, since all repairs are at the previous owner's expense. The seller knows this before selling the car and may be reluctant to offer a guarantee as a result.

Moral hazard is a more general issue and comes up in a number of contexts. In the labor market, an employer may "insure" a worker by offering to pay an hourly wage, irrespective of the amount that the worker produces during that hour. Workers who are paid time rates such as salaries (as opposed to piece rates, that compensate according to output, for example 2¢ per picked tomato) have the opportunity to work less hard, claiming that output was low for reasons beyond their control. The importance of moral hazard in the labor market context means that firms often compensate workers in ways that circumvent these problems, at least in part.[8]

The second problem is one of enforceability. Implicit in the discussion of guarantees was the notion that the buyer could easily track down the seller and make him pay the repair bill. Anyone with real world experience knows that this is easier said than done. After having made the sale, the seller may decide not to honor the guarantee, claiming, perhaps, that the particular repair lies outside the scope of the guarantee. In fact, he might use moral hazard on the buyer's part as a defense, claiming that the buyer did not take proper care of the car. The ability to renege on the guarantee may cause the separating equilibrium to break down. At the extreme, a seller of a lemon who knows that he can costlessly renege on the guarantee is always willing to offer one. Of course, buyers know that the guarantee is worthless and the equilibrium reverts to the one that held in the absence of guarantees. Lemons and good cars are pooled into the same market.

Thus, moral hazard and enforceability place limits on the extent to which contingent contracts can be used to separate the good from bad items. If these problems are sufficiently pronounced, the equilibrium that is observed in the market is likely to be a pooling one.

Contracts and Second-Best Solutions
19.4.d

Imperfect information can lead to difficulties that sometimes can be solved by contracts. A contract is an agreement, often signed before all the relevant information is obtained, that dictates behavior in various states of the world.

Contract theory has most recently been applied to the labor market to analyze quits and layoffs. The problem is this: A worker would like to demand the maximum wage that the firm would be willing to pay. A firm would like to offer the minimum wage that the worker would be willing to accept. Since those values are not known to all parties with certainty, problems can result.

To see this, consider the following model.[9] Next period, a worker will be worth M to the firm. The value of M is known to the firm, but not to the worker. Similarly, next period the worker has some other options, which dictate the amount that he is willing to accept from the firm. Denote that value A. The value of A is known to the worker, but not to the firm.

If the world were perfect, one would like the worker to work for the firm whenever $M > A$. That is, the worker should work for the firm as long as he is worth more to the firm than elsewhere. This is shown by the area below the

---

[8]See Joseph Stiglitz, "Incentives, Risk, and Information: Notes Toward a Theory of Hierarchy," *Bell Journal of Economics* 6 (Autumn 1975), pp. 552–79; and Edward P. Lazear, "Why Is There Mandatory Retirement?" *Journal of Political Economy* 87 (December 1979), pp. 1261–64.

[9]This analysis is taken from Robert E. Hall and Edward P. Lazear, "The Excess Sensitivity of Layoffs and Quits to Demand," *Journal of Labor Economics* 2 (April 1984), pp. 233–57.

45 degree line where $M = A$ in Figure 19.4.1. For example, if the worker is worth 100 to this firm and only 80 elsewhere, then both worker and firm would be made better off by having him work at 90 than not at all. Unfortunately, firms are trying to get workers to work at the lowest possible wage and workers are trying to get firms to hire them at the highest possible wage. This means that mistakes may occur that prevent work, even when such work would be beneficial. As firms and workers bicker over price, nothing gets done. An extreme form of this negotiation cost is a strike. In the previous example, the worker may believe that he is worth 90 and the firm may believe that the worker would accept 80. They may argue about the price for such a long period that nothing ends up getting done.

Both sides obviously recognize this possibility in advance. As such, they may set up a *contract,* either explicit or implicit, that allows one side to announce the wage and lets the other side take it or leave it. One frequently used arrangement awards the power to announce the wage to the firm, which is uncertain of the worker's minimum acceptable offer. (The firm may have to pay the worker something in advance for the right to do this. The way that payment is generally made is by compensating the worker at a rate greater than his productivity in the current period in anticipation of being able to exploit the worker next period.)

Although the firm does not know the minimum amount that the worker will accept, it does know how much the worker is worth to the firm. It is generally true[10] that the firm pays more, the more the worker is worth. The reason is that the firm does not want to lose the worker during boom periods when his work has a high payoff. Thus, a typical wage-offer schedule is the one shown as line OR in Figure 19.4.1.

To best understand it, suppose that after the contract has been set, it turns out that $M = 80$. The firm does not know the worker's value of A, but announces a wage of 40. If that wage exceeds the worker's acceptance wage, then the firm gets 80 units of output and only pays the worker 40 at point D, receiving a profit of

---

[10]Formally, let the firm believe that $A \sim g(A)$ with distribution function $G(A)$. The firm wants to maximize expected profit. If it announces a wage, W, that falls short of A, the worker does not accept the job. At any wage $W > A$, the worker accepts. Thus, the probability that the worker accepts at wage W is $G(W)$, since that is the probability that $A < W$.

The firm's problem then is to choose W to maximize

$$(M - W)G(W)$$

since $M - W$ is the net gain of having the worker employed, and $G(W)$ is the probability that he accepts at wage W.

The first-order condition is

$$\frac{d}{dW} = -G(W) + g(w)(M - W) = 0$$

(since $dG(W)/dW = g(W)$). Rearranging terms, we get that

$$W = M - \frac{G(W)}{g(W)}$$

Since $G(W)$ and $g(W)$ are always positive, $W < M$. The firm takes a chance on losing the worker by offering a wage that is less than his value to the firm. If the firm is lucky ($A < W$), it makes $M - W$ on the transaction. If unlucky, $A > W$.

Figure 19.4.1 Efficient Work and Optimal Wage Offer

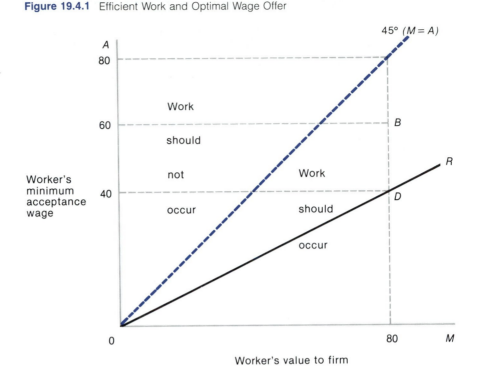

Worker's value to firm

40. Of course, there is the possibility that the worker's acceptance wage exceeds 40, for example, is equal to 60 as shown in Figure 19.4.1 at point *B*. Under these circumstances, the worker refuses to work and the firm gets nothing. It pays for the firm to take the chance, however. At the extreme, if the firm paid 80, it would induce the worker to work whenever $A < M$, but would earn no profit on the transaction. Thus, the line OR is the wage schedule that maximizes expected profit for the firm. The problem is that there are times when work should, but does not, occur. Point *B* is an example of one of those times.

An alternative arrangement allows the worker to announce a wage demand, giving the firm the option to take it or leave it. Doing so results in a wage demand schedule as shown in Figure 19.4.2. This results in firms refusing the offer of work whenever $M < W$. The firm will not hire the worker if the wage demand exceeds the value to the firm. Point *B* is one such situation. The worker knows that he can get 40 elsewhere, but demands a wage of 60, hoping that the firm will accept. Since he is only worth 55, the firm declines and work does not occur. But it should. Since the worker is worth more to this firm than he would be willing to accept, all could be made better off if work occurred. The worker's attempt to exploit the firm in this situation prevents it from occurring.

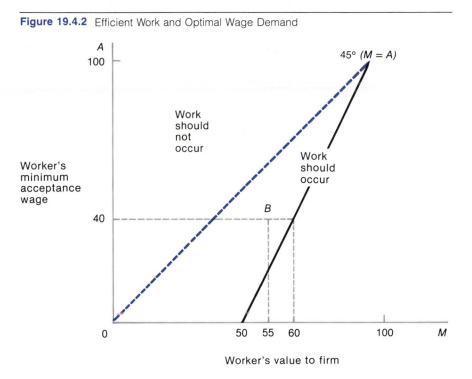

Figure 19.4.2 Efficient Work and Optimal Wage Demand

Whether the contract is set such that firms announce wage offers, workers announce wage demands, or some other arrangement, depends on which arrangement minimizes the losses associated with work that does not occur when it should. This is a "second-best" solution. The contract that awards one side the right to determine the wage is not perfect, but may be better than no contract at all. When no contract is available, parties may squander the entire period, bickering over the appropriate wage. Deciding in advance that wages are determined unilaterally conserves on strike costs and may make both parties better off as a result.

Symmetric Ignorance: Auctions and Winner's Curse 19.4.e

The information problems that have been discussed so far arise when one party knows something of which the other party is ignorant. Adverse selection and other inefficiencies may result under these circumstances. In the last example, employers knew what they were willing to pay their workers, but workers did not possess that information. In this section, we consider what happens when both sides are ignorant about some relevant value.

Consider an auction for land that may or may not have oil below it. Suppose that the land is worthless if no oil is present, and is worth the value of the oil if in fact the hole is not dry. Let the actual value be denoted V. Of course, when individuals bid on the land, they do not know V, but only have some guess of its value. The ith individuals guess can be denoted

$$V_i = V + e_i$$

where e_i is random error associated with lack of clairvoyance. The larger is the variance of e_i, the less clairvoyant and the more likely is the bidder to guess the wrong value.

"Winner's curse" is the economic analogue of an old Groucho Marx joke, in which Marx states that he would not want to be a member of any club that would accept him. The same argument goes here. On average, bidders do not want to buy any land on which they succeed in outbidding the other individuals. The reason is that the winning bid is, on average, higher than the value of the oil. This can be shown formally,[11] but the intuition is this. The individual who wins had the highest assessment of the amount of oil in the well. She had the highest e_i and that was the reason that she outbid everyone else. But this means that everyone else's guess on the value of the well is below hers, and surely the average guess is below hers. In fact, the average guess is the best estimate of the value of the oil in the well. Since the winner's bid exceeds the average bid, on average, she has paid too much for the well. Thus, there is a winner's curse: I do not want to own any well that I can buy!

The problem here is not that one bidder knows something that another bidder does not know. The problem is that ignorance on all sides works to the detriment of the market. In fact, if there were not some way out of this conundrum, auctions of this sort would not exist. No one would bid on an item when he or she knew in advance that the chances were that the winner would pay more than the good was worth.

Yet such auctions do exist in the real world. Somehow, collective ignorance does not totally disrupt these markets. How can that be the case? There are a few possible explanations.

First, bidders who understand that the winner is subject to this kind of curse can shade their bids in a way that will leave them with no loss. Instead of bidding up to V_i, they bid up to some level less than that amount to take into account winner's curse. To see this, let us pursue the oil well example.

---

[11]The formal proof follows. Consider the simplest case of only two bidders, i and j. If each bids up to her estimated value, then i wins when $V_i > V_j$ and she pays $V_j + K$, where K is the size of the bidding step (since this is where j drops out). Thus, she gets the well, worth V, and pays $V_j + K$.
The profit that she receives is

$$V - V_j - K = V - V - \varepsilon_j - K$$
$$= -\varepsilon_j - K.$$

To make things simple, suppose that e_i can take only two values, 50 or -50. Suppose that there are a large number of bidders so that on average, 1/2 see $V + 50$ and 1/2 see $V - 50$ as the value of the oil well.

Under these circumstances, if bidders were to bid up to V_i, the individual knows that if she wins, she has bid 50 more than the expected value since the winner must be drawn from the group that assesses the good at $V + 50$. Knowing this, every bidder adopts the rule that if she thinks the well is worth V_i, she will bid at most $V_i - 50$. Individuals whose estimates of the well's value were produced from $e_i = -50$ end up bidding $V_i - 50 = V - 50 - 50 = V - 100$. Individuals whose estimates of the well's value were produced from $e_i = 50$ end up bidding $V_i - 50 = V + 50 - 50 = V$. The winning bid equals V so that winner's curse is avoided. All bidders, who recognize that winner's curse plagues the auction, shade their bids by 50 and this results in a winning bid that, on average, equals the value of the well. Thus, the rational bidder always drops out of the auction at some point before the price rises to her assessed value of the good.

The reason that winner's curse is such a serious problem in this example is that the value of the well is the same to each bidder, even though those bidders do not know its exact value before buying the land. But most auctions do not have that property. This leads to the second explanation for the existence of auctions.

Suppose that the good in question were not a piece of land that might contain oil, but instead an antique table. Here the table's worth to each individual might well be known before the good is purchased. There is no ignorance on the value of the good. The auction occurs because different individuals attach different values to the table. Antique buffs might pay more for the table than those who prefer contemporary furniture. Thus, winner's curse is not an issue. The winner is certain that the good is worth to him at least as much as he pays for it. That this may exceed others' assessment of the table's value is irrelevant. All auctions need not be characterized by ignorance about the good to be sold. Generally, auctions are held because individuals have different assessments of the good's value. Auctioning the antique table is a seller's way to find the maximum value of that table. This differs from the case of the oil well, where all assess the value in the same way, but no individual knows the value with certainty before the good is purchased.

The expected value of $-\varepsilon_j$, given that i is a winner, is the expectation of $-\varepsilon_j$, given that $\varepsilon_i > \varepsilon_j$. If ε_i, $\varepsilon_j \sim f(\varepsilon)$, then this can be written as

$$E(V - V_j - K \mid \varepsilon_i > \varepsilon_j) = \int_{-\infty}^{\infty} \int_{\varepsilon_j}^{\infty} \frac{-(\varepsilon_j + K)f(\varepsilon_i)}{[1 - F(\varepsilon_j)]} f(\varepsilon_j) \, d\varepsilon_i \, d\varepsilon_j$$

$$= \int_{-\infty}^{\infty} -(\varepsilon_j + K)f(\varepsilon_j) \, d\varepsilon_j$$

$$= -K < 0.$$

Thus, winning the bidding contest is not profitable.

One of the most important ways of thinking about situations where information is imperfect is the theory of signalling, sometimes called the "screening" hypothesis. This idea, best articulated by Michael Spence,[12] holds that when information is imperfect, individuals can take steps that provide others with signals, or proxies, for the relevant variable. The idea is most frequently associated with the pursuit of formal education. The story goes that an employer does not know a worker's ability when he hires him, but he knows that individuals who complete their undergraduate degrees are more likely to perform better on the job than those who do not. More recently,[13] the same idea has been applied to the product market and advertising. There the argument goes that those firms that find it profitable to advertise believe that they are likely to remain in business longer and probably have a better product. Thus, it is rational for consumers to pay more for goods that are heavily advertised.

Signalling with Education
19.5.a

To understand how the signalling hypothesis works, we consider the example of formal education. The theory, in its purest form, holds that schooling contributes nothing to a worker's productivity. The reason that employers are willing to pay more to individuals with degrees is that they recognize that those individuals who complete school are also better workers.

In order for the signalling hypothesis to hold, two assumptions are necessary. First, it must be true that there is a positive correlation between ability to perform in school and ability to perform on the job. Second, it must be the case that the school can test performance more cheaply than the employer.

Let us consider an example to show how a signalling equilibrium is maintained. Suppose that there are only two classes of individuals in the world: quicks and slows. The quicks produce $100,000 over their work lives for the firm, whereas the slows produce only $90,000. Schooling does nothing to alter the productivity of workers, but quicks can obtain a college degree in 1/4 the time it takes a slow. If quicks and slows could be identified, then firms that bought labor in competitive factor markets would be forced to pay quicks $100,000 and slows $90,000 over their lifetimes. Our approach is suppose that employers believe that all those with college degrees are quicks and all without are slows. We then show that this belief will be self-fulfilling. Thus, a signalling equilibrium is achieved.

---

[12]A. Michael Spence, "Job Market Signalling," *Quarterly Journal of Economics* 87 (August 1973), pp. 355–374.

[13]See, for example, Benjamin Klein and Keith B. Leffler, "The Role of Market Forces in Assuring Contractual Performance," *Journal of Political Economy* 89, no. 4 (1981), pp. 615–41; and P. Milgrom and J. Roberts, "Price and Advertising Signals of Product Quality," *Journal of Political Economy* 94, no. 4 (1986), pp. 796–821.

Specifically, suppose it costs a slow $20,000 of time to obtain a degree whereas it costs a quick only $5,000 of time, because a slow has to devote more time than a quick to studying. The return to obtaining a degree is $10,000 ($100,000 − $90,000). Since this exceeds the quick's cost, all quicks finish college. But the slow's cost is $20,000, which exceeds the return. Thus, it does not pay for slows to attend college.

The employers' assumption has been validated. All quicks obtain degrees and no slows do. Thus, paying a worker with a degree $100,000 and one without $90,000 is an equilibrium strategy. No employer nor worker has an incentive to deviate from the solution.

Social Inefficiency of Signalling
19.5.b

Although employers and workers have incentives to encourage signalling, society loses as a result. The reason is that in the pure signalling world, schooling is unproductive, yet individuals waste resources on it. In the last example, suppose that the economy consisted of 10 quicks and 10 slows. With signalling, the output of the economy is

$$10(\$100,000) + 10(\$90,000) - 10(\$5,000) = \$1.85 \text{ million},$$

$5,000 being subtracted for each of the 10 quicks who uses his time in school, rather than producing output. Without signalling, the output of the economy is

$$10(\$100,000) + 10(\$90,000) = \$1.9 \text{ million}.$$

Since schooling does not alter productivity, total production does not change, except for the saving of the schooling costs.

The distribution of income is different when signalling occurs. Then quicks receive $100,000 and slows $90,000. If no signalling were permitted, quicks and slows would be indistinguishable and each individual would be paid $95,000 ($1.9 million/20 workers). It is the difference in distribution that causes employers and workers to opt to signal, even though it is socially inefficient.

If schooling were truly unproductive and served only to sort the quicks from the slows with no social good coming of it, the world would be better off without it. A law that told employers that they could not "discriminate" on the basis of education would eliminate any return to education for quicks and no schooling would be undertaken.

Criticisms of Signalling Theory
19.5.c

The last paragraph seems extreme and probably strikes most readers as a bad idea. There are a number of reasons for this, most of which have been used to criticize signalling as a model of education. The most important of these is this:

Signalling theory rules out the possibility of contingent contracts. Many have argued that although employers may not be able to sort quicks from slows initially, after some time on the job the facts will be revealed. Thus, employers could assume that all individuals were slows, paying at the low wage rate. If an individual turned out to be quick, then the employer could raise his wage enough to pay for the future and to make up for underpayment in the past. This kind of contingent contract saves schooling expenses so even quicks should prefer this kind of arrangement. Thus, if contingent contracts are feasible, they will dominate a signalling equilibrium. The feasibility of such contracts is an empirical question.

This point notwithstanding, signalling theory is at the heart of informational problems in economics. It models the behavior of maximizing agents in an imperfect world and has become an important force in modern economic theory.

SYNOPSIS 19.6

- Economic analysis is affected by the existence of imperfect information in the real world.

- Imperfect information may give rise to a distribution of prices for the same good by different sellers. When different sellers charge different prices, consumers have an incentive to search across producers for the lowest price. That incentive is greater, the greater is the dispersion in prices. The existence of search by consumers means that the distribution of announced prices by firms is different from the distribution of actual transactions prices. Since consumers search for the lowest-priced firms, transactions at low prices occur out of proportion to the number of stores who offer low prices. Although 10 percent of the firms charge the highest price, fewer than 10 percent of the sales are made at that price. Price dispersion may well reflect subtle differences in the good. Services, convenience of location, and shopping amenities may lie behind many price differences across sellers.

- When information is imperfect, firms, too, must experiment. Few firms know their demand curves perfectly and must price in a way that maximizes profit, given their ignorance. Timing of prices is important. It generally implies that prices will start high and fall as a function of time that the good remains unsold. It also implies that sellers will set prices in a way that leaves some goods unsold. The ability to change price over time means higher profits for the firm and more precise knowledge of the demand curve.

- Adverse selection can result when one party has more information than another. If buyers have less information than sellers, then price reflects lower quality that results from putting worse-than-average quality goods on the market. Because the price adjusts, buyers end up getting what they paid for, on average.

- Guarantees, which are a form of contingent contract, can minimize the impact of adverse selection. At the extreme, it creates a sorting equilibrium, so that high- and low-quality goods are sold in separate markets, with different prices and terms. Guarantees, like most forms of insurance, encourage moral hazard. In this case, buyers take less care with the good than is optimal because they know that the seller must cover the cost of repairs. Difficulties associated with enforcing the guarantees can also limit their effectiveness.

- Contracts can sometimes circumvent some difficulties that arise when information is imperfect. An agreement to avoid bickering by setting up some fixed set of terms in advance can conserve on negotiation time and increase the probability of a transaction. Contracts usually result in only second-best solutions because they cannot deal with all contingencies perfectly.

- Even when ignorance is symmetric, say in the case of many buyers bidding for a good of uncertain value, markets tend to be more complicated. In particular, the winner of a particular good would end up paying too much for it on average, unless he or she shaded his or her bid appropriately. Winner's curse does not apply when consumers have different, but known, valuations of the commodity.

- Signalling may be an important way to transmit information. For a signal to be valid, a necessary condition is that cost of acquiring the signal must be negatively correlated with the more valuable outcome. Although it may be in the interest of the private parties to acquire a signal, signalling, in its purest form, is socially inefficient. Thus, if education provided nothing more than a signal of worker productivity, a law that prohibited pay "discrimination" on the basis of education would be desirable. Few would take such an extreme view of the education process.

QUESTIONS AND EXERCISES

1. Search costs vary with the value of an individual's time. Rich people value their time more highly than poor people. This would suggest that the rich would search less than the poor. On the other hand, the rich spend more money than the poor. The more items that are purchased, the larger is the savings from having searched for the lowest price. What do these effects imply about the relationship between price paid and income?

2. Gas stations located across the street from one another often charge different prices. Can search theory rationalize this phenomenon? What else might be going on?

3. Consider an art gallery that is trying to sell a painting. Its strategy is to start with a high price, then to lower it if the painting does not sell within a month. Suppose that some individuals who come into the gallery are art collectors, whereas others are merely browsers who will not buy the painting at any price. How should the

rate of price decline vary with the number of individuals who come into the store and with the proportion of browsers to collectors? (Assume that the owner cannot tell a browser from a collector.)

SUGGESTED READINGS

Akerlof, George. "The Market for 'Lemons': Quality Uncertainty and the Market Mechanism," *Quarterly Journal of Economics* 84 (August 1970), pp. 488–500.

Hall, Robert E. "The Importance of Lifetime Jobs in the U.S. Economy," *American Economic Review* 72 (1982), pp. 716–24.

Jovanovic, Boyan. "Job Matching and the Theory of Turnover," *Journal of Political Economy* 87 (October 1979), pp. 972–90.

Klein, Benjamin, and Keith B. Leffler. "The Role of Market Forces in Assuring Contractual Performance," *Journal of Political Economy* 89, no. 4 (1981), pp. 615–41.

Lazear, Edward P. "Retail Pricing and Clearance Sales," *American Economic Review* 76, no. 1 (March 1986), pp. 14–32.

———. "Salaries and Piece Rates," *Journal of Business* 59, no. 3 (July 1986), pp. 405–31.

———. "Why Is There Mandatory Retirement?" *Journal of Political Economy* 87 (December 1979), pp. 1261–64.

Rosen, Sherwin. "Learning and Experience in the Labor Market," *Journal of Human Resources* 7, no. 3 (Summer 1972), pp. 326–42.

Spence, A. Michael. "Job Market Signalling," *Quarterly Journal of Economics* 87 (August 1973), pp. 355–74.

Stigler, George J. "The Economics of Information," *Journal of Political Economy* 69, no. 3 (June 1961), pp. 213–25.

Stiglitz, Joseph E. "Incentives, Risk, and Information: Notes Toward a Theory of Hierarchy," *Bell Journal of Economics and Management Science* 6 (Autumn 1975), pp. 552–79.

Advanced Reading

PART 1

Theory of Consumer Behavior, General
I.

Becker, Gary S. "A Theory of the Allocation of Time," *Economic Journal* 75 (1965), pp. 493–517.

Georgescu-Roegen, Nicholas. "The Pure Theory of Consumer Behavior." *Quarterly Journal of Economics* 50 (1935-36), pp. 545–93.

Hicks, John R. *Value and Capital,* 2nd. ed. Oxford: Clarendon Press, 1946, pp. 11–41, 305–11.

Hotelling, Harold. "Edgeworth's Taxation Paradox and the Nature of Demand and Supply Functions." *Journal of Political Economy* 40 (1932), pp. 577–616.

————. "Demand Functions with Limited Budgets." *Econometrica 3* (1935), pp. 66–78.

Lancaster, Kelvin J. *Consumer Demand: A New Approach.* New York: Columbia University Press, 1971.

Samuelson, Paul A. *Foundations of Economic Analysis.* Cambridge, Mass.: Harvard University Press, 1947, pp. 90–117.

Schultz, Henry. *The Theory and Measurement of Demand.* Chicago: University of Chicago Press, 1938, pp. 5–58.

Wold, Herman O. A., with **Jureen, Lars.** *Demand Analysis.* New York: John Wiley & Sons, 1953, pp. 81–139.

Complementarity and Related Goods
II.

Ferguson, C. E. "Substitution Effect in Value Theory: A Pedagogical Note." *Southern Economic Journal* 26 (1960), pp. 310–14.

Georgescu-Roegen, Nicholas. "A Diagrammatic Analysis of Complementarity." *Southern Economic Journal* 14 (1952), pp. 1–20.

Hicks, John R. *Value and Capital,* 2nd ed. Oxford: Clarendon Press, 1946, pp. 42–52, 311–14.

Ichimura, S. "A Critical Note on the Definition of Related Goods." *Review of Economic Studies,* 18 (1950–51), pp. 179–83.

Morishima, M. "A Note of Definitions of Related Goods." *Review of Economic Studies,* 23 (1955-56), pp. 132–34.

Samuelson, Paul A. *Foundations of Economic Analysis.* Cambridge, Mass.: Harvard University Press, 1947, pp. 183–89.

Schultz, Henry. *The Theory and Measurement of Demand.* Chicago: University of Chicago Press, 1938, pp. 569–85, 607–28.

Special Topics in Demand Theory
III.

Income-Compensated Demand Curves
A.

Bailey, Martin J. "The Marshallian Demand Curve." *Journal of Political Economy* 42 (1954), pp. 255–61.

Frieman, Milton. "The Marshallian Demand Curve." *Journal of Political Economy* 57 (1949), pp. 463–95.

Knight, Frank H. "Realism and Relevance in the Theory of Demand." *Journal of Political Economy* 52 (1944), pp. 289–318.

Yeager, Leland B. *"Methodenstreit* over Demand Curves." *Journal of Political Economy* 48 (1960), pp. 53–64.

Revealed Preference and Index Numbers
B.

Frisch, Ragnar. "Annual Survey of General Economic Theory: The Problem of Index Numbers." *Econometrica* 4 (1936), pp. 1–38.

Georgescu-Roegen, Nicholas. "Choice and Revealed Preference." *Southern Economic Journal* 21 (1954), pp. 119–30.

Hicks, John R. *A Revision of Demand Theory.* Oxford: Clarendon Press, 1956.

Houthakker, H. S. "Revealed Preference and the Utility Function." *Economica,* N.S., 17 (1950), pp. 159–74.

Samuelson, Paul A. "A Note on the Pure Theory of Consumer Behavior." *Economica,* N.S., 5 (1938), pp. 61–71.

————. *Foundations of Economic Analysis.* Cambridge, Mass.: Harvard University Press, 1947, pp. 144–63.

Staehle, Hans. "A Development of the Economic Theory of Price Index Numbers." *Review of Economic Studies* 2 (1935), pp. 163–88.

Cardinal Utility of Analysis of Choice Under Risk
C.

Alchian, A. A. "The Meaning of Utility Measurement." *American Economic Review* 42 (1953), pp. 26–50.

Baumol, W. J. "The Neumann-Morgenstern Utility Index — An Ordinalist View." *Journal of Political Economy* 59 (1951), pp. 61–66.

————. "The Cardinal Utility which is Ordinal." *Economic Journal* 67 (1958), pp. 665–72.

Ferguson, C. D. "An Essay on Cardinal Utility." *Southern Economic Journal* 25 (1958), pp. 11–23.

Friedman, Milton, and **Savage, L. J.** The Utility Analysis of Choices Involving Risk." *Journal of Political Economy* 56 (1948), pp. 279–304.

————. "The Expected-Utility Hypothesis and the Measurability of Utility." *Journal of Political Economy* 60 (1952), pp. 463–74.

Georgescu-Roegen, Nicholas. "Choice, Expectations and Measurability." *Quarterly Journal of Economics* 68 (1954), pp. 503–34.

Markowitz, Harry. "The Utility of Wealth." *Journal of Political Economy* 60 (1952), pp. 151–158.

Ozga, S. A. "Measurable Utility and Probability — A Simplified Rendering." *Economic Journal* 66 (1956), pp. 419–30.

Strotz, Robert H. "Cardinal Utility." *American Economic Review, Papers and Proceedings* 62 (1953), pp. 384–97.

Von Neumann, John, and **Morgenstern, Oskar.** *Theory of Games and Economic Behavior.* Princeton, N.J.: Princeton University Press, 1944, pp. 15–31, 617–32.

Market Stability
IV.

Henderson, James M., and **Quandt, Richard E.** *Microeconomic Theory: A Mathematical Approach,* 2nd ed. New York: McGraw-Hill, 1971, pp. 132–36, 191–201.

Hicks, John R. *Value and Capital,* 2nd ed. Oxford: Clarendon Press, 1946, pp. 62–77, 245–82, 315–19, 333–37.

Kuenne, Robert E. "Hick's Concept of Perfect Stability in Multiple Exchange." *Quarterly Journal of Economics* 73 (1959), pp. 309–15.

Metzler, Lloyd A. "Stability of Multiple Markets: The Hicks Conditions." *Econometrica* 13 (1945), pp. 277–92.

Samuelson, Paul A. *Foundations of Economic Analysis.* Cambridge, Mass.: Harvard University Press, 1947, pp. 17–19, 260–265, 269–76.

PART 2

The Theory of Production
I.

Arrow, Kenneth J.; Chenery, Hollis B.; Minhas, Bagicha; and **Solow, Robert M.**

"Capital-Labor Substitution and Economic Efficiency." *Review of Economics and Statistics* 43 (1961), pp. 225–50.

Borts, George H., and **Mishan, E. J.** "Exploring the 'Uneconomic Region' of the Production function." *Review of Economic Studies* 29 (1962), pp. 300–12.

Carlson, Sune. *A Study of the Pure Theory of Production.* Stockholm Economic Studies No. 9. London: P. S. King & Sons, 1939.

Cassels, John M. "On the Law of Variable Proportions." *Explorations in Economics.* New York: McGraw-Hill, 1936, pp. 223–36.

Ferguson, C. E. "Transformation curve in Production Theory: A Pedagogical Note." *Southern Economic Journal* 29 (1962), pp. 96–102.

————. *The Neoclassical Theory of Production and Distribution.* London and New York: Cambridge University Press, 1969, chaps. 2–6.

Ferguson, C. E., and **Saving, Thomas R.** "Long-Run Scale Adjustments of a Perfectly Competitive Firm and Industry." *American Economic Review* 59 (1969), pp. 774–83.

Machlup, Fritz. "On the Meaning of the Marginal Product," *Explorations in Economics.* New York: McGraw-Hill, 1936, pp. 250–63.

Samuelson, Paul A. *Foundations of Economic Analysis.* Cambridge, Mass.: Harvard University Press, 1947, pp. 57–89.

Shephard, Ronald W. *Cost and Production Functions.* Princeton, N.J.: Princeton University Press, 1953.

Stigler, George J. *Production and Distribution Theories.* New York: Macmillan, 1946.

Walters, A. A. "Production and Cost Functions: An Econometric Survey." *Econometrica* 31 (1963), pp. 1–66, with extensive bibliography.

The Theory of Cost
II.

Viner, Jacob. "Cost Curves and Supply Curves." *Zeitschrift für Nationalökonomie* 3 (1931), pp. 23–46. This is the classic reference in the field. In addition, see Ferguson, *The Neoclassical Theory of Production and Distribution* (chaps. 7 and 8); Samuelson, *Foundations of Economic Analysis;* Shephard, *Cost and Production Functions;* and Walters, "Production and Cost Functions: An Econometric Survey," listed above.

PART 4

Marginal Productivity and Input Demand
I.

Chamberlin, E. H. "Monopolistic Competition and the Productivity Theory of Distribution," *Explorations in Economics.* New York: McGraw-Hill, 1936, pp. 237–49.

Douglas, P. H. *The Theory of Wages.* New York: Macmillan, 1934.

Ferguson, C. E. "'Inferior Factors' and the Theories of Production and Input Demand." *Economica,* N.S. 35 (1968), pp.140–50.

_____. *The Neoclassical Theory of Production and Distribution.* London and New York: Cambridge University Press, 1969, Chapters 6 and 7.

_____. "Production, Prices, and the Theory of Jointly Derived Input Demand Functions." *Economica,* N.S. 33 (1966), pp. 454–61.

Ferguson, C. E., and Thomas R. Saving. "Long-Run Scale Adjustments of a Perfectly Competitive Firm and Industry." *American Economic Review* 59 (1969), pp. 774–83.

Hicks, John R. *The Theory of Wages.* 2nd ed. New York: Macmillan, 1964.

Mosak, Jacob L. "Interrelations of Production, Price and Derived Demand." *Journal of Political Economy* 46 (1938), pp. 761–87.

Pfouts, R. W. "Distribution Theory in a Certain Case of Oligopoly and Oligopsony." *Metroeconomica* 7 (1955), pp. 137–46.

Schultz, Henry. "Marginal Productivity and the General Pricing Process." *Journal of Political Economy* 37 (1929), pp. 505–51.

Stigler, George J. "Production and Distribution in the Short Run." *Journal of Political Economy* 47 (1939), pp. 305–27.

Distribution and Relative Shares
II.

Ferguson, C. E. "Neoclassical Theory of Technical Progress and Relative Factor Shares." *Southern Economic Journal* 34 (1968), pp. 490–504.

_____. *The Neoclassical Theory of Production and Distribution.* London and New York: Cambridge University Press, 1969, Chapters 11 and 12.

Robinson, Joan. "Euler's Theorem and the Problem of Distribution." *Economic Journal* 44 (1934), pp. 398–414.

Stigler, George J. *Production and Distribution Theories.* New York: Macmillan, 1941.

Name Index

Elway, John, 452
Engel, Christian Lorenz Ernst, 73, 136–37

Fama, E., 84 n, 144 n, 590
Ferguson, C. E., 125, 169, 182 n, 201 n, 206, 244, 372, 428 n, 444 n, 445 n, 446 n, 449–50, 464 n, 473, 480, 481, 556
Fisher, Irving, 43, 44, 564, 570 n, 590
Fossati, Eraldo, 492 n, 523
Friedman, Milton, 487

George, Henry, 420
Georgescu-Roegen, Nicholas, 50 n, 125
Geyskens, 134
Goldschmid, H., 384 n
Gossen, H. H., 43
Gould, J. P., 215, 383 n
Gretsky, Wayne, 452, 455
Grich, Bobby, 454
Guda, Henri, 372
Guilbault, Joseph D., 348

Hahn, F. H., 523
Hall, Robert E., 610 n
Harrod, R. F., 359, 364
Hartley-Leonard, Darryl, 348
Hayek, F. V., 534 n, 556
Healy, James J., 412 n
Henderson, James M., 56, 85, 125, 169, 206, 244, 286, 523, 557
Hicks, John R., 56, 60, 85, 94, 125, 206, 322, 421, 437, 441, 444, 450, 479, 480
Hirshleifer, J., 344 n, 563, 590
Hotelling, Harold, 60, 353, 366 n, 430
Huddle, Don, 415, 416
Hunt, Bunker, 60 n

Jackson, Reggie, 452
Jevons, W. Stanley, 43, 420

Johnson, W. E., 448

Kahn, R. F., 359
Kaplan, A. D. H., 402
Kemp, Murray C., 514 n
Kendrick, J. W., 444 n
Kenen, Peter B., 557
Keppel, Bruce, 324
Klein, Benjamin, 616 n
Knight, Frank, 162 n, 169, 286, 352, 353
Kuenne, Robert E., 523

Laffer, A., 144 n
Lancaster, Kelvin J., 122, 125, 554 n
Lanzillotti, Robert F., 384 n, 402
Lazear, Edward P., 365 n, 383 n, 542 n, 600 n, 608 n, 610 n
Leffler, Keith B., 616 n
Leonard, John, 452, 454, 455
Leontief, W. W., 492, 523
Lerner, A. P., 367 n, 384 n
Lipsey, R. G., 554 n
Lluch, 134
Lucker, Bruce, 349

Machlup, Fritz, 169, 286, 322, 372, 378
Mann, H., 384 n
Marshall, Alfred, 56, 352, 359, 420, 421, 429 n, 434 n, 437
Marx, Karl, 564, 590
Metzler, Lloyd A., 520 n
Michael, R., 542 n
Miller, Gay Sands, 372
Miller, M., 84 n, 414, 415, 590
Miller, Merton, 587
Mishan, E. J., 205
Modigliani, Franco, 587
Morgenstern, Oskar, 388, 390, 393–94, 587
Mosak, Jacob L., 480
Muelbauer, 134, 135
Mullikin, Harry, 348

Subject Index

Marginal product curve, 160–62
Marginal productivity theory of distribution, 411, 419–46
demand for a variable productive service, 421–30
  determinants of, 428–29
  individual, 425–28
  market demand, 429–30
origin of, 420
supply of a variable productive service, 430–33
Marginal rate of substitution (MRS), 50–52
definition, 51
Marginal rate of technical substitution (MRTS), 185, 193–94
diminishing, 187
input price ratio, 437–39, 441
Marginal rate of transformation, 528, 530
Marginal revenue (MR), 137–43, 256–59
calculation of, 138–41
curve below demand curve, 142
definition, 138
elasticity and, 142–43
geometry of determination, 141–42
Marginal revenue product, 458–62
Markdown, 600
Market cross elasticities, 104
Market demand, 128
firm's demand curve, 143–45
  taste determining, 145–46
income elasticity, 75–77, 136–37
marginal revenue, 137–43
price elasticity; *see* Price elasticity of demand
Market demand curve, 3, 12
Market determined (parametric) prices, 533–34
Market equilibrium, 20
barter economy, 25–28
corporate sector example, 28
definition, 21
effects of changes in demand, 23
effects of changes of supply, 24
government policies, 29–31
graphic representation, 21–23
Market franchise, 294–95
Market relation among commodities, 104

Market supply, 3
Market supply curve, 16–17
MIB (more is better), 47
Minimax principle, 395
Minimum wages, Pareto efficiencies, 548
Minnesota Mining and Manufacturing Company (3M), 293
Money income
changes in, 68–78
Engel curves, 73–78
income-consumption curve, 71–73
multiple constraints, 117–21
Money prices of goods, 61 n
Monopolistic competition, 352
ex ante competition, 365–66
excess capacity, 358–62
ex post monopoly, 365–66
Chamberlin's theory appraised, 364–65
historical perspective, 352–53
ideal output, 358–60
industries and product groups, 354–56
long-run equilibrium, 357–58
  comparisons, 362–64
product differentiation, 353–54
short-run equilibrium, 356–57
spatial equilibrium, 366–68
Monopolistic exploitation, 474
Monopoly, 290
bases of, 292
  control of raw materials, 293
  natural monopoly, 293–94
  patents, 293
block pricing, 317–20
cost and supply, 298
definition, 291–92
demand under, 295
employment, 458–66
long-run equilibrium, 306–12
  comparison with perfect competition, 309–10
  multiplant, 310–12
  single plant, 307–9
price controls, 339–40
price discrimination, 312–20
price theory, 349–69
short-run equilibrium, 298–306